Tip	Chapter
Control the colors on your desktop by customizing the Windows Color Palette.	10
Dress up your desktop by creating custom wallpaper.	11
Add sound effects to system events.	11
Make your own music by customizing Windows for MIDI output.	11
Use the Control Panel to customize your hardware.	11
Use WIN.INI options to modify your Windows environment directly.	12
Improve performance and appearance by using TrueType, raster, and plotter fonts.	13
Control screen window fonts when running DOS applications.	13
Add special characters from any font with the Character Map accessory.	13
Speed up your printouts by using downloadable and hardware fonts.	13
Speed up printing with or without the use of the Print Manager.	13
Boost performance with disk caching.	14
Speed up multitasking with swap files.	14
Control disk space used during swapping.	14
Improve throughput by defragmenting your hard disk.	14
Maximize available Windows memory with DOS 5.	15
Free up conventional memory by using upper memory blocks (UMBs) more efficiently.	15
Create a RAM disk to speed disk operations.	15
Speed up manipulations of temporary files by using the TEMP environment variable.	15
Set PIF options to maximize DOS application memory.	15
Maintain network performance when running Windows.	16
Use SYSTEM.INI settings to enhance network performance.	16
Use modems and ports successfully to maximize communications throughput.	16
Keep your system up and running by surmounting UAEs (Unrecoverable Application Errors).	18
Use diagnostic software (Dr. Watson and MSD) to find out the causes of problems.	18
Multitask more programs at once by adjusting modes, windows, and PIF settings.	19

Computer users are not all alike.
Neither are SYBEX books.

We know our customers have a variety of needs. They've told us so. And because we've listened, we've developed several distinct types of books to meet the needs of each of our customers. What are you looking for in computer help?

If you're looking for the basics, try the **ABC's** series. You'll find short, unintimidating tutorials and helpful illustrations. For a more visual approach, select **Teach Yourself,** featuring screen-by-screen illustrations of how to use your latest software purchase.

Learn Fast! books are really two books in one—a tutorial to get you off to a fast start and a reference to answer your questions when you're ready to tackle advanced tasks.

Mastering and **Understanding** titles offer you a step-by-step introduction, plus an in-depth examination of intermediate-level features, to use as you progress.

Our **Up & Running** series is designed for computer-literate consumers who want a no-nonsense overview of new programs. Just 20 basic lessons, and you're on your way.

We also publish two types of reference books. Our **Instant References** provide quick access to each of a program's commands and functions. SYBEX **Encyclopedias** and **Desktop References** provide a *comprehensive reference* and explanation of all of the commands, features, and functions of the subject software.

Our **programming** books are specifically written for a technically sophisticated audience and provide a no-nonsense value-added approach to each topic covered, with plenty of tips, tricks, and time-saving hints.

Sometimes a subject requires a special treatment that our standard series don't provide. So you'll find we have titles like **Advanced Techniques, Handbooks, Tips & Tricks,** and others that are specifically tailored to satisfy a unique need.

We carefully select our authors for their in-depth understanding of the software they're writing about, as well as their ability to write clearly and communicate effectively. Each manuscript is thoroughly reviewed by our technical staff to ensure its complete accuracy. Our production department makes sure it's easy to use. All of this adds up to the highest quality books available, consistently appearing on best-seller charts worldwide.

You'll find SYBEX publishes a variety of books on every popular software package. Looking for computer help? Help Yourself to SYBEX.

For a brochure of our best-selling publications:
SYBEX Inc., 2021 Challenger Drive, Alameda, CA 94501
Tel: (510) 523-8233/(800) 227-2346 Telex: 336311
SYBEX Fax: (510) 523-2373

SUPERCHARGING
WINDOWS

SUPERCHARGING
WINDOWS™

Judd Robbins

SYBEX®   *San Francisco   •   Paris   •   Düsseldorf   •   Soest*

Acquisitions Editor: Dianne King
Developmental and Technical Editor: Gary Masters
Editor: Richard Mills
Word Processors: Ann Dunn and Susan Trybull
Book Designer: Suzanne Albertson
Technical Art: Delia Brown and Cuong Le
Screen Graphics: Aldo Bermudez
Desktop Publishing Specialist: Dina F. Quan
Proofreader/Production Assistant: Catherine Mahoney
Indexer: Ted Laux
Cover Designer: Ingalls + Associates
Cover Photographer: Mark Johann
Screen reproductions produced with Collage Plus.

Library of Congress Card Number: 92-80097
ISBN: 0-89588-862-9

Manufactured in the United States of America
10 9 8 7 6 5 4 3 2 1

To Katana
and the rest of my wonderful family

ACKNOWLEDGMENTS

Thanks to Gary Masters, Developmental Editor, for help with the overall structure of the book. In particular, thanks for the idea for Part V and specifically for Chapter 19.

Thanks to Richard Mills, Editor, for overseeing the entire editing and production process and for shepherding this book from start to finish. Also, thanks to Doug Robert and Barbara Gordon for assisting in the editing of some chapters.

Thanks also to the following for their behind-the-scenes contributions to this book: Suzanne Albertson, book designer; Delia Brown and Cuong Le, technical artist; Aldo Bermudez, screen graphics technician; Dina Quan, desktop publishing specialist; and Catherine Mahoney, proofreader/production assistant.

Thanks to the following manufacturers for their loan of hardware during the development of this book: Compton's NewMedia, for Multimedia Encyclopedia; Grolier Electronic Publishing, for Encyclopedia on CD-ROM; Creative Labs Inc., for Sound Blaster Pro; and Iomega, Inc., for Bernoulli Transportable.

Thanks to the following vendors for providing me with versions of their excellent software during the development of this book:

MacroMind/Paracomp	Action!
Gazelle Systems	Back-It 4
Inner Media Inc.	Collage Plus
The Zuma Group	Curtain Call
Image-In Incorporated	Image-In
Software Ventures	Microphone II
Symantec Corp.	Norton Desktop for Windows
LaserTools, Inc.	PrintCache
Quarterdeck Corp.	QEMM and QEMM 386

Xyquest Corporation	Signature
Dariana Technology Group, Inc.	System Sleuth
Charles Schwab	The Equalizer
Golden Bow Systems	VOPT
Delrina Technology, Inc.	WinFax Pro

Thanks to the following software vendors for giving me permission to include copies of their excellent shareware on the disks accompanying this book:

Wilson WindowWare, Inc.	Address, Reminder, Wincheck
InfoPerfect, Inc.	Apptimer
SP Services	BackMenu, BigDesk
Soft Sale, Ltd.	Chkmodem
McAfee Associates	Clean
Dragons Eye Software	Clean, Closer, Exitw, Run
Cornfield Computing	Cpuuse
George Spafford	Cachetst
Philip Kaufman	Iconmstr
Robert Heath	Metcnvrt
Aristosoft, Inc.	Mowin
Phil Katz	Pkware
JASC, Inc.	Paintshp
Thomas Tuerke	Quote
Aryeh Goretsky	Scan, Vshield
TechSmith Corporation	SnagIt
Digital Simulations	Stop
Dave Norris	Taipei
Dave Jewell	Timefram

Data Graphics	Unicom
Stellar Technologies	Wbar
Numbers & Co.	Whiskers
David Feinleib	Winclock
Eastern Mountain Software	Winpost
Frank Bielsik	Yacht

Thanks to the following software authors for offering their freeware to the world at large, with no registration fees or permissions required: Pat Beirne, for Dirnote; Wolfgang Strobl, for Klotz; Free Software Foundation Inc., for Chess; Bill Crow, for Sysgraph; and Sergey Ryzhkov, for Winplay.

CONTENTS AT A GLANCE

	Introduction	xxxv
PART I	**Understanding Windows**	**1**
1	A Little Background: The History of Windows	3
2	Setup and Installation	33
3	The Architecture of Windows	77
4	How Windows Manages Memory	115
5	Exchanging and Sharing Data	167
6	Understanding Multimedia	205
PART II	**Running Applications**	**261**
7	Behind-the-Scenes Secrets of Running Applications	263
8	Running DOS Applications under Windows	319
9	Managing the Windows Environment	393
10	Understanding Graphics, Color, and Video Standards	431
PART III	**Customizing Windows**	**461**
11	Personalizing the Desktop and Customizing Hardware	463
12	Modifying WIN.INI and SYSTEM.INI	501
13	Managing Fonts and Printed Output	557
PART IV	**Optimizing Windows**	**595**
14	Turbocharging Your System	597
15	Fine-Tuning Your System Memory	643
16	Strategies for Networks and Communications	685

PART V   **Troubleshooting Windows**   **721**

17   Questions Most Frequently Asked   725

18   Unrecoverable Application Errors   755

19   Inside Windows Error Messages   777

PART VI   **Using Applications on the Companion Disks**   **805**

20   Productivity Tools   813

21   Tools for Personalizing Windows   881

Glossary   935

Index   977

CONTENTS

Introduction   xxxv

PART I   Understanding Windows   **1**

1   *A Little Background: The History of Windows*   3

My Personal Experience with Windows   5
A Biographer's Look at the Evolution of Windows   7
    It Began with Windows 1.0   9
    It Got Better with Windows 2.0   12
    New Processor Chips Gave Life to
    Windows /286 and /386   13
    The Marketplace Brought Us to Windows 3.0   14
    Windows 3.1 Carries the Baton Forward   15
Where Does Windows Go from Here?   22
    Point-Counterpoint: Windows vs. IBM's OS/2   24
    Point-Counterpoint: Windows on Different Processors   26

Sidebars

Large Corporations Are Making the Transition
to Windows   5
Running Windows on a Laptop   17
Overcoming the Dreaded UAE   19
The Reality of OS/2 and Windows   23
Which Is Better: A Macintosh or a PC Running
Windows?   27
Where Is the Computer Industry Headed?   29
Certain Upgrade Features Are Better
Than Others   31

2   *Setup and Installation*   33

   Preparing Your System for Windows   34
        Is Your Hardware Really Ready?   35
        Going beyond the Normal Backup Procedures   38
        Adjusting Your CONFIG.SYS File   41
   Installing or Upgrading with the Setup Program   45
        Setup Can Use a Series of Default Values   45
        What's Going On behind the Scenes?   48
   Interpreting and Making Changes to the SETUP.INF File   53
        Sections Containing Generalized Installation Information   54
        Copying Files during the DOS Portion of Setup   56
        Installing for Particular Device Types   58
        Controlling Keyboards, Code Pages, and Pointing Devices   61
        Installing Networks and Fonts   63
        Copying Files during the Windows Portion of Setup   65
        Creating and Modifying Program Manager Groups   67
        Updating Various Configuration Files   68
        Installing the Hardware-Specific Entries   70
   After Setup Is Finished   72

Sidebars

Installing Windows on Your System   **35**
Your Bootable Floppy May Not Do the Job   **39**
Setting Up CONFIG.SYS to Free Up the Most
Conventional Memory   **43**
Using QEMM with Windows   **47**
Installing Windows with Nonstandard Hardware   **53**
An Interesting Variation on Multitasking   **61**
Interrupt Conflicts with SCSI Disks   **69**
Hardware Incompatibility   **71**
Speeding Up Windows with the TEMP Setting   **75**

3   *The Architecture of Windows*   *77*

Explaining the Mysteries of System Resources   78
    How Windows Consumes Resources   79
    Internal Perspectives on Resource Usage   82
Understanding the Windows Multitasking Architecture   85
    Clarifying the Techniques of Message Passing   86
    Understanding the Windows Programming Model   88
    Protecting Data with the Share Command   92
Exploring Some Interesting Windows Connections   94
    Exploring the Nature of WINDOWS .EXE Files   94
    Enhancing DOS Programs to Run under Windows   97
    Running Windows under DESQview 386   101
Exploring the Crucial Windows Interfaces   104
    Understanding the Graphics Device Interface   104
    Understanding the Multiple Document Interface   107
    Understanding the DOS Protected Mode Interface   110

Sidebars

How to Quantify Your Application's Resource
Consumption   **81**
Keeping System Resources at a Maximum   **83**
Out of Memory or Out of System Resources?   **85**
Windows Multitasking Is Not Preemptive Multitasking   **89**
Developing Applications in Foreign Languages   **93**
Using SHARE to Prevent Data File Corruption   **95**
Tips for Writing DOS Programs That Run
under Windows   **101**
Running Windows Applications in Protected Mode   **113**

4   *How Windows Manages Memory*   *115*

Real Mode vs. Segmented Mode Addressing   116
    How Do Programs Construct Addresses in Real Mode?   117

Addressing an Extra 64K with the A20 Line 120

What Is This Thing Called Protected Mode? 122

How Do Programs Construct Addresses
in Protected Mode? 123

Mapping Logical to Physical Memory 128

Understanding the Different Types of Memory 129

Revisiting the Basics of Memory Addressing 129

Expanded Memory Addressing 133

Exploring How Windows Uses Memory 142

Using Memory in Standard Mode 142

Using Memory in 386 Enhanced Mode 146

Understanding Virtual Memory 159

Windows Uses Demand Paging in 386 Enhanced Mode 160

Swapping Creates Virtual Memory from
Hard-Disk Space 162

Sidebars

What Kind of Memory Should You Add? **117**

Using QEMM and Windows **121**

Upgrading Your System RAM **131**

RSIS Breaks the 640K Barrier for DOS Applications **137**

Gaining Memory by Changing the Windows Shell **143**

Buying New Memory Chips **147**

Regaining Conventional Memory by Using UMBs **151**

Disabling ROM Shadowing in Hardware **155**

Increasing Memory for Starting New Applications **157**

RAM Disks and Swap Files **163**

5 *Exchanging and Sharing Data* 167

Using the Clipboard to Exchange Data 169

Selecting Data to Exchange through the Clipboard 170

Capturing Screen and Window Images 174

Using the Clipboard Viewer   175
Transferring Information between Windows Applications   178
Transferring Information between DOS Applications   179
Using DDE and OLE for Application Communications   184
Understanding the Dynamic Nature of DDE   185
Taking a Look inside DDE   187
Understanding OLE's Application Connections   190
Using the Windows Packager Application   200

Sidebars

Use Cut and Delete Commands Judiciously   **173**

386 Enhanced Mode: Cut and Paste for
DOS Applications   **179**

Standard Mode: Cut and Paste for DOS Applications   **181**

Problems with Transferring Data between
Non-Windows Applications   **183**

What Good Is Object Linking and Embedding?   **197**

When to Use the Clipboard, DDE, and OLE   **199**

6   *Understanding Multimedia*   *205*

Understanding the Concepts of Multimedia   207
The Fundamentals of Multimedia Applications   208
A Historical Perspective   208
The Tools of the Trade   210
LANS and Multimedia   213
Application Ideas for Multimedia   214
Understanding the Multimedia Personal Computer   216
A CD-ROM Drive Is the Heart of the MPC   218
The Multimedia Extensions Make It All Possible   220
Selecting Your Multimedia PC Components   222
Choosing a CD-ROM Drive   223
Choosing a CD-ROM Software Application   228

Understanding Chip and Board Developments 230
Technical Underpinnings of Multimedia 232
How Do CD-ROM Disks Really Work? 232
Getting Sound On and Off CD-ROM Disks 234
Understanding MIDI 237
Understanding Data Compression 238
Understanding RIFF 240
Exciting Interactive Multimedia Applications 241
Curtain Call 242
Action! 244
IconAuthor 247
Multimedia Accessory Programs Included with Windows 250
Using the Sound Recorder 250
Using the Media Player 257

Sidebars

What Really Constitutes a Multimedia Application? **209**
LAN Users Need to Prepare for Multimedia Burdens **213**
Designing a Fancy Multimedia Workstation **215**
Constructing a Multimedia Platform **217**
Summarizing the Multimedia Extensions **219**
Data Compression Techniques for Multimedia **239**

PART II **Running Applications** **261**

7 *Behind-the-Scenes Secrets of Running Applications* 263

How to Start Your Applications 264
Issues to Consider Before Even Starting Windows 265
Contrasting Windows with Non-Windows Applications 266
Choosing Your Favorite Way to Start an Application 267
Using Drag and Drop to Load Data Files Automatically 270
Associating Data Files with Executable Files 271

Using Program Manager Properties
to Customize Execution | 275
Contrasting Standard Mode with 386 Enhanced Mode | 278
Streamlining the Windows Start-up | 282
Bypassing the Opening Windows Screen | 282
Replacing the Opening Windows Screen | 283
Controlling Window Size on Start-up | 285
Loading or Running Applications Automatically
at Start-up | 286
Specifying Your Own Windows Shell | 289
Running Your Applications Efficiently | 290
Backup Considerations Before and After
Running Applications | 290
Understanding Marked Applications | 295
Running a Single Application | 296
Preventing Monitor Burn-in | 299
Switching between Tasks | 301
Time Slicing in 386 Enhanced Mode | 306
Understanding the Concept of a Time Slice | 306
Controlling Time Allocations with Priority Settings | 308

Sidebars

Error: "Cannot Find File" | 267
Determining Existing File Associations | 273
The Two Modes of Windows 3.1 | 279
An AUTOEXEC.BAT Equivalent in WIN3 | 287
Dynamic Viewing of TEMP File Activity | 291
Reconstructing Program Manager Groups | 295
Allocating CPU Time Slices to Programs | 311

8   *Running DOS Applications under Windows* | 319

Preparing to Run DOS Applications | 322

Installing Non-Windows Applications   322
Preventing the Same DOS Applications
from Running Twice   326
Customizing an Application's Start-up   329
Iconizing Your Favorite Batch Files   331
Understanding the PIF Editor   332
Creating and Manipulating PIFs   333
Using the Default PIF Settings   335
Launching One Program with Multiple .PIF Files   338
Understanding the PIF Options Common to Both Modes   340
Entering the Program File Name   340
Entering the Window Title   341
Entering the Optional Parameters   342
Entering the Start-up Directory   343
Using Environment Variables as Option Entries   344
Understanding Standard Mode PIF Options   344
Controlling the Video Mode   345
Specifying the Conventional Memory Requirements   346
Controlling the Available Extended Memory   346
Preventing Problems That Arise from Sharing Hardware   347
Freeing Up Memory with the No Screen
Exchange Option   348
Preventing Any Program Switching   348
Closing an Application's Window on Exit   349
Saving the Screen Image   349
Reserving the Use of Certain Shortcut Keys   350
Understanding the Basic PIF Options in 386 Enhanced Mode 351
Controlling the Video Memory Settings   352
Specifying the Conventional Memory Requirements   353
Specifying the Expanded Memory Requirements   356
Controlling Available Extended Memory   357
Running a DOS Application in a Window   357
Running an Application in the Background
or in Exclusive Mode   359
Closing an Application's Window on Exit   361

Understanding the Advanced PIF Options
in 386 Enhanced Mode   362
  Controlling the Multitasking Options   363
  Controlling How DOS Applications Use Memory   365
  Using Display Options to Manage the Screen   368
  Understanding the Remaining Advanced Options   371
Running Memory-Resident DOS Applications (TSRs)   376
  Deciding When to Run a TSR   376
  Using Batch Files to Set Up a TSR Session   379
Special Considerations for Running DOS Applications   383
  Using a Mouse   383
  Avoiding Certain Commands and Programs   384
  Understanding a DOS Session's Environment   385
  Changing Execution-Time Settings   388

Sidebars

Some Common PIF Options Must Be Entered Twice   343
Alt+Tab Is Faster Than Alt+Esc or Ctrl+Esc   351
Background Communications and Faxing   361
Speeding Up 1-2-3 for DOS   367
Reducing Excess TSR Overhead   379
Initializing Windows with Your Favorite
DOS Applications   381
Loading TSRs: Memory vs. Convenience   385
Changing DOS Applications' Priority Settings
on the Fly   389

9 *Managing the Windows Environment*   393
Desktop Tips and Tricks   394
  Experimenting with the Mouse When
  Running Applications   394
  Working with the Keyboard   396

Translating between Applications with the Clipboard 398
Using the Program Manager Effectively 400
Changing an Application's Icon 400
Saving Your Program Manager Settings 402
Deleting Program Manager Groups and Icons 404
Using the File Manager Effectively 406
Finding a File Anywhere on a Disk 407
Removing Annoying Confirmation Requests 410
Using the File Manager Shortcut Keys 412
Manipulating Files Quickly 415
Pruning and Grafting Entire Directories 416
Special Features of the Copy and Move Commands 419
Tips for Using the Recorder Utility 420
Understanding the Recorder Utility 421
Automating Individual Recorder Macros 421
Tips for Using Other Utilities 425
Using the System File Editor 425
Using the Terminal Utility 427
Using the Clock Utility 429

Sidebars

Reducing Resource Consumption in the
Program Manager 395
Choosing Colorful Icons for Your Applications 403
Maintaining Your Arrangement of Program and
Group Items 405
Moving and Copying Icons between Program Groups 407
Controlling the Appearance of Confirmation
Messages 413
Selecting a Built-in Windows 3.1 Screen Saver 423

10 *Understanding Graphics, Color, and Video Standards*   431

Manipulating Screen Images   432
    Capturing Screen Images   433
    Using Graphics File Formats   434
Using and Controlling Colors   437
    Understanding the Windows Color Palette   438
    Assessing the Performance Impact of Colors
    and Resolution   442
    Changing Video Drivers   445
Understanding Video Standards   446
    Demystifying a Decade of Video Standards   447
    Selecting a Monitor for Your Windows System   449
Video Decisions That Improve Performance   453
    Which Monitor?   453
    How Many Colors?   454
    What About the Adapter's Video Memory?   456
    What About a Graphics Coprocessor?   457
    What About Continuous Edge Graphics?   458

Sidebars

Speeding Up Your Graphic Redisplays   **443**
An Impressive Video Product   **445**
Improving Readability in DOS Windows   **455**
Upgrading Your Video Board   **457**

PART III **Customizing Windows**   **461**

11 *Personalizing the Desktop and Customizing Hardware*   463

Using the Desktop Icon   464
    Dressing Up the Background of Your Desktop   465
    Switching Quickly between Applications   469

Adjusting Icon Spacing   471
Defining the Invisible Desktop Grid   472
Customizing the Program Manager Icons   474
Let Program Manager Arrange Your Icons   474
Create a Custom Group for Frequent Applications   474
Change the Look of Your Application Icons   476
Controlling Your Desktop's Colors   478
Customizing Ports, the Keyboard, and the Mouse   481
Configuring Your Serial Ports   481
Making Mouse and Keyboard Adjustments   483
Customizing Your Multimedia Hardware   486
Add the Multimedia Sound Drivers First   487
Using Sound Effects in Your System   489
Customizing MIDI Devices for Sound Effects   490
Customizing for an International Environment   497

Sidebars

Creating a New Program Item without Typing   **471**
Selecting Your Own Icons for Your Programs   **473**
Specifying a Working Directory for Any Application   **475**
Launching and Loading with One Icon   **477**
Tips for Customizing Screen Colors   **481**
Do You Have Fewer Serial Ports Than Serial Devices?   **483**

12 *Modifying WIN.INI and SYSTEM.INI*   *501*
Understanding the Basics of .INI Files   504
The Structure of a Typical .INI File   504
Documenting the Meaning of .INI Entries   506
Using Boolean Values to Turn Options On or Off   506
Understanding the WIN.INI File Settings   507
How Does Windows Use the WIN.INI File?   508
Using the [Windows] Section   511

Personalizing the Desktop Directly 519

Customizing Your File Extension Associations 520

Customizing the Country-Dependent Settings 522

Customizing Your System Ports 525

Setting Up and Editing Your System's Font Definitions 526

Managing Multimedia Sound Files 527

Customizing Your Windows Help Facility 528

Colorizing Your Windows Work Surface 529

Don't Trouble Yourself with the Remaining Sections 530

Understanding the SYSTEM.INI File Settings 532

Setting Up Customized Drivers and Devices 533

Managing the Performance of Non-Windows Applications 535

Enhancing Operations When in Standard Mode 536

Customizing Operations When in 386 Enhanced Mode 538

Sidebars

Keep Option Lines under 127 Characters **505**

Using SYSEDIT.EXE to Configure Your System **509**

Trimming the Fat from WIN.INI **511**

Removing All Traces of Applications **513**

Setting Up Associations without the File Manager **523**

Speeding Up File Access in Non-Windows Applications **555**

13 *Managing Fonts and Printed Output* *557*

Manipulating Typefaces and Fonts 558

Understanding the Terminology 559

Three Kinds of Screen Fonts 561

TrueType Fonts Are the State of the Art 564

Is TrueType Technology Really WYSIWYG? 564

Hinting Improves upon Outline Technology 566

Specifying Screen Fonts in Your Windows System   567

    Controlling Fonts in Standard Windows   567

    Controlling Fonts in Sizable DOS Application Windows   569

    Installing New Fonts in Your System   569

Using Special Characters from Any Font   571

Managing Printers and Ports   574

    Types of Printer Fonts   575

    Installing a Printer   576

    Printing to a File   582

Managing the Printing Process Itself   585

    Understanding Print Queues   587

    Controlling Printing Speed   591

Sidebars

Downloading PostScript Fonts Automatically   **573**

Enhanced PCL Printer Configuration   **575**

Creating Formatted ASCII Output Files   **579**

Using Two Printers on a Single Port   **583**

Printing Unformatted ASCII Text to a File   **585**

Using More Than One Printer   **587**

Other Ideas for Improving Printing Speed   **589**

Printing Faster Than Print Manager Allows   **591**

PART IV   **Optimizing Windows**   **595**

14   *Turbocharging Your System*   597

Boosting System Performance with Disk Caching   598

    Understanding the Concepts behind Disk Caching   600

    Using a Software-Based Disk-Caching Program   602

    Using the SMARTDRV.EXE Disk-Caching Program   606

    Using a Hardware Cache Controller   612

Better Swapping Means Faster Multitasking   614
    Improving Swapping in 386 Enhanced Mode   615
    Improving Swapping in Standard Mode   620
Improving Throughput by Enhancing Your Hard Disk   623
    Optimizing a Hard Disk by Defragmentation   625
    Maximizing Hard-Disk Space   627
    Understanding the Impact of Your Hard Disk's Interleave   632
Enhancing Operational Speed   636
    Speeding Up Your Backups   636
    Accessing Required Files More Quickly   636
    Don't Run Unnecessary Applications   638
    Improving Performance of Non-Windows Applications   638

Sidebars

Thumbnail Summary of Key Optimization Techniques   599
Beginning Efficiency Settings   611
Avoid Double Buffering Your Cache   613
Permanent vs. Temporary Swapping   617
Controlling Swapping on Your Machine   621
Defragmenting Your Hard Disk   629
You Needn't Run Applications in the Background   637
Increasing Priority Increases Speed   639

15   *Fine-Tuning Your System Memory*   643
Freeing Up Memory Before Starting Windows   645
    Using DOS 5 to Maximize Available Windows Memory   646
    Managing Extended Memory with HIMEM.SYS   647
    Maximizing Memory Settings in the CONFIG.SYS File 648
    Managing Reserved Memory with EMM386.EXE   650
Optimizing the Use of Your Upper Memory Blocks   655
    The Order of Loading High Makes a Big Difference   656
    Obtaining More UMB Space Than Appears Available   657

Fitting Large Drivers or Programs into UMBs   662
Using Alternative Memory Managers   666
Maximizing the Benefit of Available Memory   669
Using a RAM Disk   669
Save Memory by Trimming System Fat   677
Using PIFs Effectively   679
Giving DOS Applications What They Need   682

Sidebars

Optimizing Windows 3.1 by Optimizing
DOS's CONFIG.SYS   **645**
Saving Memory by Eliminating Fonts   **679**

16 *Strategies for Networks and Communications*   685

Tips for Running Windows on Any Network   686
Maintaining Network Performance   686
Install the Network before Windows   689
Use Current Driver and Shell Versions   690
Beware of Conflicts   692
Installing Windows on a Network   695
Load the Workstation, Not the Network   696
Installing Windows on Many Identical Workstations   700
Enhancing Network Performance   706
Memory Considerations for SYSTEM.INI Settings   706
Multitasking Considerations for SYSTEM.INI Settings   710
Printing on a Network   713
Connecting to a Network Printer   713
Printing from a Windows Application
to a Network Printer   714
Accessing the Network Print Queue   715

Improving Windows Communications Facilities 715
    Using a Modem under Windows 716
    Connecting to Bulletin Boards and Information Services 716
    Avoiding Interference from "Call Waiting" 717
    Losing Characters during Communications 717
    Use Your Communications Ports in Order 718
    Detecting Idle Time May Be a Mistake 718

Sidebars

Starting Up Your Network **687**
Running Windows on Diskless Workstations **689**
Networks and Non-Windows Applications **693**
Port Address, Memory, and Interrupt Conflicts **695**
Managing Directory Access on a Network **699**
Maintaining Windows on a Network **701**

PART V   **Troubleshooting Windows**   **721**

17   *Questions Most Frequently Asked*   *725*

Questions about Setting Up Windows 726
Questions about Running Windows Applications 729
Questions about Running Non-Windows Applications 731
Questions about 386 Enhanced Mode 738
Questions about Memory Management 739
Questions about Printing 741
Questions about Video Displays 744
Questions about Object Linking and Embedding 745
Questions about Networking 746
Questions about Communications 749
Questions about Performance 752

Sidebars

Having Trouble Pasting Data into a Non-Windows
Application?   **733**

Some Non-Windows Applications Must Run
Exclusively   **735**

Difficulties in Switching Applications   **737**

Solving Printer Problems   **743**

Connecting to Network Resources   **747**

Are Your Non-Windows Applications Running
Very Slowly?   **753**

18 *Unrecoverable Application Errors*   *755*

What Are UAEs?   756
What Causes UAEs and System Integrity Violations?   758
    Incompatible Software or Hardware   760
    Incorrect Version of DOS   761
    Adapter Segment Conflicts   761
    Incorrect Setup   763
    Out-of-Date Application Versions   764
    Application-Specific Problems   765
    Solving Network Crashes   766
Using Diagnostic Software   768
    Using the Dr. Watson Utility   768
    Using the MSD Utility   770

Sidebars

All Crashes Are Not Really Crashes   **757**

Identifying the Source of Unrecoverable
Application Errors   **759**

Reserved Memory Adapter Conflicts   **763**

What to Do If a Non-Windows Application Freezes Up   **765**

Use Local Reboot to Kill a Frozen Program   **769**

19 *Inside Windows Error Messages*   777

    The Major System Error Messages   779
        Difficulties Starting Windows   779
        This Application Has Violated System Integrity 780
        Insufficient Memory   781
        Insufficient Disk Space   784
    Multitasking Error Messages   784
        Clipboard Errors   785
        File Access Errors   786
        Network Errors   786
        Communications Errors   787
        Warning: Termination Is a Last Resort   789
    File-Related Error Messages   789
        Generalized File Errors   789
        Object Linking and Embedding (OLE) Errors   790
        Non-Windows Applications Errors   792
    Device Error Messages   793
        The "Application Has Been Crashed" Message   793
        Device Conflict   794
    Video Error Messages   795
        The "Cannot Initialize the Adapter" Message 795
        The "Cannot Find Necessary Files" Message   795
        The "Cannot Run in a Window" Message   796
        The "Cannot Switch to a Full Screen" Message 796
    Printing Error Messages   797
        Problems with Font Availability   797
        Problems with Obtaining a Printout   798
        Limitations on Downloaded Fonts   799
        The "Print Manager Won't Print" Message   799
    Multimedia Error Messages   800
        Configuration or Hardware Problems   801
        Problems with Accessories   801

Sidebars

Dealing with "Out of Memory" Messages **783**

Solving Network Transfer Buffer Problems **787**

PART VI   **Using Applications on the
Companion Disks**   **805**

20   *Productivity Tools*   813

The BackMenu Program   814

The BigDesk Program   819

The Cachetst Program   822

The Chkmodem Program   826

The Clean Program (Memory)   829

The Clean Program (Viruses)   830

The Closer Program   838

The Cpuuse Program   839

The Exitw Program   840

The Pkware Programs   843

The Run Program   845

The Scan Program   846

The Sysgraph Program   855

The Unicom Program   857

The Vshield Program   860

The Wbar Program   867

The Wincheck Program   870

21   *Tools for Personalizing Windows*   881

The Address Program   882

The Apptimer Program   884

The Chess Program   887

The Dirnote Program   891

xxxiii

The Iconmstr Program   893
The Klotz Program   895
The Metcnvrt Program   898
The Mowin Program   900
The Paintshp Program   903
The Quote Program   905
The Reminder Program   908
The SnagIt Program   911
The Stop Program   913
The Taipei Program   915
The Timefram Program   919
The Whiskers Program   920
The Winclock Program   923
The Winplay Program   926
The Winpost Program   928
The Yacht Program   932

Glossary   935

Index   977

INTRODUCTION

Writing this book was a toil, but you will be the beneficiary. I struggled, as you will not have to, with various system limitations, incompatibilities, and crashes. I discovered hundreds of ways to improve Windows: to make it work easier, to make it work better, to make it work at all! Everything I have learned is now in your hands.

WHOM THIS BOOK IS FOR

This book is for you if you are an advanced or an intermediate user of Windows. If you are an advanced user, you will learn a host of unique, sophisticated tips and tricks for getting the most from your system. If you are an intermediate user and would like some help understanding how Windows works and how to improve your system, you will also benefit from reading this book.

Although this book is not aimed at beginners, if you are a curious beginner, you can garner many insights into why Windows works the way it does. You will also learn how to use Windows more efficiently and how to overcome problems you may be having.

My discussions of topics presume that you have experience with the fundamental operations of Windows, such as the basics of using the Program Manager and the File Manager. However, with most topics, I present fundamental explanations before wading into deeper waters.

HOW THIS BOOK IS ORGANIZED

I've organized the book into the following parts:

Part I: Understanding Windows offers you a peek behind the scenes. You will learn about the history of Windows, the internal installation controls offered by the Setup program and its SETUP.INF file, and the architectural underpinning of Windows. You will also learn how Windows manages memory and how data is shared among applications. Finally, you will learn about the state-of-the-art developments in multimedia for Windows.

Part II: Running Applications provides a host of techniques for running your applications more efficiently. You will learn about running Windows and non-Windows applications in both standard mode and 386 enhanced mode. You will also learn about how to manage the Windows environment with the Program Manager and File Manager. Finally, you'll learn about a number of video standards and techniques to help you improve your display resolution.

Part III: Customizing Windows focuses on methods for making Windows comfortable for you. You'll learn how to customize your desktop and hardware, how to make changes to the all-important WIN.INI and SYS-TEM.INI files, and how to manage fonts (including TrueType) and printed output under Windows.

Part IV: Optimizing Windows focuses on methods for enhancing the performance of your system. Just running applications or prettying up the desktop may not be enough for you. This part shows you how to make the most of your hard disk and CPU, how to fine-tune your system's memory, and how to run Windows on a network.

Part V: Troubleshooting Windows is the part for you if you've ever had any trouble with Windows. It not only answers the most commonly asked questions about Windows but it also explains how to deal with the wide range of Windows error messages, including Unrecoverable Application Errors.

Part VI: Using Applications on the Companion Disks contains two chapters that thoroughly summarize all the applications on the disks accompanying this book. These disks, which you will find attached to the inside of the back cover, contain a number of programs that will make working with Windows easier and more fun.

The book ends with the **Glossary,** which has a complete list of Windows terms and acronyms.

SPECIAL FEATURES OF THIS BOOK

Throughout this book, you will find tips, tricks, and techniques. Many of them are incorporated into the text, but many are also found in special notes scattered throughout the chapters, interspersed among related discussions. Some of the more extensive tips and special discussions appear on right-hand pages in specially screened sidebars. If you read only the notes and sidebars, you will acquire more ability to improve your system than is available anywhere else in one place.

I

Understanding Windows

Part I provides a foundation for the rest of the book. You will learn the fundamentals of Windows and what Windows has to offer. After learning about the history of Windows in Chapter 1, you'll go on to explore the internal workings of the Setup program in Chapter 2 and the architectural underpinning of Windows in Chapter 3. In Chapter 4, you'll learn how Windows manages memory, including how it constructs virtual memory to support multitasking in 386 enhanced mode. In Chapter 5, you'll learn the fundamentals of the Clipboard, Dynamic Data Exchange, and Object Linking and Embedding. Finally, in Chapter 6, you'll learn about the latest developments in multimedia and CD-ROM.

◆

C H A P T E R

1

A Little Background:
The History of Windows

T he bottom line is that I use Microsoft Windows 3.1, and I've used Windows 3.0 since it was released in early 1990. I can't say the same thing about OS/2 or Unix. I couldn't even say the same about earlier versions of Windows. Although OS/2 and Unix are powerful enough, neither of them supports the execution of my most important applications. Earlier Windows versions ran my applications but were either unacceptably slow or frustratingly undependable, or both.

My office and home computing environments now depend on Windows. I like the current appearance of its graphical user interface (GUI). I like the power and ease of its multitasking facilities. I like the capabilities of both the Windows and third-party utility programs that I now run. I like the fact that I can still run all my earlier DOS programs that don't yet have versions for Windows.

And, now that I've figured out when and how Windows doesn't completely work, I've got a stable, supportive, and working computer system. This book will show you how to have the same with Windows.

The lessons of the past are always available to help guide the future. Many software and hardware companies have fallen by the wayside because they didn't heed the lessons of the marketplace. Windows dramatizes a unique marketplace phenomenon. Microsoft's sheer size and the focused intensity of its young chairman, Bill Gates, have enabled it to surmount years of poor press about its early-'80s fledgling version of Windows.

But ongoing reports during the late 1980s of the death of Windows were greatly exaggerated. There are many stories to tell. You probably have your own. I'll tell you mine first, then I'll tell you the Microsoft story.

Large Corporations Are Making the Transition to Windows

Many corporations are switching their employee workstations from DOS to Windows. Here are some of the most frequently heard reasons for doing this:

◆ Windows has a graphical interface that is easy to use and understand.

◆ Windows applications and equivalent applications on existing Macintosh workstations look alike.

◆ The similar look and feel of applications using the Windows interface means easier personnel training. This leverages the investment in software education.

◆ Windows makes it easier to switch between multiple applications, and, depending on the workstation's processor, makes it possible to actually multitask applications as well.

◆ Windows is a hedging step in the direction of OS/2, when and if IBM releases a version of OS/2 that successfully runs Windows alongside OS/2 applications.

◆ MY PERSONAL EXPERIENCE WITH WINDOWS

I've run DOS since IBM first released its PC more than ten years ago. I tried to use Windows 1.0 when it was released back in 1985. It was deathly slow, its setup requirements were ill-defined, and its execution was undependable. In short, I hated it, and I dropped it off my disk before the platters had a chance even to warm up.

But after years of running only one program at a time under DOS and having come to the PC world from mainframes and minicomputers, the possibility of simultaneously running multiple programs on a PC was very appealing.

I tried Unix, but at the time, it had the same cryptic interface that it had on larger computers. Additionally, versions of the most popular business software were not available for Unix.

Next, I tried OS/2 in 1987. I even wrote two books about OS/2. They were profitable intellectually but not commercially—sort of like OS/2. The program seemed to have all the power and promise of a Concorde jet. Unfortunately, as has been the problem with some commercial airlines, OS/2 didn't seem to be able to sell seats on its plane. I couldn't find my favorite applications in OS/2 versions. Furthermore, because of various incompatibilities, OS/2 couldn't even run all my DOS programs.

Since I didn't really need multitasking, I was able to successfully run and switch among my favorite DOS applications with Software Carousel. But this was still just a task switcher, not a true multitasker. When I printed a chapter from my word processor, I couldn't readily switch to another task to continue working while the computer managed the printing. The print output from the word processor stopped as soon as I switched to my spreadsheet, or to any other program I had set up for switching.

A newer version of Software Carousel addressed this problem by incorporating a print spooler. But I soon discovered that once I switched from my word processor, no more print output made its way into the print spooler. Although printing continued for a while (until the contents of the print spooler were cleared), I had to return to the word processor partition to enable further output to proceed. It was an inconvenience that would have been cured by a true multitasking environment.

◆ DETERMINING WHAT TASKS ARE RUNNING

To display a Task List, which enables you to switch to any running task, press Ctrl+Esc or double-click anywhere on the screen wallpaper. All task-switching programs must have some way to switch among tasks. When you display a Task List in Windows, you have the opportunity to do more than simply switch from one program to another. As this book will clarify further, some tasks in Windows can be frozen when you switch away from them. Other tasks can continue to run (in the *background*) when you switch to a new task (which is then said to run in the *foreground*).

Then Windows 3.0 was released. Windows versions of major software applications were available immediately. All my DOS applications worked with no adjustments. Printing proceeded whenever I switched from one application to another. I had it all. And the interface was even attractive. Within a month, I had decided to switch completely to a Windows development environment. I spent the next year writing new books on DOS 5.0 and Lotus 1-2-3 in this environment. Except for occasional and inexplicable system crashes, I was a happy convert. And I could see how increasingly popular Windows was rapidly becoming.

My next book had to be about Windows. There were plenty of books about Paintbrush, Recorder, Terminal, and the other accessory programs included in Windows. Information was plentiful about running applications under Windows. But users were increasingly frustrated with the dearth of information about how Windows really works, and what goes on behind the scenes.

This book reveals all that I've found out about the true Windows. The major parts of the book will explain how to run applications in the Windows 3.1 environment, customize your copy of Windows, optimize your entire system, and troubleshoot whatever goes wrong. But that's getting ahead of our story.

◆ A BIOGRAPHER'S LOOK AT THE EVOLUTION OF WINDOWS

To the average PC user, desktop microcomputing began in about 1981, when the first IBM PC became available. Over the next several years, a number of software developers offered operating alternatives for users who ran more than a single application on their PC. VisiCorp sold a text-based, mouse-oriented operating environment called VisiOn. It incorporated multiple business applications into a single package. However, it never had the same success as VisiCorp's earlier spreadsheet software, VisiCalc. Both packages are now a part of PC lore.

Quarterdeck Office Systems also offered a similar environment called DesQ for running multiple applications. This package has evolved into one of today's viable multitasking alternatives to Windows, called DESQview. However, it primarily enables you to run existing DOS applications simultaneously. It does not offer the wealth of graphics applications now being developed daily for Windows.

One of DESQview's major advantages is that it uses your existing DOS software. You needn't learn new programs. On the other hand, if your existing programs have to communicate with each other, it is up to you to figure out how to make that happen.

For example, you can run dBASE IV and Lotus 1-2-3 in separate windows under DESQview. However, you may want to import an inventory database from dBASE IV into Lotus 1-2-3 to analyze inventory levels and run some quarterly projections. You will have to learn the necessary commands in either Lotus 1-2-3 or dBASE IV to transfer and convert the data. Less popular marketplace programs even require that you learn import and export commands in both programs before data can be transferred.

Vendors responded to this need by developing *integrated* applications, like Framework IV from Ashton-Tate (now Borland). These software packages contain a number of unique applications, like a spreadsheet, word processor, and database, that use consistent file formats and command structures. However, these formats and structures are usually proprietary. Although it is relatively easy to use the applications and share the data contained within an integrated package, it is no easier to interface that data to other software applications.

The Windows approach took all this history into account. Just as IBM had great success by making the hardware components of its PC public, Microsoft has had similar success by making the software structures of Windows public. In so doing, it has offered an attractive environment for third-party developers. They can write independent software packages that take advantage of many of the graphical interface tools. Microsoft solved the issue of convenient data sharing between applications, using simple cut-and-paste techniques and the mouse.

IT BEGAN WITH WINDOWS 1.0

In 1983, Microsoft announced its new graphical environment called Windows. And they continued to announce and advertise their product up until it was finally available in November 1985 at the annual Comdex show. Windows' greatest achievement in those two years was to popularize the computer term *vaporware* for software that has been announced but has not been released by the manufacturer for purchase.

Finally, people could see how the old research at Xerox's research center had influenced the PC world. Macintosh users had already seen the future. GUI systems were both attractive and easy to use. The debate between satisfied Macintosh users and satisfied PC Windows users goes on. I won't settle that debate in this book. But in the next section, you will learn about some of the characteristics of Windows 3.1's predecessors. And you will begin to understand the extraordinary evolution that has been going on in the PC operating-system world.

The Windows software development engineers faced a daunting task in 1983:

- ♦ The target machine was an IBM PC, which used a relatively slow 8088 processor.

- ♦ Most PCs had no more than 256K of RAM. Many prospective purchasers of Windows had hardware that only contained 128K of memory.

- ♦ Most PC owners did not have the luxury of a hard disk; the earliest PCs had either one or two floppy drives. So the first version of Windows had to be able to run from floppies. This slowed down operations considerably.

- ♦ DOS handled file management, and Windows had to rely completely on DOS. Naturally, this two-stage dependence added to the processing burden, slowing down the computer even more.

- ♦ The top-of-the-line color displays then available for the PC were based on the early Color/Graphics Adapter (CGA) standard, which displayed 320 × 200 pixels in four colors. This was hardly an impressive standard for a graphical user interface.

The earliest version of Windows was written in the industry-standard C language. Efforts were quickly redirected toward writing in assembly language, in the hope of counterbalancing the speed slowdowns resulting from the limited hardware environment. At the same time, the Windows 1.0 memory requirement was raised from 192K to 256K. The product hadn't even been released, and the hardware requirements had been increased. As today's newest version of Windows demonstrates, the tradition continues. To make room for added features and to ensure satisfactory performance, the minimum hardware needed to run Windows satisfactorily continues to increase.

In November 1985, the day finally arrived. After some good-natured ribbing by Microsoft Chairman Bill Gates and Vice President Steve Ballmer, the Comdex attendees were handed their own shrink-wrapped copies of the real thing. Windows 1.0 had graduated from vaporware to a real product.

But what kind of a product was this first release? It was a valiant first effort, but in comparison with other graphical interfaces already on the market, it had to take a backseat. Application windows were tiled, with no option to display them overlapped. The monitors on the early PCs had much lower resolution than those of today, so forced tiling was chosen to prevent losing or confusing windows that were not full screen.

This early version had its own zoom box that enabled users to maximize an application window to full-screen size or to restore the window to its previous size. In addition, a system menu enabled users to move, size, and iconize any window.

Horizontal and vertical scroll bars were similar in action to those on the Macintosh computer and to those in Digital Research's GEM graphical user interface, but pull-down menus differed. On the Macintosh, you had to hold down the mouse button to keep a menu displayed. In GEM, you simply had to move the mouse pointer over the menu name to pull down the menu. In Windows, you could simply click to display a menu, then click again to select a menu item or some other screen object.

File management was still relatively difficult. Because Windows relied on DOS's file system, a user had to make menu choices followed by directory and file-name entries. Compared to the Macintosh's ease of use, with its icon-based capabilities, this was a major weakness. The Windows MS-DOS Executive (an early predecessor of today's Program Manager) was not icon-based and required the user to fully understand DOS's directory structures to perform the simplest of housekeeping chores.

Users of Windows 1.0 quickly learned what a minimum configuration really meant: 256K of RAM was minimum, but Windows itself used up some of that, so applications now had less memory to run than without Windows. This forced some users to buy more memory right off the bat. In fact, the swapping aspect of Windows slowed down systems so much that many users realized right away that they would need to increase their actual RAM to 640K.

◆ WHAT IS SWAPPING?

Swapping is the term applied to Windows' management of memory and hard-disk space. Windows understands that a DOS computer can only address a limited amount of memory at one time (Chapter 4 explains this in detail). To run more tasks than can fit simultaneously in memory, Windows can judiciously read in program and data information from disk whenever it needs to. The process of reading information in from disk, in order to activate one of many tasks, is called swapping. To make room for the newly read information, Windows may need to write copies of existing memory information to a disk file (called the *swap file*).

Since swapping of application program code and data is disk-based, users quickly realized how important it was to have a hard disk, even though two floppies constituted the so-called minimum configuration.

Windows 1.0 also demonstrated the enduring *event-driven* architecture that continues to be at the core of Windows' multitasking capabilities. When any computer event occurs, such as a key press or mouse button press, Windows inserts a message in its central message queue that identifies the event. Each properly written Windows application is expected to check this queue continually for event messages and then to process the messages appropriately. This continues until you switch to a different application.

Windows 1.0 implemented on PCs the concept of *device independence* for applications. The Graphics Device Interface (GDI) enabled the writers of

Windows programs to ignore the vagaries of and variations among different pieces of hardware. Unlike DOS applications, which must include drivers for all possible printers, monitors, mice, and so on, a Windows application writes output to the GDI. Windows is then responsible for sending the graphics or formatted text to the hardware in use. If Windows includes a driver for a piece of hardware, that hardware can be used by an application.

IT GOT BETTER WITH WINDOWS 2.0

Windows 1.0 wasn't really accepted in the marketplace. If a company without the resources of Microsoft had been behind the product, Windows probably would have never made it to version 2.0. But two years later, it did just that. This time, Microsoft attempted to take a technological giant step by improving its product in a number of ways.

The most significant introduction was Dynamic Data Exchange (DDE). Windows applications could now communicate with each other, exchanging data easily. Windows could even automatically link the output of one program (e.g., a spreadsheet) to the data results of another program (e.g., a word processor). This represented an important leap over facilities in the Macintosh software of the day.

Windows now adhered to more and more of IBM's SAA (Systems Application Architecture) standard for graphical interfaces. In Windows 2.0, users could now select overlapping or tiled windows, and could select buttons that enlarged windows to full-screen size or shrunk them back to their former size. The sizing box in the lower-right corner of windows in version 1.0 was replaced by dynamic window borders. Any side or corner of a Window could be selected with the mouse and expanded or contracted. Since SAA did not depend upon the existence of a mouse, menus and individual menu items could now be selected with a variety of key combinations.

Conformance to SAA standards has been most beneficial to users. New applications must now adhere to the Windows standard, thereby adhering to the consistent SAA standard. It has become easier and easier to quickly learn and use new applications. Many Windows applications have many of the same menu choices, and the methods of accessing and navigating the menus are the same.

Windows 2.0 was somewhat easier to use than its predecessor. It provided easier data sharing among applications with the DDE facility. And it attracted more developers because of its attention to the elements of SAA. But it was still a poor performer, with much of the blame going to the inadequacies of the hardware of the day. Yes, it could still be run on less, but users realized that an AT with 640K was probably a necessity. Anything less remained frustratingly slow.

NEW PROCESSOR CHIPS GAVE LIFE TO WINDOWS /286 AND /386

In the mid-'80s, IBM and Microsoft developed OS/2. They chose the high-end 80286 processor found in the AT as their chip. They were to discover that the limitations of the 80286 chip had a good deal to do with constrained performance and with both developer and user hesitations. In late 1987, Microsoft admitted this and released two new versions of Windows. The first was a somewhat modified Windows 2.0; it was called Windows/286.

Using an extra hardware address line, Windows/286 could access 64K of extended memory while still in the real mode of the processor chip. (Each address line is essentially a wire that carries an electrical signal representing one bit of an address; the voltage of the line indicates whether the bit is a 0 or a 1.) This went beyond the former limitation of 640K of conventional DOS memory. In addition, Windows now supported LIM EMS 4.0 (the Lotus-Intel-Microsoft Expanded Memory Specification), which augmented its abilities to perform more effective memory management and to juggle multiple executing tasks.

The second late-1987 release was called Windows/386 and was a major improvement. It required a computer with what was then the most powerful of Intel's chips, the 80386, and required extended memory as well. Beyond simply gaining from the enhanced speed of this new chip, Windows gained from the 80386's virtual mode. Windows/386 included its own special memory manager, which could run multiple DOS applications in what is called the *virtual 8086* mode of the processor chip.

In addition, this new memory manager could emulate expanded memory that conformed to LIM EMS 4.0. To do this, Windows used available extended RAM and could thereby make expanded memory available on demand to specific applications (like Lotus 1-2-3). It even became possible to run some, if not all, applications within windows, rather than full screen.

♦ CONFIGURE EXPANDED MEMORY AS EXTENDED MEMORY

> Most expanded memory boards have switch settings that enable you to present the memory to the operating system as either expanded memory or extended memory. In general, Windows needs extended memory for most efficient operations. When properly configured, Windows can even emulate expanded memory, using just as much extended memory as it needs or as a particular non-Windows application needs. If you have an expanded memory board, set its switches to enable the memory to be used as extended memory.

THE MARKETPLACE BROUGHT US TO WINDOWS 3.0

Between 1987 and 1990, OS/2 was the principal focus of press attention and the primary expectation of the software development community. Major vendors like Borland committed great amounts of resources to the development of their products under the umbrella of OS/2. But marketplace acceptance of OS/2 was dismal, for many reasons.

To run OS/2, users were required to spend large amounts of money to bolster existing machines. Additionally, OS/2 would not run on many IBM clones, even if they nominally contained the necessary hardware. Because of a dearth of available OS/2-specific software, users could not even run some of their DOS applications, and they certainly could not multitask the DOS applications that did actually run under OS/2. In short, the door was open for Microsoft to move in.

In May 1990, Microsoft released Windows 3.0 with the early announcement that 3.0 was merely a short-term solution while they continued to develop

OS/2. But as we now know, Microsoft and IBM have split dramatically about the future of operating-system software. Although IBM continues to develop and market OS/2, Windows has seized the imagination and pocketbooks of millions of users worldwide.

Why did Windows 3.0 succeed?

♦ It was pretty—it had a new Program Manager with icons everywhere to represent applications that could be run.

♦ It was flexible—it would run on any PC, from an 8088 in real mode to an 80486 in protected mode.

♦ It was smart—it could use any combination of conventional, expanded, and extended memory, and adjust itself automatically to do so.

♦ It was powerful—it ran older applications in real mode, it ran newer applications in extended memory on 80x86 machines, it made efficient use of extended memory for code and data, it emulated expanded memory when necessary, and it supported multitasking and virtual mode.

WINDOWS 3.1 CARRIES THE BATON FORWARD

The major step forward was the release of Windows 3.0. It pulled together all the earlier developments into the most powerful and easiest-to-use environment yet. It was so well received by users that most major developers simply abandoned their OS/2 efforts and began concentrating on Windows versions of their software. This changed the tempo of the PC marketplace race and led to the well-known rift between IBM and Microsoft.

To many users, Windows 3.1 will not appear dramatically different from Windows 3.0. These users probably already run in standard or 386 enhanced mode (real mode has been dropped in this release), do not use the Windows File Manager, and have a stable system that rarely crashes. To many others, Windows 3.1 will be a welcome relief from the frustration of sudden system crashes and the feeble File Manager.

These are some of the new features found in 3.1:

◆ Support for multimedia audio and Media Control Interface (MCI) devices

◆ Easy font changes for windowed DOS applications

◆ New multimedia accessory programs

◆ Association of sounds with system events

◆ Mouse support for windowed DOS applications

◆ Quick and easy installation

◆ Local reboot of individual applications

◆ API argument checking for developers

◆ Dramatically improved File Manager

◆ More detailed UAE (Unrecoverable Application Error) messages

◆ TrueType outline fonts

◆ Enhanced function-based DDE

◆ Powerful Object Linking and Embedding (OLE)

◆ Drag-and-drop icon management

◆ Enhanced network support

◆ More extensive printing support

◆ Built-in screen saver with password protection

◆ BACKWARD COMPATIBILITY ENDED WITH WINDOWS 3.0

Real mode has been eliminated in Windows 3.1. If your favorite DOS, or an earlier Windows 2.*x*, application requires real mode to execute, it's time to obtain an updated Windows version or switch to a competitive product.

Running Windows on a Laptop

Laptops can run Windows, but certain trade-offs warrant serious consideration. Some laptops boast great Windows performance, but weigh in at 17 or more pounds. Yes, the hard disk, gas-plasma screen, and built-in battery or modem are nice, but walking around with this extra baggage can be fatiguing—at best.

Before making a decision about which laptop to buy, find out how much the laptop weighs with all the gear that it's going to contain. Aim for under 10 pounds—the lighter the better.

Run Windows on the laptop. Make sure that the screen is easily readable when several windows are showing. A VGA screen could easily flicker, or have poor color rendering, and be less readable than an EGA screen on another laptop.

Make sure that the hard disk is large enough for all the software you'll be using. Windows software can be voluminous—both Windows itself and the typical application.

Since a great many laptops use 286 processors, be prepared to use standard mode. You will not be able to multitask any DOS applications on a 286 laptop. If multitasking is essential, you'll need to spend the extra dollars for at least a 386SX laptop.

Error Handling Is Much Improved

Microsoft has dramatically improved the handling of errors in version 3.1. A new local reboot feature enables you to press Ctrl+Alt+Del to exit from a single application, rather than having to lose your entire system because of one errant application. In addition, when Windows itself detects an error, it now displays a more detailed error box, which identifies the culprit .EXE or .DLL file that caused the error. Everyone gains from local reboot capabilities, although the improved UAE error messages are primarily useful to developers during debugging.

Since Unrecoverable Application Errors have been the bane of many a Windows user and developer, the new API services will drastically reduce the number of inexplicable problems that occur. The greatly increased number of

API service calls provides for

- ◆ Enhanced parameter validation
- ◆ Resetting the system state after errors
- ◆ Restoring resources after errors
- ◆ More specific error messages
- ◆ Single application reboot
- ◆ Enhanced dialog support

Data Sharing Has Been Enhanced

The bonuses in Windows 3.1 for developers do not stop with just this list of facilities. The new Dynamic Data Exchange Management Library (DDEML), available only in protected mode, helps to make communication between tasks easier and safer.

◆ WHAT IS PROTECTED MODE?

Protected mode is an aspect of the 80x86 processor chip family. When operating in this mode, the hardware offers a number of addressability and task protection facilities. Windows takes advantage of some of these capabilities when it runs in its two software modes: standard mode and 386 enhanced mode. Standard mode runs on any 80x86 machine, while 386 enhanced mode runs only on 80386SX and higher chips.

Message exchange between applications is now based on services rather than on application name. This puts less burden on the programmer and more burden on the new API service calls to manage the conversations between server programs (those that have the desired information) and client programs (those that want to obtain the information).

The new facility for Object Linking and Embedding (OLE, which is pronounced "oh-lay") is a major internal enhancement to Windows. As

Overcoming the Dreaded UAE

The "Unrecoverable Application Error" (UAE) message, accompanied by the dismaying message "Terminating current application," was a plague on Windows 3.0 users. Things have improved in Windows 3.1. Among many other improvements are the following:

◆ Parameter testing for API (Application Programming Interface) calls has been improved, resulting in error messages that more frequently identify the offending program and the reason for the problem.

◆ Font choices and management have been dramatically improved with the inclusion of TrueType, a group of scalable screen and printer fonts (see Chapter 13).

◆ Applications can now share data in more sophisticated ways with Object Linking and Embedding (OLE). This improves on the more limited hot-link facet of Dynamic Data Exchange (DDE), which was available in earlier versions of Windows (see Chapter 5).

◆ Many new features appear in the Program Manager and File Manager. There is faster and more secure support for multitasking and networking operations.

applications incorporate the features of OLE, users will begin to discover valuable benefits. This facility makes it easier for programs to work with the data files (called *documents*) used by applications. OLE does this by defining a format for managing compound documents, which can contain a variety of forms of data to be manipulated by multiple applications.

By using simple Clipboard cut-and-paste techniques, you can transfer data from one application to another application with a onetime technique. But no awareness or connection exists between the two applications sharing the data in this way.

DDE improves on this by enabling a client application to establish a link to the source of the shared information (the server application). Changing the data in the server can modify the data in the client application automatically.

OLE goes one step further. Two copies of the data are maintained in a client application. One copy is in a display format, which is used only to visually represent the embedded object. When you select this object, the client application can launch the server program and transfer to it the second copy of the data (this copy is in the original server format). You can then use the server application to modify the data in its original form; when you're finished, the updated data is immediately available as an updated object in the then-reactivated client application. Chapter 5 presents this topic in further detail.

Windows 3.1 Improvements Are Easy to See

Users share in the range of Windows 3.1 improvements. A new Express Install program handles all installation steps automatically. It detects the system's hardware, runs the Microsoft System Diagnostics (MSD.EXE), and automatically configures your system. Optionally, you can make custom adjustments to any or all of the detected values.

The File Manager has been significantly improved in this latest version. It is much faster than before, and child windows can now be split in two, to view a directory tree on the left side and the file contents of that directory on the right side. You can open multiple directory windows at the same time, displaying and manipulating the icons, trees, and file elements from different directories on different drives or at different sites within a network. And the File Manager remembers its state, so it will come up each time with exactly the same configuration of open directory windows that you left it in the last time you used it.

◆ 386 ENHANCED MODE IS THE MOST POPULAR

With the reduced price of 386 and 386SX processors, the majority of Windows users are now taking advantage of 386 enhanced mode. In this mode, Windows can multitask both Windows and DOS applications. It uses all available RAM and switches quickly among running tasks. When necessary, Windows can even turn disk space into virtual RAM, providing more apparent memory to your applications than really exists on your computer. In addition, this mode offers more facilities to you for supercharging your installation (Chapter 14) and fine-tuning your system memory (Chapter 15).

The Program Manager also has a new face. A built-in program group called StartUp augments the WIN.INI facility, which can run one or more programs when Windows starts up. You can simply drag a copy of an existing icon from any other group to this special group, and the associated program will be run automatically when Windows starts up. You can also define a new program item directly in this group to create the same effect.

The Accessories group provides several new and useful application packages. The Media Player allows you to easily access and play stored multimedia files on your installed multimedia equipment. The Sound Recorder offers the ability to create, edit, and mix sound files, complete with special effects. The Object Packager provides a means to create and modify the appearance and content of the new Windows 3.1 OLE objects. The Character Map provides a helpful utility program for obtaining special (e.g., mathematical and international) characters for insertion into other applications via the Clipboard.

The Control Panel now offers a built-in Screen Saver option as part of the Desktop choice. You can select from among multiple video effects, and you can easily incorporate password protection for your system. The Control Panel also sports several new icons that provide access to new multimedia capabilities. The Sound icon facilitates the association of sounds with system events. The Drivers icon makes it easy to install or update the drivers for sound and video devices. The MIDI Mapper icon provides setup and customization of MIDI equipment on your Windows 3.1 system.

Windows 3.1 also provides users with improved network and printing support. The installation process supports additional network connections with more drivers. The File Manager remembers network drives and provides easy access to files located elsewhere on the network. The Control Panel further supports network operations by offering a number of setup and modification capabilities. There are also improvements in the extent of network error checking.

Resumption of interrupted print jobs is more automatic and easier to understand. Printer configuration is also easier, more flexible, and shows improved performance.

A new dynamic link library, COMMDLG.DLL (Common Dialog Library), offers programmers a significantly easier way to program the most frequently used dialog boxes. Consequently, users will now see more consistent dialog boxes when opening and saving files, printing, searching for and replacing text, selecting fonts, and customizing colors.

Drag and Drop is a simple set of new function calls that enhance your control of operations from the File Manager. You can now select one or more files and drag them to a runnable application, either a file name in a directory window or a screen icon that represents the application. Your program receives the file name or names you selected and can perform an action with your files. New applications can easily implement this feature.

Lastly, Windows 3.1 includes the outline font technology first developed by Apple Computer as part of its System 7.0 operating software. Called True-Type, it creates scalable screen and printer fonts. You can finally see on the screen almost exactly what a final printed version of your document will look like. These TrueType fonts are visually equivalent to the 13 standard Post-Script fonts. They come in four versions—normal, bold, italic, and bold italic—of Courier, Helvetica, and Times Roman, as well as a special Symbol font. However, since Microsoft has not licensed the names Helvetica or Times Roman, it has coined its own names, Arial and Times New Roman.

◆ WHERE DOES WINDOWS GO FROM HERE?

More and more businesses appear to be adopting the Windows environment and running Windows-based applications. The transition from text-based applications to window-based applications is occurring rapidly. When queried about why, most decision makers usually cite some combination

The Reality of OS/2 and Windows

Windows is hot. OS/2 is not. That's simplistic but true. People are buying Windows in droves. Developers are producing hundreds of useful applications for Windows; OS/2 development is languishing.

Architecturally, OS/2 is a superior product. But the bottom line is that not many users care. Yes, Windows crashes more frequently than OS/2. Yes, Windows users are limited to DOS's old file system, and OS/2 users have access to the more powerful High Performance File System (HPFS). Yes, OS/2 uses the more powerful, and more structurally successful, preemptive multitasking rather than the control-yielding technique of Windows. And yes, OS/2 supports multithreading within tasks, an extremely powerful second-level capability that enables developers to assure even smoother and faster program execution.

But who cares? I just want to run my favorite word processor, spreadsheet, and communications program. I can do that now with Windows. I don't have to wait until my software vendors develop OS/2 versions, if they ever do.

of the following reasons:

- ◆ A graphical interface is easier to understand than a character-based, command-prompt interface.

- ◆ Windows makes it easier to train employees in diverse applications.

- ◆ Windows can multitask several applications, or at least switch readily among them.

- ◆ Windows makes it easy to use similar applications on the Macintosh.

- ◆ Windows is a possible step toward OS/2 2.0 or 32-bit Windows.

- ◆ Windows requires reduced user support after workstation installation of the program.

One of these reasons is most interesting, because it speaks of the continuing marketplace hedge about OS/2. IBM still promotes, develops, and touts OS/2 as the operating system of the '90s. And I agree that the current version of OS/2 is technologically superior to the current version of Windows.

However, the typical user doesn't care so much about the operating system as he does about application programs. And Windows has more available applications now.

The remainder of these reasons will only be substantiated further by ongoing Windows development. Upcoming Windows development will attempt to play catch-up technologically. And even more, new Windows extensions will try to leapfrog over IBM's OS/2 efforts. Work is under way for a 32-bit version of Windows that will not be based on DOS; rather it will directly manage your hardware from start-up. In addition, this future version of Windows will rely on preemptive multitasking, now used by OS/2 and Unix, rather than the message passing that is currently at the heart of Windows application multitasking.

Various extensions are planned in the areas of multimedia (based on CD-ROM technology), pen recognition (to allow handwriting recognition), and networking (to support more network control from Windows workstations). Continuing emphasis on object management and protocols will lead to future Windows releases that support object-oriented file systems.

POINT-COUNTERPOINT: WINDOWS VS. IBM'S OS/2

As a programmer and developer, I like the internal design of OS/2. It's more powerful than Windows, easier to program in than Windows, and considerably less subject to system failure than Windows. The OS/2 kernel is the clear winner when it comes to graceful termination of errant programs. Windows still depends on the fragile DOS operating system. The OS/2 High Performance File System is faster than DOS's file allocation table (FAT) system. The HPFS also permits longer, more descriptive file names than DOS.

Preemptive multitasking often accounts for smoother and more balanced throughput, requiring less programmer planning and user tuning to work effectively. The message passing between Windows applications places the burden for efficient operation squarely on the Windows programmer's shoulders. DOS, or non-Windows, applications bear no such responsibility for operational efficiency. Chapter 7 discusses how programs receive processing time under Windows. You will learn there that non-Windows applications each receive a fixed slice of the CPU time, while all Windows applications must cooperatively share their own single slice of time. This is not true preemptive multitasking since the burden for deciding on the slice of time to be allotted to non-Windows applications falls on you. Although Windows will allocate default amounts of CPU time to non-Windows applications, you can influence these amounts by setting up program information files (PIFs) efficiently. Chapter 8 presents this facility in depth.

◆ DOES EVERY DOS PROGRAM REALLY NEED A PIF FILE?

No. Windows contains default values for running DOS applications, stored in the file _DEFAULT.PIF in your Windows SYSTEM directory. Windows uses these values for every DOS application that you initiate, if no unique PIF file exists for that application.

Create your own special PIF files for all your DOS applications. In this way, you can later customize the execution of each one independently, since they will all no longer rely on the standard defaults found in _DEFAULT.PIF.

Finally, OS/2 supports multithreading, which enables a programmer essentially to create two levels of multiple execution. The first one is among applications, like 1-2-3 and WordPerfect. The second level is within a single application, like PageMaker for OS/2. Mutually independent code segments can simultaneously run as separate threads of execution, producing a dramatic improvement in overall speed for applications that take advantage of this unique OS/2 feature.

However, as a user, I like being able to run every single one of my favorite applications under Windows. And, in 386 enhanced mode, I can and do multitask all of them. Furthermore, with Windows 3.1, I have a program shortcut key defined for each of them, so my workplace is very comfortable.

But IBM claims that I'll be able shortly to run all my Windows applications in protected fashion on the Presentation Manager (PM) desktop. Furthermore, they'll all run faster than under Windows itself. Well, I haven't personally seen this yet, although I keep getting told by IBM that it's coming soon. If it were true, I would be one of the first to jump back on the OS/2 bandwagon. But I think that severe technological hurdles remain to be surmounted before IBM can make it work for all Windows applications.

POINT-COUNTERPOINT: WINDOWS ON DIFFERENT PROCESSORS

OK. So for the moment, you're not going to use OS/2. And since you're reading this, you're probably not going to use a Macintosh either. Windows 3.0 was the last version of Windows that could run on the old IBM PC using an 8088 chip. Because real mode is no longer supported in version 3.1, you must run in standard mode or 386 enhanced mode, and you must have at least an 80286 processor.

◆ STANDARD MODE IS FASTER

In some memory configurations, you can only run standard mode, which does not support the multitasking of DOS applications. Since this mode does not have the overhead of 386 enhanced mode's multitasking, your programs will typically run faster. If you have the choice, select standard mode to switch conveniently from one DOS application to another. However, if you really need to run multiple DOS applications simultaneously, you must run in 386 enhanced mode.

Do You Still Have an Older 80286 Around?

Few professionals would advise you to purchase an 80286 to run Windows, although there are financial reasons to do so. You can buy complete 80286 systems for only hundreds of dollars. Realistically, however, you probably will decide to use Windows with an 80286 only if you already own one. In that case, you can make the best of it, using all the optimization strategies presented in Part 4 of this book.

Some factors may help you to decide whether to use an 80286 for your work. Most word processing and spreadsheet applications work just fine with this processor. Given the typically interactive nature of these applications, an

Which Is Better: A Macintosh or a PC Running Windows?

It's getting harder and harder to tell a Macintosh and a PC running Windows apart. Considering that they both evolved from research done by Xerox on graphical user interfaces, it's no surprise.

However, there are some notable distinctions. The Macintosh has a history based on ease of use. Tasks like associating files and launching programs require more effort and knowledge in the PC-based Windows product. The Macintosh Finder knows which application created which data file. This feature is closer to OS/2's High Performance File System than the DOS-based file system still used by Windows.

Configuring your system is still much less complex on a Macintosh. The System Folder on the Mac contains all appropriate initialization files. Adding or deleting files to the Folder can control the entire start-up. Windows requires entries in the DOS-based CONFIG.SYS and AUTOEXEC.BAT files, as well as the SYSTEM.INI and WIN.INI files.

But as the lyrics of an old song once read: "If you're not with the one you love, love the one you're with." Presumably, since you're reading this book, you're with Windows. The contents of this book will show you how to successfully love it.

80286 does the job as well as any other chip. However, if you're running a computer-aided design program like AutoCAD or any equivalently complex application, you need the fastest hardware you can get.

With a 286 PC, you can run Windows in standard mode. This means that you can run and display several Windows applications at the same time, switching between them with a keystroke or a click of the mouse. Even though each non-Windows application must run in full-screen mode, you can still load several of them and easily switch among them. In these cases, increasing your system's RAM will leverage its power to the greatest extent. A 286 PC with sufficient RAM to run its applications without swapping can easily outperform a 386 PC that is burdened by an insufficient amount of RAM or a poorly designed set of optimization settings.

Architecturally, the 286 chip is now at the bottom of the Windows support hierarchy. Compared with its predecessors, it was the first chip that offered a protected mode. This is now the primary mode that Windows requires. In this mode, the processor's segment registers contain pointers to memory (descriptor) tables rather than actual base addresses for the contents of the segment. The registers use 24 bits (versus only 20 in the original PC), which enables programs to construct base addresses anywhere within a 16MB address space.

The 386 Chip Is Now the Processor of Choice

With prices falling every week, the 386 is currently the processor of choice for new computer purchases. Although all the chip's features are not always used to their fullest advantage, the price/performance ratio is the best, offering both enhanced speed and expanded power at only modest cost increases over the 286.

The 386 offers a full 32-bit data bus, enabling the processor to access data twice as fast as the original PC, which had only a 16-bit bus. Additionally, with 32 bits, programs can construct addresses that range up to 4 gigabytes (4096MB). Combined with these features is the 386's ability to manage virtual memory by paging 4K blocks of memory to disk.

This paging feature lies at the heart of the 386's enhanced multitasking facility. When memory is accessed, the 386 chip verifies whether the requested address is in physical memory or whether the 4K block that contains that address has been written to a swap file on disk. If the address is on disk, the chip interrupts the operating system and the entire 4K block is read into memory.

Furthermore, the 386 has a special mode called virtual 86 (V86), which emulates multiple 8086 processors. Consequently, multiple non-Windows applications can run simultaneously and even within windows on your desktop. So the 386 promotes a faster, more powerful, and more flexible Windows desktop.

Is the Next-Generation 486 Chip Worth Buying?

Currently, the 386 is less expensive than the next-generation 486 chip. In part, this is due to competition from other vendors who make clone 386 chips. In part, this is also due to the additional features that make the 486 chip

Where Is the Computer Industry Headed?

My first experience with microcomputers was in 1981 (an Apple running Visi-Calc). In 1982 I purchased a Televideo that ran the 8-bit CP/M operating system in 64K of memory with the limited support of a dual disk drive.

One year later, I bought a 16-bit IBM XT with a 10MB hard disk and 640K of memory. I used this machine to write my first book. That was a plush upgrade, but it didn't feel that way for long.

In 1987, I bought a Compaq Portable 386 with 3MB of memory and a 40MB hard disk to run OS/2 and write my first book about that sophisticated operating system.

I am writing this book on my new 386 system, 25MHz, with 8MB of memory on the motherboard, a 105MB hard disk dedicated to Windows software alone, and an 80MB hard disk for the rest of my software. This 32-bit processor seems to be the chip of choice for the foreseeable future, and large amounts of memory and disk space seem to be a prerequisite for effective Windows processing.

Yes. There's the obvious trend toward bigger, more, and better. From 8 bits to 16 bits to 32 bits. From 64K to 640K to 8MB of RAM. From 320K floppy systems to 10MB hard disks to 105MB hard disks. But my sister still uses the old CP/M Televideo for word processing. And my son still uses an old PC for spreadsheet work. Then again, no one uses my old slide rule from college.

perform better than most 386 chips. For the most part, a 486 will enhance performance, but not necessarily in proportion to the amount of extra money you'll have to spend on it.

In essence, an 80486 processor chip combines in one chip the facilities of the 80386 chip, a floating-point math coprocessor (i.e., 80387), a memory cache controller, and an 8K static RAM cache. The 486 executes instructions faster than a 386, and it transfers data to and from memory faster. Numerical operations are dramatically faster because of the built-in math coprocessor.

Memory is accessed frequently in Windows. Since the 486 uses an 8K onboard memory cache and an integrated controller, references to memory locations can often be satisfied from the RAM cache. Access to this memory inside the chip is much faster than access from the RAM on the motherboard. The 486 can also use its cache to rearrange both reads and writes, making more efficient use of processor cycles.

In a complex Windows environment, I'd probably be looking at buying a 486 as my next computer. But the relative costs are still somewhat out of line, so I'll wait and continue running Windows 3.1 on my 386 machines.

Regardless of which processor you choose, turn to Chapter 2 now to discover the most efficient ways to set up your system and install Windows 3.1.

Certain Upgrade Features Are Better Than Others

If you have decided to upgrade an old system rather than purchase a completely new one, consider these suggestions for the best improvements:

♦ Don't bother with a 286. Go right to a 386.

♦ Don't bother with motherboard speeds less than 25 MHz. Particularly if you intend to multitask, Windows will need the extra hardware speed to perform adequately.

♦ Even though most new motherboards come with at least 1MB of memory, select a board that allows more RAM to be installed later. Memory on the main board is typically much faster than additional memory installed on a separate board. Get a board that permits at least 8MB.

♦ Look for a motherboard that contains a static RAM cache. This feature dramatically speeds up data flow between main memory and the CPU. Aim for at least 64K.

♦ Small motherboards fit into more of the older cases. Also, the smaller boards require less power, so your older system's power supply is likely to suffice.

♦ Much of the latest software comes on high-density disks. If your older system does not have one already, you should install a 5.25" 1.2MB or a 3.5" 1.44MB high-density drive.

♦ Buy as big a hard drive as you can afford.

♦ Buy a video board meant to speed Windows screen refreshes (see Chapter 10 for details).

2

Setup and Installation

There are many steps you can take to make your Windows system more efficient, more flexible, and more useful. Most of those steps can be taken at any time, using the knowledge presented in this book to tune and optimize your system. However, you can employ many of these techniques before you ever start Windows.

In this chapter, you will first learn how to effectively prepare your computer system for running Windows. Next, you will learn a number of special techniques for using the Setup program successfully to first install or subsequently modify your Windows system. In particular, you will learn how to interpret the special Setup information file (SETUP.INF). You will also learn what sorts of files are in your WINDOWS and SYSTEM subdirectories. Lastly, you will learn how to modify the WIN.COM program to customize the opening graphic screens.

◆ PREPARING YOUR SYSTEM FOR WINDOWS

Getting your computer ready to run Windows is not unlike getting it ready for any other sophisticated application. First, you must be sure that you have sufficient and correct hardware to run the program. Second, you must be sure that your version of DOS is recent enough to run the program and has been configured properly. Third, you should back up your hard disk. Last, you must read the documentation to learn how to perform the installation.

Installing Windows on Your System

If you usually hedge your bets when you install a new version of software, take heed of the following:

♦ Use the latest versions of HIMEM.SYS, SMARTDRV.EXE, and RAMDRIVE.SYS. This requires you to verify that these versions are referenced in the relevant lines of your system's CONFIG.SYS file. This is especially important if you have upgraded both DOS and Windows within the last year, since both products include versions of these drivers. You may be using third-party drivers, such as QEMM386.SYS, instead of Windows drivers. If this is the case, you will have to be even more careful to obtain the very latest versions of these drivers. There may even be a time lag, during which you cannot use the latest version of DOS or Windows, until the third-party vendor makes its own updates available to you.

♦ Adjust your PATH command in AUTOEXEC.BAT to include a reference to the directory that contains the latest release of Windows. If you have an earlier version of Windows on your disk, this is particularly important, because it allows you to properly use the correct Windows support files.

♦ Remember that the current directory is always searched first for a required file. Be sure that the current directory is not an earlier version of Windows, unless you are purposely planning to run that earlier version. In that case, remember to temporarily change the setting of your PATH environment variable.

IS YOUR HARDWARE REALLY READY?

Not all computers can run Windows. No matter what the outside of the computer says, you must have an operating system that supports Windows, a processor chip that works with Windows, and individual pieces of hardware, such as a monitor, that are in turn supported by Windows drivers. In addition, and much less obvious, your machine's BIOS (Basic Input/Output System) must be able to support Windows' needs as well.

You must be running a version of MS-DOS or PC-DOS that is 3.1 or higher. To get the most out of Windows, you should be running DOS 5.0 on your machine.

◆ USE DOS 5 TO FREE UP MORE THAN 600K

Windows can only make use of as much conventional memory as is available when you start it up. That's probably not news. The good news is that DOS 5 is a stable version of DOS and can be set up to offer more than 600K of conventional memory.

Also, you must have at least 1MB of RAM just to run Windows in standard mode. To multitask and run in 386 enhanced mode, you must have at least 2MB of memory. As you'll discover later in this book, you may need to double these numbers to make Windows work really well as opposed to just working at all.

But that's still not enough. Your computer must have an 80286 processor chip or higher just to run in standard mode. And to run in 386 enhanced mode, your computer must have an 80386SX chip or higher. If your computer is based on an older 8088 or 8086 processor, you cannot run Windows 3.1. The last version of Windows that supported real mode and these earlier chips was version 3.0.

Your system must have at least one floppy drive and one hard disk, or your system must be a diskless workstation connected to a network. On a 286 computer that can run only in standard mode, your hard disk must have at least 4.5MB of free space. This is an absolute minimum to load up the essential Windows files for running in standard mode. More free space ensures that you can load up some optional, yet useful, files as well. On a 386 computer, the additional files related to multitasking and virtual memory require that your hard disk have at least 5.5MB of free space.

These numbers are just barely adequate, however. Because you need to have additional disk space available for program files, temporary storage, print spooling, and swapping space, you should have at least another 10MB of free space.

There is no end of choice in monitors, printers, modems, and pointing devices for your computer, but you must select a device that is supported by Windows. Your Windows documentation lists all supported devices. Although it may be possible to use one of Windows' drivers for an unlisted device, you should select a supported device if at all possible. Even if a third-party manufacturer offers their own device driver, there is no guarantee that the driver will work in future versions of Windows. There may well come a time when Windows offers an upgrade that you can't run at all until your third-party vendor upgrades its driver to work with the upgraded version of Windows.

◆ CHANGING MONITORS

When you buy a new monitor, you must adjust certain Windows settings. To change monitors or video resolution, select Windows Setup from the Program Manager's Main group. Next, choose Change System Settings from the Options pull-down menu. Modify the Display entry by clicking on the down arrow beside it. Select a new display model, then choose OK.

Even if your computer has all the latest equipment, the right chip, enough disk space, and enough memory, Windows may still not work. It may not start at all, or if it starts, it may crash when you try to use a floppy-disk drive. Or God knows what else may happen. All of these symptoms may disappear if you simply update your current BIOS. The BIOS manufacturer's latest model is more likely to recognize and understand the hardware (i.e., interrupt) demands of the latest peripheral equipment. The BIOS ROM controls the PC's start-up and its subsequent connection to a variety of peripheral devices.

The latest BIOS can enable your computer to use the latest hardware, such as a 2.88MB floppy disk, or one of the large hard drives that store hundreds of megabytes, or one of the 101-key keyboards, with all function keys active and with separate keypads. Furthermore, unlike the original AT BIOS, which supported only 15 different hard-disk types, current BIOS versions support more than three times this many drive types. Upgrading your BIOS to get Windows to work may cost less than $100, which is a lot less than a new computer.

But the success of a BIOS upgrade is not dependent solely on hardware. Many software packages, including Windows and Novell Netware, require that code modifications be made to the latest BIOS. You can call Microsoft or your individual software vendor to determine whether the BIOS in your machine is new enough to support all features of your software. The BIOS version and manufacturer appear on your screen when your machine boots up.

But caution is still advised, even if you've determined that a BIOS upgrade is necessary. Most standard PC BIOS chips are made by three companies: AMI, Award, and Phoenix. Although these chips will usually work in clone computers, many computer manufacturers create their own BIOS, with program code that is customized for a particular hardware configuration. This customization may take the form of a completely proprietary chip (as is done by Compaq and Toshiba), or it may simply be a modified BIOS from one of the three major BIOS vendors. In either case, you must be sure to obtain a BIOS that is correct for your specific computer.

GOING BEYOND THE NORMAL BACKUP PROCEDURES

Everyone agrees that backing up hard disks regularly is a good idea. But most of us do not take the time to actually follow through on this good idea.

When I am writing a new book, my daily backup consists of simply copying the day's writing onto a floppy disk. I only do complete backups occasionally, even though it only takes about ten minutes. But whenever I go to the trouble of installing new applications, thereby creating new .INI, .GRP, or .PIF files, I send a copy of these critical Windows files to another directory on my hard disk.

Occasionally, a new application will incorrectly modify one of these important Windows files. If I have a recent copy of the file, I only need to copy the old version back to the WINDOWS directory to make everything right again. This takes seconds. If I have no backup of the file, it might take minutes to hours to re-create it correctly.

Suppose that you have backed up your hard disk and then Windows or some application crashes and destroys your file allocation table. Time to use that backup, right? Right, but how do you get your backed-up files onto this

Your Bootable Floppy May Not Do the Job

OK. You do your backups conscientiously. You never work from original disks. You have created a bootable floppy with a copy of COMMAND.COM and your AUTOEXEC.BAT and CONFIG.SYS files. You're home free, right?

Pretty much. Most system crashes only require rebooting. Some system modifications (new software, new settings, attempted Windows enhancements) can modify CONFIG.SYS in a way that prevents you from booting from your hard disk. So the standard bootable floppy works fine.

But what happens when the hard disk crashes? You've heard of it happening to others; it may have already happened to you. That bootable floppy won't work because the device drivers (among other things) on the hard disk are no longer accessible. Neither is the backup/restoration software with which to reconstruct your hard disk on the replacement drive, which set your wallet back a few hundred dollars.

Here is a suggestion: Construct your bootable floppy to have COMMAND.COM and its own unique CONFIG.SYS and AUTOEXEC.BAT files. Do not use device drivers located on the hard disk. Rather, copy the necessary drivers onto the floppy and leave off the full path name in CONFIG.SYS. For example, if you normally install a Bernoulli box driver with the command DEVICE=C:\BERNOULI\RCD.SYS /F, copy the RCD.SYS file into the root directory of your boot disk (for example, A:) and include this variation as a line in the disk's CONFIG.SYS: DEVICE=RCD.SYS /F.

The same goes for your AUTOEXEC.BAT file. You can run programs directly from the AUTOEXEC.BAT on the floppy if the programs you want to run have been copied to that floppy. Make sure that you also have your backup/restoration software on that bootable floppy!

trashed disk? If you backed up the hard disk with DOS's BACKUP command, you'll need a copy of DOS's RESTORE command. Do you have that handy on a separate disk? Depending on the extent of the damage, you may need to run DOS's FDISK and FORMAT utilities as well, before you can even begin to restore your files.

If you have backed up your hard disk with one of the sophisticated third-party utilities, like Back-It 4 from Gazelle Systems, do you have a copy of

Back-It 4 on a handy disk so that you can restore from the proprietary for-matted backup file?

The easiest thing to do is to make a boot disk before you have a problem. On that boot disk, place certain key programs:

- ◆ The operating system itself (also include the FDISK and FORMAT programs)
- ◆ Appropriate CONFIG.SYS and AUTOEXEC.BAT files, refer-encing any necessary hardware drivers or TSRs (terminate-and-stay-resident programs), setting any required environment variables and running any special memory management programs
- ◆ A copy of any necessary device driver
- ◆ A copy of any necessary backup/restoration program

You can back up an entire hard disk to a streaming tape cartridge, to a remov-able hard-disk cartridge (like the Bernoulli 90MB transportable), or simply to a very large group of floppies. However, I know how infrequently you actually do make such a large-scale backup. More commonly, you probably just make copies of critical files on a single floppy.

After all, most program crashes do not result in the loss of an entire disk. In fact, many Windows crashes result in a corruption of one of Windows' init-ialization (.INI) or Program Manager group (.GRP) definition files. You can save yourself a good deal of reconstruction time by backing up just these files on a regular basis. This activity only takes seconds but can save hours of recovery time.

A power failure while Windows is running, an Unrecoverable Application Error (UAE), or the installation of a new program that doesn't work properly can corrupt one or more of these files. Simply keep a separate directory, or a floppy disk, that just contains copies of your .GRP and .INI files.

If the system fails and one of these files is corrupted, these backup files will enable you to recover quickly. You can always compare the backup file to the current version to determine whether any modifications have been made. Look for lines that have been changed, deleted, or added. Especially in the area of video, even one mistaken line change in an .INI file can account for your Windows system being unable to start again.

If you have DOS 5, use the MIRROR/PARTN command to save partition table information to your system disk.

ADJUSTING YOUR CONFIG.SYS FILE

There are several things you can do to CONFIG.SYS. If you follow some of the hints in this section, you will be on your way to improving Windows' performance as well as making more conventional memory available to both Windows and the programs you run within Windows.

First of all, your CONFIG.SYS file will become fairly complicated in short order. Windows adds some lines, typically during installation. DOS has some options, which you will typically add on your own, once you've read the DOS documentation. This is especially true if you're running DOS 5, which is particularly beneficial to Windows if you set it up properly. Furthermore, a number of optimization settings can easily be added later.

◆ SETUP MAKES DELETIONS AND CHANGES TO CONFIG.SYS

When Setup installs Windows on your system, it analyzes a number of existing entries in your CONFIG.SYS file to determine whether it should modify it. To learn more about these changes, you can read the text control file named SETUP.INF, which is located in the SYSTEM directory. In the section labeled *[compatibility]*, you will see the names of drivers whose entries will be deleted if they are found in CONFIG.SYS. In the section labeled *[lim]*, you can read the names of LIM 4.0 drivers that will be replaced with a driver supplied by Windows. In the sections labeled *[diskcache]* and *[ramdrive]*, you can determine whether any disk-caching or disk-emulation driver entries can be updated in your CONFIG.SYS file.

You should begin with the simplest possible AUTOEXEC.BAT and CON-FIG.SYS files. In this way, you can easily determine what has been done by the Setup installation program. Similarly, after you've set up your version of Windows, you can keep track of this initial setup of your CONFIG.SYS and AUTOEXEC.BAT files to compare them with any updated versions created during the installation of new software.

The following suggestions address a number of specific CONFIG.SYS options. If you make any or all of these changes, be sure to create a backup copy of CONFIG.SYS before beginning. Also, make sure that you have a boot disk, in the event that one of your changes prevents you from booting from your hard disk. I pay particular attention to those options available under DOS 5 that can greatly enhance your Windows environment. For much more detail on managing DOS 5 itself, see my book *Mastering DOS 5*, SYBEX, 1991.

◆ Retain the SETVER command as the first command in CON-FIG.SYS. If you are sure that all programs and device drivers work successfully under DOS 5, you can remove this line and recapture the memory used by SETVER. Otherwise, leave it alone.

◆ Include the line STACKS=0,0 to disable stack management. This saves 1–2K of memory, since by default DOS 5 reserves space for the stack. Unless you later receive a stack-oriented error, you will not have to adjust this line.

◆ Unless you know better, do not initially include a line for the SMARTDRV disk-caching driver from Microsoft. (Chapter 14 discusses disk caching in more depth.) Once you're sure that your system will actually perform better, not worse, with a disk cache, you can edit AUTOEXEC.BAT to set up your own disk cache. At that time, it may be Microsoft's SMARTDRV, or it may be one of the third-party disk caches that are on the market.

◆ Do not bother with DOS's FASTOPEN command. It is essentially a "poor-man's" cache. And it doesn't work as efficiently as most disk-caching programs. If you have the memory to spare, a real disk-caching program will serve both your system and Windows itself more effectively.

◆ Set BUFFERS=30 if you do not use a disk cache; set BUFFERS=10 if you do use one. You must have some buffers for DOS, and for

Setting Up CONFIG.SYS to Free Up the Most Conventional Memory

Windows 3.1 has an extended memory manager, HIMEM.SYS. So does DOS 5. Check the file creation dates on each, and use the most recent one—for example, DEVICE=C:\WINDOWS\HIMEM.SYS.

A new configuration command in DOS 5 has two optional parts. If you include the line

DOS=HIGH,UMB

the first parameter (HIGH) directs DOS 5 to place its own internal tables in the High Memory Area (HMA). The HMA is located in the first 64K of extended memory. The HIGH parameter also tells DOS to place all required buffers in that same HMA. The second parameter (UMB) establishes the necessary links between conventional memory (below 640K) and the upper memory blocks (between 640K and 1MB). If you will be using DOS 5's EMM386.EXE to manage your UMBs, this parameter is necessary.

You must also load the EMM386.EXE driver to manage the UMB area. Here is an example, although the parameters may be different on your system:

DEVICE=C:\WINDOWS\EMM386.EXE NOEMS

This example uses the NOEMS (No Expanded Memory emulation) parameter. If you need emulated expanded memory, replace the NOEMS parameter with RAM. However, be aware that this costs you 64K in page-frame space, reducing the total UMB space otherwise available to your device drivers and applications.

Now that you've established management of the upper memory blocks, you can load device drivers in this area by using the DOS 5 configuration command DEVICEHIGH instead of the standard DEVICE command. For example, to load the familiar ANSI.SYS, you enter DEVICEHIGH=C:\DOS\ANSI.SYS.

Depending on the amount of memory needed by your drivers and on contiguous space available in the UMB area, DOS 5 will satisfy each DEVICEHIGH request by loading the specified device driver in high memory if possible. Unfortunately, you will not be notified if a driver can't fit in high memory; DOS 5 will simply load it in conventional memory. So use DOS 5's MEM command or any third-party memory analyzer to determine where drivers have actually been loaded.

other programs when not running Windows. However, with an active disk cache, the buffers only result in duplication of data, extra time spent scanning the buffers to find data that may well already be in the cache, and wasted memory.

◆ Set the LASTDRIVE parameter in CONFIG.SYS equal to the last drive (hard, floppy, network, RAM) you plan to use. If you don't use this line at all, DOS defaults to drive E, even if you have only a single partition and you use no drive letter beyond C. Each drive letter beyond C consumes more memory for table space that will no longer be available to Windows partitions.

◆ Do not load a MOUSE driver, unless you must run mouse-based DOS applications. Windows has its own built-in mouse driver, which is used by Windows applications and Windows itself.

◆ Load the HIMEM.SYS driver before any other drivers that use extended memory. Load the EMM386.EXE driver with the NOEMS parameter if none of your applications need expanded memory. Use the RAM parameter instead if your programs need access to expanded memory.

◆ Use the DEVICEHIGH command to load device drivers in available upper memory blocks. Use the LOADHIGH command later in your AUTOEXEC.BAT file to load small utilities and applications in any remaining UMBs. Remember that you must include the DOS=HIGH,UMB line somewhere in CONFIG.SYS to establish DOS 5's connection with the UMB area.

◆ Do not run TSR programs before running Windows—you may crash your system. Instead, run them later from within their own Windows partitions (see Chapter 8).

◆ SETTING UP AUTOEXEC.BAT TO FREE UP THE MOST CONVENTIONAL MEMORY

After properly setting up CONFIG.SYS, you can load TSRs and other selected applications in the UMB area with a new command: LOADHIGH (or LH). For example, to load DOS 5's new disk restoration and unformatting tool in this area, enter LOADHIGH MIRROR /TC. To load the new command reentry and macro management facility, enter LOADHIGH DOSKEY.

◆ INSTALLING OR UPGRADING WITH THE SETUP PROGRAM

Windows 3.1 has a powerful Setup program on disk number 1. Not only does this program make Windows easy to install but it copies itself onto your hard disk so that you can conveniently upgrade and configure your system. With the first disk in your A drive, you need only to switch to A: from the DOS command prompt and type *SETUP* to begin the installation.

If your system already has a running version of Windows, be sure to exit from it and run the Setup program from the DOS prompt. Also, remember to run the CHKDSK/F program before installing the new version of Windows. If you are installing Windows on a network, refer to Chapter 16.

This new Setup program has an initial character-based section, followed by a graphics-based portion that completes the installation with a sequence of on-screen windows. This procedure expands the compressed Windows 3.1 files, copies them to your hard disk, and guides you through setting up your printers and applications. Because these files are compressed, you cannot simply copy the files onto your hard disk. The Windows files are not usable until Setup decompresses them.

SETUP CAN USE A SERIES OF DEFAULT VALUES

At the beginning of the Setup process, you can choose between Express Setup and Custom Setup. The former handles everything for you using a collection of defaults, and the latter allows you to customize all aspects of the installation process. Choose Express Setup if your system is fairly straightforward, and you're willing to have Windows install the program with default values.

One of the best things about Setup is that you can always run it again from the Windows Setup icon in the Main group of the Program Manager. Since Setup can automatically install Windows applications that it finds on your hard disk, you can always rerun Windows Setup when you have new applications to install.

But clicking on Windows Setup can do much more for you than simply installing new applications. Initially, you'll see five information items in the Windows Setup dialog box: Display, Keyboard, Mouse, Network, and Swap file. The last item merely tells you what kind of swap file is in use on your system—permanent or temporary—and its size. The first four items can be changed online. To do this, pull down the Options menu in the dialog box; you'll see these choices:

◆ Change System Settings

◆ Set Up Applications

◆ Add/Remove Windows Components

To change any of the first four information items displayed in the dialog box, choose Change System Settings. A new dialog box appears, which offers you the opportunity to display separate list boxes containing possible choices for each existing display, keyboard, mouse, or network setting.

To install new Windows applications from disk, choose Set Up Applications. The dialog box that appears offers two choices. The first choice directs Setup to search your hard disk for all Windows applications to install, and the second choice prompts you for additional, specific application information. You are asked to enter a specific application path and file name, and the name of the program group to which to add the newly created program item.

Choosing Add/Remove Windows Components enables you to trade off disk space for system functionality. Windows offers a large group of optionally installed utility features. By installing only those features that you want or need in your system, you can retain a larger amount of disk space for your work. You can gain disk space by removing some of the optional components of your Windows system. You can gain functionality by adding some of the optional components. Table 2.1 summarizes the major components over which you have selection control.

Using QEMM with Windows

If you have QEMM, you are probably happy with your QEMM386.SYS driver. After all, it handles both extended and expanded memory, so you probably save more space than you would with DOS 5's HIMEM.SYS and EMM386.EXE. Also, it probably gives you more optional parametric controls over how UMB space is used. But suppose you'd like to place DOS 5's own internal tables and buffers in HMA. OK. You can forget about DOS 5's UMB manager. Just use the DOS=HIGH option alone to gain the conventional memory formerly used by DOS itself.

For example, on one of my machines running DOS 5, I have this sequence in my CONFIG.SYS:

DEVICE=C:\QEMM\QEMM386.SYS RAM ROM NOEMS X=C800-C9FF

DOS=HIGH

DEVICE=C:\QEMM\LOADHI.SYS /R:1 ATDOSXL.SYS

QEMM manages the UMB, all my device drivers are loaded explicitly in one or another of the upper regions (i.e., /R:), and the X switch excludes a particular ROM area used by my Plus Hard Card's device driver, ATDOSXL.SYS.

In each case, checking an optional component's box will install it. If you install new components, you must have your original Windows 3.1 disks. Unchecking an optional component's box will direct Setup to delete the appropriate files from your hard disk. If you want to add or remove only some of

TABLE 2.1: Optional Windows Components

Name	Approximate Size (in K)
README files	150
Windows accessories	1250
Windows games	250
Screen savers	50
Background wallpaper	250
Virtual memory	System dependent

the files in each category, choose Customize beside each choice. A separate dialog box will guide you through individual selections.

WHAT'S GOING ON BEHIND THE SCENES?

Setup operates in two separate modes, DOS and Windows, to install Windows successfully. In this section, you'll take a guided tour of the steps taken by Setup to install Windows.

The DOS Portion of Setup

In the first part of the installation, Setup detects your system's hardware and copies the necessary files to your Windows directories. After drawing the opening welcome screen, Setup saves any command-line parameters you specified, such as /N for network installation. See Table 2.2 for a summary of all available switch options.

At this point, Setup also saves information about your processor type and the amount of free memory. After verifying that the SETUP.INF file is not corrupted, Setup checks your version of DOS. You must be using DOS 3.10 or higher to run Windows 3.1.

TABLE 2.2: Switch Options for the SETUP Command

Switch	Action
/N	Installs network elements
/I	No hardware detection performed
/O:*filespec*	Uses a unique Setup information file
/S:*filepath*	Specifies a directory path to the Setup disk files
/B	Displays Setup progress in monochrome
/A	Copies all files on all disks to a specific directory
/H:*filespec*	Performs an automatic installation using a specified information file
/T	Searches for existing software that is compatible with Setup

At any point, Setup may terminate the installation with a message box explaining what aspect of the installation was unsuccessful. If no problems have arisen, Setup checks your DOS PATH to determine whether version 3.1 has already been installed on your system. If it has, Setup switches to update mode and ensures that the system drivers are current. If there is no current version of Windows listed in your PATH statement, Setup verifies that sufficient conventional memory exists for the installation.

If a previous version of Windows is found, Windows asks you whether you want to install version 3.1 in the same directory. If no previous version is found, Setup uses the default directory found in the [data] section of SETUP.INF, in the *defdir* parameter. This is normally C:\WINDOWS. At this point, Setup allows you to specify a different installation directory.

If Setup is updating a previous installation of Windows, it copies just a specified set of files to your WINDOWS directory and a specified set of drivers to your SYSTEM directory. The names of the individual files are found in the SETUP.INF file. Then, Setup replaces the old WINVER.EXE file in the WINDOWS directory with the latest version. This .EXE file contains the current Windows version number. Lastly, Setup displays a closing screen, which invites you to reboot now or return to DOS for other processing.

If Setup is not simply updating an earlier version of Windows, it then checks to see whether you specified the /I switch. If you have not inhibited automatic hardware detection with this switch, Setup executes a series of routines that check for specific hardware. These routines identify your processor, display, keyboard, mouse, and network connection. In addition, Setup performs certain legitimacy checks, such as checking whether 386 enhanced mode can be run on your machine's display (EGAMONO, for example, does not support 386 enhanced mode).

◆ SETUP DIFFICULTIES?

If you are having difficulties with Setup, try entering **SETUP /?** to see the various switches that you can use. One of these switches may be all you need to solve your problem. For example, the /M switch may be necessary to set up a portable 386 machine that has a monochrome monitor.

As another example, Setup may be experiencing difficulties in detecting equipment because of extra boards in your computer (e.g., a network or fax board). Try adding the /I switch to disable Setup's automatic detection of hardware.

After completing this phase, Setup displays the configuration it found. You can make any desired adjustments, then accept the final configuration. Setup copies all necessary files and creates a simple SYSTEM.INI file, which is necessary to run the Windows portion of Setup.

Because the Windows portion of the installation must be customized according to your hardware, Setup modifies the hardware-specific lines in the [boot] and [keyboard] sections of the SYSTEM.INI file. To ensure that Setup itself is in control when the Windows portion begins, the shell= line in SYSTEM.INI is temporarily set equal to SETUP.EXE. Additionally, Setup fills the [boot.description] section with appropriate text strings that will later be used to display in clear English the current configuration.

Next, Setup copies all files listed in the [boot] section to the SYSTEM directory. These include mostly hardware drivers and font files, although they may also include dynamic link library and screen saver files. Certain other entries are modified (like the 286 and 386 grabber files), depending on which modes are supported by your configuration.

By now, the SYSTEM.INI file should be ready for initiating Windows itself to take over the remainder of the complete installation process. WIN.COM now runs, using the information gathered during the DOS portion of Setup. WIN.COM runs with certain parameters, summarized in Table 2.3, to represent the hardware configuration. The WIN.COM file is actually built by combining the WIN.CNF file with the appropriate logo files.

WIN.COM initiates the Windows portion of the Setup process, with Setup as the controlling shell. If hardware detection has failed, or if you supplied incorrect hardware information, the DOS portion of Setup may have already failed, or the upcoming Windows portion may hang up your system.

TABLE 2.3: Optional Parameters Used by Setup for Running WIN.COM

Parameter	Explanation
-2	Installs standard mode
-3	Installs 386 enhanced mode
-e	Includes EGA.SYS in CONFIG.SYS
-h:x	Defines a unique machine-dependent access to extended memory
-m	Updates a DOS mouse driver
-o	Upgrades an existing version of Windows
-u	Installs on a network

The Windows Portion of Setup

When Windows is executed, it contains its core capabilities, including all drivers, fonts, and dynamic link libraries. If you have a color monitor, the light-gray background screen color is drawn, followed by the mouse pointer when the Windows mouse driver is loaded. Then, the gradient blue Windows Setup screen appears.

If this is an initial installation, Setup will be the boot shell and will read the parameters that accompanied the WIN.COM execution line, saving their values or setting flags to guide later processing. If Setup is not the boot shell, Setup can determine this and switch to simple maintenance mode. The standard dialog box that enables you to change system settings appears. In this way, the same Setup program can continue the installation, or handle simple adjustments if you execute Setup from the Windows Setup choice in the Program Manager's Main group.

This preliminary portion of the Windows mode installation ends by displaying another dialog box. You can specify whether you want to install applications, install printers, or view the README files included with Windows 3.1. Setup saves your responses for later in the installation process.

Three sections of the SETUP.INF file control which files and applications are copied to your hard disk. With a 286 processor, the [win.copy] section specifies which files are copied. With a 386 processor or higher, the [win.copy.386] section specifies which files are copied. On a network, the [win.copy.net] section specifies which files are copied. If your machine is a 386 or higher, and you are installing on a network, [win.copy.net] is the controlling section.

After these applications are copied, Setup copies all necessary system support files, such as the appropriate grabber, mouse, and monitor drivers. It copies any additional files needed to support virtual memory, virtual display devices, and network activity. In addition, it updates all affected entries in the WIN.INI and SYSTEM.INI files. Finally, it copies all TrueType outline fonts, along with any additional appropriate system fonts that match your display's aspect ratio.

In preparation for subsequent Windows start-ups, Setup changes the shell= entry in SYSTEM.INI from *Setup* to *Progman*. In this way, the Program Manager will be the controlling shell when you run Windows later. Then Setup uses the Dynamic Data Exchange mechanism to send several messages to the Program Manager. These instructions direct the Program Manager to create all indicated groups and install appropriate program items, as indicated in the SETUP.INF file. You can see these entries in the [progman.groups] section and in the sections that immediately follow.

At this point, Setup scans your CONFIG.SYS file for driver names whose lines it will retain and for incompatible drivers whose lines it will remove. Additionally, Setup removes any existing reference to the older SMARTDRV disk-cache driver. If RAMDRIVE.SYS is already installed, Setup updates the entry; otherwise, it does not install RAMDRIVE.SYS.

During its scan of CONFIG.SYS, Setup displays a message box if any incompatible drivers are found. Additionally, it checks the FILES command line to ensure that a sufficient number of file handles are available to Windows. (A *file handle* is a numeric identifier used by the operating system and by applications for a file that is opened and in use.) Setup asks at this point whether you want any changes to be handled automatically, reviewed and edited by you, or stored in a backup file for your later review and use.

After you respond to this set of choices, Setup takes the requested actions. If you requested earlier that printers or applications be installed during this session as well, Setup runs the necessary routines to perform these chores. Finally, Setup displays a message saying that Windows is installed.

Installing Windows with Nonstandard Hardware

Your system may have a nonstandard monitor or printer that does not appear in the list of options seen when you run Setup. Often, the manufacturer of the hardware will provide you with a special driver. If this is not the case, you may still be able to run Windows successfully.

You can try selecting one of the listed options that you know resembles your equipment. If you're not sure, select the simplest choice. Alternatively, you can select an option, try out your version of Windows, and then select a different option if the first one didn't work.

You can also try selecting one of the listed choices that you know can be emulated by your own hardware. For example, many laser printers have emulation modes that can make themselves appear to be one of the HP LaserJet models. Check your printer documentation for emulation possibilities.

◆ INTERPRETING AND MAKING CHANGES TO THE SETUP.INF FILE

The SETUP.INF file controls the installation of Windows and all related data and program files. Whether you are a user, developer, or network administrator, you can adjust the contents of this file to customize your specific installation process. You can define which applications are to be installed automatically. You can direct that specific printers or display drivers be installed. You can precisely control all aspects of the Windows hardware and software configuration.

In this section, you will learn what each section of the SETUP.INF file does and how to use each one for your own purposes. You will learn what optional controls exist, from network entries to TrueType entries. As indicated in the preceding section, much of the work performed by SETUP.EXE is done by reading the various entries in SETUP.INF and manipulating files and data accordingly. These entries indicate which files are copied and installed, which Program Manager groups are created, and which Windows and DOS applications are made into iconized entries in those program groups. Setup even controls the changes made to your CONFIG.SYS file.

Each section of SETUP.INF is named in square brackets. For example, the first section is named [setup] and includes one entry:

help=setup.hlp

This entry makes available to SETUP.EXE the name of the file that contains the help text, when and if it becomes necessary to access this information during installation. Most of the other sections contain more than just one entry. Rather than just list all entries, I'll explain what a typical entry in each section looks like. You can use a text or word processor to view your actual SETUP.INF file as you read the following sections of this chapter.

SECTIONS CONTAINING GENERALIZED INSTALLATION INFORMATION

After the [setup] section, which contains the name of the file containing help text for Setup itself, comes the [run] section. You can enter the names of any executable programs that you want to run when Setup completes its installation. The programs you name here will run in the order you enter them. Place one program name per line in this section.

The next section is [dialog], which contains the text data used in the various Setup dialogs. There are a number of entries, and their use is self-evident. For example:

caption = "Windows Setup"

exit   = "Exit Windows Setup"

title   = "Installing Windows 3.1"

options = "In addition to installing Windows 3.1, you can:"

Other entries control messages that you receive during the Setup process, such as while you are waiting for events to be completed:

printwait   = "Please wait while Setup configures your printer(s)..."

copywait = "For additional information on this Windows 3.10 release, view the README.WRI file. You can view this by double-clicking the 'Read Me' icon in the Main Group."

The next section, [data], contains a series of default values used by Setup. The first group of values is used to determine whether your hard disk has sufficient free space for the installation you are proposing. For example, the entry

new386full = 10500000,8000000 ; 10.5 Mb,8.0 Mb

indicates to Setup that a full installation of all files required in a 386 processing environment requires 10.5MB. The second number, 8.0MB, indicates the absolute minimum required if none of the Windows 3.1 optional components are installed. (See below for descriptions of other sections that control the installation of optional components.)

Table 2.4 briefly describes the remaining single keyword parameters in the [data] section.

TABLE 2.4: Single Keyword Parameters in the [data]Section

Parameter	Sample Value	Meaning of Value
startup	WIN.COM	Windows start-up program
defdir	C:\WINDOWS	Default installation directory
shortname	Windows	Short name of the program being installed
welcome	"Microsoft Windows Version 3.10"	Long name of the program being installed
deflang	usa	Name of the default language driver
defxlat	437	Default code-page number
defkeydll	usadll	Default keyboard dynamic link library name
readme	"notepad /.setup readme.txt"	Command line to display online text documentation

TABLE 2.4:   Single Keyword Parameters in the [data] Section (continued)

Parameter	Sample Value	Meaning of Value
register	"regedit /s setup.reg"	Command line to run the Registration Info Editor
tutor	"tutor.exe"	Program to teach how to use a mouse with Windows
NetSetup	FALSE	Flag to indicate whether or not this is a network installation
MouseDrv	TRUE	Flag to indicate whether or not a mouse driver is needed
Version	"3.10"	Version number

The next section, called [winexec], contains another series of single keyboard entries, which provide information for the DOS portion of the Setup procedure. Depending on the hardware information discovered during this portion, this section enables Setup to copy the correct kernel file, krnl286.exe or krnl386.exe. Following this, Setup uses other entries in this section to construct the correct command line to execute for initiating the Windows portion of Setup.

COPYING FILES DURING THE DOS PORTION OF SETUP

Most of the installation proceeds by copying files from various disks to the WINDOWS and SYSTEM directories. The disk identifier zero (0) is reserved to represent the WINDOWS directory; disk numbers 1, 2, and so on represent the numbered disks that are part of your installation package. The [disks] section contains an entry for each disk that Setup will prompt for at some point during the installation. A typical entry might look like this:

3 = . ,"Microsoft Windows 3.1 Disk #3", disk3

This particular entry is for the third disk in the package. The first parameter (a period) is the special shorthand notation for the current directory, although this parameter can be any valid path to the actual disk number. The second parameter is the full text identifier for the requested disk. The final parameter is a simple one-word abbreviation that is used to prompt for the disk if it is not in the installation drive when it is needed. To do this, Microsoft places a short text file with this name (i.e., disk*n*, where *n* is the disk number) on each installation disk.

You can add additional disks of your own to install your own applications during the Setup process. Simply add another entry in this format to this section, then adjust later sections of SETUP.INF to indicate which files should be copied over during installation.

The [windows] section lists a series of required and optional files that Setup copies to your WINDOWS directory during the DOS portion of installation. Typical entries might look like

1:system.src   ,Net

1:winhelp.exe

The leading digit that precedes the colon identifies for Setup which disk number must be in the drive in order to obtain the specified file. If the required disk number (e.g., 1) is not in the drive, Setup prompts you to place the appropriate disk in the drive before continuing. Only then can Setup be sure that it can begin the copying of the needed file (e.g., WINHELP.EXE). If an entry line has the Net parameter, then the associated file name (e.g., SYS-TEM.SRC) is copied over only if this is a network installation. Remember that to install on a network, you must have used the /N switch when starting Setup.

The [windows.system] section is similar to [windows], except that it governs which files are copied to the SYSTEM directory during the DOS portion of Setup. It includes GDI.EXE and USER.EXE, as well as a series of dynamic link libraries.

◆ UNDERSTANDING THE CORE OF WINDOWS

Three main .EXE files, found in the SYSTEM directory, constitute the core of Windows operations. The GDI.EXE file manages the Graphics Device Interface, which is responsible for submitting the graphics

commands appropriate to different display devices that are necessary to create the final images. The KRNL286.EXE file (for standard
mode) and KRNL386.EXE file (for 386 enhanced mode) manage the allocation of memory, and the loading and scheduling of tasks. The
USER.EXE file creates and manages all window-oriented operations.
These include creating, sizing, moving, and removing windows. They
also include icon and cursor operations, and the processing of keyboard and mouse inputs.

The next section is [shell], which defines for Setup what program is to become
the Windows shell:

progman.exe, "Windows Program Manager"

During installation, Setup changes the shell= line in the [boot] section of
SYSTEM.INI to ensure that the Program Manager will thereafter be the controlling shell.

INSTALLING FOR PARTICULAR DEVICE TYPES

The [display] section includes the information necessary for selecting a display type and matching it to the system and OEM (Original Equipment
Manufacturer) character sets. Each entry begins with a keyword, representing
a profile of the driver, and includes a series of parameters (following the equal
sign) for the following possible entries:

- Driver
- Description of driver
- Resolution
- 286 grabber
- Logo code
- VDD
- 386 grabber

♦ ega.sys

♦ Logo data

♦ Optional work section

For example, a typical entry might look like this:

v7e=

2:v7vga.drv,

"Video Seven 1024x768, 256 colors (1Mb)",

"100,120,120",

1:vgacolor.2gr,

1:vgalogo.lgo,

1:v7vdd.386,

1:v7vga.3gr,

,

2:vgalogo.rle,

v7e

Once again, the prefixed numbers in some entries indicate the disk that contains the specified file name. In general, these numbers are crucial. However, if you install Windows from a network server that contains all necessary files in a single directory, Setup will ignore these numbers.

The single comma in the third-to-last parameter entry means that the EGA.SYS driver is unnecessary for this display type. The VGALOGO.RLE data file is really the bit map that contains Microsoft's opening logo screen. The VDD entry (e.g., v7vdd.386) is the virtual display driver that provides enhanced-mode display support. The 386 grabber entry (e.g., v7vga.3gr) supports the selection of data from a windowed DOS program when in 386 enhanced mode.

The final parameter (*v7e* in this example) is optional and exists for only some of the display entries in this section. This entry is simply a code that is used to find a succeeding section that contains expanded details. For example, the v7e parameter in this Video Seven entry points to a subsequent section that looks like this:

[v7e]

,,system.ini,v7vga.drv,"WidthXHeight=","WidthXHeight=1024x76 8"

,,system.ini,v7vga.drv,"FontSize=","FontSize=large"

Each entry in these subsequent expansion sections contains its own series of parameters. These include up to six entries:

♦ An optional support file to be copied

♦ An optional destination directory (WINDOWS is the default)

♦ An optional .INI file to be created or updated

♦ A section name in the .INI file to be scanned

♦ An old line to be removed if found

♦ A new line to add to the specified section

In the first two lines in this [v7e] section, no optional file need be copied, and the SYSTEM.INI file is to be found in the default WINDOWS directory. If a "WidthXHeight=" line is found in the [v7vga] section, it is to be deleted. If no [v7vga] section is found, it should be created. In either case, the following line will be written into the section:

WidthXHeight=1024x768

A series of .GR3 sections now appear, one for each 386 grabber indicated in the [display] section just described. These sections list the font names that must be copied to support the particular 386 enhanced mode grabber. A typical section looks like this:

[VGA.3gr]

4:CGA40WOA.FON,4:CGA40850.FON

4:CGA80WOA.FON,4:CGA80850.FON

4:EGA40WOA.FON,3:EGA40850.FON

4:EGA80WOA.FON,4:EGA80850.FON

Almost all the files are found on disk 4. The files named by the first parameter (*WOA.FON) are copied over if your system is using the default USA code page (437). Otherwise, the files named by the second

An Interesting Variation on Multitasking

Multitasking in Windows, OS/2, Unix, and in just about every other operating system is really just an illusion. It is just an elaborate method of time slicing that divides up the processsor's computational capabilities among all runnable tasks. Ideally, every task appears to progress as fast as if there were no other activities going on.

True multitasking, however, requires a separate processor for each task. Only in this way can two tasks be executed simultaneously. Except in larger-scale computers, this is not usually the case. However, because the prices of microcomputers have gone down so much, some users have chosen simply to run two inexpensive computers simultaneously. For example, when a database sort runs on one and an extensive mathematical recomputation runs on the other, they are both running simultaneously and at maximum possible speeds.

An intermediate approach is possible. Your single computer has its own monitor and keyboard. Suppose you decide to spend only a moderate amount for a second stripped-down computer. Rather than spending hundreds of dollars to buy a second monitor and keyboard, consider buying a special switching box that has an A-B switch for both monitor and keyboard jacks. This basically means three plugs for the monitor and three plugs for the keyboard. The switching box contains one plug for the monitor and one plug for the cable to each computer; the same is true for the keyboard.

Naturally, if you set up your system in this way, you have to be careful when running applications that generate output to the shared screen. It works best when you run programs that either don't output directly to the screen or can refresh the screen when you switch back to that application/computer.

parameter (*850.FON) are copied over; these support the characters in the international code page (850).

CONTROLLING KEYBOARDS, CODE PAGES, AND POINTING DEVICES

The [keyboard.drivers] section is brief and lists a series of short names used to represent actual keyboard drivers. A typical entry looks like the following:

kbd　　= 1:keyboard.drv

The short names (e.g., *kbd*) are used in a subsequent [machines] section.

The [keyboard.types] section establishes short names that represent more descriptive text. A typical entry looks like the following:

t4s0enha="Enhanced 101 or 102 key US and Non US keyboards",nodll

The optional final parameter indicates the name of a keyboard-specific dynamic link library that may need to be installed to support this type of keyboard. In fact, even if this parameter is specified, the library name is installed only if Setup is installing Windows in a USA setting. This [keyboard.types] section is specific to a type of keyboard, whereas the preceding [keyboard.drivers] section is specific to a particular machine.

In an international setting, foreign-language support can be obtained from different keyboard tables. The [keyboard.tables] section lists the particular dynamic link libraries that would be required, along with short names and descriptive text entries. A typical entry looks like

dutdll = 3:kbdne.dll , "Dutch"

International settings that do not use the USA code-page table #437 will require access to separate translation tables. The next section, [codepages], includes a number of entries, each of which includes the code-page number, the translation table file, the OEM font, the WOA font, and an appropriate description. A typical entry looks like

863 = 2:xlat863.bin, 3:vga863.fon, 3:app850.fon, "Canadian-French (863)"

The [pointing.device] section lists all devices, mostly mouse devices, that are supported by Windows. A typical entry looks like

lmouse　= 3:lmouse.drv, "Logitech", 3:lvmd.386, lmouse

The name to the left of the equal sign is a short name, or *profile name*, to be used later by Setup to refer to this particular device entry. The first parameter specifies the actual driver name and the disk number that contains the file. The second parameter is the description that will appear in the hardware configuration. The third parameter defines the name of the file that provides enhanced-mode virtual-memory support. If this parameter is in a special form, like *x:*vmd*, this indicates that no special driver file exists. Rather, the device support is built into WIN386.EXE, as it is for the conventional two-button Microsoft mouse. The final parameter, lmouse, is the name of a subsequent additional section that contains further details that are unique to this particular pointing device. For example, the lmouse section specifies, among other things, the special Logitech mouse driver name.

♦ TURN ON MOUSE TRAILS FOR LCD SCREENS

If you have an LCD screen, like that found on many portable computers, it may be difficult to locate the mouse pointer or to see it when you move your mouse. Open up the Control Panel and select Mouse. Turn on the toggle option called Mouse Trails. This will create a rapidly fading trail of mouse pointers as you move the mouse, and will make it much easier to see where the mouse is at any moment.

The next section, [dos.mouse.drivers], includes entries that enable Setup to map the Windows mouse driver to the actual DOS mouse driver on your system. A typical entry looks like

mouse.com = 4:mouse.com, "MS Dos Mouse driver .COM ver 7.XX"

INSTALLING NETWORKS AND FONTS

The following sections of SETUP.INF include a series of entries that control adjustments to be made to SYSTEM.INI and WIN.INI. The [network] section entries associate a profile name with the network driver name and with the section name to which adjustments are to be made. Each main entry contains a profile name followed by multipart information in this form:

Profile name=

Driver name and location,

Network description,

Related help file,

Optional file,

Section name to add/modify in WIN.INI,

Section name to add/modify in SYSTEM.INI,

VDD,VDD,*n*... (support files for 386 enhanced mode)

A typical entry might look like the following:

novell =

2:netware.drv,

"Novell NetWare",

2:netware.hlp,

2:nwpopup.exe,

Novell_net,

,

x:*vnetbios,2:vnetware.386,2:vipx.386

In this example, the vnetbios support is built into Windows; the two remaining files (vnetware.386 and vipx.386) must be copied from disk 2 to completely support the network in 386 enhanced mode. The section name Novell_net identifies the section in WIN.INI that must be modified. Directly following this [network] section in SETUP.INF is a series of sections that are network-specific. These sections tell Setup exactly what modifications to make to the indicated WIN.INI section.

For example, the [Novell_net] section has only one line:

Windows,load,nwpopup.exe

All the network-specific sections contain entries like this. The first parameter (in this example, *Windows*) tells Setup the section name to modify, and the next two parameters tell Setup what keyword (in this example, *load*) is to be set to what value (nwpopup.exe). This entry results in

load=nwpopup.exe

being written into the [Windows] section of WIN.INI.

The following three sections ([sysfonts], [fixedfonts], and [oemfonts]) control the fonts that are to be installed. The entries are all in the same format, which includes the font file name, its description, and its screen resolution. Setup uses the [display] section in SETUP.INF to determine the closest match between screen and display resolution. A typical entry looks like

3:vgasys.fon,"VGA (640x480) resolution System Font", "100,96,96"

COPYING FILES DURING THE WINDOWS PORTION OF SETUP

During the Windows portion of Setup, many files are copied from the installation disks to your hard disk. Depending on your hardware configuration, a different group of files is copied. In addition, you have control over the optional installation of different sets of files.

Installing the Required Files

As mentioned earlier, [win.copy] defines the files to be copied on a 286 machine, [win.copy.net] defines the files to be copied for a network installation, and [win.copy.win386] defines the files to be copied for a 386 installation of any sort (network or not).

Each entry has two parameters, which specify the file names to copy and the destination. A typical entry looks like

#win.shell, 0:

If there is more than one file to copy, a pound sign (#) indicates another section name that lists all the individual file names to copy. In this example, a section named [win.shell] appears shortly after this entry from the [win.copy.win386] section. In this following section, each entry contains a file name and an optional text description. For example, some of the entries in the [win.shell] section look like

3:PRINTMAN.EXE, "Windows Print Manager"

4:MSD.EXE,   "Microsoft Diagnostics"

3:MSD.INI

3:DOSPRMPT.PIF

3:DRWATSON.EXE

As Setup copies a file, it displays the text description so that you know which file is being installed. If there is no text string beside an entry, this means that the entry is part of a group of related files. The first file's description remains on the screen until all files have been copied. In this example, *Microsoft Diagnostics* remains on the screen while MSD.EXE, MSD.INI, DOSPRMPT.PIF, and DRWATSON.EXE are copied.

Installing the Optional Files

In Windows 3.1, there are five groups of optional programs that you can easily install or remove to control the amount of disk space consumed. During Windows operations, you can customize these groups by pulling down the Options menu from the Control Panel in the Program Manager and selecting Add/Remove Windows Components. This provides the same online opportunity to make changes that Setup offers. The next five sections in SETUP.INF define the optional groups and the files associated with the groups.

The five optional groups are the following:

win.apps	Application programs, like PACKAGER.EXE
win.games	Games, like WINMINE.EXE
win.scrs	Screen savers, like SSSTARS.SCR
win.bmps	Wallpaper bit maps, like WEAVE.BMP
win.readme	README text files, like WININI.TXT

Each group consists of a series of entries in the following sample format, which specifies the file name to install or remove:

4:PBRUSH.HLP, "Paintbrush Help" , 46242

The file name and description are the first and second parameters, the number of bytes consumed is the third parameter, and a profile string name is the last parameter. The string is used in two ways. First, it is used by Setup to look up the file name in the Program Manager sections of SETUP.INF that follow. This process enables Setup to send proper DDE messages for adding or removing this program item from a Program Manager group. Second, the profile string may be necessary to look up the names of additional files that are related to the file name on this line. The additional file names will be found in the adjacent section of SETUP.INF, named [win.dependents]. For example, there is a PBRUSH entry in [win.dependents], which specifies that the PBRUSH.DLL file must be loaded or unloaded along with PBRUSH.EXE.

Installing the Application Font Files

Setup copies over a series of raster and vector font files. For each unique display, Setup chooses the correct files from the [fonts] section. Each entry looks like this example:

5:ROMAN.FON, "Roman (Plotter)", "CONTINUOUSSCALING"

The format of all entries is similar. The three parameters contain the font file name, the text description with possible point sizes, and the resolution. This particular entry represents a scalable font.

Immediately following these fonts come the entries for the TrueType fonts, located within the [ttfonts] section. Each TrueType font entry has a similar format, consisting of four parameters. A typical entry looks like

4:ARIALBD.FOT,"Arial Bold (TrueType)",6:arialbd.ttf, "Arial0100"

The first parameter denotes the file that contains font header information. The second parameter is a font description string. The third parameter specifies the actual font containing the necessary outline information. The last parameter is a combination value. It consists of a concatenated font family name (in this example, Arial) and a set of flags (e.g., 0100). The flags can take on three values: 0000 for a normal-weight font, 0100 for a bold font, and 1000 for an italic font.

CREATING AND MODIFYING
PROGRAM MANAGER GROUPS

Once the necessary files have been copied to your hard disk, Setup creates the necessary Program Manager groups and installs the iconized program items in them. The [progman.groups] section lists the group names, with a parameter to indicate whether to leave the group open (set the parameter to 1) or minimized (do not specify a second parameter) after Setup is completed. A typical entry looks like

group7=Main,1

which indicates that group7 is to be named *Main* and left open. The items to be installed in each group appear in succeeding group sections. For example, a section titled [groups7] contains a list of items to be installed in the Main group. One such item is

"MS-DOS Prompt", DOSPRMPT.PIF, PROGMAN.EXE, 9

The first parameter in each entry is the text that appears below the representive program item icon. The second parameter is the executable file name; in this case, it is a .PIF file. The third parameter is the file containing the icon to be used for this entry; in this case, the Program Manager itself (PROGMAN.EXE) provides the icon. The fourth parameter is the offset number of the icon to be used, when the icon file contains more than one icon. A final parameter can also appear that represents a subdirectory path from the WINDOWS directory in which to find the icon file.

UPDATING VARIOUS
CONFIGURATION FILES

Setup has a [compatibility] section with information entries about drivers that can cause problems with Windows. This is simply a list of driver names, like VDISK.SYS, which Setup scans for in your CONFIG.SYS file. Setup removes any lines from CONFIG.SYS that reference any of these driver names.

The SETUP.INF file also contains two sections that alert you to a number of TSR programs that produce problems when Setup runs. You should scan the list of file names in the [incompTSR1] section and make sure to remove any of these programs before running Setup. Any of them will definitely subvert Setup processing. A second section, [incompTSR2], lists another set of TSRs that might cause problems. If at all possible, remove these from memory before running Setup. A surprising number of DOS TSRs appear in the list of incompatible programs. Be sure to avoid running any of these utilities (i.e., Print, Subst, Join, Graphics, Assign, Append) before starting Windows.

In addition to updating the CONFIG.SYS file, SETUP.INF updates the WIN.INI file with the entries in the [wininiupdate] section. However, these updates are only necessary if you are upgrading to Windows 3.1 from an earlier

Interrupt Conflicts with SCSI Disks

One of the most common causes of system freeze-up when in 386 enhanced mode is a conflict in the handling of hardware interrupts. Under Windows, this can happen with SCSI (small computer system interface) hard-disk drives that use Direct Memory Access (DMA) and with Plus Development hard cards.

Symptoms of this problem include corrupted disk files, as well as system freeze-ups when more than one non-Windows application is running. At the very least, you should check to be sure that your hard-disk driver is current. If it is a SCSI driver, make sure that it is Windows 3.1-compatible and meets the standards for virtual DMA services. Additionally, you must be sure to configure the drive to use standard DMA channels, rather than any proprietary manufacturer data transfer method.

The best defense against these problems is to make the following entry yourself in the [386Enh] section of SYSTEM.INI:

VirtualHDIrq=False

By disabling this setting, a ROM routine handles the hard-disk interrupts. This is necessarily slower than allowing Windows to intercept and handle the interrupts in RAM. But it's better to have Windows work, albeit somewhat slower, than to have it not work at all.

version 2.*x* of Windows. If so, each of the entries in this section causes a new line to be added to a particular section of WIN.INI. For example, an entry line in this portion of SETUP.INF that looks like

ports,COM4:,"9600,n,8,1"

accounts for the following new line in the [ports] section of WIN.INI:

COM4:=9600,n,8,1

Other sections found at this point include [Update.Files], which lists the names of disk files that will be updated if they already exist on the disk. Additionally, the [Installable.Drivers] section lists the file names, types, and descriptions of optional drivers that can be installed if your system contains the appropriate hardware. For example, the entry

mpu401 = 3:mpu401.drv, "MIDI", "Roland MPU401",,

provides information about the Roland MPU401 MIDI device.

Typically, at this point, you'll find a [blowaway] section in SETUP.INF. The Windows portion of Setup can stop reading the SETUP.INF file at this point, because the remaining sections are either used by the Control Panel later or were already used earlier by the DOS portion of Setup.

The next section is [ini.upd.31] and contains a series of explicit adjustments to both WIN.INI and SYSTEM.INI; these adjustments are actually handled during the DOS portion of Setup. Many older .INI entries are now obsolete and are removed. Many new Windows 3.1 .INI entries have no predecessor entry and are simply added to the proper .INI file. Each entry in the [ini.upd.31] section consists of four parameters that specify

♦ Whether to update WIN.INI or SYSTEM.INI

♦ The name of the section to affect

♦ The old line to replace

♦ The new line to add to the section

If the old line entry (parameter 3) is blank, Setup just adds the new line to the section. If the new line entry (parameter 4) is blank, then the old line is just removed from the section. A typical entry looks like

system.ini, 386Enh, "device=*vhd", "device=*blockdev"

INSTALLING THE
HARDWARE-SPECIFIC ENTRIES

The last sections of SETUP.INF control various hardware-specific aspects of your system. The [system] section maps short names to specific system driver files. In particular, this section controls the selection of drivers that vary from system to system, such as for communications or sound. Here is an example:

sound = 1:mmsound.drv

The [machine] section installs the necessary system files for different OEM equipment. Although most computers use the first entry for IBM-compatible equipment, the remaining alternatives provide information for other

Hardware Incompatibility

The Setup program is aware of the most popular hardware and software. But Setup can't take care of all cases. Many of us use equipment and programs that are not at the top of the sales charts. Hardware in particular may use proprietary parts and not even adhere to industry standards.

For example, the Complete Communicator is a single board that includes a fax, modem, and voice-mail facility. Great hardware. Fair software. But that's just my personal experience speaking. The board also has a plug for connecting the Complete Page Scanner. However, the scanner uses the same IRQ that is used by the modem.

Unfortunately, under Windows, if you use the modem first, you can't then use the scanner. The only solution is to not use the convenient miniplug, or jack, on the back of the Complete Communicator board. Instead, you must use the separate board that comes with the scanner. Then, you can set a different IRQ for the modem (on the Complete Communicator board) and the scanner. This is a pain, but otherwise you'll have to exit Windows to use the scanner after doing any modem communications.

manufacturers. Each entry has the following structure:

profile string = description, system driver, keyboard driver, keyboard type, mouse driver, display driver, sound drv, communications driver, HIMEM switch, ebios support, cookies

An example entry might look like

zenith_386 = "Zenith: all 80386 based machines", system,kbd, t4s0enha, nomouse, egahires, sound, comm, , ebios, zen386_cookz

The last entry, structurally known as a *cookie*, is merely a forward pointer to a subsequent section that contains more entries with which to update the SYSTEM.INI file. In this example, the Zenith computer's cookie entry points forward to a section named [zen386_cookz]:

system.ini,386enh,"emmexclude=E000-EFFF",

This accounts for the emmexclude entry line being added to the [386Enh] section of your SYSTEM.INI file.

The [special_adapter] section contains entries that will be added to the [386Enh] section of your SYSTEM.INI file if Setup detects specific hardware, such as a CD-ROM drive:

cdrom = 2:lanman10.386

The [ebios] section, in conjunction with the information in the [machine] section, contains entries that indicate which files need to be copied to support the computer's Extended Basic Input/Output System (EBIOS). For example, the following entry is required for most Hewlett-Packard 386 machines:

hpebios = 2:hpebios.386,x:*ebios

The [language] section installs the relevant dynamic link libraries to support international, foreign-language-specific operations. Each language driver entry has a similar form, consisting of a short name, a DLL name, a description, and a language ID. The example

dan = 3:langsca.dll , "Danish" , 1030

specifies the name of the dynamic link library that supports Danish operations.

◆ AFTER SETUP IS FINISHED

Once Windows has been installed, you'll notice that an enormous number of files have been placed in your WINDOWS and SYSTEM directories. In this section, you'll learn the responsibilities of the primary files in those directories. Table 2.5 summarizes the file types, by extension, that you'll see.

◆ DEVICE DRIVERS DO NOT HAVE TO RESIDE IN THE ROOT

Many installation procedures copy a device driver to your root directory, then automatically add a DEVICE=drivername.sys line to your CONFIG.SYS file. Unfortunately, if you later update the software yourself, you have to keep track of the driver in the root and the driver in the application software directory. How many of you actually keep a copy of HIMEM.SYS in your root *and* your C:\DOS directories?

You can leave a single copy of device drivers in the application's principal directory, and use a full path name to specify it in your CONFIG.SYS file. For example:

DEVICE=C:\QEMM\QEMM386.SYS RAM ROM NOEMS X=C800-C9FF

DEVICE=C:\QEMM\LOADHI.SYS /R:1 C:\CC\CPCSCAN.SYS 2E0 3 3

This loads an extended memory manager (located in the C:\QEMM directory) and a scanner driver (located in the C:\CC directory).

The WIN.COM file is the Windows loader. When you type *win* at a command prompt, WIN.COM determines your machine type, its memory configuration, and what device drivers have been installed. Although you can force Windows to begin in standard mode by typing *WIN /2*, or in 386 enhanced mode by typing *WIN /3*, you may not actually be able to run in the requested mode. WIN.COM starts Windows in the best mode for your hardware. To see what mode you've started in, pull down the Help menu in the Program Manager and select About Program Manager.

The WIN.COM file is actually a combination of three files. During Setup, the following copy sequence occurs:

COPY /B WIN.CNF+VGALOGO.LGO+VGALOGO.RLE C:\WINDOWS\WIN.COM

This command combines three separate files into one, the start-up WIN.COM file. The first portion (WIN.CNF) contains the hardware detection code, and the second portion (*xxx*LOGO.LGO, where *xxx* represents your type of display—mine is a VGA) contains the code needed to load and display the .RLE bit-map file listed in the third portion (VGALOGO.RLE, or any RLE screen of your own choosing).

You can create your own opening display screen by simply obtaining a new .RLE bit-map file. Then, repeat the COPY command just shown but replace VGALOGO.RLE with your own .RLE file. An .RLE file is just a compressed version of a .BMP file, so you can also use an existing .BMP file and convert it to RLE format. The Paintshop program included on the second disk at the back of this book enables you to produce and convert your own RLE-compressed bit maps.

TABLE 2.5: Windows File Types by Extension

Extension	Explanation
2GR	Grabber file for standard mode screens
3GR	Grabber file for 386 enhanced mode screens
BAT	Batch file; CP_VIRT.BAT is provided as a generic means to change the PATH when running DOS applications under Windows
BMP	Bit-map file used by Paintbrush and as desktop wallpaper
CNF	A configuration verification .COM program
COM	A memory image DOS program
CPL	Control Panel message support
DLL	Dynamic link library
DRV	Hardware-driver dynamic link library
EXE	An executable Windows application
FON	Font dynamic link library
FOT	TrueType font header file
GRP	Program Manager application group file
HLP	Application help file
INF	Information file
INI	Program initialization file
LGO	Code file for displaying the opening logo
MOD	File used to run old DOS applications
PIF	Program information file; specifies how to run non-Windows applications
REG	Registration database file
RLE	Run Length Encoded file; a bit-map format containing the actual logo bit map
TTF	TrueType font file
TXT	Textual documentation file

Speeding Up Windows with the TEMP Setting

If you have a RAM disk (for example, F:), set the TEMP environment variable to a first-level subdirectory on that drive:

SET TEMP=F:\TEMP

If you have more than one hard disk (for example, C: and D:), and you have not chosen to use any memory for a RAM disk, set the TEMP variable to a first-level subdirectory on the fastest hard drive:

SET TEMP=C:\TEMP

Don't forget to create the \TEMP directory first. It's often easiest to combine both the directory creation and the variable setting in your AUTOEXEC.BAT file; for example,

MD F:\TEMP

SET TEMP=F:\TEMP

You might ask why it is important to set a TEMP environment variable at all. The answer is that Windows and various applications frequently create temporary files. If a TEMP variable exists, it specifies the location of these temporary files. Because a RAM disk is much faster than any hard disk, you will reduce system overhead dramatically during both temporary file creation and access.

You then might want to know why you should set TEMP to a first-level subdirectory rather than the root directory. This is because DOS limits the number of files that can reside in the root directory of any drive. You can't easily know in advance how many temporary files must be created, so by using a subdirectory, you avoid the potential problem of creating too many temporary files.

Finally, you might ask if it isn't slower to access files in a first-level subdirectory than in the root. Yes, that's true, but it's a minor difference, especially on a RAM disk, and it is not nearly as important a factor as the limitation noted in the preceding paragraph.

You will find more information in Chapter 7 to help you streamline your Windows start-up. Now that you understand how the preliminaries work and how Windows starts up, read Chapter 3 to take an overall look at the underlying Windows architecture.

3

The Architecture
of Windows

Viewing a beautiful home from the outside, you can judge its appearance and the workmanship of its builders. But you have to go inside, and if possible, into the basement, before you can judge its foundation. In this chapter, you'll take a closer look at the insides of Windows. If you are just a user and are happy to learn only the more visible aspects of Windows, then move on to the next chapter. But if you want to understand more of what goes on behind the scenes, read on. You'll learn much more about the foundation on which programmers have built the Windows graphical user interface.

Many questions have arisen about the amount of system resources that Windows consumes. You'll first gain a perspective on that topic. Next, you'll further explore the message-passing approach to multitasking, which sets Windows apart from other operating environments. You'll then learn a good deal more about internal structures, such as in Windows' .EXE files. You'll learn how programmers can enhance DOS programs to run more efficiently under Windows, and you'll even explore the unique way in which DESQview users can multitask Windows. Finally, you'll learn about the technical underpinnings of Windows, exploring the concepts and implementation of the Graphics Device Interface (GDI), Multiple Document Interface (MDI), and the DOS Protected Mode Interface (DPMI).

◆ EXPLAINING THE MYSTERIES OF SYSTEM RESOURCES

Your local schools have maximums on the number of classes they can offer and the number of students they can allow in each of those classes. These constraints are due to limits on the number of classrooms and on the number of teachers. The classrooms, teachers, and such additional items as books, are called resources. When critical resources are consumed, the school cannot present another class or allow even one more student into an existing class.

In a similar way, Windows has its own set of critical resources that are consumed as you run your programs. Running low on or out of critical resources can prevent you from starting a new program or can keep existing programs from successfully continuing execution. In this section, you'll discover what constitutes Windows resources and how these resources are consumed during program operations. You'll also explore the consumption of resources from both a user's and a programmer's perspective.

HOW WINDOWS CONSUMES RESOURCES

System memory is different from system resources. Because of this technical distinction, your system can have memory to spare yet be unable to start another program because system resources have fallen to an inadequate level. But exactly what are these resources that are consumed? The simplest way to understand resources is to consider them to be a place, limited in size, to store descriptions of graphic elements. In contrast to a similarly limited factor called overall system memory, in which programs and data are stored, Windows stores descriptions of graphic screen items in small portions of memory called *heap space*.

This space is limited to 64K for each program. Some resource space is consumed by the Graphics Device Interface (GDI.EXE) program, and other resource space is consumed by the User (USER.EXE) program. These two running programs, along with the correct kernel program for your processor (286KRNL.EXE or 386KRNL.EXE), form the core of your executing Windows management software. GDI.EXE depends on a library of API (Application Programming Interface) services to create and manage screen objects, such as bit maps, fonts, regions, brushes, pens, and palettes. USER.EXE depends on another library of API services to manage entire windows and menu items, such as icons, buttons, and various screen boxes (list, dialog, and so on).

Each time that any program processes a service call to create and manage any one of these items, Windows stores information about the data structure of the item. The space required to represent the various application graphic objects comes from the limited memory designated as system resource space. In the Program Manager, you can display the percentage of available system resources by pulling down the Help menu and selecting About Program Manager. This provides you with a sense of the resource consumption of your current application.

♦ INCREASE AVAILABLE SYSTEM RESOURCES

Program groups and displayed icons consume system resources. You can increase available resources by maximizing only those program groups that contain the application icons you need most often. You can also increase available resources by grouping the applications you use most frequently into a single new program group. Place other application icons in minimized groups, which can remain at the bottom of the Program Manager window.

If your application contains child windows of any sort, close unneeded ones. Child windows that contain many graphical user elements, such as push buttons, check boxes, and list boxes, consume more system resources than other child windows.

Each new screen window and each new visible icon on your screen consume more of these limited resources. In fact, the label below each icon is treated as a separate graphic element and therefore increases the resource consumption of each displayed icon.

With this understanding, there are many ways you can enhance the efficiency of your system. In general, you should do the following:

♦ Display as few windows as you can.

♦ Display as few child windows that have many icons as you can.

How to Quantify Your Application's Resource Consumption

Using the Program Manager, you can determine the percentage of system resources that remain available to the entire Windows system. To identify the percentage of resources consumed by your application, first run Windows with just the Program Manager as the active shell and no other applications loaded or running. Select the About Program Manager option from the Help pull-down menu, and note the percentage of System Resources that remain free.

Now run your application. Immediately, switch back to the Program Manager and note again the free System Resources percentage. (Remember to pull down the Help menu and select About Program Manager once again to update the percentage value.) You can see how much of your system resources are consumed just to get your application up and running.

Continue to run your application, performing all its normal chores. Presumably, windows are opened and closed, and various internal chores are performed. Return to the Program Manager to identify the free System Resources percentage. This provides you with an indication of how much additional burden is placed on the system by your application.

Lastly, exit your application and read the free resources percentage in the Program Manager again. This should be the same as it was before you began your application. Otherwise, it suggests that your application has allocated resources that it never returned to Windows.

♦ Only open the Program Manager groups that must be open, keeping other child groups closed unless needed.

♦ Organize your program items into the smallest number of program groups.

♦ Keep the icons you need most frequently in one open group, and organize all the others into groups that you only occasionally open.

Remember, resources are consumed only when icons, windows, and so on, must actually be displayed on your screen. Until then, the descriptions of these graphic elements consume only some memory space in the application's .EXE file. This space may consume some system memory, but there is no impact on Windows' resource space until the graphic items themselves must be displayed. Only at this point do the graphic descriptions consume a visible part of your desktop display and an invisible part of your system's resource space.

A subtle extension of this thinking applies to the three initialization facilities in Windows. You can use the load= and run= lines in WIN.INI to load various applications as icons or run them in windows. You can also place program icons in a special Windows 3.1 group called StartUp; these programs will run when you first start Windows. If you don't need to have certain programs loaded or running at start-up, do not do so. It looks pretty, and it's very convenient when you finally do need to use the programs, but it consumes system resources immediately rather than when you finally need them.

◆ WHICH PROGRAMS SHOULD YOU CLOSE?

Occasionally, you'll receive a screen message that you have run out of system resources. Since resources are different from memory, you may be able to recapture larger amounts of resources by closing a small program or closing just several small on-screen windows.

Closing a small program that uses many graphic objects may enable you to start a much larger program that doesn't require as many graphic resources. In this way, you may be able to use available system memory to run the larger program. Previously, the larger program might have been unable to use available memory, just because there wasn't sufficient system resource space left to accommodate its graphic needs.

INTERNAL PERSPECTIVES ON RESOURCE USAGE

Users often ask why programs are limited in one way or another, such as in the number of items that can be displayed, stored, or otherwise manipulated. Programmers often make trade-off decisions that inevitably lead to such limitations. For example, a Windows designer may decide to institute a

Keeping System Resources at a Maximum

Each application you launch consumes resources. Each child window within an application window consumes resources. Each graphic element within a window consumes resources.

Minimizing the number of graphic screen elements that Windows must maintain will reduce the burden on system resources. Avoiding running the application completely, however, will eliminate the entire burden. Naturally, you should run your application whenever you need to do so. However, you don't necessarily need to load or run the application each time you start Windows, just for the convenience of being able to switch quickly to the application.

Reduce the number of load= or run= lines in WIN.INI. Only load or run programs that you must have when Windows starts. If you are running Windows 3.1, you also have a StartUp program group in the Program Manager. Minimize the number of icons that you place in this group for the same reason. To minimize the burden on system resources, just initiate programs that you're sure you'll need immediately.

If you have any control over which child windows are opened or which child windows remain open, make sure you display as few as possible.

limitation to produce a faster result. Remember from Chapter 1 how the hardware in the 1980s so greatly burdened the performance of Windows. Many decisions were made to optimize execution speed.

At some point, the decision was made to store information about system resources in the 64K data segments associated with USER.EXE and GDI.EXE. Within each local heap, data can be accessed faster with 16-bit direct addresses. If graphic information is stored in another segment, which would clearly enable more resources to become available, the required intersegment addressing must be done with 32-bit addressing. This requires more CPU time. However, since Microsoft has already produced a new library of efficient 32-bit service calls, this is one of the steps being taken for surmounting past constraints and enhancing future performance.

Some programs are responsible for poor use of system resources. In many cases, a program does not correctly release resource space after it is no longer needed. When this occurs, it is a programmer's fault, and only a programmer can correct it.

Let's take a brief look at the four aspects of memory consumption that a programmer must consider. After all, resource space use is only one particular form of memory management.

Inside individual programs, whenever variables or other objects must be created, space must be made for their definition, or data structure. This is called *allocation*. When a program creates any screen object, resource space is set aside for the object's definition. Windows can dynamically allocate and deallocate this space (i.e., do the work), although the individual program is responsible for issuing the correct API calls (i.e., request the work).

The question of memory accessibility brings up the concept of *visibility*, which refers to which programs can directly access the contents of memory locations. For instance, a dynamically allocated segment, such as is used by the Dynamic Data Exchange (DDE) mechanism, is accessible to all programs. This allows data sharing among applications.

The third aspect of memory consumption is called *lifetime*, which refers to the amount of time an object exists. Normally, this is the time between when an object is created (i.e., allocated) and when an object is discarded (i.e., deallocated). If the application that creates an object does not deallocate the object when it is finished, it places a burden on Windows. If it is even possible (since more than one program can reference or use a graphic object), Windows must then free up graphic and user interface objects.

Lastly, a programmer must be aware of the *overhead* involved when dynamically allocating objects. A *global memory object* is one that is created by one program but is accessible and can be possibly used by Windows and by other programs. Each global memory object has a certain number of bytes of management data, beyond the space taken up by the object itself. Because of this, programmers can write code that uses less memory by using arrays of data structures rather than by using the more traditional and easier technique of linked lists.

Out of Memory or Out of System Resources?

Free memory comes from a large pool. For example, your system may have 2MB or 4MB or 8MB of RAM; this memory is doled out to applications as they request or need it.

System resources comes from a much smaller pool, made up of *local heaps*. Each local heap is just a small area of memory, usually 64K in size, that stores information about application windows and window elements. The more icons (which are small windows, as far as Windows is concerned), radio buttons, and child windows there are, the less remaining resource space there is.

No matter which version of Windows you are using, this heap space can be used up and your program will be unable to continue. In Windows 3.0, all system resources for all applications shared the two 64K local heaps of USER.EXE and GDI.EXE. In Windows 3.1, this resource allocation is shared more evenly across the local heap space available to each running application. Nevertheless, your application may run out of room to store window resource information, even though there is system memory available.

◆ UNDERSTANDING THE WINDOWS MULTITASKING ARCHITECTURE

In this section, you'll take a closer look at three aspects of multitasking. First, you'll investigate how Windows implements multitasking by using a message-passing strategy. Then, you'll briefly explore how a programmer prepares an executable file that includes both executable code and graphic resources. Lastly, you'll see how DOS's SHARE command can help to protect important data files during multitasking operations.

CLARIFYING THE TECHNIQUES
OF MESSAGE PASSING

Every Windows program must include a block of code to analyze and redirect messages that are sent to the application by Windows. In addition, the program must have a block of code for every window that the program displays and manages. This code is in addition to that needed to perform the application's normal chores. The first code group is called a *message loop*, and the other groups (one for each window) are called *message handlers*.

Figure 3.1 depicts how message passing works in the Windows environment. All events that occur in your Windows system, as well as all actions that must be initiated, generate messages. A message is a block of data that indicates what event has occurred, or what action must be taken. Within the body of the message are additional data items that further clarify the nature of the event or action.

For example, if a key is pressed, a message is generated that contains an indication of a keystroke, as well as a code that identifies which key was struck. If the mouse is moved, the message indicates a mouse event, as well as the coordinates of the new location of the mouse pointer. If a menu item is selected or a window must be redrawn, Windows generates a message. All messages are placed in a system queue and then sent to individual application message queues.

These message queues must be processed separately by each program. The message-loop code within a Windows application must constantly check its queue for messages that are pending from Windows for that application.

When a Windows application discovers that a message is pending, it directs the message to the appropriate application for handling. After processing the message, the message loop returns to Windows to check the queue for further messages.

A properly written application message loop enables Windows to perform multitasking. If a new message is pending for this application, the loop begins again and the message is processed. However, if there are no new messages for this application, Windows checks the system queue for messages meant for another running application. If one is found, Windows passes control to the

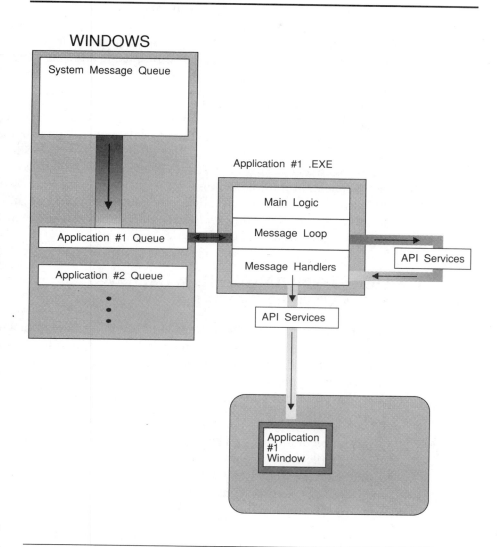

FIGURE 3.1: Windows message passing

other application. This application then checks for its message, using its own message loop. Finding a message, it reads, interprets, and acts on it, before continuing the loop by trying to read another message.

This manner of multitasking has been called "passing the baton," or *cooperative* multitasking. It works only if each Windows application uses a message loop and swiftly returns to check the system queue for more messages. One poorly written Windows application can dramatically drag down the efficiency of all other multitasking applications.

Cooperative multitasking contrasts with the *preemptive* multitasking method used by Unix and OS/2. In these environments, no one program can unduly affect any other. These operating systems will explicitly interrupt an executing application whenever its time slice expires. This ensures smooth multitasking, with an even distribution of CPU cycles. Under Windows, however, each application must consciously yield control to Windows by examining the message queue. This less efficient technique can produce an occasional stuttering effect on running applications, depending on how some programs (and Windows itself) process the various messages.

UNDERSTANDING THE WINDOWS PROGRAMMING MODEL

Programmers who write applications for the Windows environment must attend to two separate yet related processes. The first involves writing source code to carry out the chores of the application. The second, and relatively new aspect of programming in this GUI environment, involves developing the special files that contain the graphic elements of the application.

These files are called *resource* files. An executable Windows program is actually a combination of a standard executable module (a conventional source-code .EXE file) with a compiled resource file (an .RES file). You'll learn later in this chapter exactly how such a new file is structured. For now, refer to Figure 3.2 as I discuss how a programmer must follow two parallel paths to construct an executable Windows program.

All programmers must follow the path shown on the left side of Figure 3.2. Source instructions must be written in a programming language and stored in source files. These ASCII source-code files are often recognizable by the file extension used, such as a C program in a .C file or an assembler program in an .ASM file. A language compiler or an assembler then translates these source instructions into binary (or *object*) files, which typically have an

Windows Multitasking Is Not Preemptive Multitasking

In operating systems such as OS/2 and Unix, a task runs until its time slice expires, at most. At that time, it is preempted and another task is given access to the CPU for its allocated time slice. Although a task can give up control before it expires, such as during I/O waits, no task is allowed to execute for longer than its defined slice.

In Windows, however, a different method is used. It is called *message passing*. When an event occurs (such as a key press or a mouse button click), and some application action needs to be taken, Windows passes a message to your application. Applications are programmed in Windows to fetch such messages before taking action. After the action is performed, an application should return to Windows to attempt to read another message.

This request to read a message yields control back to Windows. The result may be that Windows returns control to the application to process yet another key press or mouse click, or Windows may pass control to another executing application. In this way, Windows can do its own brand of multitasking.

But if an application never yields to Windows, Windows will not readily preempt the application. This subjects Windows and all other running applications to the potential whims and bugs of an errant application. Your system will appear to run very slowly at this point. Consequently, Windows' message passing is not as effective as conventional preemptive multitasking.

.OBJ extension. Another program, called a Linker, gathers up all necessary object files, along with any externally referenced library routines, and produces an executable .EXE program.

Windows programmers must also define the various graphic resources to be used by the application. Resources include fonts, icons, menus, dialog boxes, text strings, shortcut keys, and cursors. Original data for resources can be found in many places, such as .ICO (icon) files, .BMP (bit map) files, and .DLG (dialog) files.

Resource editors are used to produce individual files for many of the resources that the application will use. A resource file (.RC) itself, however, contains

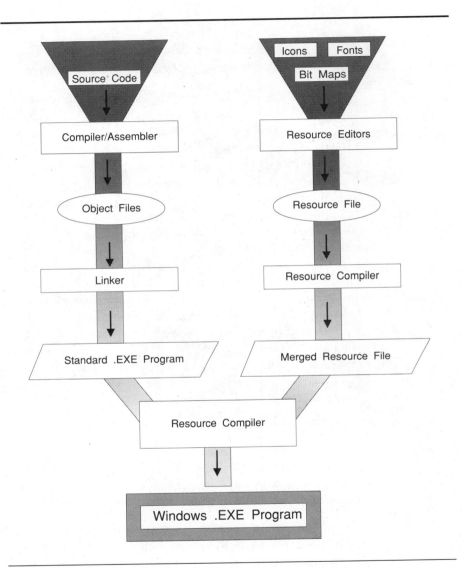

FIGURE 3.2: Building a Windows .EXE module

only simple ASCII text. In part, this text describes in English the resources used by the application.

However, only some resources can be directly described in English. These include dialog boxes, menus, text strings, and shortcut key definitions. Other resources are not so easily described in ASCII text. In part, the .RC file's text might contain the name of files (these names are then called *pointers*), which themselves contain the actual resources to be used. This is the case for icons, fonts, and bit maps. For these, the resource definitions must reside in binary fashion within separate files that are then referenced by name within the .RC resource file.

After a .RC file is created, it is compiled into a binary resource file (.RES). By converting the ASCII text entries into binary images, and then combining these with the binary data stored in any externally referenced graphic files, the resource compiler creates a single binary resource file with an .RES extension. The final step in producing an executable Windows application is to invoke the resource compiler a second time. During this last pass, the compiler combines the binary .RES file with the binary .EXE file.

There are several very good reasons why this strategy is used to produce your final executable Windows program. Most important, the various resources are not loaded into memory when you start an application. Each resource is loaded and therefore consumes resource memory only when the application explicitly loads it or when Windows itself needs it. This is why resources only burden your system when they are activated, such as when you must actually display an icon on your screen.

Also, it is very fast to compile a resource file alone. Compiling an entire application, on the other hand, can take a long time. It is not unheard of for it to take half an hour to an hour to produce the first .EXE file. However, if you change only the visual appearance of your application, you only need change the resource file, and recompile and recombine the resulting .RES file with the original .EXE file. This sequence is very quick and saves programmers considerable time during development.

Lastly, this dual process lends itself quite well to international development. You can store inside a single resource file all the text strings that are used within dialog boxes and menus. To create an executable version of your entire application, you only need to change the strings in the resource file, recompile it, and recombine it with the original .EXE file that contains the application's logic.

PROTECTING DATA WITH THE SHARE COMMAND

Multitasking applications forces users to confront a potentially dangerous situation. Unless the application running simultaneously uses completely separate data files, two or more of them may modify the same data. This can occur if multiple applications access and subsequently attempt to update the same data files, thereby compromising the integrity of those files. Because you can run the same application in two separate Windows sessions, you may accidentally modify the same data file from each session.

Unless you take special precautions or are running on a network that takes automatic precautions, accessing and updating the same files from two different Windows sessions is a prescription for disaster. Microsoft originally designed the SHARE command in DOS to protect network users from simultaneously accessing and possibly corrupting the same file. But the very same command can be used to safeguard your files when running under Windows in 386 enhanced mode.

If you are running Windows on a network node, your AUTOEXEC.BAT file probably already contains a SHARE command line. If you only run Windows some of the time, you can issue the SHARE command just before typing *WIN* to start Windows. However, if you run Windows as a matter of course when you boot up your system, you should probably include a SHARE command line in your AUTOEXEC.BAT file. Be careful to insert the SHARE command line after the PATH line and before the WIN line. This assumes that SHARE.EXE can be found in a directory that appears in your PATH statement.

How exactly does SHARE manage its magical protection role? When you load the SHARE.EXE program, it replaces the standard DOS routines that handle file opens, reads, and updates. SHARE provides the file open routine with a special area of memory (a default amount of 2048 bytes) that can store

Developing Applications in Foreign Languages

Windows applications are really built in two parts. The first part is familiar to anyone who has ever programmed in a computer language. It involves writing a series of instructions in a source language (like C++) that contains the functionality of the application. This code tells the computer what to do and in what order to do it. The code is compiled into object modules, then linked together with necessary support routines into an executable (.EXE) file.

The second part is new to graphical environments like Windows. It involves the creation of a resource file (.RES) that contains information about the visual items that appear on the screen. These elements constitute the user interface. A resource compiler can merge the conventional .EXE file with the .RES file to produce a new .EXE file that runs under Windows.

To adapt a program to a different foreign language, a programmer only needs to make adjustments to the text strings found in the graphic elements of the resource file (e.g., list boxes, dialog boxes, and menus). Then the resource compiler can merge the same original functional .EXE file with this new resource file to produce a new Windows executable file that will interface successfully with a foreign-language user.

the names of about a hundred files that it opens. It also provides the file update routine with another area of memory in which to track up to about twenty updates.

By keeping track of all program requests to update the same file, SHARE can disallow any modification requests that occur before an earlier program's update request has been completed. In this way, SHARE can use its reserved space to ensure that simultaneous updates do not take place in the same file at the same time. Although the default sizes are normally sufficient, two switches are available to enlarge the coverage. Use the /F switch to specify a larger number of bytes for tracking open files, and use the /L switch to track a larger number of simultaneous updates. For example, to enable the open and update routines to track up to 200 files and up to 50 simultaneous updates, issue the following command before starting Windows:

SHARE /F:4096 /L:50

◆ EXPLORING SOME INTERESTING WINDOWS CONNECTIONS

In this section, you'll learn more about some interesting issues regarding Windows and the applications that run under Windows. First, you'll learn about the detailed structure of a Windows .EXE file. This will further clarify the explanation in the preceding section about the Windows programming model. Next, you'll learn how DOS programmers enhance their programs to run more efficiently under Windows. Last, you'll learn about how DESQview, a major Windows competitor, has succeeded in offering a unique operating environment for Windows and DOS users.

EXPLORING THE NATURE OF WINDOWS .EXE FILES

To understand in more detail how a Windows .EXE file is structured, first take a look at the DOS .EXE file format. Figure 3.3 depicts this format, which consists of three principal sections:

◆ A *header*, which contains general program information, including such key data as the header, relocation table, and file size; minimum and maximum memory allocation numbers; initial stack pointer value; and file checksum.

◆ A *relocation table* for the entire .EXE file. This older format does not allow for the manipulation of individual segments of code or data.

◆ The actual *program code and data*, which are limited to the original DOS address space of 640K.

This structure proved to be too limiting for Windows designers. To facilitate multitasking and the efficient allocation of memory, a new, segmented .EXE format was created. In addition, the Windows designers built a special loader

Using SHARE to Prevent Data File Corruption

In a single-user DOS system, it's unusual for data file corruption to occur because of two applications attempting to update the same file. (It can happen, however, because TSRs sometimes affect the same file that is being processed by a foreground program.)

In network environments, corruption of data files is seen much more often, because users at different nodes may attempt to access and update the same file. Microsoft includes the SHARE command in DOS to protect against this situation. If you are logging onto a network, you should include the SHARE command in your AUTOEXEC.BAT file to prevent possible corruption.

Under Windows, you may corrupt data files through the use of multitasking in 386 enhanced mode and context switching in standard mode. If you plan to access, and possibly modify, the same data files from different applications under Windows, you should protect your data by running SHARE before bringing up Windows.

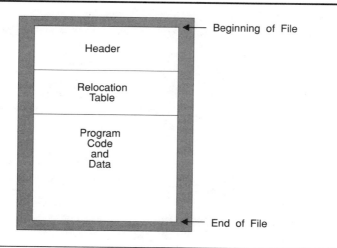

FIGURE 3.3: Structure of a DOS .EXE file

directly into Windows. When you run an .EXE file, the Windows loader determines whether or not you've loaded the old-style .EXE program or the Windows-style .EXE program.

Figure 3.4 depicts a Windows .EXE file. The file consists of two major parts: The first part is a replica of the old-style .EXE, and the second part defines a completely new structure. The new portion contains sufficient additional data to enable the program to run more efficiently within the Windows environment.

If you run this new .EXE file from the standard DOS command prompt, the standard DOS loader sees the old header at the beginning of the file. However, as part of a segmented .EXE file, the old header merely points to an extremely short block of code that displays

This program requires Microsoft Windows.

and then exits.

On the other hand, if you run this same file from Windows (e.g., with the Program Manager's Run command), the old header is quickly skipped over and

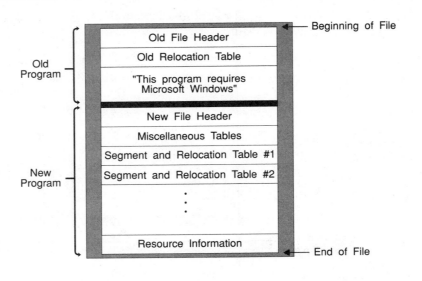

FIGURE 3.4: Structure of a Windows .EXE file

the new program portion takes control. There is a new and more detailed header portion, which contains additional data, such as

◆ A 32-bit file CRC (cyclic redundancy check)

◆ Pointers to the extra tables in the next section

◆ The number of resources stored in this file

◆ Heap and stack sizes

The next part of the file contains a series of important miscellaneous tables, containing information about segments, resources, resident names, module references, imported names, entry points, and nonresident names. This information defines the various sizes, positions, and characteristics of all the remaining information in the .EXE file.

These tables precede the heart of the new file: the actual code and data segments, with relocation tables for each segment. When the program runs, the loader does not need to load all code and data at once. It can load just a single segment, then load additional segments only when they are actually required for the continued execution of the program. In this way, Windows programs place less drain on system memory when they run. Several Windows programs can actually run simultaneously in the same amount of memory required by a single non-Windows application.

The last portion of the file contains such resources as icons, bit maps, and menus. Each resource is only loaded into memory when the application requests it. As I've pointed out, this means that your system's memory is drained only when a resource must be displayed on the screen.

ENHANCING DOS PROGRAMS TO RUN UNDER WINDOWS

Judging from the last section, you may think that it takes a good deal of new knowledge to switch from programming in the DOS environment to programming in the Windows environment. You're right. But the leap from DOS to Windows does not have to be traumatic.

As a user, you know that Windows permits you to continue running your former DOS applications without modification. (You probably had to run your DOS applications while your software vendors worked on developing Windows versions.) If you are a programmer, you can also take a step-by-step approach to moving into the Windows environment. You can learn enough about how Windows works to make your DOS text-mode programs a little more Windows-aware. In so doing, you can improve the efficiency of your DOS programs under Windows while you learn the intricacies of actually developing complete graphic Windows applications.

The next several paragraphs describe some of the programming techniques that you can employ from your DOS program while running in Windows 386 enhanced mode. Your program must first determine its own execution environment before attempting to use any of these services. Place 1600H in register AX and call interrupt 02FH. This is called the *multiplex interrupt* and is the means by which a DOS program can access the Windows API.

With this particular call, you can check the return code to determine whether or not Windows is running in 386 enhanced mode. The various return codes can even tell you the major and minor version of Windows that is running. Actual codes are beyond the scope of this book, since my intent here is to alert you to the various possibilities rather than teach you the programming details of those possibilities.

Another technique you can use to enhance the efficiency of a program is to yield the application's time slice whenever the program must wait for an event (e.g., a serial port interrupt, a keystroke, and so on). You can do this by loading 01680H into register AX and calling the multiplex interrupt 02FH. This tells Windows that the program needn't be given any more time during this time slice, and Windows can distribute the remainder of the time slice to another waiting DOS program.

You read earlier about how Windows uses a message-passing alogorithm for multitasking Windows applications. But non-Windows applications are treated differently. Chapter 7 explains this in more depth. Windows uses the priority setting for an individual DOS program to determine exactly how much CPU time to allot to the program.

But this technique is not preemptive, so each non-Windows application will waste CPU time if it is simply waiting for some event during its time slice.

Other non-Windows applications may have much CPU-intensive work to do but can only perform that work during their allotted time slice. By releasing your program's time slice when it can no longer (for the moment) use the CPU, you permit Windows to return to the other applications that are waiting for the CPU. Consequently, all programs will make faster progress.

One of the major features of Windows applications is their use of the Clipboard. Notwithstanding the increasing support of the DDE and OLE facilities, many users are quite happy with simply being able to transfer text easily from one application to another through the Clipboard. Your DOS applications can be quickly modified to support Clipboard use.

A program called WINOLDAP allows older DOS applications to use the Clipboard. WINOLDAP.MOD is actually an executable file (notwithstanding its unusual extension). It is found in the SYSTEM directory. To use WINOLDAP, you must load register AX with 01700H and call the multiplex interrupt. If WINOLDAP is available, 01700H will be replaced with version information; otherwise, AX will remain unchanged.

Working with the Windows Clipboard is much like working with a file. You open it, manipulate its contents (i.e., read, write, or erase them), and close it. There are various service calls to perform these operations. And just as with reading the contents of a file, you must have a local buffer in your program large enough to receive the contents of the Clipboard if you choose to read them.

Unlike reading a file, where you may know the size of the records you want to read, you will have to submit a special call to request the size of the data contents of the Clipboard. Once you know the size, you can dynamically create a local buffer of the right size. Writing to the buffer is similar; your write request must not only contain the size of the data block to be written but must also indicate which of the Clipboard's many formats this data is in. In this way, the Clipboard can dynamically allocate a sufficient amount of memory for storing the data in the specified format.

One last thing should be pointed out: Just as you should be careful to open a shared file for as little time as possible, you should open the Clipboard just when you need it, then close it as quickly as possible. No other program can change the contents of the Clipboard until you close it.

There are a couple of additional steps that DOS programmers can take to help smooth the transition to the Windows environment, which have no programming burden at all. First, you can create two icons for your application. If a user later installs your program under Windows, he can use one of your icons if he has a color monitor and the other icon if he has a monochrome monitor. This will help distinguish your program from other DOS applications that must suffer with the same plain-vanilla DOS rectangle icon.

Next, and very importantly, you should read about PIFs (see Chapter 8) and prepare one to accompany your application disks. After all, who knows more about what settings can make your application work best in a Windows environment? If your program does not have complex graphics, you can set the execution to windowed mode. It's a simple way to make the application look like it belongs in the Windows environment.

◆ WINDOWS PROGRAMS MUST MANAGE RESOURCES PROPERLY

A variety of graphical objects makes programming Windows applications considerably easier. In exchange for the benefits of these graphical tools, however, you must assume the responsibility for returning resources to the system after their use. If you do not, other applications suffer with diminished resources.

Many allocation routines, whose names begin with Create, Alloc, and Open, require you to return the resource to Windows with an appropriate Delete, Free, or Close routine. These include such objects as fonts, bit maps, metafiles, and palettes.

If your program releases its time slice whenever possible, you needn't check the Detect Idle Time option. Your program is already performing this function for itself. This will actually save time by reducing Windows' overhead during multitasking operations.

Lastly, if your application is normally activated by a hot key, you should specify that key combination as the Application Shortcut Key in the Advanced options portion of the .PIF file. This will further help your application to blend into the Windows environment.

Tips for Writing DOS Programs That Run under Windows

If you write DOS programs and anticipate that the programs will be run in the Windows environment, you should first use interrupt 2F (store 1600H in the AX register) to determine whether your application is running under Windows and then do the following:

◆ Release your time slice whenever you know that your program will be waiting (for example, when the computer prompts the user and waits for a keystroke or mouse press).

◆ Use WINOLDAP.MOD to enable your application to interface with the Windows Clipboard.

◆ Use the Windows API to inhibit task switching during critical code sections.

◆ Prepare an optimized .PIF file for Windows users. This will help ensure that your program uses more tailored execution values than it would receive from the default .PIF file included with Windows.

◆ Prepare a customized icon for your application.

RUNNING WINDOWS UNDER DESQVIEW 386

DESQview 386 is an excellent program, and many users successfully multitask their DOS programs with it. You may be using DESQview 386 on your system for some of the reasons discussed in this section. But you may also want to run some of the latest Windows programs. There is a way you can do both, although it does have some limitations. And to be fair, it will require a good deal of extra learning, of both Windows and DESQview.

Until recently, DESQview 386 competed with Windows as an alternative multitasking environment. However, DESQview primarily multitasks DOS applications, and Windows in 386 enhanced mode multitasks both DOS and Windows applications.

Why then do many users prefer to remain with DESQview 386? For one thing, it multitasks DOS applications faster. The overhead imposed by Windows for DOS time slicing, Windows message passing, and Windows itself is simply too much of a burden when running some DOS applications under Windows.

Furthermore, DESQview 386 is a truly preemptive multitasking environment, which has better separation between address spaces for individual DOS applications. If one DOS application crashes, it is not as likely to crash the entire DESQview environment as the entire Windows environment. You can usually just press Ctrl+Alt+Del under DESQview 386 to terminate a single misbehaving application.

This particular advantage has been drastically reduced with Windows version 3.1, which contains a local reboot facility. If an application fails under Windows, you can press Ctrl+Alt+Del to obtain these choices:

◆ Return to Windows and abort this one application.

◆ Reboot the entire machine.

◆ Return to the frozen application itself to try other attempts at resuscitation.

However, local reboot does not completely protect you against total system crashes. An errant application can still corrupt DOS, so you may not be be able to recover Windows without turning your computer off and on.

The latest versions of DESQview 386 can multitask DOS applications, and at the same time, can run Windows in standard mode. Running Windows under DESQview 386 in standard mode is just fine, since one of the major advantages of 386 enhanced mode is being able to multitask DOS applications.

By configuring your system to run DOS applications and Windows directly under DESQview 386, you gain several benefits. You can multitask your DOS applications faster, and whenever you wish, you can switch instantly to Windows. You can then run any of your Windows applications from this environment. Although there are occasional software conflicts with DESQview, it can still be a valuable package if your major applications are still DOS versions. As an example, my fax board uses proprietary DOS software that handles interrupts in a way that conflicts with DESQview 386. Consequently, I cannot run DESQview if I want to use my fax board.

DESQview 386 includes QEMM 386, which is a powerful memory management utility. It can do all the things that are now done by HIMEM.SYS and EMM386.EXE in your Windows system, and better. Since QEMM 386 is tuned to the DESQview 386 environment, you should use it in preference to the two Microsoft programs (if you are using DESQview 386). It offers greater flexibility and power in managing extended memory and in using the upper memory blocks between 640K and 1MB.

If you choose to configure your system with this combination of DESQview 386, Windows, and DOS applications, you may have some new hazards to confront. Just as Windows has a host of potential video-related problems (see Part 5 of this book), so does this combination of Windows and DESQview 386. If you discover any problems with your video display when switching between DOS and Windows applications when running under DESQview 386, set Virtualize to Yes on the DESQview 386 configuration menu.

There is yet another sophisticated way in which you can use DESQview 386 to run your DOS and Windows applications. You can create separate Windows entries on the DESQview 386 menus, with each entry set up to run a unique Windows application. In this way, you can exert DESQview 386's separate controls and configuration possibilities over each unique invocation of Windows. This is because each separate DESQview window will be running its own copy of Windows. And each of these Windows copies will be using a different shell (see Chapter 7) that runs a unique, but single, application. By applying DESQview's controls to each of these screen windows, you can fine-tune the behavior of each Windows program more than you could with just Windows itself.

It sounds like a marvelous combination. And it is, except when it doesn't quite work. The TSR support software for my fax board, for instance, is 100 percent incompatible with DESQview 386. So I have no choice, and no settings to make it work. I don't even have the option of setting up DESQview on my machine. But you might.

◆ EXPLORING THE CRUCIAL WINDOWS INTERFACES

Three interfaces are fundamental to the foundation of Windows: the GDI, the MDI, and the DPMI. In this section, you will learn the basics of each of these interfaces.

The Graphics Device Interface, or GDI, defines the manner in which applications produce device-independent output (which does not depend on any particular hardware). With this mechanism, application programmers can use device-independent API functions to request that graphical objects be drawn. The application itself does not have to take responsibility for the specific hardware commands necessary to handle the actual graphical device output.

The Multiple Document Interface, or MDI, specifies exactly how a single application manages and displays multiple individual subwindows within each application's main screen window. A spreadsheet application, for example, can display several different spreadsheets within child windows. All these child windows are restricted to the client area of the main application window. The Program Manager and the File Manager use this technique to manage windows. The SYSEDIT.EXE program, which is found in the SYSTEM directory, also uses this method to manipulate the SYSTEM.INI, WIN.INI, CONFIG.SYS, and AUTOEXEC.BAT files.

The DOS Protected Mode Interface, or DPMI, specifies how multiple protected-mode applications can successfully multitask within a DOS-based environment. It sets up rules of access to potentially problematic resources, such as extended memory, interrupts, and video adapters.

UNDERSTANDING THE GRAPHICS DEVICE INTERFACE

In this section, I will explore the important concept of device independence, but without getting bogged down in excessive programming details. One of the big pluses of the Windows environment (in contrast to the DOS environment) is that individual applications do not have to include drivers for all known pieces of hardware. This is because Windows provides drivers for many different types of hardware already. If an application adheres to the GDI, then it will issue only the generalized GDI function calls. Subsequently, Windows ensures that the appropriate driver issues the necessary hardware-specific instructions.

Each Windows application now can produce device-independent graphics on myriad devices, without having to write even one hardware-specific instruction. Essentially, the application programmer only has to learn the GDI functions to manipulate and display graphic items. Windows ensures that these device-independent requests are translated into the necessary hardware-specific instructions, using the Windows device driver. With this graphic interface, a Windows application can even run on hardware that hasn't been designed or built yet, as long as a driver for it is included later in your Windows system.

A *device context* is a special data structure that is used to connect the Windows API with a hardware-specific device driver. Your application uses a series of API service calls that are expected to perform certain graphics chores, such as drawing rectangles, lines, points, circles, and even polygons. The application further directs that these generalized drawing chores be applied to a device context, which could in reality be any output device. You can separately designate the output device as a screen window (the most common), the full screen, a printer, a plotter, or any other special-purpose hardware on your system.

Figure 3.5 depicts how the device context connects applications to hardware. At the application end, there is no dependence on the actual hardware being used. At the Windows end, the Windows device drivers perform the actual nitty-gritty instructional chores required to make an individual device satisfy a graphics request. Since it is the most common action, a device context of a particular monitor's window is called a *display context*.

Once again, the Windows design makes it easy to gain this device independence. Just as with accessing a file, which requires you to first ask the API for a file handle, you must first submit an API request for a handle to the device context. Subsequent programming commands that draw graphics or produce other kinds of output simply specify the handle (just an identifying

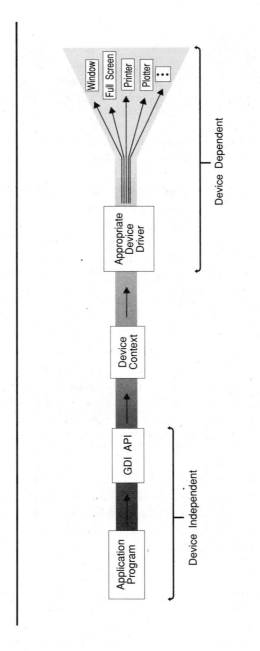

FIGURE 3.5: The device context connects applications to hardware.

number, really) and the type of output requested. Windows makes sure that the proper device driver processes the request.

Another value of this mechanism is that Windows tries to take advantage of special capabilities of your hardware. For example, the more advanced graphics adapters available now have facilities for performing bit block transfers (i.e., the bitblt API functions) extremely quickly. These functions enable an application to stretch, compress, or just move blocks of bits from memory to the screen very rapidly, in contrast to bit-by-bit transfers.

Some of these advanced adapters have special hardware facilities for generating other graphic items, like circles and ellipses. If the device driver has the capability to control these special features, Windows will help your application generate its device-independent graphics output requests in the fastest possible way.

UNDERSTANDING THE MULTIPLE DOCUMENT INTERFACE

The Multiple Document Interface, or MDI, is a specification for a single application that must manage a number of subordinate, and usually similar, objects. It was first described in IBM's Systems Application Architecture (SAA), Common User Access (CUA), Advanced Interface Design Guide. Each subordinate "document" within the client area of an application window could be a spreadsheet (e.g., in Excel for Windows), a text file (like that produced by SYSEDIT.EXE), or a Directory Tree window (as seen in the File Manager).

There is a clear parallel between how Windows handles the entire desktop, which consists of various application windows, and how an MDI application handles its own window's client area, which can consist of multiple subordinate windows. These child windows, from zero to many, can each display an individual document. And although each child window looks superficially like other screen windows, they are different.

No child window, for instance, has its own main menu. The main application window has the only Window menu, and its pull-down menus apply to all child windows. Typically, you highlight a child window, then choose an option from one of the main application's pull-down menus.

Only one child window can be active at a time, just as only one application window on your desktop can be in the foreground at a time. The active child window's title bar is highlighted, just as a foreground application's title bar on the desktop is highlighted.

There are quite a few display details to which a programmer must attend to produce an MDI application that adheres to the specifications. A user, on the other hand, only has to become aware of the menu and command options of an MDI application to take the fullest advantage of it. As I discuss some of these possibilities, you should manipulate your Program Manager window to explore each of these MDI features.

You will notice that, just like application windows, an MDI child window can be maximized or minimized. However, when such a window is maximized, it only expands to fill the workspace (or *client area*) of the application's window. A new double-headed arrow appears at the far right of the menu bar; this icon can be used to restore the document window to its former size. The title bar of the entire application now displays the application name, along with the maximized document window's name in square brackets. Also, the document window's system menu icon now appears to the left of the menu bar's choice of pull-down menu names.

You can quickly close an application window on your desktop by pressing the shortcut key combination Alt+F4. You can also close a document window in an MDI application by pressing Ctrl+F4. Just as the icon for a minimized application appears at the bottom of your desktop, the icon for a minimized document window appears at the bottom of the application window's workspace.

The next distinction doesn't affect mouse users, since it only has to do with the order of processing arrow keys when traversing the menu bar. By pressing and releasing the Alt key in any Windows application, highlighting and control are passed to the first item on the main application's menu bar. Pressing the right arrow key successively moves the highlighting from menu item to menu item, then to the system menu icon in the upper-left corner, then back to the first item on the menu bar.

In an MDI application, you similarly reach the first menu item by pressing the Alt key. However, pressing right arrow thereafter moves the highlight through each menu item, then to the document window's restore icon (if the window has been maximized), then to the overall application's system menu, then to the document window's system menu, and finally back to the first menu item.

All Windows applications offer keyboard alternatives to mouse clicks. As you would expect, MDI applications offer a keyboard method to select among the available child windows. Just as you can press Alt+Tab to cycle through all desktop applications, you can press Ctrl+F6 to cycle through all child windows. Each time you press Ctrl+F6, a subsequent child window (or child icon) is highlighted and activated.

There is no requirement that all child windows in an MDI application be the same. For example, Microsoft's Excel for Windows contains child windows for spreadsheets and charts. In such an application, the main application's menu bar will often adjust to the active child window. More or fewer choices may appear, depending on what can be done with the information in the active window. This is the responsibility of the application itself.

MDI conventions also require that all top-level menu bars have Window as their last option, unless there is a Help option available. This pull-down menu contains choices for arranging the child windows, either in cascading, tiled, or minimized icon form. The Window option also lists the names of any existing child windows. If you select any one of these, it is immediately re-displayed as the top, or active, window. If the selected window is minimized, it is opened and becomes the active window.

♦ WHEN TO USE THE MDI

Many applications are based on the simple technique of mimicking a printed form and enabling a user to simply fill in the blanks. In some applications, there are multiple forms to fill in. Windows' MDI specifies how such an application can be created. If the forms are similar, you can generate separate child windows for each form, using the same windowing procedure to handle the user interaction. Many applications already use this technique (e.g., SYSEDIT.EXE) to facilitate the interaction and handling of similar activities in multiple child windows. This not only reduces a developer's programming efforts but affords the user the convenience of window manipulations, such as tiling, overlapping, maximizing, and minimizing.

UNDERSTANDING THE DOS PROTECTED MODE INTERFACE

The DOS Protected Mode Interface, or DPMI, is a set of specifications for safely running protected-mode applications within a DOS-based multitasking environment. The DPMI essentially defines a DOS extender. Windows handles mode switching and memory management services by adhering to the DPMI.

Windows performs a sequence of steps to enable a protected-mode application to run within a real DOS environment. Many special functions are available to support the DPMI. Figure 3.6 depicts the following steps:

1. A protected-mode application makes a request for DOS or ROM BIOS services.

2. Windows intercepts the interrupt request.

3. Windows converts virtual addresses to physical addresses, as necessary.

4. Windows copies any necessary data from extended memory to conventional memory.

5. Windows switches the CPU from protected to real mode.

6. Windows reissues the original service call.

7. The DOS or ROM BIOS service is processed, and control returns to Windows.

8. Windows switches the CPU from real to protected mode.

9. Windows converts physical addresses to virtual addresses, as necessary.

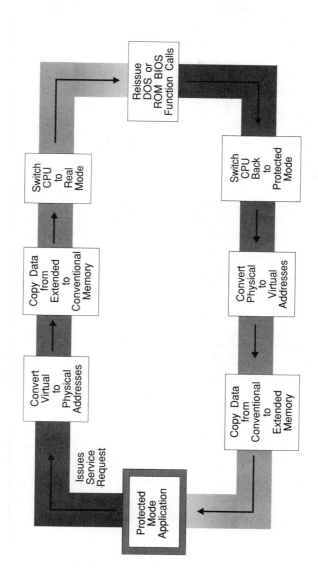

FIGURE 3.6: The DOS Protected Mode Interface procedure

10. Windows copies any necessary data from conventional memory to extended memory.

11. Windows returns control to the application that made the original request in step 1.

This mechanism is both powerful and flexible, and is available to Windows applications running on any 80286, 80386, or 80486 machine. (The details of the DPMI are available at no charge from Intel Corporation.) The wide range of service calls in this interface fall into seven categories, briefly summarized in Table 3.1.

A bit of industry history is probably appropriate to add at this point. In 1987, Quarterdeck Office Systems and Phar Lap Software jointly developed the predecessor specification to DPMI. It was called the Virtual Control Program Interface (VCPI). It was intended to enable 80386-specific memory managers and expanded memory emulators (like QEMM 386 from Quarterdeck) to coexist safely with 80386 protected-mode applications.

TABLE 3.1: DPMI Function Categories

Category	Purpose
DOS Memory Management	Connects to real-mode INT 21H services
Extended Memory Management	Allocates, releases, and resizes memory above 1MB
Interrupt Management	Handles all software/hardware interrupts
LDT Management	Supports all manipulations of local descriptor tables
Miscellaneous Services	Handles address conversions, coprocessor management, etc.
Page Management	Supports memory page locking on 80386 and 80486 machines
Translation Services	Supports procedure calls between protected and real modes

Running Windows Applications in Protected Mode

The DOS Protected Mode Interface allows Windows to run applications in protected mode, using virtual addressing, extended memory, and the hardware features of Intel's 80x86 processors. Here's a quick view of how it works:

1. While in protected mode, Windows intercepts DOS (and ROM BIOS) service requests.

2. Windows maps virtual addresses to physical memory addresses and copies extended memory locations into conventional memory, as necessary.

3. Windows switches the CPU back to real mode, then issues the service request that was intercepted in step 1.

4. After the service call is satisfied, Windows switches the CPU back to protected mode.

5. Windows maps physical memory addresses back to virtual addresses and copies conventional memory locations to extended memory, as necessary.

6. Windows returns control of the CPU to the application.

VCPI became an industry standard, later to be improved upon by Microsoft when it released Windows 3.0 in 1990. VCPI used a client-server model, where the protected-mode application is the client and the EMS emulator is the server. However, there were a number of limitations that begged for improvement. Internally, the client and server were executed at the same privilege level, which made it impossible to enforce complete protection of one protected-mode application from another.

In addition, the technical aspects of the interface made it difficult for a server to facilitate running graphics applications inside a screen window. Furthermore, VCPI was founded on the hardware concept of paging, which was only found in 80386 machines or higher. That meant that 80286 machines were unable to take advantage of VCPI. Microsoft was not about to isolate the many owners of 80286 computer systems.

By contrast, a DPMI server runs at a higher privilege level than a client program. Consequently, it provides a protection model that can use the hardware chip's capabilities to protect the kernel from the user. As a result, Windows can support demand paging for virtual memory support.

Originally, Microsoft developed DPMI as a means to run Windows applications successfully in extended memory. They broadened their design to incorporate support for all DOS-based applications that require extended memory and protected mode.

Now that you've learned about some of the architectural underpinnings of Windows, turn to Chapter 4 to take a close look at how Windows manages its most important resource: memory.

4

How Windows Manages Memory

I've been working with computers now for well over twenty years. In that time, the most common prescription for system and performance enhancement has been to buy more memory. Salesmen suggested it. System analysts suggested it. Programmers suggested it. And users often followed that suggestion, because it was nearly always the best advice. Especially in multitasking systems, more memory can result in a faster and more flexible system.

But more memory by itself is not sufficient if it is not configured and used properly. In this chapter, you will learn about the different addressing mechanisms used in the two modes (real and protected) that are built into the processing chips supported by Windows 3.1. Next, you will learn about the different types of memory that Windows can use. You will also explore how Windows 3.1 efficiently uses different types of memory, depending on whether you are operating in standard mode or 386 enhanced mode. Lastly, you will discover how Windows in 386 enhanced mode uses demand paging and swap files to construct virtual memory from hard-disk space.

◆ REAL MODE VS. SEGMENTED MODE ADDRESSING

To better understand why Windows works differently in standard mode and 386 enhanced mode, you must step back and understand some hardware issues and some history. Even though standard mode runs only on an 80286 processor or higher, these chips all have an addressing mode that replicates the design of earlier processor chips. As recently as Windows 3.0, computers based on the 8088 and 8086 chips could actually run a version of

What Kind of Memory Should You Add?

If you've decided to bolster your system with additional memory, you may be wondering what kind of memory to add. Here's how to decide:

◆ If your system does not yet have 640K of main, conventional memory, fill that in first.

◆ For previous versions of Windows only: If your system is an 8088 or 8086 system, and you're still running Windows 3.0 in real mode, you must add expanded memory. These processors cannot address extended memory.

◆ If you have an 80286 or higher processor, add extended memory. Windows uses extended memory efficiently to improve its own performance and even to emulate expanded memory if your application requires it.

◆ If your system's motherboard has memory slots left unfilled, fill these first before adding expansion boards.

Windows, called real mode. Because Windows still runs under DOS, and real-mode DOS is constrained to run within the addressing limits of the earlier processors, you will need to understand the basic addressing mechanisms.

HOW DO PROGRAMS CONSTRUCT ADDRESSES IN REAL MODE?

Minicomputers in the 1970s and microcomputers in the early 1980s used internal address registers that were 16 bits wide. This permitted memory addresses up to 2^{16}, or 64K. With 16 bits, a programmer can only directly reference individual bytes in a flat address space that ranges up to 64K.

When the first IBM PC was released in the early '80s, it used an Intel 8088 chip. This was quickly enhanced and replaced in competitors' machines by the 8086 chip, which was the primary predecessor to the 80286, 80386, and 80486 chips that Windows 3.1 uses. These early chips offered enhanced memory addressability, which Intel achieved by adding four address bits to the existing sixteen. In this way, it became possible to address up to 2^{20}, which is $2^4 * 2^{16}$, or 1024K, or 1MB, of RAM.

This enhancement was not accomplished by adjusting the size of the internal registers; they were kept at 16 bits wide. But the final memory address was to be constructed with 20 bits. This was accomplished in a technically interesting way. Intel designated four internal registers as *segment registers*; any one of these could store a 16-bit address that would represent a block, or *segment*, of memory. Since the segment register contained 16 bits, it could contain a number up to 64K itself. Consequently, the contents of a segment register could represent any one of 64K segments of memory.

The contents of a segment register pointed to the start, or *base*, address of a particular segment. Then, another register (called the *offset register*) contained another 16-bit number that represented the relative address of the desired memory byte within the particular segment. As Figure 4.1 depicts, the 16 bits within an offset register enable relative accessing of individual bytes up to a maximum of 64K within one segment.

This structure provided easy construction of memory addresses anywhere within the 1MB address space allowed by the 20 address lines. It was done by combining the contents of a segment register with the contents of an offset register, as shown in Figure 4.2.

The segment register contents must first be shifted 4 bits to the left and then added to the contents of the offset register. Using this technique, any one memory address can be denoted in a variety of ways. You can think of the entire 1MB address space as consisting of 64K segments, each one being 16 bytes long. Programmers call this 16-byte block of memory a *paragraph*.

Using this mechanism, for example, the 37th byte of memory can be addressed as segment 2, offset 4. Because computer people always count from 0, not 1, segments and offsets are counted 0, 1, 2, 3, and so on. The third segment is number 2, and the fifth byte is offset by four from the start of the segment. So the fifth byte in the third 16-byte block of memory (16 + 16 + 5 = 37) is often written and referenced in programs or articles as 0002:0004.

On the other hand, this same addressing mechanism would allow a program to reference the same memory byte as 0001:0014. In the first case, the byte is treated as an offset of four bytes into segment number 2. In the second case, the very same memory location can be treated as an offset of 0014h from the

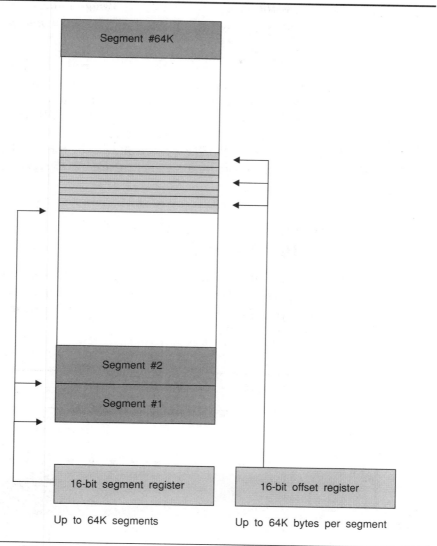

FIGURE 4.1: Maximum segment/offset register possibilities

base address of segment number 0001h. Programmers can use the *segment: offset* addressing pair to construct real addresses in a number of ways.

Some of these ways don't always work correctly. As you can see, if the two 16-bit numbers are shifted and combined improperly in Figure 4.2, it is easy to construct the wrong address. This often explains why programs and TSRs (terminate-and-stay-resident programs) in real mode sometimes crash the computer. If a program, or one of the additional TSRs that are loaded, constructs an incorrect address, it is possible to access and corrupt any address within the entire 1MB address space allowed by the 20 address bits. This includes not only the program's segment space but the space occupied by DOS itself.

ADDRESSING AN EXTRA 64K WITH THE A20 LINE

In real mode, with 20 address bits, it is physically impossible to construct an address higher than 1MB. As just pointed out, a programmer may mistakenly combine a large segment register value (say FF00h) with an offset (say 1FFFh) to produce a value that does not fit into 20 bits.

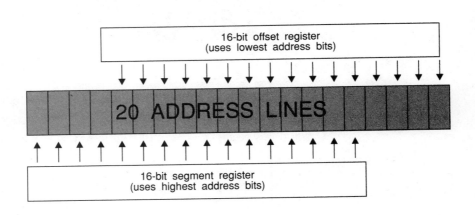

FIGURE 4.2: Each memory address combines a segment with an offset.

Using QEMM and Windows

If you have chosen to forgo the Windows high memory manager (HI-MEM.SYS) and expanded memory emulator (EMM386.SYS), you can use the QEMM386.SYS driver, available from Quarterdeck Office Systems. It performs the chores of both these products.

The good news is that QEMM386.SYS provides a more powerful and flexible set of facilities than the two Windows drivers it replaces. It offers more parameters when loading the driver to better control how memory is used. The product ships with two extremely valuable companion programs. Optimize enables you to identify what areas of upper reserved memory are available for loading drivers and programs, and helps to structure your system's initialization files (AUTOEXEC.BAT and CONFIG.SYS) most effectively. Manifest, or MFT, is a powerful tool for analyzing the exact availability and use of your system's memory.

The bad news is that each new release of Windows seems to produce some degree of incompatibility with previous versions of Quarterdeck's products. This often means that you must consider the additional expense of upgrading these products. Additionally, you may even be unable to use older versions of these products safely or successfully with the latest version of Windows. See Chapter 15 for more information about third-party memory management products.

Remember from Figure 4.2 that the segment base address must be shifted by 4 bits, or one hexadecimal character, before adding it to the offset register. Consequently, if the base in hexadecimal notation is FF00h and the offset is 1FFFh, then the following summation occurs:

FF000

+ 1FFF

———

100FFF

In this situation, the address calculation just *wraps around*, ignoring the leading 1. It uses just the 20 bits to construct a new address of 0000:0FFFh. Some programmers actually use this wraparound effect to play coding tricks, which sometimes actually work.

Newer processors, beginning with the 80286, contain an extra address line, called the *A20 line*. Normally, this line is used only in what is called *protected mode* (see the next section for further explanation). If this special line is enabled, an address can be formed that points to the first 64K of extended memory (addresses above 1MB).

Rather than wrap back to the first 64K of memory in real mode, a program can directly address this extra 64K of extended memory. As part of Microsoft's Extended Memory Specification (XMS), this specially accessible area of extended memory is called the High Memory Area (HMA). If you have installed a high memory driver, like HIMEM.SYS, your 80x86 machine can enable or disable the A20 line. Individual applications can each access this memory, and HIMEM.SYS can ensure that multiple accesses from competing programs are performed safely.

WHAT IS THIS THING CALLED PROTECTED MODE?

The newest processor chips (80286 and higher) use more bits to do more things. Additional bits are used to construct larger addresses, enabling an 80286 to access a physical address space of 16MB and an 80386/80486 to access up to 4GB (4096MB) of physical RAM. Additional bits are used to assign *privilege levels* (0, 1, 2, or 3) to every segment, with 0 being the highest and 3 the lowest. This assignment enables an operating system to restrict access to memory segments.

◆ BEWARE MEMORY MANAGEMENT BEYOND 16MB

You may be one of the few users that has installed more than 16MB of extended (XMS) memory. If so, be cautious about which extended memory manager you use. Microsoft says that you must use HIMEM.SYS.

The processor hardware generates a *protection fault* if one program (operating from an area of memory with a known privilege level) attempts to access a memory address located in a region with a higher privilege level. Application programs execute at privilege levels that are lower than the privilege levels enjoyed by the operating system. In this way, the operating system is protected from the vagaries of an executing application.

In the next section, you'll learn how memory addresses can be constructed in protected mode. Because of this unique method, each individual application is unable to erroneously access a memory address that is located in another application's address space. Consequently, during multitasking operations, each application's code and data are *protected* from other executing applications.

HOW DO PROGRAMS CONSTRUCT ADDRESSES IN PROTECTED MODE?

In protected mode, the same 16-bit segment registers you just read about in real mode are also used to construct a memory address. However, each register in protected mode does not directly contain a base address (i.e., the starting address of the segment). Instead, each register contains what is called a *selector*, as shown in Figure 4.3.

This selector technique enables programmers to construct memory addresses through an indirect method. A selector points to a special table, itself located in RAM, that contains descriptive information about the actual memory segment that is being referenced. Figure 4.3 shows how a selector points to a descriptor table, and Figures 4.4 and 4.5 (discussed later) show how the descriptor table's base address combines with the segment's offset to produce the desired memory address.

The high 13 bits of the selector in Figure 4.3 are used as an index into one of the memory tables. Thirteen bits (bits number 3 to 15) can index into 2^{13}, or 8192, table entries. The table bit (bit number 2) indicates whether the table to use is the global descriptor table (GDT), which is reserved for operating-system segments, or the current local descriptor table (LDT). Each executing application has its own LDT.

Importantly, the lowest two bits of a selector store the referencing code's Requested Privilege Level, or RPL (privilege levels are discussed in the preceding section). This is compared to the privilege level entry that is stored with

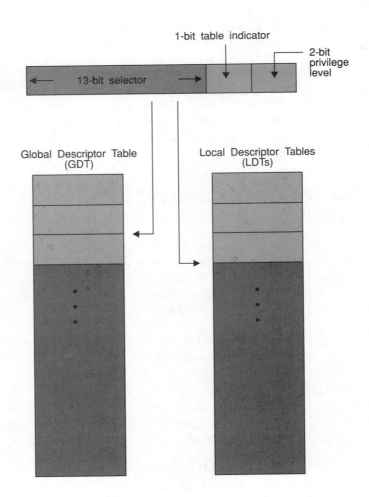

FIGURE 4.3: Segment registers store 16-bit selectors in protected mode.

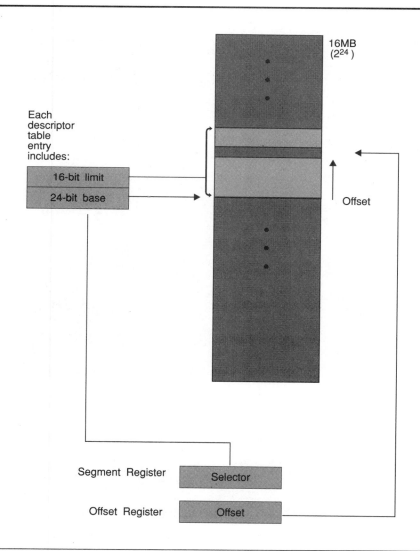

FIGURE 4.4: 80286 chips use 24-bit addressing.

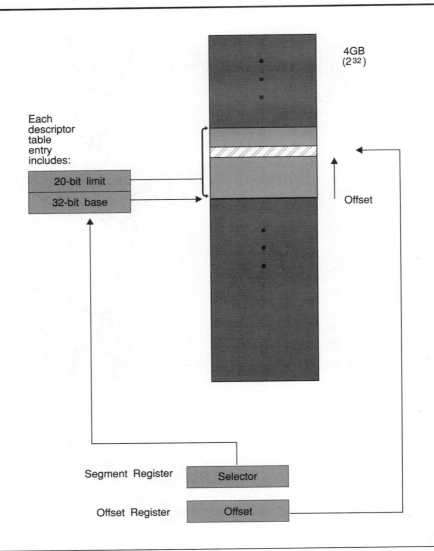

FIGURE 4.5: 80386 and 80486 chips use 32-bit addressing.

each descriptor table entry to determine whether access to that segment is allowed. As pointed out above, if the referencing selector has a privilege level that is equal to or higher than the privilege level of the memory segment being referenced, access is allowed. Otherwise, it is denied and a protection fault occurs.

The selector points to the correct descriptor table entry, and each entry is 64 bits long. On an 80286 processor, only 48 bits are used. The remaining bits must be zeroed out by a programmer for upward compatibility with 80386/80486 addressing, which uses all 64 bits. Although the detailed use of these bits is beyond the scope of this book, two key aspects of the descriptor table are worth noting.

In 80286 chip addressing, 24 bits of the descriptor table are used to construct a base segment address. This means that an 80286 can construct physical addresses within a total address space of 2^{24} bytes, or 16MB (see Figure 4.4).

Another 16 bits of an 80286 descriptor table's entry is reserved for a *limit* field. This defines the size of the segment, which is once again limited to 2^{16} bytes, or 64K. Using this limit value, the processor can further enforce protection by checking the eventual offset register's value. If the offset register contains a value that exceeds the segment limit, the resulting address would conceivably reference memory that is outside of this segment. This memory could belong to the operating system, or to another application, or to nothing. The processor disallows access to RAM addresses that are outside of the segment's limit.

In 80386 and 80486 chip addressing, 32 bits of the descriptor table are used to construct a much larger base segment address. This means that an 80386 or 80486 can construct physical addresses within a total address space of 2^{32} bytes, which is 4096MB, or 4GB (see Figure 4.5).

In the 80386/80486 descriptor table, the limit entry is expanded even further to 20 bits. This would appear to initially limit the size of the segment to no greater than 2^{20} bytes, or 1MB. The 80386 and 80486 processors use this limit value in a manner similar to that just described for the 80286 to help enforce interapplication protection. However, these processors have one more novel difference from the 80286. They have one special bit, called the *granularity bit*, which can change the interpretation of the limit on segment size.

If the granularity bit is not set, the limit field defines a segment of up to 1MB. However, if the granularity bit is set, then the limit field refers to the number of pages. Since a *page* is defined as 4096 bytes, this granularity option enables a segment size to be 4096×2^{20}, or 4GB. This is precisely the complete physical memory addressing size for a 32-bit machine, so a 386 processor with the granularity option bit set on is no longer limited to the former 64K segment size. This creates the possibility for flat addressing of segments up to 4GB, which will make programming easier in future Windows versions that use entirely 32-bit addressing.

MAPPING LOGICAL TO PHYSICAL MEMORY

One more bit in the various descriptor tables is called the *present bit*. It enables applications to write code as if they had complete access to the entire 16MB (on 80286 processors) or the entire 4GB (on 80386 and 80486 processors) address space. Theoretically, the operating system must map the larger, logical addresses within this maximum address space to the smaller, physical RAM addresses available on your particular machine. The present bit can indicate whether or not a particular block of code or data is present in physical RAM, or whether it is only available in the larger, logical address space. If the needed code/date block is not physically present, then it must be read in from the disk to a physical location, and the appropriate descriptor table entries must be adjusted.

When the present bit is set, the segment pointed to by the table entry is located in physical memory. If it is not, the operating system must first read it from disk into memory before any actual references to the RAM address can be completed. If segments are very large, it may be time consuming or just impossible to actually store a swapped copy of the information on disk. If segments are very small, the overhead of swapping them to and from a hard disk can overburden the CPU.

The 386 organizes memory into blocks of 4096 bytes to strike a consistent balance between segments that are too large and segments that are too small. In 386 enhanced mode, Windows 3.1 uses paging to swap code and data most efficiently to and from your hard disk. Chapter 14 discusses how to set up your system for most efficient swapping. The final section of this chapter discusses virtual memory and paging in much more depth.

When multiple applications run in 386 enhanced mode, each application has its own local descriptor table. Windows maintains only a small portion of the complete application's .EXE file in memory at one time, using the technique of paging to make efficient use of memory. In the next section, you'll take a closer look at the different types of memory available to applications in the Windows environment.

◆ UNDERSTANDING THE DIFFERENT TYPES OF MEMORY

Memory is your system's most fundamental resource, although you may only realize this if you don't have enough of it. It's like land; you can build houses, schools, and entire cities with enough of it. Once you've constructed your building (or computer application), you often pay no more attention to the land (or memory space) that it was built on. However, the architects and contractors (or programmers) who do the building must know more about the characteristics of the land they are working with.

This section will clarify the different types of memory in your computer. Just as different applications use different types of memory, Windows uses different types of memory at different times. In this section, you will learn the differences between conventional, expanded, extended, and virtual memory.

REVISITING THE BASICS OF MEMORY ADDRESSING

All PCs contain a certain amount of conventional memory. As you can see in Figure 4.6, *conventional memory* is a term applied to any memory installed on your machine that is below the 640K mark. When you first boot up DOS, the system typically loads some device drivers and a portion of DOS itself into the lowest part of conventional memory. What remains of conventional

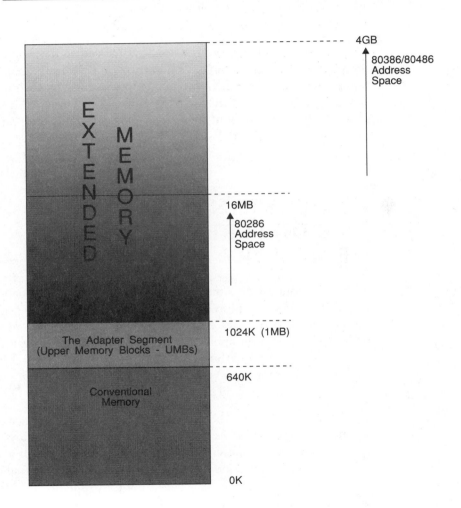

FIGURE 4.6: A linear view of memory

Upgrading Your System RAM

Windows typically performs much better as you add more RAM. Typically, you want to add extended RAM, used to augment memory addressability beyond 640K and usually well beyond 1MB. You can add new RAM in one of three ways (they are listed in order of preference):

◆ Add memory chips directly to your motherboard. Accessing motherboard memory is usually faster than any other method. Your first line of expansion should be to fill out all available chip space on the motherboard.

◆ Add a proprietary memory board designed specifically for your system, which usually has a special proprietary slot to plug into. This technique offers relatively fast access but is often more expensive than adding an equivalent amount of memory on chips.

◆ Add a third-party memory board. This is usually more expensive than the first choice but less expensive than the second one. However, it is by far the slowest method of adding memory to your system. This is because the expansion bus into which the board plugs is slower than motherboard or proprietary slot access.

memory after this initial loading process is all that subsequent programs, including Windows, have to work with.

However, many techniques exist that can maximize the amount of conventional memory available with which to begin Windows. Chapter 15 presents many memory enhancement techniques that you can use to increase available conventional memory, as well as to improve the utilization of other available memory.

◆ INCREASE CONVENTIONAL MEMORY FOR DOS APPLICATIONS

If none of your DOS applications require EMS support, you can increase available conventional memory for all your DOS applications. Simply set ReservePageFrame=No in the [386Enh] section of the SYSTEM.INI file. This tells Windows that it needn't reserve the transfer buffers in conventional memory necessary for buffering file operations when switching to real mode. This setting will only have meaning if there is no page frame already available in reserved memory (640K– 1MB). If a page frame is already set up, and there is insufficient space in reserved memory for transfer buffers, Windows uses conventional memory for these buffers. If your software doesn't need a page frame, turning off this setting allows Windows to allocate space in reserved memory for transfer buffers. Consequently, each non-Windows application will find a larger amount of conventional memory available to it when it runs.

One of the easiest techniques is to install additional physical memory to be treated as *extended memory*. This is essentially just extra RAM that can be added to your machine and smoothly addressed as a linear extension of your machine's first megabyte of address space. As seen in Figure 4.6 and as discussed earlier in this chapter, an 80286 processor can address extended memory that stretches up to the 16MB point; 80386 and higher processors can address up to 4GB of RAM.

Using extended memory is the easiest way to gain extra room to run Windows and your applications. It is also the recommended way to use the larger address spaces of the 80x86 processors. In protected mode, Windows uses the selector and descriptor table methods discussed earlier to directly address any extended memory in your machine.

Then there is something called *expanded memory*. This type of memory predates extended memory, so many earlier non-Windows applications use it. Windows does not directly use expanded memory, so if your machine has it, you may be out of luck. Some expanded memory boards are configurable; you can specify some or all of the memory on the board to be treated as extended memory. If you can do this, Windows will make more efficient use of this memory. Otherwise, expanded memory requires its own software manager, and it can only be used by your DOS applications that know how to use it.

No Windows applications use expanded memory. However, you may be running older non-Windows applications that can take advantage of expanded memory. To do so requires a more cumbersome addressing method that is considerably slower than any other method. It involves using a portion of the memory between 640K and 1MB. This upper memory area is often called the *adapter segment*, because it is usually reserved for the ROM control code used by various pieces of hardware.

However, a portion of this adapter segment can be used as a window into expanded memory. I'll discuss exactly how this works in the next section. Normally, expanded memory is added to a system as a memory board with its own special driver. But Windows (and DOS 5 as well) includes a special memory manager, EMM386.EXE, that can treat a portion of extended memory as if it were expanded memory. In this way, you can run older non-Windows applications that require expanded memory, even if your hardware does not provide expanded memory.

EXPANDED MEMORY ADDRESSING

Most DOS applications were not originally designed to take advantage of memory beyond the 640K conventional memory limit. However, quite a few—for instance, spreadsheet programs like Lotus 1-2-3 version 2.3—require additional memory in significant amounts. One approach to dealing with this problem, developed in 1985 by Lotus and Intel, was a specification for expanded memory. After viewing early presentations of their specifications, Microsoft joined Lotus and Intel to release the LIM EMS (Lotus-Intel-Microsoft Expanded Memory Specification) 3.2, which became an overnight hit.

Using Bank Switching to Expand Your Memory

Even though your desktop is physically limited in size, you can use unlimited reference materials by switching among file folders, reserving one portion of your desk as a switching area. Although your desk may contain a variety of other materials that do not change, you can access two, five, or fifty file folders during your own personal information processing, though only one of these folders is open and accessible at any given moment (see Figure 4.7).

Similarly, a computer can reserve a portion of memory as a central switching area. This area is analogous to the file folder area in the center of your desk: Any number of similarly sized (or smaller) portions of memory can be logically brought into this area. This technique is called *bank switching* (a *bank* of storage addresses in memory is a separately addressable unit). Figure 4.8 depicts this approach to memory expansion.

With LIM 3.2, all expanded memory is treated as a collection of memory banks, divided into 16K pages. Simple instructions that are part of the memory specification allow programs to switch 16K pages into and out of a 64K addressable window (i.e., the adapter segment). This area was typically carved out of an unused area of contiguous memory located in the sparsely used ROM area at the upper end of addressable memory below 1MB. The last 384K of memory, between 640K and 1MB addresses, is often called *reserved memory*, because it is reserved for hardware and system purposes and is not intended to be directly available to applications.

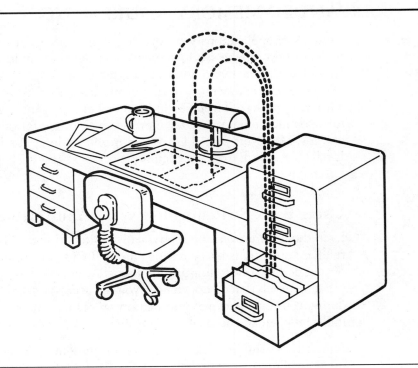

FIGURE 4.7:   A desktop analogy for memory bank switching

The LIM EMS specification contained many details of expanded memory management and of the interface between that memory and programs wanting to gain access to it. Many of these details are embodied in a program called the Expanded Memory Manager (EMM.SYS), which expanded memory systems must include as a device driver in the CONFIG.SYS file.

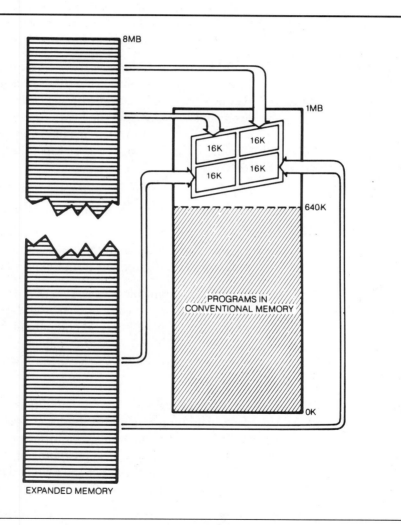

FIGURE 4.8: Bank switching addresses memory 16K at a time.

EMM.SYS is not included as a part of DOS or Windows. Instead, a version that meets the requirements of the LIM specification is normally included with each individual expanded memory board. To run DOS software that requires expanded memory, you will need to include a DEVICE command in your CONFIG.SYS file that specifies the particular memory manager included with your board. Alternatively, as you will learn shortly, you can include a DEVICE command that specifies EMM386.EXE as the driver name. This program is included with DOS 5 and Windows 3.1 and can emulate expanded memory by using a portion of your system's extended memory.

EMM.SYS provides a variety of services to a requesting program, well beyond the standard initialization and output functions of a standard device driver. EMM.SYS also provides information, through software-interrupt 67H, regarding hardware and software states and the current allocation of expanded memory pages. Diagnostic routines are available, as are routines to manage the actual mapping of logical pages out of expanded memory into physical pages in the 64K window.

Enhancing the Expanded Memory Specification

The LIM EMS specification provided the groundwork for the next generation of multitasking operating systems. But progress continued in the DOS world with the introduction of new products from industry competitors.

AST Research and Quadram have been two of the industry leaders in the production of add-on memory boards, and Ashton-Tate (acquired by Borland in 1991) is a major producer of personal computer software. Together, these three companies released their own new specifications for expanded memory use. Their enhanced version of EMS was called EEMS (Enhanced Expanded Memory Specification).

EEMS was more complex than EMS 3.2 and differed in key ways. Whereas EMS located the switching area above the DOS 640K program area, EEMS mapped expanded memory into addressable space anywhere under the 1MB address limit. This feature allowed easy switching of memory pages that contain addressable code because they could be switched into the lower memory addresses accessible by DOS programs.

EEMS also offered an expanded mapping window. Whereas EMS allowed the mapping of only four 16K logical expanded memory pages into physical

RSIS Breaks the 640K Barrier for DOS Applications

You probably know by now that Windows provides your applications with access to extended and expanded memory and that EMM386.EXE provides access to upper reserved memory blocks in the 640K–1MB range. But DOS applications can, under certain conditions, actually use an address space that falls just shy of 1MB. A number of commercial memory extenders, such as DESQview from Quarterdeck, use the Relocatable Screen Interface Specification (RSIS) to do this. RSIS specifies how an application can make use of a relocated screen buffer. Programs like DESQview and Memory Commander from V Communications adhere to the specification to share the single video buffer among several executing tasks.

In essence, the memory extender assigns a separate area of memory to each application for use as a private (and relocated by RSIS) screen buffer. When data must be written to or read from the video buffer, the memory manager transfers data between the actual video area and the private area dedicated to each application. The relocated private video buffer space is usually relocated to higher reserved block locations. Since the real video buffer is defined in the lower portion of reserved memory, this technique essentially extends the size of conventional memory beyond 640K, leaving a larger contiguous area of low memory available.

memory, EEMS allowed the mapping of 64 logical pages. EEMS also supported a minimum window size of 16K. In fact, as it turns out, the upper limit on window size was somewhat unrealistic, since much of that space ($64 \times 16K = 1MB$) is needed by DOS, application code, video buffers, and system ROMs. The new EEMS specification did, however, realistically make available all free space within the entire first megabyte of memory.

EEMS also allowed software specification of mapping areas at run time. Under EMS 3.2, you had to take great care setting the proper switches and jumpers on the memory boards to specify the mapping area. Additionally, EMS 3.2 required one contiguous 64K memory area. EEMS allowed the use of several areas that were not necessarily physically contiguous.

For a while, it was unclear which of these two heavyweight standards would emerge the winner. Microsoft's version of Windows at that time used EMS to implement its multitasking strategy, and Quarterdeck's DESQview used EEMS in its own powerful multitasking operating environment. The differing concepts and implementation strategies of these memory specifications made writing programs that ran easily under both specifications difficult. In fact, memory boards conforming to one specification did not necessarily work under the other.

The LIM EMS 4.0 Specification

Users of DOS and designers of programs in the DOS environment were gratified in 1987 by the announcement of the latest evolution of the expanded memory specifications. Known as LIM 4.0 or EMS 4.0, it specifies a new set of developer functions that support much larger DOS applications, as well as multitasking. This new specification permits the use of these improved features on all DOS machines, even the seemingly more limited 8088/8086 PC and PC/XT models.

EMS 4.0 incorporates all the best aspects of EMS 3.2, as well as the improvements made in EEMS, thus reducing confusion among program developers and setting EMS 4.0 apart as a viable standard for future program growth in the DOS world. The AST/Quadram/Ashton-Tate group has accepted the new standard.

The standard defines more than twice the number of functions and subfunctions (30 versus 15) contained in EMS 3.2. In addition, expanded memory has been increased from a maximum size of 8MB to 32MB. Incorporating some of the EEMS techniques ensures that EMS 4.0 supports the execution of any program code in expanded memory.

In addition, the LIM 4.0 specification supports a technique known as *backfilling*. Backfilling is essentially an enhanced form of bank switching that can occur in blocks of conventional memory below 640K. Whereas LIM 3.2 only allowed bank switching through a 64K window in upper reserved memory, LIM 4.0 allows programs to manipulate much larger amounts of information by permitting bank switching down to the 256K point.

By disabling memory between 256K and 640K, LIM 4.0 can then supply the memory for this extra range of addresses. Rather than having a limited single block of 384K of conventional memory (between 256K and 640K), your system can effectively switch many groups of memory into this addressable range.

EMS 4.0 directly supports multitasking. An occasional requirement of programs when they run concurrently is that they be able to share data. This new standard also specifically defines how common data access and sharing can take place.

The developers of EMS 4.0 clearly state that it is not itself a multitasking operating system. It does, however, provide a formidable array of features that allow applications to perform multitasking in expanded memory. A variety of programs, RAM disks, and print spoolers all can run simultaneously in expanded memory.

Emulating Expanded Memory

If you have no available slots in your PC for an expanded memory board, or if you choose to avoid the expense of a new expanded memory board, several solutions are available. Since Windows uses extended memory to run all programs, the solutions discussed here are only meaningful if you must continue to run DOS programs under Windows that themselves require access to expanded memory.

Since the Expanded Memory Specification is device independent, the source of the expanded memory is unimportant to applications using it. Therefore, just as surely as software can cause memory to be perceived as a RAM disk, software can cause a disk to be perceived as memory.

In fact, the same concept can be taken one step further. Expanded memory emulation software can adhere to the EMS requirements, providing memory pages not only from an expanded memory board but from any one of the sources shown in Figure 4.9.

The emulation software conforms to the expanded memory specifications, so the source of the data is irrelevant to an application making the proper EMS calls. The source could be a standard expanded memory hardware board, as shown at the top of Figure 4.9, or it could be one of the two sources (extended memory or disk file space) for emulated expanded memory, as shown at the bottom of the figure.

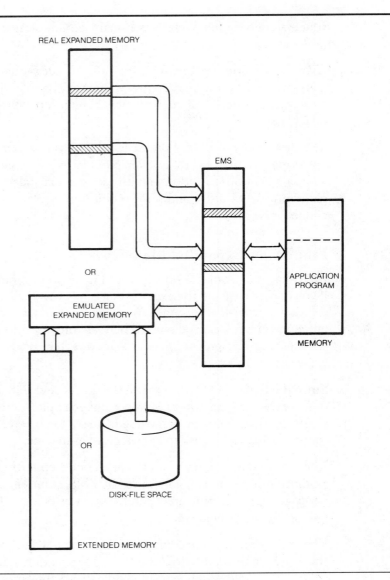

REAL EXPANDED MEMORY

EMS

OR

APPLICATION
PROGRAM

MEMORY

EMULATED
EXPANDED MEMORY

OR

DISK-FILE SPACE

EXTENDED MEMORY

FIGURE 4.9:   Sources of emulated expanded memory

If your system already includes extended memory, you can use EMM386.EXE to treat a portion of that memory as if it were expanded memory. The EMM386.EXE utility performs two significant tasks under DOS and Windows. First, it establishes a link with upper memory blocks for loading device drivers and applications into system reserved memory more efficiently. Second, it can emulate expanded memory by using extended memory you have already installed. This is only absolutely necessary if you have applications that require expanded memory in order to run.

In either case, you must include a DEVICE line in your CONFIG.SYS file. If you do not need any expanded memory emulation support, you can simply include

DEVICE=C:\DOS\EMM386.EXE NOEMS

The NOEMS parameter directs the memory manager to make upper memory blocks available but not to enable any expanded memory. Don't forget to precede this DEVICE line with a DOS=UMB command line in your CONFIG.SYS file.

If you want to establish an emulated expanded memory area, you must replace the NOEMS parameter with two new parameters. For example, you might include this line in CONFIG.SYS:

DEVICE=C:\DOS\EMM386.EXE 2048 RAM

This sample command directs EMM386 to manage the upper memory blocks and to set aside 2048K of your system's extended memory to emulate expanded memory. The RAM parameter ensures that 64K of upper reserved memory is reserved for use as an expanded memory *page frame*. This is the necessary addressable (i.e., below 1MB) window into the total expanded memory area, which is 2048K in this case.

Even if your system has no additional expanded memory installed, you still can run software that requires expanded memory. The emulation routines can create a disk file equal in size to the expanded memory that you need but don't have. The emulator handles the reading and writing of the disk file to obtain the 16K pages needed by the expanded memory manager. This solution permits you to run software in an expanded memory environment, albeit at significantly reduced speeds because of the relatively enormous disk input/output overhead. Virtually no one does this, because Windows primarily uses extended memory, which is significantly cheaper now than in previous years.

Additionally, this technique is only useful and necessary under Windows if your system has no physical expanded memory, but you must run older DOS programs that require expanded memory in standard mode.

Although emulation may seem attractive, it has some obvious drawbacks. As pointed out, using it is markedly slower than using expanded memory directly. The overhead for the software emulation is considerable, and if you are using a disk file to emulate expanded memory, the disk I/O overhead further reduces overall system performance. In addition, emulation software is not always completely compatible with programs designed to run using actual hardware boards. So even if you're willing to endure reduced performance, you still may not be able to run your favorite expanded memory program.

Naturally, the solution is to forgo expanded memory completely and run only Windows applications. However, the EMM386.EXE or third-party emulation software is the next best choice if you continue to run earlier non-Windows applications that require expanded memory.

◆ EXPLORING HOW WINDOWS USES MEMORY

Now that you've learned about the different types of physical memory, it's time to take a closer look at how Windows uses the memory it finds. On an 80286 machine, Windows runs in standard mode and can use conventional, extended, and expanded memory, but only in particular ways. On an 80386 or 80486 machine, Windows can run in 386 enhanced mode and can also use three types of memory, but very differently from standard mode.

USING MEMORY IN STANDARD MODE

When you run Windows applications in standard mode, Windows merely adds together the amount of conventional and extended memory available on your machine. It treats the sum of the two as a single, logically contiguous

Gaining Memory by Changing the Windows Shell

The Windows shell program is PROGMAN.EXE and by now is no doubt a familiar part of your Windows desktop. However, like other feature-laden, icon-based shells, it consumes more memory than a simple text-based shell. If you don't mind losing some of the graphical visual aspect of Windows, you can reduce the memory burden on your system of the shell program itself.

Use the SYSEDIT.EXE program (in your SYSTEM directory) or any other ASCII-based text editor to modify your SYSTEM.INI file. Locate the SHELL= line in the [boot] section. It is near the beginning of SYSTEM.INI and usually reads SHELL=PROGMAN.EXE.

Replace PROGMAN.EXE with any other shell program of your choosing. Windows comes with a text-based shell named MSDOS.EXE. This is actually the original Windows 2.x shell program. It is much smaller than PROGMAN.EXE and will save you space. The first disk accompanying this book has another alternative, BACKMENU.EXE, which is even smaller than MSDOS.EXE. Try them both out and use the one that you like best.

block of memory. As applications run, Windows uses the protected-mode addressing mechanisms discussed earlier to assign this memory to, then access it from, applications. In this mode, Windows cannot use expanded memory at all for its normal applications.

Using Expanded Memory in Standard Mode

When running DOS applications in Windows' standard mode, Windows uses the real-mode facilities of the processor chip. This means that all addressing is limited to the first megabyte of memory. In addition, if your machine has an expanded memory board, this memory can be made accessible to DOS programs that use it. Figure 4.10 depicts these two different ways in which Windows uses memory in standard mode.

DOS applications that run in standard mode can access expanded memory, but only if it is provided from an actual memory board. Even though the EMM386.EXE driver that comes with Windows can emulate expanded

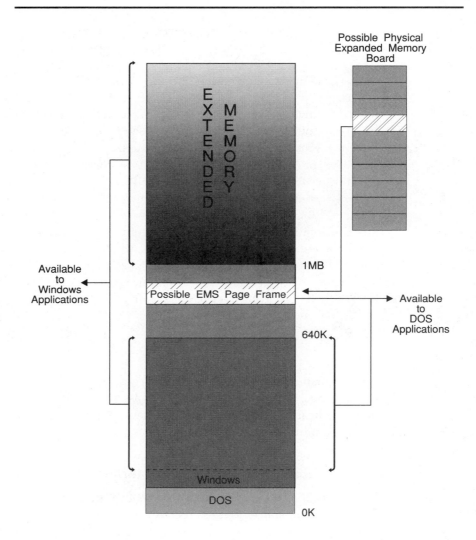

FIGURE 4.10: Using memory in standard mode

memory, it cannot provide expanded memory to DOS applications when running in standard mode. In fact, if you even install the EMM386.EXE driver, you can't start Windows in standard mode. This driver can provide emulated memory to DOS applications before starting Windows or within 386 enhanced mode, but not in standard mode.

If your system runs in standard mode, and you have an expanded memory manager, a portion of upper reserved memory is used by the manager as a windowing page frame. This is often the source of memory conflicts, which can result in Unrecoverable Application Errors. Chapter 18 further discusses expanded memory and page frame conflicts, as well as suggestions for identifying and surmounting them.

Using Extended Memory in Standard Mode

As Figure 4.10 also illustrates, Windows in standard mode can access extended memory directly. It does this through a driver, such as HIMEM.SYS, that adheres to the Extended Memory Specification (XMS). When Windows first starts up in standard mode, it requests all available extended memory from the extended memory manager. Once it has obtained it, Windows doles it out to programs as necessary. The extended memory manager is no longer needed.

If your DOS application uses extender techniques, such as those used by VCPI programs, you must be sure to specify the amount of extended memory required in the relevant .PIF file (see Chapter 8 for more details about setting up PIFs for non-Windows applications).

DOS applications that use extended memory in standard mode incur a unique additional overhead. Since Windows has already consumed all the available extended memory by its start-up call to HIMEM.SYS, there is seemingly no remaining extended memory available. At least, this is what your DOS application will be told when it makes the normal extended memory request to DOS.

To make extended memory available, Windows swaps to disk an amount of extended memory equal to that needed (as specified in your program's .PIF file) by your DOS application. Once the contents of the necessary extended memory locations are swapped out, the extended memory itself can be made available to your DOS application.

Once your DOS application has ended, or you use an application shortcut key to switch to a Windows application, the formerly swapped extended memory contents are restored from disk. If your DOS application is not yet finished, there may be additional overhead in swapping its memory contents. This swapping can be directed to hard-disk space or to a faster RAM drive. Chapter 14 explains how to set up your system most efficiently for swapping.

USING MEMORY IN 386 ENHANCED MODE

386 enhanced mode is the primary mode used by 80386 and newer processors. It can use conventional and extended memory, and can provide its own emulated expanded memory to DOS programs that require it. Most Windows users now use this mode, largely owing to the dramatic reduction in the prices of 80386 machines in the last two years. This mode is significantly more powerful and flexible than standard mode; you should use it unless you experience some unsolvable conflict that is surmountable only by running your machine in standard mode.

Using Conventional Memory in 386 Enhanced Mode

Windows treats conventional memory in 386 enhanced mode the same way as it treats it in standard mode. Windows simply adds the amount of conventional memory available to the amount of extended memory and uses the sum as a total block of available memory for Windows applications.

DOS applications will perceive a familiar amount and type of conventional memory, and possibly expanded memory as well. However, Windows in 386 enhanced mode and the EMM386.EXE driver use the power of the 386 chip to provide individual *virtual machines* to each executing DOS application. Figure 4.11 depicts how 386 enhanced mode does this.

When you first boot up your machine, you typically install DOS and one or more device drivers and TSR programs. Chapter 15 describes how memory managers can use upper reserved blocks to load some or all of your device drivers and TSRs to maximize the amount of free conventional memory. For now, you should understand the concept of how lower conventional memory

Buying New Memory Chips

When adding memory chips, be sure to purchase the correct type. Refer to your system documentation to determine exactly what you must use. You must match existing chips in the following categories:

Packaging: Older memory boards require separate chips. Newer systems use small circuit boards called SIMMs (single in-line memory modules) or SIPs (single in-line packages).

Capacity: The chips are usually 64K, 256K, or 1MB. Sometimes, the capacity is expressed as if the module consisted of four smaller chips. For instance, some 256K modules are identified as 4x64K, and some 1MB modules are identified as 4x256K.

Speed: Memory speeds are typically in the 70–120 nanosecond range, although some chips operate faster and others operate slower. The lower the number, the faster the chip. You can use faster chips than you need, but you'll be wasting your money. You cannot use slower chips. (The ultimate speed of a computer is determined by clock speed.)

Technology: This identifies the electrical characteristics of the chip. The most common type of memory is DRAM (dynamic random access memory), although some faster designs use static RAM (SRAM), video RAM, or page mode RAM.

can be consumed by DOS and any device drivers and TSRs you load into lower conventional memory.

For instance, some device drivers (like the one for a fax board) consume so much memory that you may be unable to find a contiguous block of upper reserved memory in which to place them. Consequently, even your best intentions may be thwarted, and lower conventional memory locations must be used. When Windows constructs a virtual DOS machine, it allocates enough of its memory space to run your DOS application. Up to 640K of space can be allocated for each DOS application. DOS applications do not use memory nearly as efficiently as segmented Windows application.

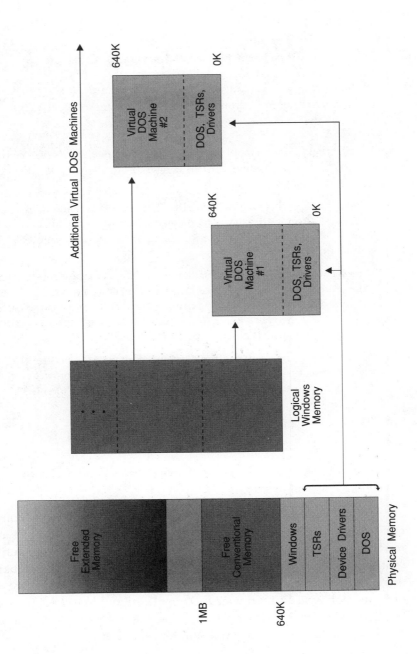

FIGURE 4.11: 386 enhanced mode creates virtual DOS machines.

Each virtual machine consists of a copy of the DOS environment, as well as a copy of the lower memory used by DOS, any device drivers, and any TSRs activated before starting Windows. Automatically receiving a copy of all existing environment variables is called *inheriting* the environment.

◆ MANAGE TSR'S EFFECTIVELY

Under DOS, you run certain TSRs to gain added functionality beyond your single application. Under Windows, you can run several programs and switch or multitask among them. TSRs no longer have to automatically share a single address space.

If a TSR is needed by all your DOS applications, you can load it before starting Windows. It will then be readily accessible to all. Additionally, starting DOS applications under Windows will not require you to construct a batch file that specifically initiates the TSR.

However, if your TSR needn't interact with any other program, you can run it in a separate DOS session. Initiate it as you would any DOS program, then switch to it when you want to access any of its capabilities. Define a hot key for the TSR that is the same as the application's normal hot key.

You can now see why it is so important to maximize the amount of free conventional memory available before starting Windows. Each virtual DOS machine that 386 enhanced mode creates for your DOS applications is reduced in size by the amount of memory taken up by these extra drivers and programs.

In fact, the actual net amount of conventional memory available to applications in 386 enhanced mode's virtual machines is just slightly less than the amount available at a command prompt before starting Windows. This is because of the small amount consumed by Windows itself when it first starts.

In other words, if your DOS configuration consumes less conventional memory, then each virtual machine will consume less conventional memory. DOS 5 is your best bet for producing the smallest *footprint* of DOS itself in conventional memory.

Similarly, each device driver and TSR that you can fit in the UMB (upper memory blocks) area means that the space taken up by each one is freed from conventional memory. The usable space in each virtual machine's apparent conventional memory area is increased. In most cases, this means that a non-Windows application has more working space for such things as spreadsheets, documents, and database files. In some cases, this larger amount of working space means that a very complex program, such as a computer-aided design program, is able to run; otherwise, it might not have sufficient space even to load.

Another factor in determining the amount of free conventional memory is the presence of the API *translation buffers*. These buffers are allocated and used by Windows in 386 enhanced mode to translate a number of DOS and network API service calls from protected mode to real mode. (The need to do this was discussed in Chapter 3.) The instruction addresses for service calls from protected mode are inaccessible to DOS itself, which can access only the first megabyte of real memory. Once the calls are translated, DOS can access the information because the translation buffers are always found in the first megabyte of memory.

Windows can place the translation buffers either in the upper reserved blocks between 640K and 1MB or in a portion of lower conventional memory below 640K. Normally, Windows uses the free locations within the UMB area for

♦ A 64K expanded memory page frame, if necessary

♦ The protected-mode API translation buffers

If you do not load any TSRs or device drivers in UMB locations, Windows will often consume all free bytes in the UMB area for these two purposes. However, DOS 5 permits the easy loading of TSRs and device drivers into UMB locations. Consequently, your system may not even have enough UMB space left to carve out a 64K expanded memory page frame, much less space for translation buffers.

Naturally, you can avoid allocating a 64K page frame in the first place. Adding the NOEMS parameter on the EMM386.EXE device-driver line does this. This method will free up additional UMB space for you to load device drivers and TSRs, or it can free up space for the API translation buffers. Of course, in either case, disabling the expanded memory page frame means that your

Regaining Conventional Memory by Using UMBs

Upper memory blocks (or UMBs) constitute the area between 640K and 1MB. This 384K area normally contains video buffers and ROM BIOS code. Occasionally, other device adapters, such as Plus Development's Hard Card, also use this area. However, although this upper memory area was reserved for such purposes and was consequently called *reserved memory,* it is not limited to these purposes alone. If you use this area wisely, you can dramatically increase the amount of conventional memory available to Windows and your applications.

Both DOS 5 and Windows now provide a program called EMM386.EXE that enables you to use any available space in the UMB area. You can and should attempt to load device drivers and some small applications in this area. To load a device driver in UMBs, simply replace the DEVICE command in your CONFIG.SYS file with DEVICEHIGH. To load an application in UMBs, run the LOADHIGH command, specifying the application name as the first parameter. But make these changes one at a time, testing your devices and applications in between each reboot to see if they will still work when loaded high.

Not all drivers or applications can work in this formerly unavailable area of memory. Some program code makes internal bit manipulation assumptions about addresses limited to below 640K. If yours doesn't work high, load the driver or program normally again. Then contact the manufacturer to determine whether newer versions are available that will work successfully when loaded high.

When I first attempted to load drivers for my fax board, hard card, and Bernoulli box in UMBs, none of them worked. But the manufacturers all had updated software available that worked perfectly in high memory locations. Loading all of them in UMBs increased the amount of conventional memory available to Windows and my applications by *more than 100K.*

DOS applications will be unable to access any form of expanded memory while running in 386 enhanced mode.

Windows will always try to allot space from UMBs for its translation buffers, but the device drivers and TSRs loaded in CONFIG.SYS may already be consuming space. And the page frame may have been reserved, taking up space as well. Whatever the reason, the translation buffers are still necessary. If space is not available in UMBs, Windows will allocate the necessary space from conventional memory below 640K.

This worst-case scenario means that every subsequent virtual DOS machine that is created will be reduced in space by the amount of memory reserved for the translation buffers. Windows allocates all translation buffer space from either UMBs or conventional memory, but not partly from both areas.

Chapter 12 explains in detail the many adjustments you can make to your Windows .INI configuration files. For now, you should be aware of a particular command line that influences the translation buffer and page frame allocations. If you include the line

ReservePageFrame=False

in the [386Enh] section of your SYSTEM.INI file, Windows will attempt to allocate translation buffers from UMBs before it attempts to allocate a possible 64K page frame. If there is enough space for the translation buffers but not enough remaining space for a possible page frame, your DOS applications will not be able to access expanded memory. On the other hand, this approach will maximize the amount of conventional memory available to your DOS applications in each virtual machine.

Using Expanded Memory in 386 Enhanced Mode

Since Windows applications can directly access extended memory, they don't need expanded memory. However, just as in standard mode, old DOS applications may require expanded memory. As you'll learn in Chapter 8, a DOS application's .PIF file specifies exactly how much expanded memory it wants. The .PIF file controls how much expanded memory is allocated to begin the program. It also can specify limits on the maximum expanded memory to emulate and make available to individual programs.

♦ RESOLVE EXPANDED MEMORY CONCERNS WITH CONFIG.SYS

Windows requires extended memory to work effectively. But some older DOS programs may require expanded memory to work. If you run those non-Windows applications from within 386 enhanced mode, place EMM386.EXE in your CONFIG.SYS file. Windows will then emulate expanded memory as needed. However, this means that if your system actually has expanded memory on a hardware board, with a separate driver, you will be unable to use it in this mode. Two drivers managing expanded memory (real and emulated) will conflict. Do not try it.

When you are not running Windows, your DOS applications can use the hardware expanded memory. In this case, you will have to reboot, using the expanded memory manager that accompanied the board rather than the EMM386.EXE file that accompanied Windows. Naturally, this requires that you use two separate files, renaming them CONFIG.SYS (from perhaps CNFWIN.SYS and CNFDOS.SYS), depending on whether you will be running the programs from within Windows or DOS.

However, standard mode only provides expanded memory to DOS applications if your system has a physical expanded memory board; 386 enhanced mode, on the other hand, emulates expanded memory that meets the LIM 4.0 specification. This means that each virtual DOS machine has large-page-frame expanded memory available to it.

Large page frame refers to the capacity for backfilling conventional memory and providing additional bank-switched expanded memory pages. This contrasts with *small page frame* expanded memory, which uses only the 64K window reserved in upper memory blocks. Most DOS programs that use expanded memory cannot even use backfilled pages and work only through the 64K UMB small page frame.

If you want to make expanded memory available to your DOS applications running in 386 enhanced mode, you must make at least a contiguous area of 64K available in the UMB region. To do this, you can attempt any or all of the following approaches:

- ◆ Reduce the number of TSR programs loaded into UMBs.
- ◆ Reduce the number of device drivers loaded into UMBs.
- ◆ Rearrange adapter memory locations (see your adapter board documentation for instructions). For example, ISA bus machines, like the IBM AT, require dip switches to be changed on the boards.

Micro Channel bus machines, like the PS/2, require a simple software modification to change the bus configuration.

♦ Reserve a page frame in UMBs by setting ReservePageFrame=True in the [386Enh] section of your SYSTEM.INI file.

Then again, the reverse situation is even more likely if you do not run any non-Windows applications that require expanded memory. You can completely remove the possibility of expanded memory emulation from 386 enhanced mode by including the following line in the [386Enh] section of your SYSTEM.INI file:

NoEMMDriver=True

In this case, no page frame is allocated, and moreover, no expanded memory driver is loaded. You free up the UMB page frame area and also recapture the space formerly taken up by 386 enhanced mode's expanded memory emulation driver.

♦ **REMOVE WALLPAPER IF MEMORY BECOMES SCARCE**

Yes, wallpaper can be pretty, or gaudy, or decorative, or impressive. But Windows stores the bit pattern and color information in memory. The more detailed and colorful the wallpaper, the more memory is consumed by it. Depending on video mode (i.e., resolution and color), a wallpaper image can consume several hundred kilobytes of space.

If you have begun to receive "Out of Memory" messages, run the Control Panel to disable wallpaper use. Select Desktop and set Pattern to <none>.

Other command lines in the [386Enh] section of your SYSTEM.INI file are important to understand as well. You may want to use the EMM-Size=<bytesize> line, which specifies a maximum amount of expanded memory to be made available. This line should be used if one of your DOS applications typically allocates all available expanded memory. If excess allocation occurs, you need to use the EMMSize line to limit the allocation; otherwise, additional virtual machines will be unable to allocate any expanded memory at all.

Disabling ROM Shadowing in Hardware

Read-only memory, or ROM, usually contains code that is not modified, such as your machine's BIOS. Special devices, such as video monitors or hard-disk cards, often include their own ROM that is mapped into upper reserved memory. But reading instructions from ROM is significantly slower than reading instructions from RAM. ROM shadowing is a technique whereby the instructions from ROM are copied once to RAM. Then the RAM is used instead of ROM.

Some hardware automatically assigns RAM to this chore of providing a fast "shadow" location for often-used ROM code. However, memory managers can do a better job of managing memory if they make all decisions about when and where ROM shadowing is to take place. Check your system documentation to determine whether you can disable ROM shadowing in hardware to enable your memory manager software to make all decisions.

Microsoft's extended memory manager, HIMEM.SYS, includes a /SHADOW switch that enables you to request that shadowing be enabled or disabled. Regardless of whether you are using Microsoft's extended memory manager or some competitor's, it is better to allow the manager to make the decisions about shadowing if possible. However, note that some hardware will not permit disabling of the shadowing facility.

By disabling ROM shadowing in hardware, more extended memory or upper memory becomes available for applications. In addition, if the memory manager itself implements ROM shadowing, it can place the shadowed code in preferred locations, making better overall use of available memory.

One of the most common causes of errors in 386 Windows systems is conflict between hardware adapter memory and Windows' use of the UMBs. Windows normally scans the UMB area for free memory. After this determination, it will use space as appropriate for transfer buffers or a page frame. However, this scan does not always work correctly, particularly if certain hardware adapters do not indicate which portions of the address space they are using.

If you know that a piece of hardware on your system uses a particular portion of the UMBs (in the hexadecimal range A000 to EFFF), you can instruct Windows to exclude those addresses from consideration. Use the EMM-Exclude line in the [386Enh] section of your SYSTEM.INI file to specify which address ranges should not be scanned by Windows or considered for Windows' purposes. Figure 4.12 demonstrates some of the more common uses of the UMB region. Check the documentation for all your hardware to ensure that Windows does not overlap its UMB use with that of any other hardware.

For example, suppose that you have a video adapter from ATI Technologies Inc. Depending on the mode in which the board operates, it may use part or all of the memory addresses in the hexadecimal range A000–C7FF. Because of a special hardware feature called a *nonmaskable interrupt* that this card uses, Windows may be unable to identify that the card actually uses all this space. To properly eliminate this address range from Windows consideration during

Hexadecimal	Decimal	Typical Usage
F000-FFFF	960-1023	ROM BIOS
E000-EFFF	896-959	Shadow RAM
D000-DFFF	832-895	Expanded Memory Page Frame
C000-CFFF	768-831	↑ TSRs and Device Drivers - Additional Video Buffers
B000-BFFF	704-767	CGA, Hercules, MDA, EGA/VGA Text
A000-AFFF	640-703	EGA/VGA

FIGURE 4.12: Typical uses of the UMB region

Increasing Memory for Starting New Applications

By employing any or all of the following methods, you will be less likely ever to see an "Out of Memory" message when attempting to initiate yet another application:

♦ Close applications that you don't need. Don't open applications until you really need them.

♦ Do not use wallpaper, even if it is pretty.

♦ Minimize windowed applications, and minimize any unneeded child windows within expanded windows.

♦ Clear the Clipboard.

♦ Run DOS applications in full-screen mode rather than in windows, if possible.

♦ Disable background execution for DOS applications if they are occasionally useful but do not have to run when you do not have them in the foreground.

♦ Replace the Program Manager with a shell that requires less memory.

♦ Load a mouse driver required by a DOS application only in the session running that DOS application, rather than before starting Windows.

its scan of the UMB region, enter this line in the [386Enh] section of your SYSTEM.INI file:

EMMExclude=A000-C7FF

If you have multiple hardware devices and multiple memory regions to exclude, you may enter several EMMExclude lines, each specifying a different UMB range.

If you discover during troubleshooting (see Chapters 17–19) that Windows is unable to find a free 64K area in the UMB area in which to locate the page frame, you can use another command in the SYSTEM.INI file. The EMM-PageFrame line allows you to set the starting address of the page frame. Use this command if you must have an expanded memory page frame and Windows could not successfully find it for you.

The most common reason for using the EMMPageFrame command is an occasional inability to successfully identify possible modes used by high-resolution graphics display adapters in the memory range between C000 and CFFF. For example, suppose that you only use your video board in normal VGA mode. However, the board itself is able to display in Super VGA mode, using the additional memory between C400 and C7FF. Since you do not plan to use Super VGA, you can be sure that the memory addresses in this range will remain available for Windows' use. If Windows does not figure this out automatically, you can enter this line in the [386Enh] section of your SYSTEM.INI file:

EMMPageFrame=C400

This line will then direct Windows to set a unique address range of C400–D3FF as the 64K expanded memory page frame.

Using Extended Memory in 386 Enhanced Mode

In one sense, extended memory is the easiest kind of memory to understand. It's just a seamless extension beyond the 1MB point of your system's conventional memory. Windows adds free conventional memory to free extended memory to determine how much memory is available to dole out to Windows applications.

Even DOS applications in 386 enhanced mode can access extended memory from a virtual DOS machine. Furthermore, DOS applications can run while the CPU is in protected mode, if they adhere to the DOS Protected Mode Interface (DPMI) specification. (This architectural definition is discussed in depth in Chapter 3.)

Extended memory used by DOS programs can even be virtualized, using the addressing and segmentation attributes of the 386 processor. But all this dependence on extended memory in 386 enhanced mode relies on an extended memory manager. When 386 enhanced mode starts up, Windows uses the extended memory manager to load itself and its various drivers into extended memory.

Virtual memory, and its reliance on 4K page management in 386 enhanced mode, is such an important topic that the next section of this chapter is devoted to it.

◆ UNDERSTANDING VIRTUAL MEMORY

If your system had unlimited amounts of physical memory, each running program would simply use actual physical memory and run smoothly. There would be no question of running out of memory. There would be no problems with multitasking one more program and squeezing it into some place in memory. There would always be a place for it.

But that's not reality. Reality says that the average computer system has no more than 2MB to 4MB of physical memory. Reality says that the average Windows application has an executable file whose size can easily range up to a megabyte in size all by itself, with an accompanying .HLP file that often is 50 to 100 percent larger. Running just a handful of these would usually consume all physical memory in your system if it weren't for Windows' ability to provide virtual memory.

◆ MEMORY: WHAT SHOULD YOU DO?

Consider the following: Don't buy just the minimum. Yes, you can run Windows with a minimum configuration, but it won't be a satisfying experience. At the very best, performance will be depressingly slow. Also, install at least 4MB. Performance in either Windows mode becomes faster. Programs can usually run quicker and switch (or multitask) quicker. Finally, use some of your available memory to take advantage of additional Windows enhancement techniques (see Chapter 15), such as using disk caches and RAM disks.

WINDOWS USES DEMAND PAGING IN 386 ENHANCED MODE

Figure 4.13 depicts the concept of virtual memory addressing in 386 enhanced mode. As you know by now, each application consists of a number of variable-length segments. In Figure 4.13, application #1 has three segments and application #2 has two segments.

In 386 enhanced mode, Windows uses the hardware paging facilities that are built into the 386 (and successor) chips. As discussed earlier in this chapter, a memory page is a 4096-byte (4K) block of information. Each program segment consists of a number of these 4K pages. This is the fundamental unit of information that is managed by the Windows Virtual Memory Manager (VMM).

Basically, for any Windows program to run, only a portion (a limited number of 4K blocks) of the application's .EXE file must be resident in physical memory. This could consist of one 4K page that contains the executing instruction and another 4K page that contains data that is being referenced by the executing instruction. The remainder of the executable program module could conceivably remain somewhere on disk until it is needed.

The concept of *demand paging* means that no pages of a program are actually copied into physical memory until they are required. These nonresident pages could be pages from the original .EXE file that have not yet been read into memory at all. Alternatively, they could be pages that were read into memory but were subsequently copied out (i.e., *paged out*) to make room for another program's executing pages.

When physical memory fills up with copies of the logical pages from executing applications, the VMM must make room for a new page. This would apply to any of pages in Figure 4.13 that are marked Not Present. To make this room, some existing pages from other applications may need to be removed from physical memory.

The concept of *swapping*, also known as paging, means that the VMM copies pages from physical memory into a disk file. This occurs to free up physical pages for the most recently executing application's demand for a Not Present page. The processor chip actually is responsible for generating an interrupt called a *page fault* to indicate that an instruction has referenced

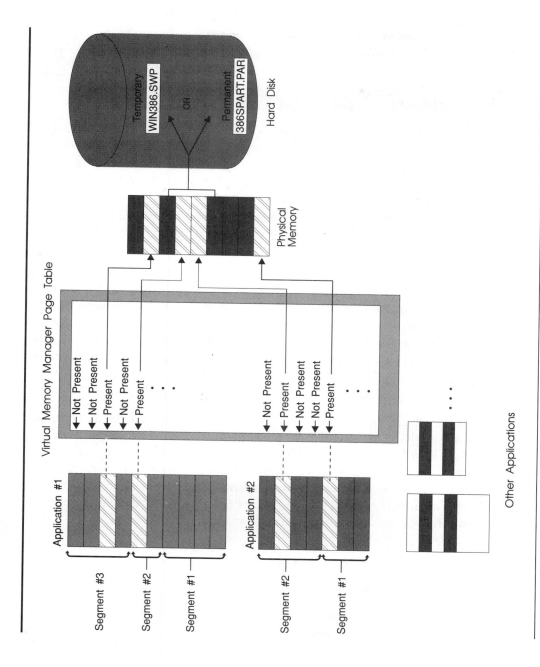

FIGURE 4.13: Virtual memory in 386 enhanced mode

a logical address that is not resident in physical memory. At this point, the VMM assumes control and decides how to satisfy this need.

◆ WHY INCUR THE OVERHEAD OF 386 ENHANCED MODE?

These are some of the advantages of running in 386 enhanced mode: The 386 processor can directly address up to 4GB of memory; that's probably more than any of your applications will ever need. Also, the 386 supports virtual memory, enabling your applications to use hard-disk space as if it were a transparent extension of physical memory. Finally, the 386 offers Windows a special virtual 8086 mode that facilitates the multitasking of both DOS and Windows applications. This underlies the ability to create virtual DOS machines.

The VMM may have an easy time of it, if there is free physical memory, since the desired page can then be directly read from disk into this space. Otherwise, the VMM will have to replace existing physical pages with copies of data for the newer, needed pages. To facilitate replacement, the VMM uses an algorithm called the Least Recently Used (LRU) algorithm to decide which pages of physical memory are copied from memory to a hard disk's swap file.

Each application performs its own segment and offset addressing, as if it actually did have access to unlimited memory resources. To sustain this fiction, the VMM keeps track of each 4K page in each running application. The VMM keeps a *page table* that indicates whether each page of an application is present in physical memory or only in virtual memory (i.e., on the hard disk somewhere). The VMM also keeps track of which physical memory pages are currently assigned to which multitasking application.

SWAPPING CREATES VIRTUAL MEMORY FROM HARD-DISK SPACE

The VMM makes sure that when an application must execute instructions or reference data in a particular 4K page, that page is actually resident in physical memory. If it is not, it is said to be located in virtual memory,

RAM Disks and Swap Files

RAM disks are created from physical memory. They emulate actual disks and have a variety of advantages. When used properly, they can significantly improve the operating efficiency of your system, but they cost you a certain amount of physical memory. Ideally, the loss of physical memory (and the possible impact on performance in a busy system) is made up for by the fast access to files that you store on and access from a RAM disk. See Chapter 15 for advice on how to best set up and use a RAM disk.

Swap files are files that contain copies of virtual pages from executing programs in 386 enhanced mode. Using swap files is critical to supporting the primary characteristic of virtual memory when multitasking applications in 386 enhanced mode.

However, if you direct Windows to place its swap file on a RAM disk, you gain nothing. In this erroneous use of memory, you give up physical memory to create a RAM disk, which reduces the amount of physical memory available to Windows to multitask programs. This means that swapping will occur sooner than it might otherwise. When this happens, and if you've set up the swap file to be on the RAM disk, Windows will use the very same physical memory for swapping (i.e., as virtual memory) that you gave up to create the RAM disk in the first place.

which is essentially another name for a portion of the hard disk. It's not real, physical memory but it's virtually as good, since an executing application doesn't see any difference. The application deals only with its own logical address space; Windows takes care of all appropriate flags and descriptor table adjustments to make the necessary pages resident in physical memory at the right times. Windows uses hard-disk space as if it were an extension of physical memory.

If a page fault occurs, and the VMM must read a new page into physical memory, it must first decide which existing page can be replaced. It uses the LRU algorithm (described below) to do this. After selecting a page to replace, it must write a copy of this page onto the hard disk. It does this by writing the page into either a temporary swap file (WIN386.SWP) or a permanent swap file (386SPART.PAR), depending on your system's configuration.

Chapter 14 discusses the trade-offs between permanent and temporary swap files in 386 enhanced mode, and explains how to control their creation and their location on the hard disk. Chapter 14 also discusses the types of swapping that can occur when you run Windows in standard mode.

After a page of physical memory has been freed up, Windows can then read into memory the application's appropriate logical page. This could be a page that is read from the original .EXE file, or it could be a formerly swapped page that was used once before and now resides in a hard-disk swap file. Windows keeps track of which pages from which applications reside at different positions within the swap file.

The Least Recently Used (LRU) algorithm uses special *flags* (i.e., assigned bits) to indicate whether each page has been read from or written to since the page was first loaded into physical memory. One flag is called the *accessed* flag, which indicates whether a page has been read or written. The second flag is called the *dirty* flag, which indicates whether the page has been modified since being loaded. Naturally, if the page is dirty, then it has also been accessed.

Although a page replacement decision often involves just a single page, it can also involve a group of pages. This might occur if the application itself requests an allocation of new memory that spans a number of 4K pages. This might also occur if the application requests that a new segment be loaded into memory, and this new segment spans several 4K pages. In both these cases, the LRU algorithm attempts to find the required number of new pages during the following procedure. The VMM follows these steps to decide which page or pages to replace:

1. The VMM scans the page table for pages that are neither accessed nor dirty. Since applications haven't referenced these pages at all, for reading or writing, these pages are prime candidates for replacement since they are the least likely to be needed in the foreseeable future. Remember that a certain number of program data and code pages are initially loaded into memory when the application starts up. Not all of these pages are necessarily accessed immediately.

   If a sufficient number of these pages is now available, the VMM swaps them to the hard disk and makes their former physical memory page locations available for new pages. During this step, and in possible preparation for step 2, the VMM clears the accessed bit from each page entry.

2. If step 1 could not identify enough pages to swap, the scan is repeated. Since step 1 clears all the accessed bits, this repeat scan should identify additional pages in physical memory that were only read from but not written to. If a sufficient number of these pages is now available, they are swapped to the hard disk. Then, make their former physical memory page locations available to the currently executing application that needs the physical memory.

   Pages that have only been read from are selected here because there is less eventual system overhead to swap them than dirty pages. Pages that have only been read from can at some later point be discarded, instead of being rewritten to disk to possibly update data files on the disk.

3. If neither step 1 nor step 2 found enough pages to swap out, the VMM simply swaps out enough pages, regardless of the status of their accessed or dirty attribute bits.

Now that you understand how Windows manages memory and multitasks applications by using memory in sophisticated ways, turn to the next chapter. In Chapter 5, you will learn much more about how multiple applications can share data and use the novel techniques for application integration available in Windows 3.1.

5

*Exchanging and
Sharing Data*

nterprocess communication, or IPC, is the formal term for describing the process of programs communicating with one another. Passing information around is a more informal way to describe it. Windows has several methods for allowing programs to share information, including using the Clipboard, Dynamic Data Exchange (DDE), and Object Linking and Embedding (OLE).

This chapter will introduce you to each of these techniques. You will learn the technical underpinnings of each, as well as how and when you can most effectively use these facilities.

The simplest, and least powerful of the three, is the Clipboard. It is similar to a message center; two communicating programs do not directly make a connection. One program can leave information on the Clipboard; another program can later pick up the information.

A step up in Windows communications is the DDE facility. It offers a unidirectional connection between two programs. Any DDE-aware Windows program can establish a one-way link to data constructed in another program. If the creating program modifies the original data (such as a spreadsheet or a graph,) the other program is automatically alerted to the changes. A user of the other program can at most make changes to a copy of the original data; the user cannot make changes to the original data itself.

The most advanced communications mechanism available in Windows 3.1 is the new OLE facility. This is a two-way communications link that involves embedding an icon within one application's data to represent a second application's data. Not only is the first application updated whenever the second application makes changes to its data, but a user can make changes to the original data by clicking on the embedded icon. This automatically runs the original program that created the data, permitting a variety of modifications before returning to the embedding application.

◆ USING THE CLIPBOARD TO EXCHANGE DATA

The Clipboard is a fiction. There is no real clipboard in your system. There is only a reserved portion of memory (named the Clipboard) whose size varies according to what sort of information, and how much of it, is to be stored there. Windows offers a number of internal API service calls that enable applications to communicate with the Clipboard.

The primary use of the Clipboard is as a temporary holding area for either text or graphics data. One program can copy or remove selected text or graphic information from its screen window and send it to the Clipboard for storage. You can then switch to another program and transfer the stored Clipboard data to a specified position in its screen window.

Generally, this facility is used to transfer text from one program to another, to avoid retyping it or to avoid using export/import techniques unique to each program. In addition, users often use this facility to copy a graphic from one program to another program that will combine the graphic with text for later printing. Graphic manipulations can also involve taking snapshots of the screen, or of a single window on the screen, and incorporating the images into a program for later processing.

Using the Clipboard is essentially a rather limited process. Once data is obtained from one source, whether it is textual or graphical, it is an unchanging version of the data at the time it was obtained. If the original data is changed later, it will not affect the contents of the Clipboard. It's a little like taking a photo: The original scene may change later, but the photo will not.

You will learn in this section how to use the Clipboard for all these purposes in your program. But before any sort of transfer can take place, you must specify exactly what it is you want to transfer.

SELECTING DATA TO EXCHANGE
THROUGH THE CLIPBOARD

It's easiest to select information to be copied to the Clipboard by using the mouse. You only need to move the mouse pointer to one corner of the screen area (text or graphics) that you want to send to the Clipboard. Press and hold the left mouse button while moving the mouse. As you move the mouse, an expanding, highlighted rectangle will appear. When you have highlighted the entire portion of data, release the mouse button. The highlighted information is said to be selected; subsequent Clipboard operations will work on this information.

Keyboard users can also readily select information to send to the Clipboard. Just move the cursor to the beginning of the information, and use one of the shortcut keystrokes. Each keystroke extends the selection highlight a prescribed number of characters in a particular direction. Many graphics applications will also accept these keystrokes, moving incremental distances within the screen graphic. Your application's documentation defines how the keystrokes work within that application.

Figure 5.1 depicts the three standard Clipboard operations, as applied to a sample block of text. Each Windows application that conforms to IBM's Systems Application Architecture (SAA) has an Edit menu that contains the following options: Cut, Copy, and Paste.

As Figure 5.1 depicts, choosing Cut removes the selected data from your application's work area and places a copy of it in the Clipboard. Choosing Copy leaves the original information intact and deposits a copy of it in the Clipboard. Choosing Paste replicates at the point of the cursor in the current application work area whatever happens to be in the Clipboard.

Although there are some restrictions, you generally first obtain data from one application's work area with Cut or Copy, depending on whether you want to leave the original data intact. Then, you switch applications, using your mouse or an application shortcut key in Windows 3.1. Alternatively, you can use the Task List, or press Alt+Tab or Alt+Esc.

Once you have switched to the new application, you typically move the cursor to the intended point of insertion for the Clipboard data. Lastly, you use the Paste command to deposit an exact copy of the Clipboard data at that

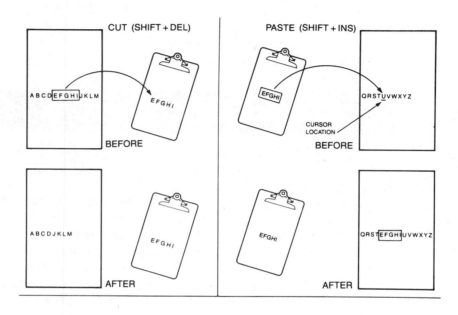

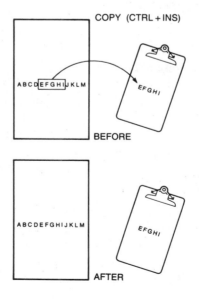

FIGURE 5.1: The three most common Clipboard operations

point. In fact, the Clipboard is a convenient way to replicate graphics or text in several places in the same application, or even in several applications. Just create the information once, and copy it to the Clipboard. Then, successively use the Paste command at each location where you'd like to insert a copy of the data.

◆ TRANSFERRING YOUR CLIPBOARD DATA TO OTHER COMPUTERS

When you are logged on to a bulletin board system (BBS) or to an information service like CompuServe, you can use the Clipboard to transfer data instead of having to type it in yourself. First, use the Edit Copy command from your Windows application to transfer a copy of the data to the Clipboard. (See later in this chapter for instructions on copying such a block from a DOS application.) Next, since you are logged on to a remote computer, you can use your communications program's Paste command to rapidly transfer the Clipboard data through your modem. When you select Paste, and you are connected properly to the remote system, the text that was in the Clipboard will be sent directly out the communications port, as if you had typed it very, very quickly.

Data that is placed in the Clipboard remains in the Clipboard until you delete it with the Clipboard Viewer (explained later in this chapter) or until you use the Cut or Copy command again. Each succeeding use of Cut or Copy causes Windows to release whatever memory was used by the Clipboard and to allocate a new block for the new information that is to be stored in the Clipboard. As you'll learn in the upcoming section on the Clipboard Viewer, you can also save the graphic or textual contents of the Clipboard to a disk file for later manipulation.

Keyboard users can also perform all Clipboard operations with shortcut keys. The SAA guidelines specify that applications interpret Shift+Del as the equivalent of pulling down the Edit menu and selecting Cut. Similarly, Ctrl+Ins is the equivalent of Copy, and Shift+Ins is the equivalent of Paste. (Ctrl+X, Ctrl+C, and Ctrl+V also work.)

Use Cut and Delete Commands Judiciously

When you select and subsequently delete (or clear) data of any sort, you throw it away irrevocably. Unless your application contains an Undo command, you will have to reenter or re-create any data that was erroneously removed. Even if your application contains some form of Undo command, you must usually specify Undo immediately after making the mistake!

When you select Cut, after highlighting some portion of your application's data, the data is similarly removed from your screen. But there's a big difference. In this case, the information is stored in the Clipboard. Typically, you use this method as a prelude to pasting the data into another application. However, you can also use it as a prelude to pasting the data elsewhere in the same application.

If you get in the habit of cutting information rather than deleting it, you can easily retrieve an inadvertent deletion. As long as you haven't moved elsewhere and activated another Cut or Copy command (which overwrites the current contents of the Clipboard), you can simply return the cursor to the point where the data should still be, and select Paste. The formerly cut data will be read from the Clipboard and rewritten back into your application.

◆ RECLAIMING MEMORY USED BY THE CLIPBOARD

Windows manages a variable-size block of memory for the Clipboard. Each time you direct Windows to delete the contents of the Clipboard, Windows releases the memory formerly used by the Clipboard. This can be a substantial amount of memory. Graphics images often consume several hundred kilobytes of memory. If your system is running low on memory, using the Clipboard Viewer to delete a no-longer-needed graphic image can have a significant impact. Then, although the effect is relatively minor, close the Clipboard Viewer itself, since it consumes several kilobytes of memory.

CAPTURING SCREEN AND WINDOW IMAGES

As a DOS user, you may be used to pressing the Print Screen key to obtain a printed copy of what appears on your screen. Under Windows, pressing Print Screen appears to do nothing. In fact, that's far from true. When you press Print Screen, Windows copies an entire graphic bit-map image (pixel by pixel) of your entire screen to the Clipboard. If you really want to use the Print Screen key to print a hard-copy image of your screen directly, you can do this only in 386 enhanced mode. For the most common 101-key keyboards, it is as easy as pressing Shift+Print Screen.

Pressing Print Screen works in both modes of Windows, although there are some unusual aspects to how it works. For example, in standard mode you cannot run a DOS application in a window. In addition, Windows is not very good at handling the copying of graphic data to or from DOS applications. Pressing Print Screen when in standard mode accurately copies a text screen but not a graphic DOS screen to the Clipboard. You can copy a DOS screen in graphics mode only when you are running in 386 enhanced mode.

There may be times when you would like to copy a single window to the Clipboard. To do this, you must first activate the window by clicking anywhere within it, by using the Task List, or by pressing any one of the task-switching keys. Once you've activated the desired window, just press Alt+Print Screen to send a copy of the entire window to the Clipboard.

Some older keyboards do not recognize the Alt+Print Screen key combination; instead, you must press Shift+Print Screen to copy an entire window to the Clipboard. If your keyboard does recognize pressing Alt+Print Screen as a means to copy a window to the Clipboard, then pressing Shift+Print Screen is a handy way to send a copy of a DOS application's text screen to the printer. This is equivalent to printing a copy of a text screen by pressing Print Screen under DOS.

Pressing Alt+Print Screen really copies a bit-map image of the complete window, in Windows .BMP format, to the Clipboard. This includes the title bar, scroll bars, and so on. You may want to use the Paintbrush utility to focus more precisely on just the work area of the window.

Furthermore, depending on where you eventually want to paste the graphic information, you may need to convert graphic formats. Since the data is stored in the Clipboard as a .BMP-formatted image, you may want to temporarily paste the image into Paintbrush or another graphics conversion program. From this middleman program, you can save the image in a different format. Lastly, you can import the image into the final destination program, which may only accept certain image formats, like the PCX format available through the Paintbrush file.

Then again, you may want to use the Snagit program available on the disks accompanying this book. The registered version of Snagit can not only capture an entire screen or window but it can also capture any rectangular portion of the screen that you specify. It can also store the image in the TIFF format.

When capturing information from a DOS application, be aware that the data will be stored in the Clipboard in a text or graphic format, according to the mode the DOS application was working in at the time. Even if the screen looks like text, it may be graphical and therefore stored as a bit map. Consult your DOS application's documentation for information about the modes in which it works. Sometimes, there is a hot key that can switch the application from text to graphics mode, or vice versa. In some applications, such as Lotus 1-2-3 Release 2.3, there is a simple menu procedure to switch from normal text display to a WYSIWYG (What You See Is What You Get) graphics mode.

USING THE CLIPBOARD VIEWER

The Clipboard Viewer is simply a Windows application (CLIPBRD.EXE) that appears as one of the main icons in the Main program group of the Program Manager. At any time, you can double-click on this icon to run the Clipboard Viewer and see what is in the Clipboard. In fact, you can leave the Clipboard Viewer open in a window on your screen. It will refresh its own display each time you perform any Clipboard manipulation from another program, such as Copy or Cut. It will also reflect any Print Screen key presses or additional Clipboard manipulations, such as those offered by the screen image capture keys of the Snagit program.

The Clipboard understands several different application formats. An application may send data to the Clipboard in several formats, which you may view with the Clipboard Viewer before pasting or storing the information. The Display pull-down menu in the Clipboard Viewer is your means of identifying all possible data formats.

When you cut or copy information from an application, that application determines what formats are to be used for sending the data to the Clipboard. By using several formats when cutting or copying, an application increases the likelihood that the information can be easily pasted into the work areas of other applications. This maximizes the compatibility of data extracted from one application.

Each application that sends information to the Clipboard conveys to the Clipboard the different formats used for the data. These formats appear on the Clipboard Viewer's Display menu. The first option is usually Auto, which is the default format used for the Clipboard Viewer's display of the data. If you want to see the data displayed in one of the other possible formats, you only need to select a different format from the menu.

The Clipboard Viewer occasionally shows some of the formats on the display in a grayed or lighter color. This means that the application that cut or copied the information was able to provide the data in more formats than the Clipboard Viewer was able to understand. Other applications can acquire the data in one of these formats because the Clipboard Viewer can store and later transfer it out, but it cannot currently display it. Microsoft Excel, for example, provides data in quite a few formats that can be passed through the Clipboard but cannot be redisplayed by the Viewer itself.

Although you'll sometimes see formats like SYLK, TIFF, and RTF, the most common formats you'll see listed on the Display menu are

> **Auto:** the default format used to display information stored in the Clipboard.
>
> **Text:** standard ASCII, null-terminated text.
>
> **OEM Text:** standard, null-terminated text. However, this format employs the character set used by the OEM application that stored the text. This is usually the default text format used when the Clipboard accepts screen text from DOS applications.

Bitmap: the most common Windows device-independent bit-map format used for graphics screen images.

Metafile: consists of a group of Graphics Device Interface (GDI) commands (see Chapter 3). These binary formatted commands usually represent drawing requests understandable to individual applications, such as drawing a circle or stretching an image.

Owner Display: a unique format provided by the originator of the information stored in the Clipboard. This option only remains available while the originating application is still running under Windows.

Once an application has stored information in the Clipboard, the source application is no longer needed. Other applications can paste the information into their workspace by using the standard Paste command. The receiving application selects the desired pasting format from those it finds in the Clipboard.

When you paste text from the Clipboard into an application, the receiving application determines the formatting of this text. Although the Rich Text Format (RTF) can retain data formatting along with the text itself, other text formats cannot. Even if the text appeared in a certain way in an originating application, the text will often change its format in the receiving application. In word processors, for example, you can often use different fonts and formats at different points in your document. The final format of the text depends on the format that is active at the point where you position the cursor before pasting new text.

You can readily save the contents of the Clipboard to a file for later use by pulling down the File menu and choosing Save As. Typically, you type in a file name with a .CLP extension to save the image in bit-map format. However, you may have text in the Clipboard that you want to save in .TXT format for eventual inclusion in a text-processing application.

Most of the time, you use the Clipboard immediately. Directly after storing information in the Clipboard, you switch to the application into which you'll paste the data. However, you may be very tight on memory in your system. Even if there is enough memory to save an image, there may not be enough memory to start another application. After saving the Clipboard contents to a disk file, you can then close the application that created the image. In this way, you may free up enough memory to start the application that will eventually receive the data.

Then again, you may have an application that creates a Clipboard image in standard mode. The application into which you want to paste the data may not run in standard mode on your system. So you may choose to save the Clipboard data until some later point when you run the receiving application in 386 enhanced mode.

◆ USE THE VIEWER TO SEE CLIPBOARD CONTENTS

Suppose that you've lost track of what data currently resides in the Clipboard. Simply switch to the Program Manager, and select Clipboard Viewer from the Main group. This runs the specialized accessory program that displays the current contents of the Clipboard.

You can keep the Clipboard Viewer open in a window on your desktop at all times. In this way, you can always see exactly what text or graphics have been extracted with Cut or Copy. You'll always know what information will be inserted as a result of the next paste operation, or what information will be lost irrevocably during the next usage of the Cut or Copy command. Additionally, you can run the Clipboard Viewer and immediately minimize (iconize) it. At any time later, you can restore it to quickly view the contents of the Clipboard.

TRANSFERRING INFORMATION BETWEEN WINDOWS APPLICATIONS

It is extremely straightforward to transfer information through the Clipboard between Windows applications. Whether it is the same application or a different one, there is generally an Edit menu that contains Cut, Copy, and Paste options. You can use these to store and retrieve information with the Clipboard. If your application does not have special move or copy abilities of its own, you can use the Windows Clipboard instead.

386 Enhanced Mode: Cut and Paste for DOS Applications

To copy (cut) text from one DOS application, press Alt+Enter to run it in a window (if you're not already running it in a window). Open the Control menu, select Edit, then select Mark. Move your mouse to the upper-left corner of the text you want to copy. Then press and hold down the left mouse button as you move the mouse to highlight the desired text. Release the button. Then select Edit from the Control menu in the window's upper-left corner. Finally, choose Copy.

To insert (paste) this text into another DOS application, switch to the other application's window. If it is running full screen, press Alt+Enter to run it in a window. Within this target application, move the cursor to the desired location for the copied text, pull down the Control menu, select Edit, and then Paste.

TRANSFERRING INFORMATION BETWEEN DOS APPLICATIONS

Transferring information through the Clipboard between non-Windows applications is more difficult. If the information is to come from a Windows application but will be copied into a non-Windows application, the source procedure is easy. Just select Cut or Copy in the Windows application to send a copy of the information to the Clipboard.

If the target application is a Windows application, but the source is a non-Windows application, the receiving procedure is easy. Just select Paste in the receiving application once the data is in the Clipboard.

The difficult part of these transfers is getting information into the Clipboard from a non-Windows application or getting information out of the Clipboard into a non-Windows application. Non-Windows applications do not have Cut, Copy, or Paste options. But with a little attention to detail, you can still perform these traditional Clipboard chores. You can even copy data from a non-Windows application and paste it into another non-Windows application.

There are some basic considerations for obtaining information from a non-Windows application. Figure 5.2 summarizes the mechanisms available to you for copying information from a non-Windows application to the Clipboard.

As Chapter 8 explains in more detail, non-Windows applications in standard mode can run only in full-screen mode. Consequently, you can only copy the full-screen image to the Clipboard. Remember that pressing Print Screen copies the full screen to the Clipboard.

However, if your system is running in 386 enhanced mode, you can run a non-Windows application in a screen window. You can copy the entire screen, the

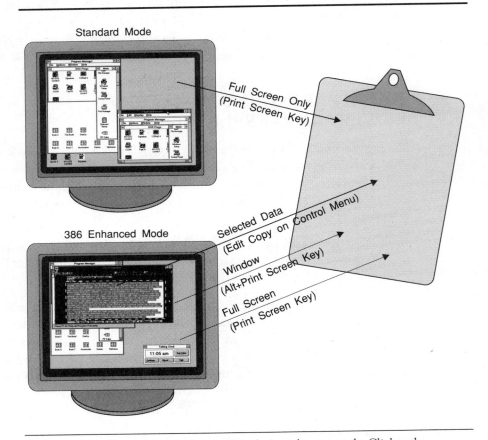

FIGURE 5.2: Copying data from a non-Windows application to the Clipboard

Standard Mode: Cut and Paste for DOS Applications

When going from DOS to Windows, when you run a DOS application in standard mode, you can press the Print Screen key to copy a DOS application's screen to the Clipboard. Once the data is in the Clipboard, you can use the Paste option on the Edit menu to insert the data in any Windows application. Afterward, you can cut any undesired portions of the copied data.

When going from DOS or Windows to DOS, you can't paste graphics directly into a DOS application. But you can paste text data from any Windows application, or another DOS program, into a full-screen DOS application. To do so, you must first move the cursor to the desired location where you would like to paste the contents of the Clipboard. Next, iconize the DOS application by pressing Alt+Tab or Alt+Esc to switch to another application.

If you wish, you can obtain data from any other application at this time. After ensuring that the desired data is in the Clipboard, select the target DOS application's icon by clicking on it once. This displays the System menu. Select Paste; this places a copy of the Clipboard's contents at the location of the cursor in the target DOS application.

entire window containing the non-Windows application, or a selected portion of data from the work area of the non-Windows application's 386 enhanced mode window. Remember that pressing Alt+Print Screen copies the active window to the Clipboard.

When a non-Windows application runs in a 386 enhanced mode window, the upper-left corner of the window has a small horizontal-bar icon. This is called the Control menu and contains several options, one of which is named Edit. If you first use mouse or keyboard techniques to select a portion of the non-Windows application's work area, the title bar displays the word Select until you do something with the selection. Typically, you open the Control menu and choose Edit, then Copy. This deposits a copy of the selected data in the Clipboard.

Once the data is in the Clipboard, you can follow different procedures for pasting the data into another DOS application. The difference depends on whether the receiving DOS application is running full screen (in standard mode or in 386 enhanced mode) or in a window (only in 386 enhanced mode). Figure 5.3 summarizes the two techniques.

In 386 enhanced mode, pasting into a DOS application's window is reasonably direct. Once you have moved the cursor to the insertion point in the receiving application's work area, you simply open the Control menu for that window and select Edit Paste. The destination location is clearly visible to you, and the results of the paste are themselves immediately visible.

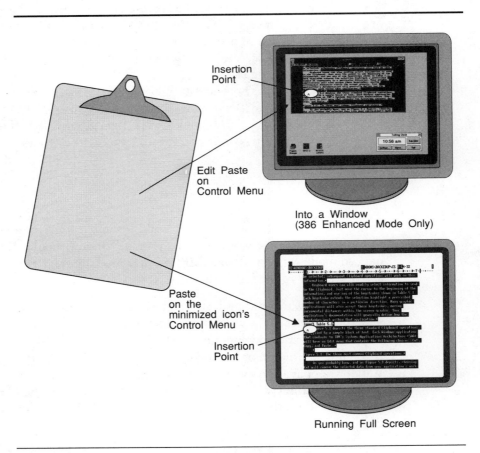

FIGURE 5.3: Pasting from the Clipboard into a DOS application

Problems with Transferring Data between Non-Windows Applications

Chapter 17 discusses a number of data transfer and Clipboard difficulties. For the moment, however, you should be aware of these possible problems:

♦ In 386 enhanced mode, you may be unable to switch back to full-screen mode from a windowed mode because you initiated a selection but did not complete the Edit Copy step. If so, the title bar of the window will show *Select*. To leave this selection mode, click mouse button 2 or press the Escape key.

♦ When you view the Control menu, the Copy command may be grayed, disallowing a transfer to the Clipboard. This is because you did not correctly complete your work area selection. If this is the case, return to the work area and repeat the selection procedure.

♦ When you view the Control menu, the Paste command may be grayed, disallowing a transfer from the Clipboard. This is because the Clipboard does not contain any information. Return to your source application, and repeat the steps to select and copy the information to the Clipboard.

♦ Copying a graphic image from a DOS application to the Clipboard may not work. This may be because you are in standard mode, which does not allow you to transfer graphic DOS images to the Clipboard.

♦ You cannot paste a graphic image into your DOS application in standard mode or 386 enhanced mode.

♦ In 386 enhanced mode, everything looks OK, but the paste does not result in the data being correctly pasted in the receiving application. This may be because the 386 enhanced mode pasting operation occurred too quickly for the application to correctly accept and process the characters. To slow the speed of data transfer from the Clipboard to your DOS application, disable the Allow Fast Paste option in the .PIF file. See Chapter 8 for further explanation.

Pasting data into a DOS application that is running in full-screen mode is the most difficult procedure. There is no Control menu for a DOS application that is running full screen. However, when running in 386 enhanced mode, you can usually put the DOS application in a window by pressing Alt+Enter. (Note that this technique will not always work for graphics applications.) Then, you can follow the instructions given before.

In standard mode, you cannot run the application in a window, so you must first iconize the DOS application to access the icon's Control menu. Transferring information from the Clipboard will then be easier.

This somewhat tricky procedure requires that you first run, or switch to, the application that is running full screen. You must move the cursor to the desired insertion point, then use one of Windows' switching keys to make a Windows application or icon active. Usually, the best way to do this is to press Alt+Tab. This cycles through all running applications, displaying their names for your selection. Release both keys when the name of a Windows application or icon is highlighted.

At this point, the insertion point in the DOS application is prepared, and the DOS application itself should be visible at the bottom of your screen as an icon. Click once on this icon to display a Control menu for your receiving application that was running full screen earlier. Select Paste (if you are running in standard mode) or Edit Paste (if you are running in 386 enhanced mode). Windows will prefix the word Paste in front of your icon's name until you next switch back to the receiving application. At that point, you will see that the Clipboard contents were correctly copied to your non-Windows application at the point where you placed the cursor.

◆ USING DDE AND OLE FOR APPLICATION COMMUNICATIONS

In the remainder of this chapter, I'll be discussing different strategies and facilities for linking and embedding information. These techniques enable you to establish automatic connections between applications, such as Microsoft's Word for Windows and Excel, or Asymetrix's ToolBook and Borland's ObjectVision, or any programs that make use of Dynamic Data Exchange and Object Linking and Embedding, offered by Windows 3.1.

It can be difficult to learn sophisticated tools in any new environment. In this particular case, it can be more difficult to learn these tools if the context for learning requires that you also understand two completely new programs. I'll explain the fundamentals of these tools by using diagrams to clarify them. You should choose two programs that you know and understand to try out these tools as you learn about them in this chapter.

As I indicated at the beginning of this chapter, Cut and Paste is a passive use of the Windows Clipboard. Dynamic Data Exchange is a messaging system within Windows that facilitates the construction of automatic one-way links between one application's data and another application's data. DDE has been an integral part of Windows in the past; the OLE facility described in the final part of this chapter was introduced in Windows 3.1 as a sophisticated extension of DDE.

UNDERSTANDING THE DYNAMIC NATURE OF DDE

Using the Clipboard is somewhat like using a mail drop. Someone drops off mail, and someone else picks it up. The mailbox itself doesn't do much. However, just as the United States Postal Service provides a convenient service to us by sending paper copies of information from one person to another, so does the Windows Clipboard provide a copying service. Just remember that the Clipboard contains only a copy of information, not the original data itself.

If you cut or copy data from a spreadsheet (e.g., a table of values) or a graphics program (e.g., a chart), you place a snapshot of that data in the Clipboard at that moment. If the spreadsheet data changes moments after you use the Cut or Copy command, those changes are not reflected in the Clipboard. The changes will appear only in the work area of the application in which you made the changes.

Using the DDE facility is a bit more like having a conversation. In fact, *conversation* is the precise term applied to any DDE transaction between two Windows programs. You can read briefly about the internal details of Windows DDE conversations in the following section. For now, realize that two programs that have DDE capabilities are able to establish active links between their data. This means that modifying the data in one program can automatically update the linked data in another program.

For example, you may have a linkage between a program that produces graphs, such as Excel or 1-2-3, and a program that can incorporate charts into text, such as Word for Windows. If the underlying data in the graphics program changes, the linked chart in the word processor's file is automatically updated. A new Windows option called *Paste Link* provides this DDE capability.

The mechanisms of DDE are nearly transparent to you as a user. If both applications understand the DDE protocols, the procedure to follow is very similar to the Cut/Copy and Paste procedure you already know. If you simply copy a chart to the Clipboard, then use Paste to insert a copy of it in Word for Windows, you insert a static snapshot of the graph. To update the report that contains this graph, you have to first delete the out-of-date graph, then repeat the entire Copy and Paste sequence involving both programs.

However, if both programs contain DDE capabilities, they will have another option on their Edit menus, Paste Link. This option establishes the linkage between the programs. You needn't do anything further. Because you've inserted a dynamic link in the word processing document, any changes to the original data in the charting program will automatically effect changes in the word processing document.

The linked data reside in the original source application's format and in a file used by it. The application that actually manages the original data is called the *server*, and the application that accepts a pasted link to that data is called the *client*. For the updating to occur automatically, both programs must be running simultaneously.

Since a link has been incorporated, the two programs use DDE messages to manage the conversation that updates the data automatically. This most common linkage is called a *hot link,* because the updating of the client's data file is automatic if the data in the server's data file changes. Some applications offer a second type of permanent link, called a *warm link,* in which the updating takes place only if the client application requests it. You will generally see a message box if your application offers warm links in addition to hot links.

Occasionally, the necessary server application is not running when you run a client application. If you attempt to open a client file that contains a linked reference, you will see a message box that either directs you to open the necessary server program or offers you the opportunity to initiate it.

To update the client program's file with the latest version of the linked server program's data, the client sends a DDE message to the server if it is running. The ensuing conversation contains the linked data range and the updated data.

DDE provides applications with protocols and a set of API service calls for establishing and maintaining conversations. Since there is no standardized interface to the DDE facility, each application may implement its own interface differently. However, the number of visual differences between programs is rapidly diminishing because of the increasing number of common library functions that Windows 3.1 now provides to applications. Nevertheless, you may have to check your application's documentation to learn all the correct commands and menu sequences for taking advantage of DDE facilities.

TAKING A LOOK INSIDE DDE

Whenever you initiate any application that supports the DDE protocols, that application sends messages about itself to other running Windows applications. Pasted links contain the name of the appropriate server application and any linked file names. Because of this, the client application can initiate a conversation by sending a requesting message directly to the server application. The server can route the message to the particular file that has been linked to the client.

Conversations go on behind the scenes all the time with DDE applications. A typical user sees only Cut, Copy, Paste, and Paste Link options. Yet, behind the scenes, it's like a telephone switchboard, with messages coming and going all the time. In fact, the same application can be the client for some data and the server for other data.

Each DDE conversation contains three key items: an application name, a topic, and a data item. The application name specifies the server's name, so the client application can construct and send a DDE message to the correct server. The topic name usually identifies the file name that contains the range of linked data. The data item identifies the particular group of data that has been linked and is to be updated.

A DDE conversation occurs between client and server applications via the standard Windows message queues. Remember from Chapter 3 how Windows has its central message queue, and messages pass to individual applications through each application's own message queue. Message-loop code in the application processes the messages found in its particular queue.

DDE conversations use the normal Windows and application queues to pass DDE-specific messages (see Table 5.1). Each application implements Dynamic Data Exchange to converse with each other by using global memory blocks and global atoms, along with these special DDE messages.

A *global memory block* is a segment of memory that is allocated from the pool of system memory. As pointed out in Chapter 4, the amount of this memory depends on how much extended memory your system contains, how much conventional memory remains when you start Windows, and the nature of the demand for memory by other programs that are running.

An allocated global memory block is represented by Windows to a requesting application by a numeric *handle,* which is later used in the service calls to identify the memory. In fact, if an application wants to access a block's contents, it must ask Windows to lock the memory block first. Locking a memory

TABLE 5.1: DDE Messages

Message	Explanation
WM_DDE_ACK	Acknowledges whether a message was received
WM_DDE_ADVISE	Requests server to advise of changes to a data item
WM_DDE_DATA	Sends a data item to a client
WM_DDE_EXECUTE	Sends a command string to a server
WM_DDE_INITIATE	Starts a client-server conversation
WM_DDE_POKE	Sends a data item to a server
WM_DDE_REQUEST	Requests a data item from a server
WM_DDE_TERMINATE	Ends a conversation
WM_DDE_UNADVISE	Requests no further change notifications about a data item

block ensures that no other application will be able to gain access to that memory. Only then will Windows return a programmer's *far pointer* for the block itself. (A far pointer is a special value that enables an instruction in one segment to access the contents of a memory address in another segment.) DDE memory blocks are allocated as shared memory, so multiple programs can access the same data.

A *global atom* is simply an ASCII string that is more easily used than a global memory block, because it is directly readable. It also requires less space to store than an entire memory block. However, each atom also requires a Windows handle to establish the standard service-call protocols. Atoms are stored in a portion of system-controlled memory that is accessible through the global descriptor table, discussed in Chapter 4.

Windows uses global atoms for the relatively short names of the server application and the linked topic. It uses a global memory block to store the linked data itself, which can be considerably larger. A typical DDE sequence, then, consists of the following steps:

1. The client program generates global atoms for the server and topic names.

2. The client program sends a message, which contains handles for itself and the two global atoms, to all open windows.

3. The correct server program acknowledges the client message by responding with handles for itself and its server/topic names. This establishes the conversation. The global atoms are no longer needed and are deleted by both programs.

4. The client program sends a message that identifies the desired data and format.

5. The server program satisfies the request by placing the desired information in a global memory block. The client program retrieves the data, using the handles sent by the server. This step is repeated for the duration of the conversation.

6. The client requests and the server acknowledges an end to the conversation.

This sequence° is in reality much more complicated, since the programmer must deal at each step with the details of the DDE messages, as well as understand and properly use the global atoms and memory blocks. This involves locking and unlocking memory blocks at the proper times, creating and deleting atoms, and acquiring and using the various handles that are created. This has been a daunting task for many a Windows programmer.

DDE is not easy for programmers to use. Even when all the DDE messaging steps are programmed perfectly, the mechanism is still subject to a number of difficulties. For example, since the linking contains the name of the linked data file, what happens if the user later changes the name of this data file? What happens if the user calls up the Task List to end one of the programs currently engaged in a DDE conversation?

In Windows 3.1, Microsoft has created a special dynamic link library that provides higher-level programming access to the DDE facilities. Called the Dynamic Data Exchange Management Library, or DDEML, it provides a number of higher-level function calls that offer traditional programming access. Rather than deal with the DDE primitive messages, a programmer can use named functions and conventional parameter specifications to manage DDE conversations. Table 5.2 summarizes this set of DDE functions.

UNDERSTANDING OLE'S APPLICATION CONNECTIONS

Microsoft also offers in Windows 3.1 a powerful extension of the DDE facility. The Object Linking and Embedding, or OLE, protocol extends the power of DDE by implementing a higher-level of connection between applications.

Using the Clipboard to cut and paste offers you the ability to insert a static copy of data from one application into another. To enable the second application to be updated dynamically when the original data changes, you must use Paste Link. In applications that support DDE, pasting a link provides a one-way updating capability. If the original data is changed by the program that created it, all links are updated. If your program is running simultaneously, you will instantly see the changes appear in your application's work area.

TABLE 5.2: DDEML Function Calls

Function	Explanation
DDEAbandonTransaction( )	Cancels DDE transaction; releases resources
DDEAccessData( )	Obtains base address and length of specific data item
DDEAddData( )	Adds new data to existing data
DDEClientTransaction( )	Specifies synchronous or asynchronous data transaction
DDECmpStringHandles( )	Compares strings associated with two handles
DDEConnect( )	Initiates a client-server conversation
DDEConnectList( )	Initiates conversations with a client and multiple servers
DDECreateDataHandle( )	Obtains a handle for a data item
DDECreateStringHandle( )	Obtains a handle for a string
DDEDisconnect( )	Terminates a conversation
DDEDisconnectList( )	Terminates a set of server conversations
DDEEnableCallback( )	Enables or disables asynchronous event notifications
DDEFreeDataHandle( )	Releases a data item handle
DDEFreeStringHandle( )	Releases a string handle
DDEGetData( )	Reads data item information into application memory
DDEGetLastError( )	Obtains explanation of most-recent DDEML error
DDEInitialize( )	Prepares the DDEML library for all other calls
DDEKeepStringHandle( )	Maintains string handle after callback exit
DDENameService( )	Maintains entry in Registration database
DDEPostAdvise( )	Notifies server of hot-linked data changes
DDEQueryConvinfo( )	Requests 32-bit application-dependent data about a client-server conversation

TABLE 5.2: DDEML Function Calls (continued)

Function	Explanation
DDEQueryNextServer( )	Sequences to next handle in a conversation list
DDEQueryString( )	Obtains a string associated with a particular handle
DDESetUserHandle( )	Sets an application-dependent 32-bit value
DDEUnaccessData()	Releases the data item pointer

OLE goes one step further, as depicted in Figure 5.4. If both the client and server programs in a conversation are OLE-aware, they can offer a two-way updating facility. The linked data can be represented by an icon in the client program. By double-clicking on the icon, the client uses OLE functions to automatically initiate the server program. All the editing facilities of the program that originally created the data are once again available to you. You can make any desired adjustments to the data, which then cause all other links to be updated as well. After the changes are completed, the client program is resumed and the server program is closed.

For example, suppose that you prepare a spreadsheet that contains a departmental budget analysis for your boss. Your boss, in turn, combines your spreadsheet with seven other departmental spreadsheets and incorporates them into a word-processing summary presentation for upper management. His management report contains pages of text, with the eight departmental spreadsheets interspersed throughout.

If your boss and upper management never made changes to the budgetary numbers, a standard DDE link would be sufficient. When you or one of the other department managers made changes to individual budgets, the final management report would be adjusted. However, the reality is that your boss would probably want to make additional adjustments to the departmental numbers before finalizing the upper-management report. The two-way linkage of OLE would be quite helpful.

His word processing document is a file that can receive the links to the original spreadsheet files. Any file that accepts data or links to data from another source is called a *container* in OLE terminology. In this example, the OLE container is a word-processing document file. It could be a Word for Windows or WordPerfect for Windows file. It could even be another consolidating spreadsheet file that the boss has on his computer.

What Is an OLE Object?

The information that originates elsewhere is part of what gets stored in an OLE container. To be complete, what is stored in a container is called an *object*.

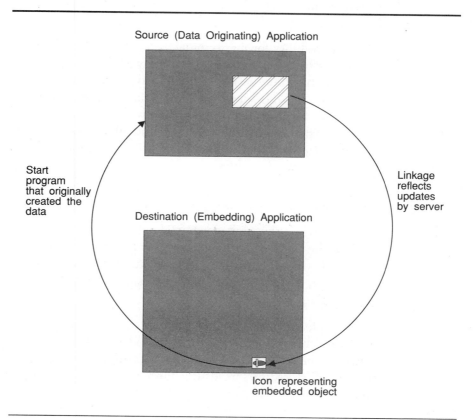

FIGURE 5.4: OLE programs offer a two-way updating capability.

It has two key aspects:

♦ Content: the data and/or linkage.

♦ Presentation: the appearance in the container of the object.

Each department manager's spreadsheet is a separate OLE object. The program that creates an OLE object is said to be the owner of the object. Each object is actually created and later can be manipulated by its originating application or owner. You may have created your department budget with 1-2-3 for Windows or Excel. Whichever program you used, it's the OLE owner of the budget objects. Your boss may be consolidating the spreadsheets in WordPerfect for Windows or Word for Windows. Whichever program is used to encapsulate the objects, that program's file is the OLE container for the budget objects.

The responsibility for managing embedded or linked data always rests with the originating application. Consequently, OLE makes it possible to construct a new file that contains many different types of data in many different types of formats. An OLE container can contain objects that otherwise would be completely incomprehensible to the encapsulating container application. Your text application needn't understand anything about graphics to easily embed a graphic object created by another application, such as Powerpoint, Excel, or Harvard Graphics.

Embedding vs. Linking

Objects can be either embedded or linked in application data files. Depending on how the application implements OLE support, it may offer choices for either or both possibilities. An object is said to be *embedded* within a file if the source data, in its original format, is actually stored in binary fashion within the container application's file.

For example, suppose you embed a range of worksheet cells in a word processing document. In addition to the name of the spreadsheet's .EXE file, the cell contents, the range information, any necessary formulas, and the cell formatting are all stored in spreadsheet format within the word processing document. Figure 5.5 depicts the process of embedding data.

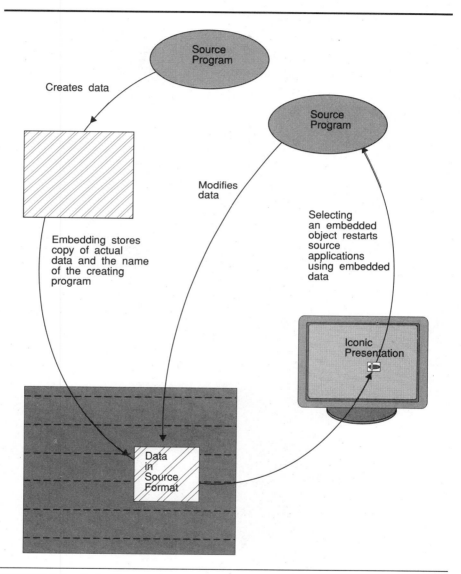

FIGURE 5.5: Embedding an object stores data in the source format.

An object is said to be *linked* if the source data is stored in its original file, and only a pointer to this original data is stored in the destination container file. Figure 5.6 depicts the process of linking data.

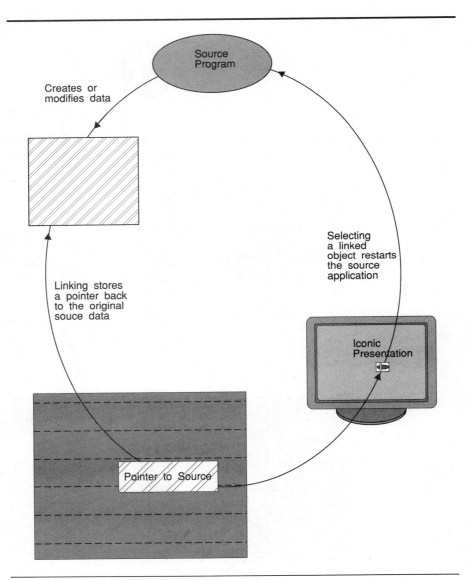

FIGURE 5.6: Linking an object stores a pointer to source data.

Notice in both Figures 5.5 and 5.6 that the presentation, or appearance, of the OLE data is the same, regardless of whether the underlying mechanism is that of linking or embedding. In either case, double-clicking or selecting the

What Good Is Object Linking and Embedding?

Here are some of OLE's advantages:

♦ Individual applications (e.g., a communications program) can specialize, knowing that other data manipulations (e.g., text preparation) can readily be performed by other specializing applications.

♦ An OLE application can print or transmit a document without any concern for the application that originally created it.

♦ Linking facilitates dynamic updating of the underlying information.

♦ Linking produces more compact files, since the underlying information is not stored in the encapsulating document.

♦ Underlying document formats are easily changed without affecting the containing document. This makes an OLE document both flexible and extensible.

presentation item (an icon) causes the source application to start up. The primary difference is that linking means that there is still only one source version of the data. If many programs link to one piece of source data, then all applications are automatically updated if the single copy of the data is changed.

In embedding, however, the container application has its own copy of the original source data. You can easily return to the source application to make changes, but in this case you are making changes to the embedded copy of the original data. This embedding technique still enables you to use the source application to update your personal copy of the data. However, no other OLE applications will be informed of the modifications made by your destination application. Of course, you can always make subsequent links from your application to other applications.

♦ IMPROVING OLE APPLICATION PERFORMANCE

An OLE client application is any program that can store and display an OLE object. In general, an OLE object is recognizable in an application as an icon. An OLE server application is any program that can begin executing an OLE object when that object is selected by double clicking in a client application. Server applications can improve overall performance by supplying application programmers with a dynamic link library, called an *object handler,* that provides rapid and specialized services to clients. These services can handle the most common requests, thus making it unnecessary to start the full-blown server application.

Manipulating Objects in OLE Applications

One of the dialog box options that an OLE application usually displays strips off the linkage and presentation aspects of the object, leaving only the original data itself. The data contents of an OLE object are operated on by the originating application. If you strip off the additional information that uniquely defines the object, the data must then be acted on by the containing application's tools.

Atomic OLE operations can be performed on objects themselves, once you've identified them. Understanding these operations will enable you to easily construct compound documents that contain multiple links to objects. Not only can one document contain several OLE objects but the referenced objects can themselves contain other OLE objects. In other words, both the source and destination containers can themselves contain links to other complex OLE objects.

To build up these compound documents easily, the OLE specification offers an enormous number of API functions. Some of these functions apply to the client application, and others apply to the server application. Some have to do with managing documents, others with handling the Clipboard, and still others with creating and managing the objects themselves.

The three fundamental operations that you can perform on OLE objects are moving, copying, and linking them. You can think of an object as an icon, much like the icons in the Program Manager. To move an object, you physically

When to Use the Clipboard, DDE, and OLE

Using the Clipboard to cut and paste is best for a onetime extraction or copying of data. I use this technique when writing about software. I copy some facet of a program once to the Clipboard, then put the copy (using the Paste command) into my word processing document (i.e., my chapter).

DDE offers a more dynamic facility. You can establish a one-way dynamic link between applications. I use this technique to prepare a monthly business report that includes financial calculations. When cell values in the linked-to spreadsheet change, the word processing document (e.g., a Microsoft Word document) automatically reflects the changes. But the data is still controlled completely by the spreadsheet program. This saves me the trouble of cutting and pasting the changing data each month.

OLE goes one step farther, offering a two-way dynamic link. I can double-click on the graphic OLE object in the linking program (i.e., the word processor), causing the originating program (i.e., the linked-to spreadsheet) to be run automatically. This linked-to program immediately activates the OLE object that was selected, enabling me to make adjustments to the spreadsheet values without having to leave the word processor.

remove the object from one container and place it in another. For example, you might move a department budget object from your consolidating Excel spreadsheet container, in which you perform some final budgetary adjustments, to your final WordPerfect document container, in which you construct your final management proposal.

To copy an object from one container to another, you replicate the entire object (data and presentation) in another container, while leaving the copied object unchanged. If the object was a linked object itself, then the newly copied object is just a newly created link. For example, to save the time of reestablishing links to the departmental spreadsheets, you might copy the spreadsheet links from the original report document to a final management proposal document.

◆ OLE APPLICATIONS MUST ADHERE TO CLIPBOARD
CONVENTIONS

To embed or link objects, both client and server applications usually pass information through the Clipboard. Users don't have to worry about this detailed information at all. Programmers must be careful to order this information properly to define the type of object they want to embed or link. Four kinds of data formats can represent the data in the Clipboard: Native, ObjectLink, OwnerLink, and Presentation. To place an embedded object in the Clipboard, you must first store the Native data, followed by the OwnerLink, any applicable Presentation/Picture, and the ObjectLink formats. To store a linked object, you must first store the OwnerLink, then any applicable Presentation/Picture, Native data, and ObjectLink formats.

The third fundamental OLE operation is simply that of linking. As I've already pointed out, a link to an object is stored in a destination container document. It contains information that specifies the source of the data, as well as the owner application that created it. This provides the destination container with sufficient information to start the originating application when requested and to provide the originating application with the correct data in its original, or native, format.

USING THE WINDOWS PACKAGER APPLICATION

A *package* is itself a type of OLE object that contains another file, part of a file, a command line, or any other object. Double-clicking on the icon that represents the contained object causes the underlying object to be activated. Applications always embed the graphic aspects of a package, whereas the data contents of a package can themselves be an embedded object or a link to an object located elsewhere.

You can use the PACKAGER.EXE program that is part of Windows 3.1 to associate an icon with any object information that is to be embedded or linked.

The Object Packager icon in the Accessories group of the Program Manager runs the PACKAGER.EXE program. Naturally, you can only use the Packager application to create or insert packages for OLE-aware applications. As you can see in Figure 5.7, the Packager application offers the opportunity to define both the appearance and the content of the package that you create.

On the right side of the Packager work area, you can display the contents of the package in either textual or graphical format, depending on what's in the package. If the package contains a bit map, for example, you can click on the Picture radio button to view the picture. You can also click on the Description radio button to view a description (e.g., "Copy of Paintbrush picture") of the package's contents.

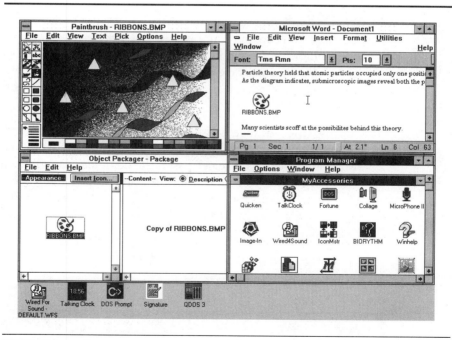

FIGURE 5.7:   PACKAGER.EXE defines the contents and appearance of a packaged object.

On the left side of the Packager work area, you can define the presentation icon that will represent this package when embedded or linked in an application. By default, Packager uses the icon from the object's source program. For example, if you are packaging a Microsoft Excel worksheet range, the default icon that appears is the Excel program icon. But you can change the icon to any other icon on your disk. To do this, click on the Insert Icon button. A dialog box appears that enables you to display all icons in any disk files and to select one of them for this package.

The File pull-down menu has several options to permit you to import any sort of graphical or textual data from other disk files into this package. It also has options for updating and saving the package data. The Edit menu has quite a few options for sending package information to the Clipboard, including Cut, Copy, Paste, and Paste Link.

Other options on the Edit menu support the unique role of the Packager application. You can add your own textual label to the package's icon by selecting the Label option, and you can use the Copy Package option to prepare your completed package for insertion in another document. Once you've prepared a package, selecting Copy Package sends a copy of the entire package to the Clipboard.

Copying the package to the Clipboard includes the contents' data, the presentation icon, and the icon's label. If you next switch to any other OLE-aware application and select Paste, the complete package will be inserted in that application. You will initially see an icon, but the OLE application will offer menu options for continuing to display it as an icon or expanding it to show as a window that displays the object contents.

You should use an application's Paste option for inserting a package, because a package is itself supposed to be embedded in the destination application. Figure 5.8 depicts this situation.

◆ USE PACKAGER TO SET UP APPLICATION HYPERLINKS

A package is an OLE object that contains other objects, such as files or commands. Use the Windows 3.1 Packager accessory to associate files and data with icons you choose. Users can later double-click on the icon to run the underlying program or display the underlying data. The

OLE libraries are responsible for activating the object within the iconized package.

Linked, as opposed to embedded, data may also be made part of a package. The linkage is stored (i.e., embedded) in the container application's document file. This means that you must make the decision about whether your data is to be linked or embedded when you actually bring the information into the Packager application. Since you always embed (i.e., paste) a package

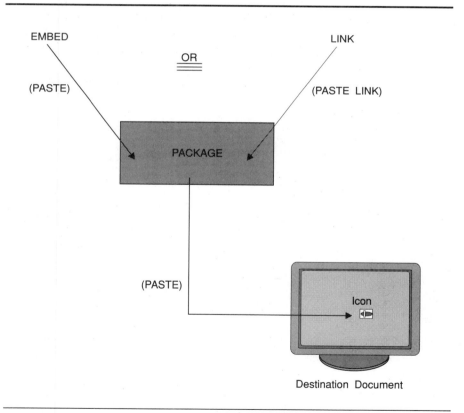

FIGURE 5.8: Using Paste to insert a package into an application

into a document, you must have defined earlier whether the package contains embedded or linked information.

Some applications do not have to use the Packager to embed a document in a package. For example, you can use the mouse or the keyboard in the File Manager to perform the necessary steps. With the mouse, you can drag the icon of the source document into a destination document. If you do this without touching the keyboard at all, you insert a package that contains an embedded file (the equivalent of Paste). If you press Ctrl+Shift while dragging the mouse, you insert a package that contains a linked file (the equivalent of Paste Link).

Now that you understand the principal ways in which applications can share data and communicate with one another, turn to Chapter 6 to discover one of the current areas in which data sharing is very important. Chapter 6 will introduce you to the hottest topics in personal computing: CD-ROM and multimedia.

C H A P T E R

6

Understanding Multimedia

♦

In the past, computers provided users with essentially static information: a table of numbers, a graph of results. In recent years, software has become available under DOS that provides a certain measure of visual animation. For example, some of these programs display bar graphs with bars that seem to grow, or display other images that appear to move around the screen, or screen shots that fade in or out, using various screen transition techniques.

Multimedia Windows is an informal term often applied to Windows 3.1. It includes support for a range of special-purpose hardware devices, as well as a host of system extensions that enable developers to more easily offer dramatically enhanced Windows programs. These programs incorporate special capabilities and effects that use animation, music, speech, video, and audio techniques.

In this chapter, you will learn the fundamental concepts of multimedia, from the historical perspective to differing viewpoints today. You will learn about the components of multimedia systems and the effects of local-area-network technology. You will read about a wide range of exciting applications available today, as well as about the many potential uses of multimedia being explored now by other developers.

This chapter explains Microsoft's extensions to its already extensive set of system service calls and how this device-independent API is organized. You will also learn how to choose a CD-ROM drive, CD-ROM software, and the hardware chips and boards that make these various applications possible.

Lastly, for the very technical among you, the chapter also explains the technical underpinning of CD-ROMs and multimedia. You will learn precisely how a CD-ROM disk is structured, how sound gets on and off such a disk, and how data of all sorts is compressed and decompressed on CD-ROMs. And you will learn a number of techniques for audio, video, and animation that are used by multimedia application developers. The technology is quite new on personal computers, and there is a wealth of new terminology. You will become acquainted with much of it in this chapter.

◆ UNDERSTANDING THE CONCEPTS OF MULTIMEDIA

The simplest way to begin to understand the term *multimedia* is to analyze its Latin roots. Basically, it just means "many ways to present information." In the strictest sense, computers have been able to present information in many ways for years. But Windows 3.1 takes a giant leap forward because it can do much more with the presentation and the packaging of information. Chapter 5 discussed OLE, so you know that various objects can be packaged and represented as icons. Everything you learn about multimedia in this chapter can be combined on your system, with appropriate application software, to construct extremely powerful and flexible application environments.

You create multimedia applications on an *authoring* platform, then later run them on a *delivery* platform. The delivery platform is your PC with appropriate support hardware. This typically includes a CD-ROM drive, with various other digital devices or boards for storing and re-creating video and sound signals. The authoring platform is essentially a similar computerized system, but it typically includes more hardware and developmental software tools.

Up until now, multimedia applications have not been created or presented on a PC platform. They may have employed a PC, but the live-action video on screen may have come from a VCR or a videodisc device. In fact, for years most professionals have combined slides with audiotape or videotape to produce presentations. Windows 3.1, along with the right hardware, can mix full-motion video with both digitally generated speech and animated graphics.

THE FUNDAMENTALS OF MULTIMEDIA APPLICATIONS

All computer applications are based fundamentally on sound and sight, but interpreting these components can become very complex. Simple sound and light combinations become true multimedia when the sound becomes real, and the sight becomes interactive. The kinds of multimedia applications that you'll learn about in this chapter can combine static artwork with text, using Windows' many fonts. This true multimedia facility can combine computer-generated graphics with sound as easily as it can combine digitized photographs or full-motion video. Further, it can combine special effects, such as cell animation of still images, multi-image displays, and various video effects like wipes, dissolves, and fades.

To develop applications with these techniques, you make use of the software packages' abilities to change the audio and visual effects, according to your inputs and choices. This interactivity is equivalent to familiar branching capabilities, but on a much more sophisticated level. Simple computer-based slide shows often provide this branching capability, but multimedia applications can add rapid linkage between on-screen selections and multimedia results. Because these connections are very much like the hypertext displays found in many help systems, some people have referred to multimedia applications used for self-paced learning as *hypermedia*.

Educational multimedia applications can combine user inputs for sequencing with logging and analysis of responses. In this way, a multimedia instructional application can both evaluate progress and control subsequent instructional decisions. Applied to this simple example of training, multimedia can dramatically improve effectiveness.

Your multimedia personal computer can output audio and video signals. Consequently, your multimedia applications can synchronize voice narration with moving video, superimpose graphics on the screen simultaneously, and incorporate a synthesized sound track.

A HISTORICAL PERSPECTIVE

Back in the 1950s, a number of manufacturers developed database applications that became known as *hypertext*. Using database indexing techniques,

What Really Constitutes a Multimedia Application?

On the computer, multimedia combines both hardware and software to offer users sight, sound, and interaction.

Sight refers to the computer's ability to display graphic images, either digitized or computer generated, along with text. In addition, it includes animation techniques, such as multi-image display and video effects (e.g., fades and wipes).

Sound refers to the computer's ability to superimpose voice or music, either digitized (on disk) or recorded (on tape), on the video display. This requires synchronization capabilities, so a sophisticated multimedia platform must have both audio and video signal output.

Interaction extends the power of multimedia output to the users of the system. It refers to the degree of influence the user can have in controlling the amount, content, nature, and sequencing of the sight and sound outputs.

they were able to jump from one textual entry to another. In various ways, the user could indicate the logical ordering of the information displays. Apple made this type of technology widely available in the 1980s with its popular HyperCard. You see this type of linked text display whenever you activate the Windows help facility.

Extending this hypertext concept to include the manipulation of graphic display segments leads to what has been called *hypermedia*. Typically associated with self-paced learning, many CD-ROM-based packages enable users to perform text-sensitive searches that result in the display of all text segments related to a specified subject.

In the latest version of Windows 3.1, multimedia applications extend hypermedia to include new data objects. The new objects that can be found by search criteria include audio, video, and animated graphics. Later in this chapter, you'll learn about a variety of specific CD-ROM-based applications, such as Compton's Multimedia Encyclopedia, that combine all these elements into highly entertaining and informative CD-ROM retrieval mechanisms.

THE TOOLS OF THE TRADE

You now have a sense of what Multimedia Windows is all about. Let's take a step further toward clarifying the different types of sounds and sights that your multimedia PC is able to manage.

Distinguishing between Analog and Digital Video Graphics

Televisions and videocassette recorders create images that are based on electrical signals and light waves. To be precise, the images are based on sine waves whose frequency and amplitude vary. Video images created from variations in these sinusoidal waves are known as *analog* images. To store an analog image requires considerable storage space, making analog signal storage a poor choice for implementing smooth animation on a PC.

Digital images are stored as and reconstructed from a pattern of binary bits whose values are 0's or 1's. Depending on how the bits are used, each screen pixel is assigned a color and an intensity. Because of the ease of manipulating files containing 0's and 1's, a digital image can be easily managed in a multimedia environment. Creating video effects and editing images are much easier than performing the same chores in an analog video environment.

Interactive video is a term that applies to the combination of digital and analog factors. It is found in training environments. You will see analog signals from laser discs or VCRs superimposed on digital images that are constructed from stored disk files. The new multimedia extensions for Windows 3.1 include support for overlay video boards, which means that combined analog and digital images will soon become a common part of many multimedia applications.

However, as the expense of computers and large hard disks continues to plummet, analog images may no longer play a part in any future applications. A new technological development called DVI (Digital Video Interactive) now facilitates the compression and decompression of digitized images in real time on a PC. The algorithms involved are described later in this chapter, but essentially they reduce the memory required to store and transmit images.

Compression algorithms often save space by replacing the image memory with simple equations. When the images must be reconstructed, the equations are used to recalculate the pixel images. Consequently, full-motion video can not only be displayed but can be readily manipulated on your PC as well. This is because it is easy to manipulate any collection of digital 0's and 1's.

DVI is being strongly promoted by Intel, who first acquired the technology from General Electric in 1988. In late 1990, Intel announced its i750 Video Processor chip set, which reduced the original GE six-board set to two VLSI (very-large-scale integration) chips. When developers and applications successfully begin to use DVI and incorporate technologies such as AVI (audio-video interleaving), you will no longer have to incur the extra expense of analog video support systems.

AVI is the state of the art. In the simplest of terms, this technology allows you to display a television picture in a window on your VGA monitor. The hardest part of this is the synchronization of the digitized full-motion picture with the sound. But this has been addressed with the new functions available in the Multimedia Extensions API, described later in this chapter.

When AVI was introduced, it wouldn't run on a minimum multimedia PC of that time. You could run stock multimedia applications on the minimum 286 system, but you couldn't support the necessary high data transfer rates demanded by an AVI application. To run AVI, you'll need at least an 80386SX processor (the new standard) along with a very fast CD-ROM drive. Specifically, the CD-ROM drive must be able to sustain data transfers at least equal to 150 kilobytes per second. In addition, the CD-ROM data transfers must not consume more than a limited portion of available CPU cycles. Only the most advanced and newest CD-ROM drives meet these demanding specifications.

Considering Analog and Digital Audio

PCs have a built-in speaker that for years has been able to produce only a feeble beep. Some new software, like Wired For Sound from Aristosoft, is able to play an extensive set of audio sounds (including simulated speech) through this simple speaker. With this particular piece of software, you can even customize your Windows environment by attaching these sounds to individual dialog boxes, screen windows, and pull-down menus.

However, the PC speaker is unable to reproduce the necessary frequency spectrum that is required for true voice and music reproduction. Various sound boards are now available that offer the necessary conversion capabilities for both recording and playing back sound in PC applications. When sound (i.e., an analog signal) is captured and stored digitally in a disk file, it is said to undergo an *analog to digital* conversion. When a stored sound file is read and converted back to audible sound, it is said to undergo a *digital to analog* conversion.

Special circuitry is necessary to perform these conversion functions. The latest sound boards have this capability, and the multimedia extensions to Windows 3.1 provide software developers easy access to sound manipulations. The Macintosh uses an 8-bit 22-kHz linear sampling rate for uncompressed sound, and Microsoft's multimedia extensions support this same audio sampling rate. But beyond this, as you will learn later in this chapter, Windows 3.1 now also offers support for interleaving sound with other hard-disk data. This means that sound can be more easily synchronized with video presentations.

What kind of sound are we talking about? Just about anything you can think of, from simple sound effects to prerecorded speech, to synthesized speech, to the audio outputs from VCRs, videodiscs, and CD-ROMs. The multimedia extensions provide additional support for the MIDI (Musical Instrument Digital Interface) format, which drives a host of electronic musical instruments.

Originally, MIDI was developed as a standard for connecting electronic instruments and music synthesizers. Importantly, it also includes an efficient format for storing music in disk files or in your computer's memory. Rather than storing the analog waveform information, MIDI specifies a series of commands. One command turns a note on, another command turns the note off, a third command changes the volume of the note, and so on.

Once again, the device-independent nature of Windows comes to the fore. The commands direct which notes to play but allow the instrument or synthesizer to decide how to make the sound. This helps to constrain the size of the sound files as well.

The digital signal processor (DSP) offers an exciting hybrid of analog and digital capability. DSP devices can easily manipulate electronic waveforms, so generating music and speech are actually feasible in your digital computer environment. You only have to obtain the proper board that contains a

LAN Users Need to Prepare for Multimedia Burdens

In earlier years, LAN users saved money by sharing expensive peripherals like laser printers and sophisticated plotters. As multimedia technology justifies the purchase of expensive audio and video computer components, LAN sharing of the hardware becomes the obvious next step.

But beware the dreaded constraints of effective bandwidth. The more traffic (data flow) around the network, the slower your PC may perform. You will need to consider several steps to ensure that your network can handle the dramatically increased data traffic associated with multimedia applications.

Speak with your network supplier about the possibilities for augmenting current hardware. Wholesale replacement should be the last possible consideration. Replacing only certain components may increase performance sufficiently to handle your new, shared multimedia applications. Also, explore data compression and decompression strategies (and new standards) for using software to reduce the actual volume of data that is being moved around the network.

DSP chip, such as the Sound Blaster Pro from Creative Labs. Since sound is no more than a collection of audible waveforms, your PC with the right sound card can play and record both music and voice.

LANS AND MULTIMEDIA

The early promise of local area networks (LANs) emphasized the sharing of expensive resources, like laser printers or expensive multicolor plotters. Although a PC can certainly be a self-contained resource that sits on one user's desk, it can potentially be more efficient when treating the multimedia components as shared resources. It is no more economical to place a CD-ROM drive on every user's desk than it is to give each user their own laser printer.

Nevertheless, there are other issues to consider when sharing resources such as multimedia components. As these issues come to the fore, so do standards for their solution. Later in this chapter, I'll be talking about some of the organizations that are springing up to establish multimedia standards.

Data compression, for example, has different proponents and different methods that can be used according to the application. All digitized video images consume a good deal of space and therefore can become a great burden on a network. Application programs, as well as communications servers, are making data compression and decompression a standard and transparent network feature.

The bandwidth of any network establishes the upper limits on the volume of data that can be transmitted per second. Ethernet speeds top out at around 10 megabits per second, while token-ring LANs top out closer to 16 megabits per second. Certain advanced graphical workstation LANs, or connective LANs that can link up token-ring or Ethernet LANs, use the 100-megabit-per-second FDDI (Fiber Distributed Data Interface) standard.

Applications that use this large bandwidth technique enjoy full color and motion video with synchronized voice and data. Nevertheless, bandwidth constraints should be among your first considerations when deciding to make multimedia equipment available to users on a network.

APPLICATION IDEAS FOR MULTIMEDIA

There is no shortage of ideas for multimedia applications. Later in this chapter, I'll discuss many applications that are now available in CD-ROM format for your multimedia PC. In this section, I'll give a brief insight into the largest categories of multimedia applications.

Corporations stand to gain a great deal by using the new facilities of the multimedia PC. Video images, with synchronized sound, can be presented easily to customers and prospects. They can just as easily be used to prepare convincing internal and external proposals and presentations. Customer information and education systems, as well as product-related information, are becoming more common on standalone PCs.

PCs have often been used to create and access extensive reference materials for employees of large corporations. You may have already used more than one document archival or retrieval system. Adding audio and visual capabilities to such systems, and possibly combining these with e-mail capabilities, will

Designing a Fancy Multimedia Workstation

Your company has lots of money and wants the best tools possible for a push into the world of multimedia training applications. What should you include in your top-of-the-line multimedia PC?

- 80386 or 80486 PC (at least 20–25 MHz)

- Windows 3.1 with 4–8MB of RAM

- 64–128K memory cache on motherboard

- CD-ROM player

- VCR and camcorder

- Video image capture board for inputs from VCR/camcorder

- 256-color Super VGA monitor and an NTSC monitor

- VGA-to-NTSC board

- Microphone, audiocassette recorder, and MIDI devices

- Audio capture board for inputs from microphone, audiocassette recorder, and MIDI devices

- Stereo speakers and audio playback board

- Scanner and scanner board

- Videodisc player and motion video board

- Input devices (e.g., keyboard, mouse, pen, trackball, touch screen)

- 100–200MB hard disk

make multimedia a major means to support the personnel in widely distributed organizations.

Interactivity makes the two-way exchange of information possible. When users make selections in a multimedia environment, the controlling application software can simultaneously collect data on user (or customer, client, and so on) preferences. So the power of the multimedia PC does not lie solely in the dramatic presentation or manipulation of audio and visual images. It can provide a broader support tool to management for decision making.

Information communications are significantly improved by easier attachment of sound to text and video. Training becomes more effective because of the addition of video and synchronization capabilities. And presentations, already a critical application in many companies, are taking on new life with the razzle-dazzle that comes from including motion video, animation, speech, and music.

◆ UNDERSTANDING THE MULTIMEDIA PERSONAL COMPUTER

Does your computer bear the MPC logo? Does that new CD-ROM sport the latest sign of the times? This special logo (see Figure 6.1) is a trademark of the Multimedia PC Marketing Council. The council consists of a number of hardware and software vendors, including Microsoft, Zenith Data Systems, Video Seven, Media Vision, and NEC Technologies. The council is a subsidiary of the Software Publishers Association, which has a seat on the board of directors of the MPC Council, along with representatives from each member vendor.

FIGURE 6.1: The MPC logo

Constructing a Multimedia Platform

Any multimedia system, whether Windows- or DOS-based, requires that you add a CD-ROM drive with audio output. You should also have an enhanced audio (often called a *sound*) board in your system that supports 8-bit, 11-kHz input and 8-bit, 11-kHz/22-kHz output.

Typically, a multimedia system includes applications that store and display extensive graphics information as well. To sustain these requirements, you will need, at a minimum, VGA graphics for the display and a 30MB hard disk for storage.

Your multimedia Windows system also requires a two-button mouse and should probably have a MIDI synthesizer and MIDI ports. Internally, your system needs the processing power of at least an 80386SX processor (although I'd recommend nothing less than an 80386DX) and at least 2MB RAM (although I wouldn't go with less than 4MB).

The MPC logo can appear on three types of products: PCs, PC upgrade kits, and software packages. However, you must realize that the council does not guarantee product compliance or compatibility. Each licensing hardware or software vendor must meet the council's specifications to obtain and maintain the license. Although the logo itself does not mean that your PC, PC upgrade kit, or software package has been tested and found to be MPC-compliant, it is likely to be the case.

The council sets standards for multimedia PCs and software that runs on them. Any PC or PC upgrade kit must meet the following minimum standards to qualify for placing the MPC logo on their product:

- ◆ A 16-MHz 80386 CPU

- ◆ 2MB of system memory

- ◆ A 30MB hard disk

- ◆ One 1.44MB floppy-disk drive

- ◆ A VGA monitor and 16-color 640 × 480 video board

- ◆ A music synthesizer with 8-bit sampling, MIDI In and Out, and on-board analog audio mixing

♦ A CD-ROM drive with audio output

♦ DOS 5.0 or above, and Microsoft Windows with Multimedia
Extensions

Some hardware products may be MPC-compatible, but they cannot use the
logo unless they provide complete MPC capability. So there may be some
products that you can still purchase even without the MPC logo, such as an
audio board, that will work just fine in your multimedia PC.

Software compliance is less demanding. To license the logo for a software
product, the software must use at least one feature (e.g., CD-ROM audio,
animation, MIDI, sound recording) of multimedia and must support the Windows Multimedia Extensions. Ideally, an MPC software product, such as one
of the many CD-ROM packages that are available, will also run on any minimum MPC hardware platform.

A CD-ROM DRIVE IS THE HEART
OF THE MPC

Yes, the compact discs that you've seen in stereo systems are virtually the
same as the ones now being touted as the heart and soul of the multimedia
revolution. They're plastic, with a shiny finish, and they store a lot of information. When used solely for audio, a compact disc can store hours of music.
When used for computer data, a compact disc can store over 600MB of data.

CD-ROM has a number of important features that make it the media of
choice for supporting the growing technology of multimedia:

Mass Storage: A single CD-ROM stores over 600MB of data. This
makes enormous amounts of information available at once on a PC.

Space Saving: One CD replaces much larger quantities of any other
paper- or PC-based storage and retrieval mechanism. This translates
into less weight, volume, shipping, and inventory expenses.

Price Reductions: CD-ROM drives are now obtainable for just a few
hundred dollars, and prices are still dropping.

Flexible Data Storage: CDs can easily contain text, graphics, sound,
still photos, or motion images.

Summarizing the Multimedia Extensions

Microsoft's multimedia extensions offer facilities that span the following key technological areas:

Animation: Has service cells for MacroMind Director files, enabling PC users to use existing animation already developed for the Macintosh.

Graphics: Has the Device Independent Bitmap (DIB), a monitor-independent format for storing and displaying graphic images.

Audio: Stores sound in hard-disk files and includes the requisite analog-to-digital and digital-to-analog conversion software; also, supports the 8-bit, 22-kHz linear sampling format for uncompressed sound.

Music: Supports the industry-standard MIDI (Musical Instrument Digital Interface) format. This provides a uniform interface to various recording devices and musical instruments.

Synchronization: Has a device-independent facility for blending audio and video outputs.

Control: Has the Media Control Interface (MCI), which offers a standard interface set of device control commands.

Information Access: Searching and retrieving information from CDs on a PC is significantly faster than performing the same tasks with print-, microfilm-, or microfiche-based information.

Unfortunately, the medium is used today solely for read-only information retrieval. All information, audio or otherwise, is actually stored on a CD-ROM in digital fashion. A laser beam is used to burn tiny pits into the surface of the CD, representing the traditional 0's and 1's of the binary storage system used by all computers.

The laser in the CD-ROM drive is reasonably affordable but is only required to read the pits and reconstruct the information stored there. The higher-powered lasers required to actually burn the pits into a CD are much more expensive. Furthermore, it becomes considerably more difficult to erase data that is physically etched into the storage medium in this way. Although other technologies do exist for reading and writing large amounts of data in this way, such as WORM (Write Once, Read Many times), they are currently too expensive.

Since many companies make CD-ROM drives, and even more companies now market CD-ROM disks, standards are very important. All conventional CD-ROMs are formatted using a standard called the ISO-9660, or High Sierra, format. The ISO, or International Standards Organization, has successfully standardized a number of aspects of the computer industry. As a result, any hardware vendor's CD-ROM drive is able to read any software vendor's CD-ROM disk.

THE MULTIMEDIA EXTENSIONS MAKE IT ALL POSSIBLE

Writing multimedia applications is considerably easier now that Windows 3.1 includes a set of device drivers and dynamic link libraries that support the control of multimedia hardware. The Windows Control Panel has an enhanced set of icons to facilitate easy configuration of your multimedia hardware. This is not a programming book, so this section will only introduce you to this array of multimedia facilities supported for programmers.

All system calls are organized into groups, with the first three or four characters of the system call indicating the group. For example, calls whose name begins with *time* denote timer services. Multimedia Windows offers a series of precise timer controls that exceed the more limited 55 milliseconds found in more conventional Windows programs.

One key system call forms its own category. The sndPlaySound call offers a variety of ways to incorporate sound into applications. It deals primarily with digitally recorded sound, which is more technically called *sampled waveform audio*. Another set of system calls that begin with *wave* enables programmers to capture and play back digitally captured sound.

The extensions offer access to the special music interface (see the "Technical Underpinnings" section later in this chapter) in a series of functions that begin with *midi*. These functions offer direct control of the MIDI ports for both input and output, as well as the opportunity to transfer control data to and from other MIDI devices.

The *joy* functions offer control facilities for your system's joystick, and the *aux* functions provide access to any additional audio hardware on your multimedia PC. This specifically includes controlling the audio output of any CD-ROM drive that includes an audio output capability.

One of the biggest difficulties that early CD-ROM drives experienced was in the area of speed. This includes not only the speed of disk access but the actual throughput of the data from the CD-ROM into an application. The *mmio* functions offer special tools for improving I/O throughput by buffering data and by both reading and writing RIFF (Resource Interchange File Format) files. I'll explain RIFF files in more detail later in this chapter.

The final major category of functions begins with *mci*, which stands for Media Control Interface (MCI). This series of functions offers developers a relatively easy text-string-based control of the multimedia hardware. The MCI itself, and consequently this set of functions, offers the most promising future for easy MPC hardware management. Previously, programmers had to write more complex, low-level computer instructions to control individual pieces of hardware.

Table 6.1 summarizes the functional categories that relate to multimedia capabilities.

TABLE 6.1: Multimedia API Categories

Category Prefix	Explanation
aux	Controls auxiliary audio hardware
joy	Calibrates and controls a joystick
mci	Offers textual interface to multimedia hardware (known as the Media Control Interface)
midi	Interfaces MIDI ports and other MIDI hardware
mmio	Accesses RIFF files and buffers I/O
mmp	Plays back movies of Macintosh Director files
snd	Plays user-defined sounds and sampled waveform audio
time	Offers precise timer services
wave	Captures and plays back sampled waveform audio

The MCI is not only easier for programming multimedia applications, it is preferable. It is easier to develop, maintain, debug, and modify multimedia applications that use the MCI commands. There are standard commands for standard devices, such as open, status, and close. There are specialized multimedia commands, such as play, seek, and stop. There are also system commands that are interpreted by the MCI rather than passed directly to the hardware. These include the sysinfo, sound, and break commands.

Most MCI commands have the standard form

<Command> <Device> [Parameters]

For example, you could issue these commands to play a prerecorded version of Prokofiev's Violin Sonata No. 1:

Open prokof-1.wav type waveaudio alias sonata

Play sonata

Close sonata

This example presumes that prokof-1.wav is a waveform file that contains the digitized version of the violin sonata. The technique of aliasing the file name is a programmer's method of making the coding more readable. The mciSend-Command can also be used to produce the same effect if the proper programming structure has been set up in advance. Personally, I prefer the text string approach to the more traditional program interface method. However, as a user, you get the same results, so the programmer's decision doesn't affect you at all.

◆ SELECTING YOUR MULTIMEDIA PC COMPONENTS

In this section, I'll concentrate in several areas. You'll learn a number of considerations for selecting a CD-ROM drive and controller, and you'll learn how to install your drive. You'll also learn about a host of CD-ROM software applications. Finally, you'll learn more about the types of specialized chips and boards that are available to support your multimedia PC.

CHOOSING A CD-ROM DRIVE

As with most other hardware devices, there are internal and external models of CD-ROM drives, each using the same driver software, which accompanies the drive. The external model usually costs more and takes up additional desktop space. However, it does not take up a drive bay and does not increase the internal heat and power drain in your main computer casing. In either model, of course, you must have a slot available for the requisite controller card.

I prefer the external CD-ROM drive. In fact, some external drives, like the CDPC from Media Vision, have a valuable extra feature. The CDPC comes with all the sound facilities of their audio board, but it only requires one slot in your PC for both CD-ROM and audio facilities. In short, you gain the advantages of both a high-quality sound device (their Audio Spectrum board) and a high-quality CD-ROM drive (a fast drive built by Sony), but at the cost of only one slot. In my rapidly expanding multimedia environment, I'm having to decide which devices to take out of my PC every time I decide to include something new. Slots are precious commodities.

The CD-ROM drive is yet another new technology where the manufacturers have made extravagant operational claims. Most hardware vendors make claims about how fast their CD-ROM drive is, or more specifically, how wonderful the data transfer rate is, or the throughput, or the burst capabilities. These factors become increasingly important as you attempt to use more sophisticated multimedia applications.

If you only use CD-ROMs that contain large amounts of textual information, and you're willing to wait several seconds for the information to be retrieved and displayed, you can purchase one of the less expensive (and probably older) models. But if you intend to play one of the more recent CD-ROMs that include both sound and video action, you'll need one of the faster drives.

Some drives provide high data transfer rates, but do not move the data evenly into and out of their buffer. This can cause jerkiness in the video pictures. A drive controller is responsible for transferring data from the physical tracks on the CD-ROM into a private portion of memory (called the driver's *buffer*) reserved by the CD-ROM driver, and then back out to DOS, Windows, and your application. The smoothness of video depends on the speed of data flow from the CD-ROM into the buffer, as well as how much time it takes the data to be transferred from the driver's buffer out to your video monitor.

Other drives can handle video sequences smoothly, because of efficient buffering and fast hardware. However, they may suffer from slow random accesses. This means that the video sequence may play smoothly, but you may have to wait a long time before the hardware can actually find the selected video clip.

The bottom line is that you ought to run your software applications on a particular CD-ROM drive before purchasing the drive. Only in this way can you be sure that the drive can handle the application's data successfully. If this is not possible, balance against price the following desirable goals in your decision:

- ◆ The fastest sustained data transfer rate
- ◆ The fastest random access time
- ◆ The lowest amount of CPU utilization

CD-ROM drive manufacturers are constantly designing and building newer models, which are usually faster, more reliable, and more efficient. This makes it difficult to suggest particular models in this book. However, I can make several observations about particular manufacturers. Naturally, there are many CD-ROM drive manufacturers that make excellent products. But I will share a little bit of experience and bias here.

I've always been impressed by the quality and reliability of Sony products. Their offerings in the CD-ROM arena are no exception to my earlier experiences. Sony has some models that use a SCSI controller (e.g., the CDU-7211) and others that use an IDE controller (e.g., the CDU-7205).

Without offering specific performance numbers (because they will probably have changed by the time you read this), I can tell you that their average access times are faster than most competitors, while their data transfer rates are in the high range. With a mean time between failures (MTBF) rating of 25,000 hours, you needn't be too concerned with downtime.

NEC also has a well-deserved reputation for quality in computer equipment. All the monitors in my office are built by NEC. They now make several CD-ROM drives. One of their earliest ones, the CDR-36, was a very popular and inexpensive portable model. It can still serve DOS users well. But their more recent Intersect CDR-73M model outperforms nearly all other competitors in both sequential and random access data throughput.

In the portable arena, CD Technology produces a model called the CD Porta-Drive that shines in both speed and reliability. For applications that require portability, this device is notably smaller and lighter than the desktop alternatives. In addition, this model offers a special adapter that permits the drive to be plugged into any computer's parallel port. This parallel-to-SCSI adapter is actually manufactured by Trantor Corporation but sold under the CD Technology name. NEC also offers the same adapter for its CD-ROM drives.

◆ BUY A PARALLEL-TO-SCSI ADAPTER FOR PORTABILITY

A parallel-to-SCSI adapter is particularly useful when you need CD-ROM support from a portable computer that does not have any available expansion slots. Even if the portable computer does have an expansion slot, it is worthwhile to use the adapter when moving the drive around. This avoids the hassle of having to jockey controller cards between computer systems. If you're planning to move the CD-ROM drive between systems, you should plan to purchase a parallel-to-SCSI adapter. Naturally, you must first select a CD-ROM drive that can run successfully when connected through the parallel port. Not all drives, even from the same manufacturer, can do this.

Selecting a Controller Card

As with many other devices, controller cards for CD-ROM drives use either a proprietary interface or the increasingly popular SCSI (small computer system interface). The most common type is the traditional proprietary interface; each manufacturer makes its own. They cost less, but they're not interchangeable and they are less flexible than SCSI.

Although SCSI controllers are usually more expensive, they are rapidly becoming an industry standard. Some computers, like the high-end PS/2 computers from IBM, come with SCSI controllers. You can just hook up a new CD-ROM to them directly.

With a SCSI controller, you can more readily change or upgrade cards later without having to give up your drive. Proprietary controller cards are more limiting and don't usually offer the daisy-chaining feature of SCSI controllers. In theory, you can plug one SCSI device into another, thereby controlling multiple SCSI devices with only one adapter card. Although it doesn't work with all SCSI devices (try before you buy!), it does address the problem of running out of slots in your PC when adding multimedia equipment.

Just as with proclaimed PC compatibility in the early '80s, some CD-ROM drive manufacturers claim SCSI drive compability now. Most CD-ROM drives that are SCSI-compatible typically have a pass-through connector and a unit-number switch. Both these features are necessary for successful daisy chaining. You can usually find them in the rear of an external SCSI device.

Getting Your CD-ROM Drive Up and Running

To get your CD-ROM drive up and running, you have to load an appropriate device driver and then run MSCDEX (Microsoft Compact Disc Extensions). You should run this TSR before you start Windows, but *after* you start any local area network you may be running. MSCDEX uses the BIOS addresses normally used by a LAN. Follow these steps:

1. Load the necessary device driver. For example, to load a device driver for a Sony CD-ROM, you might include this sample line in your CONFIG.SYS file:

   Device=C:\SONY_CDU.SYS /D:MSCD210

2. Optionally start any local area network. Be sure to install and run your network software before the Microsoft CD-ROM extensions (MSCDEX). Only then will Windows be able to recognize the CD-ROM drive as if it were another large hard disk on your system.

3. Run MSCDEX. For example, you will probably include this TSR in your AUTOEXEC.BAT file:

C:\MSCDEX /D:MSCD210 /L:F

This line assumes that the MSCDEX.EXE file is located in your root directory and specifies (with the /L switch) that the CD-ROM drive will be accessible as drive F on your system.

4. Start Windows.

◆ PROBLEMS WITH NETWORKS AND CD-ROM?

The Microsoft CD-ROM extensions use Interrupt 2F, which is also used by network services. Your system may not be on a network, yet the interrupt still must be handled. If your CD-ROM player does not seem to work under Windows, go back to the Setup program. This time, select the Network Not Installed option and specify a network driver from the displayed list (such as Microsoft Network). After you load the appropriate system disk, your CD player should work.

After successfully completing these steps, you should be able to access the CD-ROM drive from a command prompt or from the Windows File Manager, just like any other drive. A CD-ROM drive even has its own special icon on the drive line of the File Manager.

If your system already uses drive identifiers from letters A to F, remember that you must include a LASTDRIVE command in your CONFIG.SYS file. Only in this way will DOS allow you to assign an identifier beyond F to your CD-ROM drive.

Some CD-ROM installation programs automatically insert a LASTDRIVE command in your CONFIG.SYS file. However, to avoid having to figure out what other hardware your system includes, these installation programs may insert a LASTDRIVE=Z command. This wastes about 8K of memory. Check this and correct the LASTDRIVE command to identify only the last alphabetic identifier that your system actually needs.

CHOOSING A CD-ROM SOFTWARE APPLICATION

Some multimedia software applications use CD-ROM as a mere repository for large volumes of information. Other multimedia applications use the information on CD-ROM as only one piece of a creative pie, with other pieces being found in or on other multimedia hardware devices. In this section, you'll get a glimpse at some of the CD-ROM informational titles that are now available. In a later section of this chapter, you'll take a closer look at some of the most recent multimedia presentation packages, like Curtain Call and Action!.

I have children, so my first choices for CD-ROM titles were encyclopedias to help my children with school assignments.

The New Grolier Electronic Encyclopedia

This CD-ROM from Grolier Electronic Publishing Inc. (1-800-356-5590) has the entire text of the *Academic American Encyclopedia* and adds a series of historical pictures and high-resolution maps, as well as a number of music, speech, and sound clips to support the text. These typically play through the audio output jack on your CD-ROM drive.

The software interface to the information is fairly plain, but it is easy to search for data. It permits you to use Boolean operators and wildcards to construct sophisticated search criteria. It also offers the ability to view associated graphics or hear related sound bites by pressing a key.

The product also offers a hypertext facility that enables you to jump quickly from a highlighted phrase to related articles. By using multiple windows to display information, you can easily combine information from different articles, using the Clipboard or an ASCII file.

Compton's Multimedia Encyclopedia

One of the more exciting entries on the market, this CD-ROM from Compton's NewMedia (1-510-597-5555) doesn't contain as much raw textual information as the Grolier's disk, but it offers it up in a much more engaging way. It has a more familiar, icon-oriented interface that fits the

Windows environment more comfortably. Like a familiar directory tree, this offering presents a visual outline of the entire encyclopedia. You can then search through the information by navigating through the various encyclopedic categories.

As with the Grolier's CD-ROM, you can quickly find information, display related graphics, and listen to related sound bites. Beyond the hyperlink capability for looking up related information, there are selectable animation segments. These considerably extend the pleasure of reading about various scientific phenomena or historical events.

Microsoft Bookshelf for Windows

Replacing an entire bookshelf of reference material, this CD-ROM from Microsoft (1-800-426-9400) includes *Barlett's Familiar Quotations*, the *World Almanac and Book of Facts*, the *Hammond Atlas*, the *American Heritage Dictionary*, *Roget's Thesaurus*, and the *Columbia Encyclopedia*. Merging recorded national anthems, dictionary word pronunciations, and encyclopedic entry animation, this disk offers a novel way of finding out the answers to common educational questions.

The Guinness Disc of Records

This CD from Microsoft Ltd. (1-408-464-0707) offers an entertaining presentation of the well-known repository of the world's most outlandish records. The disk includes a searching capability, as well as both sound and animation to display the contained records.

National Geographic's Mammals

As dazzling on your screen as the *National Geographic* magazine is in print, this CD-ROM from the National Geographic Society (1-800-368-2728) offers both information and entertainment. There are text, color photographs, and animal sounds for more than two hundred different mammals. In addition, the product contains a number of full-motion video segments found originally on the "National Geographic" TV shows.

Multimedia Beethoven: The Ninth Symphony

The most interesting aspect of this disk from Microsoft (1-800-426-9400) is the measure-by-measure commentary on the Ninth Symphony. Text and graphics are intermixed with a digital stereo audio version of the symphony to provide a unique learning environment. The disk also includes additional information about Beethoven and music appreciation in general.

UNDERSTANDING CHIP AND BOARD DEVELOPMENTS

By now, you may be developing a sense of the demands that many multimedia applications place on any multimedia PC. This is why the hardware you select should be as powerful as you can afford if you intend to run state-of-the-art multimedia applications. However, the MPC specifications only define the minimum hardware you need. Specialized chips and boards are now being developed to bolster your computer system's ability to support and sustain multimedia applications.

There are two categories of chips available and under development in the multimedia support arena. *Fixed-function* chips are less expensive because they are designed to perform a single chore, such as image processing or video compression. *Programmable* chips are more expensive but more flexible, allowing for adjustments for different computing chores. Additionally, these chips are more likely to be able to continue providing successful service to your system as MPC standards continue to expand.

Because Windows is so graphics intensive, much work is in progress in developing processor chips that can off-load the burden of generating and maintaining your graphics screens. But in the multimedia arena particularly, full-motion video applications are the focus of the most intense chip developments. This is due to the intensive data requirements of full-motion video. Even though a CD-ROM can hold well over 600MB of information, this translates into only seconds of full-motion video storage.

Consequently, data compression, transmission, and decompression are paramount in successfully addressing the needs of any multimedia application that contains large amounts of video data. To assure some reasonable consistency in new hardware and ease of transfer of compressed images, standards have been developed.

The Joint Photographic Experts Group (JPEG) has developed a standard for compressing still images, and the Moving Pictures Experts Group (MPEG) has developed a parallel standard for full-motion video compression. Both organizations use techniques that involve some loss in image quality. However, since your eye is not going to miss the finer aspects of a picture, especially in a moving sequence of pictures, the sacrifice in precision results in a savings in storage space and in consequent transmission times.

To support the processing overhead of these programmable chips (i.e., for data compression and decompression), single chips now often include multiple processors, permitting parallel operations among themselves and with your CPU itself. Additionally, more and more boards that contain these new chips also include their own on-board, and even on-chip, memory to support the specialized operations.

But data compression and decompression is still only one requirement of multimedia support. The voluminous digital data needs to come from somewhere. Often, this originates in audio (tape or live recordings) or video signals (television or camera inputs). Converting analog sound and video to and from the digitized video storage and display formats requires chips that specialize in analog-to-digital conversion (ADC) or digital-to-analog conversion (DAC).

To output digitized sounds, many applications also rely on special audio chips that manage the reproduction of one or more sound tracks. Currently, most of the available specialized video and audio chips are available on add-in boards. This means that your processor is supplemented by these support boards, but your computer's available slots are quickly drained. Be sure that the computer you intend to use for multimedia applications has enough slots to house the specialized boards you intend to incorporate into your system.

◆ TECHNICAL UNDERPINNINGS OF MULTIMEDIA

You have now learned about the history of multimedia and the fundamentals of multimedia applications. You've also learned about the specifications for the multimedia PC, as well as the elements of the Microsoft Multimedia API Extensions and how a number of CD-ROM vendors have used them to create interesting and valuable CD-ROM applications. Now it's time to take a closer look at what goes on behind the scenes in the multimedia world.

HOW DO CD-ROM DISKS REALLY WORK?

It's an intellectually satisfying exercise to understand how CD-ROM disks really work. But more importantly, understanding these design issues also explains in part the following distinctions between CD-ROM disks and the most common hard disks:

- ◆ A CD-ROM drive costs more than a hard disk.
- ◆ A CD-ROM disk stores more than a hard disk.
- ◆ A CD-ROM drive is slower than a hard disk.

As Figure 6.2 indicates, a CD-ROM stores data as sectors located in one continuous spiral track, much like the pattern seen in old phonograph records. A hard disk stores its sectors on concentric tracks. Consequently, a hard disk can locate its sectors faster because they are always addressable by a particular track that is located at a fixed distance from the center. This by itself makes for faster random access times on a hard disk.

Another factor makes for greater expense in the CD-ROM drive's mechanics. The drive's motor must rotate the disk faster when reading sectors closer to the center. This is because CD-ROM drives use a data-encoding method known as *constant linear velocity* (CLV), and hard drives use a method known as *constant angular velocity* (CAV). Each sector on a CD-ROM takes up the

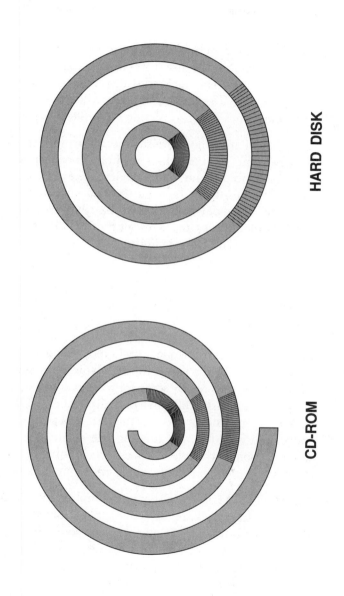

FIGURE 6.2: Storage methods on CD-ROM disks and hard disks

same amount of space on its spiral track, no matter where on the disk the track is located.

On a hard disk, each track contains the same number of sectors, so a track near the outside of the disk stores its data less densely. Each sector covers more physical space on the track, wasting physical storage that is not wasted on the CD-ROM disk. The constant angular velocity of a hard disk means that each sector consumes the space defined by a fixed angle.

A CD-ROM drive motor must constantly adjust the rotational speed to speed up (overcome inertia) when reading inner disk sectors and to slow down (overcome momentum) when reading outer disk sectors. Nevertheless, just as hard-disk access times have gotten faster and faster in recent years, you can expect the same developments in the 1990s with CD-ROM drives. Not only will drive electronics improve, but there will be ongoing improvements in the use of on-board memory, buffering techniques, transmission methods, and I/O optimization.

GETTING SOUND ON AND OFF CD-ROM DISKS

Figure 6.3 depicts the sequence whereby sound is captured, stored, and played back in a multimedia environment. Typically, sound in the form of speech or music is first captured by some form of analog-to-digital conversion circuitry. Then, it is stored digitally on a hard disk or CD-ROM disk. Finally, it is played back on command by passing the data through additional digital-to-analog conversion circuitry and sending the results out to one or more speakers. There are some other electrical aspects involved, such as filters, but I'll ignore them here for the sake of focusing on the main issue.

Since CD-ROM drives in the typical multimedia PC do not record sounds but only play them back, multimedia applications that rely on your own recordings use hard-disk files to augment the sound files found on your CD-ROM disks. These types of applications use a microphone to capture and record speech or music. Other applications may include only the playback portion of Figure 6.3, using only prerecorded sound clips found on the CD-ROM disks with the application.

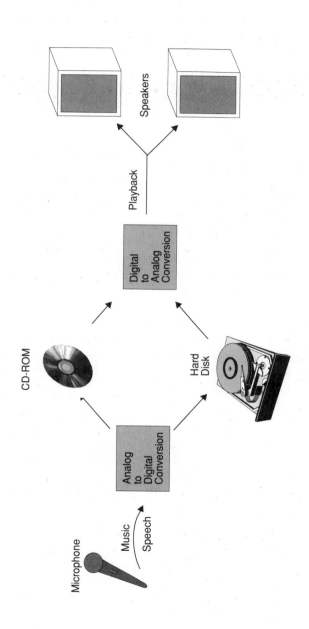

FIGURE 6.3: Capturing, storing, and playing back sound

Sound is a type of vibration that is often represented as a sine wave, as seen in Figure 6.4. The ADC chip measures the height, or *amplitude*, of the sound wave at periodic intervals. The interval of measurement is called the *sampling rate*. To be accurate, the ADC sampling rate must be at least twice the frequency of the sound that is being sampled; the rate defines how high a sound frequency can be captured accurately. Since the human ear cannot hear much beyond frequencies of 20 kHz, the sampling rate used for storing music on CDs is 44.1 kHz.

Another factor in digital sound recording and playback is the number of bits used for each sample. This factor dictates the dynamic range of the recorded sound, or the difference in volume between the loudest and the softest sounds.

The hardware specifications for a multimedia PC's sound input allow for an 11.025-kHz sampling rate with 8 bits per sample. This limits the capture of sound frequencies to about 5 kHz, with a dynamic range of 48 decibels. This allows for speech to be recorded by applications successfully, but does not allow adequate frequency ranges for music recording. This 11.025 kHz is only one-fourth of the sampling rate used by audio CDs.

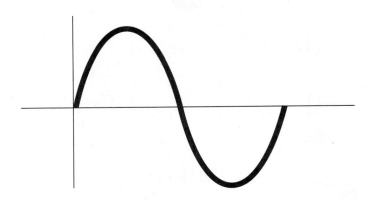

FIGURE 6.4:   A sine wave

However, the hardware specifications allow for a better range of output. There is also a 22.05-kHz sampling rate used for playing back sounds (music and speech) that have frequencies up to 10 kHz. In actual fact, audio CDs use 16 bits per sample, which provides for a dynamic range of 96 decibels. In other words, even though some CD-ROM manufacturers advertise that you can play your audio CDs through their drives, the sound reproduction may not be as good as on your audio CD player.

UNDERSTANDING MIDI

MIDI, or Musical Instrument Digital Interface, is an industry protocol for connecting and controlling devices capable of creating music. This includes synthesizers, computers, and other electronic instruments. To exercise control, the MIDI protocol specifies a one-way serial interface that transmits data at 31,250 bits per second. Since the data is organized into bytes, with one start and one stop bit, the resulting transfer rate is 3125 bytes per second.

A MIDI device may have only an output MIDI port, as in the case of a piano keyboard. Not having any form of music synthesis itself, the device sends out a message through the port each time a key is struck.

A MIDI device that has a synthesizer but no keyboard may have a MIDI In port, which receives messages from a computer or another MIDI device. Upon reception, the message is interpreted and a sound is played.

MIDI devices sometimes also have a MIDI Thru port, which simply passes through a message received at the input port. This enables you to daisy-chain more than one MIDI device. Some devices, such as an integrated keyboard and synthesizer, may have all three conventional MIDI ports: In, Out, and Thru.

Just as SCSI disk drives have drive identifier numbers, MIDI devices that are daisy-chained have channel numbers. A control message can include the channel number, which indicates which device in a MIDI chain is supposed to act on the command message.

When you activate a MIDI device—for example, when you press a piano key—the message that results identifies what is to be done. The most common MIDI messages include the following:

◆ The type of command (typically Note On or Note Off)

◆ The channel number

◆ The note and octave to play (i.e., a number from 0–127)

◆ The velocity of the note release or key press

In particular, a multimedia PC must have MIDI In and MIDI Out ports so that multimedia applications can receive and process messages from MIDI devices, as well as play music by sending messages out to a synthesizer. In addition, the MPC specification also calls for an internal MIDI synthesizer. The synthesizer must provide at least the ability to produce six simultaneous notes on each of three channels, while producing five-note percussion on a fourth channel. More complex synthesis is also defined that uses more channels for more complex polyphony.

Each of the channels produces a *voice*. Each voice is comparable to a unique instrument that may be simultaneously playing in your MIDI composition. The MIDI specification has another common command called Program Change. This command allows you to switch from one instrument, or voice, or channel to another for subsequent commands.

UNDERSTANDING DATA COMPRESSION

To store a precise replica of video, audio, and animation data, you would have to have an enormous amount of data storage. Think about it: You must re-create a simple VGA screen (640 × 480 bits), using 24-bit color reproduction (8 red bits, 8 blue bits, and 8 green bits), and you must do it 30 times per second (the American TV standard). That would allow about 20 seconds of full-motion video to be stored on a typical CD-ROM, with barely enough space left to store any application software at all.

The storage issue does not even address the transmission-time demands of the data. The data must find its way off the CD-ROM and into the application that will handle the audio and video output in some fashion. The larger the data volume is, the longer it will take to move it around your

Data Compression Techniques for Multimedia

Loss-less compression refers to techniques that remove redundant data, such as repeated blank spaces. PKZIP and LHARC are two common programs that compress data in this way. Eighty blank spaces (character bytes) might be replaced in the compressed file by two bytes, which consist of the number 80 in the first byte and the repeated space character in the second byte.

Multimedia applications that reproduce sound and motion images have a greater tolerance for slight signal degradation. Sometimes called *lossy* compression, techniques exist to remove data redundancy on a frame-by-frame basis. The Joint Photographic Experts Group (JPEG) has created a standard for compressing still images, such as those found in desktop publishing. The Motion Picture Experts Group (MPEG) has defined a similar standard for compressing successive frames of full-motion video data.

Multimedia applications require enormous amounts of space to store sufficient data to reconstruct sound and color images. Any compression technique has several immediate benefits:

◆ Less disk or CD-ROM space required to store the information

◆ Less time needed to store and retrieve the information

◆ Less time required to process and display or output the information

◆ Faster data transfer (i.e., less network traffic) when used on a local area network

computer system. Complete, detailed, and 100 percent accurate image reproduction is not going to happen. Neither is it really necessary.

Data compression techniques exist in both hardware and software. They rely on the concept that the human eye and ear will not even miss some parts of a detailed image. As mentioned previously, the JPEG sets standards for static video images. These standards apply to color desktop pictures, digital photographs, and image databases. The MPEG sets standards for compressing the data used for full-motion video.

JPEG analyzes an image and compresses segments of the picture that are the same. For example, a blue sky might consume one-third of a picture. A JPEG compression simply notes the color blue and the portion of the picture that it consumes. This can consume dramatically less space than storing each pixel in the image.

MPEG compares each successive picture in a moving video sequence to its predecessor. If portions of the successor frames do not change, MPEG notes the portions and the colors. For example, a brown wall behind two people walking is an unchanging background. The data that represents the wall does not need to be recompressed and decompressed for each frame.

These techniques produce extraordinary compression ratios. The JPEG technique usually averages about a 20-to-1 compression, while the MPEG technique is an order of magnitude larger at 200 to 1. To the typical viewer, neither technique produces any noticeable picture degradation.

UNDERSTANDING RIFF

RIFF, or the Resource Interchange File Format, is a software standard created by Microsoft and IBM, both major players in the multimedia computing game. This format enables application vendors to store different types of multimedia data consistently. Any multimedia component, whether it is a bit map, a set of MIDI commands, or a sound waveform, can be stored and retrieved consistently by using RIFF.

Each RIFF entry consists of

♦ A four-character text string for identification

♦ A 32-bit value that specifies the size of the data that follows

♦ The actual data, which may itself be stored in other unique file formats

An application can process a RIFF file by acting on only those entries that it understands, using the identifying text string. The application can skip any RIFF entries that it doesn't understand. This new RIFF format, then, is at the heart of the concept of video and audio interleaving. By sequentially storing different types of multimedia data, an application can quickly extract sound, video, and animation that have been stored sequentially on the CD-ROM.

Microsoft has used a RIFF file to establish effective audio-video interleaving, or AVI (described earlier). This methodology, when combined with standard compression methods, produces exciting on-screen animation in windows. Look to see more and more CD-ROM applications taking advantage of this technique.

◆ EXCITING INTERACTIVE MULTIMEDIA APPLICATIONS

Presentation software has been a major arena of importance for multimedia developers. Many DOS and Windows programs are available for improving the quality of corporate and personal presentations. But the latest Windows entries into this software arena take the technology far beyond its predecessors.

In this section, you'll learn about three outstanding examples of multimedia Windows software: Curtain Call from Brown-Wagh Publishing (1-408-378-3838), Action! from MacroMind Paracomp (1-415-442-0200), and Icon-Author from AimTech Corporation (1-603-883-0220). These products use the standard Windows GUI interface, with pull-down menus, on-screen display windows, and a variety of dialog boxes as necessary. But they extend conventional presentation techniques into the multimedia realm. In addition to slide-show facilities, variable fonts, and a series of screen effects, these packages allow you to easily include a wide range of video and audio effects. Yet each of these products retains an individuality that requires you to look at each before making a purchase decision.

CURTAIN CALL

Curtain Call provides a scripting mechanism for developing your presentations. As shown in Figure 6.5, a presentation consists of any number of successive frames (eight are shown in this figure). You can specify the duration of each frame and the active elements within the frame.

A Curtain Call script consists of a series of frames, each of which consists of variable-length events. You can incorporate (and even overlap) text, voice, and sound events into these frames. Each of the individual events can be prerecorded or previously prepared. A script merely references the names of existing disk files that contain the audio or visual information.

As to visual effects, Curtain Call offers many defined transition and overlay effects, not unlike other presentation programs. And as you'd expect, you can

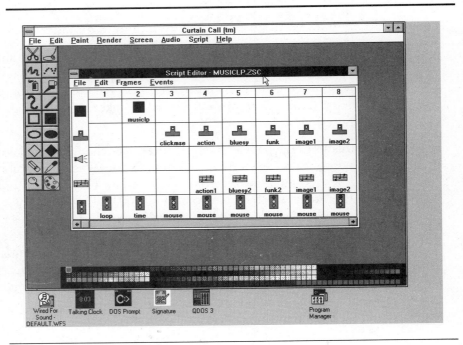

FIGURE 6.5: Curtain Call uses a frame-sequencing technique.

also preview any portion of the show at any time. You just select one or more frames and click on a Play option from a pull-down menu.

As you'd also hope for, you can import existing graphics or clip art from other programs or graphics packages. Then, you can use the tools in Curtain Call to modify the size, orientation, location, color, and general appearance of the images. Curtain Call has an unusually rich assortment of font transformation capabilities, including strobe effects, 3-D extrusions, shadows, and metallic effects. You can even use these transformation capabilities with graphic shapes or clip-art images.

If your system has a sound card installed, you can incorporate sound into your presentations. Depending on your card, you can record narration, sound effects, and music. These recordings can be stored in one or more files, then synchronized with Curtain Call images and effects during playback. But as you probably realize by now, the graphic effects and sound facilities of Curtain Call produce a drain on any CPU.

Since the product does not require a CD-ROM, you don't even have to have a minimum multimedia PC to benefit from this package. However, you must have at least a 386SX computer with 2MB of RAM; a faster computer is better. Even though the program will work with standard 16-color VGA monitors, you won't be able to appreciate some of the fine visual effects and capabilities without a Super VGA monitor and an adapter that displays 256 colors.

Curtain Call supports a number of sound and music boards, which enable you to include .VOC (Sound Blaster format, but used by all digital audio hardware supported by Curtain Call) and .WAV (Multimedia Windows) files. In addition, Curtain Call plays MIDI Type 1 files, which usually have the .MID extension.

Curtain Call also supports four common types of image formats: DIB (Device Independent Bitmap), BMP (Bit Map, defined in earlier versions of Windows), RLE (Run Length Encoded files, which contain compressed bit-map images), and PCX (one of the most common industry-standard graphic image formats). A painting facility in Curtain Call offers tools to manipulate these images. You can draw circles, lines, boxes, geometric shapes, and curves. Curtain Call also includes a standard set of drawing tools, including such things as fill tools, predefined shapes, foreground and background stencils, scissors, and a magnifying glass.

Curtain Call uses any of the new Windows 3.1 TrueType fonts or existing fonts from Adobe Type Manager, Facelift, or MoreFonts. You can define your own text styles, as well as use Curtain Call's automatic rendering capabilities for any visual elements. Unusual effects like glowing letters, gradations, and glints are only a menu choice away.

All of the Curtain Call facilities can be combined into slide shows in a variety of ways. Perhaps the simplest way is to use the built-in Clipboard support, which permits the conventional Clipboard uses discussed in Chapter 5. You can easily cut, copy, and paste to and from the Clipboard while in Curtain Call, using pictures, text, graphics, and even still-frame video (see "Action!" for possibilities using moving video). This means that you can move images and text between Curtain Call and other specialized applications.

All in all, this is an excellent product for quickly building a visually exciting presentation that incorporates colorful text and screen effects with prerecorded or digitized voice and MIDI music.

ACTION!

Although Action! is double the price of Curtain Call, the leap in power is dazzling. The amount of control over your presentation increases dramatically because of a wealth of new dialog boxes. You can create interactive multimedia presentations that combine visual and audio effects similar to those in Curtain Call, but you can also incorporate animation effects and full-motion video movies. The product is truly at the cutting edge of Windows multimedia technology. In fact, Action! is even bundled with an entire line of Compu-Add Corporation's multimedia personal computers.

As with Curtain Call, Action! seems to have been designed for users who want to create professional-looking presentations but don't want to first obtain a degree in visual arts or computer science. I especially like the time-line concept, shown in Figure 6.6. This enables you to place objects of any sort (e.g., text, voice, music, motion pictures) in the presentation at any point. You can easily control the duration of the sound or image, and you completely control the amount of overlapping or synchronization. A time line is particularly intuitive, so developing a presentation around it works very well.

The designers of Action! have given a good deal of thought to the user interface. Beyond the conventional Windows pull-down menu interface, the Timeline window is only one of the control windows. In the upper-right portion of Figure 6.6, you can see a second window, which is called the Control Panel. It sports a familiar VCR-like face, which includes recognizable push buttons for manipulating the presentation sequence: start, stop, fast and slow forward, and fast and slow reverse.

Other interface windows include the Scene Sorter, Content List, and the Tool Palette. The Tool Palette, also visible in Figure 6.6, is the vertical rectangle that appears just below the File menu (although it can be moved elsewhere on your screen). It contains a series of icon buttons that represent manipulation tools. Click on one of them, and you can instantly perform a

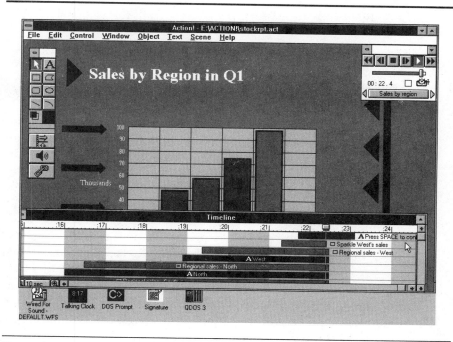

FIGURE 6.6: Action! develops presentations around a time line.

useful and powerful operation, such as pulling a prerecorded movie or sound clip into your presentation.

The Scene Sorter and Content List windows offer two different mechanisms for organizing and modifying your presentations. When the Scene Sorter is activated via the Window pull-down menu, a window appears that includes a compressed view of the individual scenes in your presentation. You can add, delete, or rearrange the scenes in the show. By clicking on individual scenes, you can set or reset a variety of scene aspects, from the actual contents to the transition effects. The Content List window is for those of you who like A-B-C-type outlines. This window lists all scenes and the visual/audio objects within them. You can quickly add objects or scenes, modify the existing elements, or rearrange any entries.

As with earlier and less powerful presentation packages, Action! can display text in a variety of ways. And you can move the text into and around the screen in different manners. Additionally, you can reinforce the textual displays with both sound and video effects. Action! includes a library of prerecorded sounds and animated graphics. You can include any of its sound and video files in your presentation, or you can directly incorporate CD-ROM music.

♦ MULTIMEDIA EXTENSIONS ARE REQUIRED FOR SOUND

Action! requires the support of the Microsoft Multimedia Extensions to play back and synchronize sound files during a scripted presentation. Remember to load MSCDEX.EXE before starting Windows if you intend to run an Action! script.

One of the most powerful aspects of Action! is its ability to use more than the usual display devices. As with many PC-based packages, you can output an Action! presentation to a VGA overhead projection panel, a projection video system, or a large screen monitor. Action! can also output its entire presentation to videotape, for later projection through any VCR playback system. However, this "printing" to videotape does require additional hardware beyond the minimum MPC specification.

Action! does not attempt to do everything by itself. As you might expect, it can import existing sound, data, and graphics files from other applications on your system. This includes more than just spreadsheet files. It extends to the incorporation of text and graphics from packages that normally output to devices that produce presentation-quality slides and overheads.

Action! was designed to run on a 286-based computer with 2MB of RAM and 16-color VGA graphics. However, as you might expect, a 386 with 4MB of RAM and Super VGA graphics will produce a much more satisfying presentation development environment. Over the years, it has become easier and cheaper to produce professional-looking presentations. If you're the sort that is creative enough to use state-of-the-art multimedia tools, you owe it to yourself to consider products like Action!.

ICONAUTHOR

IconAuthor from AimTech Corporation represents a giant step forward for presentation packages in the Windows 3.*x* world. It goes well beyond the preceding two packages; it also costs ten times as much. However, it does enable you to accomplish dramatically more with your system.

IconAuthor is a high-end authoring package with an icon-oriented interface. (Authoring packages go much farther than presentation packages.) It is a complete programming development system, using visual methods for building applications rather than using the traditional textual method of command instructions. Figure 6.7 depicts the first level of a typical application, built with IconAuthor's icon-based programming language.

As with the earlier products described, IconAuthor permits you to develop multimedia applications and presentations. As before, there is the important facility of interactivity. However, IconAuthor adds an extraordinary dimension to the idea of interaction. Beyond simply reacting to keystrokes or mouse button pushes, IconAuthor can actually capture important information about the interaction itself.

For example, if IconAuthor is used for computer-based training, it can collect information about which answers were selected or about how much time was spent in each section. It can then further control the flow of the presentation by analyzing the responses. Or it can simply provide management or the trainer with analytical summary information about the user and the interaction.

As a Windows user, you'll enjoy the comfortable graphic interface, with both indexed online help and high-resolution graphics. As a programmer, you'll definitely appreciate the visual approach to building applications. By selecting from a large number of function icons, such as those shown in Figure 6.7, you can use variables and arrays, build modules and subroutines, create looping and branching structures, and easily access the data in other packages (e.g., spreadsheets and databases) by using DDE.

As an application designer, you'll enjoy the range of fonts and text styles with easy full-screen editing. But more, you'll find it easy to blend graphic images into your textual presentations. You can easily incorporate external ASCII or bit-map graphic files into your IconAuthor applications.

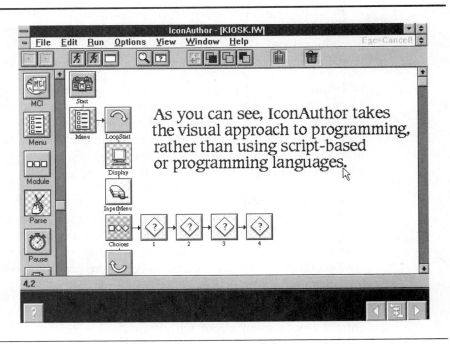

FIGURE 6.7: IconAuthor is the most powerful authoring application.

IconAuthor provides significantly enhanced video capabilities. You can merge on one screen any combination of text, graphics, and video. The graphics features include solids and natural drop shadows, as well as a variety of screen fades and blends. In addition, IconAuthor supports a number of three-dimensional animation effects to create exciting visual results from formerly static bit-map files.

The video facility includes much more. You can use videodiscs or videotape for input, as well as create your own tape-based applications. A complete VCR emulation provides easy online editing. You can display video segments in a screen window or on a full screen, and you can manipulate video segments frame by frame. This makes it easier to create video slide-shows, using a host of techniques for selection, cropping, compression, and intensity modification.

With the proper hardware cards, IconAuthor can capture video images to disk, record and play back digital audio files, and play back CD-ROM audio, wave audio, and MIDI music. The multimedia extensions for Microsoft Windows are required for some of these facilities.

This product is so powerful that it would be overkill to buy it just to develop fancy presentations. I would use Curtain Call or Action! for that purpose. It is useful to note that IconAuthor does not require a more powerful computer than the other two packages. It simply can take advantage of additional hardware boards and features.

IconAuthor is more suited to the development of information systems, such as computer-based training (CBT), point-of-sale, or interactive product demonstrations. In each of these arenas, there is much to be gained from IconAuthor's ability to present information while at the same time capturing information about a user's selections or decisions during the presentation.

This product is supposedly aimed at application experts rather than programmers. However, there are many corporations who now assign programmers to the development of interactive multimedia applications. I strongly recommend this product to those programmers and to the decision makers who have to pay for it.

◆ MULTIMEDIA ACCESSORY PROGRAMS INCLUDED WITH WINDOWS

Windows 3.1 includes two special accessory programs, Sound Recorder and Media Player, that provide multimedia services. Icons in the Accessories program group of the Program Manager offer access to both of them.

Sound Recorder enables you to record new sound files, or play existing files that were created in the .WAV format. The accessory also provides editing facilities to make a variety of adjustments to the sound files, from mixing and inserting new sounds to making speed and volume changes.

Media Player enables you to play media files on multimedia hardware, including sound files, animation files, and MIDI sequencer files. In addition, Media Player can control CD-ROM and videodisc players.

USING THE SOUND RECORDER

Sound Recorder is both fun and powerful. If your system has an appropriate sound board, you can play previously recorded waveform files. If you have properly configured a microphone with the board, you can record your own speech or music. Several sound files are included with your Windows 3.1 system. You can also customize your sound files with special audio effects, from mixing sound files together to cutting and splicing sound effects. This section explains how to use Sound Recorder for recording, editing, and playing sound files.

◆ CREATING A SOUND FILE

You can create a new sound file in several ways. You can record new sounds by pressing the microphone button in the Sound Recorder dialog box. You can also insert an existing sound file into another sound file. This can be one that you first read in or one that you are currently creating or editing. Or you can mix two sound files together so that the sounds from each will play simultaneously. In fact, you can combine all these techniques to be as creative as you like.

Recording New Waveform Files

Clicking on the Sound Recorder icon in the Program Manager's Accessories group brings up the dialog box shown in Figure 6.8.

The File menu offers options for creating a new file, opening up an existing wave file, exiting from the application, and saving a current file that you are working with. There is also an option called *Revert*. Since Sound Recorder allows you to make significant adjustments to the contents of a sound file, this option can help you to undo undesired changes.

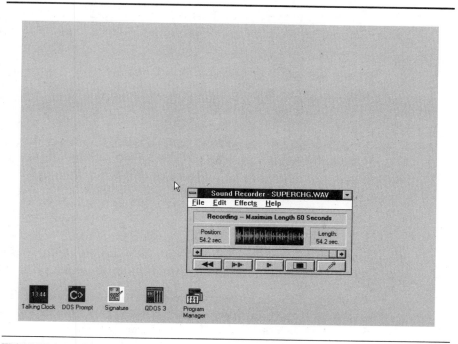

FIGURE 6.8: The Sound Recorder dialog box

Unlike an Undo option, which can reverse the effects of a single modification, Revert removes all recent updates to the file. By choosing it, you essentially revert to the last saved copy of the file. To take advantage of this facility, be sure to save your file often as you work on it.

If you are making a number of modifications, use the Save As option to save each of several successive changes to a differently named file. In this way, you are not limited to reverting to only the last version that was saved under the file's name. You can revert to any of the previously saved and separately named versions of the sound file.

To begin recording a sound file of up to one minute in length, just click on the microphone (or Record) button that is located on the bottom right of the dialog box. (In Figure 6.8, 54.2 seconds of sounds have been recorded.) The frequency spectrum of the sounds being recorded appears in the center window of the dialog box.

You can also record new sounds into an existing file. Once you've positioned the recording to a desired location, you can click on the Record button. Your microphone will record up to one minute of new sounds, and Sound Recorder will insert these into the current file that is being worked on.

To the left of the frequency spectrum window, the Position indicator tells you where the recording is occurring in the file. It is the equivalent of an indicator of where a tape head might be. The Length indicator to the right of the spectrum tells you the known length of the sound file being worked with. Since this sound file is just being recorded, the two numbers are the same. When you edit an existing file, the length will usually be greater than the playing or editing Position indicator (except when you reach the end of the sound file).

At the bottom of the dialog box, you can see buttons that are similar to those found on audiotape players. The double arrows that point left and right are Fast Reverse and Fast Forward buttons. Clicking on these buttons instantly moves the Position indicator to the beginning or the end of the sound file.

Clicking on the single right-pointing arrow is equivalent to pressing Play on a tape deck; the sound file begins to play from the current location of the Position indicator. Clicking on the solid rectangular button is equivalent to pressing Stop; the sound file retains its current position but stops playing immediately. This is useful when you want to mix other sounds into the current one, or insert other sound files at a particular point.

Playing and Editing Sound Files

Playing a sound file is as easy as clicking on the Play button at the bottom of the Sound Recorder dialog box. If you've just opened an existing file, the sound plays from the beginning. If you have been playing or editing a sound file and stopped it by clicking on the Stop button on the bottom line, it will later play from that position.

You can edit more precisely by moving the mouse pointer onto the small slider box in the scroll bar that appears just below the sound frequency window. By keeping the button depressed as you move the mouse to the left or right, you can change your current position within the sound file. Do this after you have stopped playing the sound file.

As you move the slider box, the Position indicator changes and the frequency spectrum window reflects the current sounds at that point in the file. By judiciously observing the position value, then starting and stopping the playing of the file, you can determine the exact position at which you want to make editing changes.

♦ CONTROLLING EDITING POSITION PRECISELY

In the course of inserting or mixing a new file, you can exercise control over positioning to one-tenth of a second. Moving the slider box in the scroll bar gives you a general sense of where you are. By clicking the scroll bar anywhere to the left (or right) of the slider bar, the position will decrease (or increase) by one second at a time. By clicking the right arrow (or left arrow) at the end of the scroll bar, the position will increase (or decrease) by one-tenth of a second at a time.

The Edit menu offers three primary capabilities. Two of them, although named differently, are equivalent to the techniques of cutting and pasting that you already understand. All the techniques take effect at the precise point in the sound file at which you've located the Position indicator.

By choosing Delete Before Current Position, you erase (i.e., cut) all sound data from the beginning of the sound file to the current position. The current value in the sound file's Length indicator will be reduced to reflect how much has been eliminated.

By choosing Delete After Current Position, you erase (i.e., cut) all sound data from the current position to the end of the sound file. The current value in the sound file's Length indicator will be reduced to reflect how much has been eliminated.

The Insert File option (the equivalent to Paste) allows you to select only waveform files from the dialog box that appears. The entire sound contents of the inserted file will now be heard at the current position of the file you're working with. The length of the current file will be increased to equal the sum of the two file lengths (i.e., the current one plus the inserted one).

The most interesting option is Mix With File, which blends the sounds from the selected file with the sounds in the current file. The length of the final result will be equal to the current Position value (i.e., how many seconds have been heard) plus whichever is larger between the remaining time in the current file and the time in the new file.

For example, suppose that you are at position =20 seconds in a sound file that is precisely 60 seconds in length. If you mix another file 30 seconds long into this one, the new 30 seconds of sounds will play simultaneously with the sounds in the current file that ranged from 20 to 50 seconds. The entire length of the newly mixed file will still be 60 seconds. Figure 6.9 depicts this mixing.

Suppose that the new file that you mix into the current one is 40 seconds long. Figure 6.10 depicts this scenario. The example shows a mixed file whose length exceeds the original file. As the figure demonstrates, the new file is 70 seconds long. The first 20 seconds play sounds from the original current file. The next 40 seconds play a blend of the sounds from the two files. The last 10 seconds play only the sound that was contributed from the file that was mixed in.

Adding Special Effects to Your Sounds

The Effects pull-down menu offers options that influence the entire current sound file, regardless of length. You can uniformly increase the loudness of your recording, or of any current file, each time you click on the first option: Increase Volume (By 25%). You can make the sounds softer by clicking on Decrease Volume. I find this to be a very useful tool for adjusting for variations in original recording level.

Less useful is the Increase Speed (By 100%) option. This speeds up a sound but makes no compensation for the pitch of the sound. Because the same sound is played in half the time (the file's time length is immediately cut in half), you get

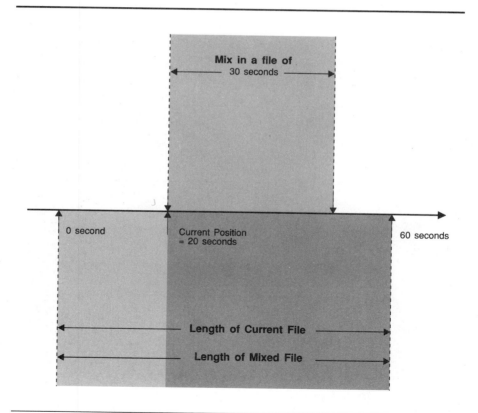

FIGURE 6.9:   Mixing a short file into the current sound file

a chipmunk effect. Try it once. If you don't like it or can't use it for anything, click on Decrease Speed to restore the sound to its former state.

The Add Echo option allows you to add an echo to the sound, producing an echo-chamber effect. It has nice resonance, and I think you'll find it pleasing as well. The Reverse option, on the other hand, is reminiscent of the stories you've heard about some rock-music groups that recorded evil things in reverse—it simply reverses the entire sound track. When you play the reversed sound file, it sounds as if you were playing the original file backward. You decide if you can use this tool for anything.

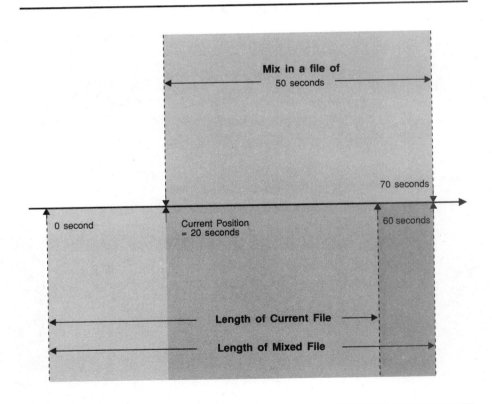

FIGURE 6.10:   Extending the length of a file during mixing

USING THE MEDIA PLAYER

The Media Player accessory program plays existing sound, animation, and MIDI sequencer files on appropriately installed and configured equipment on your system. Figure 6.11 shows the Media Player window, after the Open option was selected from the File menu.

The File menu has only an Open and an Exit option on it. When you select Open, you can limit the list box of selectable file names by first choosing one of the media types. Do that by selecting one class of media files in the List Files of Type list box in the bottom left of the Open dialog box. Once the file names are displayed, as are the .MID files in Figure 6.11, you must click on one of them before pressing OK. Only then will an actual playable file be loaded into the Media Player.

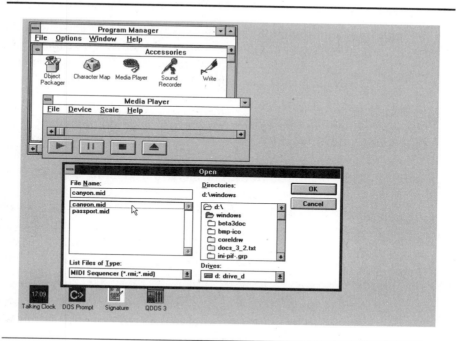

FIGURE 6.11: Opening a MIDI file for playing

The possible types of files that you can load at this point depend on the device on which you plan to play them. Remember that devices can be compound or simple. You can specify a device to the Media Player by clicking on your selection from the Device pull-down menu. You can only open and play files of a type that can be played by the currently selected device.

Remember that simple media devices play only whatever is loaded into them. They cannot accept and process the instructions in a media file. Consequently, if you've specified a simple device on the Device menu, the Open option on the File menu is grayed. Compound devices can play only media files that contain instructions appropriate to that device. If you specify a compound device, you must then use the Open option to select a file to play.

♦ **WHAT IS THE DIFFERENCE BETWEEN A COMPOUND AND SIMPLE MEDIA DEVICE?**

A simple media device plays whatever is loaded into it. A compound device plays the instructions found within a media file. You must first select the device you want to use from the Device menu. Compound device names are followed by ellipses (three periods); simple device names are not.

For example, I had already selected MIDI Sequencer on the Device menu before pulling down the File menu and selecting Open for Figure 6.11. Had I wanted to play a waveform file, I would have had to switch the device selection by clicking on the Sound choice on the Device pull-down menu. Whenever you choose a different compound device from the Device menu, the Media Player displays the equivalent of an Open dialog box, which allows you to select the particular file name you want to open for playing.

Once you've opened a media file, you can play it on the selected device by clicking on the Play button (the large right arrowhead button in the bottom left of the Media Player window). The double-bar button will temporarily pause (or continue when pressed again) the playing. The solid rectangular button is the Stop button. If you stop the playing, you'll have to press the Play button to continue later. The fourth button on the bottom row is the Eject button. It is typically grayed, although it is available for all devices that have ejectable media, such as compact discs.

As you play the media file, a scale will typically appear above the scroll bar in the center of the Media Player window. This scale can be either time-oriented or track-oriented. In Figure 6.12, for instance, the scale displays actual time durations for the two-minute-long CANYON.MID file. I find this to be the more useful scale for standard MIDI devices and straight wave-audio files.

You can select the alternative Tracks option on the Scale pull-down menu. This will display the music on a scale that depends on what track is playing. This scale is obviously more useful for devices that store and play music by track number, such as CD-audio devices.

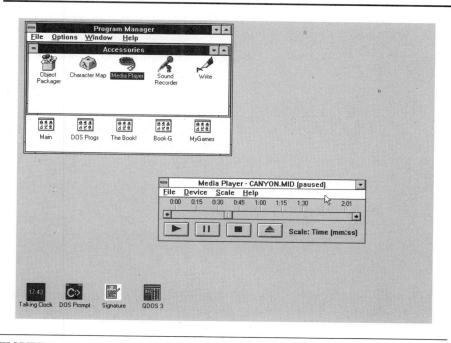

FIGURE 6.12: Playing a file with the Media Player

Multimedia and CD-ROM developments are major elements in Windows 3.1, as has been true of all the information you've read about in Part I. Turn now to Part II, and Chapter 7, to begin learning more tips and tricks about running all of your applications under Windows 3.1.

II

Running Applications

Part II presents a great many techniques for running applications in the Windows environment. In Chapter 7, you will learn how multitasking and time slicing actually work under Windows. In Chapter 8, you'll learn how to run DOS applications under Windows. In Chapter 9, you'll discover a bevy of tips and tricks for managing the Windows environment with the Program Manager and File Manager. Finally, in Chapter 10, you will learn about many aspects of the Windows graphical interface, including color and video technology.

7

Behind-the-Scenes
Secrets of
Running Applications

◆

This chapter will serve as a backdrop for the following two chapters. You will learn about many aspects of Windows that apply to running programs in general. First, you will look at some considerations for memory use and performance when running your programs in standard mode or 386 enhanced mode. You will then learn a group of techniques for streamlining the Windows start-up, such as automatically loading or executing particular programs.

You will also learn a host of methods for running applications more efficiently. This will include suggestions for protecting critical Windows files, as well as protecting data used by multiple programs. Additionally, you will learn some of the hows and whys behind custom application setups, involving such things as data and executable file associations.

Finally, you will learn a number of new facts, shortcuts, and tricks having to do with switching between tasks in either standard mode or 386 enhanced mode. And you will learn how Windows handles time slicing and priority setting.

◆ HOW TO START YOUR APPLICATIONS

Before learning any specialized techniques, you should make sure that you're aware of the many ways to actually run programs. In many cases, it doesn't even make a difference whether the program is a Windows or a non-Windows application, although I'll first contrast the two cases.

ISSUES TO CONSIDER BEFORE EVEN STARTING WINDOWS

There are two issues to consider before you even start Windows. First, you need to be aware of the differences in running TSR (terminate-and-stay-resident) applications before and during Windows. Second, you need to consider the implications of multiple programs accessing the same disk files.

Running TSRs Before Starting Windows

It is not a good idea to run TSR programs before starting Windows. Sometimes, TSRs are simply incompatible with Windows. Even if the TSR is compatible, it consumes memory that can be better put to use when placed in Windows' hands. In some cases, such as loading a mouse driver or a utility like DOSKEY, this will work all right. But even in these cases, you must make a conscious decision to trade off the memory consumed for the ready accessibility of the TSR while in Windows.

Other TSRs, like SideKick from Borland, may not enable Windows to continue running correctly if they have been loaded first. This is due to the manner in which some TSRs take control, attempting to suspend the active application when you press their hot key. If the active application is Windows, you could be in for some headaches. The severity of the problem depends greatly on how many and what applications are active.

Protecting Data Used by Multiple Programs

Chapter 3 discussed how and when to use the SHARE program for protecting the integrity of files accessed by multiple programs during Windows multitasking operations. There is sometimes confusion about the fact that DOS allows you to install the SHARE TSR application in two ways. Both ways produce equivalent operational results.

First, you can explicitly load the SHARE utility by including a command line in your AUTOEXEC.BAT file, such as

C:\DOS\SHARE

Second, you can install SHARE during initial DOS configuration by using the INSTALL command in your CONFIG.SYS file:

INSTALL=C:\DOS\SHARE.EXE

In the first case, you don't need the .EXE extension because once DOS is running, it knows to look for an .EXE extension in an executable program name. In fact, if you have the PATH properly specified on an earlier AUTO-EXEC.BAT line, you don't even need the C:\DOS prefix. In the second case, you need the C:\DOS prefix and the .EXE extension.

CONTRASTING WINDOWS WITH NON-WINDOWS APPLICATIONS

If your application was written to conform to the specifications for a Windows program, then when you run more than one application at a time, Windows will display the applications in different windows. This has the obvious advantage of graphical consistency, since all programs adhere to the GUI (graphical user interface) specifications (which include pull-down menus, control menus, and window sizing and moving capabilities).

As you'll learn later in this chapter, Windows applications are treated differently from non-Windows applications in how they receive CPU time. And the amount of time they receive can also differ according to whether you run them in standard mode or 386 enhanced mode. Furthermore, you can influence the priority and time-slicing algorithms Windows uses. You'll learn at the end of this chapter how to do this.

DOS, or non-Windows, applications are treated differently because they are quite different. The obvious difference is that they have no understanding of the Windows interface. They have no knowledge of the Windows Clipboard, so you never see a DOS program with Clipboard manipulation capabilities. However, in 386 enhanced mode, many DOS programs can access the Clipboard. You've already seen exactly how to manage this in Chapter 5. But this cut-and-paste capability offers far less power than DDE or OLE .

Furthermore, non-Windows applications cannot use the mouse in the normal Windows manner. While your DOS program uses the mouse, the Windows mouse handler is temporarily suspended.

Error: "Cannot Find File"

The "Cannot Find File" message appears when Windows attempts unsuccessfully to launch a program. The most common appearance of this message is at system start-up. To run programs or data files associated with applications automatically, representative icons can be placed in the StartUp directory. Alternatively, the application names can be placed on the Load or Run lines in the WIN.INI file.

In any of these cases, Windows may be unable to locate the specified application on your disks. This may be for any of the following reasons:

◆ The program name or the directory path has been misspelled.

◆ The specified path is invalid; for example, the file exists but is located elsewhere in the file system.

◆ A command-line switch may be interfering with Windows' ability to interpret the Load or Run entries in WIN.INI.

◆ The command line or the working directory entry is invalid in the Properties section of the File pull-down menu in the Program Manager.

Check each of these possibilities if your start-up programs fail to run.

Conversely, 386 enhanced mode users can run many non-Windows applications in full-screen windows. However, unless you use the latest version of a mouse driver, the non-Windows application will not be able to use the mouse in its usual way, because Windows will process all mouse events to the exclusion of your application. Chapter 8 discusses these distinctions and much more about running non-Windows applications in both standard mode and 386 enhanced mode.

CHOOSING YOUR FAVORITE WAY TO START AN APPLICATION

My favorite way to start an application is to set up a colorful icon for it in a Program Manager group, then double-click on the icon when I want to run the application. You can also highlight any icon, then select Open from the File pull-down menu. Figure 7.1 shows my Program Manager screen with three program groups open and visible: the icons for the programs included with this book (group name The Book!), my Windows 3.1 StartUp program group, and a group of frequently run applications in a group called MyAccessories.

The StartUp program group is a special feature of Windows 3.1. Any program icon included in this group is automatically run when Windows starts up. You can pull down the File menu and select New to add new entries to this group. Or, you can use the mouse to drag an existing icon in another group to this group. Remember that you can completely move an icon into this group by just dragging it in from another open program group. Alternatively, you can just create a copy of another icon by pressing and holding the Ctrl key while dragging the icon into the StartUp group.

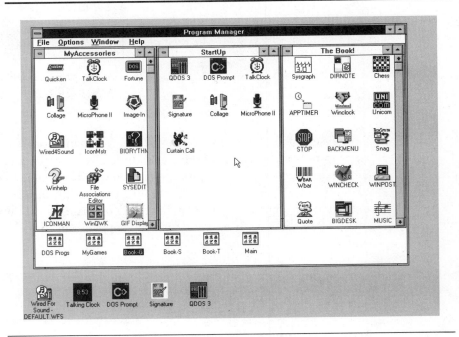

FIGURE 7.1:   The Program Manager, with three open program groups

Earlier versions of Windows use special entries (Load= and Run=) in the WIN.INI file to control start-up processing. These entries are still available. In fact, some third-party programs will actually install themselves by making adjustments to one or both of these lines in your system's WIN.INI file. The StartUp group is easier to set up and maintain, so I recommend using it for programs that you decide must be run each time you start Windows.

But I set up icons only for the most commonly run programs. To run other, less frequently needed programs, I use different methods. To test new programs on my system, I simply pull down the Program Manager's File menu and select Run, typing in the complete path name for the desired program. Windows runs it for me, using the directory containing the program as the default directory.

Finally, when I use the File Manager, I can run programs in still more ways. I can choose the Run command from the File Manager's File pull-down menu. This command operates in the same way as the Run command in the Program Manager. Alternatively, when displaying a Directory Tree window, I can simply select any executable program name (EXE, COM, BAT, or PIF) and ask Windows to run it for me.

You can select and run a program from the File Manager by double-clicking on it, or by highlighting the name, pulling down the File menu, and choosing Open. If you've selected a Windows .EXE program name, Windows immediately runs the program. If you've selected a non-Windows application, Windows starts a DOS command processor, usually COMMAND.COM, then runs your program within the environment of that command processor. This happens if you select

♦ A .COM file

♦ A DOS .EXE file

♦ A .BAT batch file that itself runs another DOS program or a series of DOS commands

♦ A special .PIF file that defines the execution parameters for running a DOS program within Windows (see Chapter 8 for further details)

USING DRAG AND DROP TO LOAD DATA FILES AUTOMATICALLY

There are additional ways to run an application that result in Windows automatically loading a data file for that application. The simpler method is for File Manager users. It involves selecting a data file name with the mouse and dragging it onto the file name of an executable program. This technique is called *drag and drop*.

Figure 7.2 depicts this situation after I selected a CorelDRAW data file (LOGO.CDR) and dragged the file name onto the executable file name (CORELDRW.EXE). As soon as you confirm such a request, Windows starts the program, passing to it the name of the initial data file to use. This technique works equally well for Windows or non-Windows applications.

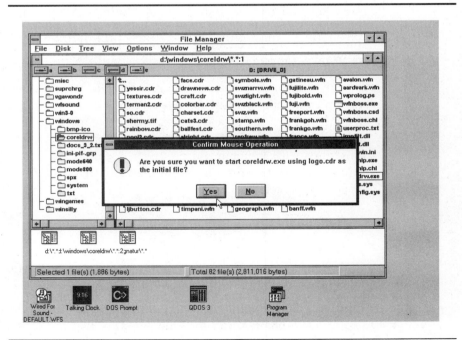

FIGURE 7.2: Using the drag-and-drop method to run applications

In the example in Figure 7.2, both the data file and the executable file are located in the same directory (D:\WINDOWS\CORELDRW). This is ideal, since there is no issue of access to the executable file, the data file, and any additional required files (such as overlays or drivers). If you use this drag-and-drop technique frequently, be sure that PATH is set to include any directories that contain required files.

Using the drag-and-drop technique to open an application with a particular data file involves no preparation whatsoever. You simply choose the data file you want to work with and bring the application icon over to the executable file name you want to run. You can select any data file and any executable program name with this method. The only requirement is that the executable program must know how to deal with the type of data file you selected. You could not, for example, drag a graphic file name onto a text-only word processor. The word processor would attempt to deal with the file in its normal manner. Rather than seeing the expected graphic, the word processor would see what appeared to be ASCII gibberish.

ASSOCIATING DATA FILES WITH EXECUTABLE FILES

There is an even better way to load specific data files when you run a particular application: You can use the Associate option on the File Manager's File pull-down menu, which enables you to specify a built-in connection between a specific executable program and any file names that have a particular extension. For example, you can associate all files that have a .WP extension with your word processor, say, Signature from Xyquest. After establishing the association, Windows will run the Signature executable application each time you open a data file whose extension is .WP.

Establishing an Association via Menu Choice

Figure 7.3 depicts the Associate dialog box that appears in the File Manager after you highlight a .WP file name, pull down the File menu, and select Associate. By typing in the full path name for the SIG.EXE file in the SIGNATUR directory and pressing Enter, Windows will know to run SIG.EXE whenever any .WP file name is selected.

As you can see in Figure 7.3, the list box offers choices of existing extension associations. You can simply select an existing entry from the list box if you wish to modify an earlier association. Your selection replaces any earlier connection. You can determine what associations exist by reading the [Extensions] section of your system's WIN.INI file. Each time you pull down the File menu and select Associate, an entry of the following sort is made or modified for you:

wp=sig.exe ^.exe

◆ ASSOCIATING PROGRAMS WITH DATA FILES

Once you've associated data files with application .EXEs, it's easy to just double-click on the data file name in the File Manager, which brings up the application with the specified data file as the initial data file. You

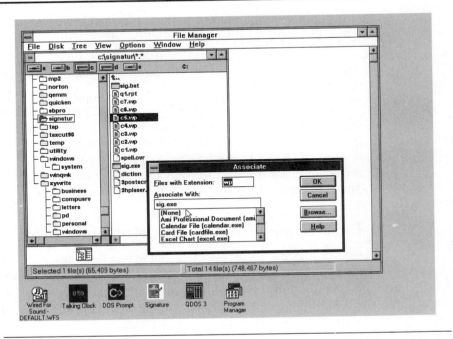

FIGURE 7.3: The Associate dialog box, which you use to load data files automatically

Determining Existing File Associations

You may wonder what associations already exist in your Windows system. Sometimes, the File Manager and other applications make adjustments to your system, setting up new associations. To find out what extensions are currently associated with applications, take a look at WIN.INI, which is in your WINDOWS directory. Find the section titled [Extensions]. You will find a series of entries that look like this:

wri=write.exe ^.wri

rec=recorder.exe ^.rec

dib=rops.exe ^.dib

txt=editor.exe ^.txt

To the left of each equal sign is the data file extension that has been associated with an .EXE file. Immediately to the right of each equal sign is the name of the .EXE file that is run when you double-click in the File Manager on any file with the specified extension.

can establish your own associations between an .EXE file and a data file (defined by the data file's extension): Highlight the data file name (or any file with the same extension) in the File Manager, then pull down the File menu and select Associate. You can then type the name of the desired application's .EXE file in the dialog box that appears. From then on, simply double-clicking on files with the specified extension will bring up the associated application.

It is also acceptable to associate multiple file extensions with the same executable program. To do this, simply repeat for each desired file extension the procedure above for associating a file extension with an executable program. Each association requires a separate line in the WIN.INI file. For example, my system has three lines that represent automatic associations between Word for Windows and .DOC, .DOT, and .RTF file extensions:

doc=winword.exe ^.doc

dot=winword.exe ^.dot

rtf=winword.exe ^.rtf

Using Program Manager Icons to Represent Associations

Since the association information is stored in the WIN.INI file, any application can learn about the connection. In particular, both the Program Manager and the File Manager can use the information. In both programs, there is a Run command on the File menu. Once an association has been created, you can enter the name of a data file in the Run field. Windows will then automatically run the associated program, passing to it the name of the data file you entered.

You can also double-click in the File Manager on the name of any data file whose extension has been associated with an executable program. Windows will start the program and open the data file. For the same result, you can create an icon to represent a data file in a Program Manager group, then double-click on the icon. The Program Manager will start the associated program and open the specified file. Use this technique when you use the same executable program (e.g., Lotus 1-2-3) to process the same files on a regular basis (e.g., WEST.WK1 and EAST.WK1).

You can use the Program Manager to set up icons that automatically start applications and open one or more data files. To automate a single data file start-and-open scenario, just pull down the File menu and select New. After specifying a program item, you can enter a Description string to identify the nature of the data file (e.g., QTR-1), then type the data file name itself in the Command Line field (e.g., Q1.RPT). Assuming that you had previously associated .RPT extensions with an executable program, such as SIG.EXE, you can just double-click on the QTR-1 icon to start the SIG.EXE program and open the Q1.RPT data file.

Some programs, such as Word for Windows, can accept the names of several data files. Constructing a single icon that initiates the executable program and several data files is a form of association. To do this with a program that can accept multiple data file names, pull down the File menu, select New, and choose Program Item. Enter any appropriate Description string (e.g., Budgets), then use the Command Line field to enter the executable program name and the names of all desired data files.

For example, suppose that you type the following in the Command Line field:

WINWORD.EXE west.doc east.doc midwest.doc

When you select this icon, Windows will start Word for Windows, and the program itself will open up three data windows to display the three budget reports from the San Francisco (west.doc), Boston (east.doc), and Chicago (midwest.doc) offices.

Creating Program Manager Icon Associations Quickly

Suppose that you've already associated a file extension with a particular program. You can easily create an associated icon in a Program Manager group with no additional typing or menu selections. To do so, use your mouse to drag the icon for a data file from a Directory Tree window in the File Manager to the desired program group in the Program Manager. If no association exists for the data file, Windows will alert you to this but will still offer you the opportunity to create the icon. You must then remember to establish the association before attempting to double-click on the icon later.

For example, suppose that you want to create the icon described above that represents the SIG.EXE program and the Q1.RPT data file. You open the program group in the Program Manager into which you would like to place the icon that will eventually represent the SIG Q1.RPT program invocation request. Then, you open the Directory Tree window in the File Manager that contains the Q1.RPT file. Next, you highlight the Q1.RPT file, hold down the left mouse button, and drag the icon into the desired Program Manager group. When you release the mouse button, Windows will spend a few moments establishing the desired icon.

USING PROGRAM MANAGER PROPERTIES TO CUSTOMIZE EXECUTION

The icons that appear in a Program Manager group will generally be the ones contained in the executable program. When you associate data files with executable files, any icons that are created will use the executable file's icon.

You can pull down the Program Manager's File menu and select Properties to learn what other characteristics lie behind the icon. When you establish an icon by the method discussed in the preceding section, Windows does all the work for you automatically. When you move an icon directly from the File Manager to a group in the Program Manager, Windows stores the full path to the data file in the Command Line field; the working directory is the directory that contains the data file.

By default, the Description field is given the base name of the data file. In that case, the description would contain *Q1*, but you can change this entry from the File Properties pull-down menu option. To make the icon label read *QTR-1*, you would simply type over the default *Q1* entry seen in the Description field of Figure 7.4.

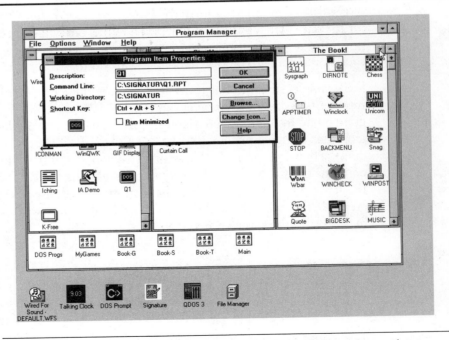

FIGURE 7.4: The Program Item Properties dialog box, which offers a shortcut-key capability

Figure 7.4 also demonstrates another special feature of Windows 3.1. You can use the Shortcut Key field to provide a quick key combination mechanism for starting any Windows or non-Windows application. If you make an entry in this field, you can quickly start a program (and any associated data files if the icon properties are defined that way) without having to make any menu choices at all.

◆ SET THE WORKING DIRECTORY FOR APPLICATIONS

Non-Windows applications have a PIF entry that allows you to specify a working directory (the Startup Directory option) for the program. This facilitates ready access to data files when the main application is executed. Without a PIF, which only helps you with DOS applications, you can still control which directory becomes the working directory. When you add a new program item with the Program Manager, the Properties dialog box offers a Working Directory choice. Enter the directory path name that you would like to be the current directory when the application runs.

To establish this quick keystroke capability, highlight the desired icon, pull down the File menu, and select Properties. Click once in the Shortcut Key field, or press Tab to move over to it. Then press any Ctrl+Alt, Ctrl+Shift, Alt+Shift, or Ctrl+Alt+Shift key combination. Later, when the Program Manager is running, you can just press the key combination and the program will start automatically. Note that at least one program group (any one will do) must be open for the shortcut key to be recognized and the indicated program to start.

Figure 7.4 shows how I have specified the Ctrl+Alt+S key combination for quick execution of the SIG.EXE program with Q1.RPT. Since the shortcut key only works when you have opened and highlighted a program group, you can use the same key combination for different icons in different program groups.

◆ HOT KEY TO ANY APPLICATION

With the Program Manager on the screen and any program group open, you can launch any Windows or non-Windows application by pressing a predefined program shortcut key. You define such a key in the Program Item Properties box that appears when you choose to define a new program item with the Program Manager. After you have launched several Windows or non-Windows applications, you can switch directly to any one of them by pressing its shortcut key.

When you attempt to use a key combination that has already been used, Windows will warn you of the existence of the other group icon using the shortcut. This warning is just in case you have made a mistake in specifying that particular key combination. You will be allowed to reuse the same shortcut key if you wish. Just be sure to open the group that contains the correct icon when you use a shortcut key that is the same in multiple groups.

◆ CONTRASTING STANDARD MODE WITH 386 ENHANCED MODE

Now that you understand how to start any application, knowing more about Windows' two execution modes will help you to more decide effectively between them and to run your applications more efficiently in whatever mode you choose.

Standard mode was originally designed to be the usual execution mode for Windows. It was designed with the 80286 processor in mind and offers access to up to 16MB of memory. This mode typically does task switching faster than 386 enhanced mode, but only if you have enough memory in your machine. If memory becomes scarce, Windows will swap inactive programs to disk, making this mode potentially slower than 386 enhanced mode.

The Two Modes of Windows 3.1

These are some of the characteristics of 386 enhanced mode:

◆ Background processing is available for DOS applications.

◆ Cooperative multitasking is used for Windows applications.

◆ DOS applications can run in windows.

◆ DPMI is available to Windows and non-Windows applications.

◆ The kernel runs in 16- and 32-bit protected mode.

◆ Multiple non-Windows applications can multitask.

◆ Preemptive multitasking is used for DOS applications.

◆ Priority adjustments are available for DOS applications.

◆ Virtual 8086 mode is available.

◆ Virtual device drivers run in 32-bit protected mode.

◆ Virtual memory is available using hard-disk space as a backup.

◆ Windows is available when DOS applications run.

◆ Windows applications run in 16-bit protected mode.

◆ Windows applications share one local descriptor table (LDT).

◆ Windows applications share one virtual machine.

These are some of the characteristics of standard mode:

◆ DOS applications can run only in full-screen mode.

◆ DOS applications can task-switch but not multitask.

◆ DPMI is available only to Windows applications.

◆ The kernel runs in 16-bit protected mode.

◆ Windows applications run in 16-bit protected mode.

◆ Windows applications share one LDT.

◆ Windows swaps itself out when DOS applications run.

As you know, 386 enhanced mode offers a virtual memory manager that provides better memory utilization for Windows than standard mode. It also offers the ability to process non-Windows applications in the background, as well as the possibility of running many non-Windows applications in a screen window.

♦ PROVIDE EXPANDED MEMORY TO DOS APPLICATIONS

In 386 enhanced mode, Windows automatically converts extended memory to expanded memory, as the need arises. In standard mode, you must take the initiative yourself. Because Windows cannot automatically provide expanded memory, you must do it before you start Windows. You can use EMM386.EXE, or some other memory manager like QEMM386.EXE, to provide expanded memory support. Check the memory manager's documentation for the necessary parameter settings.

The overhead of the code for 386 enhanced mode means that a non-Windows application will have roughly 10K less available memory than when running in standard mode. In addition, this same code to manage time slicing and background processing will usually cause slower execution of all Windows applications.

Many programs, like Norton's SysInfo, produce a comparative performance index, which relates the speed of your system to some standard system. The standard is usually the first IBM PC, which used a 4.77-MHz 16-bit processor. If you run such a benchmark at different times under Windows, you will note the following:

♦ A DOS program running alone under standard mode runs at virtually the same speed as under DOS itself.

♦ A full-screen DOS application under 386 enhanced mode runs slightly slower than under DOS itself (perhaps 5 percent slower).

♦ A windowed DOS application under 386 enhanced mode runs perceptibly slower than under DOS itself (perhaps 10–15 percent slower).

♦ A windowed DOS application under 386 enhanced mode, and running in the background as well, will run even slower (perhaps 20 percent slower). Many time-sensitive programs, such as communications programs running at higher baud rates, will not function successfully in this setting.

386 enhanced mode offers more flexible multitasking for DOS applications than does standard mode. And it offers the convenience of windowing a DOS application, with the ease of Clipboard use through the Control menu. All by themselves, these two reasons are enough for me to use 386 enhanced mode all the time.

Windows does break the 640K memory constraint, which limits DOS applications as well as earlier versions of Windows programs. (Chapter 4 discusses in depth the specific memory usage differences between the two modes.) In standard mode, Windows only provides this extra memory beyond 640K for Windows programs themselves, not for non-Windows applications. Although non-Windows applications are still limited to the standard 640K addressability, standard mode does offer a helpful task-switching capability.

♦ IS STANDARD MODE FASTER THAN 386 ENHANCED MODE?

Yes...if your system has enough extended memory to store all running applications.

Yes...if you are running only Windows applications.

No...if you wish to run DOS applications in the background.

No...if swapping occurs because of insufficient memory.

But real multitasking does not occur until you run in 386 enhanced mode. Not only can Windows applications use all available memory, but DOS applications can now use extended memory as well. However, they must do this by using the DOS Protected Mode Interface (DPMI).

Remember that the Virtual Memory Manager (VMM) in Windows 3.1 is the brain behind virtual memory in 386 enhanced mode. Each non-Windows application runs in a unique 640K address space known as a *virtual machine* (sometimes called virtual 8086, or V86). Even though V86 address spaces are not completely independent, this separateness does provide a measure of protection between applications.

◆ STREAMLINING THE WINDOWS START-UP

DOS users are familiar with the power of the AUTOEXEC.BAT file. By efficiently including commands in this start-up file, you can set up an entire execution environment each time you turn on your computer. In fact, you can even include in DOS's AUTOEXEC.BAT file the command to start up Windows.

When you start up Windows, you have another set of possibilities for initialization. Just as CONFIG.SYS and AUTOEXEC.BAT offer opportunities for customizing your DOS environment, several Windows .INI files offer opportunities for customizing your Windows environment. Chapter 12 discusses in depth the possibilities for .INI file adjustments.

In this section, you'll learn more about some specialized start-up capabilities. You'll learn how to completely bypass the opening Microsoft logo screen and how to replace the logo with your own graphic image. You'll also learn some tips and techniques for automatically initiating specific applications each time you start up Windows.

BYPASSING THE OPENING WINDOWS SCREEN

Many users want to skip Microsoft's introductory logo screen when starting Windows. There is a method, which I first discussed in Chapter 2, for replacing Microsoft's logo with your own logo or any other properly prepared bitmap image. I'll review that method in just a moment. There is also a mechanism for starting Windows so that a specifically named program is run automatically. This also will automatically suppress the opening screen. I'll show you in an upcoming section how and why you might want to use this method.

First, I'd like to discuss one of the techniques that has been proposed elsewhere for completely bypassing the logo screen. Typically, I type WIN to start Windows. Windows begins by first determining my system's hardware configuration and choosing an operating mode. In my case, 386 enhanced mode is always chosen.

If you append a space and a colon, as in

WIN :

Windows will start up as before but will completely skip the logo display step. Normally, this presents no problem, but this is not always the case. There is some additional work that is performed during this initiation phase that may prove to be a problem at times.

For example, suppose that you have two monitors and adapters. You may use a high-resolution monochrome monitor to write and edit source code, and you may use a Super VGA multiscanning monitor for final program tests. During development, you may switch back and forth between the two.

The opening logo code updates the DOS equipment flag. It must ascertain whether a color monitor is available so that switching to color graphics mode is feasible. If you start Windows from your monochrome monitor but suppress the logo code, Windows will be unable to switch to color graphics mode. The bottom line is that you should not skip the logo code. If you must do away with Microsoft's logo, you should replace it with a new image.

REPLACING THE OPENING WINDOWS SCREEN

To replace the opening Windows logo screen, you choose or create a completely new WIN.COM file that includes a new bit-map image. Because you will be unable to start Windows at all if you make a mistake, I strongly advise you to save a copy of your existing WIN.COM file. Make your WINDOWS directory the current directory, and execute this DOS command:

COPY WIN.COM WINBACK.COM

This replicates your working WIN.COM start-up command. If your new logo does not appear correctly, or if Windows does not start successfully, restore your original WIN.COM file with

COPY WINBACK.COM WIN.COM

Refer to Figure 7.5 when following the replacement procedure—it depicts the typical contents of your WIN.COM file. But since the file itself is really split into three well-defined portions, you can easily construct a new WIN.COM file that displays a different bit-map image during start-up.

FIGURE 7.5: Organization of the WIN.COM file

The first part of WIN.COM is the main program-loading portion; it is contained in a file named WIN.CNF. The second part is display-dependent. Remember that during installation, Windows copied one or more files with a .LGO extension to your hard disk. These files have such names as VGALOGO.LGO, HERCLOGO.LGO, EGALOGO.LGO, and so on. The third part is the bit-map image that will be displayed during start-up. It is in Run Length Encoded (RLE) format, which is a compressed format for bit-map files. During installation, and depending on your monitor, Windows copies one image file to your hard disk. It has a name like VGALOGO.RLE or EGALOGO.RLE.

To create the final WIN.COM file during the installation process, Windows Setup executes the equivalent of the following DOS command:

COPY /B WIN.CNF+*DisplayType*.LGO+*YourLogo*.RLE WIN.COM

When you enter this command at the DOS prompt, you replace <*Display-Type*> with the appropriate display name, such as HERCLOGO or EGA-LOGO. Also, you replace <*YourLogo*> with the base name of the RLE file you want to display.

♦ USE PAINTSHOP TO CREATE THE RLE FILE

The second disk at the back of this book contains the PAINTSHOP application, which provides graphic conversion and creation capabilities. If you have an image in some other graphic format, you can use PAINTSHOP to create the necessary RLE file.

CONTROLLING WINDOW SIZE ON START-UP

You might want to specify whether programs begin as icons, in full-screen mode, or even in particularly sized and placed screen windows. Unfortunately, you have very little control over these characteristics at start-up. Once Windows is running, you can start applications by double-clicking on an icon in the Program Manager or on the file name in a File Manager Directory Tree window. If you keep the Shift key depressed when you initiate the program in one of these ways, the application will typically start up in a minimized (iconized) state.

Beyond the initial state, it is up to the application programmer to determine the size and location of its opening window. This is done with the Create-Window function, available only to a source code programmer. The function takes four parameter values in pixels. They specify the vertical and horizontal screen position of one corner of the window, as well as the height and width of the window.

Once the window has been defined with this function, the ShowWindow function displays it on the screen. This function takes a single parameter that defines whether the window appears as an icon (minimized), as a full-screen display (maximized), or at the exact size defined by the CreateWindow function. If the programmer accepts the Windows default value for this function's parameter, the application starts up in its normal screen window. If the user presses and holds the Shift key when starting this application, Windows sets the parameter value to specify a minimized start-up.

LOADING OR RUNNING APPLICATIONS AUTOMATICALLY AT START-UP

Windows 3.1 contains a built-in program group in the Program Manager called StartUp. Any icon that you create in this group, or move or copy into this group, represents an application that will be run automatically when you start Windows. This is a convenient, graphical way to set up your desktop in a consistent manner each time Windows begins. Place your most common program icons here so that they're immediately available to you when the Windows desktop first appears.

Older versions of Window can create the same effect, running applications automatically when you include their names on the Run= line of the WIN.INI file (in the [Windows] section). Whether they are in the StartUp program group or on the Run= line, the named applications will be started. Any normal start-up steps in the programs will be executed at this point. This includes such things as loading support files or drivers, or setting up internal values.

An AUTOEXEC.BAT Equivalent in WIN3

If you would like to start one or more applications automatically when you begin Windows, you needn't wait until Windows has begun to launch applications via the File Manager or some equivalent launching program. In Windows 3.1 you can enter a program's icon in the StartUp group of the Program Manager. This will run the underlying application when you start Windows.

Users of Windows 3.1 and earlier versions can use another technique. Using a text editor or SYSEDIT.EXE, change the Load= or the Run= line in your WIN.INI file (found in the WINDOWS directory). You can start one or more programs by adding their names or associated PIF names to these lines. For example, to load and iconize at start-up both your DOS editor and your copy of Lotus 1-2-3, adjust the Load= line (found in the [WINDOWS] section of WIN.INI) to read

LOAD=EDITOR.PIF 123V23.PIF

This assumes that you've already created custom PIF files for these two sample applications. Similarly, you can use the Run= line to start Windows programs that you want to start up and activate at the same time.

In standard mode, you can run only one non-Windows application at a time. Consequently, you cannot start more than one DOS application. For example, if your StartUp group or the Run= line specifies the DOS applications QD3.EXE and SIG.EXE, as in

Run=QD3.EXE SIG.EXE

only QD3.EXE will actually run. In 386 enhanced mode, this is no problem and both applications will start up and run normally.

Multiple programs in 386 enhanced mode use a form of CPU cycle sharing, or *time slicing*, that is explained later in this chapter. Even though you can start two or more non-Windows applications with the Run command or in the StartUp group, each will initially run only for a limited amount of time. This may not be enough to complete the application's normal start-up processing. If you want the application to complete all normal start-up processing, you must be sure to check the Background box in the program's PIF. In this way, Windows will be sure to continue to allot time slices to that application, even if you don't immediately bring it to the foreground.

Running a program automatically is different from simply loading the application. The WIN.INI file contains a Load= line, on which you can also specify the names of programs to initiate. This also helps to set up the desktop but does not take as much time to complete as running the application itself at start-up. When loading, Windows merely establishes the initial memory consumption for the application and sets up a minimized icon for the application on your desktop. Only when you double-click the icon does Windows actually start up the application itself.

Nevertheless, automatic loading or running of programs at start-up takes longer than not loading or running programs. In one respect, it's just a convenience to avoid having to individually start each program. But it still takes a finite amount of time. So load or run just the applications you need at start-up.

In the first place, loading or running just what you need avoids the extra waiting for programs that you may actually never need during the current Windows session. In the second place, this reduces the number of active programs that Windows must manage. In that case, you will probably improve the performance and throughput of all other programs that you really do access and use.

◆ RUNNING OUT OF MEMORY AT START-UP

If you receive "Out of Memory" messages when starting applications, try rearranging the order in which you load and run these applications. All applications share the same limited resource space. This space is not available memory; it is the heap space in the Windows core.

Some applications will run with less initial resource space, so they will successfully load if they are initiated later than others. However, they may consume more resource space than they need if they are loaded prior to other less demanding applications. This may leave insufficient space for other applications to even begin.

SPECIFYING YOUR OWN
WINDOWS SHELL

You know about using the StartUp group in the Program Manager, or the Load and Run lines in WIN.INI, for launching applications each time you start up Windows. These techniques offer a relatively permanent customization of your Windows environment.

Occasionally, you will want to run a particular application when you start Windows. You may even want to use a particular file with a particular application. There are several variations on this theme, all of which can be controlled by the way you start Windows at the command line.

To start Windows and immediately invoke (for this one time) a specific application (e.g., SIG.EXE), just type its name after WIN:

WIN SIG

If you know the particular data file you want to work with, you can start Windows in two ways, depending on whether the data file's extension has been associated with the desired application.

If the [Extensions] section of WIN.INI reflects an association between a particular file extension and a specific application, you can bring up Windows and the application automatically by specifying a data file name. For example, to bring up Windows and use Notepad to edit SYSTEM.INI, type the following at the DOS prompt:

WIN C:\WINDOWS\SYSTEM.INI

If no association exists, just enter the names of both the application and the data file, for example,

WIN EDITOR TEST.DTA

The application that you start in this way will be run in addition to any other programs included in your StartUp group or on the Load= and Run= lines of WIN.INI. You can use this one-time-only program start-up with either Windows or non-Windows applications. If you are going to pass a data file name to an application, the application must be able to accept such a name as a command-line parameter.

◆ RUNNING YOUR APPLICATIONS EFFICIENTLY

This section has a number of useful suggestions for running applications more efficiently.

BACKUP CONSIDERATIONS BEFORE AND AFTER RUNNING APPLICATIONS

Backing up your files is a suggestion that appears in nearly every computer software text. New applications typically include instructions for backing up the source disks. Backup software is increasingly commonplace in computer installations. In this section, I'll offer some advice and information about backing up not only entire disks that contain your Windows software but also backing up the most crucial Windows files.

Backing Up Your Entire Disk

You've heard it so many times. Back up everything. Buy a tape drive and back up everything. Or buy a removable hard-disk cartridge, like the Bernoulli 90MB Transportable, and back up everything on your hard disk. Or if expense is an issue, just use as many floppy disks as you need to back up everything.

I'm not going to belabor the obvious. Hard disks crash. Even though it doesn't happen often, and it may never happen to you, it does happen. You and your disk could be the victim. It has happened to me several times, for different reasons. Other books discuss how and when to back up. I'm going to point out some backup facts that are unique to your Windows environment.

First of all, do not use a DOS-based backup application from within Windows. Even though you can theoretically run such a program in a DOS session under Windows, the outcome may be quite upsetting. Many DOS backup applications read the disk directly, rather than use DOS service calls, to speed up the backup process. Under DOS, when nothing else is going on, this is perfectly

Dynamic Viewing of TEMP File Activity

While multiple programs run, many files are created temporarily in the directory that the TEMP variable points to. My system's TEMP variable points to a 2MB RAM disk (F:). Depending on how you use your system, it can be simply interesting, or very satisfying, or critical to know what's going on in your TEMP directory.

If you compile programs frequently, it can be a learning experience to know what files are created in the TEMP directory. You may print large amounts of data and be astonished to discover how large the spooled files can be. Then again, you may discover that your TEMP directory fills up, explaining previously inexplicable performance drop-offs. An application will be forced to wait, or even terminate, if required TEMP space is unavailable. This could be because a RAM disk is too small or because your hard disk does not have as much free space as the application really needs.

To dynamically see all file creations, deletions, and updates, follow these steps:

1. Set the FileSysChange=On parameter line in the [386Enh] section of SYSTEM.INI.

2. Restart Windows for this change to take effect.

3. Start the File Manager and open a window into the TEMP directory, wherever it is on your system.

4. Run an application that may use the TEMP directory. The window in the File Manager will automatically be redrawn whenever any change occurs to the directory.

You can use this technique to display the activity level in any directory on any disk.

acceptable, and even desirable for the purposes of getting the backup procedure over and done with faster.

Under Windows, however, other disk activity may be going on. Files to be backed up may be modified by one of the applications that Windows is multitasking. The DOS backup application won't know this and may write an incorrect version of the file.

Furthermore, Windows may be using the disk for virtual memory. This has two ramifications. First, the execution status of many application and data files may be unclear, and multiple files may be incorrectly read or written. Second, you may have installed a caching utility like SMARTDRV. This means that the actual contents of individual disk files will be incorrect, since the backup software will be directly reading the disk rather than the cache. The cache contains the correct and most recent version of the affected files, and the backup software will be reading the older and out-of-date disk versions of your files.

The potential problems go beyond even these issues, however. Windows normally controls all direct memory access (DMA). Since DOS backup applications assume that nothing else is going on in the computer, they sometimes temporarily reprogram the computer's DMA controller chips. If Windows attempts to access files through these reprogrammed controller chips, your disk is in for some hard times.

Another problem can occur with some DOS backup programs. Some backup programs execute a file by file copy, which produces a more easily readable backup. This is a slower mechanism than if the backup program makes an image copy of the disk. In this technique, a track-by-track copy is made of your disk's contents. Unfortunately, since Windows may still be writing new files or modifying old files on the disk, you could wind up with a completely trashed file allocation table (FAT). This is because the actual FAT when the backup ends will be different from the FAT that is read by the backup program when the backup procedure begins.

♦ DO NOT RUN DOS BACKUP PROGRAMS FROM WITHIN WINDOWS

Backing up a disk from within Windows can be very tricky and very dangerous. Some Windows backup programs, such as the Norton Desktop for Windows, are designed to handle such tasks, even when running in the background. But the typical DOS-based backup program is not prepared for the multiplicity of activities that occur when Windows operates.

Most DOS backup programs use speedup techniques that make the assumption that no other program is currently operating. For example, Back-It 4 from Gazelle Systems uses direct disk reads and DMA transfers to improve performance. If you run such a program from a DOS session under Windows, you are asking for trouble. Gazelle's backup program for Windows, while slower than its DOS counterpart (like many other applications), has no problems running simultaneously with other Windows applications.

Protecting Your Critical Windows Files

Full-scale backups, like the ones discussed in the preceding section, are most useful when you've lost an entire disk. Consequently, you probably don't create such backups very often. After all, you're only trying to protect yourself against a catastrophic hard-disk loss.

In most cases, you can also use a complete backup to restore just a few files. However, when you do this, it takes a long time to restore an individual file. So for individual files, I usually just make a quick disk copy for safekeeping. That's how I usually back up each day's writings.

But there is another arena where individual file backups can pay off. Since Windows is so dependent on its special .INI files, it makes sense to keep individual copies of them. The .INI files are so important that Chapter 12 is devoted to explaining each one's contents and functions.

Some writers suggest that you simply make .BAK (or .IN2) copies of each .INI file in your WINDOWS directory. That's fine and will work OK, but it involves both copying and renaming the files. I have a subdirectory under WINDOWS called BACKUPS, which contains all my critical Windows files.

It's easiest to copy all .INI and .GRP files from the WINDOWS directory to the BACKUPS subdirectory. In this way, if a third-party application or Windows itself accidentally destroys or corrupts one of these important files, you can easily restore the original copy. For example, after creating the BACKUPS subdirectory, you can save copies of your original files with these commands:

CD \WINDOWS

COPY *.INI BACKUPS

COPY *.GRP BACKUPS

If you discover that any file has become corrupted, you can easily restore the original from the backup file (of the same name) that you've stored in the BACKUPS subdirectory. For example, suppose that you install a new application and your WIN.INI file becomes corrupted. (Don't forget that sometimes you are the cause of the corruption. Making any of the changes discussed in Chapter 12 can account for such a result. WIN.INI is in fact the initialization file corrupted most often, with SYSTEM.INI a close second.) To restore your saved version of WIN.INI, you can enter these commands:

CD \WINDOWS

COPY BACKUPS\WIN.INI

This command sequence overwrites the corrupted version of WIN.INI found in the WINDOWS directory with the former version found in the BACK-UPS subdirectory.

You may wonder why I've included the .GRP files in this suggested backup sequence. The PROGMAN.INI file contains the names of all the .GRP files that represent Program Manager groups. These files contain the properties information for every iconic entry in the group:

> Description
>
> Command Line
>
> Working Directory
>
> Shortcut Key
>
> Run Minimized flag
>
> Actual copy of the icon to be used

♦ PROTECT PROGRAM MANAGER GROUPS FROM CHANGE

To ensure that no one else can delete or add icons to one of your Program Manager groups, make the appropriate .GRP file a read-only

Reconstructing Program Manager Groups

Suppose that you've made changes to your Program Manager groups. Suppose further that one of these changes was a Program Manager group deletion that you regret. If you restore the saved version of the PROGMAN.INI file, you'll get back the deleted group, but all your other changes will be lost. The saved version of PROG-MAN.INI will not reflect any of the other changes that you'd like to keep.

Relax. You can restore just a single group with the following procedure. First, copy to the WINDOWS directory the deleted .GRP file, say, BOOK.GRP. Then pull down the File menu in the Program Manager and select New. Choose the Program Group radio button and choose OK. In the New Program Object dialog box, type a description for the group, then type the name of the .GRP file you're restoring (e.g., BOOK.GRP) in the Program Group field. Select OK and the Program Manager will quickly re-create the entire graphic group, using all the properties information stored in the .GRP file itself.

file. You can do this from the File Manager by turning on the Read Only toggle after choosing Properties from the File menu.

It can be a time-consuming process to re-create each Program Manager group. It is even more time-consuming if you have laboriously replaced default icons with customized icons that are stored in different disk files. Having a convenient backup for the .GRP files will dramatically reduce your frustration level if you must re-create one or more of them.

UNDERSTANDING MARKED APPLICATIONS

Marking is a technique used to distinguish Windows 3.*x* applications from earlier Windows 2.*x* applications. Two bits stored in an .EXE file indicate which Windows version the program was designed for. Although many earlier programs will still work in Windows 3.*x*, some applications will not.

Some developers use a utility called MARK.EXE to set these two indicator bits. One bit controls whether or not a warning dialog box appears to inform you that the application you are about to run was designed for an earlier version of Windows. Generally, I prefer to see this message, because it alerts me to possible danger in running the application. The second bit allows the application to use the improved font capabilities of Windows 3.x. However, since the program was not designed with these resources in mind, it is definitely not a sure thing that the program will work correctly.

It's not usually a problem to run such applications, because the earlier programs simply couldn't and didn't do as much as the newer ones, which are designed specifically to take advantage of Windows 3.x API service calls. However, I'm personally reluctant to run earlier programs unless I know more about what they really do behind the scenes.

♦ OLD APPLICATIONS NO LONGER WORK

Some older applications simply do not work under the latest version of Windows. If your application worked before upgrading, you should call the manufacturer of the software in question. They will advise you of a modification to your Windows environment or will inform you of an available upgrade to their own software.

Developers often use the MARK utility to hide the fact that you are really using an older Windows 2.x program. If you have a Windows 2.x program that forces Windows to display warning messages, do not use the MARK utility yourself. Instead, contact the software vendor to obtain an updated version of the program that was written for Windows 3.x.

RUNNING A SINGLE APPLICATION

Do you run Windows to run one special application? If so, you needn't run the Program Manager or File Manager at all. The Program Manager is actually only a shell that enables you to tap the power of Windows through a series of utility programs. These programs are often called *applets*, which is a diminutive for the little applications that are included in Windows 3.1.

You needn't accept this default shell application. In the first place, you may have purchased a more powerful or flexible shell. You may prefer faster response and want to use a text-based shell, like the BackMenu program included on this book's first disk. Many other shell programs like this one offer a faster response to menu selections and consume fewer system resources than the Program Manager.

In the [boot] section of your SYSTEM.INI file, you will find the following line:

shell=progman.exe

You can direct Windows to use a different program as the shell by merely substituting the program's name on this line. When you replace PROG-MAN.EXE with another executable program name, Windows will run that program as the main access to your system. Figure 7.6 depicts the possibilities.

On the left is the normal Windows environment. The middle portion depicts the replacement of the Program Manager with the BACKMENU.EXE program. To make this replacement, you must replace the shell= line in your SYSTEM.INI file with

shell=backmenu.exe

BackMenu provides a small program that requires very little memory to present a textual series of pop-up menu screens. Through these menus, you can gain access to any executable disk programs by name. You lose the familiar Program Manager windows and icons, but reduce the drain on memory and other system resources.

The right portion of Figure 7.6 depicts a situation where you've used the shell= line in SYSTEM.INI to give up the traditional shell capabilities entirely. By changing the shell= line to

shell=*YourProg.exe*

you can start up Windows with the YOURPROG.EXE file in charge. Unless YOURPROG.EXE offers some form of execution access to other programs, you will be completely unable to do anything else but run YourProg. You should use this mechanism only when you are sure that you only want to use YourProg's functionality. If you don't use some form of traditional shell, like the Program Manager or BackMenu, you won't be able to launch other applications.

You can't even exit from YourProg back to Windows. Just as you return to the DOS prompt when you exit from the Program Manager, you return to the DOS prompt when you exit from any program named on the shell= line.

The normal Windows environment expects a traditional shell, and most programs assume that they are being launched from a traditional shell. If you replace the Program Manager with another shell, the replacement program may not fully work. This is only a concern if the replacement program was not designed as a true replacement shell. If your substitution produces a single-application Windows shell environment that does not completely work, you

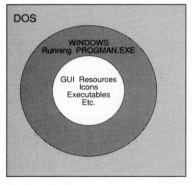

Normal Shell

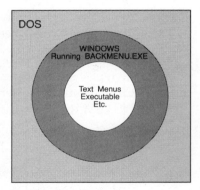

Replacement Shell

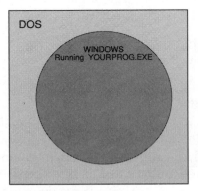

Single Program Shell

FIGURE 7.6: The Program Manager is only one possible Windows shell.

should revert back to the normal SYSTEM.INI line:

shell=progman.exe

You may have to use a text editor or word processor from the DOS command prompt to restore your SYSTEM.INI file to its former state. Once you've restored the shell= line, you can restart Windows and the Program Manager will once again be in control.

PREVENTING MONITOR BURN-IN

Windows 3.1 offers a set of screen saver choices in the Desktop portion of the Control Panel. Figure 7.7 shows the list box containing the names of selectable screen savers in Windows 3.1. Each screen saver offers a delay time. If

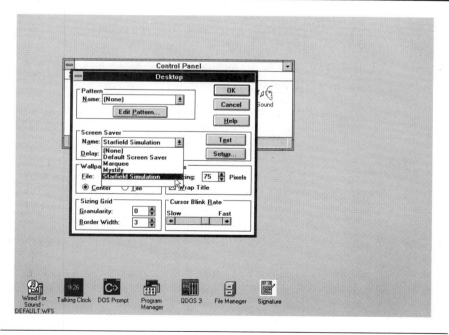

FIGURE 7.7: The Desktop dialog box in Windows 3.1, with screen-saving choices

you delay using either the keyboard or the mouse for for this specified amount of time, Windows will start the screen-saving display that you select from the list box.

There are several attractive displays. If you're a fan of the "Star Trek" series, you may prefer the Starfield Simulation display. Take a moment now on your system and try out each of the screen saver choices. You can choose one from the list box, then click on the Test button to see what it will look like.

Once you've selected one that you like, choose Setup and customize the saver screen. This customization is different for each saver module. You can adjust the number of stars in one saver, the number of lines in another, the colors, the speed, and so on. You can even define a password protection string with the Setup option.

If you decide to add password protection, you will have to remember the password. Normally, a screen saver restores the prior screen display whenever you press a key or move the mouse. If you've instituted a password via this Setup option, Windows will display an Exclamation box. You will have to enter the correct password or the screen-saving display will not disappear. This offers screen protection for your monitor and data protection for your system while you are gone.

These screen-saving modules work only while you are in Windows. They offer no protection before you start or after you exit Windows. In fact, the screen savers will not even work while you are in a DOS session within Windows. That's too bad. To obtain combination DOS/Windows screen-saving protection, you will have to obtain a third-party program like After Dark from Berkeley Systems, Inc. This application includes both DOS and Windows screen-saving components.

The DOS screen-saving component is a traditional TSR that can be run automatically from your AUTOEXEC.BAT file. Because it works in concert with Windows, it can also monitor for inactivity while Windows is running a DOS session. When you are running a DOS program under DOS but outside of Windows, inactivity leads to a black screen-saving display. When you are running a DOS program under Windows, inactivity activates the colorful and graphic Windows screen-saving display.

◆ HELP YOUR SCREEN SAVER DO ITS JOB

> Most screen savers require that you leave the screen in a Windows application. If you leave your computer while a full-screen DOS application is running, your screen saver will probably be unable to do the job. Either switch to a Windows application before leaving your system, or buy a third-party screen saver that can protect your monitor regardless of whether the active task is a Windows or a non-Windows application.

If you just run Windows applications, the built-in tools of the Control Panel's Desktop icon will be enough for you. But if you run DOS applications under Windows, you will be somewhat frustrated by the inability of Windows to initiate screen saving (and password!) operations when you leave your system while non-Windows applications are running.

If this is the case, take a look at After Dark. It gets high marks for its graphics options and some powerful behind-the-scenes capabilities. For example, you can easily animate a favorite bit-map file. After Dark can also adjust its own processing demands to minimize its impact on other operating programs, while still providing its fundamental password and screen-saving functions.

◆ SWITCHING BETWEEN TASKS

When you use one of the many available techniques for switching between executing programs, there is no obvious indication of what happens to the program you switched from. If there is enough memory in your system, all executing programs may have their own memory space. Switching just tells Windows to use a different portion of memory that already contains the desired code and data for a different program.

If there is not enough memory for all your applications, Windows will usually swap applications. The hows and whys of swapping are discussed more fully in Chapters 12 and 14. For now, it is only important to realize that swapping is transparent. It is done when necessary to switch from one program to another. Program switching can occur either automatically or on demand. When multitasking is going on, Windows automatically switches from one executing application to another to assure continued processing in all multitasking applications.

Windows programs are always able to multitask, since they all cooperatively pass control. Non-Windows applications, on the other hand, do not always multitask. In fact, in standard mode, they cannot multitask. Only one non-Windows application can execute at a time; all other non-Windows applications are frozen in the background. You must issue some form of program-switching request to bring one of them to the active, foreground position.

In 386 enhanced mode, on the other hand, you can specify in the PIF (see Chapter 8) whether or not Windows should multitask a non-Windows application in the background. As you'll learn, you can pull down the Control menu from a windowed DOS application in 386 enhanced mode and select Settings to activate background multitasking.

When multiple application windows have been opened, the window in which you are currently working is called the *active window*. If you're not sure which window is active, look at the title bars of all windows. The active window's title bar is typically displayed in a unique color or intensity. Also, the active window always appears in the screen foreground; that is, it may obscure other windows, but no other window will ever obscure your view of it.

If you can see the window containing the program you want to switch to, click on it with your mouse. However, there are a number of keyboard methods by which you can switch another program to the foreground. In the next section, you'll learn about the keystrokes to do this. Later in this chapter, you'll learn how the foreground or background position of a window influences the amount of processing time allotted to a program's execution.

Using Key Combinations for Rapid Switching

Whether or not multitasking is occurring, you can still force program switches in a variety of ways once you have opened or started more than one task. Table 7.1 lists the keyboard shortcuts for switching among tasks. The most common and recognizable key combination is Ctrl+Esc, which displays

TABLE 7.1: Primary Shortcut Keys for Task Switching

Key	Result
Ctrl+Esc	Displays the Task List
Alt+Enter	Switches a DOS application between windowed and full-screen modes
Alt+Esc	Changes the screen focus to the next application icon or window
Alt+F4	Closes the current screen application window
Alt+Tab	Switches back to the most recently active application
Alt+Tab repeatedly	Displays the name or icon of other possible applications to switch to

the Task List. It lists all open applications by name, permitting you to switch to any one of them, as well as perform a number of other on-screen activities.

The Alt+Tab key combination deserves special note. The unique variation on this keystroke, seen at the bottom of Table 7.1, is my personal favorite. I use it all the time, in lieu of the Task List, to switch from one application to another. Each time you press the Tab key, if you keep the Alt key depressed, Windows displays a title bar or icon or small window in the center of your screen that represents another possible task to which you can switch.

Release the Alt key when you see the task name to which you want to switch. This offers very fast switching since there is virtually no time consumed in reconstructing the entire screen for each application. It's even faster still if the other open applications are iconized. The Alt+Esc key combination is slower because it really does switch to a different application, redisplaying the entire screen in the process.

Windows offers a number of mouse- and keyboard-oriented methods for controlling applications and windows. Table 7.2 summarizes all the quick techniques for managing your desktop screen.

This table may be too simplistic for those of you who are experienced with Windows. I've included it here for completeness. Regardless of your experience level with Windows, take a quick look through the table to see if you

TABLE 7.2: Controlling Desktop Windows

Action	Result
Click Control-menu box	Opens Control menu
Click minimized application icon	Opens Control menu
Click title bar	Switches focus to that window
Double-click COMMAND.COM file name or DOS Prompt icon	Starts DOS command prompt session
Double-click minimized desktop icon	Restores application's screen window
Double-click application's Control menu	Closes application
Double-click on desktop	Opens Task List
Double-click window's title bar	Maximizes window or restores it to former size
Press Alt+F4	Closes application's window; quits Windows if you do this from the Program Manager (or other shell program)
Press Alt+spacebar	Opens application's Control menu
Press Alt+hyphen	Opens child window's Control menu
Press Ctrl+Esc	Opens Task List
Press Esc	Closes any open dialog box; also cancels any menu or command choice
Press Enter	Starts a program directly or a program associated with the document file selected
Press Shift+F4	Tiles all open program groups in the Program Manager
Press Shift+F5	Cascades all open program groups in the Program Manager

know all these mouse and key actions. I learned a new one myself (the Alt+hyphen key press) when I researched all the possibilities for this table.

◆ DOUBLE CLICKING PERFORMS COMMON CHORES QUICKLY

To rapidly close any Windows application, just double-click in the Control-menu box in the upper-left corner of the window. To rapidly maximize any normally sized window, double-click on any portion of the title bar. To rapidly restore any window to its normal size, double-click on any portion of the title bar, or double-click on any minimized icon.

Why Do Keystrokes Seem to Get Lost Sometimes?

In standard mode, it appears that the first few keystrokes processed after you switch to a DOS application are occasionally lost. Even in 386 enhanced mode, fast typists can hang up a DOS application by typing too fast, anticipating that the application is ready to process keystrokes immediately. This problem occurs in standard mode.

Each keystroke results in an interrupt, and each interrupt must eventually be processed by some application. If the new application to which you've switched is not yet truly active, the keystroke cannot be processed immediately. The problem becomes annoying when the application screen to which you've switched does in fact appear, but the application does not seem to respond instantly to your keystrokes.

In response to a DOS application task switch, Windows must first save the current contents of the lower 640K of memory. It stores this information in a hidden read-only file. When Windows saves the current contents of the lower 640K of memory, the screen blanks out. Now that the current memory contents, along with any necessary video buffer information, have been saved, Windows can continue processing the switch. It rereads the hidden read-only file that reflects the former memory image of the standard mode non-Windows application to which you have directed Windows to switch.

After rereading this file, Windows reloads the video buffer, which enables the screen image to be restored quickly. You see the non-Windows application screen and can begin to consider what to do next. Note that the application you've switched to is not ready to do anything for you yet. Once the video buffer has been restored, Windows reloads the low DOS memory with the previously frozen DOS application memory.

Then, after resetting the current disk and directory, Windows resets the interrupt vectors. This last step is what enables the DOS application to respond correctly to hardware interrupts, such as from the keyboard or the mouse. And this sequence explains why you will see the application to which you switch before the application is truly active and ready to respond to key presses or mouse movements.

◆ TIME SLICING IN 386 ENHANCED MODE

You learned in Chapter 3 how Windows facilitates multitasking with its cooperative execution model. In standard mode, you can run one DOS application in full-screen mode while Windows cooperatively multitasks all open Windows applications. But multitasking is the order of the day in 386 enhanced mode. Subject to some memory constraints, you can multitask any number of Windows and non-Windows applications.

UNDERSTANDING THE CONCEPT OF A TIME SLICE

It is fascinating to discover how Windows allocates CPU cycles to itself and all running applications. To understand this mechanism, first take a look at Figure 7.8. It depicts all available CPU time as a pie-like circle, with each wedge (or *time slice*) representing the minimum block of time allocated to a single application. The default size of a time slice is 20 milliseconds.

Based on a priority algorithm, which is described below, Windows actually allocates one or more of these time slices to each application. You can control the relative priority of both Windows and non-Windows applications. As you'll soon see, this enables Windows to assign more CPU time to more important applications. And you control this prioritization whether the application is running in the foreground or in the background.

Because your computer is quite fast, Windows can rapidly allocate time slices to different applications, switching from one to another fast enough to create the illusion that all applications are running concurrently. This process is called *time slicing*, and the rapid switching is what we call *multitasking*.

In fact, the Windows kernel is treated as a single sophisticated application. If there are no DOS applications running, the Windows kernel oversees the distribution of all available CPU time slices. Some of the time slices are used by

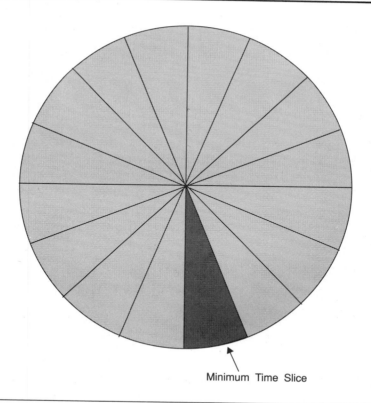

Minimum Time Slice

FIGURE 7.8: CPU time is divided into minimum time slices.

the kernel itself for management operations, but virtually all slices are used for the cooperative multitasking of any open Windows applications.

The situation is more interesting when there are DOS applications running. According to the priority mechanism described below, each DOS application receives a certain number of time slices from all available CPU time. The number is variable, and the amount of time allotted during multitasking depends on a number of factors. You can control the amount in several ways, which I'll discuss shortly. Here are some generalizations:

♦ The more DOS applications running under Windows, the slower the apparent throughput and processing efficiency of any one application.

♦ If a DOS application is in the foreground, it will seem to run faster because it receives more CPU time by default. It will in fact be running faster.

For the purposes of explanation, take a look at Figure 7.9. It depicts one or more Windows applications running in 386 enhanced mode with two DOS applications.

According to the priority settings, the number of actual CPU cycles devoted to the Windows kernel will change. Similarly, the number of actual CPU cycles devoted to each of the DOS applications will change. But, all told, the two DOS applications and the Windows kernel create a time-slicing environment in which you can identify three principal segments, each of which receives a variable number of time slices.

CONTROLLING TIME ALLOCATIONS WITH PRIORITY SETTINGS

The 386 enhanced mode icon in the Control Panel offers you control over two key aspects of time allocations. As you can see in Figure 7.10, you can set the actual minimum amount of a time slice. The default is 20 milliseconds and generally works quite well. You can vary the number in the text box entry field from 1 to 10,000.

If you reduce the number much below 20, Windows will attempt to automatically switch between open applications more often. This may create the illusion of smoother multitasking, but the overhead of the switching itself will actually reduce each application's throughput.

If you increase the number much above 20, each application may gain in throughput, because it will have the CPU for a longer period of time. However, this will only be true when it finally gets the CPU, after other applications get their increased amount of time also. This leads to reduced smoothness in multitasking, characterized by an occasional jerkiness in individual program execution.

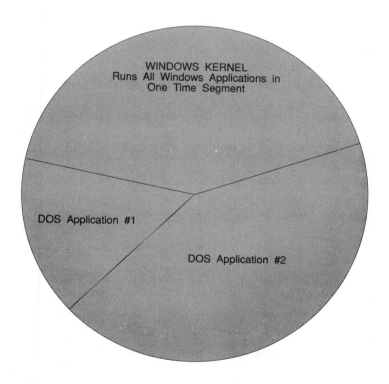

FIGURE 7.9: Two DOS applications and one or more Windows applications

In the following sections, I'll first tell you how you can control the actual priority settings for Windows and non-Windows applications. Then, I'll explain how Windows uses the priority numbers to determine actual time allocations.

Controlling Windows Application Priorities

The Control Panel also offers text entry fields for the scheduling of Windows applications. The entries Windows in Foreground and Windows in Background in the Scheduling portion of the 386 Enhanced dialog box control the priority values of Windows applications. By setting these numbers, you can control the proportion of time allotted to the Windows kernel.

If you are running any Windows application in the foreground, Windows uses the first number to determine how much time to allot to the Windows kernel.

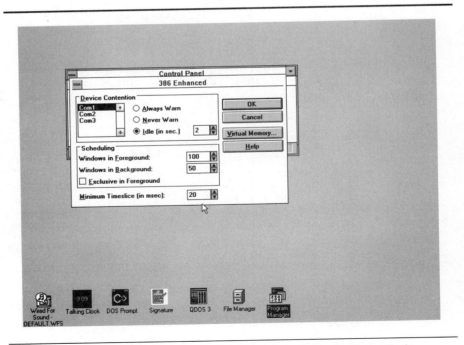

FIGURE 7.10: The Control Panel's 386 Enhanced dialog box, which controls the minimum time slice

Allocating CPU Time Slices to Programs

In 386 enhanced mode, you can control the relative priority of your executing applications. This represents an important customization facility, which enables you to control Windows' allocation of available processing power.

For Windows applications, to control the background and foreground priority values, open the Control Panel and select the 386 Enhanced icon. Make entries in the priority settings here. All Windows applications (including the kernel) share a single time slice.

For Non-Windows applications, to permanently set or change background and foreground priority values, make entries in the Advanced section of the application's PIF file. To temporarily set or change priority values, make entries in the Settings portion of the application's Control menu.

If you are running a non-Windows application in the foreground, Windows uses the second number to determine how much time to allot to the Windows kernel.

Controlling Non-Windows Application Priorities

Windows also enables you to set values for the background and foreground priorities for non-Windows applications. If you do nothing else, Windows will use the priority values found in the _DEFAULT.PIF file. Chapter 8 explains exactly how to use the Windows PIF Editor to edit this file or to create your own customized PIF for non-Windows applications.

If you run a specific DOS application, Windows uses the values found in _DEFAULT.PIF. But you can and should use the techniques found in Chapter 8 to build a customized PIF for your DOS applications. In this way, you can adjust the foreground and background priorities for each separate non-Windows application. When you run such a program by opening the PIF name in the File Manager or by selecting a Program Manager icon whose command line entry is the PIF name, Windows uses the unique priority values found in that PIF.

Regardless of whether the start-up priority values for a non-Windows application come from the default or a customized PIF, you can adjust them on the fly. In 386 enhanced mode, you can always run any non-Windows application in a window by pressing Alt-spacebar to display the Control menu. If the application is currently running in full-screen mode, Windows will first switch it into a window before displaying the Control menu.

By selecting the Settings options on the Control menu, you see the dialog box shown in Figure 7.11. This dialog box controls a number of execution-time parameters. You'll learn about the rest of them in the next chapter. If you want to change the priority values for this application for the rest of the current session, just change either or both of the numbers.

The changes are not permanent; you would have to use the PIF Editor to change the actual numbers stored in the PIF. Only then would the changes become permanent. They would then take effect when you run this program

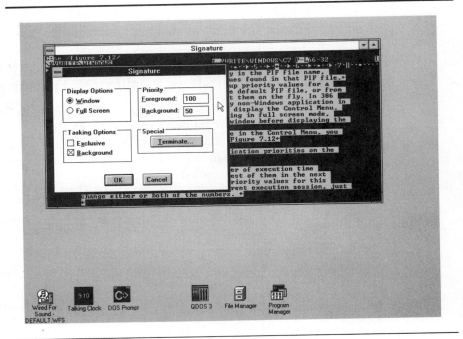

FIGURE 7.11: You can change DOS application priorities on the fly.

later. Changes that you make on the fly through the Settings dialog box are effective immediately but only last until the program terminates and the session ends.

Understanding the Windows Priority Algorithm

Let's look at a typical example now to clarify how Windows uses priorities to determine how much CPU cycle time to give to different applications.

Assume that you are running two DOS applications and three Windows applications on your system. Let's say that your Windows applications are Microphone II (an excellent communications program), PageMaker 4 (a powerful and flexible desktop publishing program), and 1-2-3 for Windows (one of the most popular spreadsheet programs). Let's also say that the two DOS applications are Signature (a powerful word processing program) and a DOS prompt. Once you've gone to the DOS prompt, Windows treats it as a DOS session whether or not you are actually running a conventional application. In fact, you are running COMMAND.COM, which may be idle or may be explicitly running a non-Windows application. From this prompt, you can run any DOS application.

You can see in Figures 7.10 and 7.11 that it is easy to adjust up and down the foreground and background priority numbers for any program. You can decide later, for your specific system, whether or not to adjust these values individually to improve the performance of particular programs or of the overall system.

◆ SET PRIORITIES TO AFFECT SPECIFIC APPLICATIONS

Remember that adjusting the Windows kernel priority values (through the 386 Enhanced icon of the Control Panel) affects the time allotted to the Windows kernel itself and all running Windows applications. Adjusting the DOS application priorities can affect each individual DOS application, if you make the change in the PIFs created for each application. However, you can adjust the priority values for all DOS applications at one time by changing the priority numbers in the _DEFAULT.PIF file. If you execute a non-Windows application through a unique PIF, that file's customized settings will override the default settings stored in _DEFAULT.PIF.

In this example, I'll assume that you've left the foreground and background priority values for the Windows kernel set at the default numbers: 100 for foreground and 50 for background. But I'll also assume that you've changed the values for the non-Windows applications to the following: For Signature, foreground priority is 75 and background priority is 30; for the DOS prompt, foreground priority is 125 and background priority is 60.

Suppose now that you have switched to your communications program, Microphone II. While this Windows program has the main screen focus, the Windows kernel is said to be in the foreground. Microphone II shares the kernel's time allotment with 1-2-3 for Windows and PageMaker. When the Windows kernel's time allotment is completed, Windows switches to the DOS prompt for its time allotment, then to Signature for its time allotment. The amount of CPU time given to each application during each allotment depends directly on the priority values assigned.

In particular, when a Windows application like Microphone II is running in the foreground, Windows notes that the kernel's foreground priority is 100. It also notes that there are two DOS applications running in the background, with background priority values of 30 and 60. This means that the total allotment of priority numbers is 100 + 30 + 60, or 190. The Windows kernel receives a proportional amount of the total CPU time by receiving $^{100}/190$, or 52.63 percent, of all available CPU cycles. In the same fashion, Signature has a background priority of 30, so it receives $^{30}/190$, or 15.79 percent, of all CPU cycles. The DOS prompt, and whatever program, if any, is running in this session, receives $^{60}/190$, or 31.58 percent, of all CPU cycles. Figure 7.12 summarizes this result.

Now suppose that you use any of the switching methods to make Signature the foreground application. Without changing any of the priority numbers, Windows makes a new allocation determination. Windows notes that Signature is now in the foreground and therefore should receive CPU time according to its foreground priority value, 75.

While Signature is in the foreground, all other applications are in the background. The entire Windows kernel runs at a background priority of 50, while the DOS prompt session runs at a background priority of 60. Therefore, the total allotment of CPU cycles in this execution configuration is 75 + 50 + 60, or 185.

Since it is in the foreground, Signature now receives $^{75}/_{185}$, or 40.54 percent, of the CPU cycles. This is nearly triple what it received when in the background. The DOS prompt receives $^{60}/_{185}$, or 32.43 percent, of available CPU cycles. All Windows applications must cooperatively share the remaining $^{50}/_{185}$, or 27.03 percent, of the CPU time. Figure 7.13 summarizes this result.

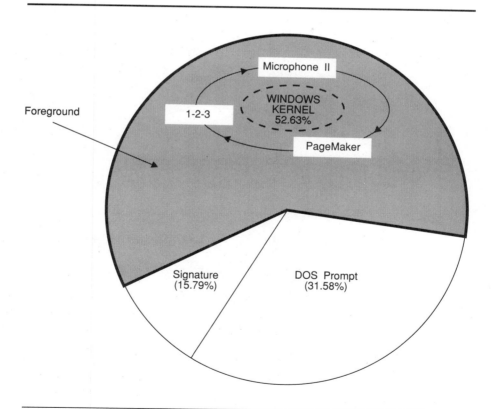

FIGURE 7.12:   Running a Windows application in the foreground

◆ GIVE AN APPLICATION ALL AVAILABLE TIME SLICES

You can force Windows to assign nearly all CPU time to a particular DOS application. To do this, if you run the application from a PIF file, you must click the Exclusive button in the Execution section of the PIF Editor. When this application runs, all other background tasks will be suspended.

You can likewise assign all CPU time slices to the Windows kernel. To do this, you must choose the Exclusive in Foreground option in the

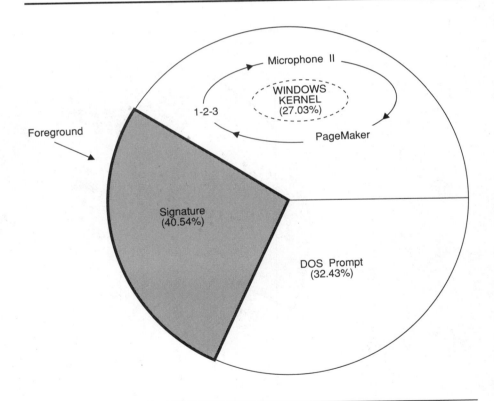

FIGURE 7.13: Running a DOS application in the foreground

Scheduling section of the 386 Enhanced part of the Control Panel. When you switch a Windows application to the foreground, all DOS applications will be suspended. Regardless of any other settings, each DOS application will run only when you switch it to the foreground.

Now that you understand some of the relationships between Windows and DOS applications, turn to the next two chapters. You will learn a host of specialized techniques and tricks for running DOS applications in Chapter 8, and you will learn much more about running Windows applications in Chapter 9.

C H A P T E R

8

*Running DOS Applications
under Windows*

More and more applications are written every day that are designed to run under Windows. They use the Clipboard, which means that they can more easily share data with one another. They use Dynamic Data Exchange (DDE) and Object Linking and Embedding (OLE), which means that different Windows programs can work together cooperatively. You learned in Chapter 5 how you can dynamically link data in more than one application, using DDE options. You also learned that Windows can automatically start up the program that created data originally, using OLE, even when you are running a different program that is just using the data.

Unfortunately, with the exception of sharing data through the Clipboard in 386 enhanced mode, you can't use these facilities with your DOS applications. Programs that were written to run directly under DOS are called *non-Windows applications*. They do not use the specialized API libraries that provide Windows programs with the many GUI capabilities and the ability to use DDE and OLE. However, until your favorite application becomes available in a Windows version, it's nice to know that you can continue to run your DOS version within Windows.

You learned in the preceding chapter a number of ways to run any program, whether it is a Windows or a non-Windows application. This chapter will teach you how to run your non-Windows applications in the most efficient manner. In large part, this involves creating or modifying a program information file, or *PIF*. PIFs govern the way in which Windows runs non-Windows, or DOS, applications. You will learn how to use the PIF Editor, available from the Main program group in the Program Manager, to create and customize your PIFs.

PIFs differ according to whether you are running your non-Windows applications in standard mode or 386 enhanced mode. I'll explain the various options in standard mode, as well as the basic and advanced options available when you run non-Windows applications in 386 enhanced mode. But this chapter goes far beyond just explaining PIF options.

In addition to PIFs, this chapter presents tips and techniques for running memory-resident programs, also known as TSRs, under Windows. It also presents some sophisticated techniques for using batch files in Windows and for directly running non-Windows applications at the DOS command prompt.

Finally, you will discover a host of special considerations for running DOS applications in either Windows mode. These include using a mouse, changing execution-time settings, passing parameters to DOS applications, and much more. In 386 enhanced mode, you will learn a number of special techniques for such things as running DOS applications within windows, switching between DOS applications, and managing simultaneous device contention.

◆ **"PROGRAM CANNOT BE RUN FROM DOS MODE"**

You've seen this message, you say? It appears whenever you try to run a Windows application from the DOS command prompt. But you thought that Windows had only two modes (standard and 386 enhanced)? Well, you're right. It's just misleading phraseology. But the message is still accurate, even if the DOS prompt (or mode) is one that you initiated from within Windows.

If you receive this message, you must return to Windows. The program you've tried to initiate can be launched or run only from Windows.

Although some of this chapter's PIF options deal with performance issues, you should also read the discussion in Chapter 14 for more details on performance considerations for running DOS programs under Windows. And even though some of the discussion in this chapter addresses the correct settings of a number of options, you should also look at the information in Chapters 17–19. Those chapters specifically address many of the problems that crop up when running non-Windows applications.

◆ PREPARING TO RUN DOS APPLICATIONS

This section covers a number of interesting aspects of preparing to run non-Windows applications, from the initial installation to the final iconization of the application in a Program Manager group. I'll also cover some unique issues that should be addressed before starting certain programs. For example, I'll explain how some DOS programs can access expanded memory. And I'll demonstrate a technique for preventing yourself from even attempting to use the same data files with the same DOS program, which you can theoretically run multiple times under Windows.

INSTALLING NON-WINDOWS APPLICATIONS

I find it easiest to create program icons in the Program Manager for every application that I run more than once. During the initial setup, when you install Windows or update your version of Windows, the Setup program automatically creates program icons for every Windows program it finds. It also attempts to recognize and set up program icons for the most popular non-Windows applications.

During this initial procedure, Setup lists all possible application names and asks you to select the ones you'd like it to install. If you choose, Setup also offers the option to automatically install all applications at once. It creates one or more application groups with icons for your applications. If you accept some of these choices, you should check them after installation. Sometimes, the selections are not correct. This is because more than one program may have the same .EXE name. Your disk may have a FORTRAN compiler and a word processing format conversion program, both named FC.EXE. Setup may actually install the word processing format conversion program but call it a FORTRAN compiler.

Besides similar program names, there are a number of applications that may be included with your system, like QBASIC.EXE with DOS 5. If you have no intention of using such applications, don't bother creating icons and installing them in the Program Manager. They will drain resources when the icon group is open, and they'll make it harder to quickly see and select icons. It's easy to add an icon anytime later.

In Windows 3.1 and 3.0, you can add a new icon at any time. The New option on the Program Manager's File pull-down menu enables you to create an icon for any Windows or non-Windows application. Figure 8.1 shows the Program Item Properties dialog box after creation of an icon for Quicken 5, a DOS program.

You first saw this dialog box in Chapter 7. It offers the same choices for setting up icons for Windows or non-Windows applications. For either, you can specify the label that will appear below the icon (in this example, Quicken 5), the name of the actual program that will be executed when you select the icon (Q.EXE), the working directory (C:\QUICKEN), and a shortcut key (Ctrl+Alt+5).

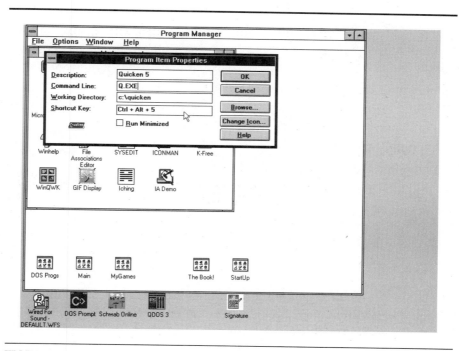

FIGURE 8.1: The Program Item Properties dialog box, used for creating a Program Manager icon

When you're in the Program Manager, Windows programs are represented by the icon that is embedded in the Windows .EXE file itself. But for DOS programs, you'll only see the bland DOS rectangular icon. I make it a practice to replace this plain DOS icon with a unique icon for each of my DOS programs. To do this, I've acquired a group of extra prepared icons. Many packages are available, both in commercial and shareware versions, that include many colorful and customized icons.

◆ BUILD CUSTOMIZED ICONS WITH ICONMSTR.EXE

The second disk accompanying this book contains the ICON-MSTR.EXE program. This Windows application has all the tools necessary to view existing icons on your disk, extract icons from existing .EXE files, and to build customized icons from scratch.

Notice in Figure 8.1 that a custom icon appears in the lower-left corner of the dialog box. This icon is not a part of the Quicken 5 program (Q.EXE). Instead, it resides in a special icon file named QUICKEN.ICO. DOS programs cannot contain icons. To tie a custom icon to a DOS program, as I've done here, you must click on the Change Icon button. When you first do this, Windows will display an exclamation box that says

Cannot find any icons in this file.

Just click on OK; the Change Icon dialog box (Figure 8.2) will appear. Since your DOS program does not have any icons within it, Windows will let you use one of the icons stored in the Program Manager file itself (PROG-MAN.EXE); .EXE files can contain multiple icons.

To choose one of the existing Program Manager icons, just use the scroll bar to highlight the one you want. Then choose OK and the Program Item Properties dialog box will reappear with the icon you chose appearing in the lower-left corner. Choose OK again and your Program Manager group will be updated with all the properties seen in the dialog box, including your selected icon.

If you want to attach a different icon to your DOS program, you can enter a different name in the File Name field of the Change Icon dialog box. Choosing OK once will then display all icons found in this file. Highlight the one you want and choose OK again. If you have a collection of specialized icon files, they probably have an .ICO extension. Type in the icon file name and choose OK to see the icon before attaching it to your DOS file. Choose OK twice more to return to the Program Item Properties dialog box and update the Program Manager group entry.

If you merely want to explore icons in a variety of files, use the Browse button to select other files. As you graphically find and select a file name, Windows will display in the File Name field the name of each selected file. Use this technique if you don't explicitly know the name of the .EXE or .ICO file that contains a desired icon.

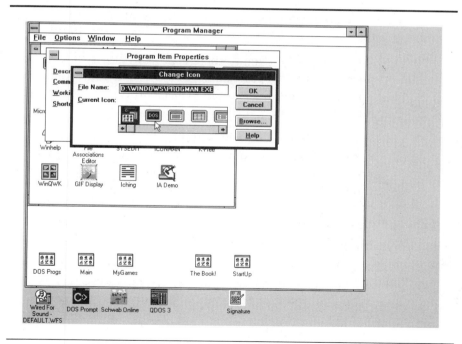

FIGURE 8.2: The Change Icon dialog box

PREVENTING THE SAME DOS APPLICATIONS FROM RUNNING TWICE

You have learned about the potential problems of multiple access to the same data file. On networks, this can occur because users on different nodes access the same data file on a server. Under Windows, this can occur because you can start more than one application that accesses the same data file. You have learned that the SHARE.EXE program can help to allow multiple access but still protect against inadvertent modification to the same data.

What about when you double-click on the same program icon more than once, bringing up a new version of an application that may already be running? Suppose that this particular icon not only brings up a particular application but also opens a data file. When a programmer develops a Windows application, the Windows API allows him to check a PrevInstance parameter to discover whether the application has already been started. The programmer can then prevent the application from restarting.

But with DOS programs, there is no such facility. If you click on a DOS application icon, the program itself cannot determine from an API call whether it is already running. You can in fact start two instances of the same DOS application. This may at times be desirable.

For example, you may still be using a DOS version of 1-2-3, in which you can work with only one worksheet in memory at a time. You can easily create two unique 1-2-3 icons, each with their own shortcut key but both actually running 1-2-3. If you always work with the same two data files, you can incorporate them directly into the start-up icons as well. (I'll review how to do this shortly.) When you later want to work with both data files, you can start two instances of the 1-2-3 program by successively double-clicking on each icon.

In 386 enhanced mode, you can quickly switch between both instances of 1-2-3 by pressing the shortcut key combinations. As I wrote this book (with my DOS version of Signature), I actually had one version of Signature open to work on the chapter text, while another instance of Signature was available (with its own 640K of memory) to contain the large glossary. It simply became too cramped in 640K to work with chapters, figures, tables, *and* all the glossary material.

But what if running two instances of the same DOS application is not desirable? Suppose the DOS program has the responsibility of maintaining the seating charts for a concert hall or the master status of a customer list. You can use a DOS batch file to protect yourself from your own forgetfulness. By running a batch file rather than the application itself, you can ensure that no more than one instance of any DOS application has a chance to execute.

As an example, suppose that you actually want to prohibit yourself from running more than one instance of the SIG.EXE program. The batch file shown in Figure 8.3 demonstrates how to do this.

The line numbers shown at the left of each line are for reference only in this text; you should not include them when you create your own batch file. You can easily use this same batch file on your system by replacing the references to SIG in lines 1, 7, and 11 with the actual name of your application. Don't forget to change the drive and directory references in lines 3 and 4 to appropriate entries.

The technique used here to prevent an application from running more than once involves using a programming device known as a *semaphore*, or a *flag*. This device is used as a communications or signaling technique. Sometimes a flag is set to one value or another. At other times, as is done here, the existence or nonexistence of a file is treated as the On or Off status of the flag.

A disk file, named *flag.sig* here although you could use any file name, is created whenever you run the actual .EXE file. It is deleted immediately after

```
 1   @Rem RUNONCE.BAT prohibits a second instance of SIG.EXE
 2   Echo off
 3   C:
 4   CD \SIGNATUR
 5   IF EXIST %TEMP%\flag.sig GOTO whoops
 6   ECHO %0 > %TEMP%\flag.sig
 7   SIG %1 %2 %3 %4 %5 %6 %7 %8 %9
 8   ERASE %TEMP%\flag.sig
 9   GOTO end
10   :whoops
11   ECHO The SIG.EXE program is running now.
12   PAUSE
13   :END
```

FIGURE 8.3: RUNONCE.BAT permits only one instance of a DOS program.

the application runs. When you attempt to run the batch file, it tests whether or not this flag file exists. If it does, you receive a screen message to that effect. If it does not, the batch file invokes the SIG.EXE program.

In this batch file, line 6 creates the flag.sig semaphore, by using the ECHO command and the technique of redirection. The flag file is created in your system's TEMP directory, using the contents of the environment's TEMP variable. In any batch file, %TEMP% is replaced by the actual contents of the TEMP environment variable. This is often a path to a faster hard disk, or to a RAM disk, such as E:\TEMP. When the flag file is created, it contains the text string *RUNONCE.BAT*, which is the name of the batch file (%0 when a batch file line is interpreted).

Line 5 actually tests for the existence of this file. If the flag file already exists, lines 6–9 are skipped and control is transferred directly to the label on line 10. The batch file displays the echoed line

The SIG.EXE program is running now.

and then pauses. A second instance of SIG.EXE would not be allowed to start, and you would be alerted to your attempt to do so.

If the flag file is determined in line 5 to not exist, then lines 6–9 are executed. Line 6 first creates the flag file, which will remain in the TEMP directory until the SIG.EXE program is completed. Line 7 actually runs SIG.EXE, passing any of up to nine variable parameters to it. When SIG.EXE ends normally, line 8 erases the flag file and control passes immediately to the end of the batch file. Since the flag file no longer exists, and SIG.EXE is no longer running, running RUNONCE.BAT will start up a single version of the SIG.EXE program.

Lines 3 and 4 in this batch file ensure that you execute SIG.EXE from its own special directory. This may or may not be necessary or convenient for your particular application, depending on what defaults are set or what assumptions are made when your application runs.

There is one more thing to consider. If your TEMP variable is set to a hard-disk directory rather than a RAM-disk directory, you must be alert to the possibility that your system may crash, or you may choose to reboot the system before SIG.EXE (or your application) is completed. Either of these cases leaves the flag file still in place, but the batch file will no longer be executing when your system reboots. To ensure that during a reboot, your system does not erroneously assume that the SIG.EXE application is still running, add the following to your AUTOEXEC.BAT file:

IF EXIST %temp%\flag.sig ERASE %temp%\flag.sig

Replace *flag.sig* with the flag file name that you've chosen.

CUSTOMIZING AN APPLICATION'S START-UP

In this section, I'm going to clarify how to perform some of the same initialization functions under Windows that you may have gotten used to under DOS. Some of the DOS programs that you run accept parameters and switches. These additional pieces of information tell the DOS application how to get started. For example, in the command line

FORMAT B: /Q /S

there is one parameter (B:) and there are two switches (/Q and /S).

Now that you see how easy it is to create a program icon for a DOS application, you may be wondering how to pass parameters and switches to the application when it starts. Actually, it's quite easy. When you create or modify a program item, you work with the dialog box shown in Figure 8.1. The simplest thing to do is to type any parameters or switches you need in the Command Line entry field.

For example, it may be as simple as passing the name of a data file as the first parameter. In my system, I typically want to open my GLOSSARY.DTA file at the same time as I bring up my Signature word processor. To do so, I can type

SIG glossary.dta

in the Command Line field of the Program Item Properties dialog box. However, this technique requires some care and understanding. In the first place, to just type SIG instead of the full path name C:\SIGNATUR\SIG, I must have placed the C:\SIGNATUR directory name in my DOS PATH environment variable. Furthermore, to reference GLOSSARY.DTA, the data file must be located in the current disk directory, which must be C:\SIGNATUR.

The safest approach is to specify a full path name for both the program you want to execute and the data file you want to open. For example:

C:\SIGNATUR\SIG C:\SIGNATUR\GLOSSARY.DTA

Depending on your application, you can follow the application name itself with one or more parameters like this, or with one or more command-line switches. You should consult your application documentation for information about the possibilities when you first start the program.

As another example, Microsoft Word for DOS enables you to start up with the most recently edited data file. To do this, you must simply start the program using the /I switch. For example:

C:\WORD\WORD /I

If you use multiple switches and parameters, just leave a space between each of them on the command line. They will then work just as if you had started the program at the DOS command prompt. Suppose that you still have only the DOS version of WordPerfect on your system. When it starts, suppose that you want to open the BUDGET.RPT text file, run WordPerfect in monochrome mode, and execute the special updating macro named ANALYZE. If the WordPerfect directory (in your PATH) contains WP.EXE, the budget report, and the macro, you can simply type the following into the Command Line field of the appropriate Program Manager icon:

WP BUDGET.RPT /MONO /M-ANALYZE

♦ PROBLEMS WITH DOS PROGRAM START-UP SCREENS

Some text-based non-Windows applications have graphic opening screens. If your PIF settings are optimized for text displays, you may be unable to start such an application in a window. If you face this problem, adjust the .PIF file to begin the application in full-screen mode. You can later press Alt+Enter to switch execution into a window (in 386 enhanced mode). Alternatively, your application may offer command-line parameters that will launch the program without attempting to display the graphic start-up screen.

ICONIZING YOUR FAVORITE BATCH FILES

You can iconize your favorite batch files, but what about setting up an environment in which the program can execute? When you are in DOS, you can execute a number of preliminary commands before actually invoking any program. You can change drives and directories; you can run a TSR; you can set environment variables. How can you accomplish the same chores when running a DOS program under Windows?

The answer is to prepare a batch file that, when run, executes all the preparatory commands and then executes the desired .EXE program as well. Figure 8.4 shows just such a batch file.

As you can see in lines 2–4, the RUN-SIG.BAT file sets a current drive (C:) and directory (C:\UTILITY), and sets the value of an environment variable (SIGLOC). Before actually running the SIG.EXE program on line 6, RUN-SIG.BAT launches the F11F12.EXE program, a TSR, in line 5. This F11F12 utility sets up the F11 and F12 keys for two frequent spell-checking operations.

After using a word processor to prepare the RUN-SIG.BAT file, I can attach it to a Program Manager icon by simply typing RUN-SIG.BAT into the Command Line field of the Program Item Properties dialog box. You must place the batch file in a directory that is accessible from your PATH, or else you must use a full path name.

As you'll soon learn, you can obtain the same customized start-up capabilities by creating a special PIF for each DOS program. Doing so gives you all the

```
1   Rem RUN-SIG.BAT
2   C:
3   SET SIGLOC=C:\UTILITY
4   CD \SIGNATUR\WINDOWS
5   F11F12 /1=CALL C:\SIG\PERSONAL.SPL /2=LOAD C:\SIG\PERSONAL.SPL
6   SIG
```

FIGURE 8.4: Use a batch file to run a DOS application in a particular environment.

advantages discussed in this section, as well as a host of other customized settings that affect such things as background processing, memory usage, and video performance. To gain these extra features, you'll have to do the extra work associated with a onetime setup of a PIF. But running a PIF that itself specifies a .BAT file is the most powerful and comprehensive way to automate any of your DOS programs under Windows.

◆ EXERCISE CONTROL OVER WHAT RUNS IN A DOS SESSION

For the easiest icon setup of a DOS program, type an .EXE file name in the Command Line field of the Program Item Properties dialog box. For greater control over the environment within which the .EXE file runs, make the entry a .BAT file. To exercise the greatest customization over the execution of any DOS program, make the Command Line entry a .PIF name.

◆ UNDERSTANDING THE PIF EDITOR

The PIF Editor is a program that enables you to create or modify program information files, or PIFs. Although Microsoft provides the _DEFAULT.PIF file, which contains a set of default values for running any DOS program, you should create your own unique PIFs for each DOS application that you plan to run on a regular basis.

Windows provides a PIF Editor icon in the Main group of the Program Manager. When you double-click on this icon to bring up the PIFEDIT program, you will see either the dialog box shown in Figure 8.5 (if you are running Windows in standard mode) or the dialog box shown in Figure 8.6 (if you are running Windows in 386 enhanced mode). In fact, Windows allows settings for both modes to be stored in a single PIF. When you open an application, Windows first determines which operating mode is running. It then uses the appropriate set of options from the PIF.

As you can see, some options are the same in both modes and others are different. In addition, the 386 enhanced mode PIF Editor contains a button called Advanced, which displays an additional screen of special options. You'll learn about them later in this chapter.

CREATING AND
MANIPULATING PIFS

Actually, you may be running Windows in one of these modes but may want to prepare a PIF for later use when running in the other mode. To do this, pull down the Mode menu and simply choose the desired mode. Windows will alert you that you are choosing a different mode. That's OK, as long as you plan to use the PIF later when in the other mode.

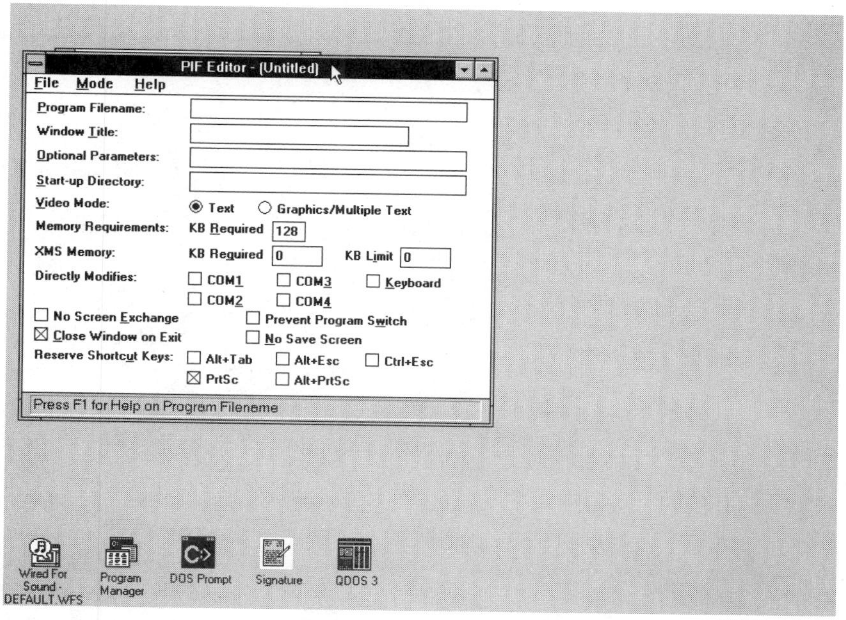

FIGURE 8.5: The PIF Editor in standard mode

To manipulate PIFs, pull down the File menu, which displays familiar options: New, Open, Save, Save As, and Exit. Choosing New clears all option values, and allows you to enter new settings from scratch for all possibilities. Choosing Open displays a Directory Tree box that enables you to locate an existing PIF that you want to modify with the PIF Editor. The current values in this PIF then appear on your screen, and you can make any modifications you wish.

When you choose the Save option, the PIF Editor saves all option values in the PIF file name you opened most recently. If you create a new PIF, the PIF Editor asks you for the name of a file to create.

In a similar fashion, you can select Save As to store the contents of the PIF you're editing in a completely new PIF. Use this choice to make changes to one PIF and store the modified PIF under a new name. As you'll see below, this option is the one you'll use when creating multiple PIFs to control the

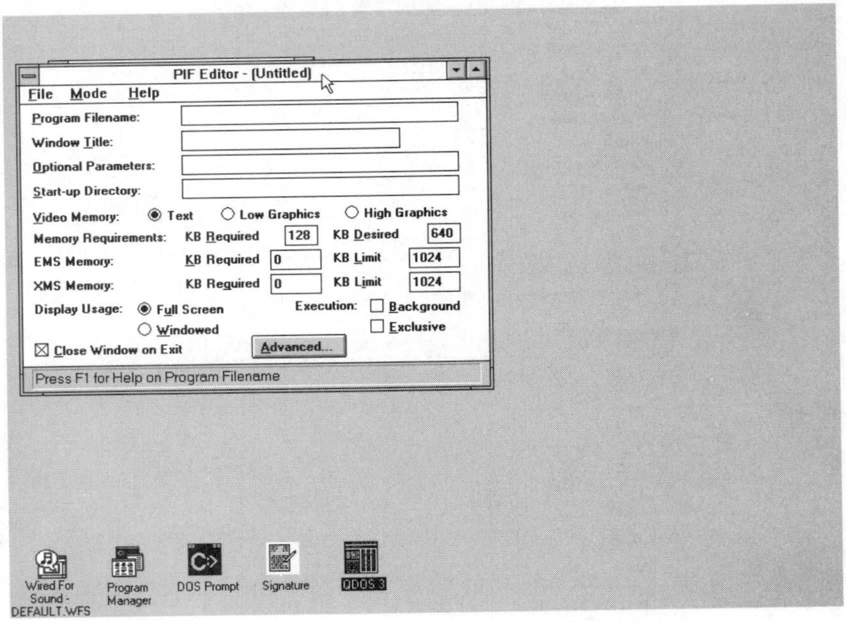

FIGURE 8.6: The PIF Editor in 386 enhanced mode

execution-time environment of a particular program. For instance, you may create and use 123.PIF. Later, you may open the 123.PIF file, make some slight modifications to the Expanded Memory Required option values, then use the Save As option to create a new PIF called 123EMS.PIF.

As always, choosing the Exit option exits you from the PIF Editor and closes its window. If you have any unsaved changes, you're asked whether you want to save or abandon them.

I'll first discuss the options you can control in standard mode, because most of the options found in standard mode are also found in 386 enhanced mode. Additionally, since there are quite a few advanced options available only in 386 enhanced mode, I'll explain those in a separate section.

USING THE DEFAULT PIF SETTINGS

When you use any of the methods discussed earlier for running a DOS application from within Windows, Windows will first look in the Windows directory and then in the PATH for an executable file with the name you gave. Note that Windows finds .EXE file names before it finds .PIF file names. If, for example, you only enter SIG in the Run field on the File menu of the Program Manager, Windows will first look for SIG.EXE. If SIG.EXE is found, even if you've explicitly created a SIG.PIF with customized settings, the values found within it won't be used. Instead, Windows will use the values from the _DEFAULT.PIF file. Table 8.1 lists these values for standard mode. Table 8.2 lists the basic option settings for 386 enhanced mode. Table 8.3 lists the advanced option settings for 386 enhanced mode.

These values are not optimized for anything; they are merely a best guess as to the safest combination of settings for most DOS programs that you might run. You can almost always obtain better system performance by creating your own customized PIF for each DOS application. It is interesting to note the default entry for the program file-name field. Some entry is required, but because _DEFAULT.PIF is used only for its other option settings (when there is no customized PIF to use), the program file-name field is actually ignored.

So if Windows does not find the .EXE file name you entered, either in the WINDOWS directory or in the PATH, it will look for a PIF file with the same

TABLE 8.1: Default PIF Settings in Standard Mode

Option Name	Default Value
Program Filename	_DEFAULT.BAT
Window Title	None
Optional Parameters	None
Start-up Directory	Current
Video Mode	Text
Conventional Memory Required	128K
Extended Memory (XMS) Required	0K
XMS Memory Limit	0K
Directly Modifies	Nothing
No Screen Exchange	No
Prevent Program Switch	No
Close Windows on Exit	Yes
No Save Screen	Off
Reserve Shortcut Keys	All Off

name. For example, if Windows can't find SIG.EXE after you enter SIG, Windows looks for a file named SIG.PIF. If it finds this file, Windows uses all the option values within the file.

♦ USE PATH FOR EASY PIF NAMING

If your application's PIF has the same base name as the .EXE file, you have to consider whether Windows will run the .PIF or the .EXE file. If they are both in the same directory, Windows will use the .EXE file and ignore the .PIF file. If they are in different directories, the file selected depends on your PATH.

Suppose that you want to use the same base name for the executable file and the PIF, and you want Windows to execute the PIF. You

TABLE 8.2: Basic PIF Option Settings in 386 Enhanced Mode

Option Name	Default Value
Program Filename	_DEFAULT.BAT
Window Title	None
Optional Parameters	None
Start-up Directory	Current
Video Mode	High Graphics
Conventional Memory Required	128K
Conventional Memory Desired	640K
Expanded Memory (EMS) Required	0K
XMS Memory Limit	1024K
Extended Memory (XMS) Required	0K
XMS Memory Limit	1024K
Display Usage	Full Screen
Execution	Background
Close Window on Exit	Yes

can create a special directory for PIFs and place its name in the PATH before the directory containing the application's .EXE file.

Since one of the options is the program file-name to run, you don't really have to run SIG.EXE within a PIF named SIG.PIF. You could actually run MONEY.EXE or some other program. Naturally, you should have a good reason to do so, such as wanting a measure of added security for your files.

Actually, you should always use PIFs for running DOS applications. Since you can specify the exact program name you want to run, while at the same time specifying the entire execution environment in which it runs, you have total control by doing it this way. Furthermore, as discussed above, you can even run a DOS batch file as the "program" in a PIF, so you can control the total environment in which an entire series of DOS commands executes.

TABLE 8.3:   Advanced PIF Option Settings in 386 Enhanced Mode

Option Name	Default Value
Background Priority	50
Foreground Priority	100
Detect Idle Time	No
EMS Memory Locked	No
XMS Memory Locked	No
Uses High Memory Area	Yes
Lock Application Memory	No
Monitor Ports	High Graphics
Emulate Text Mode	Yes
Retain Video Memory	No
Allow Fast Paste	No
Allow Close When Active	No
Reserve Shortcut Keys	None
Application Shortcut Key	None

Since the default values for both modes are contained in the _DEFAULT.PIF file, you can use the PIF Editor to make changes to this PIF. In that case, any DOS program that you run later (that does not have its own PIF) will use the new values in _DEFAULT.PIF. You may decide, based on the discussion in the upcoming sections, that you want to apply a series of default values to nearly all DOS programs. To do so, just update the _DEFAULT.PIF file. You can then create customized PIFs for just a handful of specific DOS programs that require more unique settings.

LAUNCHING ONE PROGRAM WITH MULTIPLE .PIF FILES

You now have a better sense of how valuable a .PIF file can be for controlling the DOS environment. Before I take a close look at the individual settings in PIFs, there is one more possibility you should consider. It's obvious that multiple PIFs can run multiple programs, each with its own customized settings. It is not so obvious that multiple PIFs can run the same program.

Why would you bother to set up more than one PIF for an application? How about when different people run the same program on your system, and each person uses a different start-up directory? How about when you need more or less memory for a program, depending on the data that is to be processed? How about when the video demands of the program vary, depending on whether or not you'll be generating graphics?

As you can see, there are many possible situations that could explain why the same program could have different option values. By constructing different PIFs for these different situations, and by creating different Program Manager icons that run the different PIFs, you can more efficiently manage the resources of your system.

In some cases, multiple PIFs simply result in a smoother operating environment. At other (busier system) times, a more efficient PIF may even allow your program to run, where otherwise it might have to wait for sufficient system memory or resources. For example, your DOS 1-2-3 spreadsheet application may at times demand 640K of conventional memory, as well as another 512K of expanded memory. If your 386 enhanced mode system uses 512K of extended memory to emulate the needed expanded memory, this loss of 512K could make it impossible to start another DOS application.

Since this extraordinary demand for system memory may only occur when you work with one particular .WK1 worksheet file, you should create two special PIFs. The first one should specify that no expanded memory is needed, and the second PIF should specify that 512K of expanded memory is needed. Use the first PIF most of the time, and only use the second PIF occasionally. For instance, you might use only the second PIF when you update a very large worksheet that spills over into the expanded memory region that is supported by earlier DOS versions of 1-2-3.

Try to name your PIFs in some meaningful way. If you have a number of DOS programs that you use regularly, WP.PIF probably runs your word processor, and 123.PIF probably runs your spreadsheet. If you customize more than one PIF for different circumstances, it is a good idea to incorporate the customization into the name. For instance, the PIF that runs 123.EXE and requires extra expanded memory could be named 123EMS.EXE.

◆ UNDERSTANDING THE PIF OPTIONS COMMON TO BOTH MODES

Regardless of the mode in which Windows is operating, there are certain fields that do precisely the same job. In either standard or 386 enhanced mode, you can specify a program file-name, a window title, optional parameters, and a start-up directory. Other fields are similar in each mode, while still others are unique in each mode. In this section, I'll discuss the first four common fields. Subsequent sections will address the remaining options in both modes.

In either standard or 386 enhanced mode, there are several options that serve the same purpose. However, the PIF Editor must actually be in the correct mode when you save the PIF option values. For instance, you can specify one or more optional parameters when the PIF Editor is in standard mode. If you later run the program in 386 enhanced mode, Windows will not supply these optional parameters to the program. If you expect to run a program in both modes of Windows, remember to use the Mode pull-down menu when in the PIF Editor. After switching to the other mode, you should enter any changed or additional parameters to be used when you run the program in that other mode. After entering all possible parameters, in one or both PIF Editor modes, you should then save the PIF.

Only some of the common options that are seen in both standard mode and 386 enhanced mode are carried over automatically when you switch modes with the Mode pull-down menu. Of the most common options, Program Filename, Window Title, and Start-up Directory are automatically repeated for you in the alternate mode.

ENTERING THE PROGRAM FILE NAME

When you explicitly use a .PIF file, Windows actually runs the program that is specified in the PIF's Program Filename field. Remember that you can create an icon for a program item in the Program Manager, and the icon can refer to an actual PIF name. Additionally, if you attempt to run a file name without an extension from the Run pull-down menu, Windows will first look for an .EXE file by that name. If it doesn't first find an .EXE file with that base name, it will then look for a PIF bearing that name. If the PIF is used, the actual program that Windows runs will be the one whose name is found in this Program Filename field.

Naturally, if the program file-name is in a directory that appears in the PATH, you needn't enter a full path name in this field. However, it is safest to explicitly enter a full path name here. You will avoid any confusion about which program is to execute if the PATH is modified or if two programs with the same name somehow make their way into your PATH.

ENTERING THE WINDOW TITLE

Windows identifies running applications in two ways. If the application is iconized, a label appears below the icon. If the application runs in a sizable or maximized window, the application name appears in the title bar of the window. In both places, the identifying label is known as the *window title*.

In standard mode, you cannot run a DOS application in a window, but occasionally you will see the application represented by a desktop icon. This occurs when you switch to any other screen view showing the desktop and existing windows or icons. When a DOS application is represented as a desktop icon in standard mode or 386 enhanced mode, the window title appears below the icon.

A second place where icons have labels is in a program group of the Program Manager. Each icon has a name that should not be confused with the window title. An icon's label in a Program Manager window represents a selectable application, but one which is not necessarily running. A desktop icon's label represents an application that is actually running under Windows.

The name used for an icon's label in the Program Manager is actually a property of the icon itself and is stored in the .GRP file for the group. It is created and easily changed via the Program Item Properties dialog box. By contrast, the window title used for minimized desktop icons (not in a Program Manager group) are considered resources and are stored in the actual .EXE file.

If you do not make an entry in the Window Title field, Windows will use the PIF's base file name as a window title. You will see this name as the label underneath any minimized icon, or on the title bar of a screen window, if you run the DOS application in 386 enhanced mode.

ENTERING THE OPTIONAL PARAMETERS

Use the Optional Parameters field for parameter values or switches you want to pass to an application when it starts. For instance, if you run your Word for DOS program and always want to start up with the last document file edited, enter /I in this field.

Suppose that you're writing a very large book, and you want to open the book file each time you start up your word processor. Since writing a book usually takes months to complete, you can take a moment to change the contents of this field. If the book's file name is BOOK.SIG, and you're running the SIG.EXE word processor, then you would enter BOOK.SIG in the Optional Parameters field. At the command prompt, you would see the same result as if you had entered

SIG BOOK.SIG

Then again, suppose that your book contains 20 chapters, and you'd rather be able to simply enter the chapter name each time the PIF is used to initiate the SIG.EXE word processor. When you enter a question mark in the Optional Parameters field, Windows pauses each time it runs the application named in the Program Filename field. You will see a special dialog box that includes a single field (named *Parameters*). You can type in any parameters, including any desired start-up switches, and then press Enter to continue with the execution of the application itself.

For example, you might use this technique if you wanted to specify a different chapter each time you started your word processor. One time, you might enter CHAP12.DTA in the Parameters dialog box; another time, you might enter CHAP16.DTA in the Parameters dialog box. Naturally, if you consider another, less demanding line of work, you might enter RESUME.TXT in the same field. That day, you might just work on your resume, instead of your book.

Some Common PIF Options Must Be Entered Twice

Some of the common options are carried over automatically from standard mode to 386 enhanced mode, and vice versa. The Mode pull-down menu in the PIF Editor enables you to enter or modify the PIF option values for standard or 386 enhanced mode.

Suppose that you create a PIF while your system is in 386 enhanced mode but later use the PIF when your system is in standard mode. The Program Filename, Window Title, and Start-Up Directory entries will be the same. However, most of the other entries, such as Optional Parameters or Memory Required, must be reentered.

To ensure that a PIF accurately represents the desired settings for a program that you may run in both standard and 386 enhanced modes, you must use the Mode pull-down menu. After switching modes in the PIF Editor, reenter values for all important option settings.

◆ PROMPT FOR PARAMETERS EACH TIME

Normally, you start a customized non-Windows application with fixed parameters (in the appropriate .PIF file). However, if you run the non-Windows application in a variety of ways, you may want to change the start-up parameters when you run the program. To do so, merely place a question mark in the .PIF file's Optional Parameters field. Windows will display a dialog box each time you start the program, in which it will prompt for the parameters to use during this invocation.

ENTERING THE START-UP DIRECTORY

Use the Start-up directory field to change the current directory to a specific directory. Otherwise, Windows uses the directory that contains your PIF as the current directory. If your application requires data files, overlay files, configuration files, and so on, you must typically execute the program from the directory that contains these files. By starting the application in the directory that contains all necessary files, you ensure that the application has ready access to all required support files. Enter the complete directory path to this execution-time directory in this field.

USING ENVIRONMENT VARIABLES AS OPTION ENTRIES

In each of these PIF options, you can enter an environment variable's name (surrounded by percent signs). In this way, you can use the SET command from DOS before starting Windows to initialize the variable to any value. You could even put in your AUTOEXEC.BAT file a series of SET commands that some of your PIFs will use.

For example, suppose that you reorganize your disk structure from time to time. For now, you store all your games files in the C:\GAMES directory. So you use the variable %GAMES% in the Start-up Directory field of any PIF file that you create for a game. Later, if you reorganize your disk so that all games are now stored in C:\APS\GAMES, you needn't modify each of 40 PIF files that you created for running your DOS game programs. You only need to change the one SET statement that you probably placed in your AUTOEXEC.BAT file:

SET GAMES=C:\APS\GAMES

Even though some of the other options appear in both standard mode and 386 enhanced mode, there are a number of important distinctions. I'll discuss these other options separately in the appropriate upcoming sections.

◆ UNDERSTANDING STANDARD MODE PIF OPTIONS

Now that the first four field options in Figure 8.5 have been explained, this section will explain the meaning of the rest of the options. Although some of the options perform similar tasks regardless of which mode you run the program in, standard mode is sufficiently different from 386 enhanced mode to warrant separate discussions.

CONTROLLING THE VIDEO MODE

The Video Mode option consists of two buttons. Because of the way video memory is used in the UMBs (upper memory blocks) beyond 640K, this option was designed to enhance performance of EGA and VGA systems. Each radio button indicates a different amount of memory to allocate for saving or restoring the display, as well as copying the display to the Windows Clipboard. The saved video image is what Windows uses when it restores an application's display after switching away from it.

The Text setting for this option reserves the least amount of memory for a video option (approximately 4K). Use this setting whenever possible because it leaves the maximum amount of conventional memory available for the application itself to use. If you know that your application uses only text displays, you should choose the Text radio button.

The Graphics/Multiple Text radio button reserves a larger amount of memory for more demanding display demands. If your application actually displays graphics, it is safest to choose this button. Although it reduces the amount of memory your application has to work with, it increases the likelihood that you will be able to switch to and from this DOS application and your Windows applications with no display difficulties.

The Multiple Text aspect of this second radio button refers to the fact that there are actually up to eight video memory pages (a total of up to 32K) that can be used by certain sophisticated text management programs. These additional pages can be used to instantly switch from page to page in a text document. Even if your application never displays graphics, it may still need to have this button turned on if the application uses more than one video page.

Suppose you choose a text video mode, guaranteeing only a 4K save area for display information. If your application then needs more memory to save a graphics screen, Windows will refuse to switch from the application. To switch from the DOS application to Windows, you will have to exit the application. If this occurs, you should definitely change the PIF setting from Text to Graphics/Multiple Text.

SPECIFYING THE CONVENTIONAL MEMORY REQUIREMENTS

In standard mode, the Memory Requirements specify only a single value. The default value is 128K but can be adjusted up or down according to your application's needs. Very few business applications require less, and most require more. If you have a small utility, game, or TSR program that can execute in less memory, you will want to specify a smaller value. A later section of this chapter deals with the special treatment for running TSRs under Windows.

This option specifies the minimum amount of conventional memory that must be available for Windows even to bother loading the program. If the amount you specify here does not exist, Windows will alert you with an exclamation box that says there is "insufficient memory to run the application." This amount of memory is not necessarily a reasonable amount for your particular application to use; it is only a minimum amount to get your application going.

As an example, your word processor or spreadsheet application may be able to load with only 128K. However, the program itself may be unable to load a serious report or a useful spreadsheet if there is not a lot more memory available. Since you can only run one DOS session in standard mode, Windows actually allocates all available conventional memory to the DOS application when it starts. So it hardly makes any difference what you specify here, although the number must be less than the amount of conventional memory that is available once Windows starts.

CONTROLLING THE AVAILABLE EXTENDED MEMORY

Some DOS applications, such as Lotus 1-2-3 version 3.x, are able to use extended memory directly. They do so according to the Lotus-Intel-Microsoft-AST Extended Memory Specification. Leave both of the XMS memory entries equal to zero, unless you know that your application must have extended memory to run.

The KB Required field indicates how much extended memory must be free before Windows will even attempt to start your application. Unless the program must have extended memory when it starts, leave this value at zero. Entering a nonzero value will slow down Windows drastically when you switch between this application and other applications. This is because a program switch requires significantly more time to write the contents of extended memory out to the application's swap file.

The KB Limit field indicates the maximum amount of extended memory the application can use. You must use this field if your application requires extended memory, but it will consume all available extended memory unless you place limits on its use. Leaving this value at zero will restrict extended memory use totally, while setting this value to −1 will enable the application to obtain as much extended memory as it requests, up to the maximum available amount.

PREVENTING PROBLEMS THAT ARISE FROM SHARING HARDWARE

Some DOS applications require exclusive use of communications ports or the keyboard. That's not surprising because traditionally a DOS application could legitimately expect that it had exclusive use of all system hardware. DOS was not designed to offer multitasking.

Under Windows, however, it is entirely possible that multiple applications may be trying to send or receive information through the same serial ports (COM1 through COM4). Doing this at the same time can compromise the integrity of the data received or transmitted by your DOS application. If you know that your DOS program accesses one or more serial ports, click on the appropriate COM port option in this section.

The same situation may exist if your DOS application requires exclusive access to the keyboard. This technique reads characters directly from the keyboard's buffer. If you know that your DOS application completely monitors and interprets all keystrokes, you can click on the Keyboard option.

By turning on any of these five Directly Modifies options, you have allowed your DOS program to use the keyboard and the communications ports in a nonmultitasking manner. No other program will be allowed to access those hardware devices. To do this, Windows disallows any program switching, which means that you must exit from your DOS application if you want to return to Windows or to another application.

FREEING UP MEMORY WITH THE NO SCREEN EXCHANGE OPTION

Remember that pressing Print Screen or Alt+Print Screen sends a copy of the screen to the Clipboard. If you do not intend to use this mechanism, you can tell Windows not to allocate memory to store the data copy by checking the No Screen Exchange box. Since this memory is a system resource, selecting this check box has a beneficial result throughout your system.

Selecting No Screen Exchange has both positive and negative results. On the good side, checking this box frees up several kilobytes of system memory that become available for all Windows applications. On the bad side, this DOS program will no longer be able to copy data to the Windows Clipboard.

PREVENTING ANY PROGRAM SWITCHING

The Prevent Program Switch option is only used rarely. Since Windows is designed to be a multitasking environment, you will typically want to be able to switch quickly from one application to another. If you check this box, you will be restricted from switching away from this application. To execute any other program, you will have to exit from your DOS application.

You might consider checking this option if your system is extremely tight on memory. Windows allocates a block of memory to restore an application's execution context. It uses the information stored in the application's swap file for this purpose. If you never switch away from your DOS application, and therefore never need to switch back to it again, Windows need never allocate the memory needed to store the application context.

CLOSING AN APPLICATION'S WINDOW ON EXIT

Generally, when you exit from a DOS application, Windows closes the application completely and restores the desktop appearance. Under normal conditions, this produces no problems. Occasionally, however, a DOS application displays some final output on the screen. Since Windows automatically restores the Windows desktop, you won't have enough time to read this output.

Furthermore, if you start a DOS application that immediately terminates, you won't be able to read the termination messages. Often, these will describe what was wrong with the input parameters or switches, or what might be amiss with the hardware environment. These messages are unique to each application and depend on how much error checking is done.

To see any text messages that are displayed during controlled exits from a DOS application, you must uncheck the Close Window on Exit option. Once this option is unchecked, Windows will not immediately restore the desktop screen. Instead, Windows will display all final messages from the DOS session in a window.

You can read any information that is displayed and then choose to return to the Windows desktop. If your application was in text mode, you will receive an advisory message to press any key to return to the Windows desktop. In graphics mode, the message will not appear, but pressing any key will similarly return you to the Windows desktop.

SAVING THE SCREEN IMAGE

For a screen image to be restored properly after a program switch, a copy of the original screen must be saved, or the application that created the screen must be capable of reconstructing the screen on demand. Generally, Windows uses some memory to store a screen image. When you switch away from this application and then return to it, Windows can quickly restore the video information by copying the saved image back to the screen.

If Windows did not save this screen information, it would be unable to correctly restore the DOS application's screen image. If you know that your application itself has the capability of maintaining or easily restoring its own screen status, you can check the No Save Screen option. If you do, Windows will not allocate any memory for a copy of the screen image. This frees up memory for other applications, contributing to higher overall Windows performance.

RESERVING THE USE OF CERTAIN SHORTCUT KEYS

Some DOS applications use their own group of hot keys that are the same as special-purpose Windows shortcut keys. For example, my word processor (Signature) when run under DOS uses Alt+Tab to display the Tab and Margin Selection menu. Under Windows, however, the Alt+Tab key switches programs immediately. The key combination is immediately processed by Windows and is not even passed along to the application.

If your application uses any one of the special-purpose Windows shortcut keys, you should consider placing an X in one or more of the check boxes in the last section of the .PIF file. You must decide whether it is more important for your application to use the shortcut keys than it is for Windows to use them. Personally, I know of other ways to obtain the tab and margin settings in my word processor, so I don't check any of these reserve shortcut key options. However, your DOS application may not have alternate ways to perform certain functions, so you may be forced to check off one or more of these keys.

Each key combination that you choose will be ignored by Windows if you press it when this DOS application executes. The keystroke will be passed on to the DOS application. Remember that if you don't check a particular key combination, the normal Windows action will take place when you press the keystroke:

♦ Alt+Tab and Alt+Esc perform program-switching chores that are discussed in Chapter 7.

♦ Ctrl+Esc displays the Task List, which is also discussed in Chapter 7.

♦ Print Screen copies the full-screen image to the Clipboard.

♦ Alt+Print Screen also copies the full-screen image to the Clipboard.

Alt+Tab Is Faster Than Alt+Esc or Ctrl+Esc

You can switch out of a full-screen DOS application by pressing any one of three Windows shortcut keys or by pressing the shortcut key associated with another DOS application. You would have had to define this special shortcut key in the PIF of another DOS application.

Press the Alt key and keep it depressed while you successively press the Tab key. This merely cycles through the names of all other running tasks. The name of the application will appear either at the top or in the center of your screen. Release the Alt key when the name of your desired application appears. Windows will switch you to it immediately.

Pressing Alt+Esc is slower because it switches completely to successive applications. This can involve the time-consuming loading of an application's code and data, as well as the redisplaying of an entire Windows screen. Pressing Ctrl+Esc merely displays the Windows Task List, from which you will have to select the other desired application. And displaying the Task List usually involves refreshing a complete screen, which typically includes the time needed to redraw other windows and icons.

Some of the standard mode PIF options are related to one other. For instance, if you checked off the No Screen Save option earlier, then the Print Screen and Alt+Print Screen key combinations are disabled. You cannot then copy a full screen to the Clipboard with either key.

◆ UNDERSTANDING THE BASIC PIF OPTIONS IN 386 ENHANCED MODE

There is more going on behind the scenes in 386 enhanced mode than in standard mode. Consequently, there are additional execution-time options for DOS applications that you can control or influence with a PIF. As you saw earlier in Figure 8.6, a PIF for 386 enhanced mode is similar to a PIF for standard mode.

The first four parameters—Program Filename, Window Title, Optional Parameters, and Start-up Directory—are all used in exactly the same manner. Refer to the discussion above under "Understanding the Common PIF Options in Both Modes" for explanations of these parameter entries. As I pointed out then, you can switch the PIF Editor mode to specify the option values to use when the DOS application runs in either standard or 386 enhanced mode.

To change PIF modes, just pull down the Mode menu and choose the desired mode. Where there are duplicated options in the two modes (with the exception of the Optional Parameters field), the PIF Editor carries over any entries you've made in the other mode. For example, if you check off the Alt+Tab reserve shortcut key while in the PIF Editor's standard mode, then switch to 386 enhanced mode, the Alt+Tab keystroke will also appear checked off.

CONTROLLING THE VIDEO MEMORY SETTINGS

In 386 enhanced mode, the PIF Editor offers three radio buttons for controlling the initial appearance of a DOS application. In each case, the option determines how much memory Windows will reserve to initially display the application.

If your application primarily uses text mode, choose the Text radio button. This reserves less than 16K of memory for displaying the application's opening screen. Low-resolution graphics applications using CGA require closer to 32K of video memory. Choose Low Graphics if your application displays graphics but only of the lowest possible resolution.

Some adapters, like CGA or Hercules, have only one possible graphics mode. Consequently, neither of these devices demands more than Low Graphics. However, EGA and VGA adapters have several higher resolution modes that require as much as 128K of video memory. Choose High Graphics if your application will initially display a high-resolution graphics screen.

This setting only affects the initial reservation of memory for the application. Once the application is running, Windows dynamically allocates or deallocates memory according to the application's current video mode. This is fine if the application starts out in a high graphics mode and then switches to a lower graphics, or even text, mode. When you switch to a mode that requires less memory, Windows frees up the extra video memory for use by other applications, improving overall system performance.

However, suppose that you start a DOS application in text mode and then attempt to switch to high-resolution graphics mode. Windows will automatically try to obtain additional system memory for displaying the additional graphics information. If not enough additional memory is available, your application may appear to completely or partially lose its graphic image. To prevent this from happening, choose High Graphics. If you know that your application will sometimes use this resolution, choosing this option will ensure that the application starts up with enough video memory.

SPECIFYING THE CONVENTIONAL MEMORY REQUIREMENTS

In 386 enhanced mode, you can control the allocation of conventional memory to a DOS application with two fields: KB Required and KB Desired (they appear next to Memory Requirements in Figure 8.6). The default value of the first is 128K, and the default value of the second is 640K.

Controlling the Minimum Memory Reserved for a DOS Program

The KB Required value specifies the minimum amount of conventional memory that must be available for Windows even to bother loading the program. If the amount you specify is unavailable, Windows will alert you with an exclamation box that says there is "insufficient memory to run the application." This amount of memory is not necessarily a reasonable amount for your particular application to use; it is only a minimum amount to get your application going.

Your application can actually receive more memory when running than the KB Required value indicates. Change this value from the default 128K only if you know that your application requires more memory to begin to run successfully. If you try to start this DOS application and receive an insufficient memory message, try to close other applications to free up enough memory for this application to run.

By setting the KB Required value, you guarantee that a minimum amount of memory will be reserved for the exclusive use of this DOS application. In a multitasking environment, try to set this option to as small a value as possible that will allow your application to get going. Because the memory you assign here is lost to other possible Windows uses, entering too large a number reduces overall system performance.

Of course, if your application definitely needs more than the minimum to get going, increase this number. If your application is very demanding, as are some computer-aided design programs, you can set KB Required equal to −1. This assigns all available conventional memory to the application, up to the limit that is available or is specified in the next field, KB Desired.

Controlling the Maximum Memory Reserved for a DOS Program

Whereas the KB Required field specifies the lower boundary of reserved memory, the KB Desired field specifies the upper boundary. If your application will work successfully with less than 640K, set the KB Desired value to something less than the default 640K. This will ensure that more memory remains available to Windows for use by other programs.

If sufficient memory is available to satisfy your entry in the KB Desired field, Windows reserves this amount for the exclusive use of your application. This memory is then unavailable to any other applications for as long as your DOS application is active. Naturally, 386 enhanced mode can use hard-disk space for virtual memory if it runs out of physical memory, but this burdens your system's performance. By reducing the demand made by each DOS application for memory, you will put off the time at which virtual memory swapping begins.

However, there is a trade-off here. Suppose that you know that your application can still work just fine with only 384K. For example, some DOS applications like WordPerfect and dBASE IV can use up to 640K to more efficiently manage their files, but they can also perform their chores with less memory. This may mean that the DOS application itself runs more slowly, but Windows in general will perform better.

For example, suppose that you set to 384K the upper limit on conventional memory assigned (remember that conventional memory in 386 enhanced mode is really virtualized). In this case, the difference between 640K and 384K is 256K. This means that this 256K of memory remains available for Windows to use in other ways.

◆ MEMORY REQUIREMENTS AFFECT OVERALL WINDOWS PERFORMANCE

When you specify the two Memory Requirements values in a .PIF file in 386 enhanced mode, your decision will have an impact on overall Windows performance. Reduce the KB Required value to the minimum you discover is necessary for starting your application. Reduce the KB Desired value to a number that allows your application to perform its required chores.

Minimum values for both fields will reduce the memory drain on available Windows memory. While your DOS application runs, these values control how much conventional memory is assigned to your application. Remember that the term *conventional memory* in 386 enhanced mode is somewhat of a misnomer. For any particular application, its "conventional" memory may be part conventional, part extended, and even part virtual (i.e., disk space) memory. No matter what it really is, the application sees a certain amount of addressable space that acts just as conventional memory typically used to when the application ran directly under DOS. The more memory that is exclusively reserved for your application, the less memory remains for Windows to perform multitasking without having to resort to 386 enhanced mode virtual memory.

SPECIFYING THE EXPANDED
MEMORY REQUIREMENTS

In 386 enhanced mode, Windows does not permit any DOS program to use actual expanded memory. Instead, if a program requires expanded memory, Windows will simulate expanded memory by using an equivalent amount of extended memory. The EMM386.EXE program that you include on a DEVICE= line in your CONFIG.SYS file performs this emulation of expanded memory.

You cannot use the EMM386.EXE driver if you run Windows in standard mode. However, applications in standard mode can still use expanded memory if your system has actual expanded memory and a special-purpose expanded memory driver that has been included in your CONFIG.SYS file.

Not many DOS applications actually require expanded memory, although some applications can run more effectively if it is available. One important exception is version 2.*x* of Lotus 1-2-3, which can handle large worksheets by spilling excess cell data into expanded memory. However, to obtain access to such memory in 386 enhanced mode, you must set the EMS Memory fields properly.

As with conventional memory, you can think of the KB Required and KB Limit field values as minimum and maximum levels. Set the KB Required value to the least amount of expanded memory you want to be made available to your application. Your application will not even start if this much expanded memory is not available initially. If this value is greater than zero, you have ensured that your application will have at least this much expanded memory available when it runs. Set KB Limit to the most amount of expanded memory that you want your application ever to use under Windows. Since some DOS applications request as much expanded memory as they find available, the KB Limit value is important. Setting it too high will permit some applications to confiscate more expanded memory than they can efficiently use. Since this expanded memory is really carved out of your system's extended memory, your system's performance will once again suffer if you allow too much memory to be acquired by any one DOS application.

To guarantee that no emulated expanded memory is made available to an application, set both EMS Memory fields equal to zero. Although the default limit is 1024, any number in this field represents the largest amount of expanded memory that will be provided to your application (subject to memory availability). As your application requests expanded memory, Windows will provide up to but not more than the limit amount.

CONTROLLING AVAILABLE EXTENDED MEMORY

Some DOS applications, such as Lotus 1-2-3 version 3.*x*, can use extended memory directly. They do so according to the Lotus-Intel-Microsoft-AST Extended Memory Specification. Leave both XMS Memory fields equal to zero unless you know that your application must have extended memory to run. These settings ensure that no extended memory is allocated to your DOS application; all extended memory then remains available for Windows to support efficient multitasking.

The KB Required field indicates how much extended memory must be free before Windows will even attempt to start your application. Unless the application must have extended memory when it starts, leave this value at zero. A nonzero value may slow down Windows when you switch between this application and other applications. This is because, in tight memory situations, a program switch will require the added time to swap pages out to the 386 enhanced mode swap file.

The KB Limit field indicates the maximum amount of extended memory to allow the application to use. You should use this field if your application requires extended memory but will consume all available extended memory if limits are not imposed. Leaving this value at zero will restrict extended memory use totally. Setting this value to −1 will enable the application to obtain as much extended memory as it requests, up to the maximum available amount.

RUNNING A DOS APPLICATION IN A WINDOW

In 386 enhanced mode, you can run most DOS applications within windows. The Display Usage section of the PIF Editor screen, shown in Figure 8.6, contains two radio buttons: Full Screen and Windowed. Choosing Full Screen directs Windows to use the full screen when it initially runs the application, and choosing Windowed directs Windows to run the application in a window.

Some applications are unable to begin if you choose the Windowed button. In particular, most graphic DOS applications write directly to video memory instead of using the Graphics Device Interface commands required by the Windows API. Windows cannot remap these types of programs into a screen window, and these programs will not run in a window.

Some applications, however, can be started successfully in full-screen mode and then switched to run in a window. If you are unable to start a program in windowed mode, choose Full Screen and later try the Alt+Enter method to switch execution to windowed mode.

When you run a DOS application in a window, you gain several benefits. Most notably, you have access to the Control menu in the upper-left corner of the window. On this menu, you will find standard window manipulation commands, such as Size, Move, Maximize, and Minimize. You will also find an Edit submenu, which allows you to mark text for copying and pasting to and from the Clipboard. This permits a measure of communications between Windows applications and your DOS application.

Furthermore, as I'll discuss later in this chapter, there is a powerful Settings menu for controlling execution-time parameters that dynamically govern how your DOS application executes in 386 enhanced mode. It's convenient to run a DOS application in a window because you can see it along with any other executing applications. As with your Windows applications, you can use the Task List (press Ctrl+Esc) to tile or cascade this DOS window with any other running Windows applications.

One downside to running a DOS application in a window is that Windows allocates several kilobytes of memory to manage the windowed execution. This is a minor but potentially significant drain on memory. If your memory usage is already high, this may be all it takes to prevent another application from running. An even greater burden affects the execution speed of the DOS application itself. Invariably, running a DOS application in a 386 enhanced mode window uses extra processing cycles. DOS applications run noticeably, and sometimes painfully, slower when run in a window.

Consequently, I never run DOS applications in screen windows, except when I want to use the Clipboard for intertask text or information sharing. At these times, I just press Alt+Enter to switch into windowed mode, use the Control menu for Clipboard manipulations, and press Alt+Enter again to switch back to full-screen mode.

♦ PROS AND CONS OF RUNNING DOS PROGRAMS IN WINDOWS

After starting any full-screen DOS program from within Windows, you can press Alt+Enter to switch it into a window. Press Alt+Enter once again to return it to full-screen mode. The good news is that, when a DOS program runs in a 386 enhanced mode window, Windows can support Clipboard-oriented mouse operations (i.e., sharing information). The bad news is that your DOS program can only use a mouse for its own purposes when the program runs in a full screen. Also, more memory is consumed when a DOS program runs in windowed mode, and the processing overhead is greater. Consequently, DOS programs usually run more slowly when run in 386 enhanced mode windows.

RUNNING AN APPLICATION IN THE BACKGROUND OR IN EXCLUSIVE MODE

The two Execution check boxes control how and when your DOS application multitasks. There are two possible execution statuses controlled by these two check boxes. If your application has the screen focus (i.e., it is running in full-screen mode, or you can see its title bar highlighted), it is in the foreground. Otherwise, some other application is in the foreground and your DOS application is one of perhaps many applications that are considered to be in the background.

The Background check box determines whether or not your application will receive any CPU cycles at all when it is in the background. The Exclusive check box determines whether or not any other applications will receive CPU cycles when your DOS application is in the foreground.

Notice that the default setting in Figure 8.6 for both of the execution options is unchecked. With Background unchecked, your DOS application will run only when it is in the foreground. Leave it unchecked if your application only does useful work when you are personally interacting with it. For example, you may use your spreadsheet program for quick and simple analyses. If you're not directly working with a spreadsheet, it won't need any CPU cycles.

By leaving Background unchecked, you will reduce Windows' CPU requirements (explained at the end of Chapter 7). Your DOS application will be suspended whenever you switch away from it to work with another program. When you are not actually using such an application, and the Background box is not checked, all other applications will progress and perform better.

However, if your DOS application can continue to perform useful work while you are working with another application, by all means check the Background box. In this way, your DOS application will continue to get its share of the time-sliced CPU cycles. It can continue to operate (e.g., to manage serial communications or printing) while other applications execute.

Some DOS programs are extremely demanding and cannot tolerate any other simultaneously executing programs. Although I strongly recommend that you find replacements for such programs as soon as possible, you may have no choice but to run them. My proprietary fax software requires that I run with the Exclusive check box marked.

When the Exclusive box is checked, all other applications are suspended when this application is in the foreground. Naturally, you can run other applications in your Windows environment. However, when you decide to run this particular DOS application, your one application will now receive virtually all CPU cycles. Even if you have checked the Background box in other DOS applications, they will not receive any CPU cycles when a PIF directs that a DOS application is to be run exclusively.

You should almost always run an exclusive application in full-screen mode. After all, why should you slow it down by running it in a window, which requires memory and extra CPU time for unimportant Windows and windowing activities. By checking Exclusive, you are effectively saying that no other applications are important until this particular one has completed its work.

Background Communications and Faxing

Fax boards often arrive with their own software. Sometimes, the vendor directs you to load its software as a TSR before Windows starts up. This usually consumes a large amount of memory—sometimes as much as 100K. If the lost memory does not affect your other applications, there is no problem. If it does, you can use an upper-memory-block manager to load all or part of the TSR software in the memory blocks between 640K and 1MB. Alternatively, you can load small drivers and TSRs in the upper memory blocks (UMBs), freeing up conventional memory for the faxing software.

Even if the memory consumption does not present an insurmountable problem, you may discover a more serious difficulty. When a background fax is received, the software may attempt to pop up a window on your screen. Unfortunately, if Windows is running, this DOS TSR pop-up may not work properly. In fact, it may simply destroy your current screen image and freeze your system until the fax reception is complete.

You can try another solution if your system can run 386 enhanced mode and your hardware is fast enough. Carefully create a .PIF file for the TSR and run it as a background application. Once started, iconize it to make background reception possible. Foreground sending is then readily available by simply clicking on the TSR's icon.

CLOSING AN APPLICATION'S WINDOW ON EXIT

Generally, when you exit from a DOS application, Windows closes the application completely and restores the desktop appearance. Under normal conditions, this produces no problems. Occasionally, however, a DOS application displays some final output on the screen. Since Windows automatically restores the Windows desktop, you won't have enough time to read this output.

Furthermore, if you start a DOS application that immediately terminates, you won't be able to read the abnormal termination messages. Often, these will describe what was wrong with the input parameters or switches, or what might be amiss with the hardware environment. These messages are unique to each application and depend on how much error checking is done.

To see any text messages that are displayed during controlled exits from a DOS application, you must uncheck the Close Window on Exit option. Once it is unchecked, Windows will not immediately close the DOS session that the application completes.

If you direct Windows not to close a window on exit, you will be able to read any final output that is displayed. Regardless of whether you were running the application in full-screen or windowed mode, Windows will display the final state of your application in a screen window labeled *Inactive*, followed by the window title you specified in the PIF. Afterward, you can choose to return to the Windows desktop by selecting Close on the inactive window's Control menu.

◆ USING AN INACTIVE WINDOW TO VIEW CLOSING MESSAGES

Normally, Windows automatically closes a running non-Windows application when you exit from it. However, if such an application displays any closing messages, you cannot read them because they only appear momentarily before Windows erases them and redisplays its desktop. To read such messages, you should uncheck the Close Window on Exit option in the PIF for the application. Then, when you exit such an application, Windows switches the application into a window with the label *Inactive.* You can read the final displayed message text, then close the window to remove it from the screen.

◆ UNDERSTANDING THE ADVANCED PIF OPTIONS IN 386 ENHANCED MODE

Figure 8.7 shows the dialog box that appears when you choose Advanced at the bottom of the basic PIF Editor window. These options represent a wide range of additional controls that you can exercise over how your DOS applications execute. You can accept the default values, or you can enter your own customized values for controlling time slicing, memory allocation, display management, and task switching.

CONTROLLING THE MULTITASKING OPTIONS

The Multitasking Options section has two priority settings and a check box for detecting idle processing time. These three options provide a high degree of control over when and for how long your DOS application will execute.

Setting Background and Foreground Priority

You learned in Chapter 7 how an application's priority setting (it can range from 0 to 10,000) determines how many of a processor's CPU cycles the

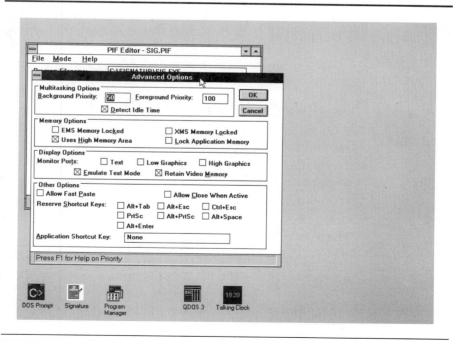

FIGURE 8.7: The Advanced Options dialog box for the PIF Editor in 386 enhanced mode

application receives. Refer there for a precise explanation of how priority affects the time-slicing algorithm.

The higher the background priority, the more CPU cycles an application receives, but only when the application is running in the background. According to the Windows time-slicing algorithm, the Background Priority value is used to compute the application's CPU allocation when it is running in the background. Therefore, this value only has meaning to this application if Background has been checked on the PIF Editor's basic options screen (see the preceding section).

The higher the foreground priority, the more CPU cycles an application receives, but only when the application is running in the foreground. Your application's Foreground Priority value is used to compute the application's CPU cycles when it is running in the foreground. If Exclusive was checked on the basic options screen, this Foreground priority value is not needed.

Normally, all application's priority values are set initially to the defaults of 100 for foreground and 50 for background. This gives slightly more time to the application you are focusing on, enabling it to proceed more quickly. Generally, I leave most PIF settings at these defaults, except for my communications programs. I typically double these values for programs that must handle serial-port data movements, both in the background and foreground.

Detecting Idle Time in an Application

The Windows time-slicing algorithm by itself assigns a fixed number of CPU cycles to your DOS application. Sometimes, however, your DOS application will waste these cycles. This will be particularly true if your application relies heavily on keystrokes or mouse inputs. If Windows can correctly determine when your DOS application is wasting time by idly waiting for input, it can reassign the time to other applications. This improves the overall performance of your system.

The Detect Idle Time option is usually checked. When it is checked, Windows attempts to discover when an application is wasting time within its time slice. This sometimes happens when an application is waiting for a keystroke or some other user entry. If your application is not using its CPU time and

Windows notices this, the remainder of the time slice can go back into the time-slice pie. All other applications benefit from this.

However, there are situations in which you would not want to check the Detect Idle Time box. Unfortunately, you need to know something about how the application is programmed to be absolutely sure of these cases. I'm not going to get overly technical about intermittent event timings or 2F interrupts—just note whether your program seems to run unusually slowly. If Windows thinks that your program is doing nothing but waiting for input, it could be reassigning CPU cycles incorrectly. The result is that your program may become starved for CPU cycles and appear to run very slowly. If you notice this occurring, come back to this PIF and uncheck the Detect Idle Time box.

CONTROLLING HOW DOS APPLICATIONS USE MEMORY

Windows is a consummate juggler of available memory. In 386 enhanced mode, Windows manages all available conventional memory and extended memory. When necessary or requested, Windows temporarily uses some of the extended memory to simulate expanded memory and provide it to DOS applications. When memory is used up, Windows smoothly uses disk space to simulate memory, providing additional memory for multitasking. However, this virtualization procedure involves swapping of memory images and can produce a heavy operating burden.

If you only run programs in available memory, each program runs faster in a multitasking environment, because there is no extra overhead in swapping applications in and out of memory. However, the number of applications that can multitask is limited. So the trade-off is between having fewer applications in physical memory but running faster and having more applications in a swapping environment but running slowly.

Preventing Swapping by Locking Memory

On an individual basis, you can attempt to influence your DOS applications by checking one or more of the options in the Memory Options section of the Advanced Options dialog box. Locking one type of memory means that Windows will not swap that memory portion of your application to disk. Consequently, switching to and from this application will be faster. The memory you lock remains immediately available to the application.

Any application memory that is locked, however, is not available to Windows for any other purpose. Locking memory may even make it impossible for Windows to start new applications. Locked memory reduces the overall pool of memory that Windows uses to juggle. Overall memory is needed by Windows to start new applications or to provide needed memory to running applications.

If you reserve some of your system's memory for a particular application, all remaining applications will be forced to swap more quickly. The performance of these other applications will suffer unless your system has more than enough memory to go around. In this case, locking memory is no issue at all because all running applications have the memory they need, and no swapping is necessary.

If memory is a concern on your system, you can improve the performance of an individual DOS application (at the expense of overall system performance) by checking the Lock Application Memory option. This option affects only the virtualized conventional memory that the application uses. If your application directly attempts to access expanded memory or extended memory, you can similarly reserve or lock these types of memory as well. To do this, check the EMS Memory Locked or XMS Memory Locked box.

◆ PERFORMANCE ENHANCEMENT FOR INDIVIDUAL DOS APPLICATIONS

In 386 enhanced mode, the Advanced portion of the .PIF file contains a Memory Options section. A check box within this part is called Lock Application Memory. Typically, you should not check this option because it will slow down your overall Windows performance.

This option is provided to enable you to force Windows to keep a running application in memory. If the option is selected, Windows will not swap it to disk to more efficiently use its memory space. This means that it is able to continue processing more quickly when it is its turn again, since there is no disk I/O (input/output) overhead to bring it back into memory. However, while doing this speeds up an individual DOS

Speeding Up 1-2-3 for DOS

If you have a large worksheet and recalculation consumes an unusual amount of time, you may have the following problem. Version 2.x of 1-2-3 uses expanded memory for very large worksheets. However, in 386 enhanced mode, Windows emulates expanded memory with extended memory. Part of the worksheet may reside in conventional memory and part may reside in what 1-2-3 thinks is expanded memory.

In reality, this expanded memory may really be swapped to disk. To minimize the extraordinary overhead of swapping, turn on the Lock Application Memory option in the Advanced section of your 1-2-3 PIF. This forces the emulated expanded memory to remain in its extended memory locations rather than being swapped to disk.

Be aware that this technique will speed up 1-2-3 but will slow down other non-Windows applications. You also have the option of buying 1-2-3 for Windows.

application, overall system performance suffers, because Windows has less overall memory remaining for other applications to use.

All three of these boxes are generally unchecked, because the system cost of locking memory is very high. Check one of these boxes only if your application uses one or more types of memory and cannot perform its chores successfully under normal swapping conditions.

Using the High Memory Area for 64K More Conventional Memory

In Chapter 4, you learned about memory addressability. The High Memory Area, or HMA, is the first 64K of extended memory. By using a special extra address line, certain DOS programs can actually make use of this usually inaccessible portion of extended memory (between 1024K and 1088K). In fact, if no program has consumed the HMA before Windows starts, Windows itself will allocate the addressable equivalent of a private HMA to each DOS application that requests it.

Generally, you should leave the Uses High Memory Area option checked, which is the default setting. In this case, Windows will make a private 64K HMA available if your application asks for it; this can improve the efficiency of your DOS application. If your application does not use the HMA at all, Windows does not allocate any memory, so there is no burden.

Some TSRs, such as network TSRs, are executed before Windows and use the HMA first. In this case, the HMA will be unavailable to all DOS applications running under Windows. To reduce the overhead required by the HMA code in Windows, you should then clear this check box for all PIFs.

USING DISPLAY OPTIONS TO MANAGE THE SCREEN

There are three display options that affect the appearance of your application on the screen. To an extent, these options also affect how Windows uses memory and consumes CPU resources when displaying your program's output on the screen.

Monitoring Video Operations

The Monitor Ports options are actually three separate check boxes. Each identifies a video mode that your application may be using at one time or another. Since some DOS applications change the video mode used by your monitor's video adapter, Windows may not always know what the current mode is. In particular, some of the more recent video adapters perform automatic mode switching. This can happen if your DOS application writes directly to a hardware port address to change to a desired video mode.

Windows reads the mode setting in the BIOS, which may occasionally be different from the actual video mode currently used by the display adapter. This can cause a problem if you put the DOS application in the background. When you attempt to switch back to the application, Windows may be unable to restore the screen correctly.

To avoid this problem, Windows offers these three monitoring options. Usually, you won't need to choose any of them, unless you find that Windows has difficulties restoring the display after a switch. If this is the case, choose only the option that corresponds to the video mode in which Windows has a problem restoring the screen.

You may have to experiment somewhat to discover the correct check box. As before, the Text option corresponds to an application running in text mode, the Low Graphics option corresponds to an application running in low-resolution CGA mode, and the High Graphics option corresponds to an application running in EGA or VGA mode.

◆ TUNE PERFORMANCE WITH THE MONITOR PORTS OPTIONS

The Monitor Ports options are provided as a tuning feature. If Windows has no trouble restoring your application's display or you experience no video display problems, you don't need to set any of them. Windows' performance will be faster.

Most problems involve the High Graphics option. You can try this one first if you are having a problem. Just realize that checking this last option minimizes the likelihood of your having a problem but uses resources to monitor the video hardware. Since this monitoring is time consuming, your DOS application will always slow down if you check any of the Monitor Ports options. So don't bother checking any of them unless you first encounter problems with the display.

Speeding Up Your Application by Emulating Text Mode

The Emulate Text Mode option is another control the PIF Editor provides for enhancing your application's video display. In general, you should leave this option checked because it will more often speed up your application than hurt it in any way. Uncheck the option only if your application's text display becomes muddled, the cursor becomes lost, or you lose control of the mouse pointer.

This option can help speed up your application if the application uses graphics mode to display text characters. If the application uses the normal

ROM BIOS calls to display text, and you have this option checked, Windows can use faster text mode routines to send the text to the screen.

For example, by emulating text mode, scrolling a single line on the screen does not have to involve a complete graphic redraw. It can be more quickly accomplished by a driver that understands how to send out predefined character blocks. Drawing text is almost always faster (because it involves a more limited number of character images) than drawing large numbers of pixels in an infinite number of possible configurations.

Ensuring Display Integrity by Retaining Video Memory

Earlier in this chapter, in the section on basic options for 386 enhanced mode, you learned about three Video Memory buttons: Text, Low Graphics, and High Graphics. These radio buttons control the initial amount of video memory allocated to your application. You learned that you should select the button that corresponds to the video mode your application uses. However, these buttons ensure only that your application starts up with enough video memory.

Once your application gets going, Windows can dynamically allocate and deallocate video memory. It does this according to the video demands of your application. If your application switches from high graphics mode to a lower graphics mode or a text mode, Windows frees up the unneeded video memory for use by other applications. This is never a problem by itself and is an intelligent redistribution of memory.

However, suppose that your system is low on memory. Suppose further that your application changes video modes from High Graphics to Text and then attempts to change back to High Graphics. In the interim, Windows may have redistributed the extra video memory to another application and may now be unable to use it again. For instance, some other application may have locked that memory.

In these types of low memory situations, you may want to check the Retain Video Memory option. If the application obtains a certain amount of video memory in the first place, Windows will never redistribute that memory to any other application. The memory will always be retained for use by your application, making it easy to switch back immediately to the application and restore its display image.

Consequently, the basic Video Memory options discussed above ensure that your application will be able to display itself if there is enough memory to start it. The advanced Retain Video Memory option ensures that any video memory that is obtained will never be released to other applications; you can always safely switch away and then back to your program.

In both cases, however, the video memory consumed is not available to any other applications. This has a detrimental impact on overall system performance that is similar to locking the application's conventional, expanded, or extended memory.

UNDERSTANDING THE REMAINING ADVANCED OPTIONS

There are a few remaining options in 386 enhanced mode (grouped at the bottom of the Advanced Options dialog box in the Other Options section). They enable you to further customize the way Windows runs your DOS program.

Sending Data to the Clipboard

When you run a DOS application in a 386 enhanced mode window, you can open the Control menu and use the Edit command to copy data to the Clipboard or paste data into your application from the Clipboard. When pasting data into a DOS application from the Clipboard, Windows can only paste text, not graphics. Windows can use two different methods of transferring text. In general, Windows tries to use the fast method because it usually works, and the data transfer takes the least amount of time.

However, some older applications cannot accept text faster than a certain speed. This generally occurs when the application uses a technique for reading the text that is based on the assumption that it will always be coming from the relatively slow keyboard.

Even if your application cannot accept the text at the fastest possible transfer rate, Windows will often but not always discover this and switch automatically to the slower speed. You may find that your application displays garbled text characters after pasting information from the Clipboard. Or you may discover that your application does not seem to accept any characters from the Edit Paste command.

In those cases, return to the PIF and uncheck the Allow Fast Paste option. Windows will then always use the slower method of transferring text characters from the Clipboard to your application. Refer to Chapter 5 for information on how to transfer data to and from the Clipboard and your DOS applications.

Closing DOS Applications

When you want to close a Windows application, you can open the Control menu and select Close, or you can do it through the Task List. In either case, Windows sends the application the appropriate DDE messages and the application shuts down. Sometimes, this shutdown process involves a polite reminder that you have not saved your recent work. Sometimes, the shutdown process automatically saves your work and even saves information about what you were doing. The next time the Windows application starts up, it can pick up where you left off.

As you learned in Chapter 5, a DOS application can't accept DDE messages. Consequently, it can't initiate any shutdown sequences just because you tried to close its window. In fact, the Close option on a windowed DOS application's Control menu is normally grayed. You can't even select it.

And that's the way it usually should be. Closing a DOS application's session, windowed or not, does not mean that Windows will properly close any open files. In fact, Windows will never do this. It assumes that your DOS application is correctly managing its own files.

You should adhere to each DOS application's unique shutdown procedure, which typically involves its own reminder about saving files or work in progress. Make sure that the Allow Close When Active option is not checked. Windows will not shut itself down or allow you to use any Windows method to close a DOS application's window. You will have to switch back to the DOS application and exit from it using its own exit procedure.

However, some DOS applications don't open files and don't have to go through any special shutdown procedures. You may be using a disk management application, like QDOS 3, in lieu of the Windows File Manager program. It would be easier to use the Windows termination commands to end such a program. In fact, if you just want to exit from the Program Manager, and know that no DOS application has any important open files, it would be nice not to have to go back to each active DOS program just to say good-bye.

You can check the Allow Close When Active option to do this. If this option is checked, Windows will enable you to close the DOS session without returning to it and explicitly shutting it down. But do this only if you are 100 percent sure that the application will never have any files open. If the application does have open files, you can be sure that there will come a time when you forget about them and leave Windows. Don't make that assumption.

Even if you check this box and later attempt to close the application, Windows will still display a confirmation box. Windows gives you one last chance to abort the requested closure by displaying the name of the DOS application you are requesting be closed and this message:

Application still active;

Choose OK to end it.

Press Enter or click on OK to tell Windows to actually end the running DOS session. Choose Cancel to tell Windows to ignore the request.

Reserving the Use of Certain Shortcut Keys

Some DOS applications use their own group of hot keys that are the same as special-purpose Windows shortcut keys. For example, my word processor (Signature), when run under DOS, uses Alt+Tab to display the Tab and Margin Selection menu. Under Windows, however, Alt+Tab switches programs immediately. The key combination is immediately processed by Windows and is not even passed along to the application.

If your application uses any one of the special-purpose Windows shortcut keys, you should consider placing an X in one or more of the check boxes in the last section of the .PIF file. You must decide whether it is more important for your application to use the shortcut keys than it is for Windows to use them. Personally, I know of other ways to obtain the tab and margin settings in my word processor, so I don't check any of these reserve shortcut key options. However, your DOS application may not have alternate ways to perform certain functions, so you may be forced to choose one or more of these keys.

Each key combination that you choose will be ignored by Windows if you press it when this DOS application executes. The keystroke will be passed on to the DOS application. Remember that if you don't check a particular key combination, a usual Windows action will take place when you press the keystroke:

- ◆ Alt+Tab and Alt+Esc perform program-switching chores that are discussed in Chapter 7.
- ◆ Ctrl+Esc displays the Task List, which is also discussed in Chapter 7.
- ◆ Print Screen copies the full-screen image to the Clipboard.
- ◆ Alt+Print Screen also copies the full-screen image to the Clipboard.
- ◆ Alt+spacebar activates a window's Control menu. If the application is running full screen, this key also switches the session into windowed mode.
- ◆ Alt+Enter toggles a DOS session between windowed mode and full-screen mode. If the DOS program cannot be run in a window, you will receive a message box to this effect.

Conversely, you should always choose any key combination that you want to reserve for your DOS application's use. I suggest you do this for any key that you are used to pressing during a DOS session. For example, if you are used to obtaining printed copies of your screen while a particular DOS program runs, check the PrtSc box. This enables the DOS session to send a screen copy to the printer. If you still want to communicate with the Clipboard, you can always use the alternate key combination Alt+Print Screen to send a screen copy to the Clipboard.

Defining an Application Hot Key

An application shortcut key, or *hot key*, is any key combination involving the Ctrl or Alt keys that instantly switches you to an application. You can define

Ctrl+ another key, Alt+ another key, or Alt+Ctrl+ another key. The other key in each case may not be Escape, Enter, Tab, spacebar, Print Screen, or Backspace. No matter what other application is running at the time you press such a key combination, Windows immediately switches the associated application to the foreground.

The application to which you've assigned a shortcut key must already be loaded for Windows to successfully switch to it when you press the shortcut key. However, you should be cautious in assigning shortcut keys because they are interpreted first for switching purposes. These keystrokes are never passed along for any other purpose to Windows itself, any Windows application, or any other DOS application.

◆ SPEED UP YOUR WORK WITH DOS APPLICATIONS

Yes, you can multitask many DOS applications in their own windows. But task switching among the DOS applications by using an application shortcut key is dramatically faster when the DOS applications are running full screen. In addition, overall Windows processing can be measurably faster as well. Keystrokes are received and treated with much less delay when your DOS application is running full screen. Check it out yourself by running several programs, then trying out some standard operations in your DOS application—first in full-screen mode and then in windowed mode.

You learned in Chapter 7 that you can specify an application shortcut key for any Windows or non-Windows application in the Program Item Properties box of the Program Manager. Now you see that for DOS applications you can also specify an application shortcut key in this last advanced option in 386 enhanced mode. Realize, however, that this DOS application shortcut key will not switch to the application unless it has already been started by one of the techniques discussed in the preceding chapter.

◆ HOTKEY FOR NON-WINDOWS (DOS) PROGRAMS

In 386 enhanced mode, you can define an application shortcut key
(often called a *hot key*). Once it is defined, you can quickly activate your
favorite DOS application at any time by pressing this hot key. To set up
this capability, create or modify the application's PIF with the PIF Editor
located in the Main group of the Program Manager. Click on Advanced
and choose Application Shortcut Key. Press the desired key combination, then select OK. Pull down the File menu and save the PIF.

◆ RUNNING MEMORY-RESIDENT DOS APPLICATIONS (TSR'S)

If you are used to running memory-resident applications in a DOS environment, you probably have a number of questions about running them under
Windows. This section explains some of the considerations. I'll discuss some
of the alternatives for deciding when to run a DOS TSR (terminate-and-stay-
resident program). I'll also give some examples of TSR use with Windows and
explain some of the trade-offs.

DECIDING WHEN TO RUN A TSR

Under DOS, you are probably used to loading up one or more TSRs before
running your main application. When you want to access the special features
of your TSR, you just press the appropriate hot key. If you followed the same
approach before loading Windows, your system might look something like
Figure 8.8.

Unfortunately, each TSR that you load before you load Windows reduces the
amount of conventional memory available to each DOS session that later
runs under Windows. In addition, attempting to access a TSR through its hot

key from within Windows can be frustrating. Sometimes, the key press is never passed through to the DOS TSR at all. Other times, the key press makes it through, but the TSR suspends Windows, with fairly severe consequences.

In 386 enhanced mode, you can readily run separate DOS sessions for each TSR. In the first place, this means that the conventional memory formerly consumed by the sum of the TSRs (before Windows started) is once again available to Windows. Each DOS session under Windows then gains this equivalent amount of conventional memory. Chapter 4 explains this trade-off between available conventional memory when Windows starts and the size of DOS sessions within Windows. I'll discuss shortly the trade-offs between

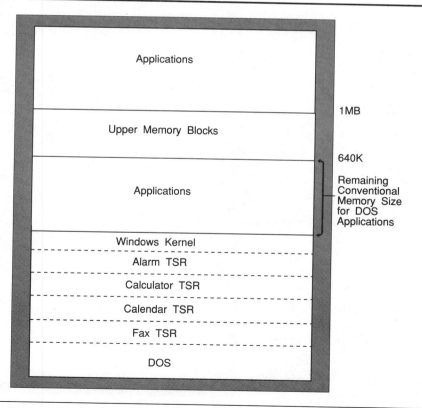

FIGURE 8.8: Loading TSRs before starting Windows

running multiple TSRs in separate DOS sessions under Windows and running a group of TSRs in a single DOS session.

In the second place, the ability to run separate DOS sessions means that you can run each DOS TSR in its own virtual DOS machine. Figure 8.9 depicts this scenario. By using the Application Shortcut Key field in the Advanced section of the PIF, you can set up a hot key (ideally the same one as the application specifies for use under DOS) to activate each unique application.

This has the major advantage that each TSR is individually accessible by hot key, just as before when it ran under DOS directly. In addition, since each session

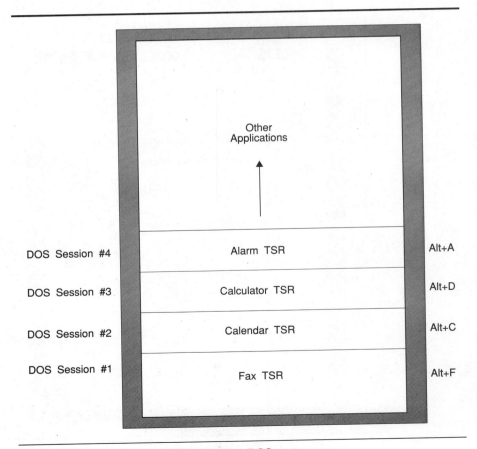

FIGURE 8.9: Running each TSR in its own DOS session

Reducing Excess TSR Overhead

Some of us load TSRs for such things as function key redefinition. But TSRs don't have to be loaded before starting Windows. Suppose that you only use a particular TSR to open a Send menu for your fax board. Instead of loading SEND.COM before running Windows, you can load it in a batch file that actually runs the non-Windows fax software. For example, the batch file might include

SEND

CD \FAXCOMM

FAX

The memory overhead for the pop-up software is consumed only when you run this particular DOS application. Other non-Windows applications are not burdened by the loss of conventional memory required by SEND.

Remember that under DOS 5, you can load programs like SEND.COM in upper memory blocks with the LOADHIGH command.

is separated from each other one, there is less likelihood than before of any one TSR affecting any other TSR. Doing it this way ensures that your DOS and Windows system is actually safer than before.

USING BATCH FILES TO SET UP A TSR SESSION

Creating separate DOS sessions for each TSR means that you have to create separate PIFs for each TSR. To minimize either processing time or memory consumption, you will have to set all the various options discussed above for the 386 enhanced mode PIF carefully. Doing that correctly may not be easy. Personally, I prefer another approach.

As Figure 8.10 depicts, you can also collect all your TSRs in one DOS session under Windows. You can first write a batch file that properly starts all the desired TSRs. Then you can create a PIF that has the batch file name as the program file-name to execute when you attempt to run the PIF.

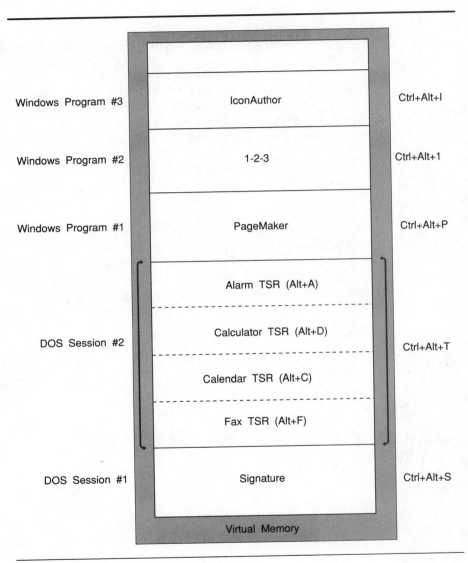

FIGURE 8.10: Running TSRs in one session

Initializing Windows with Your Favorite DOS Applications

You can bring up Windows with any of your non-Windows applications ready to go. For example, start 1-2-3 version 2.3, or your DOS modem program, iconized and ready to go, by including a Load= line in your WIN.INI file. Modify WIN.INI (found in your WINDOWS directory) to load applications into memory at start-up by naming the file to run. Preferably, create a customized .PIF file for each application.

For example, on one of my systems, I have the following entry in the [windows] section of my WIN.INI file:

LOAD=SIG.PIF 123R23.PIF COMMAND.PIF

This line ensures that Windows starts up with my word processor, spreadsheet, and the DOS command prompt, all available at the press of a customized hot key. You can edit the Load= line in your WIN.INI file with the Windows Notepad, the Sysedit program, or your own ASCII-based word processor.

In the example shown in Figure 8.10, pressing Ctrl+Alt+T switches you to DOS session #2. Once you are there, each of the four individual TSR hot keys are active. For instance, pressing Alt+A activates the alarm TSR.

In fact, you can use the same technique when you want to install one or more TSRs in addition to a single DOS application. For example, when I bring up my Signature word processor, I actually bring it up with a SIG.PIF file. Inside that PIF, I have specified all the PIF options to work most efficiently with my Windows environment. But SIG.PIF itself specifies a SIGNATUR.BAT file as the program file-name to execute. This file consists of the following lines:

```
c:
cd \signatur\windows
f11f12 /1=call personal.spl /2=load personal.spl
sig
```

This batch file changes the current drive and directory, loads the F11F12.EXE program (a TSR), and loads the SIG.EXE program. Because of the application shortcut key, I can switch at any time to my word processor by pressing

Ctrl+Alt+S. Once in the word processor, I can press F11 or F12, which are the two hot keys recognized and processed by the F11F12.EXE program. If I want access to additional TSR programs, I can include them on lines in the batch file before the last line, which runs the SIG.EXE program.

Suppose that you like the idea of a single DOS session that includes all your TSRs. Wouldn't it be nice if you could ask Windows to automatically load the entire session for you when Windows first starts up. Of course, there is a way to do this. Assume that you've created a START.BAT file that contains all the initiation commands for your group of TSR programs. You can use the Load= command in the WIN.INI file to run START.BAT automatically each time you load Windows.

After preparing a START.PIF file that runs this START.BAT batch file, you can modify the Load= line in the WIN.INI file to read

Load=START.PIF

Assuming that START.PIF is located in the WINDOWS directory or in the PATH statement, Windows will load up and iconize this special TSR session. At any time after Windows starts up, you can press the application shortcut key defined in START.PIF to switch to this special TSR DOS session.

◆ LOAD A TSR SESSION AUTOMATICALLY UNDER WINDOWS

If you've prepared a PIF that runs a batch file that initiates a series of TSR programs, you can automatically load the entire session when Windows starts: Just modify the Load= line in your WIN.INI file to read the following: Load=<PIF filename>. Replace <PIF filename> with the name of your PIF (e.g., Load=SIG.PIF). If you have other file names on the Load= line, just add your PIF name to the list. Make sure that you've defined an application shortcut key in the PIF so that you can quickly switch to the DOS session that contains all your TSRs. Also make sure that the Program Filename field in the PIF specifies the name of the batch file that contains the TSR program names.

◆ SPECIAL CONSIDERATIONS FOR RUNNING DOS APPLICATIONS

In this section, you will learn some important considerations for running DOS applications under Windows. Some of these issues apply regardless of whether you run them in standard mode or 386 enhanced mode. Other issues will be relevant only for the more advanced 386 enhanced mode environment.

USING A MOUSE

One of the most common problems you are likely to encounter when running DOS applications has to do with the mouse. Naturally, Windows uses a mouse for managing the mouse pointer on the desktop. However, some DOS applications also use a mouse for certain activities when they run. With Windows 3.1, you can finally have it both ways. Just be sure to use the latest mouse drivers that come with 3.1.

If you want Windows to manage the mouse, just use the desktop normally. If there are windows visible, Windows handles the mouse. It does this by using a built-in mouse driver, called MOUSE.DRV, that you can find in the SYSTEM directory. On the other hand, if you want your DOS application to be able to use the mouse, you must be sure to have loaded a mouse driver first.

Normally, if you run a DOS application that uses a mouse, you must load a DOS mouse driver to manage the interrupts from the device. This driver is typically MOUSE.COM, which can be loaded from the DOS prompt, or MOUSE.SYS, which can be loaded from the CONFIG.SYS file. See Chapter 15 for further explanations about conserving memory by loading the DOS mouse driver in upper memory blocks.

Be sure to use the latest version of whichever mouse driver you use, and follow any special instructions for running that mouse with Windows. Also, be sure to use the mouse driver that came with your particular mouse, rather than a generic mouse driver that came with your DOS application software.

If you run MOUSE.COM under DOS, you can load it as a TSR during AUTOEXEC.BAT file processing. If you must run your particular mouse driver before starting Windows, this is a good place to load it.

However, by loading it before starting Windows, you give up the memory (10–15K) required by the driver for the entire Windows session. A better alternative is to create a separate batch file, as discussed in the preceding section, for each DOS application that uses a mouse. In the batch file, precede the executable name of the DOS application with a line that loads the MOUSE.COM program. Then, run the batch file from a PIF.

When the DOS application runs, it will have access to the mouse driver, just as if it you had loaded the mouse driver before starting Windows. However, when the DOS application ends, the memory consumed by both the application and the mouse driver will be returned to Windows.

AVOIDING CERTAIN COMMANDS AND PROGRAMS

In Chapter 7, I discussed some important and useful techniques for backing up the Windows .GRP and .INI files. In the course of that discussion, I emphasized the dangers involved with using a backup program that was originally designed for use under DOS.

There are many programs that should never be run under Windows, even though it would appear to be easy to do so in 386 enhanced mode. As previously discussed, you should not run DOS backup programs that use Direct Memory Access (DMA). You should also avoid running all programs or commands that make changes to a hard disk's file allocation table (FAT). Since the FAT defines how to find files on your disk, you should never allow one program to modify it while other programs (including Windows itself) are still using it. If you must run such a program or command, exit from Windows and run it from a standard command prompt.

All disk optimization programs fall into this category. I use the VOPT.EXE program to defragment my hard disk, but I always exit from Windows before using it! If I tried to run this program from a DOS session within Windows, Windows would probably crash before it finished and I would probably cry a lot. A common DOS command is CHKDSK, which should never be run from

Loading TSRs: Memory vs. Convenience

If you use a TSR or a driver (e.g., a mouse driver) for several applications, you need to load it once only—before you load Windows. It will then be available to all applications under Windows, but it will consume space that Windows might profitably be able to use in some other manner. That may be just fine with you. For example, I load a mouse driver in upper reserved memory before running Windows. It's available to all my full-screen DOS applications while in Windows.

On the other hand, you may want to use upper reserved memory blocks for other purposes. And you may not want to reduce conventional memory by the size of the TSR or driver. Consequently, you can choose to run each DOS application that requires a mouse via a command prompt or a via a batch file that first loads the mouse driver.

In general, you should run any desired TSR program first, followed by the appropriate DOS application. In this way, only one DOS session is burdened by the size requirements of the TSR software.

within Windows with the /F switch because it makes corrective changes to the disk's FAT.

UNDERSTANDING A DOS SESSION'S ENVIRONMENT

The environment is a reserved area of conventional memory that DOS uses to store the values assigned to certain system variables. For example, the list of directory names that will be searched to find an executable file is in an environment variable called PATH. The directory that contains the reloadable portion of the COMMAND.COM command interpreter is in an environment variable called COMSPEC.

You can use the SET command at any DOS command prompt to discover the current variables in use. By typing SET and pressing Enter, you will see a list similar to this:

TEMP=F:\TEMP

```
COMSPEC=F:\COMMAND.COM
QDOS=C:\UTILITY
SOUND=C:\SBPRO
BLASTER=A220 I2 D1 T2
PATH=D:\WINDOWS;C:\DOS;C:\;C:\UTILITY;C:\SIGNATUR
windir=D:\WINDOWS
```

In this example, my TEMP and COMSPEC variables point to a RAM disk. Specific applications set up their own variables (QDOS, SOUND, and BLASTER) during installation. I set up the values for PATH and PROMPT in my AUTOEXEC.BAT file. And Windows itself sets up the value of the *windir* variable so that it can later easily determine the location of the main Windows directory.

The SET command offers an easy way to discover what variables have been named and what values have been assigned to them. In fact, using the SET command one or more times enables you to specify values for different variables. For instance, many people incorporate a customized version of the PROMPT command into their AUTOEXEC.BAT file, such as this:

SET PROMPT=$e[1m$p$g

This uses a special sequence of escape codes to produce intensified characters on the screen, which some people find easier to read. You can use the PROMPT command to create a multicolored command prompt, in lieu of the simple C> prompt, that contains information about your system, such as the date, time, or current directory. Many people use this command to redefine the command prompt so that it is immediately obvious that a DOS session under Windows is running, rather than a DOS command prompt outside of Windows. You can also display your own customized information prompt in a fixed position on the screen rather than on the next available screen line. Refer to my book *Mastering DOS 5* (SYBEX, 1991) for complete details on using this powerful command.

When Windows starts up, it uses all existing environment variables. For each DOS session, Windows assigns as many bytes as necessary (rounded up to a multiple of 256 bytes) to store the environment values that are currently in use. If you later try to define new values, you may run out of room in the environment.

Unfortunately, it is not easy to figure out how many bytes are taken up by your environment. DOS limits the size of the environment when you first start DOS itself. If you know that your system is going to require extra space, you can use the SHELL command in CONFIG.SYS to enlarge the environment.

Even before considering Windows, you can include this line in CONFIG.SYS to ask for a 512-byte environment:

SHELL=C:\DOS\COMMAND.COM /E:512 /P

This example assumes that COMMAND.COM is in a DOS directory on the C drive. It specifies a permanent command processor (the /P switch) and indicates that 512 bytes be reserved for the environment (the /E switch). You can change 512 to some larger number if you have a complex system that defines more environment variables. By specifying a permanent command processor, COMMAND.COM will consume space for itself that it will never give back up. In particular, the EXIT command under DOS will no longer have any effect on this invocation of COMMAND.COM.

But this SHELL command applies to your overall DOS system. When you start Windows, each DOS session within Windows will typically receive less environment space than existed in DOS. Actually, Windows doesn't look at the environment space that was reserved under DOS. When Windows starts, it looks to see how many bytes have already been used. Rounding this number up to a multiple of 256, it then determines how big to make the DOS session's environment.

You may need more bytes for a particular DOS session's environment. This will often happen if you run a PIF that specifies a batch file that includes several SET commands before running an .EXE file. There are two primary ways to enlarge the environment of a particular DOS session under Windows. Both ways depend on the entries you make for the Program Filename and Optional Parameters fields in the PIF.

First, suppose that you simply want to run a DOS command prompt under Windows. Perhaps you want to run one or more DOS commands, or perhaps you want to test some TSRs together in the same session. If you discover that you need more environment space, you can set up a PIF named DOS.PIF that specifies at least two entries, along with any other options you like. Type COMMAND.COM in the Program Filename field, and type /E:512 in the Optional Parameters field.

Not only do I have a PIF like this on my system but I have also created a program item icon in the STARTUP program group of Program Manager. In this way, I always have immediate access to the DOS command prompt within Windows. I've defined an application shortcut key (Ctrl+Alt+D) to switch to this session whenever I want.

But I've discovered that some programs require even more environment space. The DOS version of Charles Schwab's Equalizer portfolio software requires a 1024-byte environment. So I have a similar setup to run that program. Since you can also run a DOS program at the same time as starting up a COMMAND.COM session with an expanded environment, I use these entries in my SCHWAB.PIF file: COMMAND.COM and /E:1024 /C C:\EQUAL2\EQ.EXE.

This allocates 1024 bytes to the command processor's environment and then runs the EQ.EXE program found in the EQUAL2 directory. So even though you have to run COMMAND.COM as the program to execute, you can still use the optional parameters to specify the application name that you want to run.

CHANGING EXECUTION-TIME SETTINGS

The PIF enables you to specify many options that govern how your DOS application executes under Windows. Once it is running, you can still adjust some of these settings. To do so, you must use the dialog box that appears when you select Settings from the DOS application's Control menu. Remember that the Control menu is available by clicking on the horizontal-bar icon in the upper-left corner of a window. If the DOS application is minimized, the Control menu also appears when you click on the desktop icon.

The Settings option appears only in the Control menu of a DOS application, as does the Edit option, which I discussed in the context of sharing data through the Clipboard (see Chapter 5). Figure 8.11 shows the Settings dialog box for my QDOS 3 application.

You can control the most important and visible aspects of your DOS application through this dialog box. However, any changes you make here apply only to the current execution of your program. The next time you run your DOS

Changing DOS Applications' Priority Settings on the Fly

You probably know by now that pressing Alt+Enter toggles a DOS application between full-screen mode and windowed mode. But did you know that pressing Alt+spacebar, while a DOS application is in the foreground, will display a Control menu that includes a Settings option? If your DOS application is running full screen, pressing Alt+spacebar puts it in a window, then displays the Control menu. If your DOS application is already in a window, pressing Alt+spacebar simply displays the Control menu.

Once the Control menu is displayed for a DOS application, you can select Settings, which offers a number of special-purpose options. Foreground and background priority settings are among these options. You can adjust the CPU attention and time-slicing factors by changing these numbers at this time. However, when done this way, note that the adjustments are temporary only.

For example, suppose that you use a DOS application for serial communications. For some reason, when you run the application in the background, you discover that it can't keep up with the data transfer rate. Increase its background priority until transmission speed settles out and data is received successfully.

As a second example, suppose that you use a DOS printing program to print more than one output page on each piece of paper—TJET is such a program; with it, you can save a considerable amount of paper by printing text at one-quarter size. But when run in the background, such a DOS program may slow down noticeably. Even if you are spooling your printed output, your printer may become bogged down while waiting for the spooled output to arrive. Use the technique discussed above to give the DOS window more processing cycles by increasing its background priority value.

The adjusted values apply only to this DOS task for its current activation. To permanently adjust the relative priority of multiple coexisting tasks, you should read the text in this chapter about the Advanced Priority option in the DOS application's PIF.

application, the PIF option values once again will take effect. The PIF represents the semipermanent start-up execution values, and the Settings dialog box represents the on-the-fly values, which can be modified.

You can click on the Window or the Full Screen radio button to change instantly from one presentation method to another. But personally, I find it easier just to press Alt+Enter whenever I want to switch display methods.

Similarly, choosing the Terminate button is one way to close a DOS application that has gone haywire. If your application freezes up, and you can't even get to this Control Menu Settings dialog box, choosing Terminate is one step away from a Windows closure of the DOS session. However, in Windows 3.1, I find it easier just to press Ctrl+Alt+Del, followed by the Enter key, to forcibly close an errant DOS application. In either case, remember that Windows will not save any work in progress or properly close any open files.

The other two controls in this Settings dialog box are the ones that you will use more often. The Tasking Options section has the same two check boxes as described for the PIF. The Exclusive check box applies only when your

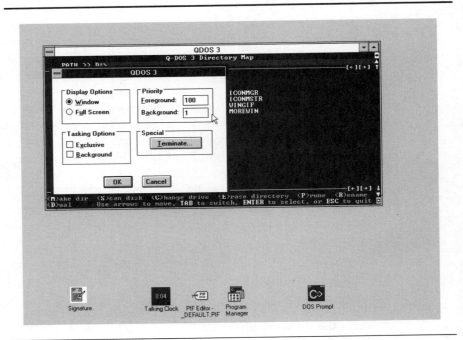

FIGURE 8.11: The Settings dialog box for QDOS3, which controls execution options on the fly

program is running in the foreground. The Background check box applies only when your application is running in the background.

Check the Exclusive box to suspend all other applications when your program is in the foreground. Check the Background box to enable your application to receive a proportional share of CPU cycles when it is running in the background.

The number of CPU cycles received by your application when it is in the background or the foreground depends on its priority number and on the sum of the priority numbers of all other applications. (I explain the algorithm that governs this determination in Chapter 7.) The Priority section allows you to fine-tune the number of CPU cycles received by your DOS application.

If your application is running too slowly when you are working with it in the foreground, increase its Foreground priority number. If the application makes too little progress while it is running in the background with other applications, increase its Background priority number. In fact, it's a good idea to adjust the Priority values in the Settings dialog box on the fly. In this way, you can more readily determine the best values to place in the application's PIF.

In this chapter, you have learned the meaning of all the PIF options that you can control when running a DOS application under Windows. Now turn to Chapter 9, which will discuss issues that relate to improving the execution of your Windows applications.

9

Managing the Windows Environment

I n Chapter 7, you learned a wide range of tips and techniques for running applications under Windows. In Chapter 8, you focused on specifically how to run DOS applications under Windows. In this chapter, you'll concentrate on improving the execution of your Windows applications. The first section of this chapter focuses on some general techniques for enhancing Windows applications. The remaining sections present specific methods that you can apply to the primary applications contained within Windows. The two major emphases in this chapter are the Program Manager and the File Manager. However, you will also discover a number of unique techniques to use when running other applications, including the Recorder and Sysedit.

◆ DESKTOP TIPS AND TRICKS

This section explains a few general tricks for running Windows applications. You'll learn a number of techniques for using the mouse to manage actions and using your keyboard as a mouse alternative. You'll even learn about how to use the Clipboard as a convenient data translator between applications.

EXPERIMENTING WITH THE MOUSE WHEN RUNNING APPLICATIONS

You are probably familiar with many aspects of using the mouse on your desktop. But have you stopped to think about some of the consistencies (or inconsistencies) of mouse clicking? A single click usually selects the item

Reducing Resource Consumption in the Program Manager

The following guidelines summarize techniques for reducing the resources required by the Program Manager. The fewer visible screen elements, the less drain on internal storage space for information about these elements.

◆ Reduce the number of open program groups. Fewer groups open means fewer icons visible.

◆ Reduce the number of icons in each program group. In this way, there is less impact whenever you open a group.

◆ Start up and maintain program groups in a minimized state.

◆ Remove unused icons from existing program groups.

◆ Delete program groups you never use.

◆ Group icons together for programs that you use at approximately the same time.

◆ Run programs automatically so that you don't have to open a program group each time to launch only one iconized application within it.

◆ Run programs from within the File Manager by establishing associations. This removes the burden completely from the Program Manager and allows you the convenience of specifying a particular data file to use.

below the mouse pointer, but not always. All applications do not necessarily implement the Systems Application Architecture (SAA) specifications faithfully.

Double clicking usually combines highlighting a selection with a choice (as if you had pressed Enter after highlighting your selection). If you double-click on an item in a list box, you've both highlighted it and made it the active choice.

In a similar way, double-clicking on an icon in the Program Manager activates the program and opens its window on screen, making it the foreground program. In an OLE-aware program, double-clicking on a representative icon will activate the original program that created the data that underlies the icon.

When in the File Manager, double-clicking on a file name usually runs a program. But this occurs only in certain circumstances. In the WIN.INI file, the Programs= line specifies the extensions of all executable programs. Generally, it will read

Programs=exe com bat pif

which means that any file name with any one of these four extensions is executable.

You learned in the preceding chapter that a .PIF file name controls the execution-time aspects of a DOS application running in a special DOS session under Windows. In addition, you learned that you can associate any other extension with an executable file name. For instance, you can associate all files with .WP or .TXT extensions with your word processor executable file, such as WP.EXE or SIG.EXE. The [Extensions] section of your WIN.INI file contains the details of these associations. Once finished, you can then double-click on a file name with that extension and Windows will automatically run the associated executable program.

Single clicking, by itself or in conjunction with certain keys, usually does something interesting as well. For example, single clicking in the File Manager highlights a file name, turning off the highlighting of other files. However, if you hold down the Shift key when you click on a file name, all names between any previously selected file name and this one are highlighted. If you hold down the Ctrl key, all previously highlighted names remain selected and highlighted, adding this latest one to the existing group.

There is no best way to make selections and choices in Windows. Sometimes, the mouse offers the most intuitive approach. At other times, the keyboard is actually easier and less time-consuming for some operations. It is best to learn both mouse and keyboard alternatives so that you can decide for yourself what combination of techniques works most efficiently.

WORKING WITH THE KEYBOARD

Discovering menu choices with a mouse can be quite slow. Its main advantage is that you needn't know anything about command alternatives. You can just access the menu bar with Alt, then find the desired option by using the arrow keys. A faster method is to use *accelerator keys*.

An accelerator key is any key that is underlined on a menu bar or pull-down menu. By pressing the Alt key, you merely highlight an item on the menu bar. But by pressing the Alt key plus the accelerator key, you immediately pull down the selected menu. Pressing Alt+W usually pulls down the Window menu in all Windows programs.

Similarly, you can see accelerator keys on each pull-down menu; they are also underlined. By pressing the accelerator key, you instantly highlight the menu item with that key underlined. You needn't press arrow keys until that item is highlighted.

Sometimes, a menu bar may have two items with the same accelerator key underlined. Or, a pull-down menu may have two or more choices with the same accelerator key underlined. When this is the case, you must simply press the accelerator key again and the next item with that key underlined will be highlighted. As before, you can press Enter when the proper menu item has been highlighted to actually choose the action or operation.

Finally, and this is my personal favorite for replacing the mouse, many menu items have shortcut keys. When a shortcut key has been defined for an application, you can circumvent the requirement of pulling down any menu, highlighting any item, and finally choosing the highlighted action. Press the shortcut key, and a specific menu item is automatically selected. For example, if you want to display or modify the program file name, or icon, or any other property that is attached to a Program Manager program item, you can pull down the File menu and select Properties. The Program Item Properties dialog box appears.

Alternatively, you can just press the Alt+Enter shortcut key. The same Program Item Properties dialog box appears for the program item that happens to have been highlighted at the time. Figure 9.1 depicts the key techniques just described.

You can see in this figure that each menu bar item has one underlined letter, as does each menu item on the File pull-down menu. In addition, where an application has defined a complete shortcut key, such as Alt+Enter to reach the Properties dialog box, you can read the shortcut key to the right of the menu choice itself. Although the shortcut key is no longer active when you've reached the menu (press the underlined character instead), the shortcut key is included as a reminder that you can reach the desired menu choice even faster the next time you want to reach this operation.

TRANSLATING BETWEEN APPLICATIONS WITH THE CLIPBOARD

Chapter 5 explains how the Clipboard can serve as a central storage area for data. You can extract data from one application and store it in the Clipboard. You can later import data from the Clipboard into a completely different application. In most cases, except with some DOS applications, you can export and import either text or graphics by using the Clipboard.

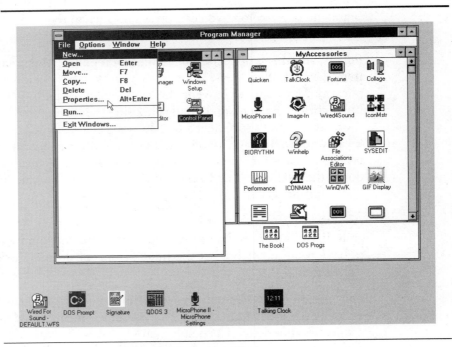

FIGURE 9.1: Using keyboard techniques in Windows

However, Chapter 5 only briefly touches on the Clipboard's ability to store data in multiple formats. Some applications actually store ten to fifteen different versions of the same information in the Clipboard. Consequently, the Clipboard can provide a unique and easy opportunity to translate between otherwise incompatible formats.

In some cases, an application will offer menu choices to select the format in which to send data to the Clipboard. In other cases, the application will offer a pull-down menu that displays the names of the formats in which the data is currently being stored in the Clipboard. You only need to choose the desired formats.

For example, suppose that your word processor can read a bit-map file, such as wallpaper, but cannot understand files in the industry-standard .GIF format. You can copy such a .GIF file directly to the Clipboard from your graphics application.

During copying, this application may store a .GIF and a .BMP version of your data. Your word processor can incorporate the .BMP version, thanks to the automatic data translation services of the Clipboard. The Paste command can automatically read the appropriate format.

◆ UNDERSTANDING THE GRAYED ENTRIES IN THE CLIPBOARD

The Clipboard's Display menu displays the names of data formats that represent information stored in the Clipboard. The Clipboard itself, however, cannot always display these formats. If a name is grayed, it means that some application has stored data that is now available to other applications, but the Clipboard is unable to display the data. For example, Excel can store data in RTF or SYLK format, but the Clipboard cannot display the data.

◆ USING THE PROGRAM MANAGER EFFECTIVELY

The Program Manager is probably the Windows application you use most frequently, if only because you probably use it as the shell to reach all other applications. In this section, I'll present a number of special techniques that can enhance how the Program Manager deals with program items, program groups, resources, icons, and applications themselves.

CHANGING AN APPLICATION'S ICON

In the last chapter, you learned that all DOS applications are generally represented by the same plain DOS rectangular icon. You also learned how to change that icon to another one. You can also change the icon used to represent a Windows application, even though each Windows application already has an icon embedded in its .EXE file. Remember that the ICONMSTR program included on this book's second disk offers you the ability to create from scratch any icon you like. The technique explained in this section enables you to attach such icons to any application.

To change the icon that appears in a Program Manager group, first highlight the existing icon and press Alt+Enter, which is the shortcut key to display an icon's Program Item Properties dialog box. In the dialog box, you will see the current icon displayed in the lower-left corner. On the right side, click on the Change Icon button to display the Change Icon dialog box (Figure 9.2).

For Windows applications, this dialog box displays the current file name containing the program icon. Usually, the current icon is highlighted in the center of the dialog box, and the file name that contains this icon's pixel data appears in the File Name field. Some file names contain more than one icon, such as the MP2.EXE file shown in Figure 9.2. You can use the horizontal scroll bar to view different icons.

Alternatively, you can click on the Browse button to display a small Directory Tree window. You can browse through other files on any disk to view other icons. Once you've found another file that may contain other icons, click on OK to display the icons in the Current Icon window. If the file you've chosen contains no icons, you'll see a dialog box that says

Cannot find any icons in this file

Just click on OK and the Change Icon dialog box will reappear. You can either browse some more, or type in a specific file name in the File Name field.

After you've selected a different icon, either in the current .EXE file or in any other file, you can click OK in the dialog box. This restores the Program Item Properties dialog box, with the new icon shown in the lower-left corner. Click OK in this box to update the Program Manager's group entry. Your newly selected icon will now appear in Program Manager displays.

It's worth hunting around your disk for files that contain many icons. Even if you don't have many .ICO icon files, your .EXE files may have a surprising

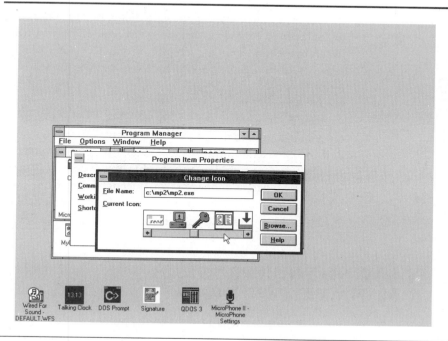

FIGURE 9.2:   The Change Icon dialog box

wealth of icons. The Program Manager itself (PROGMAN.EXE) contains a handful of choices. Many of the programs contained on this book's disks contain icons.

Some of your own applications may surprise you. When I looked at the .EXE file for my communications program, Microphone II, I was pleased to discover a large number of very well done icons that I now know I can use with other applications. When you change an icon in the Program Manager, remember that you are only copying the icon pixels from the specified source file into the .GRP file of the Program Manager. Once you've attached the icon to the Program Manager group, you don't need the source file anymore. If you have a directory that contains 3MB of icon files, you really don't have to keep it around after you've selected and attached the icons you want to Program Manager groups.

♦ SAVE DISK SPACE BY ERASING ICON FILES

When you use the Change Icon dialog box to change the icon used to represent a Program Manager item, you can select from .EXE files (often containing multiple icons) or from .ICO files (usually containing only one icon). Even though there are other files that can contain icons, these files may only be important to you as sources of new icons for your Program Manager items.

Once you've attached an icon to a Program Manager item, you no longer have to keep the source file available on your disk. You can erase it (if you have a backup copy) to free up disk space, or you can rearrange the disk, without having to fear that the Program Manager may no longer be able to find the icon. You only need a specific source file if you later want to extract this or any other icon from that particular source file.

SAVING YOUR PROGRAM MANAGER SETTINGS

After you've used your system for a while, you know which program groups contain the icons you use most often. You probably use the Window pull-down

Choosing Colorful Icons for Your Applications

Some applications have dull icons. All DOS applications use the boring DOS icon unless you direct Windows to use a different icon. The icon that appears when a window is minimized is a property of the application under Windows.

To change an application's icon, follow this procedure:

1. Run the Program Manager and click on the application icon that you want to change.

2. Pull down the File menu and select Properties.

3. Choose Change Icon.

4. Type into the File Name field the name of the .EXE or .ICO file that contains the icon you want to use.

5. Use the scroll bar to highlight the icon.

6. Choose OK.

menu to cascade or tile windows, or you just arrange the icons in your favorite way. Wouldn't it be nice if this arrangement appeared every time you started Windows?

The Options pull-down menu contains just what you need. If the Save Settings on Exit option on this menu is checked, Windows will save information about the current configuration of your program group icons and child windows. When you next start Windows, the Program Manager configuration will appear exactly as it was when you last shut down.

After exiting from Windows once, with the Program Manager configuration set up as you would like it to appear, you can uncheck the Save Settings on Exit option. The Program Manager won't save any other temporary configuration when you exit from Windows.

When you exit Windows, a message is sent to all running Windows applications to ensure that any open files are closed. If a Windows application has a file open or has a private configuration file whose settings have changed, the

application is supposed to display a dialog box that asks you whether or not
the relevant file should be updated.

The same is not true for a DOS application. If a DOS application is running,
Windows merely displays a dialog box that says

Application still active;

exit the application and then try closing Windows

This gives you a chance to abort the termination process but does not actually
close Windows. Follow this procedure to store your current Program Manager
configuration on disk:

1. Start up any DOS application. You can just run COMMAND.COM
   if you have no other DOS application that you want to run.

2. Switch back to the Program Manager and press Alt+F, then X. The
   Exit Windows dialog box appears.

3. Choose OK.

4. Since a DOS application is running, Windows will direct you to exit
   from it directly before you can actually shut down Windows: Choose
   OK. You don't actually have to exit the DOS application, but Windows saved the Program Manager configuration already.

5. Remove the check mark from the Save Settings on Exit option on
   the Options pull-down menu. In the future, Windows will start up
   with the current configuration, even if you make more changes
   during the current session.

DELETING PROGRAM MANAGER GROUPS AND ICONS

OK. You've switched from 1-2-3 to Excel, or from Word to WordPerfect. Or
you've installed all the programs from this book's disks. In any case, you may
now want to clean up your Program Manager configuration by deleting individual icons or entire groups. How do you go about this?

It's easy to create a new program item or program group. You just click on one
of the two radio buttons that appear when you select New from the File menu.

Maintaining Your Arrangement of Program and Group Items

To control the arrangement of group and program items, the Program Manager offers two toggle switches. They are located on the Options pull-down menu and provide these facilities:

Save Settings On Exit: When turned on, this toggle saves information about both the contents and positions of all open program groups and icons.

Auto Arrange: When turned on, this toggle rearranges all program item icons whenever the size of a group window changes.

I keep both of these toggles turned on. However, if you like to save your visual configuration once and start up your system each time with that appearance, you must first turn on the Save Settings toggle, arrange your program groups to your liking, then exit from Windows once to save the arrangement. When you restart Windows, you can then remove the check from beside the Save Settings toggle. Each subsequent start-up of Windows will have your favorite arrangement.

To delete a program item, just open any group, and highlight the program icon you want to delete. Then press the Delete key, or pull down the File menu and choose Delete.

But how do you delete an entire group of icons? And can you delete an entire group when there are program item icons within the group? To delete a program group, you must first iconize the group, then highlight the group icon itself. Then you can press Delete or select the Delete option on the File menu to erase the program group completely.

To iconize a program group, remember that you must click on the Minimize button in the upper-right portion of the title bar, or select Minimize from the group's Control menu. Be cautious when deleting a program group. If you haven't highlighted the group icon when you press Delete, you may be about to delete a program item icon instead. In either case, a confirmation box appears that specifies exactly what is to be deleted if you choose Yes. Be sure to read the message to confirm whether an item or a group is going to be deleted.

◆ USING THE FILE MANAGER EFFECTIVELY

You've already learned a number of special aspects of the File Manager at earlier points in this book. For example, you learned how to run any program by merely double-clicking on its name in a File Manager directory listing. You also learned in Chapter 7 about associations. Table 9.1 lists the built-in extension associations that Windows automatically includes for you.

Many applications add new associations during their installation procedure. At any time, you can also add new associations for your own purposes. After highlighting any file name in a File Manager display, you can create a new association for that file name's extension through the Associate option on the File menu. You can see the current list of all associations in the [Extensions] section of your WIN.INI file.

In this section, you'll learn a number of additional techniques that enhance your use of the File Manager. They include using the menus more effectively, using the available shortcut keys more frequently, and controlling the amount of automatic confirmation that occurs during file operations.

TABLE 9.1:   Default Extension Associations

Extension	Associated Application
BMP	Paintbrush
CAL	Calendar
CRD	Cardfile
INI	Notepad
PCX	Paintbrush
REC	Recorder
TRM	Terminal
TXT	Notepad
WRI	Write
HLP	Winhelp

Moving and Copying Icons between Program Groups

To customize your own StartUp group in Windows 3.1, you will want to copy some icons from other groups into this specialized Program Manager group. You can use the File pull-down menu, but using your mouse is much faster. Just press the Ctrl key, then move the mouse pointer to the desired icon. Hold down the left mouse button one. While keeping the Ctrl key and the mouse button depressed, move the mouse pointer to the StartUp group. Then release both, and a new copy of the selected icon will appear in the StartUp group.

If you want to use a similar technique to reorganize the icons in one or more groups, you can move icons just as easily. First, move the mouse pointer to the desired icon in one group. Simply hold down the left mouse button as you move the mouse pointer to the target group. The selected icon is removed from the source group and moved completely into the new target group.

If you begin either the move or the copy sequence, then change your mind, just move the mouse pointer to any screen position that is not within a legitimate target directory window. Release the left button and the operation will be canceled.

FINDING A FILE ANYWHERE ON A DISK

How many times have you tried to find a file that you know was lurking somewhere on a disk. Generally, you look for the file in two or three directories before getting frustrated. If your system has a hard-disk management program, like the File Manager, you can almost always issue some form of searching command that will look for a file by name.

The File Manager has a Search command on its File pull-down menu. Figure 9.3 depicts the dialog box that appears when you select this option.

In the File Manager, you can open several Directory Tree windows at the same time. When you pull down the File menu and open the Search dialog box, the File Manager uses the current drive and directory as the starting point of the search. In Figure 9.3, the current drive is D: and the current directory is WINDOWS. The Start From field in the dialog box is automatically filled in with D:\WINDOWS, although you can move the cursor to that field and type in an alternative drive/directory combination.

♦ CONTROLLING THE CONTENT OF FILE WINDOWS

The default display of a directory includes file name, size, attributes, and date/time of last modification. If not all of this information interests you, you can easily tell Windows to display only some of it. This enables you to have smaller child windows in the File Manager, potentially allowing you to see more directories on the screen at once.

To select which file characteristics should appear, pull down the View menu and select Partial Details. Remove the default check mark beside any toggle option that you no longer want to see when calling up new child windows for other directories.

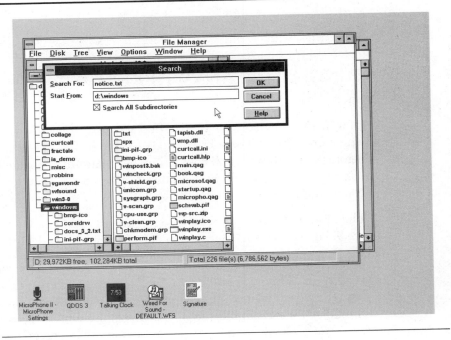

FIGURE 9.3: The Search dialog box

Similarly, type into the Search For field the name of the file names you want to find. Wildcards are permitted, so you could, for example, enter *.TXT to find all text files. The Search All Subdirectories toggle switch enables you to limit the search to a single directory (clear this toggle) or to allow the search to go down through the entire directory branch below the starting directory. To search an entire disk drive, specify the root directory (i.e., C:\) in the Start From field, and check the Search All Subdirectories box.

The File Manager displays the result of its search in a separate child window named Search Results. Both files and directories are listed if they meet the specification entered in the Search For field. Different mini-icons appear beside each found name, depending on whether it is an executable file or a data file, a directory, or a system or hidden file.

The File Manager uses a rectangular icon with a simulated title bar for executable applications. It uses a dog-eared page of paper for data file icons; if the data file extension has been associated with an application, the paper icon has simulated text drawn in it. A file folder icon indicates a directory, and a dog-eared paper icon with an exclamation mark in it indicates hidden files.

Yes, the search mechanism will find hidden files. Also, if you have the proper associations set up, you can double-click on an entry in the Search Results window and automatically run the associated program to deal with the found file. But the File Manager will display only one Search Results window at a time. Each succeeding request to search for a file specification will reuse the single Search Results child window.

◆ FIND HIDDEN FILES ON YOUR DISKS

The File Manager's Search option can locate hidden files on your disk. Specify *.* as the Search For field entry. Enter the root directory (i.e., C:\) in the Start From field. Check the Search All Subdirectories box, and click on OK.

The Search Results child window will list all files on your disk. Each file will have an identifying icon beside it. You will see all the familiar File Manager icons, from a rectangle to indicate an executable file, to a dog-eared page to indicate a data file. Hidden files can be quickly identified by the exclamation-point symbol that appears inside the file's mini-icon.

On color monitors, the exclamation point is red. In either case, you can rapidly scroll through the file names to find the hidden files.

REMOVING ANNOYING CONFIRMATION REQUESTS

Personally, I never remove any confirmation boxes on my system. If I ask the File Manager to delete a file or an entire subtree, or to replace a file through a copy or move operation, I want it to ask me whether I know what I'm doing. Sometimes, after working for five or seven or eleven straight hours, the simple fact is that I no longer know what I'm doing.

It's too easy to make a big mistake, and it's too time-consuming to correct such a mistake. Someone once said that computers just enable you to make the same mistakes as before, only much faster. So I put up with the confirmation messages that appear on my screen. But you may be unwilling to do so.

You can instruct the File Manager to skip displaying some or all of its confirmation message boxes. Figure 9.4 shows the dialog box that appears when you select Confirmation from the File Manager's Options pull-down menu.

Windows can provide automatic confirmation of up to five types of operations that affect files. Each of these can result in the erasure or overwriting of an existing file. If you mark a check box in Figure 9.4, you are asking the File Manager to warn you of an operation that can lead to lost data. If you don't want to receive a confirming request from the File Manager at such times, uncheck the appropriate box.

Table 9.2 summarizes the file operations that will be confirmed if you check each of the boxes in the Confirmation dialog box.

The choices you make will remain in effect until you shut down the File Manager or until you return to the Confirmation dialog box and change the settings. If you want your confirmation choices to apply each time you restart the File Manager, you must place a check mark beside the Save Settings on Exit option. This option can also be found on the Options pull-down menu. When you close the File Manager, all your confirmation options will be stored on disk and reused when you next start the File Manager.

TABLE 9.2: Confirmation Options

Confirm On	Protects Against
File Delete	Direct file deletion requests
Directory Delete	Direct directory deletion requests
File Replace	Copy or move commands that would overwrite an existing file
Mouse Action	Overwriting a file by dragging a file with the mouse
Disk Commands	Formatting or copying a disk

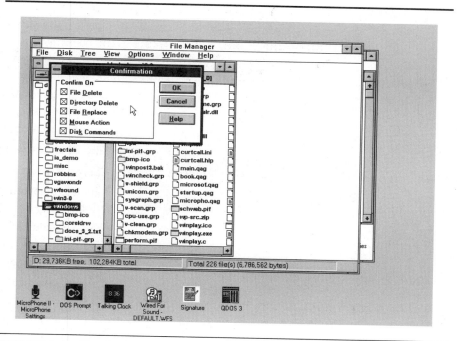

FIGURE 9.4: The Confirmation Options dialog box

USING THE FILE MANAGER SHORTCUT KEYS

In this section, you'll learn about the shortcut keys available in the File Manager. Table 9.3 organizes the keys into three areas: directory tree, directory window, and general shortcut keys.

TABLE 9.3: File Manager Shortcut Keys

	Keystroke	Action
General Shortcuts	Ctrl+Tab (Ctrl+F6)	Switches to next document window
	End	Switches to last file or directory
	Enter	Opens highlighted file or directory
	F7	Moves highlighted files or directories
	F8	Copies highlighted files or directories
	Home	Switches to root directory
	Shift+F4	Tiles directory windows
	Shift+F5	Cascades directory windows
Directory Tree Shortcuts	*	Expands selected directory's full branch
	+	Expands selected directory only
	–	Collapses selected directory
	Ctrl+↓	Selects next directory at this level
	Ctrl+↑	Selects previous directory at this level
	End	Selects last directory
	Home	Selects root directory

Controlling the Appearance of Confirmation Messages

The File Manager protects you from a number of inadvertent mistakes by requesting confirmation of certain requests. The appearance of certain confirmation dialog boxes can be time consuming and annoying, although the intended goal of protecting you from yourself is laudable.

You can decide for yourself which, if any, of the possible confirmation mechanisms you want to remain in place during File Manager operations. Pull down the Options menu and select Confirmation. A dialog box will appear that contains five toggle switches. Remove the check mark beside any action that you wish. No subsequent confirmation box will appear.

But exercise some caution here. Some of these options are more serious than others. DOS 5 users can undelete a file that has been deleted, so Confirm on Delete is not as critical as Confirm on Subtree Delete, since no easy method exists to restore an entire subdirectory of files and other directories.

TABLE 9.3: File Manager Shortcut Keys (continued)

	Keystroke	Action
Directory Tree Shortcuts (cont.)	←	Selects previous directory at next level up
	→	Selects first subdirectory of selected directory
	Tab	Selects current disk drive
Directory Window Shortcuts	↓	Selects next file or directory down the list
	End	Selects last file or directory in the list
	Home	Selects first file or directory in the list
	↑	Selects next file or directory up the list

◆ MOVING UP THE DISK HIERARCHY

When you are in a directory tree, you can press the Backspace key to change quickly from the current directory to a directory's parent. A few quick presses of Backspace brings you right to the root directory of any drive. At that point, it may be easier to navigate forward and down the directory structure than to wend your way sideways or back up.

Each child window in the File Manager displays a directory tree on the left side, with the files in the currently highlighted directory window shown on the right side. The directory tree keys apply when the focus is in the hierarchical tree area on the left side of any child window. The directory window keys apply when the screen focus is located in the file display portion of a File Manager child window. The general keys apply to the File Manager as a whole, usually acting as shortcuts for pull-down menu options.

◆ CONTROLLING DETAILS IN A DIRECTORY TREE

Each child window in the Windows 3.1 File Manager shows a directory tree on the left and the files within the current directory on the right. Pull down the Tree menu to exercise control over the detail that will be visible in the directory tree portion of each child window.

If you check the Indicate Expandable Branches option, the File Manager will show a plus sign in the icon beside any directory's name that contains subdirectories that are not currently being shown. Double-click on this folder icon and the File Manager will expand the directory tree immediately, placing a minus symbol inside the now-expanded directory tree branch.

If you want to expand all branches fully, select Expand All from the Tree pull-down menu. Alternatively, use the shortcut key Ctrl+asterisk, which is the same as Ctrl+Shift+8.

MANIPULATING FILES QUICKLY

You will perform some operations over and over again with the File Manager, so it pays to discover the fastest ways to perform these operations. For example, suppose that you have multiple drives. Most of you have at least one floppy-disk drive and one hard drive. But more and more systems have a second hard drive, which usually means frequent switching between the hard drives.

You can move the mouse to the drive bar and click on the drive identifier that you want. Or you can quickly change the active drive by holding down the Ctrl key while you press the letter of the desired drive. For example, pressing Ctrl+C makes drive C the active drive in the current File Manager child window.

When a child window appears, you can quickly change directories by clicking on a different directory name in the Directory Tree portion. You can also change directories by double-clicking on the directory name as it appears in the file list.

If you double-click on a file name, the File Manager will attempt to open the file. This means that the file will be run if it is executable. Alternatively, an associated program will be run if one has been associated with the file name that you double-clicked. Otherwise, you'll just receive a message box saying that the file cannot be executed and that no application is associated with this data file.

◆ LOADING A WINDOWS APPLICATION AS AN ICON

You may want to successively load several applications while using the File Manager or some equivalent program. If you keep the Shift key depressed while double-clicking on a Windows application file name, the application will be loaded and its icon will be displayed at the bottom of your screen.

In preparation for using any of the pull-down menu options, you must select (or highlight) one or more file names. To select a single file (or directory), you can just click on its name. To select a group of adjacent files (or directories), highlight the first item. Then, hold down the Shift key while you either press arrow keys to reach the last item in the adjacent list or move the mouse pointer and click on the last item. All list items between the first and last ones will be highlighted.

To highlight nonadjacent files or directories, you follow a similar procedure, except that you use the Ctrl key. Highlight the first item by clicking on it. Then hold down the Ctrl key while you move the mouse pointer to the next nonadjacent item; click on it. Each time you click on a new item, while you keep the Ctrl key depressed, all previously highlighted items remain highlighted. The latest file name or directory name clicked on is simply added to the group of noncontiguously highlighted items.

Once you've highlighted one or more files, you can use the Move and Copy commands on the menus to perform standard file movement. These two operations are probably not new to you, but the Windows 3.1 File Manager can perform these operations on directories as well as files.

♦ **PRINTING TEXT FILES QUICKLY**

Text files typically have a .TXT extension. You can print such files from the File Manager without having to open a word processing or text processing application. You only need to select the files first, then pull down the File menu and choose Print.

PRUNING AND GRAFTING ENTIRE DIRECTORIES

The File Manager can restructure your disk hierarchy for you without your having to go to the trouble of creating new directories, copying files, deleting files, and deleting directories. You can *prune and graft* a directory by moving it from its disk location to a new location. You simply use the move capabilities of the File Manager. Although you can prune and graft with an option on the Move pull-down menu, it is easier to use the mouse.

When the object of a move is a directory, or one or more directories, the File Manager essentially re-creates the old directory structure at a new location of your choice. To prune and graft a directory branch (one or more directories and any subdirectories located within them), follow these steps:

1. In the Directory Tree window, highlight the directory name whose branch is to be moved.

2. Hold down the left mouse button while you drag the directory name onto another directory name. Figure 9.5 depicts this point in time, after the BIX directory was highlighted and dragged down to the MINIBBS directory location. You can drag an icon directly onto a new directory location or anywhere on the same horizontal line as the new directory's name.

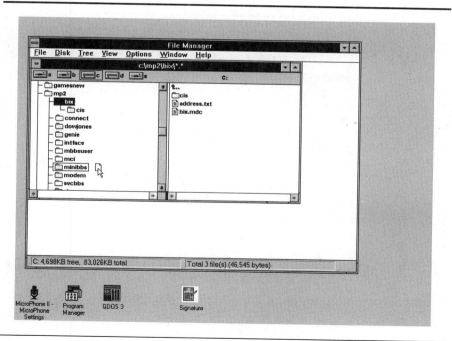

FIGURE 9.5:   Dragging to prune and graft directories

3. As you move the paper icon, the destination directory appears to be enclosed within a thin rectangle, as shown in Figure 9.5.

4. If Confirmations are enabled, you will see an appropriate confirmation message box. Answer Yes to confirm the move. The File Manager will automatically perform all directory restructuring. The result of moving BIX in this example is shown in Figure 9.6. Notice that the File Manager also moved the CIS subdirectory.

This example shows how to use the mouse to move a directory from one location to another. If you simply want to re-create a directory branch somewhere else (i.e., copy the branch), you must hold down the Ctrl key while you drag the directory icon to its destination. Be careful not to release the Ctrl key before you release the mouse button. If you do, the File Manager will interpret the request as a move rather than a copy.

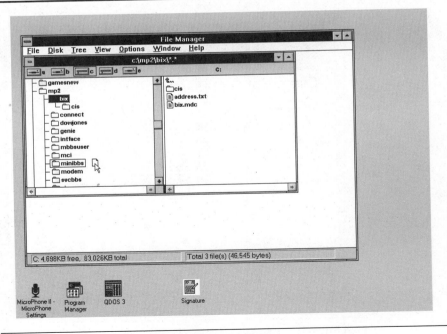

FIGURE 9.6: Moving a directory moves the entire branch.

You can move or copy a file just as easily with the mouse. Just highlight the file in the Directory Tree window on the right, press the Ctrl key (if you are copying), and drag the file icon to the destination directory in the Directory Tree window on the left. After any confirmations, the file is moved or copied to its new directory location.

◆ MOVING FILES ACROSS DRIVES

To move a file across drives, you must hold down the Alt key while dragging the mouse. If you don't, the file will be copied instead of moved.

It's interesting to observe how the File Manager handles pruning and grafting. When the File Manager restructures a directory hierarchy by moving (or copying) a directory, its subdirectories, and all files within that specified branch, it actually performs a sequence of three operations:

1. It creates a directory with the same name.

2. It moves (or copies) all files within the old directory to the new one.

3. It repeats steps 1 and 2 for each subdirectory.

4. It deletes all source directories and files.

SPECIAL FEATURES OF THE COPY AND MOVE COMMANDS

Copying and moving is very easy for mouse users, and I find it to be significantly faster than using pull-down menus and keystrokes. However, there is a benefit to using the pull-down menu approach: You can rename a file at the same time you move or copy it. First highlight the file you want to move or copy, then select Move or Copy from the File pull-down menu. Next, type in the To box the new path and file name. Finally, select OK; Windows will copy or move the file to the new path location and rename it.

Windows 3.1's ability to link and embed objects is evident when you use the Copy option on the File menu. There is a new radio button called Copy to Clipboard. If you do not specify a destination path name in the To field, as has always been the default case, you can alternatively click on this Copy to Clipboard button.

If you click on this button rather than enter anything in the To field, Windows will copy the icon view of the file to the Clipboard so that you can later link or embed it in an OLE application file. You will not be able to display the copied file with the Clipboard Viewer, but an OLE-aware application will be able to paste the file's OLE icon. Refer to Chapter 5 for more details about object linking and embedding.

◆ TIPS FOR USING THE RECORDER UTILITY

The best advice I can give you about the Recorder utility is to never use the mouse when recording a macro. Because the Recorder replicates each key press, mouse movement, and mouse button push, it depends heavily on the location (and even size) of screen objects. A Recorder macro's ability to work correctly depends on window size because the size affects whether information has to be scrolled to appear. The macro depends on the exact size and contents of list boxes and menu lists, as well as which program has the screen focus when you execute the macro.

In short, Recorder macros can be very useful but require you to take great care when you create them to assure consistent execution each time you run them. Keyboard selection of menu options and the definition of accelerator and shortcut keys are typically more reproducible than most mouse-dependent screen objects. Consequently, you should use the keyboard to define your macros.

This section is not designed to teach you how to use the Recorder utility. To learn the basics of using Recorder and the other Windows utility programs, you can read Robert Cowart's *Mastering Windows 3.1*, SYBEX, 1992.

UNDERSTANDING THE RECORDER UTILITY

The Recorder utility offers a powerful method for automating almost any repetitive Windows activity. The Recorder creates macros, each of which is similar to a DOS batch file. You can define a macro that contains a sequence of instructions; the instructions can involve keyboard or mouse sequences. DOS batch files can only contain keyboard sequences.

When the Recorder utility is active, you use the Record command on the Macro pull-down menu to record individual instruction sequences. You can later use the Run command on this menu to quickly execute the named, stored sequence of instructions. However, there are faster and better ways to rerun stored macros; I'll show them to you in the next section.

Figure 9.7 depicts a saved Recorder file. The illustration is meant to indicate how a single file can contain any number of defined macros. As you record and define macros, the workspace area in the Recorder displays the shortcut key combinations and the name you've assigned to each macro. When you are ready to store a group of macros, you use the Save (or the Save As) option on the File menu.

AUTOMATING INDIVIDUAL RECORDER MACROS

The .REC extension is associated with the Windows Recorder utility. If you've already defined a Recorder file, such as BEGIN.REC in Figure 9.7, you can define this set of macros when you first start Windows. To run the Recorder utility, minimize it, define the macros in the BEGIN.REC file, and adjust the Load= line in your WIN.INI file:

Load=BEGIN.REC

If your Load= line already contains entries, just add BEGIN.REC to the list.

Executing a Recorder Macro at Start-up

Adding a macro to the Load= line in WIN.INI only defines the macros and makes them available for use. Suppose you want to execute a specific macro at start-up, such as a macro that runs the Colors icon from the Control Panel and specifies a particular combination of desktop colors on your system.

Figure 9.7 indicates that the Colors macro was originally defined to have the shortcut key Ctrl+F12, distinguishing this macro from any others that may exist in the BEGIN.REC file. To run this macro at start-up, you could enter the following at a DOS command prompt:

WIN RECORDER -H ^F12 BEGIN.REC

You can see that *WIN* brings up Windows, and the first parameter on this line forces Windows to run the Recorder utility. The Recorder utility itself receives the second parameter, which is -H. This special character sequence

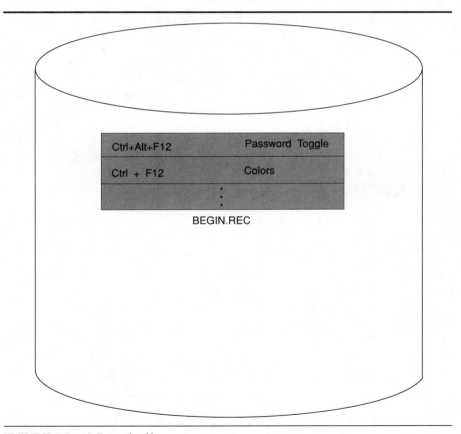

FIGURE 9.7: A Recorder file can contain one or more macros.

Selecting a Built-in Windows 3.1 Screen Saver

Windows now offers a choice of automated screen savers. From the Desktop choice in the Control Panel, choose Screen Saver. Click on the list-box down arrow to display available screen savers and select one of them.

To specify how long you want Windows to wait (with no user input) before invoking the screen saver, click on the up or down arrow beside the Delay field. This increases or decreases the number of minutes by one at each click. To adjust various aspects of the screen saver images themselves, click on Setup and make any adjustments to screen characteristics.

You can also password-protect your system when you leave it. Turn on password protection in the Password Options section of Setup. Whenever the screen saver runs, no one (including you—don't forget your password) will be able to resume Windows until the password is entered. Whenever any user input occurs, a dialog box will appear on the screen saver image to request that the password be entered.

indicates that the Recorder is to run a particular macro from a particular file. The next two parameters define which macro is to be run (^F12 stands for the Ctrl+F12 macro) and the recorder file (BEGIN.REC) where the macro can be found.

The only part of this sequence that requires further explanation is how key combinations are represented on a command line like this one. As you can see, the Ctrl key is represented by a carat (^) symbol. The other two possible special keys are the Shift key and the Alt key. They are represented by the plus (+) sign and the percent (%) sign, respectively.

Suppose that you wanted to run a macro whose shortcut key was Ctrl+Alt+Shift+J. To run Windows and this particular macro at start-up, you would enter ^%+J as the shortcut key indicator on a command line. For example:

WIN RECORDER -h ^%+J BEGIN.REC

Preventing Percent-Sign Confusion

There is one caution to note here. It has to do with DOS's use of the percent-sign symbol (%) in batch files. Suppose you typically start Windows from a DOS batch file. If you decide to define a macro and run the Recorder when you start Windows, you may be in for a surprise. The command line just shown will not work unless you use double percent signs:

WIN RECORDER -h ^%%+J BEGIN.REC

The double percent sign in a batch file enables DOS to treat the symbol differently, properly passing the indication for an Alt key to the Recorder utility. If you don't use the double percent sign, DOS may confuse its meaning. DOS already uses a single percent sign for other purposes.

Running Recorder Macros from Icons

Don't forget that you can run *any* program from a Program Manager icon, including the Recorder. On my system, I leave the computer on all the time because I have a fax board constantly monitoring my fax phone line. Normally, I use a screen saver in Windows 3.1 that is password-protected. However, when I'm in the office during the day, I don't want to be bothered entering the password if I stop working on the computer for several minutes.

So I defined a Password Toggle macro, activated by Ctrl+Alt+F12 and located in my BEGIN.REC file. Furthermore, I created an icon in my Accessories program group. The Command Line field in the Program Item Properties dialog box for this icon contains

RECORDER -H ^%F12 BEGIN.REC

Whenever I click on this icon, the macro quickly opens the Control Panel, selects Desktop, tabs down to the screen saver section, chooses Setup, tabs down to the Password Protected check box, and presses the spacebar to toggle this switch. After several appropriate OK entries, everything is back to where it was and the password protection has either been activated (just before I leave for the evening) or deactivated (sometime early in the day).

◆ TIPS FOR USING OTHER UTILITIES

There are many more helpful utilities that come with your Windows system. In this section, you'll learn several tips about using them.

Some utilities, like Winhelp, are simply worth exploring on your own. With this utility, for instance, you can directly read the help files that come with nearly all Windows utility programs.

◆ SEARCHING HELP FILES WITHOUT STARTING APPLICATIONS

Nearly all Windows applications have their own help files, accessible through the main menu's Help option. You can access and read these .HLP files directly, without running the related application, by running the single program WINHELP.EXE, located in the WINDOWS directory. Once you've launched this program, you can pull down its File menu and select Open. All .HLP file names in the current directory appear in a window. Also, Winhelp offers you the opportunity to switch directories and drives if you want to open a help file located elsewhere.

USING THE SYSTEM FILE EDITOR

The System Configuration Editor, or Sysedit, is shown in Figure 9.8. It offers a customizable environment in which to view or modify the entries in four important and influential text files.

Although the editing facilities in this program are not particularly special, you are not burdened with even the effort of specifying the file name you want to edit. This program is designed to open the current versions of the two principal Windows initialization files, WIN.INI and SYSTEM.INI, as well as the current versions of the two principal DOS start-up files, AUTOEXEC.BAT and CONFIG.SYS.

Once this program starts, you can use standard mouse techniques to switch rapidly between any of the four predefined child windows. You can also use standard window techniques for cascading or tiling the appearance of the four files in the Sysedit workspace.

The Sysedit utility offers a couple of important features that may not be readily available or may be inconvenient to use in your word processor. Because these particular files must be edited and saved in strictly ASCII format, Sysedit automatically saves files in this format. If you use the document mode of a non-ASCII word processor to edit and save these files, it may store control characters along with the text, making the resulting file unusable to DOS or Windows. When you use your own word processor to edit these files, save them in plain ASCII format.

Additionally, Sysedit has an Undo option on its Edit menu. If you make a mistake during editing, you can easily back up and withdraw your last change.

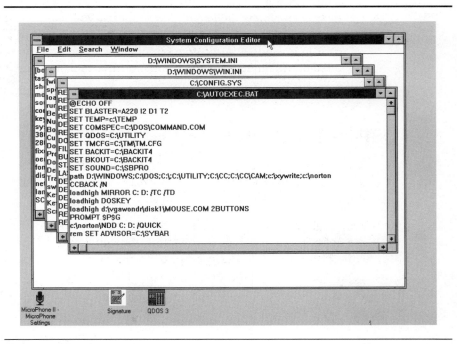

FIGURE 9.8: The Sysedit utility

Unfortunately, the edits are not stacked, so you can only recover the most recent change.

♦ COLORS CAN AFFECT SPEED

If your Windows system commonly displays many windows, it can be difficult to look quickly at the screen and determine which window is active. Normally, the default color scheme displays all windows with the same border, even though the active window typically shows an enhanced title bar. Personally, I like to change the default color scheme so that active and inactive window borders are displayed in different colors. However, Windows can redisplay the desktop faster if you use the same color for both the active and inactive borders, and you select only a solid color for these desktop elements. Choose the Colors icon in the Control Panel to access and modify any of your desktop colors.

USING THE TERMINAL UTILITY

One of the most common complaints from people who use terminal emulators with modems is that a lot of time is wasted scrolling down or to the right on the screen. This is typically because more information is received than can be seen at one time on your monitor. The more information that can be displayed on a single screen, the better most people feel—especially if they're paying a premium for connection time to a communications service, such as CompuServe.

To display more information on your screen with the Terminal utility, first, pull down the Settings menu and select Terminal Preferences. This displays the dialog box shown in Figure 9.9.

This dialog box offers two ways to increase the amount of information displayed on your screen. You can click on the 132 button in the Columns portion to expand the number of columns from the default of 80 to a maximum of 132. If your video hardware can display all 132 columns, you will instantly see the additional columns of data, if there are any. Most bulletin boards and communications services transmit the more common 80 columns of data.

The options in the Terminal Font portion of the dialog box can affect both the number of columns and the number of lines that appear. To see more information, just select a display font that is smaller than the default 15 points. As with any other program, you can always maximize the window to full-screen size to see the most information without having to scroll.

♦ REDUCING EYESTRAIN WHEN USING A COMMUNICATIONS PROGRAM

If you suffer from eyestrain when using your terminal emulator program, try using a larger font. The Terminal utility's Terminal Preferences dialog box, accessed through the Settings menu, has a choice of screen fonts, with different point sizes.

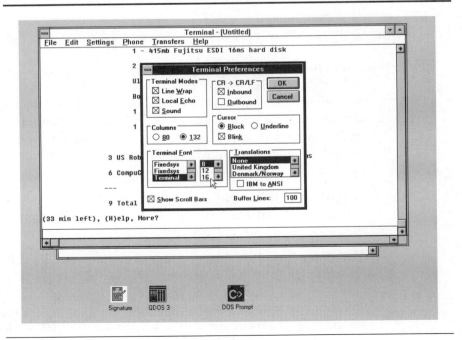

FIGURE 9.9: The Terminal Preferences dialog box

USING THE CLOCK UTILITY

The disks accompanying this book contain a number of programs that track time and date information. These programs can either display the information or use it in different ways, or both, using a variety of options. See Chapter 21 for detailed explanations of Winclock, Timefram, Apptimer, and Reminder.

Windows includes its own very simple date and time program. CLOCK.EXE displays the time of day in either analog or digital fashion, using selections available from the Settings menu. Personally, I've used so many digital-clock programs and devices over the years that I'm ready for a clock that just shows hands that sweep around a good old circle.

◆ ICONIZING THE CLOCK

The Clock program works in a window or in an icon. When you minimize the clock window, Windows will keep track of time within the icon at the bottom of your screen. You can start Windows with an iconized Clock by using the Load= line in the WIN.INI file.

When you display the Clock program in a sizable window, you can see hours, minutes, and seconds in whatever format you choose. If you minimize the Clock, it displays only hours and minutes. However, the neat thing about this program is that it keeps track of the time when minimized, even if you're looking at an analog watch face with hands for the hours and minutes.

In the last three chapters, you've learned a great many tips and tricks for running Windows and non-Windows applications more efficiently. In Chapter 10, you'll learn about video standards and some special techniques for dealing more successfully with the Windows graphical interface.

10

Understanding Graphics, Color, and Video Standards

I n the preceding three chapters, you learned a good deal about running your programs under Windows. But I said nothing about the appearance of those programs on your screen. In fact, each program can appear differently from computer to computer. Each program's appearance depends heavily on the video adapter in your system, the monitor you've connected to it, and the video mode in use by that adapter/ monitor combination.

In this chapter, I'll explain video standards, as well as present a number of tips for controlling performance and influencing screen resolution on your system. Additionally, you'll learn some tricks for using and controlling colors on your desktop.

This chapter also covers issues related to graphics applications. I'll present information about capturing whole screens, whole windows, and specific portions of a screen. You'll learn about the many graphics file formats used by different programs to store graphic images on disk. Understanding these formats will help you to manage graphical data more effectively in your applications. Understanding how to capture screen images can help you to incorporate desktop images into your documentation or presentations.

◆ MANIPULATING SCREEN IMAGES

Unfortunately, there is no commonly agreed-upon disk format for storing graphic images. Consequently, programs that generate graphics files frequently use incompatible formats. This requires a greater level of understanding before you can successfully work with more than one graphics format. In this section, you'll learn about screen capture techniques, graphics file formats, and graphics format conversions.

CAPTURING SCREEN IMAGES

Who captures screen images? Writers and publishers do for their books. Trainers do for their classes. Speakers often do for their presentations. Computer magazines do for their articles. Advertisers do for their layouts. Students do for their reports. And that's just the serious stuff.

Some people capture a sequence of humorous screen images, then bundle them into animated birthday cards for friends. Other people capture images of spreadsheet analyses to display rapidly on their screens when the boss comes by, to cover up the video game they're playing.

You learned in Chapter 5 that Windows offers you the ability to send to the Clipboard a copy of the full screen (you press Print Screen) or the active window (you press Alt+Print Screen). Once the image is in the Clipboard, you can import the image into the Paintbrush accessory program for further manipulations. Of course, the Paintbrush is not a very sophisticated program. Beyond this constraint, the Windows capturing capabilities send only a bit map to the Clipboard. This is inherently a limited format, doing a poor job of converting screen colors into shades of gray.

◆ CAPTURING ALL OR PART OF YOUR SCREEN

Press the Print Screen key to capture a bit-map image of your entire screen to the Clipboard. Press the Alt+Print Screen key combination to capture just the active window or dialog box to the Clipboard.

You may want to augment Windows capabilities with additional programs. The second disk accompanying this book offers the Snagit program for capturing screen images, converting file formats, and printing images. You'll also find the Paintshop program, which offers additional graphic manipulation tools for managing your screen images, as well as converting between formats. There are a number of expensive and extensive commercial products available

for managing screen images. The screens in this book, for example, were captured with Collage Plus from Inner Media Inc.

Windows' ability to grab a full-screen image is fairly limited. Almost all
screen-grabbing programs are more versatile, allowing you to capture a
specified portion of the screen. Once it has been captured to a file, you can
then use other tools to expand, contract, or change the video elements of the
picture for presentation purposes.

Capturing a portion of a screen means that you can easily capture child windows within an application, or capture interesting icons directly from the
screen. One nice touch in Collage Plus is its countdown timer. Depending on
how complex a screen sequence is, I can specify exactly how much time I want
to be given, after requesting the screen capture, to set up the window and
pointer positioning. Additionally, Collage Plus automatically removes itself
from the screen while the capture is taking place.

Between the Windows Paintbrush and this book's Paintshop program, you
will probably have sufficient ability to manipulate your images once you've
captured them. You may also have sufficient ability to convert them between
formats, which is especially important if you will be exporting the images to
another application.

USING GRAPHICS FILE FORMATS

Windows offers a powerful environment for sharing data. As you learned in
Chapter 5, the Clipboard and the DDE and OLE facilities make communications and information sharing between programs both powerful and dynamic.
However, since there are so many programs producing graphic data in so
many formats, exporting, importing, and converting graphics still requires
extra effort.

Although you could argue that one format is better or worse than another, you
must accept that different formats do different jobs. However, they can all be
grouped into two major categories: vector-based and bit-map-based. A vector-
based image is mathematically defined, and a bit-map-based image consists of
a specified group of pixels.

A vector graphic image usually consists of a collection of mathematically
defined objects. For example, one of these objects might be a circle whose

center ($x1,y1$) and radius (2 inches) are defined. The image of this object depends on the output device. If you output such a vector object to a laser printer, you might see the circle generated on a grid of 300 dots per inch (dpi).

If you send the same mathematical definition to a typesetting device, the circle will appear more highly resolved because it is created at 1200 dots per inch. In fact, if you send the same vector graphic to a pen plotter, the circle will be drawn with a continuous pen motion, creating the equivalent (i.e., a solid circular line) of an infinite number of dots.

On the other hand, a bit-map graphic relies on the construction of the graphic image as a collection of individual dots, or pixels. Once an image has been captured, its quality is fixed. If the image is captured on screen at EGA resolution, the information is limited to the source resolution (a total of 640×350 dots). Even if you later print the image at 300 dpi or 1200 dpi, or even on a continuous pen plotter, the output device can no longer compensate for the constrained source-image definition.

As you can see, the method for capturing (or creating) images has a good deal to do with how you plan to use those images. By definition, screen captures must be in some form of bit-map graphics. After all, you are only capturing the status of the screen pixels (i.e., which ones are on or off, and what the color is). But individual applications can create the images in either vector or bit-map format. If the output device is a screen, then even a vector graphic image will be converted during output to the necessary collection of pixels.

Because vector graphic images are defined mathematically, the memory or disk space needed to define them is inherently smaller than most bit-map images. The equation that defines such a vector image requires only a few bytes of storage. When the image must be reconstructed, the equation is used to calculate which bits must be turned on or off. There is simply more raw data required to define and store a bit map.

Beyond this, there is an additional subtlety. The quality of a vector image is limited only by the nature of the output device. The quality of a bit-map image is limited by the nature of the original captured bit map or by the application that is creating the image. If the original or generated image is a 200-dpi scanned image, you cannot improve the quality by outputting it on a 1200-dpi typesetting device. Although the total number of dots per inch will increase, the amount of information (i.e., the amount of detail) in the image will be no greater than in the original.

When an application attempts to export or import a graphic image, the extension you choose for the file name is used to indicate the format of the data. Table 10.1 lists some of the most common types of formats used by Windows applications.

Generally, you will only find vector graphics supported by the more sophisticated CAD and drawing programs, such as CorelDRAW and Arts & Letters. Not only can these programs manipulate each mathematically defined object individually but they allow groups of objects to be combined and then separated again quite easily.

Such programs offer a number of tools based on the mathematical object definitions. It becomes quite easy to readjust the size of a circle or line and zoom in or out. At any moment and at any level of zooming, the program can

TABLE 10.1: Common File Formats

Extension	Format
BMP	Standard Windows bit map
CDR	CorelDRAW (vector)
CGM	Computer Graphics Metafile
CLP	Internal Windows Clipboard
DXF	Data Exchange Format
EPS	Encapsulated PostScript
GIF	Graphics Interchange Format
HPGL	Hewlett-Packard Graphics Language (vector)
IMG	GEM Image
PCL	HP Printer Control Language
PCX	ZSoft PaintBrush
PIC	Dr. Halo
RTF	Rich Text Format
TIF	Tagged Image File
WMF	Windows Metafile (vector)

take full advantage of the resolution of your monitor. Furthermore, if your system has a math coprocessor, the vector equation calculations can be done even faster. Consequently, all redraws occur much faster than with bit-map graphics.

This speedup doesn't always occur. Some video adapters can't handle any increased data speeds. In effect, then, they create a new bottleneck even after the math coprocessor improves performance past the capacity of the CPU.

Bit-map applications generally include all screen capture applications, as well as most typical paint, scanning, and faxing programs. Once you've captured an image, a paint program can touch it up before exporting it to another program. Unfortunately, since there are no mathematical vectors to process in manipulating the image, you won't benefit from a math coprocessor.

If your system contains data in both bit-map and vector graphic formats, you will be limited in how readily you can convert between the two. Although it can be done, it is not always a precise process. Converting from a vector to a bit-map image is the easier of the two and the more precise. Converting from a bit-map to a vector image typically requires more touching up to assure the accuracy of the final image file.

Most conversion programs, like Snagit or Collage Plus, support only a few file formats. Be sure to check out which formats you'll need in your environment.

◆ USING AND CONTROLLING COLORS

As Figure 10.1 shows, you can select Color from the Windows Control Panel to display the Color dialog box shown on the right. From this dialog box, you can specify one of several predefined color schemes for all visual elements of your desktop. As I'll explain in this section, there are two conceptual approaches to defining and customizing the colors for any portion of a video image. In the first approach, you mix a differing amount of red, green, and blue to achieve a final color. I'll explain that approach first.

UNDERSTANDING THE WINDOWS COLOR PALETTE

If you want to customize your desktop even more than a predefined color scheme will allow, you can choose the Color Palette button to reveal the Basic Colors and Custom Colors portions of the dialog box, which are shown in Figure 10.1. You can also choose the Define Custom Colors button, which is visible at the bottom right of the Color dialog box. This displays the Custom Color Selector dialog box, which is on the left side of the desktop in Figure 10.1.

You can use this dialog box to truly customize any aspect of your desktop. And you can use one of two mechanisms to define your custom colors. You can make entries in the Hue, Sat (i.e., saturation), and Lum (i.e., luminosity) fields. Or you can make entries in the Red, Green, and Blue fields. Or you can

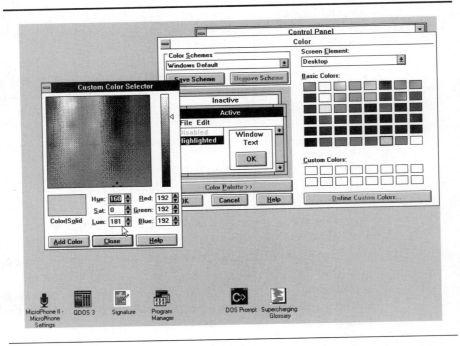

FIGURE 10.1: Customizing colors on the desktop

click your mouse anywhere in the colored square workspace, and Windows will adjust the six fields according to what colored portion of the workspace you clicked on.

The easier mechanism to understand is the red-green-blue (RGB) model, because it corresponds directly to the three electron guns that some video monitors use to generate colored pixels. Each pixel on your monitor is some combination of the output from these three colored light sources. Figure 10.2 shows a color cube designed to represent how the three colors can be combined to produce different colors.

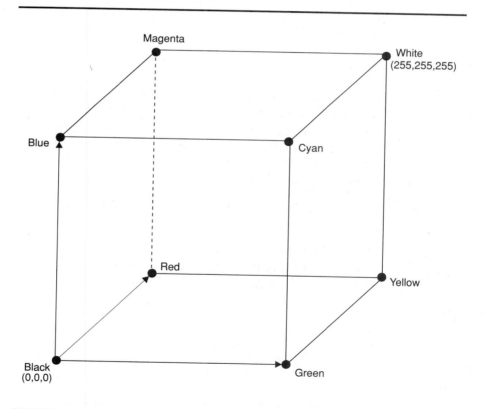

FIGURE 10.2:   The color cube model for understanding how video colors are produced

If a point on the screen receives no contributing red, green, or blue color, the result is black. This forms the starting point (in the lower-left corner of the cube) for constructing any color. The three arrows leading to the Red, Green, and Blue corners of the cube indicate that you can contribute a variable amount of each of these three colors to any final desired color.

For example, if you contribute the maximum possible amount of blue (moving you to the top of the cube) and the maximum possible amount of green (moving you to the right side of the cube), but contribute no amount of red (leaving you at the front face of the cube), then the resulting color is cyan (at the top, right, front point of the cube). You can create all possible colors of the rainbow by adjusting the contributing amount of blue, green, and red. The final result will always be some location (representing a color) within this three-dimensional cube.

Windows can use up to 8 bits to represent the intensity level of each color component of a single pixel. Although this range is constrained by the capabilities of your video board and monitor, you can see the idea. You can divide up the contribution of each primary color in 256 ways (a value from 0 to 255). A zero contribution from all three sources is represented in coordinate geometry as (0,0,0) and results in a black pixel (i.e., no light). A maximum contribution from all three sources (255,255,255) results in a total blending of the colors, producing a white pixel.

Table 10.2 summarizes the 16 most commonly used colors and the red-green-blue values needed to produce them.

If you create your own custom colors using the Control Panel, you'll notice that the Hue, Saturation, and Luminosity field values automatically change as you make changes to the Red, Green, and Blue fields. The reverse is also true.

This connection exists because these are equivalent approaches for specifying the colors to be outputted on your video monitor. In both cases, you will see cross hairs moving the target point in the colored square workspace of the window.

The three value entries for hue, saturation, and luminosity also have ranges, but they differ from the red-green-blue model because the meaning of these three factors differs. *Hue* is the primary wavelength of the light, much as you

TABLE 10.2: Red-Green-Blue Combinations for Common Colors

Red	Green	Blue	Color Produced
0	0	0	Black
0	0	128	Dark Blue
0	0	255	Bright Blue
0	128	0	Dark Green
0	255	0	Bright Green
128	0	0	Dark Red
255	0	0	Bright Red
0	128	128	Aqua
128	0	128	Purple
128	128	0	Dark Yellow
128	128	128	Dark Gray
192	192	192	Light Gray
0	255	255	Cyan
255	0	255	Magenta
255	255	0	Bright Yellow
255	255	255	White

can see differing colors in a rainbow or a prism. Each color has a different wavelength. Hue varies from 0 to 239; when you go past 239 by one, the hue wraps back to 0. In fact, if you do this, the cross hairs simply move from the right side of the square (which is red) back to the leftmost side (which is also red).

Saturation is the depth of the color; that is, how much color of a particular wavelength is to be contributed to the final pixel color. Saturation can vary from a value of 0 (which represents a grayish shade) to a value of 240 (which represents the deepest possible color).

Luminosity is the degree of brightness. You can think of this field like a window shade; that is, the closer this value is to 240, the higher up the shade is. Maximum luminosity produces white; minimum luminosity produces black. Luminosity varies along the diagonal of the cube shown in Figure 10.2.

In the next chapter, you'll learn how to control the colors of a number of desktop objects that cannot otherwise be set through the Control Panel.

ASSESSING THE PERFORMANCE IMPACT OF COLORS AND RESOLUTION

This section explains how your choice of display drivers can affect your system's performance. I'll discuss the impact on performance of two major aspects of a display driver choice: resolution and colors.

When your screen must be updated, the video driver must manage a variable number of bytes. Although the next section will discuss different ways in which the video board you choose can more effectively manage this memory, the raw number of bytes establishes the data transfer requirements. In essence, the more colors you want to see, the more data must be transferred and the slower the screen is drawn. Similarly, the higher the screen resolution is, the more overhead there is and the slower the screen draws.

The amount of memory depends on the specific number of pixels you ask your adapter and monitor to display, and on the number of different colors you want to use. VGA (640 × 480 resolution) is currently the most common standard for IBM-compatible PCs. Increasingly often, newer systems are using Super VGA (800 × 600) or 8514 (1024 × 768) resolution. Although Windows supports both higher and lower resolutions, I'll present some specific numbers for these three standards. If you're considering other possibilities, you can easily figure out the overhead involved by using the techniques explained in this section.

To represent a color, a certain number of bits are assigned to each screen pixel. The most common color alternatives for display monitors are 16 and 256. Many monitors and adapters can handle varying resolutions, as well as different numbers of colors. You make the choice based on a number of factors, from performance impact to application requirements.

If you choose a video driver that can handle 16 colors, it will use 4 bits for each pixel (i.e., $2^4 = 16$). If you choose a video driver that can handle 256 colors, it will use 8 bits for each pixel (i.e., $2^8 = 256$). By multiplying the number of bits by the number of pixels, you can determine how many bits the driver will

Speeding Up Your Graphic Redisplays

You may have your monitor set to display up to 256 colors. But if 16 colors are sufficient for you and your applications, throttle down to 16-color mode to speed things up.

If you currently use 1024 × 786 resolution, perhaps you should also consider backing down to 800 × 600 or 640 × 480. If lower resolution still works for your specific applications, you will discover a pleasing speedup in your graphic displays. The screen redisplays will appear faster, which will make everything appear to run faster.

If you don't need higher resolution or more colors, switch back to the lower resolution mode. But don't just stop there. Use a different driver that supports only the lower resolution. Simpler drivers will run faster because of less code that has to execute to decide what to do and how to do it on your screen. Typically, the simpler driver is one of the standard ones included with your Windows package rather than one that is available from your board manufacturer.

have to manage to redraw an entire Windows desktop screen. Because there are 8 bits in a byte and 1024 bytes in a kilobyte, it's easy to calculate the video memory overhead in terms of kilobytes.

For example, the most common VGA screen has 640 columns and 480 rows and uses 16 colors. Since 4 bits are required to display 16 colors, the number of bits required can be calculated as follows:

Number of bits = 640 columns * 480 rows * 4 bits

= 1,228,800 bits

= 1,228,800 / 8 bytes

= 153,600 bytes

= 153,600 / 1024 kilobytes

= 150K

Table 10.3 demonstrates a similar analysis for VGA, Super VGA, and 8514 resolutions for both 16 and 256 colors.

SUPERCHARGING WINDOWS

TABLE 10.3:   Memory Impact of Colors

Type of Display	No. of Colors	No. of Bits per Pixel	Columns × Rows	Video Memory Required
VGA	16	4	640 × 480	150K
VGA	256	8	640 × 480	300K
Super VGA	16	4	800 × 600	234.375K
Super VGA	256	8	800 × 600	468.75K
8514	16	4	800 × 600	384K
8514	256	8	1024 × 768	768K

You can discover some interesting relationships by studying Table 10.3. First, you can see that the decision to use 256-color mode always doubles the video memory overhead. A VGA screen requires 150K when the driver is displaying 16 colors, but requires 300K to show 256 colors.

♦ THE EFFECT OF AVAILABLE VIDEO RAM

The more video RAM your adapter card carries, the more opportunity you will have to use higher-resolution screen modes, like Super VGA or 8514. Additionally, with more video RAM, the card can display a larger number of colors for your applications. On the other hand, using this extra memory will slow down Windows while the video driver and the adapter card manage the extra memory.

Increasing the resolution does not have as drastic an impact on the video memory required, but it is still significant. Moving from VGA to Super VGA increases video memory overhead by 56 percent. Moving from Super VGA to 8514 resolution causes another 64 percent increase. So you will have to decide if the overhead, and subsequent slower video redraws, is worth the higher resolution or greater number of colors.

An Impressive Video Product

I like a product called More Windows from Aristosoft (510-426-5355) in Pleasanton, California. After you install it, this product replaces your current DIS-PLAY.DRV file in SYSTEM.INI. Suppose you'd like 800 × 600 screen resolution but your video card doesn't support it, or you don't like the smaller window images that appear if you install the SUPERVGA.DRV that comes as part of Windows.

I installed the driver from More Windows and suddenly, I was able to pan around an 800 × 600 screen. Only some of the screen was visible at a time, but the visible part was at the easier-to-read size of standard VGA. The panning was immediate because all the pixels are stored in system memory. The higher resolutions require extended memory to store the screen.

I like their product a lot for the video enhancement of straight VGA. There's an obvious trade-off. You can't see the larger display area at one time (i.e., all 800 × 600 pixels). But what you can see is much easier on the eyes and the panning is extremely quick. Furthermore, I could play this little trick with less expensive video boards.

CHANGING VIDEO DRIVERS

The Windows Setup option in the Main program group of the Program Manager enables you to install drivers for both differing resolutions and numbers of colors. However, it can be a burden to go through this process each time you want to switch video drivers. Once you've installed the different drivers on your hard disk, the Windows Setup procedure will make the appropriate adjustments to the Windows initialization files. Unfortunately, you'll still have to restart Windows for the changes to take effect.

A number of reasons exist, from increasing system performance to meeting individual application requirements, for why you may wish to switch screen modes regularly. It can be burdensome to follow the Windows Setup procedures each time you want to switch.

Try this process instead. Set up your system in the first mode (say, 640 × 480 VGA) that you want to use. Then create a subdirectory of your WINDOWS directory called MODE640 and copy all .INI files to that directory:

COPY C:\WINDOWS*.INI C:\WINDOWS\MODE640

Now create a batch file called RUN640.BAT and include the following two lines in it (modify the drive identifier if your WINDOWS directory is not on drive C):

COPY C:\WINDOWS\MODE640*.INI C:\WINDOWS

WIN

Repeat this process for each additional mode you plan to use, copying .INI files to other newly created subdirectories (i.e., MODE800 or MODE1024) and changing the batch file name appropriately (i.e., RUN800.BAT or RUN1024.BAT). Don't forget to change the command line in the batch file to copy .INI files from the appropriate subdirectory.

Whenever you want to run Windows in standard VGA mode, you only need to type RUN640 at the DOS command prompt. If you want to run 800 × 600 Super VGA mode, type RUN800. Don't forget to place the batch files in a directory that can be found in your DOS PATH.

◆ UNDERSTANDING VIDEO STANDARDS

In the past ten years, video standards have made great strides. In this section, you'll learn about the improvements in monitors, adapters, and video standards that have accompanied the evolution of Windows, leading to version 3.1. Table 10.4 summarizes the principal video standards that have been used by computers.

The previous section discussed issues having to do with color display, resolution, and memory. As it turns out, the latest in video adapter technology can actually minimize the impact of these issues. Although few have spent the money to acquire these latest adapter boards, it's important to know how valuable the boards can be to the performance of a Windows system.

TABLE 10.4: Summary of Video Standards

Standard	Year Introduced	Common Resolution in Pixels	Number of Colors
MDA (Monochrome Display Adapter)	1981	720 × 350	1
CGA (Color/Graphics Adapter)	1981	640 × 200	2
MGA (Hercules Monochrome Graphics Adapter)	1982	720 × 348	1
EGA (Enhanced Graphics Adapter)	1984	640 × 350	16
PGA (Professional Graphics Adapter)	1984	640 × 480	256
VGA (Video Graphics Array)	1987	640 × 480	16
MCGA (Multicolor Graphics Array)	1987	640 × 480	2
8514/A	1987	1024 × 768	256
SVGA (Super Video Graphics Array)	1989	800 × 600	16
XGA (Extended Graphics Array)	1990	1024 × 768	256
CEG (Continuous Edge Graphics)	1991	2048 × 1536	700,000

DEMYSTIFYING A DECADE OF VIDEO STANDARDS

You may have never heard of some of these so-called standards. And with good reason. Some of these standards were introduced as much for marketing reasons as for technological reasons. Computers used both MDA and CGA for a number of years. People who primarily worked with text and numbers chose the monochrome adapter because it used more pixels (9 × 14) to display each character. But it only displayed text. People who worked with graphics, such as drawings, spreadsheet graphs, or time charts, chose the color adapter. It could also display text but only in a hard-to-read 8 × 8 character box.

Nevertheless, CGA was the first graphics adapter used by the early Windows software. It permitted colorful screen displays, which became increasingly popular with users through the 1980s. As an interim improvement, Hercules Technologies developed a new adapter that could display graphics on an IBM monochrome monitor, as well as show text in more readable resolutions.

In the mid-1980s, CGA gave way to EGA, which could display both graphics and text in a readable and colorful manner. It was preferable to CGA because of its higher text resolution and ability to display more colors. But in 1987, VGA almost instantly became the preferred video standard, keeping that position into the early 1990s. It is still the most popular adapter standard for the majority of programs.

Currently, SVGA is fast becoming the most popular display standard for Windows systems. It represents a balance of increased resolution and color palette capabilities. Because the latest video adapter and driver development is aimed at these Super VGA displays, improved resolution reduces performance mimimally. However, as you might expect, the cost is in dollars rather than in system performance.

There are a number of standards shown in Table 10.4 that improve upon even SVGA. However, the burden on your system is so great that you almost certainly would require newer video adapters to make efficient use of the higher video standards. The most promising current technology is Continuous Edge Graphics, originally developed by Edsun Laboratories. This technology enhances the apparent (but not actual) screen resolution by using a technique called *anti-aliasing*. This technology not only offers a greater number of available colors but mixes the colors more effectively to produce smoother transitions between pixels. As a result, curved lines on your monitor appear smoother and more visually pleasing.

SELECTING A MONITOR FOR YOUR WINDOWS SYSTEM

Video drivers can affect your system by how they handle video memory and colors. But what about the monitor itself? You should be aware of how Windows will be affected by your monitor's dot pitch, its refresh rates, and even the video standards that it can handle.

The Impact of Dot Pitch

Just as character pitch refers to the number of characters that you can fit per inch on the printed page, *dot pitch* refers to the number of dots (or pixels) that you can fit per inch on your video monitor. To be precise, dot pitch represents the actual diameter of an individual screen dot. At any fixed screen size, the higher the screen resolution you choose, the more pixels must somehow be squeezed onto that screen.

Although the dot pitch on monitors varies greatly, you'll find that the better monitors have dots that are no larger than 0.31 millimeters each. This enables them to display Super VGA mode successfully.

Suppose you have a 14-inch monitor, which is currently the most common size. This is a diagonal measurement, so the actual horizontal width of your screen is closer to 10 inches. If you attempt to display VGA on this monitor, the adapter will attempt to display 640 dots in 10 horizontal inches, or 64 dots per inch. Since there are approximately 25.4 millimeters per inch, there are $64/25.4$, or just over 2.5, dots per millimeter.

Inverting this number leads us to the conclusion that a standard VGA monitor can have a dot pitch no greater than $1/2.5$, or 0.40, millimeters. If your monitor's dot pitch is greater than this value, you will not be able to fit a 640×480 VGA screen on it. Table 10.5 shows the same calculations for a 14-inch monitor for the three most common screen modes.

This table shows the dependence that Windows has on your monitor's capacity to display the number of pixels demanded by differing modes. To even consider using your adapter's ability to display Super VGA mode, your monitor must have a dot pitch no greater than 0.32 mm. To go beyond this

TABLE 10.5: Approximate Dot Pitch Requirements for a 14-Inch Monitor

Video Mode	Horizontal Dots per Inch	Dots per Millimeter	Maximum Pitch (in mm)
VGA (640 × 480)	64	2.52	0.40
SVGA (800 × 600)	80	3.15	0.32
8514	102	4.03	0.25

to 8514 resolution, your monitor must have a dot pitch no greater than 0.25 mm.

There are other considerations with dot pitch. While it's true that a smaller dot pitch will make the higher screen resolutions possible, your eyes may have difficulty reading the display. How many dots per inch can your eyes comfortably resolve? If you want to use the higher resolution screen modes and achieve the same readability as before, you will have no choice but to buy a larger monitor. If you attempt to use the same 14-inch monitor as before, at higher screen resolutions, there will simply be more dots per inch, and it will be harder to read.

The reason that text becomes harder to read at higher screen resolutions is that each text character in a particular font is formed from a fixed number of pixels. A VGA monitor typically constructs a text character from an array of pixels that is 9 pixels wide and 16 pixels high. When you increase screen resolution, the pixels get closer together, so the same text character (9 × 16 pixels) appears more cramped. The character takes up less area on the screen, appearing visually smaller and consequently more difficult to read. Chapter 13 discusses screen fonts and explains how to increase the size of the characters to make them more readable. A larger monitor at the higher resolutions can spread out the larger number of pixels over a larger screen, making the images larger.

Also, the smaller the dot pitch, the more separation between dots. Since adjacent dots will often have different colors, there will be less fuzziness because of visual blending of colors. Consequently, colors on a monitor with a lower dot pitch will often appear to be clearer.

The Impact of Refresh Rates

Besides considering what appears on your screen, you must also be aware of how your eye perceives the contents of your screen. In fact, it is your eye that accounts for a good deal of comfort or discomfort when you view high-resolution Windows images. The final screen appearance depends on everything I've discussed so far, and more. Your video adapter is responsible for more than just *what* appears on the screen; it also decides exactly *how* to display all those pixels.

Assuming that your monitor can handle the signals sent from the display adapter, it is the adapter's circuitry that accounts for how fast the horizontal lines are generated (the *horizontal scan rate*) and how frequently the screen is refreshed (the *vertical refresh rate*). Both of these factors, in conjunction with a biological phenomenon called *persistence of vision*, account for how "solid" (i.e., flicker-free) your screen image appears.

Your mind actually retains images for brief periods of time. This explains why a television picture appears to be a continuous image, when in reality it is only a series of 24 images, or frames, per second. This frame rate is sufficient for your brain, because each image persists for $1/24$ second, to believe that the moving picture is continuous.

Similarly, on your monitor, the entire screen is not really a solid image. Electron beams move from left to right, illuminating successive pixels with the correct color. After each row is completed, another row is begun. If your monitor is *interlaced*, all even rows are completed first before the screen's group of odd-numbered rows are begun. If your monitor is *noninterlaced*, a screenful of pixels is completely displayed in one vertical refreshing cycle.

Interlaced monitors are generally less expensive, partly because the frame rate is halved. Since the scanning beam makes two passes to create each single image, the monitor requires only half the bandwidth because it displays only half as much information during each pass. Each of these odd and even scan lines is called a *field*. Because the lines are interlaced to create a single screen image, the method is called *interlacing*.

Interlacing by itself does not have to cause flicker. However, the phosphors in the monitor must persist long enough to create a continuous image from frame to frame. In addition, the monitor must synchronize the odd and even fields properly without any overlapping. The quality of the monitor's electronics is directly responsible for the quality of the Windows desktop image.

Noninterlaced monitors create an entire screen image in one pass, reducing the reliance on synchronization and phosphor persistence. But flickering occurs even on these monitors if the frame rate is too low. The present trend is toward higher frame rates, in large part because Multimedia Windows now offers the opportunity for applications to display video on the PC. This places even more burden on the adapter and monitor to create and maintain solid screen images. Table 10.6 summarizes the current standards for scan and refresh rates.

TABLE 10.6: Video Standards for Analog Video Monitors

Video Standard	Resolution	Vertical Refresh Rate	Horizontal Scan Rate
VGA	640 × 480	60/70 Hz	31.5 kHz
SVGA	800 × 600	72 Hz	48 kHz
VESA Standard	1024 × 768	60 Hz	48 kHz
8514 and XGA	1024 × 768	88 Hz	35.5 kHz

The acronym VESA in the table stands for Video Electronics Standards Association. Formed in 1988 by NEC, it involved all major manufacturers of video cards, monitors, and computers in the setting of video standards. In addition to setting standards for current and future monitors, VESA specifies agreed-upon standards for older monitors as well.

VESA currently recommends 72 Hz as the Super VGA monitor refresh rate, but it also has defined guidelines for the new, larger monitors and higher resolutions that will become increasingly prevalent through the 1990s.

◆ VIDEO DECISIONS THAT IMPROVE PERFORMANCE

This section will place the earlier discussions in perspective. In addition to emphasizing the performance impact of each aspect already discussed, I'll explain a bit more about some of the technological features now making their way into state-of-the-art video (sometimes called *accelerator*) boards.

The term *performance* in this section refers to speed, comfort, and ease of use. You'll have to make your own decisions about cost. The recommendations in this section don't consider cost.

WHICH MONITOR?

The greater the desired screen resolution, the greater the monitor size you should consider. Trying to see 800 × 600 pixels, or 1024 × 768 pixels, on the common 14-inch screen can lead to eyestrain and headaches. Trust me, I spend a lot of time in front of my video monitor. If you can afford to upgrade, do so. If you use the higher resolution modes with Windows, you can see more windows and more of the desktop, and you will have an easier time managing your environment. But you'll need a 16-inch, 17-inch, or 19-inch monitor to avoid trading in your eyes.

◆ YOU CAN SWITCH BETWEEN TWO DISPLAYS

You can attach two monitors to your system. For example, if you are using a desktop publishing application, one can be a standard VGA or Super VGA color display (for most common applications), and the other can be a high-resolution black-and-white page display. If you are using a CAD application, one monitor can be a very high resolution color display. You do not have to reinstall Windows to switch from one application and monitor to another.

To switch monitors, select Windows Setup from the Main group in the Program Manager. Pull down the Options menu and choose Change

System Settings. At this point, you can change the settings for the display, keyboard, mouse, and network. Click on the drop-down arrow beside Display to see the list of known display drivers. Highlight the driver name you want to use, and click OK.

When you look for a replacement monitor, the best bet is to buy a noninterlaced multiscanning monitor. Look for a monitor with a broad range of scanning frequencies that cover the expected frequency standards (see Table 10.6).

◆ READABILITY ON AN LCD DISPLAY

Black characters on a white background can be difficult to see on some LCD displays. Use white characters on a black background.

HOW MANY COLORS?

Remember from the discussion earlier that the more colors you want, the more bytes must be available on your adapter card. If you're handling only black and white or gray-scale images, the less expensive cards are probably adequate. Even if you're handling simple color output, the standard VGA cards are probably adequate.

Refer to Table 10.3 to make sure that your video card has sufficient video memory to handle the number of colors you want to display. The most common video cards in use today contain 512K of video memory. This is sufficient to display 256 colors at standard VGA resolution. However, upping the resolution to 1024 × 768 means that 512K is only sufficient to display 16 colors.

◆ ADAPTER CARDS WITH 1MB OF VIDEO MEMORY ARE BETTER

One megabyte of display memory offers the greatest flexibility for using all video modes, as well as displaying up to 256 colors. Even at

Improving Readability in DOS Windows

If you've taken advantage of high-resolution video adapters to achieve 1024 × 768 Super VGA resolution but are still using a smaller monitor, you may have difficulty reading the text in a DOS application running within a 386 enhanced mode window. You can enlarge the size of the font used within a DOS application's window in two ways.

The first way is available only to Windows 3.1 users. Open your application's Control menu, choose Fonts, and select a larger screen font.

The second method requires more work but is useful for users of earlier Windows versions. First, make a backup copy of the SYSTEM.INI file. There are many vagaries associated with video monitors and boards. If this technique does not work on your system, restore the old version of SYSTEM.INI.

You'll have to obtain three files from your Windows installation disks if they are not already in your SYSTEM directory. You can use the EXPAND.EXE utility to decompress the necessary files (8514*.FON). Then, use an ASCII editor (like SYSEDIT.EXE) to modify three lines in your SYSTEM.INI file.

In the [Boot] section, make this change:

oemfont=8514oem.fon

In the [386Enh] section, make this change:

cga80woa.fon=8514fix.fon

ega80woa.fon=8514fix.fon

lower resolutions or using fewer colors, Windows 3.1 video drivers (when optimized) can take advantage of unused video memory. Large bit maps, located off screen, can be cached in this extra video memory to improve display performance.

Earlier, I discussed only 16-color (requiring 4 bits per pixel) and 256-color (requiring 8 bits per pixel) adapters. The number of bits per pixel that are required to specify a color is sometimes called the *pixel depth*. Currently, these

16- and 256-color adapters are the most common boards. However, there are boards available that can display over 16 million colors. They use 24 bits per pixel, are quite expensive, and are used only by a limited (but growing) number of Windows applications. Sometimes called *true color cards*, they are used by magazine and book publishers to provide the most accurate reproductions of color images.

The cards that use 24 bits per pixel will probably become increasingly prevalent as multimedia applications rely on improved video reproductions. However, they represent the high end of both performance and cost. Personally, I have trouble picking out the colors of my ties, so 16-color boards will probably be good enough for me for a while.

WHAT ABOUT THE ADAPTER'S VIDEO MEMORY?

So far, I've talked only about the amount of video memory required to create a certain screen resolution or to apply a particular color to a particular pixel. As your screen is refreshed, the screen image actually resides in the video memory on your adapter card. The frame rate (e.g., 72 Hz, or 72 times per second) specifies how many times per second the data in your card's video memory is transmitted from the PC to the screen.

There are fast RAM chips, and there are slow RAM chips. This is just as true for video board RAM as for motherboard RAM. The most common, and least expensive, RAM is dynamic RAM, or DRAM. The least common, and most expensive alternative, is video RAM, or VRAM.

RAM chips require a voltage pulse from the adapter card to maintain the integrity of the information stored on the card. On a DRAM chip, data cannot be read or written during the voltage pulse cycle. This means that there will be unused waiting time, increasing the total time needed to redraw any Windows screen.

VRAM, on the other hand, uses a special, dual-ported architecture, which allows the card's controller to access data even while the voltage pulse is being supplied. Consequently, VRAM chips eliminate the DRAM data bottleneck. If you are moving toward using high-resolution Windows modes or enhanced

Upgrading Your Video Board

Windows is intensively graphical. Consequently, selecting the right video board for your monitor has a dramatic impact on the quality of your display. Consider these issues as you decide on a new video board to improve your Windows system:

♦ Make sure the drivers are optimized for Windows 3.1. This latest release can improve performance by permitting available memory to cache off-screen bit maps.

♦ Make sure the board supports 1MB of on-board display memory. This will sustain the current highest PC display resolution of 1024 × 768 with 256 colors.

♦ Minimize flicker by choosing a board that supports the VESA standard 72-MHz refresh rate.

♦ Select boards that use VRAM rather than the slower DRAM.

♦ Select a graphics accelerator card that includes a graphics coprocessor or other circuitry that is enhanced for managing common graphics commands. This is the most expensive option but the one that can most significantly improve graphic redisplays.

color applications, make sure that your video adapter card uses VRAM chips. But be prepared to spend some bucks.

WHAT ABOUT A GRAPHICS COPROCESSOR?

Depending on your application, you can experience dramatic gains if your video card has its own coprocessor. This is particularly true for applications that create, use, or display the vector graphic images discussed earlier in this chapter.

Why can a graphics coprocessor be so beneficial in many graphical environments? Because the graphics coprocessor is optimized for certain graphical tasks, such as computing the pixels that must be illuminated to display a circle, a line, or other mathematically defined geometric objects. CAD programs often fill solid objects and transform graphic images by rotating, bending, or stretching them. If the video board contains a coprocessor, your CPU does not have to do this work.

If the video card does not have its own coprocessor, the CPU must not only generate all images but it must send all the generated pixels to the video board's memory. This typically occurs on a slow, 16-bit, 8-MHz bus. It's better to let the CPU get on with other multitasking chores while the coprocessor handles drawing chores.

Remember that the graphics coprocessor is a relatively new enhancement in the Windows environment. The board may have a coprocessor but your application may not know how to use it. Be sure that your applications have the necessary drivers to use a coprocessor.

WHAT ABOUT CONTINUOUS EDGE GRAPHICS?

Continuous Edge Graphics (CEG) is one of the latest buzzwords in the Windows arena. A number of board manufacturers are beginning to incorporate this new technology, first developed by Edsun Laboratories. Although CEG does not enhance speed, it does enhance appearance. For example, you may be familiar with the staircase effect that occurs with graphics that have curves. Since a video monitor actually displays all images as a set of pixels, this means that all curves are represented on your monitor as a group of carefully specified dots.

The greater the curvature of the line that is to be drawn, the greater the likelihood that the image's boundaries, or edges, will appear jagged. These rough edges are dramatically improved by Edsun's anti-aliasing technology, which blends the colors of all pixels that are located on the image's edges. Careful selection of the colors along an image's edges can create a smoother appearance.

For example, you can make a black curved line on a white background appear smoother by using a blended gray color for pixels along the rounded edges. Continuous Edge Graphics boards can create much smoother screen images with no other impact on performance. If your applications rely on high-quality presentations, look for a CEG-based board.

This finishes the second part of this book, in which I concentrated on running applications and displaying Windows screens most effectively. Now turn to Part III, which offers a number of tips and techniques for customizing the environment in which you run your applications.

P   A   R   T

Customizing
Windows

Part III has all you need to know to customize Windows to suit your own tastes. Chapter 11 discusses techniques to personalize your desktop and customize your hardware. Chapter 12 offers a wide range of techniques for controlling the Windows environment by making changes to the WIN.INI and SYSTEM.INI files. Chapter 13 focuses on issues related to fonts (including TrueType) and printing.

◆

C H A P T E R

11

*Personalizing the Desktop
and Customizing Hardware*

This chapter focuses on making the Windows desktop a personal place. You will learn many tricks, primarily available through the Control Panel facilities, for making your work environment a unique one. This will include information about colors, icons, windows, and much more. The Control Panel is shown in Figure 11.1. You will also learn how to use your system's multimedia hardware to incorporate special effects into your desktop.

◆ USING THE DESKTOP ICON

Some of us like messy desks; others must have neat desks. In the Windows environment, some people like to have only one window open at a time to be able to concentrate on one application. Others like multiple windows to stare them in the face, separately positioned and sized. For them, the ability to switch quickly from one open window to another may also be important. Furthermore, some people like to cascade their open windows, and other people like to tile their windows. The choices are yours. This section discusses some of the special customization options for windows and icons.

Selecting the Desktop icon from the Control Panel brings up the dialog box shown in Figure 11.2. It controls many useful aspects of your desktop's configuration and appearance. I'll discuss some of the less obvious aspects of this icon in this section. I'll also explain the image of Yosemite that appears in the background of the desktop shown in Figure 11.2.

DRESSING UP THE BACKGROUND OF YOUR DESKTOP

The first section, Pattern, of the Desktop dialog box offers you the opportunity to replace the plain solid background on your desktop with a repeating pattern. The fourth section, Wallpaper, offers you the opportunity to replace the solid background with a detailed graphic image found in a bit-map file. Using a pattern requires less memory and takes less time to be generated than a detailed bit-map image.

Displaying a Two-Color Pattern as the Screen Background

To choose one of Windows' existing patterns, just click on the down arrow to the right of the Name field in the Pattern section. A list box will appear that

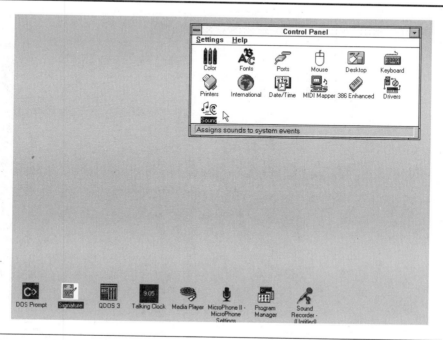

FIGURE 11.1: The Control Panel

contains all Windows 3.1 patterns on your system. Instead of just selecting and accepting one of these patterns, you can click on the Edit Pattern button if you wish to edit an existing pattern or create a completely new one. Figure 11.3 shows the Edit Pattern dialog box that appears when you click on the Edit Pattern button.

After creating or editing the pattern, click on the Add button to add your newly edited pattern to the list of available patterns and to make it the currently selected one. A pattern such as Checkmarks in Figure 11.3 can use only two colors. The pattern's background color takes on the desktop color, and the pattern's foreground color takes on the color of Window Text. (This is the color used by Windows to display text characters in an application window.) Later in this chapter, you'll learn how to adjust the colors of all portions of your screen. There are many more screen elements beyond Desktop and Window Text to which you can assign colors.

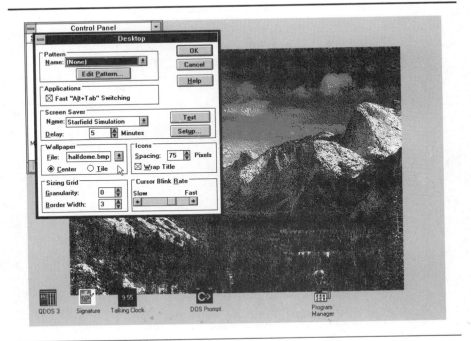

FIGURE 11.2: The Desktop dialog box

As Figure 11.3 suggests, the pattern you create or edit in the center of the Edit Pattern dialog box will be repeated over and over again on your desktop behind any application windows. A sample repeating image is shown on the left side of the dialog box.

Displaying a Multicolor Image as the Screen Background

The Wallpaper section of the Desktop dialog box enables you to use any existing .BMP file as a screen background. Remember that the Windows Paintbrush accessory program can create color bit-map images from scratch. Additionally, the Paintshop program included with this book's second disk can convert graphic image files from other formats into the required .BMP format. Furthermore, remember that you must store all .BMP files that you want to use as wallpaper in your WINDOWS directory.

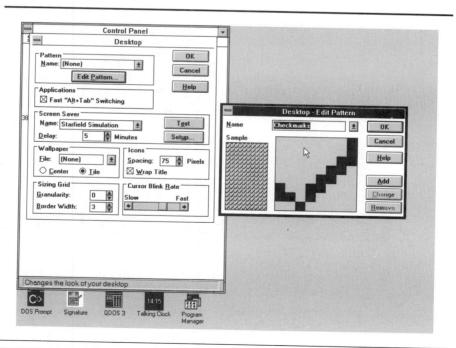

FIGURE 11.3: The Edit Pattern dialog box

Whether you create or acquire a graphic image file, you will sometimes have the opportunity to specify the height and width of the image. To create or convert an image in the best proportions for your screen, you have to know how many pixels are used in your video system. Table 11.1 summarizes the standard graphic image sizes in the most common video configurations.

TABLE 11.1: Common Graphic Image Sizes

Video Configuration	Width × Height (in pixels)
8514	1024 × 768
CGA	640 × 200
EGA	640 × 350
Hercules	720 × 348
MCGA	320 × 200
Super VGA	800 × 600
VGA	640 × 480

To select a bit-map file to use as wallpaper, click on the list-box down arrow to the right of the File field in the Wallpaper section. Highlight any .BMP file name you would want to use in the list that appears. After closing the Desktop dialog box by clicking on OK, the solid desktop will be replaced by your selected graphic image. If you choose the Center radio button, the graphic will appear only once in the center of the screen. If you choose Tile, the graphic image will be repeated as many times as necessary to cover the entire desktop.

◆ MAKE A BIT-MAP FILE INTO WALLPAPER

You can turn any bit-map file into centered or tiled wallpaper. The easiest way to do this is to begin by copying or moving the .BMP file into the WINDOWS directory. Then, open the Control Panel in the Main group of the Program Manager. Double-click on Desktop and enter a name for the file in the Wallpaper File field. (You can click on the down arrow to display a list box that contains the names of all .BMP files in the

> WINDOWS directory.) Click on OK and your newly selected wallpaper immediately appears on your desktop.

Notice in Figure 11.2 how I've already selected the HALFDOME.BMP file as my desktop's wallpaper file. Since the image was originally created as a 640 × 480 VGA image, it doesn't fill my entire 800 × 600 Super VGA screen. To ensure that a wallpaper image completely fills your screen, you must create or obtain an image in the exact size of your screen. Alternatively, you can select a simple image that will look all right when repeated; then choose the Tile button.

But using wallpaper is not without cost. An entire bit-map image consumes a chunk of memory, whose size depends on the detail and color of the image. Also, the larger the original image or the more colors used (e.g., 256 instead of 16), the more memory will be required to restore the image during screen redraws. Reproducing detailed images takes more time than merely producing a solid background. As I pointed out in Chapter 10, you can also use the Color icon in the Control Panel to produce a solid, colored background that will not burden your system in either time or memory.

SWITCHING QUICKLY BETWEEN APPLICATIONS

Windows 3.1 offers a special Applications section near the top of the Desktop dialog box. It contains one check box, which controls which method is used to switch between tasks when you press the Alt+Tab key combination. If the box is unchecked, then pressing Alt+Tab cycles among all active tasks. The title bar of the application appears, or a minimized icon is highlighted. Releasing the Alt key automatically switches you to the application whose name or icon label was last displayed.

In previous versions of Windows, this technique was the fastest one available for switching from one application to another. The new method is faster still. When the Fast "Alt+Tab" Switching box is checked, you can cycle through the active tasks by holding down the Alt key and pressing Tab successively. This produces a small window in the center of your screen that

SUPERCHARGING WINDOWS

successively lists the names of the active tasks and displays each one's desktop icon. Figure 11.4 shows an example.

This technique only works if you are actively using a Windows application when you begin the Alt+Tab sequence. If you are using a DOS application when you start an Alt+Tab sequence, you see the same pattern of highlighted title bars as you do in Windows 3.0. However, in either case, you can decide to return to the active application by simply pressing Escape before releasing the Alt key.

♦ HOT KEY TO YOUR FAVORITE WINDOWS APPLICATION

In Windows 3.1 you can set up a shortcut (hot) key to switch quickly from one task to another. This includes both non-Windows applications and

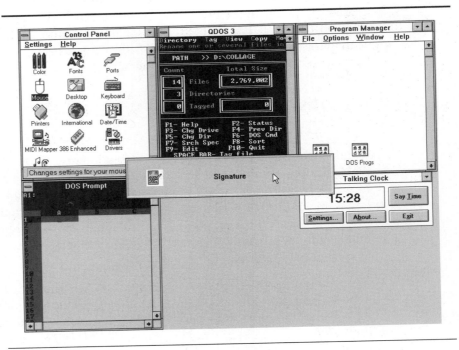

FIGURE 11.4: Fast application switching in Windows 3.1

Creating a New Program Item without Typing

No, you needn't type anything to establish new program item icons in the Program Manager. You can use the File Manager to help you do it. Follow these instructions:

1. Minimize all applications except the Program Manager and File Manager.

2. In the File Manager, highlight any .PIF, .EXE, .BAT, or .COM file names in any directory.

3. Display the Windows Task List (press Ctrl+Esc), then choose Tile. This splits the screen between the File Manager and Program Manager.

4. Move the mouse pointer to the highlighted file name in the File Manager, hold down the left mouse button, and drag the file's reverse video icon into any group you like in the Program Manager's window.

5. Release the mouse button and Windows does the rest. It creates a new program item, along with all necessary field entries.

Windows applications. Earlier versions of Windows offered this feature for DOS applications only in 386 enhanced mode, via the Advanced portion of a PIF. To assign a shortcut key to any task, you only need to click in the Shortcut Key field of the Program Item Properties dialog box and press any desired hot key combination. Click on OK. Whenever the program for this icon runs, you can switch to it by pressing your specified shortcut key.

ADJUSTING ICON SPACING

There are two reasons for wanting to change the spacing of desktop icons. First, you may have a lot of them and want them all to appear on the bottom row of your screen. If the space between each icon is too great, and they cannot fit on the bottom row, Windows will simply start a new row of icons just above the existing one. This reduces your total usable desktop. You can reduce the separation between icons by lowering the Spacing value in the Icons section of the Desktop dialog box.

On the other hand, if you have long labels, reducing the space between icons may cause some labels to overlap. You can partially deal with this by checking the Wrap Title box in the Icons section. This tells Windows to use more than one line for an icon's label, as necessary. You may have to adjust the icon spacing, as well as some of your icon titles, to obtain a satisfactory screen appearance.

The settings will affect both the desktop icons and the icons in the Program Manager's program groups. You can adjust spacing from as little as 32 pixels (i.e., the width of an icon) to as many as 512 pixels. Naturally, if you make the spacing too narrow, the icons will be smashed up against each other and all titles will be difficult to read. If you make the spacing too great, you'll wind up with very few icons per line and lots of wasted space on your desktop. It pays to experiment.

The new spacing will appear on the desktop after you select Arrange Icons from the Task List. The new spacing will appear inside each Program Manager's program group after you pull down the Window menu and select Arrange Icons for that group.

DEFINING THE INVISIBLE DESKTOP GRID

The Sizing Grid section at the bottom of the Desktop dialog box has two important settings, which influence both appearance and speed. The Granularity setting is normally equal to zero, which allows you to move desktop windows and icons anywhere on the screen. This setting applies only to application windows and icons; it does not apply to child (or document) windows within applications.

When Granularity is set to something other than zero, an invisible grid is placed on your screen. When you move or size windows and icons, they will automatically be positioned on the closest grid lines. This is called *snapping* to the grid, a technique often used in computer-aided design applications, in which precise alignment of elements is critical.

Selecting Your Own Icons for Your Programs

Some applications come with their own colorful icons. However, others do not, and the Program Manager usually assigns default icons to these applications. You can change the default icon by pulling down the File menu, selecting Properties, then choosing Change Icon from the Program Item Properties dialog box.

If the current file from which the existing icon was chosen (most often PROG-MAN.EXE) has other icons, you can scroll through them to choose a new one for your application. You can also choose a new icon from any other disk file that contains a usable icon. Just type in a different entry in the File Name field, including a complete path to the file if it cannot be found in the current PATH. Select OK and the Program Manager will display all icons that are in the file you specify.

After you highlight one of these displayed icons and choose OK, the Program Manager will replace the existing program item icon with the icon you just selected. This procedure has no effect on the file that provides the icon. A copy of the selected icon is simply attached to the program item entry in the Program Manager group.

The granularity number can be adjusted from 0 to 49, with each numeric increase representing an additional eight pixels in grid separation. A granularity value of 3, for instance, means that all icons and windows will align themselves on the invisible grid lines that are laid across the screen at separations of 24 pixels (3 × 8).

◆ SPEED UP WINDOW MOVES

Internally, Windows uses bit block transfers when you move a window on the screen. This particular operation proceeds much faster if windows are aligned on byte boundaries (i.e., every eight pixels). Windows needn't perform any bit shifting within display bytes. To make your window moving faster and smoother, open Desktop from the Control Panel, set the Granularity option to 1, and click on OK. This improvement will be most noticeable if you have a very high resolution monitor.

The Border Width field in the Sizing Grid section controls the thickness of window borders. If you do a lot of window sizing, thicker borders can make it easier to place your mouse pointer on the borders to size the windows.

◆ CUSTOMIZING THE PROGRAM MANAGER ICONS

This section offers some clever and helpful techniques for personalizing your Program Manager window.

LET PROGRAM MANAGER ARRANGE YOUR ICONS

You can always arrange your own icons, both on the desktop and in the Program Manager. However, if you frequently move icons and size windows, you will save yourself effort by letting the Program Manager arrange your program group icons. Just check the Auto Arrange option on the Option pull-down menu. Whenever you open any program group or resize a group window, the Program Manager will lay out all icons in neat rows and columns. This will often enable you to see and access an icon that might not even be visible in a smaller group window.

CREATE A CUSTOM GROUP FOR FREQUENT APPLICATIONS

After you use Windows for a while, you'll probably know which applications you use most. Put these in one program group so that you can quickly select them, since all the icons will appear in a single window.

If you use more than one data file with a particular application, create a separate icon for each file and application combination. In that way, your custom group offers an easy way to start not only a favorite application but a frequently used data file as well.

Specifying a Working Directory for Any Application

In Windows 3.1 you can explicitly define a working directory for any application. This includes both non-Windows applications and Windows applications.

To specify a working directory for an application that is run from a Program Manager icon, you only need to make an entry in the Working Directory field of the Program Item Properties dialog box. This box appears whenever you add a new program item from the File menu of the Program Manager, or whenever you select Properties for an existing program item icon.

Click on the Working Directory field, or tab to it, and type in the path name to the desired directory. Click on OK and you're done. Whenever the underlying program for this icon runs, the Program Manager will ensure that the current directory is the one you entered.

If you use an earlier version of Windows, you can, with a little effort, create the same effect. Assuming that the application itself can be found in the PATH, you enter into the Command Line field the name of the application, but prefixed by the desired working directory. For example, to set the working directory to C:\BUSINESS but actually run the WRITE.EXE program, you enter C:\BUSINESS\WRITE.EXE in the Command Line field of the earlier Windows dialog box.

As your favorite applications and data files change, keep this custom group updated. Delete icons that are no longer necessary, and update the program item properties as necessary.

◆ SHORTEN ICON NAMES

Why clutter your desktop with icons whose descriptions are long, tedious, and unnecessary? Reduce the number of characters in an icon's label, both in the Program Manager and on the desktop. To shorten an icon name, find the icon in its group within the Program Manager. Pull down the File menu, select Properties, type a shorter name in the Descriptions field, and click on OK.

CHANGE THE LOOK OF YOUR APPLICATION ICONS

Icons are fun. By themselves, they're no big deal. But many people simply enjoy using a computer that has a colorful screen interface. The work gets done by applications, and you can start them in a variety of ways. If you're like me, it's simply more entertaining to represent the applications with colorful icons. You hardly even have to read the icon label to know which one to click on.

This book's second disk includes the very useful ICONMSTR.EXE program. With this program, you can create new icons from scratch or modify existing ones. The program offers a wide range of tools for displaying icons (in separate .ICO files or within .EXE files) as well as editing them.

ICONMSTR.EXE also offers the ability to extract one or more icons from existing .EXE files and then create individualized .ICO files. This opens up a unique opportunity. Your Windows system includes a large number of hidden icons that can be used to create new program item icons in the Program Manager. These icons are within a number of Windows .EXE files, such as the Accessory program files.

Most accessories, like CALC.EXE or CALENDAR.EXE, contain only one icon. However, four .EXE files contain multiple icons: PROGMAN.EXE, SETUP.EXE, TUTOR.EXE, and WINFILE.EXE. Remember that you can attach any icon found in an .EXE or .ICO file to a new program item in a Program Manager group.

Although you can use the Browse feature of the Program Item Properties dialog box, it would be easier if all icons were separated into individually named .ICO files. You can do that with the IconMaster program. To demonstrate the results, I created a WINICONS directory on my disk and used ICONMSTR.EXE to extract all the hidden icons from my Windows files

Launching and Loading with One Icon

Do you typically use the same file with a particular Windows application? If so, why bother loading that file each time you run the application. Create a unique icon in the Program Manager that both runs the application and simultaneously loads the file.

Pull down the File menu, select New, and choose Program Item. In the Command Line field, type the name of the application and the name of the data file. For example, to load the REPORT.WRI file when running WRITE.EXE, type

WRITE.EXE REPORT.WRI

Depending on how your PATH is set up, and the location of both the executable program and the data file, you may need to prefix one or both of these names with drive and path-name information. For example:

D:\WINDOWS\WRITE.EXE C:\BUSINESS\REPORT.WRI

into separately named .ICO files. Figure 11.5 depicts the IconMaster display of more than 75 hidden Windows icons that can be used.

To create each of these separate icons, I first used the Open EXE/DLL command found on IconMaster's File menu. Then, upon discovering Windows .EXE files that contained multiple icons, I successively highlighted each icon. Next, I used the Copy To command on the Icon menu to create a uniquely named .ICO file that contained only that single icon. Finally, to display Figure 11.5, I opened all the newly created .ICO files in the WINICONS directory.

You can spend a few minutes on your own system to follow the same procedure. Afterward, you'll have ready access to each of these colorful icons for creating your own useful and entertaining program groups. Furthermore, as you develop your program groups in Windows 3.1, you can assign application shortcut keys to any (Windows or non-Windows) application to facilitate quick switching.

◆ CONTROLLING YOUR DESKTOP'S COLORS

If you do nothing special, many of the standard aspects of your desktop will appear in plain black, gray, or white. This is true even if you have a color monitor. The primary way in which you can make color changes is to select the Color icon in the Control Panel, which displays the Color dialog box shown in Figure 11.6. In Chapter 10 you learned how to create custom colors for any aspect of your desktop by clicking on the Color Palette button at the bottom of the Color dialog box. This permits you to select one of the existing Windows colors or to create your own red-green-blue custom color.

It's simple to change the tone of your screen by applying a different predefined scheme of colors to your desktop. To apply a scheme of colors to all desktop

FIGURE 11.5: Windows contains many hidden icons.

colors, you can choose one of the predefined color sets from the Color Schemes drop-down list box (in the upper-left corner).

But you may want your desktop to be unique—you can apply personally selected colors to separate desktop elements. First, notice that on the left side of the Color dialog box, there is a simulated screen display. This miniaturized display has an active and inactive window, as well as certain window features, like a menu bar and a scroll bar.

To assign a different color to a particular screen element, you can just click on the element in the miniaturized screen area, then click on the desired color in the right side of the window. Do this for every screen element, then click on the OK button. The desktop will be redrawn with your color combination, which will be retained for subsequent Windows sessions (they are stored in your WIN.INI file). You'll learn more about these stored settings in the next chapter.

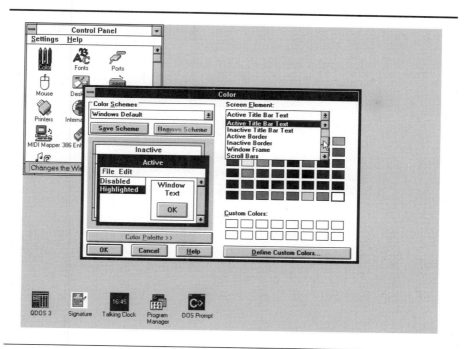

FIGURE 11.6: The Color dialog box

If you don't like the new colors, just select the Color icon from the Control Panel again and change colors. You can restore the original desktop colors by choosing Windows Default from the list box in the Color Schemes section.

On the other hand, if you've created a nice combination of screen colors, you can save it under a new name. Just click on the Save Scheme button near the upper-left portion of the dialog box. You'll be asked to type in a name (or you can type over an existing name.) Then click the OK button.

If you would rather not click on a screen element on the left side of the Color dialog box, you can also open up the list box in the Screen Element section, which displays the name of each screen element. When you select one of these names, the screen element in the miniaturized screen is highlighted, just as if you had clicked on it directly. In fact, this method is somewhat easier because it can be cumbersome to select between certain screen elements in the miniaturized display.

In particular, if you click on the word Highlighted more than once, Windows will alternate between selecting the highlighted text characters themselves and the background color behind the highlighted text. The Highlighted Text screen element applies to both highlighted text and menu commands. The screen element named Highlight represents the color assigned to the background pixels that lie behind highlighted text or menu commands.

When you click, the name of the selected screen element will appear in the Screen Element list box. In a similar way, you can click on the OK button in the miniaturized screen. (Be careful not to click on the OK button at the bottom of the Color dialog box. This will exit you from the dialog box.) As you click, Windows will alternate between selecting colors for the button's face, its shadow, its background pixels, and its text.

In the next chapter, you'll learn that each of these separate screen elements is assigned a keyword. You can discover the precise numeric settings for these screen colors by looking in the [colors] section of the WIN.INI file. This is actually where your selections are stored between sessions.

Tips for Customizing Screen Colors

Here are some tips for customizing the colors on your screen:

◆ Select only solid colors for your screen elements. Windows will be able to update your screen faster. The Windows Default color scheme uses only solid colors.

◆ Use an LCD scheme for laptop computers that have LCD displays. This prevents reverse video difficulties in viewing certain screen elements.

◆ Use a Plasma Power Saver color scheme for plasma displays. The darker colors in this scheme draw less power than livelier colors.

◆ To speed up screen redraws, choose the same color for both active and inactive borders. Note, however, that this will make it more difficult to tell at a glance which application is in the foreground.

◆ CUSTOMIZING PORTS, THE KEYBOARD, AND THE MOUSE

Three remaining icons in the Control Panel enable you to customize the settings of some of your system's hardware. To adjust your mouse, keyboard, and serial ports, just click on the appropriate icon and make any adjustments. You may only use these controls occasionally, so you will probably set them only once.

CONFIGURING YOUR SERIAL PORTS

Serial ports under DOS are used for a variety of communications devices. On my system I use one port for my modem, a second for a mouse, a third for a plotter, and a fourth for a fax card. On a DOS system, you can use no more than four ports, named COM1 to COM4. To configure your serial port for your equipment, choose the Ports icon from the Control Panel. Figure 11.7 shows the Advanced Settings for COM1 dialog box.

Nearly every serial device has its own unique requirements. The standard settings are displayed in the Settings box and include such things as the baud rate and the number of data bits, parity bits, and stop bits. The documentation for your serial device includes the values that you should set here. For example, a modem might have a baud rate of 2400, and a plotter might have a rate of 9600.

If you have a plain-vanilla system, without many add-in boards, the advanced settings are probably OK. However, when you start adding extra boards to the typical DOS system, you will often need to adjust the settings in the Advanced Settings dialog box. The documentation for your add-in board or external serial device contains the specifications for your device.

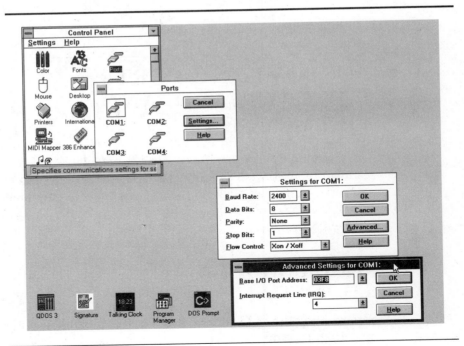

FIGURE 11.7: The Advanced Settings for COM1 dialog box, which allows you to customize serial port settings

Do You Have Fewer Serial Ports Than Serial Devices?

Suppose that you have one serial port and share it between a printer and a modem, or between a mouse and a plotter in a DOS CAD session. In each case, you can successfully use the serial port for the two separate devices at different times. This probably requires switching cables or using a switch box.

Does this situation apply to you? Not everybody can afford to add another serial port. Sometimes, you don't have another slot. Or you may not have an available interrupt for another COM port and may be forced into sharing ports.

Individual serial port programs usually have their own communications settings. Since these will override the values set in the Control Panel, you can set the Control Panel for one device and then set the individual program's serial port values for the other device. When you switch to the program that uses the serial port in a different way, it will temporarily change the port values. The values will revert to those specified in the Control Panel when the overriding program closes.

One of the most common problems when installing new serial equipment has to do with overlapping use of interrupts. Check your device's documentation to be sure of the base port I/O address used by the device's driver. Then check what interrupt it will use. Next, bring up the Advanced Settings box to be sure that the Windows default is correct for your device.

If the device's standard port address or IRQ (interrupt request) assignment is already being used by another device, you may need to make changes in this dialog box. In addition, you may need to make adjustments to your hardware itself. Refer to your serial device's documentation for explanations of whether you must make hardware switch or jumper changes. You may be able to make changes through some utility program included with your equipment.

MAKING MOUSE AND KEYBOARD ADJUSTMENTS

Although I ignored it earlier when I first discussed the Desktop dialog box, you can also adjust the cursor blink rate. To do so, in the Cursor Blink Rate section, just move the slider box to the right or to the left to speed up or to slow down the rate at which your screen cursor blinks.

There are separate icons in the Control Panel for customizing your mouse and your keyboard. Choosing the Keyboard icon brings up the Keyboard dialog box, shown in Figure 11.8. This dialog box controls how fast Windows processes repetitive key presses. When you hold down a key, there is usually a time lag before you begin to see repetitions on the screen of the character pressed. This is called Delay Before First Repeat. Once a key begins repeating, it repeats at a certain rate (number of characters per second). This is called Repeat Rate. You can adjust both of these values by moving the appropriate slider box in the dialog box. The Test field is provided for you to test your settings. Just click in the Test field and then type any keyboard character. You

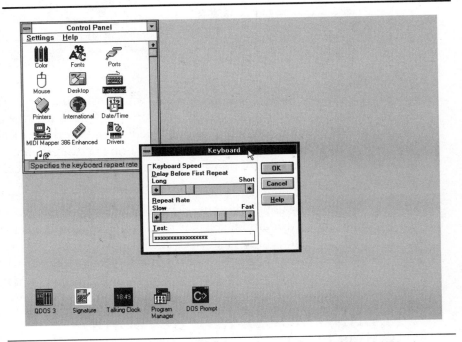

FIGURE 11.8: The Keyboard dialog box, which allows you to adjust the keyboard's repeat rate

will immediately be able to see how long it takes before repetitions begin (the delay time) and how much time occurs before each automatically repeated character appears (the repetition rate).

In a similar way, you can customize the settings for your pointing device. Selecting the Mouse icon in the Control Panel displays the Mouse dialog box, shown in Figure 11.9. The contents of this dialog box vary according to the type of mouse in your system. Figure 11.9 shows the standard set of options available for a Microsoft-compatible mouse.

The most frequently used option in this dialog box is the check box marked Swap Left/Right Buttons. By checking this box, you can reverse the functionality of the mouse buttons: The primary button for selecting and dragging becomes the right one instead of the left one. Many people who are left-handed prefer to swap buttons.

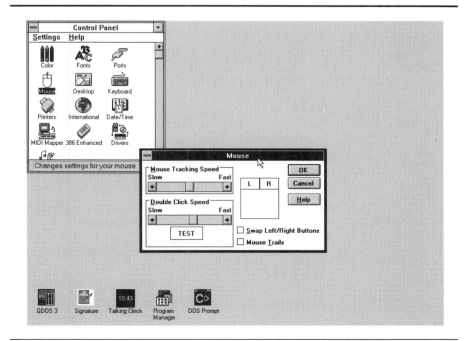

FIGURE 11.9: The Mouse dialog box

You can control how fast the screen mouse pointer reacts to the movement of your mouse on the desk surface by adjusting the slider box in the Mouse Tracking Speed field. You can similarly adjust the amount of time required to identify a double click by moving the slider box in the Double Click Speed field. Try this now by first trying to double-click in the Test rectangle. If your clicks are recognized as a legitimate double click, the Test box will reverse colors (text and background will switch). How sensitive Windows is to the time between the two successive clicks is set here. If your finger speed is on the slow side, you should move the slider box to the left so that Windows will still be able to recognize your double clicks.

The Mouse Trails check box is a useful toggle if you have a screen that makes it difficult to easily identify the location of the mouse (this is especially true with LCD monitors). As soon as you check this box, you will begin to see a trail of mouse pointer icons behind the actual position of the mouse as you move it around the screen.

◆ CUSTOMIZING YOUR MULTIMEDIA HARDWARE

In Windows 3.1, there are two new multimedia accessory programs, known as the Sound Recorder and the Media Player (you learned about them in Chapter 6). In this section, you'll learn about some of the additional facilities found in the Control Panel for manipulating sounds in your Windows system. Exactly which icons appear and what customizing capability you have depends on your hardware.

During your Windows Setup procedure, the installation program determines as much about your hardware as possible. However, not all hardware is recognized and configured for Windows automatically. Furthermore, you will probably be adding new equipment from time to time. For example, on my computer there are no free slots. My Sound Blaster Pro card was the last one I added, and it was difficult to decide which devices would use which interrupts. This was a problem because the Sound Blaster card's default values were already in use by other equipment.

ADD THE MULTIMEDIA SOUND DRIVERS FIRST

To make the Sound Blaster Pro card work, I first had to add a driver to Windows. Windows 3.1 includes a choice of drivers, but you must add and configure the ones for your hardware. After selecting the Drivers icon in the Control Panel, the Drivers dialog box appears (shown in the upper-left portion of Figure 11.10). It shows a list of already installed drivers. At this point, you can choose the Add button to install additional drivers, as shown in the Add dialog box.

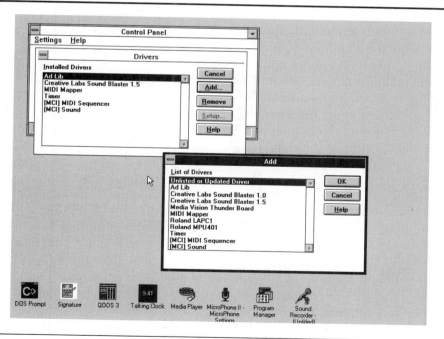

FIGURE 11.10: Adding a sound card driver

You can choose the first entry, Unlisted or Updated Driver, to install a driver that is not listed here or to install a newer driver than the one found in your Windows 3.1 system. But do not remove any of the drivers that you already find listed in the Drivers dialog box. These are automatically installed by the Setup program and are needed by Windows 3.1.

Other drivers for MIDI devices appear on this list. Select each device that is connected to your system. After adding a driver for each device, you can configure that device by choosing the Setup button in the Drivers dialog box when the desired driver name is highlighted.

As an example, Figure 11.11 depicts the dialog box that appears when you set up a Sound Blaster card. You must specify which one of several possible port addresses is being used, as well as which of several possible interrupts will be used. This is essential to do if you have changed the hardware settings of these values from the device's defaults.

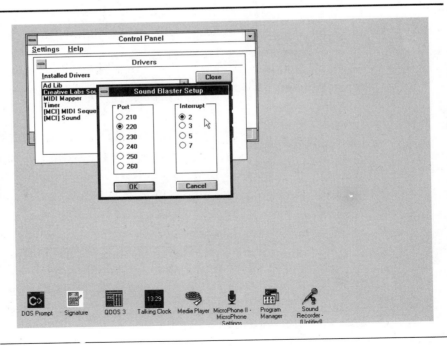

FIGURE 11.11: Configuring an individual driver

In a similar way, setting up the MCI Sound driver name will display a dialog box titled MCI Waveform Driver Setup. You indicate how many seconds of audio data are to be buffered during playback or record operations. Your choice has a direct impact on memory, since the more seconds of sound information you retain, the more memory is required to store it. Each driver has its own unique setup dialog box.

USING SOUND EFFECTS IN YOUR SYSTEM

One of the most useful and entertaining aspects of Windows 3.1 multimedia support has to do with using sound. Once you have properly installed a sound board, and installed and configured the necessary Windows driver, you can assign different sound effects to different system or application events. For example, you can ask Windows to sound a musical chord each time an Exclamation box appears. Figure 11.12 shows the Sound dialog box, which appears when you select the Sound icon from the Control Panel.

Sound effects are stored in .WAV files and are used by both Windows and your applications. As you can see in Figure 11.12, you can assign a sound effect to be played automatically each time Windows starts up and each time you exit from Windows. In addition, five separate events can have associated sound effects. These events mark Windows actions, such as critical stops or the display of Exclamation boxes. At other times, an application can play a sound effect that is assigned to one of these system events. This often happens when an application triggers a warning event. Typically, this sounds only a single beep through the PC speaker. Now you can dress up your Windows system with a variety of interesting sound effects.

To enable system sound effects, check the box labeled Enable System Sounds in the Sound dialog box. If this box is unchecked, all Windows sounds will be inhibited.

To assign individual sounds to specific events, first click on the desired event, then click on the desired sound-wave file. Finally, click on OK. Try it yourself now if you have a sound card on your system. You can click on the Test button to immediately hear each sound effect through the board. If you later wish to turn off the sound effects for a particular event only, you should select the desired event in the Sound dialog box, but choose <none> in the Files list box.

CUSTOMIZING MIDI DEVICES FOR SOUND EFFECTS

During your Windows installation, Setup installs a series of standard MIDI device settings. These standards adhere to the guidelines put forth by Microsoft for MIDI synthesizers, and include values for channel settings, instrument patch settings, and key assignments. The MIDI Mapper icon in the Control Panel enables you to modify these default assignments in a variety of ways. This will be necessary if your system includes an external MIDI synthesizer that does not support the General MIDI guidelines.

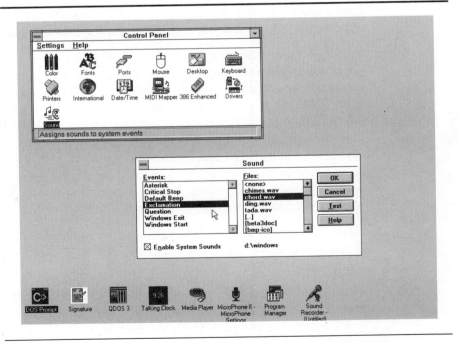

FIGURE 11.12: The Sound dialog box, which you use to assign sound effects to system events

Selecting a Standard MIDI Setup

If you will be running MIDI applications, you should already understand MIDI concepts and terminology. This book does not go any further than the discussions in this chapter and in Chapter 6 toward explaining MIDI operations under Windows 3.1. In Chapter 6, you learned how to use the Media Player. In this section, you will learn how to customize your Windows system for running multimedia applications.

To play MIDI files, you will need to first select a MIDI setup for your synthesizer. To do this, first choose the MIDI Mapper icon from the Control Panel. Then, after making sure that the radio button to the left of Setups is selected, click on the Name list box arrow. This opens up the available setups, as shown in Figure 11.13. Select one to use and click on the list-box scroll arrow again. The description for that setup will automatically appear below the name.

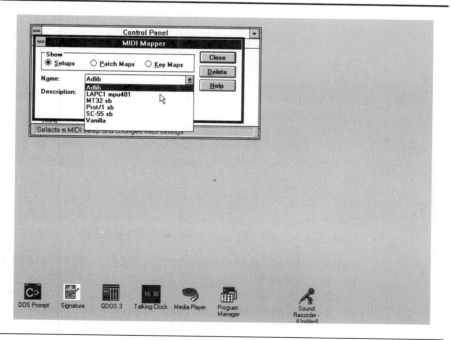

FIGURE 11.13: The MIDI Mapper dialog box

Creating a Custom MIDI Setup

If you are using a MIDI synthesizer that supports the General MIDI specifications, you're finished after you select the appropriate name in the preceding section. However, you may need to create a custom MIDI setup in either of two cases:

◆ If your synthesizer does not support General MIDI

◆ If you use a sound board with its own built-in synthesizer, and Windows does not offer a setup for that particular synthesizer

First, you must set up your synthesizer hardware so that it can receive MIDI messages on multiple channels. Consult your synthesizer documentation for instructions on how to do this. Next, you must use the MIDI Mapper service discussed here to specify the following:

◆ At least one key map (one for percussion instruments and maybe another for melodic instruments)

◆ Two patch maps (one for percussion and one for melodic instruments)

◆ A channel mapping

The next few sections explain how to do a custom setup. Before you begin, however, you will need to know something about how your synthesizer works to make channel assignments properly. A *base-level* synthesizer can simultaneously play six notes on three melodic instruments while also playing up to three notes on three percussion instruments. An *extended-level* synthesizer can simultaneously play sixteen notes on eight percussion instruments while also playing sixteen notes on up to nine melodic instruments.

Creating or Editing a MIDI Key Map

Figure 11.14 shows the dialog box (in the upper-left corner) that appears after you select the MIDI Mapper icon in the Control Panel. Depending on your hardware, you can make adjustments in one of three areas for each named MIDI setup. First, you must click on one of the three radio buttons (Setups, Patch Maps, or Key Maps). Then, you can create a new entry by entering a particular name, then selecting New. Or, you can edit one of the existing setup names by choosing Edit.

In Figure 11.14, Key Maps is already selected for the Setup named *+1 octave*. The MIDI Key Map dialog box, which appears after you select Edit, is on the right side of the figure. It enables you to create a new key map or to edit an existing one. This particular example shows the dialog box that defines the percussion sounds used by source keys 35 to 81. This range adheres to the General MIDI specifications; you can use the scroll bar to see the keys not shown.

You should use this dialog box to create or edit a key map for a synthesizer that does not support General MIDI or that plays sounds at different registrations. The Src Key column is unchanging, representing the key values that can appear in MIDI file messages. The Src Key Name column contains the percussion instrument names generally associated with the first column's source

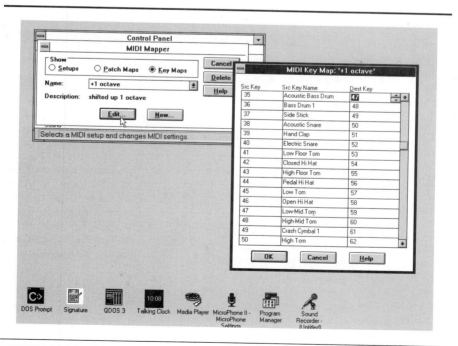

FIGURE 11.14: Editing a MIDI key map

keys. You can use this column as a reference, or you can ignore it if you are only adjusting registration values for melodic instruments.

The final column, Dest Key, is the primary one you make adjustments to. The numbers you enter in this column represent the actual keys that will be played on your synthesizer when an application or MIDI file references the related source key number. You can change any Dest Key entry by typing a new number into the field or by clicking on the up or down scroll arrows that appear when you move the highlight to a particular field.

Creating a Customized Patch Map

Figure 11.15 depicts the MIDI Patch Map dialog box for the MT32 setup, which appears after you select the Patch Maps radio button, then Edit, in the MIDI Mapper dialog box.

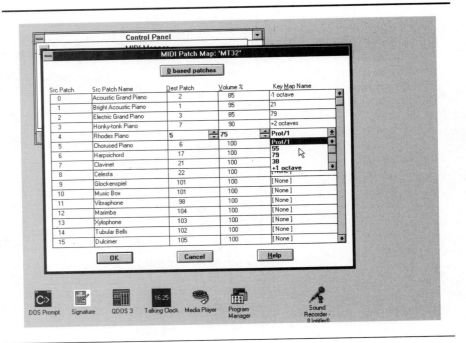

FIGURE 11.15: The MIDI Patch Map dialog box

You can also select one of the existing patch maps by choosing New instead of Edit. A new dialog box appears, which allows you to type in a name and description for your customized patch map. In either case, you can then edit the specifications of your map by making adjustments to the MIDI Patch Map dialog box.

General MIDI defines sounds for source patches numbered from 0 to 127. You can specify any of the entries in the rightmost three columns: the destination patch, the patch volume as a percentage, and the key map to use for each patch. As before, you can move the highlight to any field and type in a new entry. To change the destination patch and volume percentage, you can click on the up or down arrow. To make changes to the Key Map Name field, open up the list box of names by clicking on the arrow, and select from among the defined key maps.

The first two columns are unchangeable. The Src Patch column simply lists the numbers that occur within MIDI file messages. The Src Patch Name column contains the reference names for melodic channels. You can ignore these entries if you are creating a patch file for percussion instruments.

The Dest Patch column contains the numbers that your synthesizer will use to match the instrument sounds listed in the Src Patch Name column. For percussion instruments, change all values to correspond to your synthesizer's percussion numbers.

The Volume % column allows you to make the sounds specified in the MIDI file softer or louder. At 100 percent, the patch will play at the volume indicated in the MIDI file. Use numbers less than 100 to decrease the volume, and use numbers greater than 100 to increase the volume.

The Key Map column connects each patch map to a particular key map. For melodic instruments, choose a key map that appropriately maps keys to the correct registration for each sound's patch. For percussion instruments, choose a key map for all source patches that was created specifically for percussion.

Defining the Channel Mapping

The last step necessary for customizing your new MIDI setup is to define melodic and percussion channels for base-level or extended-level synthesizers. Table 11.2 summarizes the Microsoft guidelines for channel usage.

SUPERCHARGING WINDOWS

TABLE 11.2:   Microsoft Authoring Guidelines for Channel Maps

Channel Number	Base Level	Extended Level
1–9		Melodic
10		Percussive
13–15	Melodic	
16	Percussive	

If you must make changes to an existing setup or create a new one, click on the Setups radio button in the MIDI Mapper Show box, then select New or Edit. Figure 11.16 shows a modified Adlib setup. Adjustments have been made to the channel mapping for source channels 1 and 2.

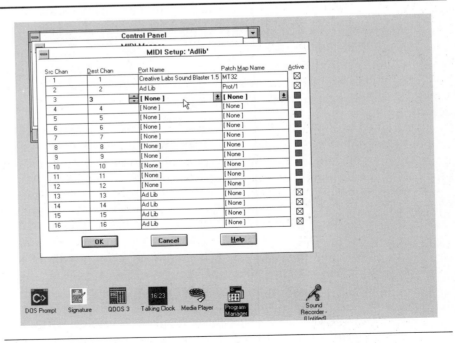

FIGURE 11.16:   Defining customized channel mapping

In Figure 11.16, only the Src Chan column is unchangeable. In the Dest Chan column, you should make any necessary adjustments to indicate which channel your synthesizer will use for playing sounds coming from the source channel.

Set the Port Name column value to the MIDI output port name to which you want Windows to send the sound output for each source channel. In my setup, shown in Figure 11.16, I can send source channel output on channel 1 to my Sound Blaster port, while simultaneous output on source channel 2 goes to an AdLib port. When you select a particular port name, the Active box is checked automatically. This indicates that MIDI data for a source channel will now be sent to the defined port.

Set the Patch Map Name column value equal to the name of a patch map that you want to use with an individual channel. Remember to use a patch map that was created for melodic or percussion instruments, depending on whether the source channel is melodic or percussive.

◆ CUSTOMIZING FOR AN INTERNATIONAL ENVIRONMENT

Many people in many countries use Windows. They are not forced to use the standard American settings for such things as currency, numbers, date, time, and measurements. Choosing the International icon in the Control Panel opens up the International dialog box, which offers a variety of customizations, as shown in Figure 11.17.

Most of the adjustments in this dialog box are tied to your selection of a country in the first field. By opening up the list box, you can select the name of the country in which you will be using Windows. Windows will automatically adjust the date, time, currency, and number formats. In addition, the standard of measurement (English or metric) and the typical separator symbol (used for lists of words or numbers) for that country will also be changed automatically. Even though it is not visible in this dialog box, changing the

Country setting will also adjust the Paper Size option in Print Setup to conform to the usual paper format in that particular country.

Each one of these six fields can be individually modified, but most of the time, the automatic adjustments will be sufficient. The Language and Keyboard Layout fields are not connected automatically to the Country field. You will have to change these individually because there is a greater variety of languages and keyboard layouts in use around the world. Even in one country, there can be several standards for keyboard and language.

The actual language used in the country affects such things as the sort order of file names and the way your applications treat words and phrases. For example, many foreign languages use special accent characters. Specifying a language in the Language field affects this aspect of Windows; it does not change

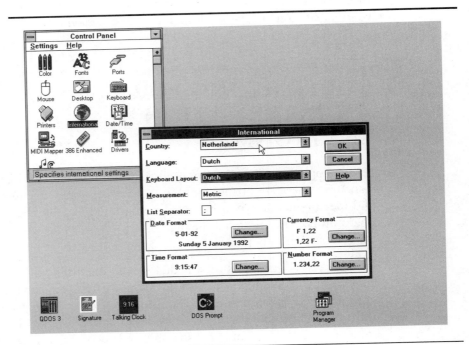

FIGURE 11.17: The International dialog box

the actual language of the words that appear in dialog boxes and menus. You must buy a completely different language version of Windows for this—see your dealer.

In this chapter, you learned how to use many facets of the Control Panel to personalize your desktop. Turn now to Chapter 12 to learn the internal facilities available to you for customizing Windows by adjusting keywords and parameters in the system's primary initialization (.INI) files.

C H A P T E R

12

*Modifying WIN.INI
and SYSTEM.INI*

◆

After you first boot up your PC, the environment in which all programs execute is determined by the CONFIG.SYS and AUTOEXEC.BAT files. You have probably made changes to these at various times to customize your DOS environment.

When you first start Windows, there are similar files that influence the initial environment in which all executing programs will run. Some of these files are created when Setup first installs Windows for you. You can easily view them as text files. You can find them in your WINDOWS directory with .INI extensions.

Many applications create and maintain their own .INI files. These private .INI files have a similar purpose. They contain initial values for the applications. Occasionally, you will choose certain menu options or make dialog box entries that change the execution environment for an application. The application often will store the changes in its .INI file.

Windows does the same thing. Some of the programs supplied with Windows have their own .INI files. For example, when you make changes to the contents of your Program Manager groups, the PROGMAN.EXE program stores the new configuration in an .INI file named PROGMAN.INI. When you run the Control Panel and make changes to the color schemes, pattern selections, multimedia drivers, or screen savers, the new configuration you specify is stored in the CONTROL.INI file.

Accessory programs often create and manage their own .INI files as well. For example, the Media Player stores its settings in the MPLAYER.INI file, and the File Manager stores its settings in the WINFILE.INI file. As I'll discuss shortly, some applications store their initialization and status information in specially named sections of the WIN.INI file.

WIN.INI is one of two primary start-up files that store information about your Windows system, your principal applications, and your hardware settings. Much of the information in this file, and in the SYSTEM.INI file, is maintained automatically by Windows. Occasionally, one of your applications or one of Windows' accessory programs will make entries or changes in one of these files.

You also can make changes to the entry lines in one or both of these files. In fact, if you know what an .INI file does and how its individual command lines work, you can directly customize any of the execution-time aspects that it controls.

This chapter focuses on explaining the purpose of all the major sections and of most of the option lines in your WIN.INI and SYSTEM.INI files. These two files cover the broadest range of Windows features. Knowing what each option can do will enable you to customize Windows to your liking and to fine-tune Windows performance for your particular mix of programs.

♦ LEARN EVEN MORE DETAILS ABOUT WIN.INI AND SYSTEM.INI

Your WINDOWS directory contains a number of text files that go into particular detail about all the exotic options discussed in this chapter. A careful reading of the WININI.WRI and SYSINI.WRI files will answer many questions and suggest many possibilities. Use the Windows Write accessory program to scan through these files for more details.

However, even if you know how to change entries in these files, it is safest to make as many changes as possible through the Control Panel or other menu-oriented mechanisms. Let Windows adjust the files if possible. Use the information in this chapter to understand what Windows is doing or to make only those changes that Windows does not offer through the Control Panel.

◆ UNDERSTANDING THE BASICS OF .INI FILES

All initialization files resemble one another in important ways. Beyond the fact that they contain only ASCII text, they are always arranged into logically related groups of options, called *sections*. The section name is always surrounded by square brackets, occupies its own line, and precedes all option lines that pertain to the group.

THE STRUCTURE OF A TYPICAL .INI FILE

To understand the structure of a typical .INI file, take a look at a sample [Devices] section of the MPLAYER.INI file:

[Devices]

cdaudio=0,

Sequencer=22, MIDI Sequencer

WaveAudio=22, Sound

Without looking at any documentation, this section can be understood. Each line specifies something about a multimedia device. The first line specifies that there is no CD audio player in the system, and the second and third lines specify information about the two other devices that are available from the menu bar of the Media Player.

Each line in an .INI file has the following format:

Keyword=parameter value(s)

One or more unique and meaningful parameter values are assigned by each option line to a keyword. Each keyword usually controls an operational aspect or specifies an environmental or execution-time setting. If there is more than one value to specify, you can separate the values with commas or spaces. You will see both separator techniques used in your system's .INI files.

Keep Option Lines under 127 Characters

Option lines in the initialization files must be no longer than 127 characters. With the exception of the Load and Run lines, this is no problem. In Windows 3.1, the existence of the StartUp program group means that you don't even have to worry about the Run command. If you have many programs to run at start-up, just create icons for them and place those icons in the StartUp group.

If you want to run and iconize a number of applications at start-up, however, you'll still have to use the Load line in WIN.INI. And, as you may discover, some third-party applications actually modify your WIN.INI file's Run line as well. In both cases, your WIN.INI file may end up with a Run or Load line that exceeds 127 characters. Unfortunately, only the first 127 characters will be processed.

To keep the Load and Run lines from exceeding 127 characters, use any or all of the following suggestions:

◆ If your [Extensions] section indicates that certain extensions (like .EXE or .COM) are executable programs, you needn't waste space by typing the extension with the program's base name. For example, Run=CLOCK DRWATSON NOTEPAD works just fine.

◆ If the subdirectories that contain third-party applications have long names, you can shorten them to reduce the number of characters needed to specify full path names. For instance, if you install this book's disks, you'll have a directory called SYBEX2 with two subdirectories named REMINDER and ADDRESS for those particular applications. You could just as well rename SYBEX2 to S2, and rename REMINDER and ADDRESS to RM and AD. Loading these two programs alone would reduce the characters required from

Load=C:\SYBEX2\REMINDER\Reminder C:\SYBEX2\ADDRESS\Address

to

Load=C:\S2\RM\Reminder C:\S2\AD\Address

◆ Spread your start-up applications across the two Load and Run lines and the STARTUP directory so that neither the Load nor the Run line exceeds 127 characters. Remember that an icon in the STARTUP directory is equivalent to an entry on the Run line. And the only difference between starting entries with Run (or in the STARTUP directory) and starting entries with Load is that using Load guarantees that the application will start minimized.

DOCUMENTING THE MEANING
OF .INI ENTRIES

Many programming languages have a special character or sequence at the
beginning of each line that explains the purpose of this line. You can see such
a technique in the AUTOEXEC.BAT file of most DOS systems. Any line that
begins with the word REM is treated as a remark rather than a command.
Such lines are inserted by the creator of the file.

In Windows .INI files, the equivalent technique for including comments is to
start the line with a semicolon. For example, you may occasionally see a comment line such as the following that precedes an option that is not immediately clear:

;Exclude BIOS addresses for PLUS HardCard

EMMExclude=C800–C9FF

If you add a special address-exclusion line in your SYSTEM.INI file, which requires the EMMExclude= line, you should also include a comment line before
the EMMExclude= line. The comment line will help to remind you later, or
to explain to someone else, why the specific range of addresses was excluded
as parameter values.

USING BOOLEAN VALUES TO
TURN OPTIONS ON OR OFF

Using Boolean values is just a fancy mathematical way of saying Yes or No,
On or Off, True or False, 1 or 0. In other words, Boolean representation is
binary: It represents one of two possible values. You will see many keywords
set to Boolean values. Windows allows all these possible ways of expressing
Boolean values. In this way, you can more readily read and understand an
option-line entry.

For example, my WIN.INI file contains the following Boolean settings:

TTEnable=1

Beep=Yes

Both of these settings are equivalent ways of turning on Windows options: On
the first line, I enabled the use of TrueType fonts, and on the second line, I

activated the use of sound.

My SYSTEM.INI file contains similar Boolean settings:

FileSysChange=Off

VirtualHDIRQ=False

These lines are also ways of turning off system settings. The first line improves performance by not wasting time with DDE messages to the File Manager whenever one of my applications makes disk file and directory changes. The second line slows down performance by directing that hard-disk interrupts be handled by a ROM routine when Windows is running in 386 enhanced mode.

♦ SYNONYMS IN .INI FILES

Have you ever wondered why documentation, actual files, and occasional magazine articles seem to conflict in what they say about .INI settings? Certain settings can take on only one of two values. Microsoft allows the various initialization files to employ several conventional alternatives. You can use True or False, 1 or 0, Yes or No, or even other words that just begin with the letters *Y* or *N*, even in lowercase. For example, you can enter Spooler=Yes in the WIN.INI file, or you can just enter spooler=1.

If you make changes to any of the Boolean settings in WIN.INI or SYSTEM.INI, feel free to use whichever technique you prefer for specifying values. Choose the one that will be most easily understood by you later.

♦ UNDERSTANDING THE WIN.INI FILE SETTINGS

Before you begin to learn the exact meaning of the settings in the WIN.INI file, you should understand how Windows uses this file. In this way, you may prevent losing data by mishandling the file.

HOW DOES WINDOWS USE THE WIN.INI FILE?

When Windows starts up, it first reads into memory a copy of the WIN.INI file. Windows can then rapidly access WIN.INI settings from this memory area whenever it needs to. However, if you make changes to the WIN.INI file with SYSEDIT.EXE or some other text/word processor, you are actually changing the original disk version of WIN.INI. Your application does not make changes to the copy in memory, which Windows uses to determine its own environment. Figure 12.1 depicts this scenario.

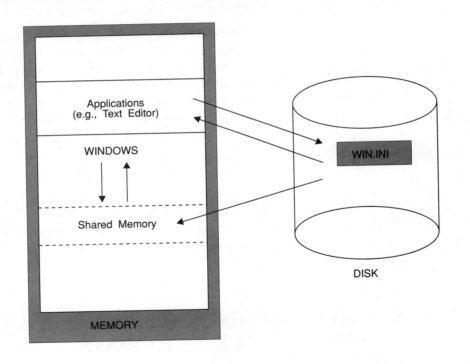

FIGURE 12.1: Windows uses a memory copy of the WIN.INI file.

Using SYSEDIT.EXE to Configure Your System

You are probably familiar with how to adjust the contents of your CONFIG.SYS and AUTOEXEC.BAT files. You may use your own word processor to do this, or even the DOS 5 full-screen EDIT command. But do you know about the existence of the SYSEDIT.EXE program in Windows? Located in the SYSTEM directory, it offers a safe and convenient way to quickly modify these ASCII files in Windows. (If you use your own word processor, be sure to save the WIN.INI or SYSTEM.INI file as an ASCII text file!)

This same program enables you to edit SYSTEM.INI and WIN.INI. In short, this one, barely documented application offers a convenient way to modify all four ASCII files that affect the initialization and configuration of your Windows environment.

Furthermore, each time you save a changed version of one of these four files from the SYSEDIT.EXE program, it saves the previous version of the file in a .SYD file. This can make restoration of the former, working version easy if your changes do not work as successfully as you hoped.

This explains why changes to WIN.INI do not take effect immediately. You have made changes only to the disk file. Windows will not use any of your changes until it reads the disk file into memory again. This may not be until you restart Windows; it can be sooner if something forces Windows to reread the disk file. In fact, this is what happens each time you make choices in the Control Panel. Not only is the memory version changed but Windows also updates the disk file. After all, only Windows has direct access to the memory version, so only Windows can change both the memory and disk versions.

♦ WARNING: DO NOT USE CONTROL PANEL WHILE EDITING WIN.INI

The Control Panel can change the memory and disk versions of WIN.INI. This is normally no problem but can become one if you are editing the disk version of WIN.INI directly. If Windows updates the disk file before your text editor saves your updates, these adjustments will overwrite the Control Panel's changes. Be aware of this possible double access to the WIN.INI disk file. It can be insidious because many of the direct changes that you make (for performance purposes) will not have an easily noticeable effect.

This brings up an interesting possibility. Suppose that you read a copy of WIN.INI into your text editor, intending to change a line. But before you actually use your text editor's Save command to update the disk version of WIN.INI, you make a Control Panel adjustment. If your adjustment causes Windows to update your disk version of WIN.INI, then the subsequent use of Save from your text editor will overwrite these changes.

The same problem can occur if any application causes changes to be made to WIN.INI. Many applications can make requests to Windows that WIN.INI be changed. These requests are allowed, and as a result, Windows updates its memory version and the disk version of WIN.INI. You must be sure that nothing like this is going on while you make editing changes directly to the disk version of WIN.INI.

Table 12.1 summarizes the names and purposes of the major sections in the WIN.INI file; the order in which they appear in the file is unimportant. The next several sections of this chapter explain the possible entries in these WIN.INI sections. The order of these entries is also unimportant, but each entry must be included in its appropriate section. In each section, I present information about all possible options, including both their purposes and defaults. To avoid being tedious, I only discuss in more depth the more interesting and useful of the command entries.

◆ UPDATE WIN.INI SETTINGS IMMEDIATELY

Normally, when you make changes to the WIN.INI or SYSTEM.INI file with an ASCII editor, like SYSEDIT.EXE, you must shut down Windows and restart it for the changes to take effect. This can be annoying if you have several programs running and have to restore each of them to where you want them.

Trimming the Fat from WIN.INI

Many applications make changes to WIN.INI, often storing their own initialization values in a private section. A private section usually begins with the name of the application itself in square brackets, such as [Taipei] or [Unicom]. Since these settings are often modified, either automatically or by user request, there is a certain degree of system overhead in just writing and rewriting the contents of WIN.INI.

You can reduce this burden on disk activity in two ways, both of which require you to use an ASCII editor to change the WIN.INI file. First, some people like to remove all comment lines. Since the comment lines are ignored by both Windows and your applications, they merely get in the way of actual instruction processing and require more time to read and write. But this is false economy. These lines offer valuable information and you shouldn't discard them so readily.

Second, you can prune entire sections of WIN.INI that you no longer need. When you install a program, it may add an entire section of initialization settings. If you later remove the program from your disk, this section in WIN.INI is not typically removed. It can slow down your system, so just edit it out.

In some cases, you can force Windows to make your changes by using the Control Panel in the Main group of the Program Manager. Simply select an option, like Fonts or Ports, then choose OK from the dialog box that appears. Windows will reread WIN.INI from the disk, using *most* of the changes you made to this file.

USING THE [WINDOWS] SECTION

The [Windows] section of WIN.INI has one of the largest range of possible option lines. You will see most of these settings in your own WIN.INI file. Table 12.2 explains each of them briefly.

The [Windows] section controls the most general aspects of your Windows environment, including the keyboard, mouse, and printing settings. Many of the settings are straightforward, and the brief explanations in Table 12.2 are sufficient for you to decide whether or not you want to use them. However,

TABLE 12.1: The Primary WIN.INI Sections

Section Name	Purpose
[Colors]	Sets colors of different screen elements
[Desktop]	Controls appearance and arrangement of windows and icons
[Devices]	Lists printer information for older Windows 2.x programs
[Embedding]	Lists OLE server object information
[Extensions]	Lists associations between extensions and executable files
[Fonts]	Lists information about all loaded screen fonts
[Fontsubstitutes]	Lists acceptable alternative font pairs
[Intl]	Specifies country-dependent display information
[MCI Extensions]	Lists associations between file extensions and MCI devices
[Networks]	Indicates network settings and connections
[Ports]	Lists available output port names
[PrinterPorts]	Lists driver-name, port, and timeout information
[Programs]	Lists additional path information to locate application files
[Sounds]	Specifies sound file names corresponding to system events
[TrueType]	Specifies options for displaying TrueType fonts
[Windows]	Lists option settings that affect the overall system
[Windows Help]	Defines characteristics of Windows Help application

even if you want to make adjustments to many of these settings, you should use an appropriate Control Panel icon. You can control most important settings by making simple dialog box entries in the Control Panel.

For example, the Beep setting controls basic sound effects. But you can make adjustments in the Sound dialog box in the Control Panel to automatically

Removing All Traces of Applications

So you've decided to erase all aspects of an old application, or perhaps a new application that you tried but didn't like. In Windows, you must do more work than simply deleting disk files. Follow these steps:

1. Run SYSEDIT.EXE to remove any lines that were added to WIN.INI by the application.

2. Look at CONFIG.SYS and AUTOEXEC.BAT to see if any lines were added there. Remove them, but remember to retain a backup to each of these important files in case you've made an error and some other application actually added the lines you're removing.

3. Look for an .INI file with the same base name as your application. It may have been created to house all initialization information for the application. Microsoft now recommends to all developers that they use private .INI files rather than update the WIN.INI file.

4. Run Program Manager to delete a program item icon or program group icon that may have been added by the application or by you.

5. Run the File Manager to erase the files and directories that constitute the application.

turn this option on or off in the WIN.INI file. Also, the Keyboard dialog box directly updates the KeyboardDelay and KeyboardSpeed entries, which manage the keyboard repetition delay and repetition rate. If your system is connected to a network, the Control Panel will include a Network icon. Choose this icon to control automatically whether warning messages are displayed (with the NetWarn setting).

Some settings in the WIN.INI file are for internal Windows use. Although they are available to you, you shouldn't change them unless you are an experienced programmer. Even then, you should know precisely how Windows will respond to your modifications before making any changes to the defaults listed in Table 12.2. The [Windows] section only contains one setting that is for Windows' internal use: DefaultQueueSize.

TABLE 12.2: Setting in the [Windows] Section of WIN.INI

Name	Default	Purpose
Beep	Yes	Sounds warning beep for invalid actions
BorderWidth	3	Sets thickness for most window borders (in pixels)
CoolSwitch	1	Turns fast Alt+Tab switching on (1) or off (0)
CursorBlinkRate	530	Defines time in milliseconds between cursor blinks
DefaultQueueSize	8	Limits number of application queue messages
Device	None	Specifies default system printer
DeviceNot-SelectedTimeout	15	Defines waiting time in seconds for a device to be turned on
Documents	None	Defines additional document files
DosPrint	No	Toggles whether or not to print using DOS interrupts
DoubleClick-Height	4	Limits vertical mouse movement (in pixels) during a double click
DoubleClickSpeed	452	Limits elapsed time (in milliseconds) during a double click
DoubleClickWidth	4	Limits horizontal mouse movement (in pixels) during a double click
DragFullWindows	0	Toggles full window drags on (1) or off (0)
KeyboardDelay	2	Sets delay time (in milliseconds) before key repetitions begin
KeyboardSpeed	31	Sets repetition rate (in milliseconds) for held key presses

TABLE 12.2:   Settings in the [Windows] Section of WIN.INI (continued)

Name	Default	Purpose
Load	None	Lists programs to run and iconize at start-up
MenuDrop-Alignment	0	Aligns pull-down menus to right (1) or left (0)
MouseSpeed	1	Permits (1) or denies (0) accelerated pointer motion
MouseThreshold1	5	Sets threshold for double mouse pointer movement (in pixels)
MouseThreshold2	10	Sets threshold for quadruple mouse pointer movement (in pixels)
MouseTrails	–7	Sets number of trailing mouse pointers
NetWarn	1	Displays warning message if expected network is not up
NullPort	None	Defines name for null port
Programs	com exe bat pif	Specifies extensions to be treated as programs
Run	None	Lists programs to be executed at start-up
ScreenSaveActive	0	Enables (1) or disables (0) a screen saver
ScreenSave-TimeOut	120	Sets idle time (in milliseconds) before a screen saver is activated
Spooler	Yes	Toggles whether or not to print through Print Manager
SwapMouse-Buttons	0	Sets primary mouse button to left (0) or right (1)
Transmission-RetryTimeout	90 (PostScript); 45 otherwise	Limits time (in seconds) within which to successively reattempt retransmissions

Customizing the Desktop

The Desktop dialog box in the Control Panel controls the BorderWidth, CoolSwitch, and CursorBlinkRate settings. Your entries will automatically adjust the settings in these next three lines. The Desktop icon also controls the setting of ScreenSaveActive and ScreenSaveTimeOut.

If you enable a screen saver by setting ScreenSaveActive to 1 or by selecting a screen saver's name in the relevant Desktop list box, Windows will use the ScreenSaveTimeOut value to determine when to activate the saver screen. Windows will obtain the name of the screen saver you selected from the SCRNSAVE.EXE entry in the [Boot] section of the SYSTEM.INI file.

Managing the Printer Settings

The Printers dialog box in the Control Panel automatically adjusts the entries on the Device, DeviceNotSelectedTimeout, DosPrint, Spooler, and TransmissionRetryTimeout lines. If you are using the Print Manager, you can alternatively select the Printer Setup command on the Options menu to similarly affect these settings.

The Device line has three parameters:

Device=<output-device-name>,<device-driver>,<port-connection>

The first parameter must be one of the device names found in the [Devices] section of WIN.INI, and the third parameter must be one of the port names found in the [Ports] section. The second parameter gives the file name of the device driver, without an extension.

Depending on your printer's initial response time, you may wish to modify the default value for DeviceNotSelectedTimeout. This setting usually specifies how long Windows will wait for a device to be switched on before giving up. Click on the Connect button to find the dialog box entries that change this setting, TransmissionRetryTimeout, or DosPrint.

Uncheck Fast Printing Direct to Port if you want to print by using DOS interrupts. Unchecking the box sets the DosPrint option to Yes in the WIN.INI file, which causes slower printing than if print output is sent directly to the port. If everything works OK with direct output to a print port, keep it that way. Change this setting only if you have trouble printing.

The Print Manager is a Windows accessory that provides print spooling. Most computer systems perform better when printed output is spooled. This is primarily because a fast CPU can send output to a slow printer and your task will not have to wait until printing is finished before being able to go on with other work.

However, there is another important function performed by the Print Manager. In a network or multitasking environment, the Print Manager has the important role of ordering the print requests from tasks that are competing for your printer. All print output from individual tasks are gathered up by the Print Manager for subsequent printing. The Print Manager will submit all the pages from a single task's output requests as a group. If multiple tasks send output directly to the port, you will probably have sequential pages from one task printed in the middle of another task's output pages.

Checking the Use Print Manager box in the Printers dialog box sets the Spooler option in WIN.INI to Yes. Unless you print from only one program at a time, your system will perform better if you use the Print Manager. Because it does bear a certain overhead burden, you can output faster from a single program if you go directly to the printer port and turn the Spooler option off.

Controlling the Mouse Settings

The Mouse dialog box in the Control Panel controls the DoubleClickSpeed, MouseSpeed, MouseThreshold1, MouseThreshold2, MouseTrails, and Swap-MouseButtons settings, which you've already learned about. You can customize a number of other settings in this dialog box that affect the sensitivity of the mouse to your hand movements during double clicks. Use the Double-ClickHeight and DoubleClickWidth entries to manage these adjustments.

The values for MouseSpeed are somewhat obscure. In the Control Panel, you simply move a slider box labeled Mouse Tracking Speed from slow to fast. However, Windows takes the position of your slider box and sets the Mouse-Speed entry to a value of 0, 1, or 2. At 0, the mouse pointer moves at a fixed rate. At values of 1 or 2, the pointer accelerates according to the threshold settings. See Figure 12.2 for a clarification of the relationship between these three settings.

You can set MouseTrails to a number from 1 to 7, which indicates the number of mouse pointers to be displayed as the mouse moves around the screen. The Mouse dialog box may simply display a check box, allowing you to turn mouse trails on or off. To specify exactly how many mouse pointers appear, you have to edit this entry in the WIN.INI file. A negative number means that the mouse trails option has not been enabled.

Controlling Minor Appearance Options

The Documents line allows you to specify the extensions of files that you want Windows to consider as documents. For example, if the data files created by

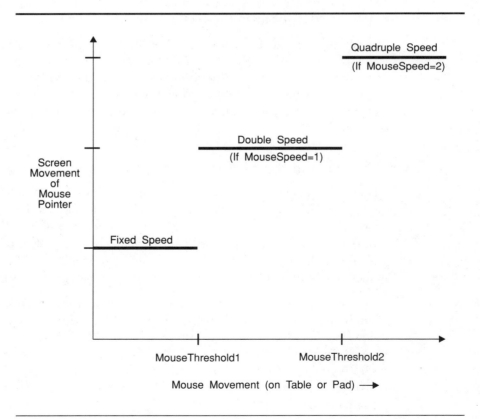

FIGURE 12.2: Accelerating the screen's mouse pointer movement

the DOS Signature program all have the extension .SIG, this line can be edited to read

Documents=SIG

Programs like the File Manager can then understand that .SIG files are document files. The File Manager would be able to select the correct icon to represent the file type. This command applies only to file extensions that do not already appear in the [Extensions] section. Files in [Extensions] are assumed to be document files.

The MenuDropAlignment setting is a simple appearance option. If its value is 0, all menus open with their entries aligned with the left side of the menu title. If the value is 1, menus open with the entries aligned on the right side.

♦ **DON'T DRAG AN ENTIRE WINDOW**

You can set the DragFullWindows option to 1 to see an entire window move on the screen when you drag it. This may look better but it will drastically slow down your video refreshes. If you don't mind seeing just an outline box moving, accept the default value of 0.

Load and Run Are Less Important Now

The Load and Run lines were more important in earlier versions of Windows. Now that a StartUp group in the Program Manager controls which programs run automatically when Windows starts, you hardly need the Run command at all. The Run and Load lines both consist of a list of applications or documents with associated extensions. If a name appears on the Run list, it will be executed when Windows starts. If a name appears on the Load list, it will be executed and immediately minimized to an icon on the desktop.

PERSONALIZING THE DESKTOP DIRECTLY

The Desktop section controls a number of options that influence the appearance of windows, icons, and the screen background. You will see most of these settings in your own WIN.INI file. Table 12.3 explains each of them briefly.

Once again, many of these options can be controlled through the Control Panel. (I explained many of them in Chapter 11.) For example, the Grid-Granularity value is based on your entry in the Granularity field of the Desktop dialog box's Sizing Grid section. The Desktop dialog box also controls the following options: IconSpacing, IconTitleWrap, Pattern, TileWallpaper, and Wallpaper. Personally, I never bother to set any of these options directly; rather, I simply click the Desktop icon, make changes in the dialog box, and let Windows update WIN.INI for me.

This section does offer some extra customizing options. If you find the font used for icon titles difficult to read, you can change both the label's size (using IconTitleSize) and its font style (bold or regular). If your system frequently displays more than one row of icons, you can adjust the amount of empty space between rows with the IconVerticalSpacing option.

In this section, you can affect two factors that have to do with display timing: MenuHideDelay controls the amount of time Windows waits before hiding a cascaded menu, and MenuShowDelay controls the amount of time Windows waits before displaying a cascaded menu. You can adjust these parameters according to the speed of your computer and video board.

Finally, WallpaperOriginX and WallpaperOriginY are simply pixel offsets to use for tiling your wallpaper. Generally, the default—the upper-left corner of the screen (0, 0)—is most effective for tiling. However, if your wallpaper is unique, you may want to begin the tiling elsewhere on the screen to produce a special visual effect.

CUSTOMIZING YOUR FILE EXTENSION ASSOCIATIONS

The [Extensions] section is merely a repeated sequence of lines that specify file-name associations. (You learned in Chapter 7 about associating file extensions with executable programs.) There is no limit to the number of entries in this section; each entry has the following format:

<extension>=<DOS command line>

TABLE 12.3:   Settings in the [Desktop] Section of WIN.INI

Name	Default	Purpose
GridGranularity	0	Sets size of invisible desktop alignment grid
IconSpacing	77	Limits horizontal number of pixels between icons
IconTitleFaceName	MS Sans Serif	Sets typeface for icon labels
IconTitleSize	8	Sets type size for icon labels
IconTitleStyle	0	Toggles bold (1) or regular (0) icon label text
IconTitleWrap	1	Toggles word wrap for icon labels on (1) or off (0)
IconVerticalSpacing	Variable	Sets vertical number of pixels between icons
MenuHideDelay	0	Sets waiting time (in milliseconds) to hide a cascading menu
MenuShowDelay	0 (386 machines); 400 (286 machines)	Sets waiting time (in milliseconds) to display a cascading menu
Pattern	None	Sets pixel pattern for screen background
TileWallpaper	0	Toggles wallpaper tiling (0) or centering (1)
Wallpaper	None	Names bit-map file to use as wallpaper
WallpaperOriginX	0	Sets pixel offset from left side of screen for tiling
WallpaperOriginY	0	Sets pixel offset from top of screen for tiling

All of the entries in this section are generally created automatically by Windows when you select the Associate option on the File menu in the File Manager. You can, of course, edit the WIN.INI file directly to add or remove associations: Just replace <extension> with the file extension (one to three characters), and replace <DOS command line> with the command line you want to run when a document file with your selected extension is opened.

For example, suppose that you decide to use the ICONMSTR program, included on this book's second disk, to manipulate all icon files with an .ICO extension. You would add the following line in the [Extensions] section:

ICO=ICONMSTR.EXE ^.ICO

If the ICONMSTR program is in your PATH, this entry will be sufficient to run that program, using the actual document file name as the DOS command line's first parameter. If you open a file whose name is CHESS.ICO, Windows will recognize the ICO extension and replace the carat (^) with the file's base name (i.e., CHESS). Consequently, the following DOS command line is run by Windows:

ICONMSTR CHESS.ICO

Knowing how this mechanism works means that you can bypass the Associate sequence from the File Manager and create more complex associations. For instance, you can add any number of parameters or switches to the <DOS Command Line> field if you use an editor to enter the line.

As an example, suppose that you use a word processor that automatically calls up the last document you worked on. Suppose that a /I switch is all that you must add. You may wish to associate .TXT files with your word processor but, if you use the Associate option in the File Manager, you will have to edit the entry in this section to incorporate the necessary switch to direct the program to start up with the last document you worked on. You might therefore edit the line so that it reads

TXT=WORD.EXE ^.TXT /I

This kind of customization is only available to you when you directly edit the individual lines in the [Extensions] section.

CUSTOMIZING THE COUNTRY-DEPENDENT SETTINGS

The meanings of most of the settings in the [Intl] section are obvious. As shown in Table 12.4, these settings control the appearance on screen of

Setting Up Associations without the File Manager

You can directly associate executable programs with a file extension by editing or adding entries in the [Extensions] section of your WIN.INI file. For example, to process all .TXT files with your own word processing program, replace the Notepad association line with your own:

txt=editor.exe ^.txt

Several hints about associations come to mind here:

♦ You can associate any executable program with a data file extension. This includes .EXEs, .PIFs, .BATs, and .COMs.

♦ You can associate both Windows and non-Windows applications with data file extensions.

♦ You can precede the executable file name with a directory path, so the executable file itself does not even have to be in your system PATH.

♦ You can speed up things even more by placing the executable file on a RAM disk.

country-dependent items, such as currencies, dates, times, and units of measure, and are most readily accessible by choosing the International icon in the Control Panel. In fact, you will probably understand them more easily in the Control Panel than in the WIN.INI file.

For example, the iCurrency line can be set from 0 to 3, which controls where to place the selected currency symbol. If the value is 0, a two-dollar amount appears on the screen as $2. If the value is 1, a two-dollar amount appears as 2$. If the value is 2, a space appears between the symbol and the number (i.e., $ 2). Lastly, if the value is 3, no symbol appears (i.e., 2).

Many entries in this section are stored in a similar manner. My advice is to ignore the values stored in WIN.INI and change them using the Control Panel, where you can see complete information rather than obscure codes.

TABLE 12.4: Settings in the [Intl] Section of WIN.INI

Name	Default	Purpose
iCountry	1	Sets country code
iCurrDigits	2	Sets number of digits after separator for currency
iCurrency	0	Specifies one of four currency formats
iDate	0	Specifies one of three date formats (for Windows 2.x)
iDigits	2	Sets number of digits after separator for numbers
iLZero	0	Toggles leading zeros in decimal numbers on (1) or off (0)
iMeasure	1	Toggles English (1) or metric (0) measurements
iNegCurr	0	Specifies one of ten formats for negative numbers
iTime	0	Toggles 12-hour (0) or 24-hour (1) clock
iTLZero	0	Toggles leading zeros in time on (1) or off (0)
s1159	AM	Sets text to follow morning times in 12-hour format
s2359	PM	Sets text to follow afternoon/evening times in 12-hour format, or all times in 24-hour format
sCountry	United States	Sets default settings for a particular country
sCurrency	$	Sets desired currency symbol
sDecimal	.	Sets symbol to use for separating decimal places
sLanguage	usa	Sets language to use for certain tasks
sList	,	Sets list separator symbol
sLongDate	dddd, MMMM dd, yyyy	Specifies expanded format for date display

TABLE 12.4: Settings in the [Intl] Section of WIN.INI (continued)

Name	Default	Purpose
sShortDate	M/d/yy	Specifies abbreviated format for date display
sThousand	,	Sets thousands-place separator symbol
sTime	:	Sets symbol to separate parts of the time

CUSTOMIZING YOUR SYSTEM PORTS

The Ports dialog box in the Control Panel enables you to create entries only for the four COM ports supported by DOS. For other ports, you must edit the [Ports] section of WIN.INI. Each entry defines a unique available output port, although you can only have up to ten such entries. Windows ignores any additional lines.

Each entry has the following format, although most entries do not use all the possible parameters:

<portname: ¦ filename>=

   <Baud Rate>,<Parity>,<Word Length>,<Stop Bits>[[,p]]

There are several different ports available in a typical system. Your [Ports] section probably includes some lines like this:

LPT1:=

COM1:=2400,n,8,1,x

COM2:=9600,n,8,1,x

FILE:=

LPT1.DOS=

In this example, there is one standard parallel port (LPT1). There could be up to two others (LPT2 and LPT3); they do not require any parameters.

This example also shows one serial port, COM1, set to 2400 baud for a modem, and a second serial port, COM2, set to 9600 baud for a plotter. There could be up to two other serial port lines in this section.

The FILE:= line provides you with the option of sending printed output to a file. You will be able to redirect Windows output to the FILE choice in the list box that appears when you run Connect in the Printers dialog box. If you do so, Windows will ask you to enter an output file name when you're finally ready to print.

The last line uses a file name to the left of the equal sign. Output is directed to that particular file instead of to a physical port. In the Connect portion of the Printers dialog box, you will see a list of all the possibilities seen in this section to the left of the equal signs. You may want to occasionally redirect printed output to a file for printing or for transmission to another site for printing.

SETTING UP AND EDITING YOUR SYSTEM'S FONT DEFINITIONS

Three sections of the WIN.INI file control the appearance of fonts on your screen: [TrueType] (which I'll explain shortly), [Fonts], and [Fontsubstitutes].

The [Fonts] section defines the names of files containing display fonts that Windows loads at start-up. Each entry looks like

<Font Name>=<Font File>

The <Font Name> entry represents a text description of the installed font, and the <Font File> entry represents the name of the file that contains the font data. A typical entry might look like

Arial Bold (TrueType)=ARIALBD.FOT

Typically, you use the Fonts icon from the Control Panel to install fonts. The appropriate entry in this section is then automatically created for you. But you could easily install your own private font files by adding a new line in this format.

You may have created documents using an earlier version of Windows, using fonts that are no longer supported by Windows 3.1. The [Fontsubstitutes] section defines fonts that represent equivalent typefaces. Each entry has the following format:

<Font Name>=<Font Name>

Place the older typeface name on the left and the newer one on the right. Windows will display all older text fonts in the typeface specified by the newer font. For example, an entry in my [Fontsubstitutes] section is

Helvetica=Arial

Helvetica was available in Windows 3.0 but is no longer known by that name. If a document uses Helvetica, Windows will now display it using Arial.

The [TrueType] section contains three possible entry lines that affect the inclusion and appearance of TrueType fonts in Windows applications. Each entry line is some variation of

[nonTTCaps ¦ TTEnable ¦ TTOnly] = <0 ¦ 1>

You can only change the first option by using a text editor. If nonTTCaps is set to 1, then font names that are not TrueType will appear as all capital letters on your application's dialog boxes. Setting this value to 0 (which is the default value) uses standard, first-letter-capitalized format for non-TrueType fonts.

The second and third options can be set automatically via the Fonts icon from the Control Panel. Just select the TrueType button and you'll see two check boxes that directly control these options. If TTEnable is set to 1, TrueType fonts are available to Windows applications. If TTOnly is set to 1, only True-Type fonts will be listed as available to Windows applications.

MANAGING MULTIMEDIA SOUND FILES

The [MCI Extensions] section is similar to the standard [Extensions] section in that it defines which associations have been made. This section connects media files to the appropriate Multimedia Command Interface driver. Each entry has the same format:

<Extension>=<MCI Driver Name>

For example, my system contains these three lines:

rmi=sequencer

mid=sequencer

wav=waveaudio

When I bring up the Media Player, I can play files with any of three extensions: .RMI, .MID, or .WAV. Files with an .RMI or a .MID extension will be played by the MIDI sequencer driver, and files with a .WAV extension will be played by the wave-audio driver.

The [Sound] section defines the correspondence between system events and specified sound files. Each entry has the following syntax:

<System Event>=<Filename>,<Description>

There are seven system events that can have associated sounds. These entries are made and updated by simply completing the entries in the Sound dialog box. At each possible system event (such as the display of a Question or Exclamation box), the sound driver will play the specified <Filename>. On my system, for example, two different sounds are played when the system starts and when I exit to DOS:

SystemExit=CHARGE.WAV,Windows Exit

SystemStart=TADA.WAV,Windows Start

CUSTOMIZING YOUR WINDOWS
HELP FACILITY

The help system is always at your fingertips in Windows. Press F1 and a Help window appears with context-sensitive information, or select the Help option from any Windows application to obtain the same window. Several entries in the [Windows Help] section define the initial size and position of the main Help window, as well as the History, Annotate, and Copy dialog boxes. These WindowPosition entries (each preceded by a letter identifying the window, such as M_ for main, H_ for history, A_ for annotate, and C_ for copy) are automatically set and reset whenever you move or size the main Help window or the relevant dialog boxes.

Five other settings are possible in the [Windows Help] section. Each of them allows you to customize the colors of portions of the Help window. Each entry has the same syntax:

<Option Name>=<Red> <Green> <Blue>

Remember from Chapter 11 that the red, green, and blue components of a color are numeric values that range from a minimum value of 0 to a maximum of 255. The first possible option name is JumpColor, which sets the text color for window entries that lead to new help panels when selected. The MacroColor option sets the color of text that runs a help macro. PopupColor sets the color of text entries that display a pop-up panel. IFJumpColor sets the text color that leads to a different help file's panel of information. IFPopupColor sets the text color that leads to a different help file's pop-up panel.

COLORIZING YOUR WINDOWS WORK SURFACE

Every conceivable portion of the Windows screen, from menus to buttons to the screen background itself, can be individually colored. Table 12.5 explains all the options that appear in the [Colors] section of the WIN.INI file.

Each entry in this section has the same format:

<Screen Element>=<Red> <Green> <Blue>

You can specify the intensity of each red, green, and blue component in a particular screen element. But, once again, it's just as easy to use the Color dialog box in the Control Panel. Windows will create and update these entries for you.

TABLE 12.5: Settings in the [Colors] Section of WIN.INI

Name	Default	Purpose
ActiveBorder	192 192 192	Sets color for active window's border
ActiveTitle	0 0 128	Sets color for active title bar
AppWorkspace	255 255 255	Sets color for Windows application's workspace
Background	192 192 192	Set color for screen background
ButtonFace	192 192 192	Sets color for face of all window buttons
ButtonHilight	255 255 255	Sets color for highlight on top and left sides of screen buttons
ButtonShadow	128 128 128	Sets color for shadow behind screen buttons

TABLE 12.5: Settings in the [Colors] Section of WIN.INI (continued)

Name	Default	Purpose
ButtonText	0 0 0	Sets color for text in screen buttons
GrayText	192 192 192	Sets color for unavailable (dimmed) screen options
Hilight	0 0 128	Sets color for background of highlighted text
HilightText	255 255 255	Sets color for all highlighted text
InactiveBorder	192 192 192	Sets color for border of inactive window
InactiveTitle	255 255 255	Sets color for title bar in inactive window
InactiveTitleText	0 0 0	Sets color for title bar text in inactive window
Menu	255 255 255	Sets color for menu backgrounds
MenuText	0 0 0	Sets color for menu text
Scrollbar	192 192 192	Sets color for all scroll bars
TitleText	255 255 255	Sets color for title bar text
Window	255 255 255	Sets color for workspace in window
WindowFrame	0 0 0	Sets color for window frame
WindowText	0 0 0	Sets color for window text

DON'T TROUBLE YOURSELF WITH THE REMAINING SECTIONS

A number of remaining WIN.INI sections are maintained automatically by Windows, based on your entries or responses in various dialog boxes. Unless there is some compelling reason for you to make adjustments, don't bother.

There are three WIN.INI file settings in the [Network] section that affect printing from Windows on a network. All three are maintained via the Printers dialog box in the Control Panel or the Network Connections command on the Options menu of the Print Manager. Once again, it is best to simply use the dialog boxes to change these settings. Chapter 16 discusses the possible controls and settings that have to do with running Windows on a network.

The [Embedding] section describes OLE objects, lists the programs used to create them, and shows the file format that the objects are stored in. The Registration Info Editor (REGEDIT.EXE) is the Windows tool to register applications as being OLE-compliant. It also makes all necessary adjustments to the entries in this section.

The [PrinterPorts] section specifies the possible printers that have been installed in Windows. Windows can only use a printer after an entry has been made in this section. For every device name, each entry defines a printer driver name, the port used, and a sequence of timeout values. Choosing the Printers icon leads you to the dialog boxes that acquire this information from you; Windows then updates the [PrinterPorts] entries.

Similarly, the Printers icon also establishes entries in a [Devices] section. This information is similar to the [PrinterPorts] section, without timeout information, but is included only to make Windows 2.*x* applications workable.

There is also a section named [Programs], which specifies path names in which to search for an application. These entries are only needed when you attempt to open a document file that has been associated with an application that Windows cannot find in the DOS PATH. If this occurs, Windows will ask you to tell it where the necessary application file is located. Personally, I'd suggest that you consider changing your PATH statement, or move the referenced application file to the WINDOWS directory, or somewhere else in the PATH.

◆ UNDERSTANDING THE SYSTEM.INI FILE SETTINGS

The WIN.INI file controls a number of aspects of your Windows environment. You can influence the appearance and the ease of use of your Windows system by making the changes discussed so far in this chapter.

The SYSTEM.INI file is more concerned with the hardware in your system. Making adjustments to your SYSTEM.INI entries can not only ensure that Windows works properly on your computer but can also dramatically enhance the performance of your system. Table 12.6 explains the various sections of the SYSTEM.INI file.

Because the settings in SYSTEM.INI directly influence how Windows deals with your hardware, it is even more imperative than with WIN.INI that you exercise extreme care in making changes to the file. In fact, before any modification, make sure that you save a backup copy of SYSTEM.INI in the event that you must restore the original to make Windows work again. Often, you can compare the older version with the current copy of SYSTEM.INI to determine what lines have changed to help you correct a problem.

TABLE 12.6: The Primary SYSTEM.INI Sections

Section Name	Purpose
[386Enh]	Sets execution parameters for 386 enhanced mode
[Boot]	Lists drivers and start-up files
[Boot.description]	Lists devices modifiable from Setup
[Drivers]	Lists names assigned to installable driver files
[Keyboard]	Specifies information about installed keyboard
[Mci]	Lists MCI drivers
[NonWindowsApp]	Lists acceptable alternative font pairs
[Standard]	Lists information about all loaded screen fonts

SETTING UP CUSTOMIZED DRIVERS AND DEVICES

The [Boot] section includes an extensive list of device driver, font, executable, and library names that Windows uses each time it starts. Table 12.7 summarizes the entries in this section. They are all straightforward, and nearly all of them are automatically initialized by the Setup program.

Although most of the entries are obvious from the descriptions in Table 12.7, one of them is not. The CachedFileHandles option defines the limit of open .EXE and .DLL files. This number should sometimes be lowered (but only if you experience a problem) when you run Windows on a network that has a limited number of files that can be open on the disk server.

The [Boot.description] section is a short list of devices that appear when you run the Setup program. These represent the devices that you can modify from Setup. Don't bother changing these entries. The section is created automatically, and making changes will only interfere with future use of Setup.

The [Drivers] section is also unlikely to require modification. Typically, a setup program for a new driver will update this section. Each entry defines an alias that can be used for a device whenever the device driver includes parameters. The driver then can be referenced by its new alias in the [Boot] section. The entries all look like

<Alias Name>=<Driver Filename> [Parameters]

For example, when I set up the channel map in the MIDI section of Chapter 11, the MIDI Sequencer installed new MIDI device drivers on my system, automatically adding these lines to this section:

MIDI=sndblst2.drv

MIDI1=adlib.drv

This enables me to use the two aliases MIDI and MIDI1 to output MIDI instructions to Sound Blaster and an Adlib device.

The [Keyboard] section contains another group of four entries that clearly define different aspects of your keyboard, such as the layout dynamic link library (KEYBOARD.DLL), the code-page translation tables file for non-United States OEM character sets (OEMANSI.BIN), as well as the keyboard type and subtype.

TABLE 12.7: Settings in the [Boot] Section of SYSTEM.INI

Name	Default	Purpose
286grabber	None	Specifies driver to restore DOS application screen in standard mode
386grabber	None	Specifies driver to restore DOS application screen in 386 enhanced mode
CachedFileHandles	12	Limits number of open .EXE and .DLL files
comm.drv	None	Names serial communications driver file
display.drv	None	Names display driver file
drivers	None	Sets alias names for installable drivers
fixedfon.fon	None	Specifies fixed system font file for Windows 2.x applications
fonts.fon	None	Specifies proportional system font file
keyboard.drv	None	Names keyboard driver file
language.dll	None	Names language-specific dynamic link library
mouse.drv	None	Names mouse driver file
network.drv	None	Names network driver file
oemfonts.fon	None	Names OEM character set font file
scrnsave.exe	Variable	Names currently selected screen saver file
shell	progman.exe	Names main program run by Windows at start-up
sound.drv	None	Names sound driver file
system.drv	None	Names hardware driver file
TaskMan.Exe	taskman.exe	Names task switcher that pressing Ctrl+Esc runs

Finally, the [MCI] section includes a list of driver names installed by Setup that will be used to play MCI media files. These entries are also obvious when you look at your SYSTEM.INI file.

MANAGING THE PERFORMANCE OF NON-WINDOWS APPLICATIONS

You can affect the performance of DOS applications when run under Windows, regardless of whether you are using standard mode or 386 enhanced mode. Table 12.8 lists the settings that appear in the [NonWindowsApp] section of SYSTEM.INI. Some of these options improve execution speed and others affect ease of use.

TABLE 12.8: Settings in the [NonWindowsApp] Section of SYSTEM.INI

Name	Default	Purpose
Disable-PositionSave	0	Saves (1) or ignores (0) position and font used in windowed DOS application
FontChange-Enable	1 (Windows 3.1); 0 (Windows 3.0)	Enables font change capability on earlier systems
GlobalHeapSize	0	Sets size of a conventional memory buffer for sharing data among DOS applications in standard mode
Mousein-DosBox	1	Enables mouse support when running in a window
NetAsynch-Switching	0	Allows or disallows switching away from an application in standard mode while an asynchronous network BIOS call is processed
ScreenLines	25	Sets number of screen lines for DOS applications
SwapDisk	Variable	Specifies disk drive and directory for standard mode swap files

The first option, DisablePositionSave, controls whether or not Windows saves information about the screen position and font used by a DOS application's window in 386 enhanced mode. Windows will save this information in the DOSAPP.INI file if this option is set to 0. In addition, Windows will save this information if the option is enabled but you've overridden it by checking the Save Settings On Exit box in the Font Selection dialog box. Remember that the Control menu of a non-Windows application has a Fonts option. Choosing this option displays a dialog box that controls the selection of a font to use in the application's window.

In Windows 3.1, the latest versions of some mouse drivers support the use of a mouse by a non-Windows application when it runs in a window. If you are using a mouse driver that does support using a mouse in a DOS window, you may still need to enable appropriate screen support by setting MouseinDOSBox=1.

The SwapDisk option controls the drive and directory for swapping of non-Windows applications in standard mode. The default is the drive and directory specified by your TEMP variable, which is usually set in the AUTO-EXEC.BAT file. If you have not set TEMP, Windows will use the root directory of the first hard drive on your system for swapping.

♦ USE SWAPDISK TO BOOST EFFICIENCY

Use the SwapDisk setting in the [NonWindowsApp] section of SYS-TEM.INI to enhance your control of performance settings in standard mode. Windows uses this setting to determine where to swap a non-Windows application when switching away from it. If you have more than one hard disk on your system, use this setting to direct Windows to swap to the fastest hard drive.

ENHANCING OPERATIONS WHEN IN STANDARD MODE

Depending on your hardware, you may be running Windows in standard mode (or, after reading the next two sections, you may choose to run in standard mode even though you could run in 386 enhanced mode). The options listed in Table 12.9 control many aspects of Windows execution when you are running in standard mode.

Other than the FasterModeSwitch option, which is unique to two non-IBM computers (see Table 12.9), the rest of the options are all programmer-oriented. Don't bother changing any of them unless you are a programmer yourself and fully understand the implications of the change.

The NetHeapSize option requires a brief explanation. Usually, an 8K buffer is sufficient for transferring data over a network. In fact, if your system is not running on a network, this setting is ignored and no memory is consumed. If a network application does not seem to be running properly, you may need a larger buffer for data transfer. Increasing this entry will increase the amount of conventional memory used for this buffer. Consequently, all applications will suffer to some extent from the loss of this memory.

TABLE 12.9: Settings in the [Standard] Section of SYSTEM.INI

Name	Default	Purpose
FasterModeSwitch	0	Unique to Zenith Z-248 and Olivetti M-250-E computers
Int28Filter	10	Controls percentage of INT28h pass-through to memory-resident software loaded before Windows
NetHeapSize	8	Sets size of standard mode network data transfer buffer in K
PadCodeSegments	0	Enables (1) or disables (0) padding of code segments with 16 bytes
Stacks	12	Sets number of standard mode DOSX interrupt reflector stacks
StackSize	384	Sets individual DOSX reflector stack size in K

CUSTOMIZING OPERATIONS WHEN IN 386 ENHANCED MODE

By far, the largest section of any .INI file is the one labeled [386Enh]. As Table 12.10 indicates, this section contains options that control or directly affect Windows performance.

TABLE 12.10: Settings in the [386Enh] Section of SYSTEM.INI

Name	Default	Purpose
A20EnableCount	Variable	Sets starting A20-line enable count
AllEMSLocked	False	Locks expanded memory contents in memory if True
AllVMsExclusive	False	Forces exclusive full-screen mode on DOS applications if True
AllXMSLocked	False	Locks extended memory contents in memory if True
AltKeyDelay	.005	Defines the wait time (in seconds) for interpreting a keyboard interrupt that follows an Alt-key interrupt
AltPasteDelay	.025	Defines wait time (in seconds) after Alt key is struck before pasting characters
AutoRestore-Screen	True	If True, requires Windows or the DOS application itself (if False) to restore screen display when the application moves to the foreground
AutoRestore-Windows	False	If True, requires Windows to repaint screen display when switching from DOS application to Windows application
BkGndNotify-AtPFault	True (VGA); False (8514)	Notifies applications (if False) not to access display

TABLE 12.10:   Settings in the [386Enh] Section of SYSTEM.INI (continued)

Name	Default	Purpose
CGA40WOA.FON	None	Specifies fixed-pitch display font file for DOS applications using 40-column screen sizes and 25 lines or fewer
CGA80WOA.FON	None	Specifies fixed-pitch display font file for DOS applications using 80-column screen sizes and 25 lines or fewer
CGANoSnow	No	Eliminates (if Yes) snow on IBM CGA display
COM1AutoAssign–COM4AutoAssign	2	Specifies serial port contention detection values
COM1Base, COM3Base	3F8h	Defines base addresses for serial ports 1 and 3
COM2Base, COM4Base	2F8h	Defines base addresses for serial ports 2 and 4
COMBoostTime	2	Defines time (in milliseconds) for a DOS program to process a COM interrupt
COM1Buffer–COM4Buffer	128	Defines buffer size for incoming serial data on COM1 through COM4
COMdrv30	False	Toggles whether or not the Virtual COM driver uses a private copy of the serial communications driver's interrupt handler
COM1FIFO–COM4FIFO	True	Enables or disables the FIFO buffer in any existing 16550 UART (Universal Asynchronous Receiver Transmitter) on COM1 through COM4
COM1IRQ, COM3IRQ	4	Defines interrupt lines used by COM1 and COM3

TABLE 12.10: Settings in the [386Enh] Section of SYSTEM.INI (continued)

Name	Default	Purpose
COM21IRQ, COM4IRQ	3	Defines interrupt lines used by COM2 and COM4
COMIRQSharing	True (EISA and Micro Channel); False otherwise	Enables or disables interrupt sharing
COM1Protocol– COM4Protocol		Stops virtual character transmission to COM1–COM4 virtual machines after receiving XOFF if set to XOFF
Device	None	Defines virtual devices in 386 enhanced mode
Display	None	Defines a display device in 386 enhanced mode
DMABufferIn1MB	No	Places DMA buffer memory in first megabyte, or not
DMABufferSize	16	Sets size of DMA buffer in K
DOSPrompt-ExitInstruc	Yes	Enables or disables opening DOS prompt message lines
DualDisplay	False	Enables (if True) use by Windows of video memory in range B000:0000 to B7FF:000F
EBIOS	None	Defines extended BIOS device for 386 enhanced mode
EGA40WOA.FON	None	Specifies fixed-pitch display font file for DOS applications using 40-column screen sizes and more than 25 lines
EGA80WOA.FON	None	Specifies fixed-pitch display font file for DOS applications using 80-column screen sizes and more than 25 lines
EISADMA	0,8; 1,8; 2,8; 3,8; 5,16w; 6,16w; 7,16w	Sets EISA machine modes for extended DMA channel

TABLE 12.10: Settings in the [386Enh] Section of SYSTEM.INI (continued)

Name	Default	Purpose
EMMExclude	None	Restricts Windows from searching a memory range for unused addresses
EMMInclude	None	Directs Windows to search a memory range for unused addresses
EMMPageFrame	None	Defines beginning paragraph of 64K page frame
EMMSize	65,536	Limits the amount of mappable expanded memory in bytes
FileSysChange	On	Enables File Manager reception of messages indicating creation, renaming, or deletion of disk files
Global	All devices	Specifies names of global DOS devices
HardDisk-DMABuffer	0 (AT); 64 (Micro Channel)	Sets DMA buffer memory size
HighFloppy Reads	Yes	If Yes, converts DMA verify to area above E000 into a read
IdleVM-WakeUpTime	8	Forces timer interrupts (in seconds) to occur in idle virtual machines
Ignore-InstalledEMM	No	If Yes, starts Windows in 386 enhanced mode when there is an installed memory manager supporting physical EMS hardware
InDOSPolling	No	Supports critical section exclusivity for memory-resident software

TABLE 12.10: Settings in the [386Enh] Section of SYSTEM.INI (continued)

Name	Default	Purpose
INT28Critical	True	Enables (if True) a critical section for handling memory-resident software's INT28h interrupts
IRQ9Global	No	Converts IRQ9 masks to global if Yes
Keyboard	None	Defines the 386 enhanced mode keyboard driver
KeyBoostTime	.001	Increases application priority after a keystroke (in seconds)
KeyBufferDelay	.2	Slows down pasting once the keyboard buffer fills (in seconds)
KeyIdleDelay	.5	Speeds up keyboard input by ignoring idle calls (in seconds)
KeyPaste-CRSkipCount	10	Controls speed of Clipboard fast pasting after a Return key press is received
KeyPasteDelay	.003	Controls speed of subsequent pasting after each key is pasted
KeyPaste-SkipCount	10	Controls speed of Clipboard fast pasting after a key is pressed
KeyPasteTimeout	1	Sets limit for application to read fast paste keystrokes before switching to slow paste (in seconds)
KybdPasswd	True (PS/2s); False otherwise	Implements password security on PS/2 keyboards
KybdReboot	True	Enables (if True) rebooting via a keyboard controller command, or (if False) requires Ctrl+Alt+Del

TABLE 12.10: Settings in the [386Enh] Section of SYSTEM.INI (continued)

Name	Default	Purpose
Local	None	Specifies device drivers to be made local to each virtual machine
LocalLoadHigh	False	If True, makes UMB area available to each virtual machine
LPTxAutoAssign	60	Sets parallel port timing (in seconds) for Windows 3.0 systems only
LRULowRateMult	10	Sets multiplier for determining low paging rate sweep frequency
LRURate-ChngTime	10,000	Sets time to switch paging rate techniques
LRUSweepFreq	250	Sets high paging rate sweep frequency (in milliseconds)
LRUSweepLen	1024	Sets size (in pages) of region swept on each LRU pass
LRUSweep-LowWater	24	Sets number of remaining free pages when LRU sweep is activated
LRUSweepReset	500	Sets time (in milliseconds) for ACC bit reset
MapPhysAddress	None	Sets memory range for page-table entries
MaxBPs	200	Sets maximum break points for transferring control to Windows
MaxCOMPort	4	Sets number of supported COM ports
MaxDMAPG-Address	0FFFh (non-EISA); 0FFFFFh (EISA)	Defines maximum physical page address for DMA
MaxPaging-FileSize	None	Sets maximum size (in K) for temporary swap file

TABLE 12.10: Settings in the [386Enh] Section of SYSTEM.INI (continued)

Name	Default	Purpose
MaxPhysPage	Variable	Sets maximum manageable physical page number
MCADMA	True (MCA machines); False otherwise	Controls use of MCA extensions to DMA
MinTimeSlice	20	Sets minimum virtual-machine time slice (in milliseconds)
MinUnlockMem	40	Defines required amount of unlocked memory (in K) when switching back to one of several running virtual machines
MinUser-DiskSpace	500	Limits size (in K) of temporary swap file
Mouse	None	Defines virtual device driver for mouse
MouseSoftInit	True	Enables use of mouse with DOS application in a window
NetAsynch-Fallback	False	Specifies how to react to failing NetBIOS request
NetAsynch-Timeout	5.0	Sets timeout period for enabled NetAsynchFallback critical sections (in seconds)
NetDMASize	32 (Micro Channel); 0 otherwise	Sets DMA buffer size for network use
NetHeapSize	12	Sets data transfer buffer size (in K)
Network	None	Defines network in use
NIMReboot	No	Defines response to nonmaskable interrupt
NoEMMDriver	False	Controls whether EMM driver is installed

TABLE 12.10: Settings in the [386Enh] Section of SYSTEM.INI (continued)

Name	Default	Purpose
OverlappedIO	On	Controls whether more than one virtual machine can make overlapping disk reads and writes
PageOverCommit	4	Sets multiplier for computing address space to be managed (in MB)
Paging	Yes	Enables (Yes) or disables (No) virtual memory
PagingDrive	None	Defines drive to contain any temporary swap file
PerformBackfill	True	Enables or disables automatic backfilling of conventional memory
PermSwap-DOSDrive	C	Sets drive used for a permanent swap file
PermSwapSizeK	Variable	Sets size of a permanent swap file
PermVMFiles	10	Defines how many file handles to allocate to each virtual machine
PSPIncrement	2	Determines additional memory to reserve when UniqueDOSPSP setting is on
ReflectDosInt2A	False	Passes through (True) or processes (False) all INT 2A interrupts
Reserved-HighArea	None	Eliminates a range of memory from Windows' scan for unused address space
Reserve-PageFrame	True	Determines whether EMS page frame can be used for allocating transfer buffers
Reserve-VideoROM	False	Sets video ROM in pages C6 and C7 if True

TABLE 12.10: Settings in the [386Enh] Section of SYSTEM.INI (continued)

Name	Default	Purpose
ROMScan-Threshold	20	Sets number of scans used to determine if memory is ROM
SGrabLPT	None	Sends printer output directly to screen
SyncTime	True	Forces synchronization with system clock
SystemROM-BreakPoint	True	Enables or disables use of ROM between F000:0000 and 1MB for break point
SystemVMPriority	100,50	Defines initial background and foreground priority values for virtual machines
SysVMEMSLimit	2048	Limits amount of usable expanded memory (in K)
SysVMEMS-Locked	No	Enables or disables swapping of expanded memory
SysVMEMS-Required	0	Defines minimum expanded memory space required to start Windows
SysVMV86Locked	False	Controls locking of virtual conventional memory
SysVMXMSLimit	2048	Controls amount of extended memory (in K) allocated to virtual machines
SysVMXMS-Required	0	Defines minimum extended memory space required to start Windows
TimerCritical-Section	0	Sets up critical sections around timer interrupt code (in milliseconds)
TokenRingSearch	True	Enables or disables recognition of token-ring network adapter card

TABLE 12.10: Settings in the [386Enh] Section of SYSTEM.INI (continued)

Name	Default	Purpose
TranslateScans	No	Converts nonstandard scan codes
TrapTimerPorts	True	Enables or disables Windows' interception of timer port reads and writes
UniqueDOSPSP	True (Microsoft Network or LAN Manager); False otherwise	Enables or disables starting of each application at unique addresses
UseableHighArea	None	Defines memory range to scan for usable addresses
UseInstFile	False	Compatibility setting for older Windows versions
UseROMFont	True	Enables or disables use of ROM font for full-screen DOS applications
VCPIWarning	True	Enables or disables warning messages when applications use VCPI
VGAMonoText	True	Enables or disables use of monochrome adapter video addresses (B000h-B7FF)
Video-BackgroundMsg	True	Enables or disables warning messages when video memory is low
VideoSuspend-Disable	False	Controls whether background applications are suspended when available video memory becomes too low
VirtualHDIrq	True	Enables or disables bypassing of ROM interrupt handler for hard-disk controller interrupts
WindowKB-Required	256	Defines minimum size (in K) of conventional memory that must be free to start Windows

TABLE 12.10: Settings in the [386Enh] Section of SYSTEM.INI (continued)

Name	Default	Purpose
WindowMemSize	−1	Controls amount of conventional memory Windows uses for itself
Window-UpdateTime	50	Defines the wait time (in milliseconds) before updating DOS application's display in window
WinExclusive	No	Enables or disables exclusive use of CPU by Windows when Windows application is in foreground
WinTimeSlice	100,50	Sets foreground and background priority values for Windows applications
WOAFont	DOSAPP.FON	Defines font files for DOS applications
XlatBufferSize	4	Defines size (in K) of mapping buffer for translating DOS calls when in protected mode
XMSUMBInitCalls	Variable	Controls whether Windows uses an extended memory manager's UMB routines

In this final section, I will concentrate on the [386Enh] options that are not obvious from the explanations in Table 12.10. I'll also further explain some of the options that can affect multimedia operations. In general, the default values for most parameters will work best for your system. The defaults tend to minimize the use of conventional memory, which maximizes the virtual memory available to each DOS application. The defaults also tend to minimize application favoritism by balancing system load and creating smoother multitasking.

Before making changes to a setting, you must understand what you will gain, and most important, what it may cost your system in efficiency, responsiveness, or ease of use. Some of these options are adjusted automatically by Windows when you make changes in the 386 Enhanced dialog box in the Control Panel. Windows adjusts other option values after running the Setup command. Still other options are maintained by the settings you enter in a DOS application's PIF, discussed in Chapter 8. The majority of options, however, require that you make direct edits in SYSTEM.INI.

Enhancing Interrupt Processing

Certain options are required to compensate for limitations in some applications. For example, the AltKeyDelay setting can slow down Alt-key interrupt processing by Windows. Although this may be necessary for some applications that cannot deal correctly with the fast interrupt handling in 386 enhanced mode, it will slow down your operations if you raise this default value.

The AltPasteDelay option has a similar purpose. When necessary, you can raise this value to slow down Alt-key recognition before pasting characters to an application.

When your system runs several background applications, the total time allocated to each application is reduced. This can occasionally impair a particular application's performance because it may not have enough time to process keystrokes. Use the KeyBoostTime option to temporarily increase the application's priority to improve responsiveness to keystrokes.

◆ IMPROVING RESPONSE TO KEYSTROKES

Fast typists sometimes notice that Windows doesn't process their keystrokes as fast as they type them. This is particularly true if the application is running in a window. And it's even more true if there are several background tasks running.

The easiest answer is to boost foreground priority, but that's simplistic because it reduces the remaining time available to other applications running in the background. A more efficient approach is to

> increase the KeyBoostTime setting in SYSTEM.INI. This temporarily in-
> creases the priority of a foreground application each time you press any
> key. Increase the value from the default of 0.001 seconds to at least 0.01.

Look at other options in Table 12.10 that begin with the prefix *Key.* Adjusting them can improve individual application performance. Do this only as
necessary to enhance a program that seems to be having problems dealing
with key interrupts under the default settings.

Hard disks are an important part of any Windows system, and processing the
interrupts from your hard disk correctly is essential. The VirtualHDIRQ option is typically set to True, which means that in 386 enhanced mode, Windows will handle the hard-disk controller interrupts. By bypassing the slower
ROM routine that would otherwise handle the interrupts, Windows can improve performance across the board. Unfortunately, this doesn't work for all
hard disks. Check your hard disk's documentation to determine whether this
option must be disabled, as in

VirtualHDIRQ=False

My Plus Hard Card requires this adjustment. Consequently, the slower ROM
routine from the Plus Card handles this hard card's interrupts. I have to admit,
however, that although I know that my entire system suffers from slightly
worse performance, I don't really notice the difference.

Redrawing the Video Screen

Two settings can affect screen redraws. If AutoRestoreScreen is set to the
default value of True, Windows will save display information for DOS applications in memory. This makes restoration of the screen very quick, but costs
memory. If you do not mind slower screen restoration, you can disable this option. This frees up memory for other purposes but requires your DOS application to bear the burden of repainting the screen when you switch back to it.
If your non-Windows application can even do this, it will probably do it
slower than Windows can. Additionally, you'll have to be the one who initiates the redraw through some menu selection or shortcut key in your DOS
application.

When switching to a Windows application from a DOS application, the AutoRestoreWindows setting controls the speed of screen restoration. The default value of False, which applies only to VGA screens, means that a Windows screen is similarly saved in memory. This allows rapid restoration of a screen without the overhead of repainting. Once again, this costs your entire system a certain amount of memory. If you need the memory and don't mind the slower screen restorations, you can change the setting to True.

♦ DISPLAY PROBLEMS IN 386 ENHANCED MODE

> If your system has difficulties when attempting to run two or more separate non-Windows applications, you may need to add the following line to the [386Enh] section of SYSTEM.INI: Local=EGA$. This forces Windows to keep a separate copy of the driver in each virtual 8086 machine, with separate status information about each non-Windows application.

The Effects of Exclusivity and Locking on Your System

Certain options reserve memory or CPU time. When an application is given exclusive use of the CPU or memory, that application alone usually benefits; the rest of your Windows system usually suffers. This is a trade-off that you will occasionally want to make as you fine-tune your system's performance.

For example, you may judge that a DOS application requires no CPU time if it is not the foreground task. Each DOS application will run fastest under Windows if it runs in full-screen mode and is given exclusive execution status. Although you could turn on the Full Screen and Exclusive check boxes in each application's PIF, you would then have to remember to do so in every new PIF that you create. The AllVMsExclusive option can be enabled to automatically ensure that each application will run in exclusive full-screen mode.

The two locking options, AllEMSLocked (for expanded memory) and AllXMSLocked (for extended memory), are similar. They each inhibit Windows from swapping to disk a particular type of memory that may be used by both Windows and non-Windows applications. Since DOS applications can control these factors via PIF entries, the setting in SYSTEM.INI will override the PIF settings.

Customizing the Display Fonts

The Setup program normally updates several SYSTEM.INI entries that specify fonts to use in non-Windows applications when they run in a screen window. You can use the Setup program from the DOS prompt and modify the Codepage or Display setting. Be sure to exit Windows first.

CGA screens are limited to 25 lines or fewer, and the other graphics modes can display more lines. The CGA40WOA.FON and CGA80WOA.FON options control 40- and 80-column fixed-pitch CGA screen fonts, and the EGA40WOA.FON and EGA80WOA.FON options control 40- and 80-column fixed-pitch EGA and VGA screen fonts.

Although you can directly change these settings, it is much easier to use the Font dialog box that appears when you select Fonts on the DOS application's Control menu. Just select a different font size, and you will immediately see a preview of the window shape and the application's characters using the new font. Choose OK to accept the new selection and continue. Remember that if you exit the application while it is still running in a window, Windows will save information about the font being used in the DOSAPP.INI file. When you next run the application in a window, Windows will use your selected font.

Managing Your Customized Serial Port Settings

You learned in the last chapter that the Ports icon in the Control Panel gives you access to a number of serial port communications settings. When you change the advanced settings for port address values in the BIOS area, Windows adjusts the COM*x*Base entries in SYSTEM.INI, where *x* is 1, 2, 3 or 4.

The COM*x*AutoAssign values are set automatically from the 386 Enhanced icon in the Control Panel. In this panel, you are actually shown three radio buttons. If you choose the Always Warn button, Windows sets the COM*x*-AutoAssign value to −1 and will always display a warning message when two applications try to access the same port. You will be asked to choose which application should be allowed to access the port.

If you choose Never Warn, Windows will set the value to zero, which means that you will receive no warning of two applications contending for the same port. Any program can access the port at any time. If you set each port's Auto assignment value equal to a fixed number of seconds, Windows will inhibit all other applications from accessing the port for this many seconds after any application stops using the device.

If you find that your communications program seems to be losing keyboard characters, it may be unable to process its COM port interrupts. Increasing the COMBoostTime value temporarily increases the program's priority to allow it more time to process those interrupts.

A communications program sometimes has difficulty processing characters that are received at high baud rates. If this is the case on your machine, there are several steps you can take. First, set the values for the COM*x*Protocol options to XOFF. As a result, Windows will respond better to an XOFF control character that is received with the data, pausing all virtual machine processing until an XOFF character is received.

If this still does not improve high-speed data processing, you can use the COM*x*Buffer options, which control how many characters are buffered. When you choose to buffer incoming characters, as shown in Figure 12.3, Windows reserves an area of memory to store the characters. The application can subsequently process the characters at its own workable (usually slower) speed. The buffer has to be large enough to store characters without running out of buffer space, until the application can get around to processing them.

Several other serial port settings will improve overall system performance. If set to True, the COMdrv30 option provides a separate (private) copy of the serial driver's interrupt handler for every DOS application that uses the port. This setting is generally unnecessary with the Windows 3.1 serial communications driver, but is necessary if your system uses an older Windows serial communications driver.

Some serial ports have a speedup device known as a 16550 Universal Asynchronous Receiver Transmitter (UART). Setting COM*x*FIFO to True will invariably enhance Windows' ability to process character transmissions at high speeds.

Depending on what serial devices you are using and their required (or alternative) interrupt numbers, the COMxIRQ options specify which interrupt line is being used. Remember that the Ports option in the Control Panel updates these entries. If you can share interrupts between more than one device or serial port, you can set COMIRQSharing to True. This is automatically done on Micro Channel and EISA machines.

Customizing for Adapter Conflicts

The EMMExclude option is extremely important for minimizing problems that arise from adapter conflicts. The upper memory adddresses above 640K

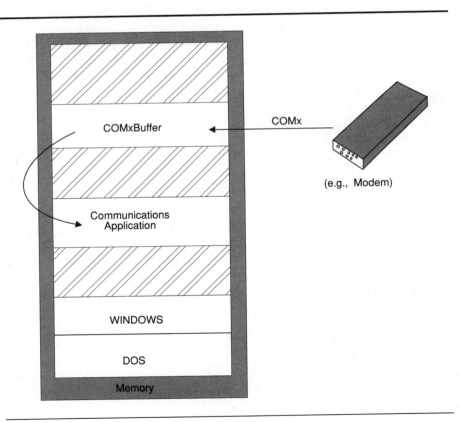

FIGURE 12.3: Buffering on serial ports

Speeding Up File Access in Non-Windows Applications

The [386Enh] section of SYSTEM.INI contains a setting that controls how Windows deals with changes to the file system. In general, you should turn this setting off:

FileSysChange=Off

If this setting is off, then each time you create a new file or change an existing file, Windows will not bother to notify the File Manager. This will speed up the throughput of all your applications.

Just remember that, once you've turned off the FileSysChange setting, the File Manager's directory and file windows will not necessarily reflect the current state of your drives. You must remember to update the File Manager windows by selecting Refresh on the Window pull-down menu or by pressing the F5 shortcut key.

are typically used by the ROM adapters for special devices, like hard disks and video cards. In addition, Windows attempts to ascertain what memory addresses are not used by any devices. It does this to more efficiently use those free memory addresses.

If Windows uses memory addresses that are actually in use by an adapter, you can be sure that your system will crash. Most devices that use adapter memory will tell you in their documentation what range is used. You must be sure to add EMMExclude lines in the SYSTEM.INI file to exclude these ranges. Each such line looks like the following example from my SYSTEM.INI file:

EMMExclude=C800–C9FF

This line excludes from Windows' scan for free space the paragraph range of addresses that are used by my system's Plus Hard Card. There is no possibility that Windows or any other application will use these addresses; the Plus Hard Card's adapter can use them safely.

Customizing for Enhanced Swapping Operations

Swapping, or paging, is the heart and soul of any multitasking operating environment. If you have plenty of memory, you may never experience any swapping to disk. Typically, however, your multitasking Windows environment in 386 enhanced mode relies on swapping activities to run more programs than available physical memory can support.

The Paging option in the [386Enh] section of SYSTEM.INI enables or disables virtual memory (i.e., swapping) in 386 enhanced mode. Unless you are extremely low on disk space and need the space that would be used by a temporary swap file, do not disable this setting.

The PagingDrive option defines the disk drive that Windows uses for its temporary swap file (obviously, this setting will be ignored if you've set up your system to have a permanent swap file). See Chapter 14 for an explanation of how to set up a permanent swap file on your system. If PagingDrive is not set or is set to an invalid drive, the drive containing your Windows system is used.

♦ DOCUMENTATION ABOUNDS

> Beyond the text files (SYSINI.WRI and WININI.WRI) that offer brief explanations of WIN.INI and SYSTEM.INI, Windows comes with a number of other text files. After installing Windows, take a look in your Windows directories for .TXT and .WRI files. You will be surprised to discover undocumented information about 3270 emulation, printers, and networks, along with general system information.

You've learned in this chapter how to directly control most of the parameters and options that affect how Windows relates to your system's hardware. Because of its special importance to most applications, customizing your printing operations and font usage is treated separately in Chapter 13.

13

Managing Fonts and Printed Output

If you use a computer, the bottom line is getting results. And getting results involves seeing them on the screen or on the printed page. This chapter concentrates on issues that affect the appearance of your output.

The first portion of this chapter deals with understanding fonts and typefaces. This information provides a backdrop for understanding how Windows displays information on screen. You will learn about typographical concepts and how they are implemented in Windows. You will also learn about installing and sizing fonts, and how TrueType fonts offer the latest version of What-You-See-Is-What-You-Get capability in Windows 3.1.

The second portion of the chapter explains how Windows manages printers and printer ports. It offers a number of special tips and tricks for selecting and connecting printers to ports, for using special characters in your documents, and for printing from either Windows or DOS applications.

The last part of this chapter deals with how to use the Windows Print Manager efficiently. You will learn about print queues and how to manage them. You will also learn techniques for improving printing speed, from enhancing how the Print Manager runs to circumventing the Print Manager.

◆ MANIPULATING TYPEFACES AND FONTS

This section explains much about the construction of characters on your screen and on your printer. First, I'll bring you up to speed on the terminology used and then I'll explain further some of the special aspects of font management under Windows 3.1.

UNDERSTANDING THE TERMINOLOGY

A *typeface* is a group of designed characters. A font is the set of all characters in a given typeface at a specific size and with a specific weight, such as boldface or italic. For example, Arial is a typeface and 14-point Arial Bold Italic is a font. There are four type weights, sometimes called *attributes*: regular (sometimes called roman, in which the letters are straight up and down), bold, italic, and bold italic.

Figure 13.1 depicts several lines of text using the Arial typeface. Arial is Windows' own version of the popular Helvetica typeface. There are several facets of typefaces that influence which one is appropriate for a particular purpose. From the point of view of appearance alone, some typefaces, like Arial,

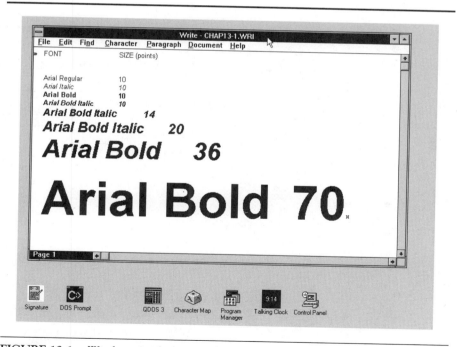

FIGURE 13.1: Windows Arial is comparable to the Helvetica typeface.

are known as *sans serif*. These typefaces contain smooth characters that have no frills around the edges.

In addition to sans serif typefaces, such as Arial, Windows has serif typefaces, such as Times Roman and Courier New. A serif typeface contains characters that have decorative frills at the edges. Figure 13.2 depicts the entire character set available in the Courier New typeface. Later in this chapter, I'll explain the Character Map window shown in this figure.

Each individual character, regardless of the font it comes from, has a number of distinguishing attributes. Each character has width and height. The width specifies whether the character is in normal proportions, or whether it has been compressed or expanded horizontally. More characters will fit in any location if you use a condensed font. The height of a character can be confusing, because some characters are lowercase and others are uppercase, and some of the lowercase characters have descenders. A *descender* is a portion of

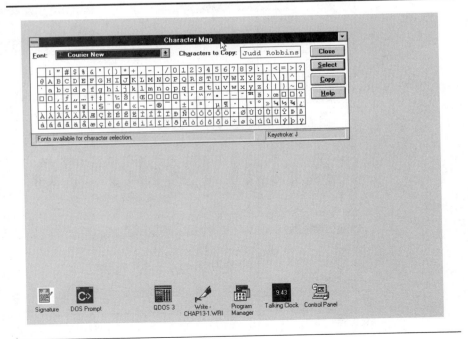

FIGURE 13.2: The Courier New character set

a character that extends below the line on which the character appears (like the bottom portion of the letter *g*).

A typographical *point* is ¹⁄₇₂ inch. A character's *point size* is the number of points that can be measured from the bottom of the font's lowercase descenders to the top of the capital letters. Sometimes, an attribute called *x height* is used to represent the number of points in the lowercase letters only.

Most typefaces offer proportional spacing, in which each character can use a different amount of horizontal space. The wider letters, like *A*, occupy more horizontal space than the narrower letters, like *i*. You can see this effect in Figure 13.1. By contrast, other typefaces like Courier offer fixed spacing (or *fixed pitch*), in which each character takes up the same amount of horizontal space on a line. The appearance of text in fixed-pitch fonts seems uneven because the amount of white space between the characters varies according to the amount of space required to produce the character.

Many dot-matrix printers only support fixed-pitch fonts. The word *pitch* is only used to describe an attribute of a fixed-spacing font.

◆ MEASURING FONT SIZES ON DOT-MATRIX PRINTERS

Windows defines font sizes by the number of points in the height of a font. The majority of dot-matrix printers use characters per inch (cpi) as the controlling factor in font size. On these printers, different fonts often have the same height but differing widths.

Applications that offer lists of font choices for dot-matrix printers typically offer two list boxes: one for the font name and one for the font's point size. A Windows font choice, therefore, may have a different name (e.g., Times Roman 8cpi or Times Roman 15cpi) but the same point size (e.g., 10).

THREE KINDS OF SCREEN FONTS

Windows supports three kinds of screen fonts: raster, plotter, and TrueType. Table 13.1 lists the names and sizes of each Windows 3.1 font, as well as which type of font it represents and the disk file (on my system) that contains the font definition information.

TABLE 13.1: Available Windows 3.1 Fonts

Font	Sizes	Type	Disk File
MS Sans Serif	8, 10, 12, 14, 18, 24	Raster	SSERIFx.FON
MS Serif	8, 10, 12, 14, 18, 24	Raster	SERIFx.FON
Symbol	8, 10, 12, 14, 18, 24	Raster	SYMBOLx.FON
Small	Display-dependent	Raster	SMALLx.FON
Roman	Scalable	Plotter	ROMAN.FON
Modern	Scalable	Plotter	MODERN.FON
Courier	10, 12, 15	Raster	COURx.FON
Script	Scalable	Plotter	SCRIPT.FON
Arial	Scalable	TrueType	ARIAL.FOT
Arial Bold	Scalable	TrueType	ARIALBD.FOT
Arial Bold Italic	Scalable	TrueType	ARIALBI.FOT
Arial Italic	Scalable	TrueType	ARIALI.FOT
Courier New	Scalable	TrueType	COUR.FOT
Courier New Bold	Scalable	TrueType	COURBD.FOT
Courier New Bold Italic	Scalable	TrueType	COURBI.FOT
Courier New Italic	Scalable	TrueType	COURI.FOT
Times New Roman	Scalable	TrueType	TIMES.FOT
Times New Roman Bold	Scalable	TrueType	TIMESBD.FOT
Times New Roman Bold Italic	Scalable	TrueType	TIMESBI.FOT
Times New Roman Italic	Scalable	TrueType	TIMESI.FOT
Symbol	Scalable	TrueType	SYMBOL.FOT
Small Fonts	Display-dependent	Raster	SMALLx.FON

A *raster font* is a bit map tuned for specific sizes on different monitors. As you can tell from the size column in Table 13.1, Windows supplies the raster fonts in specific point sizes. For example, MS Serif is available on my system in VGA resolution in 6-point sizes from 8-point to 24-point, while Courier is available only in point sizes of 10, 12, and 15. Raster fonts are just a collection of bits, so they become jagged if you ask Windows to adjust the size to anything other than the original choices.

Because raster fonts are dependent on the intended screen resolution, Windows includes different sets of bit maps for different device resolutions. These resource files each have a recognizable base name with a suffix (*x* in Table 13.1) that defines the screen's aspect ratio and resolution, and an extension of .FON. As Table 13.2 indicates, the suffix letters range from A to F.

On my system, the installed raster font files are in VGA resolution and are named SSERIFE.FON, SERIFE.FON, SYMBOLE.FON, and so on.

Plotter fonts, sometimes called vector fonts, are a collection of lines drawn between points. (Computer plotters are pen-based and draw everything as a series of such lines.) Since plotter fonts are just a collection of relative coordinates that represent each character in the font, it is easy to scale such a font on different devices. The coordinate information for these fonts is stored in a .FON file in your SYSTEM directory.

Although they do not usually look as good as raster fonts at the optimum VGA resolution, plotter fonts typically look better than bit-map fonts at large

TABLE 13.2: Raster Font Set Suffixes

Suffix	Aspect Ratio (Horizontal to Vertical)	Horizontal Resolution in dpi	Vertical Resolution in dpi
A	2:1 (CGA)	96	96
B	4:3 (EGA)	96	72
C	5:6	60	72
D	5:3	120	72
E	1:1 (VGA)	96	96
F	1:1 (8514)	120	120

point sizes. Some graphics programs actually have the ability to switch automatically from raster to plotter fonts at large point sizes.

◆ IMPROVING FONT APPEARANCE AT LARGE POINT SIZES

Check your software's documentation for a setting that enables automatic switching from raster to plotter (or TrueType) fonts at large point sizes. PageMaker, for instance, offers a Vector Above setting that controls the point size at which raster fonts are replaced automatically with plotter fonts.

Bit maps are fixed in terms of the pixels that are turned on or off. Plotter line segments must still be converted into pixels, but the starting point is a series of straight lines. Line segments are notoriously pesky when you try to create characters that have curves in them.

◆ TRUETYPE FONTS ARE THE STATE OF THE ART

TrueType is really a programming language, specially designed to describe the character shapes in a font by defining the outline of each character. TrueType, or *outline*, fonts, mathematically define each character as a series of straight lines *and* curves. The contours of a character define the inside and outside of the character, and once converted into a series of points can be readily and very smoothly scaled up or down in size.

IS TRUETYPE TECHNOLOGY REALLY WYSIWYG?

TrueType technology promises true What You See Is What You Get, or WYSIWYG. Although TrueType fonts certainly come much closer to this goal than raster or plotter fonts, printed text is still not truly an exact replica of what you see on the screen. For example, Figure 13.3 is a printed version of the Arial TrueType sample seen in screen resolutions in Figure 13.1. Notice how the 70-point line is very close in appearance in both the screen and printed versions. This is what passes for WYSIWYG nowadays. Although you can't expect 96-dpi VGA resolution to be able to match 300-dpi laser printer output, the TrueType technology does take a pretty good shot at it.

When you ask Windows to use a TrueType font to display text on screen or to print it on your printer, the same process occurs, which produces a close match between the display and the printed output. Windows uses a built-in module called the *TrueType rasterizer* to manage the conversion of the outline information into the necessary graphic bit map for a particular device. Windows sends the name of the selected font, the character chosen, the specified size, and information about the intended output device to the rasterizer. The rasterizer creates a bit map of dots that fall within the outline for that device's resolution and sends the resulting bit map back to Windows for transmission to the output device.

FONT	SIZE (points)
Arial Regular	10
Arial Italic	10
Arial Bold	10
Arial Bold Italic	10
Arial Bold Italic	14
Arial Bold Italic	20
Arial Bold	36
Arial Bold	70

FIGURE 13.3: Printout of the file shown in Figure 13.1

HINTING IMPROVES UPON
OUTLINE TECHNOLOGY

At lower resolutions, the number of dots (or pixels) per inch that fall within an outline can vary. In particular, some characters with serifs or parallel stems (like the letters *m* and *w*) can end up looking unbalanced (see the left side of Figure 13.4).

The TrueType rasterizer uses special instructions, called *hints*, that are contained in each TrueType font. These hints provide information to reshape the outline of a font for particular characters at particular sizes to enhance the eventual selection of dots that will make up the final character image. These hints are particularly important for producing good-looking characters at lower resolutions.

For example, Figure 13.4 depicts a sample letter *n* created from a TrueType outline font definition. On the left side, the normal first-pass TrueType outline rasterization produces unbalanced stems on the left and right side of the letter, as well as an unequal number of dots in the otherwise equivalent serifs at the bottoms of the stems.

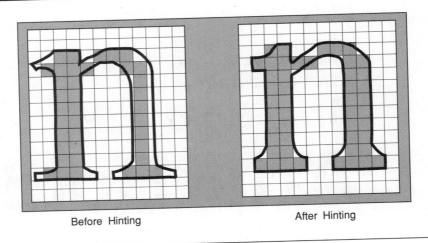

Before Hinting   After Hinting

FIGURE 13.4: Hinting improves TrueType font output.

On the right side of Figure 13.4, you see the result of applying TrueType hints. The TrueType rasterizer moves the two stems slightly apart and adjusts the serifs to ensure an even smoother and more balanced appearance.

The TrueType rasterizer is an integral part of the Windows 3.1 Graphics Device Interface (GDI). In essence, an application only needs to send its requests for screen or printed output to the GDI. Windows finds the correct TrueType file and sends the necessary information about the characters selected and the output device to the rasterizer. After the rasterizer converts the outlines and any appropriate hints for a particular device, the GDI once again takes over, sending output commands directly to the screen or printer.

This is a very efficient process in Windows 3.1. The GDI also uses RAM for dynamic font caching, which results in faster printing and faster screen scrolling. TrueType technology also minimizes downloading time to printers because only the characters actually to be printed are sent to the printer. Previous techniques downloaded an entire font before any characters were printed.

◆ SPECIFYING SCREEN FONTS IN YOUR WINDOWS SYSTEM

Beyond the fonts used by applications, Windows itself uses certain font files for regular purposes. In the typical window, title bars, menus, and general text must be displayed in some font. In the specialized window that contains a DOS application running in 386 enhanced mode, a different font is used.

CONTROLLING FONTS IN STANDARD WINDOWS

The [Boot] section of the SYSTEM.INI file contains three option lines that control the use of fonts on your screen during general window processing.

In my system, these lines are

oemfonts.fon=vgaoem.fon

fixedfon.fon=vgafix.fon

fonts.fon=vgasys.fon

Each setting specifies the name of a font file used for a particular screen purpose. The OEMFONTS.FON option defines the font file used to obtain special extended characters. It is also used by the Terminal program. The FIXEDFON.FON option defines a monospaced (fixed-space) font used by the Notepad accessory program. The FONTS.FON option is the primary file used to obtain characters for displaying menus, title bars, and normal text in Windows.

Understanding these settings can enable you to make proper adjustments when you change video resolutions. For example, you may have changed to a higher-resolution or larger monitor (or both). When you use a higher-resolution monitor, text on menus and elsewhere appears smaller and less readable. You can switch to a more readable, larger font by simply adjusting the three entries in your SYSTEM.INI file.

For example, you can use the fonts designed for the high-resolution 8514 displays to present more readable screen displays. First, copy the EXPAND.EXE utility from Disk 1 of your Windows installation disk set. Then, use it to decompress the 8514 font files from your Windows installation disks:

EXPAND A:8514*.FON \WINDOWS\SYSTEM

After expanding the 8514 font files from your installation disks, you can simply rewrite the appropriate option lines in the SYSTEM.INI file:

oemfonts.fon=8514oem.fon

fixedfon.fon=8514fix.fon

fonts.fon=8514sys.fon

When you next start Windows, these new font specifications will control the character sizes in your screen windows.

CONTROLLING FONTS IN SIZABLE DOS APPLICATION WINDOWS

In 386 enhanced mode, you can run DOS applications in sizable windows. In the most common, 80-column screen mode, the fonts used by default to display text can be found in the file specified by the EGA80WOA.FON option:

ega80woa.fon=EGA80WOA.FON

As you learned in the preceding chapter, similarly named options also appear in the [386Enh] section to specify fonts for a CGA screen in 80-column mode (CGA80WOA.FON) and in 40-column modes (EGA40WOA.FON and CGA40WOA.FON).

Windows 3.1 provides an easy, online way to adjust the fonts used while running a DOS application in a sizable window. There is an option named Fonts on the Control menu of every window that contains a DOS application. By selecting that entry, the Font Selection dialog box, shown in Figure 13.5, appears.

As you can see in the DOS application running behind the dialog box, I've already chosen a 10×18 font. The characters in this window are much larger and easier to read than they typically are at the standard size.

INSTALLING NEW FONTS IN YOUR SYSTEM

Choosing the Fonts icon in the Control Panel is the straightforward way to install new fonts in Windows. Although Setup defines an initial group of fonts, as indicated in Table 13.1, you will often come across new fonts that you want to add to your system. Once you've added them via the Fonts icon, they will be available to any of your applications.

For example, suppose that you get a new set of TrueType fonts. Figure 13.6 shows the Fonts dialog box, which appears after you choose the Fonts icon in the Control Panel.

By clicking on the Add button, the Add Fonts dialog box appears, as shown in the upper-left corner of Figure 13.6. By then specifying the B drive and selecting two fonts from that drive, I am able to load the calligraphic and handwriting fonts highlighted in Figure 13.6. Selecting OK loads both of them into my system. The Add Fonts dialog box disappears and both fonts then appear in the list box of the Fonts dialog box. They will also appear now in all font selection lists found in applications, such as the one used in Microsoft Write (see Figure 13.7).

♦ WHAT IF A FONT DOESN'T APPEAR ON SCREEN?

The most common explanation for why a known font does not appear on screen is that it hasn't been installed. Open up the Fonts section of the Control Panel and select Add. Find the font files you need and choose OK to install them.

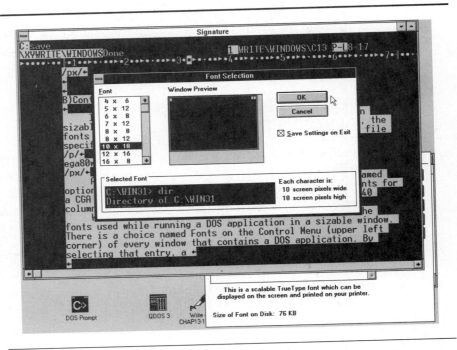

FIGURE 13.5: Controlling fonts in a sizable DOS window

Occasionally, a font file becomes corrupted in some way. This also may explain display difficulties and may require that you reinstall the font from the original disks.

◆ USING SPECIAL CHARACTERS FROM ANY FONT

In the past, you had to have a printout of all available characters in all available fonts before you could attempt to include special characters in your documents. In particular, you had to know the Alt key combination that produced

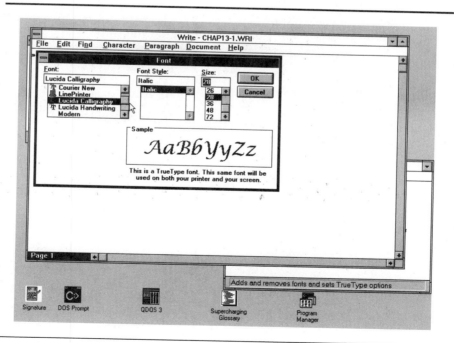

FIGURE 13.6: Installing new fonts in your system

international accented characters or special graphic or mathematical symbols. In Windows 3.1, you no longer have to suffer this burden because you can use the Character Map accessory program.

The Character Map program can be run through the Accessories group of the Program Manager. Figure 13.8 depicts one of the particular advantages of this accessory.

When you run the Character Map, you can select any available font by selecting it from the Font list box in the upper-left corner of the workspace. All available characters in the font are then displayed in the window. You can look closely at each character by clicking on it and holding down the mouse button. The Character Map program will enlarge that particular character for you to view. At the same time, it will display the particular Alt key combination code in the lower-right portion of the window for your future reference.

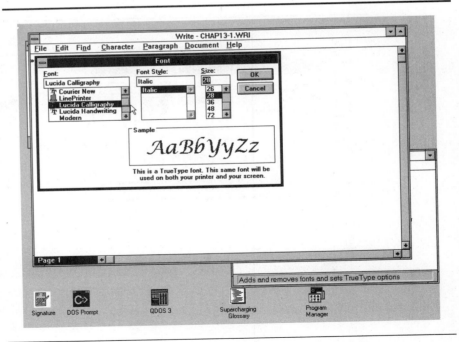

FIGURE 13.7: Newly added fonts are immediately available to applications.

Downloading PostScript Fonts Automatically

To download PostScript fonts automatically when needed during printing, you must include path information for both the printer font metric (PFM) files and the physical (type 1 soft) font files (PFB) themselves. Make sure that the PostScript section of WIN.INI looks something like this:

[PostScript,COM1]

sfdir=C:\POSTFONT

softfonts=1

softfont1=C:\POSTFONT\font1.PFM,C:\POSTFONT\font1.PFB

This sample entry specifies the location and name of the directory containing the printer fonts, the number of soft fonts to download, and location/name information about the actual printer font and printer font metric files.

Most important, you do not have to type any Alt key combination to obtain the special characters in each font that are not readily obtainable with a single key press. You can merely double-click on the characters themselves in the Character Map window. Each character will be placed in the special box labeled Characters to Copy in the upper-right portion of the Character Map window.

After selecting any character string, as I've done in Figure 13.8, you can click on the Copy button. All the selected characters will be copied to the Clipboard. Once they're on the Clipboard, it's an easy matter in any application to select Paste from the Edit menu. The special characters selected visually in the Character Map will be instantly entered in your existing text.

The only real limitation is that the font you use in the Character Map must be the same as the font you are using in the Windows application at the time of the paste. Naturally, you can use different fonts in different places in a document. Just be sure to synchronize your choices of fonts before copying special characters from the Character Map into your document. However, it's no big problem if you forget. You'll notice the results right away, because you'll get the wrong characters inserted in your document. You'll get the characters from the second font, which have the same ASCII identifying number as the characters you really wanted from the first font.

◆ MANAGING PRINTERS AND PORTS

There are unique considerations when outputting to a printer or a screen. As you just learned, TrueType technology makes things much easier. There are still a broad array of questions to deal with when setting up your printers.

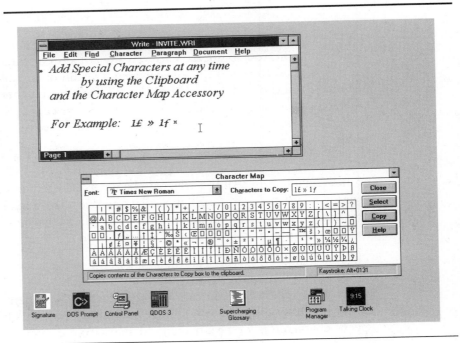

FIGURE 13.8: Obtaining font characters from the Character Map accessory

Enhanced PCL Printer Configuration

The native instruction language of the Hewlett-Packard series of printers is called PCL (Printer Control Language). If you use permanently downloaded fonts or macros, you can improve your system's configuration by adding two lines to the WIN.INI file:

MemReserve=<Amount to Set Aside>

This command defines how many kilobytes of printer memory to reserve for permanent soft fonts.

ResetPrinter=<0 ¦ 1 ¦ 2>

Set this option to 0 if you want the driver to reset printer memory when available printer memory gets low. Available memory is defined as total physical memory less the amount reserved by the MemReserve option. Set this option to 1 if you want to reset after each page is printed. Use this value if your document contains a lot of graphics. Set this option to 2 if you do not want the driver ever to reset printer memory.

TYPES OF PRINTER FONTS

TrueType fonts are essentially printable screen fonts; they can be readily translated into printer output by using GDI commands. Both TrueType and plotter fonts are examples of fonts that are convertible to either screen or printable bit maps. Printers offer a number of alternative methods for printing different fonts. Some printers can use some, but not all, of these methods.

A *downloadable font* is a file on your hard disk that contains character data. All characters from such a font must be first transmitted to, then stored in, the memory of your printer. Subsequent requests to print characters in that font use the data available in printer memory.

Downloadable fonts, sometimes called *soft* fonts, can be either temporary or permanent. These are most commonly used in the Hewlett-Packard series of laser printers and in a host of compatible printers. *Temporary* fonts are ones that are downloaded only when the printer driver must format text in that particular font. When the print job is finished, all temporary fonts are erased from the printer's memory. *Permanent* fonts are ones that will remain resident in printer memory until the printer's power is shut off. To speed up printing, you should load frequently used fonts as permanent fonts so that the characters are available as necessary during the printing of different jobs.

◆ PRINTING DOCUMENTS WITH MANY FONTS

Have you been unable to print a document that contains many fonts? Usually, the reason is an insufficient amount of printer memory to store all necessary fonts in the document. If this is the case, you may still be able to print the document if you download, then immediately erase (i.e., flush from printer memory) just the fonts needed for each page.

If possible, for greatest efficiency, you should manually download those fonts in heaviest use throughout your document. Keep these in memory for the entire session. Then, auto-download all other fonts as needed per page.

A *hardware font*, sometimes called a device font, is one that actually resides in the printer hardware. You will have to check your printer's documentation to determine which fonts are available in your printer. A device font is either built into the device or is contained in a plug-in font cartridge. Each device driver installed by Setup knows what built-in hardware fonts and what plug-in hardware font cartridges are possible for a specific printer.

Each of these alternative printer font methods requires its own installation sequence for your printer. The next section of this chapter discusses how to best use the Printers icon in the Control Panel to install printers and fonts.

INSTALLING A PRINTER

I've given you good reasons to use TrueType fonts for all your application output: They look better than many other fonts, and they scale up and down more easily. Especially after scaling, they will usually still look good on both the screen and on the printed page.

However, you still need to establish the proper printer connections through Windows before you can successfully print any of the fonts you've learned about in this chapter. The Printers dialog box, available through the Printers icon in the Control Panel, is your primary mechanism for performing the necessary steps. However, it can appear somewhat intimidating at first glance. Figure 13.9 visually summarizes the correlation between what you must do and what the Control Panel will help you to do.

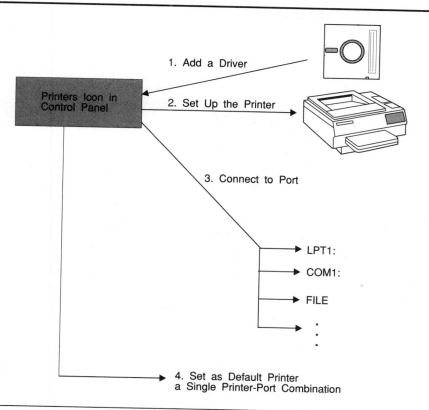

FIGURE 13.9: Selecting and connecting a printer

Adding and Installing a Printer Driver

Printer drivers are the hardware-dependent feature of your system that helps
Windows and your applications in particular to avoid having to contain information about every possible printer. The driver software includes all necessary information about the available printer features, the hardware interface,
any built-in font support, character translation capabilities, and all control
codes supported. You must install a printer driver before you can do anything
at all from Windows with that printer.

By first clicking on the Add button, the entire lower half of the Printers dialog
box opens up. As shown in Figure 13.10, this displays a list box that contains
the names of known printers. If you are installing a printer for which Windows does not already have a driver on its installation disks, choose the first
option that appears at the top of the scrolling list (Install Unlisted or Updated
Printer).

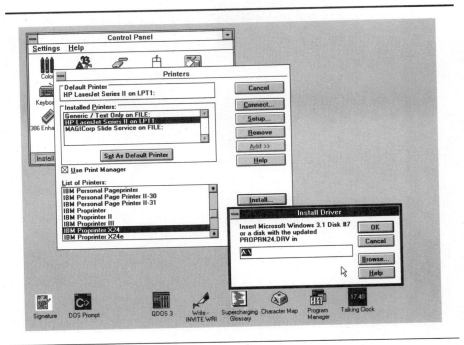

FIGURE 13.10: Adding a new printer driver to your Windows system

Creating Formatted ASCII Output Files

You can output printable ASCII text from any Windows application by printing to an installed printer that has been connected to a port called FILE. Such a file will contain the actual ASCII text with embedded print commands, specific to the printer you're outputting to. Use this technique for deferred printing, either at more convenient times of the day (when the printer load is reduced) or after transmission elsewhere on a network.

To establish this kind of connection, open the Control Panel and double-click on Printers. Click on Connect and select the port named FILE from the list box. Confirm by choosing OK. When you actually print to the connected printer, Windows will pause to ask you for the file name in which to output the formatted data.

By printing to FILE, Windows enables you to store printed output in files named differently. If you want your output to always go to the same file, you can modify WIN.INI. Add the following entry to the [ports] section:

ASCIITXT.PRN=

Although you can change the base name, ASCIITXT, the principle here is that Windows won't ask you to enter a new file name each time you print. If you've connected your output printer to this specified port/file name, each print job will be sent to the file, erasing any previous output stored in that file.

In either case, you must first highlight the appropriate option for the printer you want to install, then click on the Install button. Windows displays the Install Driver dialog box, shown in the lower-right corner of Figure 13.10. In this example, the IBM Proprinter X24 printer is highlighted in the List of Printers box, and Windows is prompting for insertion of the correct disk containing the required driver (in this case, PROPRN24.DRV).

After you click on OK in this dialog box, Windows reads the driver and then asks for additional disks to be placed in drive A. Whether or not the additional disks are requested depends on the fonts that this printer can use and whether your system already has all necessary font information. If it does not, you may be asked to place the disks containing the needed .FON files in the A drive. After all driver and font file data is read, the newly installed printer will be added to the list of installed printers in the center of the Printers dialog box.

Preparing and Connecting the Printer Hardware

All printers can be customized. By clicking on the Setup button in the Printers dialog box, you gain access to subsequent dialog boxes that enable you to customize your printer.

♦ SWITCHING BETWEEN LANDSCAPE AND PORTRAIT MODES

Many applications offer the ability to send control codes to a printer to direct it to switch between landscape and portrait modes. If your printer offers this facility but your software does not, you can still switch by using the Printers dialog box. Choose Setup and click on the Portrait or Landscape radio button in the Orientation section. Windows will print in this specified mode until you change the orientation.

As Figure 13.11 indicates, you can control the IBM Proprinter's resolution, paper size, paper source, and orientation from the initial dialog box that appears. Advanced options appear when you click on the Options dialog box. The contents of the Setup dialog box vary according to the capabilities of each printer.

One powerful technique for speeding up printing is dependent on both you and your application. In particular, this technique can have a dramatic impact when you print multiple copies of a document that uses downloadable fonts. Unless directed otherwise, most applications will download the necessary fonts just before sending the document to the printer. Unfortunately, the application repeats this entire process for every copy of the document, wasting an enormous amount of time.

Generally, the more sophisticated printing applications enable you to print multiple copies of the same document more efficiently. Your part in this is simply to find a COPIES box for the application. By directing the application to produce a specified number of copies, it can download the necessary fonts only once, then send the document to the printer the required number of times. You can usually find this COPIES option in the Printer Setup dialog box, reachable from the application's File menu. If the option is not there, you may also find it via the Printers icon in the Control Panel.

Connecting Your Printer to a Port

Once you've set up your hardware, you can click on the Connect button in the Printers dialog box, which presents a list of alternative ports to which you can connect your printer (see Figure 13.12). Applications will send printed output to what is known as the default printer. The default printer consists of an installed physical printer in tandem with a logical port that you've connected that printer to. The way Windows implements this mechanism, you can actually install any number of printers and connect any one of them to one or more unique ports. Whichever tandem combination is selected as the

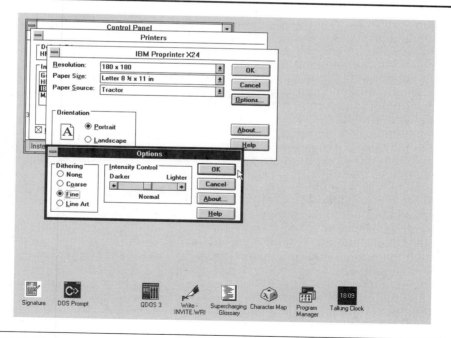

FIGURE 13.11:   Setting up an individual printer

default printer is the one that typically receives printed output from your applications.

PRINTING TO A FILE

Connecting one or more printers to a specific port offers a number of interesting opportunities. You can use more than one printer in your system and select from an application the one to which you want to print. You do this in the application by either choosing Print on the application's File menu (to print to the default printer) or choosing Print Setup on the File menu to display a list of alternative installed printers.

You can also prepare printed output without necessarily having the actual printer connected to your system. You first use the Connect option in the Printers dialog box to connect the installed printer to a port named FILE.

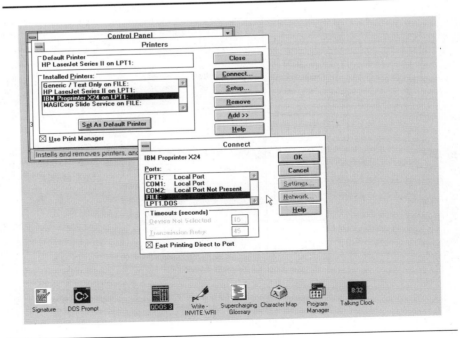

FIGURE 13.12: Connecting a printer to a specific port

Using Two Printers on a Single Port

If you have only one output port (usually LPT1) but two printers, you can print to either printer through Windows. But you need to perform several steps during hardware and software installation.

Hardware: Run a cable from your printer port to the I/O port of a standard A-B switch box. Run cables from the A and the B connectors on the switch box to each printer's input port. Turn the A-B switch to the printer you want to receive output from the computer.

Software: Simply install the appropriate printer drivers for each printer, then connect each printer to the same port name. When you want to print to a particular printer, choose Print Setup in the application to select a particular printer-port combination (if it is not currently the default printer). Alternatively, if your application does not offer Print Setup, you can go back to the Control Panel, highlight the desired driver in the list of installed printers, and click on the Set As Default Printer button. Return to your application and then request your printout.

When you later send printed output to that printer, Windows will display a Print To File dialog box that requests the name of the file into which you want printed output to go. When you eventually have the desired printer on your system or when you want to print the file on another system, you can later use a DOS command to send the specially formatted output directly to the port.

For example, suppose that I'm still waiting on the delivery of the IBM Proprinter that I installed in the last section. But my branch office in Boston already has the printer and I need to prepare a detailed report, complete with spreadsheet graphics, as well as an invitation to the annual stockholders' meeting, to send to them. After connecting the printer to the FILE port, as shown in Figure 13.12, I create a file called INVITE.WRI with Microsoft Write.

On my system, the default printer is an HP LaserJet Series II, so Write is typically configured to print to that device. But sending printed output to different devices is no problem. In any Windows application, the File menu contains a Print Setup option, which, when selected, brings up a dialog box similar to the one shown in Figure 13.13.

From the Printer Setup dialog box, you can redirect printed output from the default printer to any other printer-port combination that your system has (in the list of installed printers). By changing my setup for the Write program, all subsequent output via the Print command on the File menu will go to the FILE port connected to the IBM Proprinter driver.

When I later attempt to use the Print menu option to print the INVITE.WRI file, I will enter a unique name in the Print To File dialog box. If I enter IN-VITE.PRO as that file name, I can print this file on the IBM Proprinter (presumably connected to an LPT1 port) by entering this command at the DOS prompt:

COPY /B INVITE.PRO LPT1:

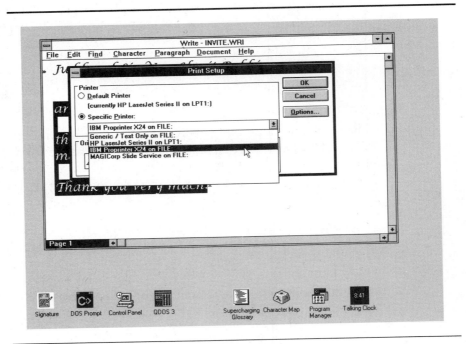

FIGURE 13.13: Printing to a nondefault printer

Printing Unformatted ASCII Text to a File

To produce a plain-vanilla text file, you must use a special printer driver. To install this required driver, first run the Control Panel and choose the Printers icon. Select the Add button, choose Install, and select Generic/Text Only. Insert the disk containing the necessary TTY.DRV printer driver, and click on OK.

After installing this printer driver, you must then connect it to the FILE port so that output via this driver will be stored in plain ASCII format in a disk file. To do this, highlight the Generic/Text Only option in the list of installed printers, choose Connect, and select File from the list of available ports.

Lastly, you must activate this particular combination of printer driver and connected port. To do this, highlight Generic/Text Only on FILE from the list of installed printers, and click on the Set As Default Printer button. Then choose the Close button in the Printers dialog box.

◆ INSTALLING A POSTSCRIPT DRIVER

If you use the services of a print shop that has very high resolution equipment, such as a 1000-dpi Linotype 3000 typesetting machine, you should consider installing a PostScript printer driver on your system. You can connect the driver to a file, which can then be given to your print shop. The results can be very high quality masters for your presentation or your customer/stockholder report.

◆ MANAGING THE PRINTING PROCESS ITSELF

The Print Manager is the primary utility program used to manage the flow of printed information from Windows applications to your printer. This section considers some aspects of printing through the Print Manager. Non-Windows applications do not use the Print Manager at all. Instead, they typically send printed data directly to a port. If you would like to use some of the Print Manager capabilities discussed in this section for your DOS program print output, you first have to transfer the file to a Windows application and print it from there.

◆ POWER UP BEFORE BOOTING UP

Your AUTOEXEC.BAT and CONFIG.SYS files control the initiation of many aspects of your Windows and DOS system. For example, you may have a Bernoulli disk driver in your CONFIG.SYS file, and you may send a PostScript header to your printer as part of your AUTOEXEC.BAT file. In both cases, you must remember to power up the appropriate devices (Bernoulli and printer in this example) before turning on your computer. If you do not have devices both powered up and online, a device may not be enabled by the driver software, or a device may never receive the necessary start-up instructions.

Alternatively, you can buy a third-party product, like PrintCache from Laser-Tools Corporation in Emeryville, California. This spooling program can work with Print Manager or replace it completely. (Replacing the Print Manager is advisable for some printers whose drivers are relatively inefficient.) The LaserTools print-spooling algorithms are very fast.

PrintCache can supplement the Print Manager by working in tandem with it to accept output very quickly from your application, allowing you to get on with your application's work. It can then allow the Windows Print Manager to manage the printing to devices that may have efficient drivers installed. Because PrintCache also spools output from DOS applications under Windows, I recommend this utility to anyone who even occasionally sends printed output from a non-Windows application to the system printer.

Using More Than One Printer

You can install multiple printers with Windows. These printers can be local to your computer, or they can be located elsewhere on a local area network. For example, you may have an inexpensive draft-quality dot-matrix printer next to your computer and a high-speed proof-quality laser printer at another network node.

You can also install multiple drivers for the same printer. For example, you may have a Kyocera laser printer with several emulation modes. You may want to print to this printer in each of several modes. To do so, you install different drivers for the different modes.

In both these cases, you must first install the necessary printer driver in the Printers section (choose Add) of the Control Panel. Then, you must connect that printer to a particular output port. Lastly, before printing from an application, you must select which printer-port combination will receive your application's output. Do this by clicking on the Set As Default Printer button in the Printers dialog box.

UNDERSTANDING PRINT QUEUES

When Windows applications send printed output to any installed printer, the Print Manager ensures that printed pages from multiple applications do not accidentally become interspersed at the printer. It does this by creating and managing separate *queues*, or lists, of documents to print for each physical printer.

Distinguishing between Local and Network Queues

A *local queue* contains names of files to be printed on a printer attached directly to your computer. A *network queue* contains file names to be printed on a network print server. Typically, the Windows Print Manager manages the printing of files on a local printer only. The Print Manager's window, however, can display information about the status of jobs on the network printer. The actual management of those network print jobs, however, is the task of the network print manager.

When you initiate printing to a local printer, the Print Manager icon appears at the bottom of your Windows screen. If you enlarge the window, it shows the status of all jobs on all printers. For local jobs, you can pause the printing of one or more jobs, cancel them completely, or just reorder the printing sequence. Figure 13.14 shows a typical Print Manager window after several print requests have been sent to an HP LaserJet printer.

The Print Manager window is automatically updated (by DDE messages) so that it always accurately reflects the system status of the print queues. Notice in Figure 13.14 that the line for the HP LaserJet printer is highlighted. All print jobs that are queued up for that printer are indented and listed below that printer. If other printers were also receiving output on the local, or on a network, printer, there would be other groups of file names displayed as well.

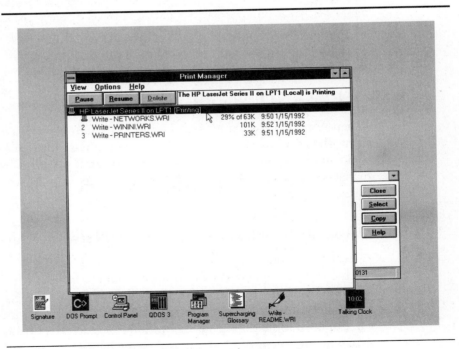

FIGURE 13.14: The Print Manager controls local printing requests.

Other Ideas for Improving Printing Speed

Here are some additional techniques you can employ to improve printing speed under Windows:

♦ Set up a RAM disk, create a directory, and point the system's TEMP environment variable to that directory. For example, if your RAM disk is F:, you can include the line SET TEMP=F:\TEMP in your AUTOEXEC.BAT file.

♦ Avoid using the Print Manager and either print directly to a port or use a replacement print spooler.

♦ Run DOS applications in exclusive mode if this is feasible on your system. You must not be running anything critical in the background, such as a communications program.

Pausing and Resuming a Printer Queue

If you highlight the line that displays the printer name, as is done in Figure 13.14, the Pause and Resume buttons are activated. Pressing Pause ceases output to that printer temporarily, and pressing Resume continues sending output. If you highlight any file-name line that is printing or to be printed, the Pause and Resume buttons are grayed (because they are meaningless in this context), and the Delete button is activated.

Removing an Entry from the Queue

Pressing the Delete button removes an entry from the queue. You will first be asked if you really want to stop printing the file. If you choose OK, the file is removed from the queue. The print output is lost; if you later want to print the information, you'll have to run the Windows application again.

The Delete button works almost the same for any file in the queue. Jobs that haven't started printing produce no output. Item 2 (WININI.WRI) and item 3 (PRINTERS.WRI) in the queue of Figure 13.14 fall into this category. However, what about deleting a print job that has already begun?

The small printer icon beside the first item in a queue indicates that the entry is either printing or waiting for a paused printer to become ready again. If you delete a queue entry that has already begun printing, the Print Manager will stop sending output immediately and erase the remainder of the print data. This may leave some data in the printer's buffer. Before sending any additional printout to that printer, you should eject a page or use form feed to clear the current page.

◆ DELETING FILES FROM A PRINT QUEUE

Choose Delete in the Print Manager window to remove a file from a local print queue. Be careful, however, when deleting a file that is currently printing. If the file is printing in graphics mode, you may need to reset your printer manually. To do this, and to clear any data still in the printer's buffer, press the printer's Reset button or turn the printer off and then back on. If the file is printing in text mode, a partial page may have been sent to the buffer. Sending a form-feed character or pressing the Form Feed button may be necessary to clear the printer and ready it for subsequent text output.

Rearranging the Order of the Queue

Occasionally, you will want to rearrange the order of the jobs in the print queue. For example, suppose in Figure 13.14 that you look at the queue and realize that the third queue entry (PRINTERS.WRI) is much smaller than the second entry (WININI.WRI). Perhaps you'd like to begin reading the PRINTERS.WRI file while the printer chugs along printing the larger WININI.WRI file.

To move a queue entry, just click on its name and hold down the mouse button as you move the mouse in the list. As you move the mouse, a horizontal line of dashes appears between successive queue entries. When the dashed line appears at the location in the list where you would like to reposition the highlighted file entry, just release the mouse button. The Print Manager immediately rearranges the queue with your highlighted file in its new position.

Printing Faster Than Print Manager Allows

Yes, the Print Manager can sometimes be surprisingly slow. You can buy faster spooling programs, but you can also try a trick within Windows itself. Open the Control Panel and select Printers. Choose Connect to link your output printer to the LPT1.DOS port rather than the more common LPT1 port. This directs Windows to bypass the Print Manager, send output to a file named LPT1.DOS, then ask DOS to output the file directly to the printer.

The good news is that printing will be dramatically faster for complex, long, or graphic output. Do this if the printout is your most important application.

The bad news is that all other applications will be slowed down for the duration of printing. You can counter this delay for specific background applications by adjusting their priorities to higher values.

CONTROLLING PRINTING SPEED

The Options menu in the Print Manager displays a number of optional control facilities. The most interesting ones are the options labeled Low Priority, Medium Priority, and High Priority. By checking one of these, you direct that more or less system CPU time be dedicated to the Print Manager itself. This is not unlike changing the priority of an application.

If you select Low Priority on this menu, the Print Manager uses fewer CPU cycles to control printing. This frees up more time for other running applications, so they will perform better. However, the output managed by the Print Manager might take a longer time to be printed.

If you select High Priority, Windows assigns additional CPU time to the Print Manager and printing is faster. All other applications, however, will obtain less CPU time while printing occurs.

The Medium Priority option is the default, representing a balance of CPU time distribution. Leave this setting unless you understand the trade-offs of the other two settings and want to implement a different proportioning of CPU cycles.

There are other options for controlling the speed of printing. For example, you can choose a draft-quality option in many word processors, which sends less data to the printer, requiring less time to print a page.

Also, you can use the Printers icon in the Control Panel to set up some printers to print everything at lower resolution. For example, the HP LaserJet drivers offer an option to specify the resolution in dots per inch. Although the driver can support 300 dpi, printing will be faster if you use 150 dpi.

Suppose that you are printing to a network printer. You could send printed output directly to that printer. By bypassing the Print Manager completely, you remove one unnecessary step from the process needed to obtain your final printout.

As mentioned earlier, you can also often obtain faster printing performance by using a replacement spooling program, such as PrintCache. This is certainly true if you are printing from non-Windows applications in a virtual 386 enhanced mode machine.

Additionally, you can buy a third-party print spooler program that is customized for network operations. For example, the PrintQ LAN program from Software Directions provides intelligent network printing. In addition to providing a sophisticated range of queue controls, the program can enhance an important and sometimes overlooked aspect of print output. Whereas most print spoolers wait to print until an entire print job is received and spooled to disk, PrintQ LAN begins to print the pages of a print job as soon as the first page is received. If the printer is available, you will no longer see an idle printer while the CPU waits to receive the entire print job and spool it to disk.

◆ PRINTING WITHOUT USING THE PRINT MANAGER

To avoid using the Windows Print Manager, you must go to the Printers dialog box and remove the check mark beside the Use Print Manager option. You can do this if your application manages its own printing, if you've installed an alternative print spooler, or if you simply want to print through DOS.

However, if you choose not to use the Print Manager and have not installed a replacement print spooler, you will have to wait for each printing job to finish before starting another one. If multiple applications attempt to output to the printer, Windows will notify you that the second print job cannot begin.

Turn now to Chapter 14, which focuses solely on a wide range of techniques for enhancing your entire Windows system.

Optimizing Windows

Part IV focuses on ways to fine-tune your system. You will learn techniques that enhance not only the operation of Windows but DOS as well. In Chapter 14, you'll learn how to use swapping and disk caches to improve performance. In Chapter 15, you'll learn how to make more efficient use of your system memory. Finally, in Chapter 16, you'll learn how to optimize Windows' performance on a network.

◆

14

Turbocharging Your System

omputer users are usually hungry for faster systems. This desire to "make it faster, make it better" pervades the Windows marketplace.

In this chapter, you will learn techniques for improving performance that depend on making more efficient use of your system's hard disk and CPU. I'll start with the technique of disk caching, explaining hardware and software methods for implementing disk caches. I'll move on to explain how swapping helps multitasking, as well as throughput, and how you can customize swapping to suit your needs.

Because so much data is constantly being transferred to and from the hard disk, you will often see dramatic improvements by enhancing the performance of your hard disk. Beyond using a caching scheme, you can improve file layout and access techniques. You can also tweak Windows settings, such as those in the WIN.INI and SYSTEM.INI files, so that Windows manages hard-disk data more efficiently. Some of these settings enhance hard-disk access, while other settings enhance the distribution of CPU cycles among executing applications. I'll present a wide range of techniques for improving the CPU and hard-disk performance of both Windows and non-Windows applications.

◆ BOOSTING SYSTEM PERFORMANCE WITH DISK CACHING

It's simple. I've said it before, and you'll probably hear it again: The more memory your system has, the better it will perform. Windows can access memory in a matter of nanoseconds. This is a lot faster than accessing data from any

Thumbnail Summary of Key Optimization Techniques

To enhance the hard disk:

♦ Adjust the disk's interleave.

♦ Defragment the disks.

♦ Allocate space for a permanent swap file.

To enhance the configuration:

♦ Install a RAM disk.

♦ Install a disk cache.

♦ Set the TEMP environment variable to a RAM disk or to a fast hard disk.

To enhance memory (see Chapter 15):

♦ Install more extended memory.

♦ Minimize the use of expanded memory.

♦ Maximize available memory before starting Windows.

disk, which typically does its chores in milliseconds (this is fast, but not as fast as the CPU). If you have enough RAM, you can configure Windows to do most of its work in RAM. The disk will rarely need to be accessed.

From time to time, Windows reads into memory different parts of a program's code or data. From time to time, Windows makes room in memory for a new program by moving portions of executing programs out to specially designed files on the disk. And from time to time, Windows will read new information for its own purposes into memory. Every disk read or disk write reduces overall system performance. Any technique that reduces the average time necessary for disk reads or writes will make Windows and your applications run faster. This section begins the discussion on disk improvements by explaining how to use a technique called disk caching to speed up overall disk input and output.

UNDERSTANDING THE CONCEPTS
BEHIND DISK CACHING

Disk caching is the best direct improvement you can make to a hard disk's performance. A *cache* is simply an area of memory that replicates disk data. By using the data in memory, programs can access the data at RAM speeds instead of at disk speeds.

As Figure 14.1 depicts, a disk cache can be constructed in hardware or in software. Both methods offer improvements in performance. Software cache programs are inexpensive and use memory that already exists in your system. They result in a significant speed boost. Hardware caching controllers are significantly more expensive, but offer a noticeable jump in performance even when compared with software cache programs. In large part, this results because the hardware board provides its own cache memory. Because of this, the cache does not reduce available Windows memory, thereby reducing the performance impact on all remaining Windows activities. Additionally, hardware cache boards usually include their own processor chip to manage the cache. Consequently, your system's processor chip is freed up from caching chores to concentrate on other tasks, thereby improving your system's performance even more.

In both types of caches, there is additional overhead involved in creating, filling, and maintaining the cache. If data were read or written only once, a disk cache would not provide any speedup. But disk caching provides significant performance improvements; I'll discuss why this is invariably true as I explain both types of caches.

Windows 3.1 comes with version 4.0 of the SMARTDrive utility (SMART-DRV.EXE), a disk-caching program that significantly improves Windows response. It is software-based, so to gain the performance improvement possible with a cache, you must allocate some of your extended memory to the cache. If your system is short on memory, you should allocate a proportionally smaller amount of memory to the cache, or you should add more memory.

All software caches work in roughly the same way. The disk cache program intercepts all disk read and write requests, which come from Windows itself and applications. The cache program attempts to satisfy the disk requests by locating a copy of the disk data in the RAM-based cache. If the disk data has

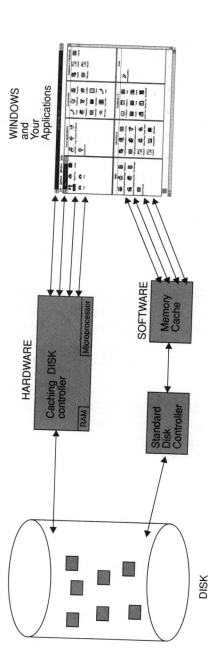

FIGURE 14.1: Disk caches come in hardware and software versions.

already been read from the disk once, for instance, the data will be found in the cache. If the same data is requested more than once, it can be provided to Windows or your application much more quickly from the RAM cache in which it is held than it can by rereading it from its disk location over and over again.

Some competitive software cache programs are more efficient than Windows' SMARTDRV program. These programs have more effective algorithms for managing the memory assigned to the cache and for reading data from and writing data to a disk. If all other things were equal, I'd suggest getting the smartest and most effective cache program on the market.

On the other hand, SMARTDRV comes with Windows and is therefore always compatible with the current version of Windows. Nearly every other competitive cache program is potentially incompatible with each new Windows release. Typically, the cache vendors must release new versions of their programs each time Windows releases a new version.

At the very least, this entails a time lag during which you may have to spend time without a disk cache (or go to the trouble of installing SMARTDRV). It typically entails an additional expense because upgrades cost money. But there is more. I always have a nagging suspicion that the competitive program has additional incompatibilities that may put my hard disk's data at risk.

I may be somewhat conservative, but I strongly recommend installing SMARTDRV. Read the next two sections, however, to learn what other possibilities there are for improving on SMARTDRV. You can then decide for yourself whether or not to buy into the possible improvements in exchange for the additional cost, possible incompatibilities, and extra effort of learning and installing the competitive program.

USING A SOFTWARE-BASED DISK-CACHING PROGRAM

You must load software cache programs at the time you start your system. You load some disk caches as device drivers in your CONFIG.SYS file, and you load others, like Windows' SMARTDRV.EXE program, from the command prompt, perhaps in AUTOEXEC.BAT. When a disk-caching program is first loaded, it reserves for itself a portion of available memory. SMARTDRV starts out by allocating a portion of extended memory, although

Windows and SMARTDRV work in tandem to increase or decrease this amount dynamically as Windows' needs for memory vary.

This technique can be quite efficient. Some other cache programs allocate a fixed amount of memory. Still others allocate all available memory, releasing it only when applications request it for other purposes.

Caching Disk Read Requests

Once installed, a disk-caching program is activated each time that any executing program makes a disk request. The cache program intercepts the read request and checks to see whether the requested data already resides in the cache. If so, the request is satisfied from the data in the cache. If not, the data is read from the disk and placed in the cache. Again the request is satisfied from data in the cache. Note that the next time the data is requested, it is returned from the cache and no disk read is necessary.

Typically, more data is read from the disk at a time than is requested. The portion of the cache that holds this extra information is sometimes called a *read-ahead*, or *look-ahead*, buffer. Figure 14.2 depicts this caching scenario.

This constitutes intelligent guessing by the disk cache program about upcoming read requests.

Usually, the extra information is simply data from adjacent sectors on the same track as the requested sector. This presumes that data in nearby sectors is related to the actual data requested. This logic works best if your disk is unfragmented (see later in this chapter) and adjacent sectors do in fact represent related portions of the same file.

When your application makes disk requests, the cache program intercepts the requests again. This time, however, the requested data may be found within the read-ahead buffer. If so, the application's read request is satisfied, saving time when compared to a slower disk read. If it is not already in the cache, it is read into the cache from disk, along with some extra sectors to increase the possibility of satisfying subsequent read requests without having to incur subsequent disk reads.

After a certain time, the disk cache will fill up with copies of disk data. Some of this information will be from earlier application requests. To make room in the cache for new data, some portions of the cache holding the data least recently used are freed up. New sectors of information can be stored in these sectors. This logic assumes that whatever data has been stored in the cache for the longest amount of time, without having been accessed, is the least likely to be needed in the immediate future.

The smarter the algorithm in the disk cache program, the more likely the memory cache will actually contain sectors that will satisfy upcoming disk information requests. The more often that disk requests are satisfied from the cache rather than from new physical disk reads, the faster your system will be.

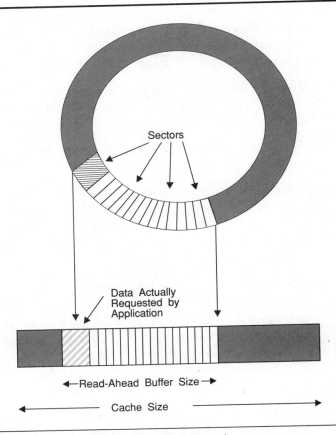

FIGURE 14.2: Disk caching anticipates upcoming read requests.

In addition, an intelligent disk cache program can intercept CPU memory management requests as well as disk requests. If disk requests are not a bottleneck, the software can free up some of its temporarily underutilized disk cache memory. This gives Windows more memory for improving the performance of tasks, such as spreadsheet recalculations or database sorting.

Caching Disk Write Requests

The preceding section explains how disk caching can improve performance by reducing disk reads. But what about disk writes? Once again, the disk-caching software can have a dramatic impact on performance. However, some caching programs do not intercept write requests at all. Theoretically, this ensures that all requested writes are made directly to your disk. If you have a power outage, you can be sure that all requested disk writes were done.

However, some applications write very small amounts of data. Under normal, uncached conditions, this means that multiple write requests will result in multiple physical disk writes. Once again, though, if those writes are made to adjacent sectors in the same file located in the same unfragmented track, an obvious optimization is possible with caching. A smart caching program can collect all the writes in adjacent cache memory locations. Periodically, a group of updates to the affected file could be made with a single physical disk write.

If physical disk writes are not done when immediately requested by applications, there is the possibility that the file itself will not always contain the changes made to it. If power is lost, your file's integrity could be compromised. Some reviewers claim that the period of time during which this problem can occur is so small that it's not worth worrying about. The performance improvement can be substantial, so go with it, they say. But power brownouts and blackouts are regular enough that I'm queasy about relying on delayed write-backs to a disk, unless my system is plugged into a battery backup device.

I have to marvel, however, at the ingenuity demonstrated by caching techniques. Because the overall time savings can be substantial, you should weigh the trade-offs in using disk caches for both reading and writing.

Pending writes can be done at fixed, periodic times or when a certain number of sectors' worth of data accumulates to be written from the cache. Or they can be done a certain amount of time after an application actually writes the data into the cache. Or they can be done at times when the cache program determines that the CPU is idle. Each program makes its own decisions about trade-offs in CPU usage and disk/memory efficiency.

There are also advanced techniques that defer writing of data until certain percentages of individual tracks must be updated and rewritten. Some caching programs even analyze the pending writes and reorder them according to the type of disk you have. If the movement of the disk heads is considered when the writes are performed, this overhead can also be minimized. Reducing physical disk write time results in a more efficient Windows system.

Smart caching logic also compares write requests from applications to existing sector data currently in the cache. There are a couple of powerful algorithms that can be employed here. First, suppose that the caching program determines that a new write request does not change data that has already been written to the disk. In this case, the new write request will simply be ignored.

Next, suppose that a new write request causes changes to occur to data that is still being held in the cache (i.e., it has not yet undergone its delayed, or *staged*, write). The caching program can simply throw away the earlier request to the affected data sector, replacing it with this more current write request. This means that multiple application requests to write the same data will take dramatically less time because only the final write request has to be written to the disk.

All these techniques can further reduce the overhead of disk accessing. Since no one caching program implements all of them, you really have no way of knowing which program to buy, but you now know why there are differences among the programs. Most differences lie in the degree of intelligence in each program's caching logic.

USING THE SMARTDRV.EXE DISK-CACHING PROGRAM

Both DOS and Windows include a version of SMARTDRV (also called SMARTDrive). You should always use the newer version. Windows 3.1 was released after DOS 5.0, so you should use the SMARTDRV.EXE program from Windows instead of the SMARTDRV.SYS program from DOS.

Because SMARTDRV almost always improves performance, you should make sure that the SMARTDRV command line is in your AUTOEXEC.BAT file. When you first install Windows 3.1, Setup includes a single line at the beginning of AUTOEXEC.BAT that specifies the SMARTDRV.EXE program:

C:\WINDOWS\SMARTDRV.EXE

This line accepts all the default settings, which typically work just fine for your system. However, this version of SMARTDRV has a number of optional settings that you can use to optimize your particular environment.

Customizing Your Version of SMARTDRV

To install SMARTDRV with customized settings, you can issue the following command line:

[*pathname*]SMARTDRV.EXE *options*

where *pathname* indicates where the SMARTDRV.EXE program resides. The options can be any or all of the following:

Drive[+ | –]...   Each *drive* entry specifies a disk drive to be cached. You can specify multiple drives, separated by spaces. If you do not specify a particular drive, SMARTDRV will automatically set its own level of caching for drives not indicated. It will cache read requests only for floppy disks, will cache read and write requests for hard disks, and will ignore both read and write requests for CD-ROM and network drives. You can follow each drive identifier with a plus or a minus sign. Appending a plus sign enables read and write caching on that drive. Appending a minus sign disables read and write caching. Entering a drive letter but not appending either a plus or a minus sign enables read caching but disables write caching.

InitCacheSize	Defines how many kilobytes are to be initially reserved for a SMARTDRV cache. Because the cache is actually set up when DOS alone is active, the amount of the cache may drop when Windows runs. The difference between InitCacheSize and WinCacheSize represents the amount of memory reduction that Windows will be allowed if it needs to reduce cache usage to satisfy other memory needs. Table 14.1 summarizes the default values used by SMARTDRV for this initial cache size.
WinCacheSize	Defines the minimum size that Windows must retain for SMARTDRV if it decides to reduce the memory allocation to enhance Windows operations. In general, Windows and SMARTDRV cooperatively expand and contract the cache during multitasking. WinCacheSize controls the minimum cache size, just as InitCacheSize controls the maximum cache size. When you exit Windows, the cache is restored to the InitCacheSize amount.
/E:elementsize	Each *element* defines how many bytes of memory constitute the smallest amount of information that is processed at a single time by SMARTDRV. By default, an 8K element is used, although any element size can be chosen that represents a power of two (2^n).
/B:buffersize	*Buffersize* defines how many bytes are to be in SMARTDRV's look-ahead buffer. Regardless of how many bytes are actually requested during a disk read request, SMARTDRV will read the specified number of bytes into its memory cache. The default buffersize is 16K, but it can be any multiple of *elementsize*.

/C	Clears all delayed write data from the cache out to disk. Normally, SMARTDRV delays writing data from the cache memory until other disk activity has been completed.
/L	Forces SMARTDRV to load itself into low memory (below 640K). This option applies only in DOS 5.0 and if you have enabled the upper memory blocks (UMB) region with the EMM386.EXE program.
/Q	Prevents the display of SMARTDRV information messages on your monitor.
/R	Restarts SMARTDRV, after first taking care of any delayed writes out to disk.
/S	Displays extra status information about SMARTDRV.
/?	Displays help text about the SMARTDRV utility and its command options.

Setting the SMARTDRV options to their optimum values is not a precise science. As Table 14.1 suggests, there is no specific percentage of available extended memory that works all the time. Under Windows, the defaults used by SMARTDRV use a larger proportion of extended memory as the amount of

TABLE 14.1: Default SMARTDRV Settings

Amount of Extended Memory (x)	InitCacheSize	WinCacheSize
$x < 1MB$	Uses all extended memory	0
$1MB \leq x < 2MB$	1MB	256K
$2MB \leq x < 4MB$	1MB	512K
$4MB \leq x < 6MB$	2MB	1MB
$x \geq 6MB$	2MB	2MB

available extended memory increases. This is reasonable because once the memory needed by applications is satisfied, the remaining memory can be used by SMARTDRV to satisfy disk requests more efficiently.

Analyzing the Performance of SMARTDRV

At first glance, you would think that the larger the cache, the more frequently requested data would be found in the cache. In fact, on my system, approximately 70 percent of all disk data requests were satisfied from the cache (see Figure 14.3). Finding the desired data in the memory cache is called a *cache hit*, and having to access the disk is called a *cache miss*.

Although you should adjust your cache-size values according to your particular mix of applications, my 70 percent hit rate was obtained using a cache size

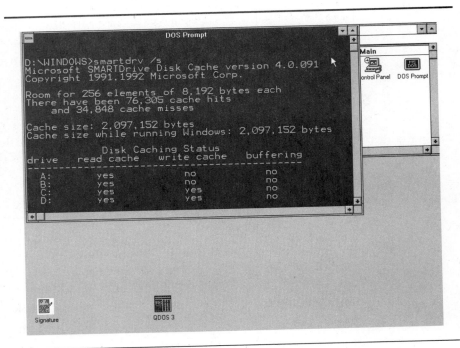

FIGURE 14.3: Obtaining SMARTDRV status information online

Beginning Efficiency Settings

There is no best size for any of the key performance facilities: swap files, RAM disks, and disk caches. Each of them depends on a number of variables and will be different depending on your system. The following factors may influence your decisions:

◆ Amount of memory

◆ Amount of free disk space

◆ Number and type of running applications

◆ Size of running applications

◆ Mix of DOS and Windows applications

Many adjustments require that you experiment to determine the best mix of settings for your particular combination of hardware and software. Here are some guidelines for settings to get you started:

◆ RAM disk (e.g., RAMDRIVE.SYS): One-fourth of your total physical memory.

◆ Disk cache (e.g., SMARTDRV.EXE): One-fourth of your total physical memory.

◆ Permanent swap file: One-fourth of your available hard-disk space.

of 2MB. This was my starting cache size; Figure 14.3 shows that the cache size while running Windows is still equal to 2MB. My own rule of thumb is to specify a starting cache of one-fourth of available memory. I let Windows work that size down as necessary in response to application demands.

As you can also see in Figure 14.3, the entire 2MB is still available. This confirms that Windows is not feeling pressed to reduce cache size to satisfy other applications' needs. This even suggests that, for my particular mix of multitasking programs, I should be able to improve the percentage of cache hits by enlarging the initial size of the cache.

There is almost no end to the number of suggestions that I could make about specifying cache sizes. What sizes to use depend greatly on your mix of applications and how you use them. For example, suppose that you open and run new applications frequently and open and close documents frequently. In both cases, your disk is accessed frequently. A disk cache will be very helpful. In this case, you will probably want to increase your cache's size.

On the other hand, suppose that you run certain applications regularly, leaving them open on the desktop once you've started them. Particularly if you use certain documents repeatedly, Windows will be better able to use the cache memory if it can assign it to the applications. In this case, a smaller disk cache will probably be better for your system.

Is Unnecessary Buffering Occurring in Your System?

At the bottom of the window in Figure 14.3, you can see a column of information that indicates no buffering is being done for any of my four drives (A to D). This means that my particular computer is relatively new, has a correct BIOS, and can work with virtual memory. If your equipment is older and cannot handle the requirements of the SMARTDRV program, Setup inserts the following line in your CONFIG.SYS file:

Device=smartdrv.exe /double_buffer

This implements an extra level of *buffering*, which may be necessary for some equipment. However, Setup may not always be able to assess the capabilities of your equipment correctly. If you run SMARTDRV at the command prompt with the /S option, and all the entries in the "buffering" column are NO, then you do not need this extra buffering. If the Device=smartdrv.exe line appears in CONFIG.SYS, you should exit Windows, remove the line from CONFIG.SYS, and reboot. Your system will perform more efficiently without double buffering.

USING A HARDWARE CACHE CONTROLLER

Using a hardware disk cache is more efficient but much more costly than using a software disk cache. A disk controller that has caching capabilities includes a

Avoid Double Buffering Your Cache

A software cache, like SMARTDRV, provides a form of memory buffer for data. It is a more intelligent buffer than the standard DOS buffers. Algorithmic decisions about the contents of the cache can dramatically speed up both disk reads and writes, depending on the intelligence built into the software cache driver.

A hardware cache, such as the kind found on an Adaptec controller board, offers similar capabilities but is built into the electronics on the board. Caching in hardware is normally faster than caching in software and frees up your CPU to perform other chores at the same time. Additionally, the space consumed by the software cache can be released for other uses.

If you're not careful, however, you may install a hardware cache controller board and a software cache program. In this instance, you may be asking your system to maintain two copies of all cached data. This is wasteful. If your hardware supports its own caching, discontinue software caching.

microprocessor and RAM on the board. The microprocessor manages the cache reads and writes, and the RAM on the controller card handles the job formerly done by a part of your system's extended memory.

If your system includes a hardware cache controller, you can remove the software cache program to free up memory. You will have more UMB space available for other TSRs or device drivers, or more low memory available for virtual machines when running DOS applications under Windows.

Because a hardware controller contains a separate microprocessor, it can perform its disk-sector caching duties while your system's CPU carries out other chores. Consequently, your CPU is used more efficiently, and Windows can use the freed-up RAM more efficiently—your entire system benefits. Particularly in multitasking environments and in heavily burdened network environments, a hard-disk cache controller will frequently account for noticeable improvements in overall system performance.

Because of the expense of hardware cache controllers, they are probably most worthwhile in networking environments, where the speed improvements can benefit many users. In addition, realize that the RAM on a cache controller card cannot be used for other system purposes if, for instance, your applications are CPU-intensive and disk efficiencies are not your system's bottle-neck area.

◆ BETTER SWAPPING MEANS FASTER MULTITASKING

In Chapter 4, you learned how Windows uses disk space to support the efficient use of memory. Refer to Chapter 4 for more extensive details on the implementation of swapping in both operating modes of Windows. This section concentrates on some of the performance-oriented implications of the swapping facility. You will learn methods to improve swapping speed, which will improve the performance of your Windows system.

When memory must be reassigned from one application to another, Windows temporarily makes a copy of the memory to be swapped before freeing it up for a different application's use. If your system is running in 386 enhanced mode, these memory images are stored on disk in a file known as the *swap file*. If your system is running in standard mode, these images are stored for non-Windows applications only in individual *application swap files*. Windows applications in standard mode are not swapped, so when you run out of physical memory, you simply cannot start another application until memory is freed up.

◆ PERFORMANCE AND THE SWAP FILE

If you run out of space on your swap disk, Windows will be unable to swap out an application. Your overall system performance will suffer in a number of ways. Perhaps a new application will be unable to begin or a current application will be unable to continue. Make sure that you're not tight on disk space for swapping. Specify a different disk, if necessary, that has plenty of free space.

IMPROVING SWAPPING IN 386 ENHANCED MODE

In 386 enhanced mode, Windows uses a single file for memory copied (i.e., swapped) to disk during multitasking. If you have established a permanent swap file, this file's name is 386SPART.PAR. It is a hidden file and is usually stored in the root directory of your system's boot drive. If there is no permanent swap file, Windows will create a temporary one in your WINDOWS directory as necessary, named WIN386.SWP. Figure 14.4 depicts this situation.

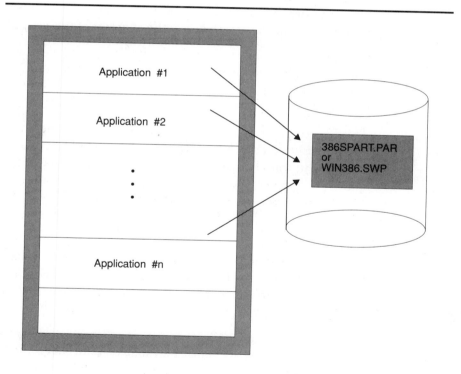

One Hidden Swap File

FIGURE 14.4: 386 enhanced mode uses a single swap file.

Should You Use a Permanent or a Temporary Swap File?

When you first install Windows, the Setup program decides whether or not to set up a permanent swap file, a temporary one, or none at all. If it can, it will always attempt to carve out a permanent swap file. For several reasons, it is always more efficient to use a permanent swap file because Windows will run faster.

First, Windows can use direct disk reads and writes to a permanent swap file (i.e., specific track and sector addresses are used), because it will know exactly where on the disk the permanent file is located. Windows will have exclusive use of this disk space. Windows will not then incur the overhead of standard DOS file system requests to access the contents of the swap file.

Second, if a temporary swap file is created each time you start Windows, you must incur a certain amount of extra overhead each time Windows starts. If you start Windows in 386 enhanced mode with a permanent swap file, you don't have this burden.

Third, a temporary swap file might be located anywhere on the disk, so it might consist of a number of separate, or fragmented, parts. (See the discussion later in this chapter on fragmentation.) This fragmentation is not possible with a permanent swap file because Windows ensures that such a file is only created from contiguous sectors. Because of the way caching works, a permanent swap file results in a higher percentage of cache hits and a more efficient system.

Fourth, a permanent swap file is always the same size unless you change it yourself. This means that your system has a consistent amount of virtual memory, guaranteeing that Windows will have enough disk space to create virtual memory if your system runs out of physical memory.

With a temporary swap file, the amount of virtual memory varies according to how much disk space remains available at any given time. Windows can only allocate temporary swap space out of available disk space. This may translate into an ability to run varying numbers of programs in each Windows session. One time, you may be able to run a particular group of applications simultaneously; the next time, you may not be able to do so because there is less disk space available for swapping.

Permanent vs. Temporary Swapping

In 386 enhanced mode, you have the option of using a permanent swap file or allowing Windows to create and maintain a temporary file as necessary. Windows only creates a temporary file if you have not explicitly created a permanent one and if sufficient disk space remains available.

These are the advantages of a permanent swap file:

♦ Windows runs faster because it reads the reserved disk space directly rather than going through the DOS file management system.

♦ Windows starts up faster because it doesn't have to create a temporary swap file.

♦ Multitasking can proceed more smoothly because disk space is guaranteed to be available for virtual memory if your system runs out of actual physical memory.

The disadvantage of a permanent swap file is that free disk space is reduced because of the space that Windows reserves. Even when Windows is not running, this space is unavailable to other programs.

The only advantage of a temporary swap file is that a large portion of your hard disk is not made permanently unavailable. For example, if your hard disk has 20MB of available contiguous storage when you run Setup, roughly 10MB will be reserved for a hidden 386SPART.PAR permanent swap file. Even when Windows is not running, this space will be unavailable to you for any other purposes.

Even if Setup can create a permanent swap file on your system, you may choose to create a temporary swap file to reclaim the otherwise unusable 10MB of disk space. Windows will then only consume as much disk space as it needs to support swapping for your particular mix of applications.

Modifying the Default Swap File Settings

Then again, you may decide that you don't want to use swapping at all. First, you may have more than enough physical memory to run all your applications. Disabling swapping will not affect your applications, and you will not even incur the internal Windows overhead relating to swapping.

Second, you may be limited in available disk space. Rather than allow Windows to consume any of it, you can disable both temporary and permanent swapping, but you will be able to run fewer applications. This runs counter to the benefits of 386 enhanced mode, but the applications that do run will have more available disk space to use.

Regardless of whether you want to disable swapping, specify a temporary swap file, or define the precise size of a permanent swap file, the 386 Enhanced icon in the Control Panel is your ticket. After selecting the icon, you should click on the Virtual Memory button to bring up the dialog box shown in Figure 14.5.

Your system's current settings appear in the upper-left box. They indicate the drive on which the swap file, if any, resides, as well as the size and type of the file. If you have a permanent swap file, the size represents the actual amount of reserved disk space that is unavailable for any other purposes. As a reminder to you, Windows indicates that a permanent swap file uses fast and direct 32-bit disk access. If the swap file were temporary, Windows would remind you that the slower accessing technique would be through the MS-DOS file system.

If you have specified a temporary swap file, the size value only represents the maximum space that Windows might possibly use, depending on need, during multitasking. A temporary swap file can expand during multitasking operations. If Windows does not need this much space for your application mix, the temporary WIN386.SWP file will not grow and the extra disk space will remain available for other purposes.

To change the type of swapping on your system, click on the down arrow beside the Type list box in the New Settings section of the dialog box and select Permanent, Temporary, or None. In each case, Windows displays the current space available on your chosen drive. If there is not enough space on one drive, just click on the down arrow beside the Drive list box to select a different drive for your swap file.

If you disable swapping completely by choosing None in the Type box, the New Size field is grayed. You can only view the amount of space available on the drive. Choose OK to accept the disabling of virtual memory on your system.

If you specify a temporary swap file by choosing Temporary in the Type box, Windows displays a line below Space Available that defines Recommended Maximum Size. This will be roughly half of your available disk space. You can constrain the amount of virtual memory by typing in a smaller number in the New Size field.

If you specify a permanent swap file by choosing Permanent in the Type box, Windows will display the maximum possible size of that swap file, as shown

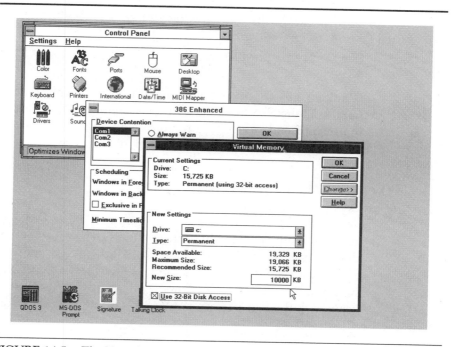

FIGURE 14.5: The Virtual Memory dialog box, which controls virtual memory in 386 enhanced mode

in Figure 14.5. This represents the largest contiguous block of disk space that can be found on the selected drive. Be sure to defragment your disk before attempting to create a new or larger permanent swap file. When defragmented, Windows will offer you the largest possible contiguous block of disk space from which to allocate your permanent swap file.

◆ CONTROLLING DISK SPACE CONSUMED BY SWAPPING

By specifying a permanent swap file in 386 enhanced mode, you can precisely define the amount of disk space that Windows will use in support of its paging activities. But a permanent (and hidden) swap file always consumes that amount of disk space, even if Windows is not running. If you do not define a permanent swap file, Windows will create a temporary one each time Windows starts. You can define the maximum size of a temporary swap file. By explicitly setting a limit in this way, Windows will only use what it needs. You only use disk space when Windows is running. The temporary swap file is deleted when Windows is terminated.

Windows will also recommend a size to use, and place that recommended number in the New Size field for your acceptance. As before, you can override the recommendation by typing in a smaller number in the New Size field. Choose OK to accept your final selections.

IMPROVING SWAPPING IN STANDARD MODE

When you run Windows in standard mode, there is no 386 Enhanced icon in the Control Panel. Swapping in standard mode affects only non-Windows applications. As Figure 14.6 indicates, Windows will create a separate hidden swap file for each non-Windows application that you start. These files all begin with the four characters ~WOA and end with the extension .TMP.

When you switch away from a non-Windows application, Windows writes all or part of the application's memory out to its private swap file. Later, when

Controlling Swapping on Your Machine

You can disable swapping in 386 enhanced mode by specifying the swap file type *None* in the Virtual Memory dialog box. Alternatively, in the [386Enh] section of SYSTEM.INI, you can set Paging=No to disable paging completely. You might do this for a number of reasons:

♦ You are tight on disk space and don't want Windows to use any space for paging activities.

♦ You want to improve the performance of active applications at the expense of new applications. Newer applications may not be able to run at all if existing applications cannot be swapped to disk. However, currently running applications will run and switch faster because all switching will be memory-based, involving no disk swapping of any application memory segments.

♦ Your system has more memory than it needs for your mix of applications.

By disabling swapping, you gain more memory for applications because no memory is consumed by the internal tables maintained by Windows to manage the pages of the swap file. You also gain more disk space for applications because no swap space is allocated on the disk. Finally, processing is faster because the internal Windows overhead for managing the swapping process is eliminated.

you switch back to the application, Windows rereads the data from the swap file back into memory, restoring the application. When the application ends, Windows erases the swap file completely.

You can control swapping speed in your standard mode system by maximizing the rate at which Windows accesses swap files. The best way to do this is to ensure that Windows swaps to your system's fastest hard disk. In addition, you can gain slightly by making sure that the swap file is in the root directory of this disk.

If a second, slower disk drive has a much larger amount of free space, it will usually be better to use this drive. Because of the free space, the swap files will be more likely to reside in contiguous disk addresses (i.e., they will be less fragmented). This will minimize disk head movement during swapping and will make for faster switching to and from non-Windows applications.

To specify a particular disk and directory for application swap files in standard mode, include a Swapdisk= entry in the [NonWindowsApp] section of SYS-TEM.INI. For example, suppose that your C drive has a 28-millisecond access time, but your D drive is a Plus Hard Card with a 9-millisecond access time. You would probably want to include this line in SYSTEM.INI:

Swapdisk=D:

You may still benefit from swapping to your fastest drive if you have speci-fied a TEMP environment variable. Usually, you place this setting in

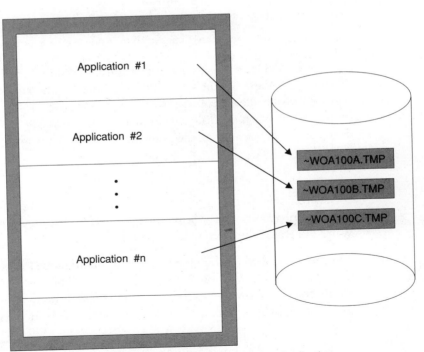

FIGURE 14.6: Controlling virtual memory in standard mode

AUTOEXEC.BAT. If you do not include a Swapdisk= entry in SYS-TEM.INI, Windows sends its application swap files out to the disk specified in the TEMP setting. If you haven't set TEMP before running Windows, that's still OK; Windows will use the root directory of your boot drive.

There may be a problem, however, if you don't explicitly specify your system's swapping location in standard mode. If your system has a RAM disk, the TEMP variable usually points to that disk. Using one portion of memory (i.e., a RAM disk) to swap memory images from an executing application is inefficient and a mistake. You incur the overhead of swapping, but because the RAM disk consumes memory itself, you do not gain any memory for other applications. Figure 14.7 depicts this self-defeating process.

To create the RAM disk in the first place, you have to allocate some of your system's extended memory, which reduces the amount of memory available for other applications. Consequently, when Windows swaps a DOS application out to its swapping drive, it only regains the memory formerly given up to create the RAM disk. The net gain is zero, and the net cost is the overall burden of swapping.

There is one situation, however, in which you can benefit from setting a RAM disk to be your standard-mode swap disk. This is useful if your system has more memory than is necessary for your Windows applications. If there is enough excess memory to create a RAM disk without taking away from memory that would better be left for Windows, you can improve switching time to and from a DOS application. But this is a special, and relatively rare, case.

◆ IMPROVING THROUGHPUT BY ENHANCING YOUR HARD DISK

Earlier in this chapter, you learned a good deal about disk caching and about swapping. In both cases, the techniques are aimed at improving the speed at which information is stored on or retrieved from your disks. Both techniques

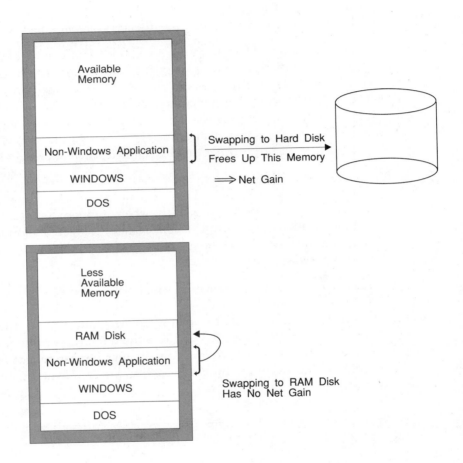

FIGURE 14.7: Why you should not use a RAM disk for a swap disk

enhance system facilities that use your hard disk. In a sense, they make hard-disk access more efficient, but they do not directly improve your hard disk's efficiency.

There are two areas in which you can make adjustments that result in a noticeable improvement in your hard disk's (and consequently Windows') performance. First, I'll discuss the concept of *defragmentation*. Even though it is only a single technique for enhancing disk performance, it is sometimes called *disk optimization*. Second, I'll discuss methods for freeing up large amounts of disk space on your system.

OPTIMIZING A HARD DISK BY DEFRAGMENTATION

As hard disks fill up, you and your applications will often delete older files to make space for the latest files. DOS manages the actual storage and retrieval of files on your disks. When it cannot store a large file in a single contiguous area of the disk, it stores the file in pieces around the disk.

When a file is split up into more than a single storage unit, it is said to be *fragmented*. All the file's contents are intact, but the disk's mechanical heads must move to multiple disk locations to read or write the contents of the file. The more fragmented the file, the longer the time spent accessing its contents. Take a look at Figure 14.8.

The graphic at the right side of this figure represents a view of my C drive before optimization. Neither DOS nor Windows contains a utility for eliminating natural fragmentation. Programs that can reduce fragmentation carefully move pieces of files around the disk to combine the parts into contiguous areas. Such programs are sometimes called disk optimizers, disk compaction utilities, disk organizers, or defragmentation utilities.

I use the VOPT program from Golden Bow Systems to rearrange the files on my fragmented disks. Figure 14.8 shows how broken up the files on a disk can get. The details on the left side of the figure show that 48 files, occupying more than 5000 disk clusters, are fragmented. Figure 14.9 shows the same drive, several minutes later, after the defragmentation program has compacted the fragmented files.

If a disk contains no fragmented files, the mechanical overhead caused by fragmentation is eliminated. In a Windows multitasking environment, where the disk is accessed constantly, having an unfragmented disk means you will have faster response from your applications. This is true because all files are contiguous and can be read or written with fewer mechanical disk head movements. You enjoy the following benefits:

◆ The information in individual files can be retrieved more quickly.

◆ New files can be written to more quickly.

◆ Swap files in standard mode can be written to and read from more quickly.

◆ A temporary swap file in 386 enhanced mode can be written to and read from more quickly.

◆ Your disk-caching utility performs even more efficiently because the cache is used more effectively. When you access the tracks on an optimized disk, the cache is more likely to be able to fulfill upcoming disk requests. This is because nearby sectors are more likely to contain data from the same file as the preceding sectors.

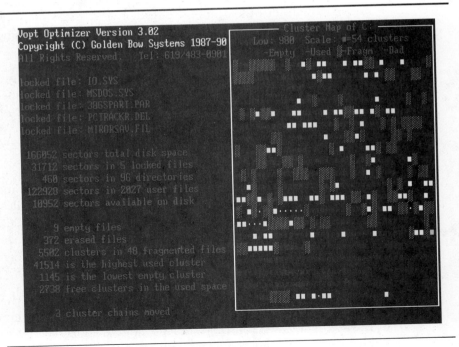

FIGURE 14.8: A fragmented disk before optimization

If you use a defragmentation utility, you should follow these important steps:

1. Exit Windows first!

2. Run the CHKDSK /F utility at the DOS prompt (but not from within Windows).

3. Remove any TSR that may attempt to use your hard disk during optimization.

4. Execute the compaction program.

MAXIMIZING HARD-DISK SPACE

In the course of writing this book, as I became more and more involved with Windows applications, I was astonished at the growth in the size and number of my disk's files. I first outgrew a 40MB hard disk and replaced it with an

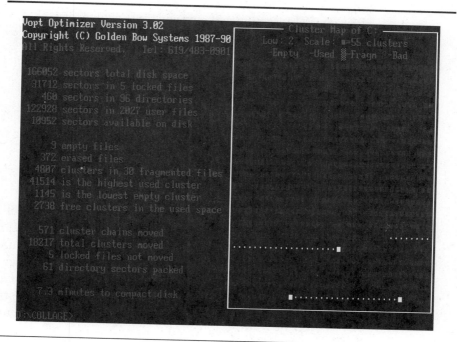

FIGURE 14.9: The optimized disk after defragmentation

80MB disk. Next, I added a 105MB Hard Card. Finally, I bought a Bernoulli transportable drive with 90MB removable cartridges. That ought to take care of all my needs for a while.

However, that also took care of a lot of money that I can't use for other purposes. You may decide to save some money and make more effective use of your available hard-disk space. I have to admit that when I install new programs, I install everything from text files to optional modules. Everyone goes through the agony from time to time of having to decide which files to delete from a hard disk to free up space for new files.

An alternative to adding hard drives is to install a compression program like Stacker. This program automatically decompresses files when they are read and compresses them when they are written. The result is that you roughly double your hard-disk space.

Naturally, you can use available disk space for new programs. But as I've discussed in this chapter, Windows can also use available disk space for swapping. It's up to you to decide which applications and which directories to eliminate. This section will give you some guidance about how to reduce the burden on your disk from the many optional modules installed by Windows.

Installing and Removing Optional Windows Components

To control the installation and removal of the many optional Windows file modules, select the Windows Setup icon in the Main group of the Program Manager. Then pull down the Options menu and choose Add/Remove Windows Components. You see the Windows Setup dialog box, shown in Figure 14.10.

This dialog box provides easy access to the megabytes of disk space that are consumed by optional files under Windows. As you can see, my disk is burdened with more than 2MB of optional components. By removing the X beside any component name, I can free up the amount of space indicated. For example, by removing the X beside the Readme Files and Games entries, I would free up more than half a megabyte. If I never use the optional Windows accessory programs, like Notepad and Write, I could free up more than a megabyte by removing the X beside the Accessories choice.

Defragmenting Your Hard Disk

Disk-optimizing programs reduce disk fragmentation and are consequently called *defraggers* by many people. You should defragment your hard disk on a regular basis; Windows can run noticeably faster if your disk is optimized. How often should you do it? Monthly at worst. Weekly is a good plan, but also anytime just after you've deleted a large number of files on your disk.

Remember to back up your disk just before starting defragmentation. To speed up the backup process, delete all temporary and unnecessary files from your disk.

Also, before compacting your disk, you should fix or delete lost clusters (but *not* from within Windows). Use the CHKDSK/F command to reclaim wasted clusters that are taking up valuable disk space.

Caution: Unless your disk optimizer specifically says that it works from within Windows, run it only from the DOS prompt after exiting Windows.

You can be even more precise by removing some, but not all, of the files within a Windows optional category. Just click on the Files button on the right side of each component line. For example, clicking on Files to the right of Wallpapers, Misc. brings up the dialog box shown in Figure 14.11. To eliminate only some of the files (e.g., certain wallpaper bit maps that are never used), just click on their names, choose Remove, and choose OK. This returns you to the Windows Setup dialog box. Choose OK to complete this procedure.

Cleaning Up Unnecessary Disk Files

There are some files that can be removed that are not so obvious. The safest way to determine which files these are is to exit Windows first.

When you are at the DOS prompt, change to the TEMP directory. If you use a RAM disk for a TEMP directory, ignore this step. All unnecessary files located there will disappear the next time you turn off your system. But if you use a hard-disk directory for a TEMP directory, you can probably delete all files in this directory now. You have left Windows to ensure that no TEMP directory files are still in use. If you have active TSR programs, be sure not to erase any TEMP files required by them.

A temporary swap file in 386 enhanced mode is usually deleted when Windows shuts down. Similarly, application swap files are usually deleted when you exit from non-Windows applications in standard mode. However, sometimes your system crashes and sometimes your computer loses power and you must reboot. In these situations, a temporary swap file may be left taking up space on your disk. You can erase any of these files if you're no longer in Windows.

Rearranging Information on Your Disk

I recommended earlier that, before defragmenting your disk, you run the DOS utility CHKDSK with the /F option. At the time, I didn't give a reason for doing this. The real purpose of this command is to locate and fix any disk clusters that have somehow become disassociated from real disk files.

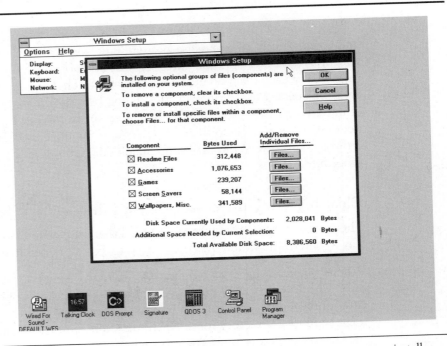

FIGURE 14.10: The Windows Setup dialog box, which you use to remove or install optional Windows components

Disassociated disk clusters waste space. By running the CHKDSK /F command, you can reclaim this space on your disk. By running this command before defragmenting your disk, the disassociated clusters become part of the freed-up contiguous space.

The CHKDSK command can collect lost clusters. But you can control a certain degree of file organization yourself. The fewer unnecessary files that you have in your WINDOWS directory, the faster DOS will be able to access any individual files in the directory, and the faster Windows will execute.

After installation, many programs leave files in the WINDOWS directory. You can speed up disk access by reorganizing these files. Once they are reorganized, you may have to adjust the directory locations in the applications themselves.

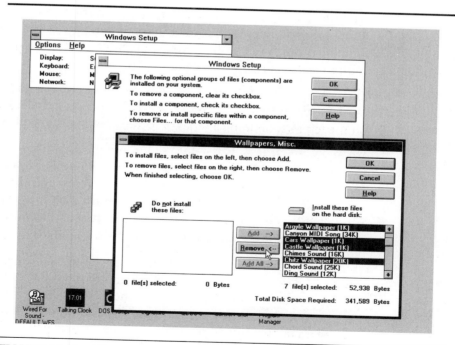

FIGURE 14.11: The Wallpapers, Misc. dialog box, which allows you to remove certain files

For example, you may keep .BMP files in the WINDOWS directory itself. Instead, you could create a subdirectory that contains only these occasionally used files. As a second example, if you use Excel, you may allow your .XL and macro files to accumulate within the WINDOWS directory. Instead, you can place them in a new subdirectory, called FILES or DATA.

UNDERSTANDING THE IMPACT OF YOUR HARD DISK'S INTERLEAVE

So far, I've talked about disk efficiencies that result from optimized organization of files on a disk. If all the sectors for a particular file are defragmented and on the same track, for instance, you should be able to access the information faster. The disk heads don't have to spend any additional time moving to tracks and sectors elsewhere on the disk.

But there is another facet of disk information retrieval that has nothing to do with DOS or Windows. You usually have no control over it at all. This section explains this to you and gives you enough information to discover whether you can make additional big gains in performance.

On each track of a disk, there are a number of sectors of data (the exact number depends on your disk). Take a look at Figure 14.12. It depicts a typical file on the left as containing a series of sectors that logically follow one another.

When the file is stored on a disk, you would think that it is stored as you see it in case 1 in the figure. This arrangement places each logical sector from a file in consecutive physical sectors on a disk track. This discussion assumes that no other file is contending for space on the disk. (It's true that on fragmented disks, the physical sectors of a track often contain interspersed pieces of more than a single file, but I won't consider that here.)

Actually, the file system keeps track of which sectors belong to which files. The hard-disk controller merely stores and retrieves information on tracks and sectors, not caring what you place there. The issue of interleaving arises from the question about whether a hard disk's controller can actually respond to a system request for information on a track fast enough to pick up disk data located on contiguous sectors.

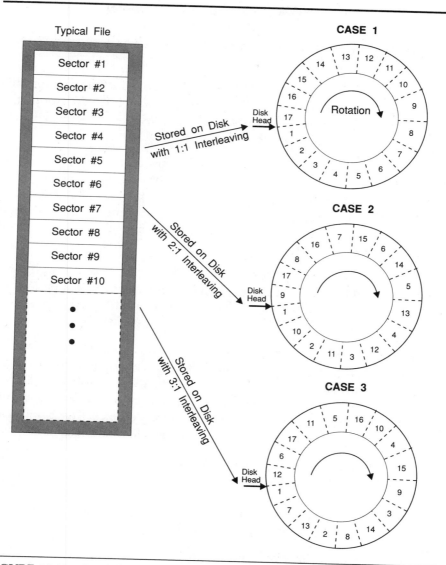

FIGURE 14.12: Interleaving greatly affects hard-disk performance.

Imagine for a moment those highway workers at the end of a day of working on the road. One worker drives a pickup truck slowly down a lane while another worker reaches down to pick up an orange marking cone. While the truck continues to move forward, the worker who picked up the cone has to control the cone, reach back into the truck, carefully stack the cone over others that he has picked up, then reach back outside the truck to ready himself to pick up the next cone.

In the same way, a disk head has to read data from a sector while the disk platter is rotating. The disk controller is responsible for storing the data, transferring it back to a requester (DOS or Windows), then readying itself to get the next sector's worth of data.

What if the truck is moving too fast for the physical skills of the worker in the rear? By the time the worker has stacked the first cone and leaned out for the next one, the truck may have driven by a second cone. Similarly, what if the disk controller cannot read, store, and transfer an entire sector's worth of data before the disk platter has moved the next sector past the disk's read/write head?

One solution is to slow down the truck to match the physical capabilities of the worker who picks up the cones (the equivalent of slowing down the disk drive to match a slow controller's capabilities). This wastes time. There are better ways.

Another solution is to hire a faster, more agile worker to pick up the cones while the truck maintains a faster pace. This is a more efficient use of personnel and resources. Similarly, a faster disk controller should be able to keep up with today's faster hard-disk drive rotation. I'll use the sample layout shown in Figure 14.12, which has 17 sectors per track. That's common but not necessary. The principle will hold for any disk, however.

Ideally, case 1 in Figure 14.12 would match a drive with a controller that would be able to read sector 1, process the information within the sector, and be ready to read sector 2 before the start of the sector reaches the read/write head. There is a small, intersector gap on each track, which accounts for a small amount of time during which the preceding sector's data can be dealt with.

As you have no doubt guessed, not all disk controllers can keep up with rotational speed. If the sequential sector numbering seen in case 1 were maintained, a slower disk controller would have to wait until the entire platter rotated completely. Only then would it be able to read sector 2, having missed it the first time around. In this mismatched drive/controller environment, it would require 17 rotations to read all 17 sectors on a single track.

Interleaving is a solution to this problem—it physically reorders sectors on a track. In a 2:1 interleaving pattern, each successively numbered sector is actually placed two sectors away from its predecessor, rather than one (see case 2 in Figure 14.12). In a 3:1 interleaving pattern, each successively numbered sector is actually placed three sectors away from its predecessor, rather than one (see case 3 in Figure 14.12).

If your drive/controller combination cannot handle 1:1 interleaving, 2:1 interleaving will require only one extra disk rotation to read all sectors on the track. This is not as bad as 17 times, so interleaving is an intelligent solution to the problem of mismatched capabilities.

As an example, take a look at case 2 in Figure 14.12. After sector 1 is read, it is processed by the controller while the disk continues to rotate. An entire sector (number 10 out of 17) is ignored. When the controller is ready to read another sector, it is labeled number 2. While this is being processed, sector 11 passes the disk head and is ignored. The next sector is number 3, and so on. In two complete rotations, the disk controller will process sectors numbered from 1 to 17. During the first rotation, sectors 1 to 9 are read; during the second rotation, sectors 10 to 17 are read. Even though the sectors are not physically contiguous, they are numbered and read (and data is stored in them) in logically contiguous order.

Naturally, slower and less capable controllers that are matched with faster disk drives may require 3:1 or even 4:1 interleaving. If your disk's interleave is not set accurately, you may be doubling or tripling the disk access time for all operations.

On the one hand, using an incorrect interleave can completely negate everything else that you do to enhance performance. On the other hand, it is possible to obtain a fantastic boost to your entire computer system by simply improving your hard disk's interleave. Interleaving is a low-level facility and is set by the hard-disk manufacturer. By the time the disk finds its way into your computer and is matched with a controller card, the original interleaving may not be optimum.

Programs like CALIBRAT (found in Norton Utilities) or SPINRITE II can test and change the interleaving of most hard disks. Because of the possible benefits of doing so, you should run out to obtain one of these programs. Before you run it, however, be sure to back up your entire disk.

◆ ENHANCING OPERATIONAL SPEED

All the techniques presented so far aim at improving the efficiency of the Windows environment. A technique that improves hard-disk efficiency will improve any application that uses the hard disk. A technique that improves virtual memory usage will improve the speed of all applications. In this section, I'll present some techniques that can enhance specific operations more directly.

SPEEDING UP YOUR BACKUPS

Do you use a permanent swap file in Windows? Do you run a backup program from time to time? If so, you may be wasting time by making a copy of the swap file.

Many backup programs offer a way to ignore files during the backup process. Some backup programs do not automatically copy hidden files. Other backup programs contain configurations that you can set up once to ensure that certain files or directories are copied or ignored, according to your instructions.

To save time, run your backup program so that your Windows swap file is not copied. See earlier in this chapter for the names of the affected swap files.

ACCESSING REQUIRED FILES MORE QUICKLY

Windows currently performs nearly all disk requests through DOS. Remember that Windows directly reads and writes disk tracks and sectors for a permanent swap file in 386 enhanced mode. For all file searches, DOS checks the

You Needn't Run Applications in the Background

Some non-Windows applications needn't run concurrently in the background while you are running a different application in the foreground. For example, a TSR in its own session or your favorite DOS disk manager will typically have no need for processing time except when you've switched it to the foreground.

Save time, save memory, and make Windows operate more smoothly by unchecking the box beside background execution in the specific PIF file. You can also uncheck this setting in _DEFAULT.PIF, which applies to all non-Windows applications that do not have their own PIFs. In this case, you get the time- and memory-saving benefits for all non-Windows applications.

Occasionally, you may want to activate background processing for a particular program. Do this in 386 enhanced mode by running the program in a window (press Alt+spacebar), opening up the Control menu, and clicking the Background check box in the Settings dialog box.

current directory first, then checks each directory in the PATH in order. If the files you use frequently are found in a directory that appears late in the PATH, Windows will seem to slow down. This is part of a deficiency in the layered design of Windows (i.e., Windows runs on top of and depends on DOS).

Here are some guidelines on the best use of the PATH statement in DOS when you are running Windows:

- After creating a RAM disk and storing important files in its root directory, make the RAM disk's root directory the first directory in the PATH.

- Make the WINDOWS directory the second directory in the PATH, since WINDOWS is constantly accessing its own files.

- Make the DOS directory the third directory in the PATH.

- Make the UTILITY directory the next directory if you have grouped your most common utilities in one directory.

♦ Order the remaining directories according to how frequently you run applications that access the files within those directories.

♦ Remember that only one PATH statement is used: the last one executed. Your AUTOEXEC.BAT file's PATH statement is overridden if you execute a new PATH statement within a DOS session under Windows.

♦ Remember that the PATH environment variable is limited to 128 characters. You cannot include directories in the PATH that will force the variable to exceed this length. All characters after the 128th will be ignored. If you must include a large number of directories in the PATH, try renaming these directories with smaller names so that fewer characters will be required.

DON'T RUN UNNECESSARY APPLICATIONS

There is only a finite amount of CPU time to go around. The fewer applications that are running, the more time for each one, and the faster each one will complete its tasks.

Make more time available for your important and necessary applications by running only them. Don't run frivolous applications all the time (like fish that move around on your desktop). And don't leave useful applications running all the time when you only need the information from them once in a while (like system monitoring programs). Run such programs when you specifically need them. Remember that besides the potential slowdown, each program consumes a certain amount of memory resources that are no longer available to the rest of your Windows system.

IMPROVING PERFORMANCE OF NON-WINDOWS APPLICATIONS

Everything you've learned in this chapter so far can improve the performance of Windows overall. This section specifically discusses performance enhancement for non-Windows applications. I'll revisit some of the specific PIF settings that bear directly on performance.

Increasing Priority Increases Speed

You can specify two priority values for any non-Windows application: one to control its priority when it runs in the background and the other for when it runs in the foreground. Knowing exactly what values to use for the foreground and background priorities is not a precise science. Here are some guidelines:

◆ Set initial background priority to 50 and foreground priority to 100.

◆ If you want an application to run faster than others, adjust these values, retaining the ratio by keeping the foreground priority equal to double the background priority (e.g., background=100, foreground=200)

◆ If you want more visible progress in your application when you switch to it, triple or quadruple the foreground value as compared to the background value (e.g., background=50, foreground=200).

◆ If your application is very CPU-bound, as in engineering, mathematical, and compiling applications, increase both the background and foreground values dramatically (e.g., background=1000, foreground=4000). However, you should typically run these types of applications in the background and do something else in the foreground.

You can also apply many of these same guidelines to setting the Windows priority values in 386 enhanced mode. Make adjustments to the Scheduling settings in the 386 Enhanced dialog box when you are trying to improve the performance of Windows applications in an environment that mixes Windows and non-Windows applications.

In Chapter 12, you learned about the myriad of possible customization options that exist in the WIN.INI and SYSTEM.INI files. Many of these special settings have important effects on your system's performance. In this section, I'll also selectively organize and briefly discuss the most important of these settings.

If you have a non-Windows application that is running slowly, open its Control menu and boost its priority setting. If it is running in the foreground, boost the foreground priority. If it is running in the background, and you want it to proceed relatively faster, boost its background priority.

If you want to maximize its speed, when no other program must absolutely continue running (such as a communications program in the background), you can check the Exclusive box. If these adjustments work effectively for your environment, you can make them permanent by using the PIF Editor.

Don't forget that any DOS program runs noticeably faster if you run it in full-screen mode. You can always press Alt+Enter to switch it back (in 386 enhanced mode) to windowed mode if you wish, or you can press Alt+spacebar to open up the Control menu as well as switch a full-screen DOS application to windowed mode.

♦ RUNNING FULL SCREEN SPEEDS UP NON-WINDOWS APPLICATIONS

In 386 enhanced mode, you can choose to run a non-Windows applications in full-screen mode or in a window. Running in a window offers a number of advantages, such as the ability to change fonts, to move and size the window, and to cut and paste text through the Clipboard. However, if these considerations are not important, you can boost speed immediately by switching the application to full-screen mode. You will notice an instant improvement in just the processing of keystrokes, but all processing requirements of your application will receive more CPU time.

Remember that the Monitor Ports check boxes in the Advanced section of a 386 enhanced mode PIF can slow down your application. If your application works fine (especially when switching to and from it) with these check boxes cleared, leave them cleared to boost a DOS application's performance.

In the Memory Options section of a PIF, be sure to carefully specify maximum values. They should be no more than you really need for the application, otherwise you may be consuming memory that could be better used by other applications. Anytime that you waste memory, you increase the likelihood that Windows performance will be slowed.

Although it biases Windows toward your particular DOS application, you can clear the Detect Idle Time option in the Advanced Options dialog box in 386 enhanced mode. This ensures that your DOS application receives its complete time allotment, even if it does not use it all. There is usually some time wasted, but your individual application keeps the CPU's attention, thereby increasing its own throughput.

Lastly, in the Display Options section, you can clear the Retain Video Memory option. This releases video memory to the system when you switch away from the application, making Windows more efficient. In theory, this will make your application and every other application work that much better. In practice, this can occasionally have a negative impact on your application if it is unable to obtain the video memory when eventually switching back to it.

This chapter focused on techniques for enhancing your overall system performance. The methods discussed work effectively for both Windows and non-Windows applications. But I largely concentrated on disk-oriented enhancements. Turn to Chapter 15 now to learn more enhancement possibilities, which focus primarily on memory.

C H A P T E R

15

*Fine-Tuning Your
System Memory*

Tuning your car involves a number of factors, from spark plugs to engine timing. Tuning your Windows system likewise involves many different factors, from specifying your individual application's priorities to optimizing your hard disk's caching parameters. You've already learned about execution optimization. In this chapter, I'll focus on those aspects of DOS, Windows, and your applications that specifically affect memory availability and usage.

Available memory determines how many applications can run simultaneously under Windows. It also determines how much information each application can store and process. The more memory you can make available to Windows and your applications, the faster and more efficiently Windows and your applications will run.

First, you'll learn how to use the HIMEM.SYS driver to manage extended memory and the EMM386.EXE program to emulate expanded memory. Then you'll learn how to free up the most possible memory before even starting Windows. Refer back to Chapter 4 for in-depth discussions of the types of memory used by Windows at different times.

The tips in these opening sections will concentrate on optimizing the evironment within which Windows itself runs: the DOS environment. These tips are normally covered in DOS books, such as my own *Mastering DOS 5* (Sybex, 1991), so I'll be brief; I'll explain how to best optimize your CONFIG.SYS and AUTOEXEC.BAT files for running Windows. I'll also explain the value of a RAM disk, and how to install and use one most effectively in your Windows environment.

You'll also learn how to maximize your available memory by adjusting system settings effectively, and by trimming the fat in several important areas like the WIN.INI file. Lastly, you'll revisit the many aspects of running DOS applications under Windows. This will include the parameters that can be set in a

Optimizing Windows 3.1 by Optimizing DOS's CONFIG.SYS

◆ Install a high memory manager, like HIMEM.SYS.

◆ Include an upper reserved blocks manager, like EMM386.EXE.

◆ Include a DOS=HIGH line to load portions of DOS 5 in the high memory area (HMA).

◆ Include a DOS=HIGH,UMB line if you wish to load portions of DOS 5 in the High Memory Area, as well as be able to load device drivers and TSRs in upper memory.

◆ Use SMARTDRV.SYS to establish disk caching.

◆ Use RAMDRIVE.SYS to create a RAM disk.

◆ Set BUFFERS=10 and FILES=30, unless one of your application programs requires that they be set higher.

◆ Use DEVICEHIGH commands to load device drivers into upper reserved memory blocks.

◆ Remove any drivers that will be unnecessary to Windows, like MOUSE.SYS, unless you plan to run applications outside of Windows.

DOS application's PIF, as well as providing expanded memory and extra environment space to your non-Windows applications.

◆ FREEING UP MEMORY BEFORE STARTING WINDOWS

You can enhance the amount of memory that Windows can use by making some good decisions prior to ever starting Windows. In particular, you can optimize your DOS environment in several ways. DOS itself, particularly

DOS 5, has many options for configuring memory efficiently. The more you do before Windows starts, the better your Windows applications will perform.

Extended memory is essential for running Windows. To optimize your use of extended memory under Windows, you must begin by optimizing DOS's management of memory prior to starting Windows. The 80286, 80386, and 80486 (and SX) models provide hardware access to that memory, but you must configure your DOS system properly to actually use it. The HIMEM.SYS device driver offers system support to manage extended memory.

In addition to extended memory, DOS and Windows each provide a version of the EMM386.EXE program. This driver can perform two chores. First, it can manage the region of memory located between 640K and 1MB, which is called reserved memory (or the upper memory blocks, or UMB, region). Second, this program can emulate expanded memory for DOS applications that run in 386 enhanced mode. I'll discuss these two services in this section as well.

USING DOS 5 TO MAXIMIZE AVAILABLE WINDOWS MEMORY

When Windows first starts up, it always has less than 640K of conventional memory available for applications. Exactly how much less depends on many factors, not the least of which is simply the version of DOS you are using. The remainder of this chapter will go into these factors in more depth. This opening section is meant to provide an overview and a context for upcoming discussions.

First of all, get DOS 5 if you haven't already. It offers a number of significant memory- and performance-oriented enhancement possibilities that are simply not available in earlier versions of DOS:

◆ It requires less conventional memory to run than earlier versions of DOS.

◆ It permits part of DOS to be placed in extended memory.

◆ It can manage extended memory, emulate expanded memory, and load device drivers and TSRs in upper reserved memory blocks (between 640K and 1MB).

Pay careful attention to how you configure your entire system. Various entries in CONFIG.SYS can greatly affect the amount of memory that remains when you start Windows 3.1. This in turn can impact the overall performance of Windows. See the CONFIG.SYS sidebar for a summary of applicable techniques.

You can effectively start (or refrain from starting) many programs and environment variables in your AUTOEXEC.BAT file:

♦ Remove any TSRs that can be run from within a DOS session under Windows.

♦ Remove any TSRs whose graphics handling techniques are incompatible with Windows. Run these separately after exiting Windows if you still need to run them.

♦ Use LOADHIGH commands to load TSRs or small application programs into upper reserved memory blocks.

Remember to reboot your system after making any changes to CONFIG.SYS and AUTOEXEC.BAT.

MANAGING EXTENDED MEMORY WITH HIMEM.SYS

The HIMEM.SYS extended memory manager must be loaded in your CONFIG.SYS before any applications or other device drivers that must access extended memory. (You can replace HIMEM.SYS with competitive memory managers. I'll discuss some alternatives shortly.)

To install HIMEM.SYS (which comes with Windows as well as with DOS), you must include a DEVICE line in CONFIG.SYS:

Device=[path]HIMEM.SYS [options]

where [options] can be any or all of the optional settings summarized in Table 15.1. Refer to my *Mastering DOS 5* book, or to your system documentation, for more extensive details about each option. Be sure to use the version of HIMEM.SYS that comes with the version of Windows that you are using.

TABLE 15.1: Optional Parameters for HIMEM.SYS

Parameter	Explanation
/a20control:*on* |*off*	Toggles control by HIMEM.SYS of the HMA A20 line
/cpuclock:*on* |*off*	Toggles clock-speed management by HIMEM.SYS
/hmamin=*m*	Sets *m* kilobytes as the requirement for access to HMA
/int15=*xxxxx*	Defines how many kilobytes are reserved for Interrupt 15 handling
/machine:*name*	Explicitly defines the computer type
/numhandles=*n*	Specifies *n* as the maximum number of simultaneous extended memory block handles
/shadowram:*on* |*off*	Toggles shadow RAM on or off

MAXIMIZING MEMORY SETTINGS IN THE CONFIG.SYS FILE

DOS 5 offers a number of CONFIG.SYS settings that impact memory usage. This section will offer specific advice for using these settings to maximize the conventional memory prior to starting Windows.

Loading DOS Itself into Extended Memory

Once you've started HIMEM.SYS from your CONFIG.SYS file, you can improve the efficiency of your system by using the extended memory that HIMEM.SYS now manages. Start by including the following command line in your CONFIG.SYS file:

DOS=HIGH

This enables DOS to place a number of its own internal tables and buffers in memory areas beyond 1MB, thereby freeing up additional conventional memory. This one line directs most of the command processor itself (COMMAND.COM), the DOS kernel, all buffers, and all code-page information to use space from the 64K HMA, or High Memory Area. Remember from Chapter 4 that this is the first 64K of your system's available extended memory, and it is addressable because of the extra address line (A20).

♦ **REDUCE THE SIZE OF DOS 5 IN CONVENTIONAL MEMORY**

Use DOS 5's DOS=HIGH command in your CONFIG.SYS file. After using this command, the conventional-memory burden of DOS 5 itself is less than 20K.

More available conventional memory means faster processing by applications that may swap to disk. This is because the extra memory will be used by Windows to minimize the need for swapping.

By retaining more low memory for programs, you enable your system to use overall memory more efficiently. In many cases, this technique even lets you consider running programs that couldn't run before because they required more physical memory to run than was available in your system. Remember also that the greater the conventional memory that remains available when Windows starts, the more the overall memory that will be available to each non-Windows application that you run in a 386 enhanced mode virtual machine.

Best Settings for DOS 5 CONFIG.SYS Values

The FILES command in your CONFIG.SYS determines how many file handles (essentially equivalent to the number of files used by your applications) will be allocated to be managed by DOS 5. To run Windows well, you should set this value to at least 30:

FILES=30

However, any one of your applications may require access to more file handles. This depends on the application. Use a number equal to the largest suggestion in your applications' documentation.

The BUFFERS command can be a problem if you're not careful. To run Windows without a disk cache, you need at least 30 buffers. However, if you install a disk cache (as discussed with SMARTDRV in the last chapter), you do not need that many buffers. The disk cache takes care of the same buffering chore to a large extent, so you can reduce the buffers consumed to 10:

BUFFERS=10

On the down side of memory consumption, those of you who run standard mode with an EGA monitor need a special support driver. You must make sure you have the following line in your CONFIG.SYS file to support this special case:

Device=C:\WINDOWS\EGA.SYS

In fact, the Setup program will insert this line for you during installation if you are installing Windows on a system with an EGA monitor.

Configure your SHELL command to use only as much environment space as you actually need. Many writers suggest that you blindly specify a SHELL command with a /E switch that allocates a 1024-byte environment. While this is often needed for some systems, it is not generally required, and represents a burden of one kilobyte of conventional memory.

The default environment space is usually enough. Unless you determine that you need extra space, don't bother to use the /E switch. If you discover that you do need extra space, refer to the section "Giving DOS Applications What They Need" near the end of this chapter for an explanation of how to provide it.

MANAGING RESERVED MEMORY
WITH EMM386.EXE

You load HIMEM.SYS to manage extended memory, and you use the DOS=HIGH configuration command to direct DOS to use some of this memory for its own internal needs. But there is still the problem of TSRs and drivers consuming conventional memory, leaving less memory available to virtual machines under Windows.

If you could load one or more TSRs or device drivers somewhere other than conventional memory, you would have more conventional memory remaining available when you start Windows. The EMM386.EXE program enables you to do this. This program lets you use any available space in the reserved memory area between 640K and 1MB. Rather than consuming precious conventional memory, you will be able to load some or all of your system's device drivers and TSRs into upper memory blocks. Whatever you load in the UMB region will still be available to your system, regardless of what Windows is doing.

There are some operating concerns that you must have in loading drivers and programs in this High Memory Area. I touched on these issues in Chapters 7 and 8. There are two main issues: (1) Does the device driver or TSR operate correctly when placed in the formerly unavailable reserved memory (640K–1MB) addresses? (2) Does the TSR even need to be loaded before Windows anymore? Remember to consider the possibilities discussed in Chapter 8 about loading TSRs in one or more virtual machines in 386 enhanced mode.

Installing the Reserved Memory Manager

You should first direct DOS to use reserved memory areas by including

DOS=UMB

in your CONFIG.SYS file. The UMB parameter stands for upper memory blocks, which is what the addressable portions of this reserved system memory area are called. If you already have included a DOS=HIGH line, you can combine these two lines into one command that both loads DOS into the HMA and connects low memory with the upper memory blocks:

DOS=HIGH,UMB

To be more precise, the UMB parameter in this command directs DOS 5 to include in the total free memory pool all the available upper memory blocks that EMM386.EXE now provides. The pool is now enlarged to include both conventional memory and reserved memory. The DOS program loader now has a larger total memory space within which to load programs.

Once you've included the DOS=UMB command line, you can then load the special UMB manager by including the line

DEVICE=EMM386.EXE [options]

in your CONFIG.SYS file.

◆ EMM386.EXE AND STANDARD/ENHANCED MODES

> To run Windows in standard mode, you must not run the EMM-386.EXE program. This means that you will be unable to use the UMB area for drivers or memory-resident software.
>
> To maximize the amount of conventional memory in virtual machines in 386 enhanced mode, you must be sure to include a DEVICE=EMM386.EXE line in your CONFIG.SYS file. This gains for you the ability to load TSRs and device drivers in the UMB region (i.e., to load them high).

There are many options available for customizing your installation of EMM386.EXE. They are summarized in Table 15.2 and are explained in more detail in *Mastering DOS 5* (Sybex, 1991) and in your system documentation. The most common option to specify is either RAM or NOEMS.

If you have no need for expanded memory in your non-Windows applications, use the NOEMS parameter:

Device=EMM386.EXE NOEMS

In this way, your system will have access to the UMB region, but will not need or reserve a 64K EMS page frame. This 64K region will thus be available to your memory managers from the UMB region.

If you specify RAM instead of NOEMS, the EMM386.EXE memory manager will provide both UMB management and a 64K EMS page frame.

Loading Device Drivers and TSRs in Upper Memory Blocks

Normally, device drivers as well as applications load into low memory. However, with EMM386.EXE, you can now load most device drivers in UMB. After EMM386.EXE has been installed, you can include a DEVICEHIGH command in your configuration file to load a device driver into this reserved memory area. (First, though, you might check to make sure the device driver is recent enough to work in the UMB region.)

TABLE 15.2: Optional Parameters for EMM386.EXE

Parameter	Explanation
/p*mmmm*	Defines page frame address
/p*n=address*	Defines segment *address* for a specific page *n*
a=*numberRegSets*	Allocates a number of fast alternate registers to EMM386.EXE
b=*address*	Defines the lowest address to use for EMS bank switching
d=*nnn*	Reserves *nnn* kilobytes for buffered DMA
frame=*address*	Defines starting address of 64K page frame
h=*handles*	Defines number of handles usable by EMM386.EXE
i=*mmmm-nnnn*	Includes the specified range as allowable memory addresses
L=*XMSKeep*	Defines how much extended memory to leave available after loading EMM386.EXE
MemSize	Defines how much extended memory EMM386.EXE is to use for emulating expanded memory
m*x*	Specifies one of 14 possible predefined page-frame addresses
noems	Enables UMB access but disables LIM3.2 expanded memory
ram	Enables both UMB access and expanded memory
Status	Toggles EMM386 status *on*, *off*, or *auto*
w=*on* l *off*	Toggles Weitek Coprocessor support on or off
x=*mmmm-nnnn*	Excludes an address range from use by EMM386.EXE

Generally, all that you must do is change existing DEVICE statements to DEVICEHIGH statements, but I suggest that you take a little extra time to do this one statement at a time. Naturally, you can change all DEVICE statements at once and only follow a more cautious procedure if something doesn't work. The more cautious procedure is to change one statement at a time and then reboot your system and verify that everything is working as before. If there is a problem, you may have to run the driver in low memory, or you may have to obtain a different version that can work in upper memory.

Once you've configured your system to use the upper memory blocks in the reserved area, you can even load applications into that area as well. Assuming that they are small enough and will fit there, you can load an application into reserved memory with the LOADHIGH command at a command prompt. For example, suppose that your scanner device comes with a special Optical Character Recognition (OCR) software program. If it fits, you can request that DOS load it into reserved memory with this command:

LOADHIGH OCR.EXE

Finding Out Where Programs and Drivers Are Loaded

If a program that you try to load high requires more reserved memory than is available, DOS will automatically load it into conventional memory without informing you. However, DOS 5 includes a MEM command that will display the names and locations of all loaded drivers and programs. To display this information on screen, type

MEM/C ¦ MORE

at a command prompt prior to starting Windows. This will display useful information that will enable you to learn not only what is loaded where, but what amount of memory remains (and where it is) for possible optimization. To obtain a printout of the same information, such as the example shown in Figure 15.1, just send the results of the MEM command on your system to the printer:

MEM/C > PRN:

◆ HOW TO LOAD TSR'S AND DEVICE DRIVERS INTO
RESERVED MEMORY

Use LOADHIGH in your AUTOEXEC.BAT file to load short, memory-resident programs or TSRs into upper memory blocks. Use

DEVICEHIGH in your CONFIG.SYS file to load device drivers into available UMB space.

◆ OPTIMIZING THE USE OF YOUR UPPER MEMORY BLOCKS

The UMB region can at first appear to be a confusing collection of different things, from video adapter buffers to EMS page frames to BIOS buffers. To be

```
Conventional Memory :

   Name              Size in Decimal        Size in Hex
------------        --------------------    -------------
   MSDOS                21648    ( 21.1K)        5490
   HIMEM                 1072    (  1.0K)         430
   EMM386                3216    (  3.1K)         C90
   COMMAND               3392    (  3.3K)         D40
   SMARTDRV             11712    ( 11.4K)        2DC0
   FREE                    64    (  0.1K)          40
   FREE                614016    (599.6K)       95E80

Total   FREE :         614080    (599.7K)

Upper Memory :

   Name              Size in Decimal        Size in Hex
------------        --------------------    -------------
   SYSTEM              200224    (195.5K)       30E20
   SMARTDRV            16384    ( 16.0K)        4000
   ATDOSXL              9520    (  9.3K)        2530
   ANSI                 4192    (  4.1K)        1060
   RCD                 12912    ( 12.6K)        3270
   CPCSCAN              9264    (  9.0K)        2430
   FREE                 9520    (  9.3K)        2530

Total   FREE :          9520    (  9.3K)

Total bytes available to programs (Conventional+Upper) :    623600    (609.0K)
Largest executable program size :                           613744    (599.4K)
Largest available upper memory block :                        9520    (  9.3K)

    7340032 bytes total contiguous extended memory
          0 bytes available contiguous extended memory
    5005312 bytes available XMS memory
            MS-DOS resident in High Memory Area
```

FIGURE 15.1: Viewing the DOS 5 memory load map (MEM/C)

able to use the available chunks of memory in this region will mean savings in conventional memory space. This will translate directly into extra memory for Windows to use, both in multitasking and in enlarging each DOS virtual machine in 386 enhanced mode. To gain the most from the management services of EMM386.EXE, you should consider a number of optimization factors.

THE ORDER OF LOADING HIGH MAKES A BIG DIFFERENCE

Available UMBs are not usually contiguous. This is why the available upper memory is treated as blocks with separate memory ranges. Remember that this reserved memory area is also known as the adapter segment, a name that derives from its use by different hardware device adapters. The address ranges used by the separate devices are independent of one another and rarely occupy contiguous blocks.

Programs and drivers that load high must fit into one or more available blocks of memory, and each will probably be a different length. Since the programs that you load high are themselves different in length, it's a little like packing a suitcase or the trunk of a car. Items can sometimes fit in one way and not another. You would typically load the largest item into your trunk first, then fit smaller remaining items around it. In fact, this is precisely the technique used by DOS 5.

As each LOADHIGH or DEVICEHIGH is processed, DOS 5 looks at the remaining blocks and tries to place the new program or driver into the largest remaining block. This normally works out best for fitting all your requests successfully into UMBs.

However, a problem sometimes arises because the memory initially required to load some drivers or programs is greater than that required to actually run them after loading. For example, the DOS 5 MIRROR command can be loaded high and only requires 6K of space. However, during loading it consumes approximately 20K. This means that in order to successfully load it in reserved memory, there must be at least one block of 20K or more available when its LOADHIGH command is processed.

Because the loading burden of some programs is greater than others, the order in which you submit LOADHIGH or DEVICEHIGH can sometimes affect your success in fitting your requests into the UMB region. As an example, take a look at Figure 15.2. In this example, I'll try to load MIRROR.EXE and MOUSE.COM into a single UMB that consists of 25K. The previous paragraph defined the needs of the MIRROR command. The MOUSE command varies according to manufacturer, but my MOUSE.COM consumes 11K. That will be enough to demonstrate my point.

On the left side of the figure, I've loaded the MIRROR command first:

LOADHIGH MIRROR.EXE

LOADHIGH MOUSE.COM

After MIRROR completes loading, it consumes 6K, leaving 19K. This is more than enough to load MOUSE.COM, which after loading consumes only 11K. Both programs have loaded high, avoiding any impact on conventional memory. But suppose you tried to load these two programs in the reverse order:

LOADHIGH MOUSE.COM

LOADHIGH MIRROR.EXE

In this case, the MOUSE program loads and consumes 11K. However, when it's finished loading, only 14K remains. While this might be enough for MIR-ROR after it's loaded, it is insufficient for MIRROR's initial memory requirements. Consequently, DOS 5 just loads it into conventional memory without giving you any indication. You only discover it later when you realize that every virtual machine under Windows has less memory available.

OBTAINING MORE UMB SPACE THAN APPEARS AVAILABLE

When you first try to squeeze device drivers or TSRs into reserved memory, you might find that there are no large blocks of space available. My fax board requires that a device driver of 86K be loaded somewhere. As you could see in Figure 15.1, I already used up all but 9.3K of my available upper memory region. Conventional memory has only 599.7K available. To run my fax board means that my conventional memory will drop to close to 500K. That's not a pleasant prospect, but it seems to be the only choice if I wish to continue running all the equipment that I've installed in my system.

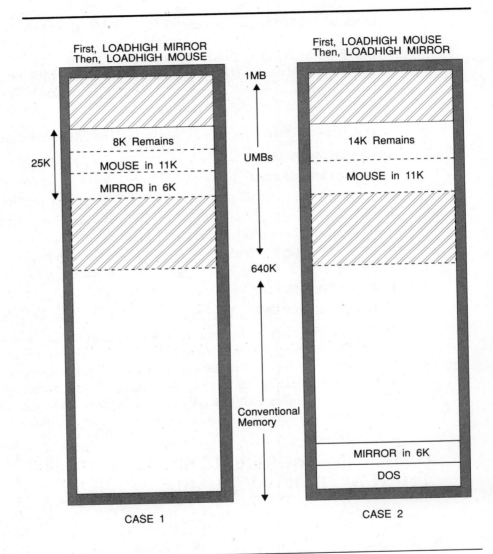

FIGURE 15.2: The order of loading high affects the results.

Increase UMB Space by 64K

Or is it really the only solution? No, it's not. On my system, and perhaps on yours, the amount of free UMB memory can be increased by 64K by simply adding the M9 parameter to the DEVICE=EMM386.EXE command line in your AUTOEXEC.BAT file.

Although this technique works on most AT-compatible systems, it doesn't work on all machines. In particular, it doesn't work on IBM's PS/2 computer systems. If you add M9 to your EMM386.EXE line, you'll receive a warning message about optional ROM or RAM being detected in the page frame area. If you receive that message on your computer after adding the M9 parameter, you should immediately remove the parameter from the CONFIG.SYS line and reboot.

On my AT system, I changed the initiation line in my CONFIG.SYS to the following:

DEVICE=D:\WINDOWS\EMM386.EXE NOEMS X=A000-CFFF M9

Even though I'm running EMM386.EXE with the NOEMS parameter and didn't wish to reserve any EMS memory, you'll see that this technique still made 64K of extra memory available on my system. In Windows 3.1, the NOEMS parameter disables access only to LIM 3.2 expanded memory. LIM 4.0 expanded memory is still available in 386 enhanced mode, so the page frame is still initially reserved.

By convention, the upper memory block that begins at hexadecimal address D000 is used for the normal page frame. The M9 parameter moves the starting address up to E000, extending whatever UMB ended at D000 by this now freed-up 64K of extra space.

Running the MEM/C command after making this simple change produced the results seen in Figure 15.3. As you can now see, there are two visible results. Formerly, there was 599.7K available in conventional memory, and only 9.3K seemingly left free in the UMB region. In addition, the SMARTDRV disk cache program had to split itself into two chunks (a 16.0K data segment in upper memory, and an 11.4K chunk for program and environment space in lower memory).

After rebooting my system with the M9 parameter on the EMM386.EXE line, the UMB region gained 64K of usable space. SMARTDRV immediately used

11.4K of that, loading all of itself into UMBs. This meant an immediate increase of 11K in available conventional memory. Additionally, there is still more than 60K available in upper memory. Previously, there was scarcely enough space left in upper memory for anything else. New drivers and programs would almost certainly have had to load in lower memory.

If I required no other programs to load high, this simple exercise would have at the very least gained more conventional memory for my system. This would translate directly into larger DOS sessions when running virtual machines in Windows' 386 enhanced mode. At the very most, I have over 60K within which to load additional device drivers or TSRs before having any further impact on conventional memory.

```
Conventional Memory :

    Name              Size in Decimal        Size in Hex
    ----              --------------         -----------
    MSDOS             21648    ( 21.1K)         5490
    HIMEM             1072     (  1.0K)         430
    EMM386            3216     (  3.1K)         C90
    COMMAND           3392     (  3.3K)         D40
    FREE              64       (  0.1K)         40
    FREE              625760   (611.1K)         98C60

Total  FREE :         625824   (611.2K)

Upper Memory :

    Name              Size in Decimal        Size in Hex
    ----              --------------         -----------
    SYSTEM            200224   (195.5K)         30E20
    ATDOSXL           9520     (  9.3K)         2530
    ANSI              4192     (  4.1K)         1060
    RCD               12912    ( 12.6K)         3270
    CPCSCAN           9264     (  9.0K)         2430
    SMARTDRV          28064    ( 27.4K)         6DA0
    FREE              63360    ( 61.9K)         F780

Total  FREE :         63360    ( 61.9K)

Total bytes available to programs (Conventional+Upper) :   689184   (673.0K)
Largest executable program size :                          625488   (610.8K)
Largest available upper memory block :                     63360    ( 61.9K)

    7340032 bytes total contiguous extended memory
          0 bytes available contiguous extended memory
    4939776 bytes available XMS memory
            MS-DOS resident in High Memory Area
```

FIGURE 15.3: The M9 parameter in EMM386.EXE can gain 64K of UMB space.

Use Video Adapter Space

The 64K page frame area is a large block of obtainable space in many computer systems. Some additional portions of your UMB area may also be obtainable, but you'll have to put a little effort into the task. Remember from the discussion in Chapter 4 that video adapter ROM consumes a large initial memory area in the upper memory region.

In fact, the EMM386.EXE program does not automatically even look in the area below hexadecimal address C800 for available memory in which to load TSRs and drivers. However, suppose that you know exactly which video modes your system uses and doesn't use. You can direct EMM386.EXE to explicitly include specific addresses in memory space that is otherwise ignored. The I, or Include, parameter on the EMM386.EXE device line in your CONFIG.SYS file will give you this facility.

For example, a monochrome display adapter uses only the addresses from B000 to B7FF (ROM hexadecimal). The same goes for a Hercules adapter's Video Page 1, or it might be used by a VGA adapter that is using 256 colors. If you are not using any of these, you can direct EMM386.EXE to gain that 32K by adding the explicit address range with the I, or Include, switch:

```
DEVICE=D:\WINDOWS\EMM386.EXE NOEMS X=A000–AFFF X=B800–CFFF
   M9 I=B000–B7FF
```

To avoid an overlap of addresses, I had to adjust the X parameter to exclude two separate UMBs. This is because the B000–B7FF area falls right in the middle of the formerly excluded A000–CFFF range. Naturally, making these types of adjustments requires great care, and a reasonable degree of knowledge. You can begin by calling your video board manufacturer to discover the address ranges the adapter uses, and under what application circumstances those ranges are used.

If you make this kind of setting adjustment, be cautious for a while until you verify that your system continues to work reliably. When you run your applications, back up your work even more frequently than usual to be sure of minimizing any data loss. If you were wrong in the address range you specified, and your video adapter does in fact use certain addresses (that you have now loaded another driver or TSR into), you will be very likely to encounter a system crash.

EMM386.EXE also ignores all memory above the hexadecimal address DFFF. Thus, if you are sure that no program, driver, or system function uses some portion of these highest UMB addresses, you can also use the I switch to enlarge the usable UMB ranges even further. Be even more cautious up here. Since the system BIOS is located at the top of the UMB area, you must really know what is going on up there before you make use of those higher address ranges.

FITTING LARGE DRIVERS OR PROGRAMS INTO UMBS

Now that you've learned some techniques for obtaining even more UMB space, let's take a look at some methods for using the UMB space you end up with. Regardless of whether your system has 30K of UMBs or you've used the techniques in the preceding section to make 100K available, the following approaches can result in significant improvements both in space and in the way your programs use the space.

The Order of Loading Can Save Memory

On the system I've been using for my examples, I can now juggle the order of loading to make most efficient use of the remaining space and still load my fax driver. I discussed the concept earlier in connection with Figure 15.2. Here, you'll look at an example of putting the concept to work in practice.

As I mentioned previously, the fax driver on my computer consumes approximately 86K in two pieces (named CCBACK and CCBACK2). If I simply add DEVICEHIGH and LOADHIGH statements after all the ones you saw loaded in Figure 15.3, the driver would not be able to load into UMBs; thus all 86K would be housed in lower memory. However, by loading it just prior to SMARTDRV, it efficiently uses nearly all of the UMB space available. This forces SMARTDRV to load completely in lower memory, but conventional memory is then reduced by only 27K rather than 86K, and upper memory is more efficiently used. Figure 15.4 shows the final result after adjusting the loading order of my DOS 5 startup files.

You can exercise some judgment in the loading order, as well as whether or not you even use LOADHIGH and DEVICEHIGH commands. Adjusting the order of load-high requests works fine if you are just changing a sequence of LOADHIGH or DEVICEHIGH requests. Typically, device drivers are processed in the CONFIG.SYS file first. Only then is the sequence of LOAD-HIGH requests processed in your AUTOEXEC.BAT file.

Use Conventional Memory to Save Conventional Memory

Sometimes you have to give up a little to gain a lot. You can wisely load a device driver into lower memory if, by so doing, you gain just enough UMB space to squeeze an even larger TSR into upper memory space.

There may be times when you have to not only adjust the order of load-high requests, but replace a DEVICEHIGH command with a DEVICE request.

```
Conventional Memory :

    Name            Size in Decimal        Size in Hex
------------      ---------------------    -------------
    MSDOS            21648    ( 21.1K)          5490
    HIMEM             1072    (  1.0K)           430
    EMM386            3216    (  3.1K)           C90
    COMMAND           3392    (  3.3K)           D40
    SMARTDRV         28160    ( 27.5K)          6E00
    FREE                64    (  0.1K)            40
    FREE            597568    (583.6K)         91E40

Total  FREE :      597632    (583.6K)

Upper Memory :

    Name            Size in Decimal        Size in Hex
------------      ---------------------    -------------
    SYSTEM          200224    (195.5K)         30E20
    ATDOSXL           9520    (  9.3K)          2530
    ANSI              4192    (  4.1K)          1060
    RCD              12912    ( 12.6K)          3270
    CPCSCAN           9264    (  9.0K)          2430
    CCBACK            5456    (  5.3K)          1550
    CCBACK2          82640    ( 80.7K)         142D0
    FREE              3296    (  3.2K)           CE0

Total  FREE :        3296    (  3.2K)

Total bytes available to programs (Conventional+Upper) :   600928   (586.8K)
Largest executable program size :                          597296   (583.3K)
Largest available upper memory block :                       3296   (  3.2K)

    7340032 bytes total contiguous extended memory
          0 bytes available contiguous extended memory
    4939776 bytes available XMS memory
            MS-DOS resident in High Memory Area
```

FIGURE 15.4: Change the loading order to minimize the burden on conventional memory

This latter operation explicitly requests that a particular device driver be loaded into conventional memory rather than in UMBs. You would only do this if you've determined that the space required by a small driver is just the right amount, when added to free UMB space, to allow a large TSR or large other driver to load into the UMB area.

For example, suppose that my fax driver required 90K instead of 86K to load. Just changing the order of LOADHIGH requests for SMARTDRV and CCBACK would not have been sufficient to enable CCBACK to load high. You can see this in Figure 15.4: even though a mere four additional kilobytes are required, there aren't that many remaining available in the UMB region. And the other four entries that I've loaded high are all device drivers loaded high in the CONFIG.SYS file. They were all placed there by DEVICEHIGH statements in CONFIG.SYS before the LOADHIGH commands for SMARTDRV and CCBACK were even read in the AUTOEXEC.BAT file.

The solution would be to select one of the device drivers and change DEVICEHIGH to DEVICE. For example, changing

DEVICEHIGH = C:\ATDOSXL.SYS

to

DEVICE = C:\ATDOSXL.SYS

would cost 9K in conventional memory (by loading the Plus Hard Card driver, ATDOSXL, low), but would free up just enough UMB space to allow the theoretical 90K driver to load into UMB space.

Use Upper Memory Space to Save Upper Memory Space

Earlier, you learned how to use the /I switch with the EMM386.EXE driver to include a memory range (B000-B7FF) from video adapter ROM that EMM386 would otherwise ignore. By using this switch, I expanded the apparent UMB space by using portions of UMBs that would otherwise be ignored because of standard conventions. Those conventions may not apply to your system.

In the preceding example, I was able to place an 86K driver in upper memory blocks by moving the page frame address. This freed 64K, which my fax driver happily consumed. And I was happy to retain that amount of conventional memory. However, I still had to give up 27K for the SMARTDRV driver. By further tuning the EMM386.EXE line on my system, I included the 32K video ROM block and consequently saved even more conventional memory. Figure 15.5 shows the result the next time I rebooted my system.

This demonstrates an interesting aspect of DOS 5's UMB facility. There are limits on what you can get. Its algorithm for fitting drivers and TSRs into the largest block first will occasionally produce a result that is not as good as possible. Even though the I=B000-C7FF parameter gained 32K, the entire SMARTDRV driver does not fit neatly into that 32K block. By the time

```
Conventional Memory :

    Name            Size in Decimal        Size in Hex
-------------       -------------------    -------------
    MSDOS             21648    ( 21.1K)        5490
    HIMEM              1072    (  1.0K)         430
    EMM386             3216    (  3.1K)         C90
    COMMAND            3392    (  3.3K)         D40
    SMARTDRV          11776    ( 11.5K)        2E00
    FREE                 64    (  0.1K)          40
    FREE             613952    (599.6K)       95E40

Total  FREE :        614016    (599.6K)

Upper Memory :

    Name            Size in Decimal        Size in Hex
-------------       -------------------    -------------
    SYSTEM           167488    (163.6K)       28E40
    SMARTDRV          16384    ( 16.0K)        4000
    CCBACK             5456    (  5.3K)        1550
    CCBACK2           82640    ( 80.7K)       142D0
    ATDOSXL            9520    (  9.3K)        2530
    ANSI               4192    (  4.1K)        1060
    RCD               12912    ( 12.6K)        3270
    CPCSCAN            9264    (  9.0K)        2430
    FREE              12400    ( 12.1K)        3070
    FREE               7200    (  7.0K)        1C20

Total  FREE :         19600    ( 19.1K)

Total bytes available to programs (Conventional+Upper) :     633616    (618.8K)
Largest executable program size :                            613680    (599.3K)
Largest available upper memory block :                        12400    ( 12.1K)

    7340032 bytes total contiguous extended memory
          0 bytes available contiguous extended memory
    4907008 bytes available XMS memory
            MS-DOS resident in High Memory Area
```

FIGURE 15.5: Using the EMM386.EXE /I switch increases UMB space.

DOS 5 got around to loading the SMARTDRV.EXE program from my AUTOEXEC.BAT file, it had already loaded the other device drivers in such a way that only the 16K data segment of SMARTDRV could still fit into an available UMB. The remaining 11K was forced once again to load into low memory.

The final result in Figure 15.5, when compared to the starting point in Figure 15.1, demonstrates an important principle. Note that back in Figure 15.1, before any of this chapter's techniques were applied, there was only 9K available in UMBs for additional programs or drivers.

By judiciously manipulating the ordering of drivers, and by judiciously controlling the initial EMM386.EXE device settings, I was able to accomplish a significant memory enhancement. First, my system retained roughly the same amount of conventional memory as before. Second, I was able to load a previously unloadable (in the High Memory Area) 86K fax driver. Third, there is more than double the remaining UMB space for additional loading, even after loading this extraordinarily large driver into UMBs.

USING ALTERNATIVE MEMORY MANAGERS

DOS 5 and Windows offer a pair of programs to manage memory. You can manage extended memory and the HMA with the HIMEM.SYS driver, and you can manage upper memory blocks with the EMM386.EXE manager program. Personally, I use both of these facilities all the time now.

I Use HIMEM.SYS and EMM386.EXE

When I first started using Windows, I succumbed to the publicity surrounding alternate memory-management products. I compared the features and reputation of several and decided to use QEMM-386 from Quarterdeck Office Systems, although it was a tough final decision between that and 386Max from Qualitas Corporation. Both are excellent programs and both offer significant advantages over DOS 5's management facilities.

When DOS 5 was released, I had difficulties with my earlier versions of QEMM 386. I was forced to upgrade. In fact, since I was a Beta tester for

Microsoft during the development of DOS 5, I was forced to upgrade more than once. When I began testing the Beta versions of Windows 3.1, I once again ran into incompatibilities between QEMM 386 and new versions of Windows. After several rounds of system crashes, due largely to software incompatibilities rather than bugs, I decided to revert to HIMEM.SYS and EMM386.EXE.

As you might know, Windows and now DOS as well come solely from Microsoft. Consequently, you can trust that there will be no new incompatibilities between the two.

But many people stick to third-party memory-management software. Why is that? After all, HIMEM.SYS and EMM386.EXE are included at no additional cost as part of both DOS 5 and Windows 3.1. The cost of any third-party memory-management software is additional.

To begin with, the better products offer much more control than DOS 5 does over UMB loading. In QEMM 386, for example, each separate UMB is uniquely numbered. The QEMM LOADHI.EXE program (the equivalent of DOS 5's LOADHIGH command) has a /R (Region) switch, which enables me to control precisely which UMB region to load a program into. In DOS 5, I can control the order of load-high requests, but I can't control which UMB a particular program actually goes into. LOADHI /R in QEMM 386 offers precise control over program and driver placement. The situation seen in Figure 15.5, in which an 11.5K entry was made into low memory when 19.1K remained in upper memory, would not have to occur with the more powerful QEMM 386 program.

On the other hand, it is harder to learn how to use a third-party memory manager. To configure QEMM 386 to do what I just described required a good deal of personal study and effort, much more than that required to get the two DOS 5 products up and running. Because such products as QEMM do more, they require more effort to use correctly and well. They do come with optimizing programs that assist you in coming up with the best ordering of load-high requests and the best use of the UMB regions. However, it's no simple chore even to use the optimization routines that are supplied.

If You Decide to Use a Third-Party Memory Manager

Regardless of the trade-offs mentioned above, I've made my decision based solely on compatibility. I upgrade my DOS, Windows, and application software environments as often as the software changes. I try to minimize the pain and suffering that invariably attend upgrading software. If you have a more stable environment, you may wish to use the extra facilities of these more sophisticated memory managers. If you do so, consider the following issues.

If you use a third-party memory manager, you should no longer include references in your CONFIG.SYS file to either HIMEM.SYS or EMM386.EXE. Neither should you include the DOS=UMB line in CONFIG.SYS, although you should retain DOS=HIGH in order to use the HMA for DOS buffers and part of the kernel. You should also remove all references to DEVICEHIGH in the CONFIG.SYS file, and to LOADHIGH in your AUTOEXEC.BAT file.

In place of all these DOS 5 program references, you must substitute the appropriate program and command references for the program you've selected. For example, both HIMEM.SYS and EMM386.EXE are replaced by Quarterdeck's product QEMM386.SYS, which you must load with a DEVICE command in your CONFIG.SYS file. This memory manager, like EMM-386.EXE, is sometimes called a *UMB provider* because it creates the available upper memory blocks after determining what else is occupying the region above 640K.

Each DEVICEHIGH command must be replaced by a new device driver (the LOADHI.SYS driver). Each LOADHIGH command must be replaced with a LOADHI.COM command configured to work correctly with Quarterdeck's QEMM386.SYS driver. Both the LOADHI.SYS and the LOADHI.COM modules are sometimes called *UMB loaders*, because they assign memory block address ranges to drivers or TSRs that you specify.

For example, when I was using QEMM, I used the following line in my CONFIG.SYS file to precisely control the creation of upper memory blocks:

```
DEVICE=C:\QEMM\QEMM386.SYS RAM ROM NOEMS
    X=A000–C7FF X=C800–C9FF X=E000–FFFF
```

I then included a series of loader lines like this one:

DEVICE = C:\QEMM\LOADHI.SYS /R:1 C:\ATDOSXL.SYS

Each line loaded a specific driver into a specifically mapped region of UMBs. Prior to doing this, I used other Quarterdeck software to accurately map out and analyze the upper memory region. The software is quite powerful, and when I finally understood it completely, it was quite successful in making efficient use of my system's UMB area.

In my AUTOEXEC.BAT file, I used a series of LOADHI lines like these to load UMBs with specific TSRs:

C:\QEMM\LOADHI /R:1 FILES=+69

C:\QEMM\LOADHI /R:2 F11F12 /1=DOSSHELL /2=EXIT

C:\QEMM\LOADHI /R:3 MIRROR C: D: /TC /TD

This example sequence demonstrates yet another powerful aspect of using Quarterdeck's UMB loader. It can obtain memory from UMBs for DOS 5 "FILES" support; DOS 5 itself always obtains this space from conventional memory. The LOADHI program also offers precise location control for whatever it loads into UMBs.

◆ MAXIMIZING THE BENEFIT OF AVAILABLE MEMORY

In the preceding sections you've learned how to maximize conventional memory most effectively and how to use upper reserved memory most efficiently. In this section, you'll learn a number of techniques for taking full advantage of whatever memory you actually end up with.

USING A RAM DISK

DOS 5 and Windows 3.1 include a device driver that can create a *RAM disk* (sometimes called a *virtual disk*). The RAM disk is not really a disk; it is an area in memory that simulates an additional disk drive. If your system has enough memory to assign to this purpose, and you use the resulting RAM disk effectively, it can be one of the best ways to trade memory for system performance.

Although the technique makes very different use of memory space than a disk cache, you can potentially gain more in terms of enhanced system performance. However, a RAM disk will improve efficiency only if it is used appropriately. If you have limited memory on your system, establishing a disk cache instead of a RAM disk will improve system efficiency more easily and for more of the time, since so much of a system's operation depends on disk reads and writes.

It takes more effort and understanding to make sure that a RAM disk contains the right programs, that the applications use those versions, and, when necessary, that the information on the RAM disk is properly copied elsewhere. The bottom line here is that I suggest you establish a disk cache first, and only then consider whether or not you have sufficient extra memory to use for a RAM disk.

The critical aspect of the RAM disk concept is that any files placed on the RAM disk are really memory-resident. They can therefore be retrieved at the speed of memory, which is usually microseconds or nanoseconds. File access on mechanical disk drives is slower, usually in the millisecond range. First, I'll briefly review how to create a RAM disk. Then, more importantly, I'll discuss the best ways to use it.

Creating a RAM Disk

Usually, you allocate some of your *extended* memory for RAM disk space, thereby reserving as much low memory as possible for your programs while gaining the performance benefits of a RAM disk. If you do not have extended memory to spare, forget about using a RAM disk. Although the driver can create a RAM disk in conventional memory, it would affect Windows 3.1's performance so adversely that it would be counterproductive.

As to the size of the RAM disk, that depends on too many factors. If you have lots of memory, and you've already established a disk cache, start out with a RAM drive equal to one-fourth of your total memory. As you use your system, pay attention to how you use the RAM disk (see next section) and whether you actually need this much space. If you don't need the space, reduce the size and allow Windows to use the memory for other purposes. If you find that you can profitably use a larger RAM disk, and your Windows performance hasn't suffered, then expand the size and see what happens.

♦ **RAM DISKS ARE COUNTERPRODUCTIVE IN LIMITED MEMORY SITUATIONS**

Memory reserved for use as a RAM disk is no longer available for use by Windows 3.1. If you use too much space for a RAM disk, there may not be enough remaining memory for Windows 3.1 to work efficiently.

Remember that swapping only occurs when Windows 3.1 runs out of physical memory. If you create a RAM disk to enhance performance, but force time-consuming swapping operations that otherwise would not have occurred, the overall effect will be slower Windows 3.1 operations.

The RAM disk seen in Figure 15.6 can be implemented simply by including the following DEVICE line in your CONFIG.SYS:

DEVICE=C:\WINDOWS\RAMDRIVE.SYS 1024 /E

This statement first loads the RAM disk driver into memory. In this example, the RAMDRIVE.SYS file itself is located on drive C in the WINDOWS directory. The parameter value of 1024 in this example indicates that a total simulated disk of 1024K, or 1MB, should be created from the available extended memory. See the next section for advice on determining the size of your RAM disk, and on how to use it most efficiently.

You can use two switches with this device driver command, depending on whether you wish to use extended or expanded memory for the RAM disk created. I've used the /E switch to use extended memory. For this command to work properly, you must have preceded this line with a DEVICE line for an extended memory manager, like HIMEM.SYS.

If you were to use the /A switch instead of /E, you could install your RAM disk in expanded memory. In this case, of course, you must precede the RAMDRIVE.SYS line with an appropriate DEVICE command for an expanded memory manager. If your system has an expanded memory board

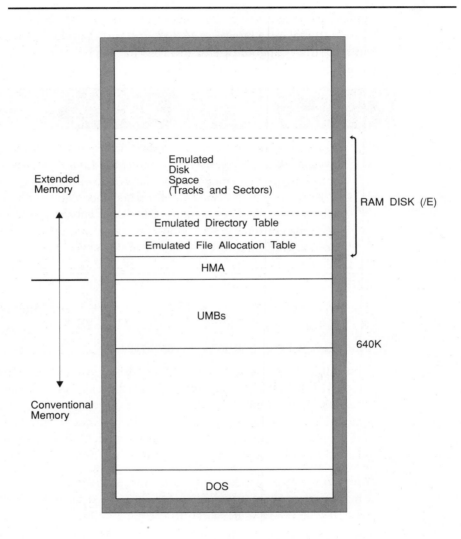

FIGURE 15.6: RAM disk use of physical memory

installed, and you must use the memory *as* expanded memory (as opposed to configuring it as extended memory), remember to use the driver that accompanied the physical expanded memory board.

You should usually install a RAM drive in extended memory (using the /E switch). If you do not specify either /A or /E, RAMDRIVE.SYS will attempt to install your RAM disk in conventional memory, which isn't recommended; use one of the two switches. For those of you who wish to exercise even greater control over the creation of a RAM disk on your system, use the following detailed syntax:

Device=[path]ramdrive.sys [Size [SectorSize [Entries]]] [/E|/A]

[Path] defines the full path to the RAMDRIVE.SYS file. The other parameter/switch possibilities are explained briefly in Table 15.3.

Although you can use an expanded-memory emulator, such as EMM386.EXE, to obtain expanded memory for a RAM disk, it is inadvisable because of the inefficiencies associated with emulating expanded memory. Windows 3.1 includes the emulation program to work with any 386 or 486 computer system; however, it does so mainly to enable you to run older applications that require expanded memory.

♦ DON'T INSTALL A RAM DRIVE IN EMULATED EXPANDED MEMORY

It is inefficient to use a RAM disk in emulated expanded memory, such as that provided by EMM386.EXE in 386 enhanced mode.

TABLE 15.3: Optional Parameters for RAMDRIVE.SYS

Parameter	Explanation
/a	Uses expanded memory for the RAM drive
/e	Uses extended memory for the RAM drive
Entries	Sets maximum number of file and directory entries in the RAM drive's root directory
SectorSize	Sets the size of each emulated disk sector
Size	Sets the number of kilobytes to allocate for the RAM drive

If you intend to use disk drives with drive identifiers beyond the letter E, DOS requires a LASTDRIVE statement to be included in your configuration file. This additional statement must be of the form

LASTDRIVE=x

where *x* is the last valid alphabetic character that DOS will use for a drive identifier.

Don't forget that changes you make to the CONFIG.SYS file don't take effect until the DOS system is rebooted.

Advice for Efficient Use of a RAM Disk

Now that you know how to create a RAM disk, you need to know how to use it to its best advantage. Here are some suggestions for using your RAM disk.

Place a copy of COMMAND.COM on your RAM disk. Then perform the following to inform DOS that COMMAND.COM is located on the RAM disk. Assuming your RAM disk is on drive E (substitute the appropriate letter on your system), include the following command in your system's AUTO-EXEC.BAT file:

SET COMSPEC=E:\COMMAND.COM

This will speed up all programs that execute DOS commands from within themselves, such as Framework IV or QDOS III. These programs work by loading a second copy of the command processor (COMMAND.COM). This command will also speed up application software that overwrites the command-processor portion of DOS.

Further suggestions for RAM disk use: Load the files for frequently used DOS commands onto your RAM disk. Consider loading EDIT.COM if you use the DOS editor often to edit small text files. Place your favorite batch files and disk-resident utility programs (shareware, public-domain, or purchased, like the Norton Utilities) on the RAM disk if you use them frequently.

Load any text files that are used frequently but are not changed. Load any large support files (like spelling dictionaries or a thesaurus file) that your word processor or integrated software may need. Or place index-type files (generated by many database management systems) on the RAM disk for faster data access, especially if you must search through many records in large data files.

Place overlay files on your RAM disk to speed up execution of software that references such overlay modules. These overlays contain portions of your application that couldn't fit into memory and that are normally read into a special part of memory only when needed. Note that you will need to make your RAM disk the default DOS disk before invoking your application, so that it will look for the overlay file on the RAM disk and not on the standard drive. Alternatively, put the location of the files in the PATH statement.

Remember to set your PATH properly so DOS can find your main applications. Set the RAM disk at or near the front of the PATH specification so that the files that were copied onto the RAM drive are accessed first, rather than the original files that may also be accessible from directories on the path.

Before you follow the above suggestions for using your RAM disk effectively, you should learn how to use it safely. As you know, using a RAM disk is much faster than using real disks. Programs that formerly took hours to run may take minutes, minutes can become seconds, and waiting time can disappear. When RAM disks are used improperly, however, hours of work can also disappear in seconds.

Since a RAM disk exists in memory, any information stored on it will vanish when the computer is turned off. You gain great advantage by storing and accessing the right files on a RAM disk, but you must remember that these files are destroyed when any of the following events occur: you turn off the power, a power failure or brownout occurs, your computer plug comes out of the wall, or you simply reboot your system with Ctrl+Alt+Del.

If you place and update important data files on a RAM disk for the sake of rapid access, save copies of them to a real disk before you turn off the power. Also back up copies of them to a real disk at frequent intervals to avoid losing all your work.

◆ BACK UP RAM DISK FILES

If you use a RAM disk to work more efficiently with permanent files, remember to back up these files to a real disk frequently.

Setting the TEMP Environment Variable

Many Windows applications create temporary files during their operations. For example, compiling and print spooling are notorious for generating them—I say "notorious" because they are a burden on your system. You can speed up operations greatly by first creating a RAM disk and then setting the TEMP variable to point to a directory on the RAM disk.

Because there is a design limit on the number of file names a root directory can hold, use a subdirectory (like E:\TEMP if your RAM disk is known as drive E:). You can't easily know in advance how many files will be temporarily created by your applications. If you choose to gain speed by setting TEMP to a RAM disk, you must also be sure to have created a sufficiently large RAM disk. Some programs will fail if they try to write to a disk that is out of space. RAM disks are usually much smaller than the space available on a hard disk, so you are more likely to encounter problems if your RAM disk is not large enough. Because many printing jobs consume large amounts of space, you should not assign the TEMP variable to a RAM disk location unless you have at least 2MB to spare for your RAM disk. (If you do not use a RAM disk location, you can and should still use the TEMP variable to enhance system performance by pointing it to a fast hard disk.)

Set up your RAM-disk TEMP connection with these commands in your AUTOEXEC.BAT file:

MD E:\TEMP

SET TEMP=E:\TEMP

Note that some programs (like a C compiler) may use a different environment variable (like TMP) for the same purpose as the more common TEMP. Read your application's documentation to discover the name of any environment variables used for this purpose. In these cases, you would simply include an additional SET command in your AUTOEXEC.BAT to point the application's environment variable to your RAM disk location.

SAVE MEMORY BY TRIMMING SYSTEM FAT

Several features of Windows consume variable amounts of memory. It is not even obvious in some cases that the memory is being consumed. This section will point out some of the areas that, once managed, can yield surprising gains for your system.

Wallpaper Is Not Free

The more detailed your wallpaper bit map is, the more memory it consumes. In order to redisplay your desktop, including the background wallpaper, a copy is made of your entire wallpaper file in memory. I occasionally use a beautiful, peaceful mountain scene for wallpaper background on my 8MB system. When I do, I also occasionally receive an "Out of Memory" message.

If Windows sends you this message too often, try a less detailed .BMP image. Or eliminate wallpaper completely by setting Wallpaper to None in the Desktop section of the Control Panel. Remember that wallpaper images consume memory equivalent to their bit-map size, which in the case of graphics can be several hundred kilobytes.

Don't Load Unnecessary Drivers

There is a temptation to load small device drivers (of the .COM or .EXE file type) and TSRs prior to starting Windows. Even though it is clearly less efficient, and uses extra conventional memory, it is easier to load them once in an AUTOEXEC.BAT file. The alternative is to run DOS applications under Windows from customized batch files run from PIFs. This may be the most efficient way to do it, but it is still an extra effort.

If you are just running Windows applications, you needn't load a mouse driver at all. Only if you run DOS applications that require a mouse must you even consider loading a mouse driver in addition to the one that Windows includes. That is because Windows manages your mouse during all Windows operations, except when running full-screen DOS applications.

Similarly, although it may be tempting to use DOS 5's ability to load drivers and TSRs in upper memory blocks, don't do it just as a matter of course. After all, small TSRs from DOS itself (like MIRROR and DOSKEY) are useful and don't take up much room, right? Wrong. This whole chapter is about getting 5K here, 10K there, 32K another place. Every conventional memory program that can be placed in UMBs, and every buffer that can be moved into extended memory, frees up more conventional memory. This in turn improves Windows' overall efficiency.

Reduce the Size of WIN.INI

Reducing the size of WIN.INI can not only reclaim memory for your system but can also improve overall performance. While Windows is executing, a portion of memory is reserved to hold a copy of the WIN.INI configuration settings. By making WIN.INI smaller, you reduce the necessary amount of memory that must be reserved. This will make extra memory available to Windows for other uses, not to mention reducing the time it takes to load and later update the WIN.INI file itself. Try any or all of these techniques to reduce WIN.INI file size:

◆ First make a backup copy elsewhere for safety, readability, and ease of restoration.

◆ Remove all comment lines. (These all begin with a semicolon.)

◆ Remove all blank lines.

◆ Remove all initialization sections for applications you no longer need or use.

◆ Remove all lines in the [ports] section for any ports your hardware does not have, or that your software will not use.

◆ Remove lines in the [fonts] and [TrueType] sections for fonts you do not expect to use.

◆ Remove lines in the [extensions] section for associated programs that you do not typically expect to run via the associated data file.

Saving Memory by Eliminating Fonts

If you eliminate access to fonts from within Windows 3.1, you are not necessarily erasing them from the disk. You are merely freeing up the memory that Windows would otherwise use in providing font selections to your applications.

Select the Fonts icon in the Control Panel to display the Fonts dialog box. You can use this box to save memory in three ways:

♦ If none of your applications use TrueType fonts, remove the mark beside the Use TrueType check box.

♦ If *all* of your applications use TrueType fonts *only,* turn on the mark beside the TrueType Only check box.

♦ If you know you have fonts that are not used by Windows or any of your applications, remove them. You can always restore them later by selecting Add from this same screen and then telling Windows to add from the list of fonts found in the SYSTEM directory.

♦ Remove all entries from the [intl] section except those that override (are not equal to) the default values.

♦ If you don't expect to print from multiple programs at once, you may not need the Print Manager. Setting Spooler=False in the [Windows] section will retain memory otherwise assigned to the Print Manager.

USING PIFS EFFECTIVELY

As you learned in Chapter 8, you can customize the operation of your non-Windows applications by modifying the entries in each program's PIF. This section will revisit the most important PIF settings that influence memory availability.

Saving Memory in Standard Mode

All of the settings suggested in this section can have a measurable impact in standard mode on the amount of free memory available. As always, this memory can then be used by either your application or Windows to share among other running tasks.

♦ Select the No Screen Exchange option, but only if you have no intention of copying full-screen or windowed images onto the Clipboard.

♦ Do not check the Directly Modifies Keyboard option, unless you are sure that your application must have complete control of the keyboard.

♦ Select Prevent Program Switch, if you are willing to exit the application in order to switch to other applications.

♦ Set KB Required in Memory Requirements to as low a value as possible. Windows will require this much memory to be free before starting your application.

♦ Set the video mode to text mode, if possible. It requires the least amount of memory for storing and restoring the application's display. If graphics are required, select Low if your application's screen can be properly restored after a tasking switch.

♦ Set EMS Memory to 0 if your application does not explicitly need or know how to use expanded memory.

♦ Set XMS Memory to 0 if your application does not explicitly need or know how to use extended memory.

Saving Memory in 386 Enhanced Mode

All of the settings suggested in this section can have a measurable impact in 386 enhanced mode on the amount of free memory available. As always, this memory can then be used by either your application or Windows to share among other running tasks.

♦ If it is not necessary to ensure correct execution, do not turn on any Lock Memory options. Although locking memory can speed up an individual application's execution, it retains that memory for this one application, thereby keeping Windows from swapping the space and using it for other running applications.

◆ Do not select Retain Video Memory, unless Windows has difficulty restoring your application's display. Although selecting this option helps to ensure correct video redisplay, the memory consumed will never be released to Windows for alternate use.

◆ Set KB Required in Memory Requirements to as low a value as possible. Windows will require this much memory to be free before starting your application. Use this setting to restrict this memory, if you're sure that your application can run successfully with less than 640K. By so doing, you will consume physical memory at a slower rate, still be able to run your favorite applications, and lessen the likelihood of receiving "Out of Memory" messages.

◆ Set the video mode to text mode, if possible. It requires the least amount of memory for storing and restoring the application's display. If graphics are required, select Low if your application's screen can be properly restored after a tasking switch.

◆ Set EMS Memory to 0 if your application does not explicitly need or know how to use expanded memory.

◆ Set XMS Memory to 0 if your application does not explicitly need or know how to use extended memory.

◆ LOCK EXPANDED MEMORY IN 386 ENHANCED MODE

You may have noticed that a particular non-Windows application that uses expanded memory (e.g., Lotus 1-2-3) in 386 enhanced mode is running extremely slowly. This could be due to insufficient free physical memory and consequent paging of the application's memory out to disk. If the part of memory that is paged is expanded memory, then Windows is, first, emulating expanded memory (from extended memory) and, second, paging it out to disk. This is now equivalent to a very slow, but functional, disk-based expanded-memory emulator.

To prevent such a dramatic slowdown in an important non-Windows application, mark the Locked check box beside the EMS Memory option in the Advanced Options portion of an application's .PIF file. This retains the expanded memory area that is assigned to your application in physical memory, and avoids the disk-based slowdown in its operations.

Freeing Up Conventional Memory for TSR-Burdened Applications

Non-Windows applications are still constrained to run within the usual 640K limit. So are TSR programs. Even though Windows-compliant programs can now access the larger addressable memory spaces of a 80x86 processor (memory beyond 640K), older DOS programs cannot. So even though the About field of the Program Manager's Help pull-down menu says you have a lot of memory available, it's not truly available to older programs.

Nevertheless, because you can set up multiple DOS sessions under Windows, you can separate your TSRs from each other and from other non-Windows applications. Unless one or more TSRs must be run in the same session, or in combination with an application, create a separate .PIF file for each TSR and run the TSRs in separate non-Windows partitions.

Running them in this way means that the sum of all the TSRs you run can exceed 640K, and applications that formerly were squeezed by having TSRs in their addressable space can now have more conventional memory available for their own use.

GIVING DOS APPLICATIONS WHAT THEY NEED

Non-Windows applications are sometimes a demanding lot. They expect to have an entire system's resources available to them. This section deals with providing memory-related resources, like expanded memory and environment space, that they occasionally need in order to run successfully.

Managing Environment Space

Do you use up most of the space in your DOS's default environment? If you've changed your DOS Shell command (in CONFIG.SYS), you may think that you've increased the environment size—and in fact, you have—but only in DOS, not in Windows.

To enlarge the environment space, you added the /e:*nnnn* switch to increase the available environment to *nnnn* bytes. But once you start Windows, each DOS session you start (i.e., each DOS shell that you spawn), and each DOS PIF that you use to launch a DOS application, consumes an additional *nnnn* bytes of environment space.

Some DOS applications require additional environmental variable space beyond what is initially used. If the available space is exceeded, the application may erroneously attempt to use addressable locations that it should not or can not, and the application may freeze up, or worse.

You must use one of the following techniques to ensure that your non-Windows applications receive a larger environment. There are two ways to launch a DOS application with more than the default number of environment bytes:

◆ *To launch DOS applications from a DOS prompt that you bring up via the DOS Prompt icon in the Main group of the Program Manager:* Open up the Main subgroup in the Program Manager. Highlight the DOS Prompt icon. Then pull down the File menu, and select Properties. Change the Command Line field entry from COMMAND.COM to

COMMAND.COM /e:1024

or any other size that you'd like.

◆ *To launch DOS applications from their own customized .PIF files:* Run the PIF Editor from the Accessories subgroup in the Program Manager. In the Program Filename field, enter COMMAND.COM. In the Optional Parameters field, type the environment size specification (e.g., /e:1024), followed by a /C and the name of the program you actually wish to run. For example, to run 123.EXE, you might enter in this field

/e:1024 /c c:\123r23\123.exe

In either of these two cases, the extra environment size will ensure more successful execution of your program. And the memory consumed is only a temporary burden on that particular DOS session under Windows. When the

DOS application ends, the environment memory is freed up along with all other memory that was specific to this single DOS session under Windows.

Providing Expanded Memory

As a rule, you should configure any expanded memory in your system as extended memory. Follow the instructions that accompanied your expanded memory board for doing this.

When running in 386 enhanced mode, Windows can use the EMM386.EXE device driver to emulate expanded memory whenever necessary for your non-Windows applications. Consequently, your system needs no actual expanded memory in order to satisfy the occasional expanded-memory needs of a non-Windows application. Maximizing the available extended memory is the best use of any physical expanded memory in your system.

If you run non-Windows applications in 386 enhanced mode, but none of those applications requires expanded memory support, you should enter or modify the following line in the [386Enh] section of your SYSTEM.INI file:

ReservePageFrame=No

Turning this setting off frees up conventional memory. Since the page frame in upper reserved blocks (between 640K and 1MB) is no longer reserved for EMS support, Windows can now use this space for other purposes, such as allocating DOS transfer buffers when necessary.

When running in standard mode, configure your expanded memory board to provide as expanded memory only as much of its memory as is needed by your non-Windows applications. For most efficient Windows operations, the remainder of the board's memory should be configured as extended memory.

These last two chapters concentrated on optimizing your system. While Chapter 14 concentrated on performance, this chapter focused on maximizing memory. Naturally, the two are closely intertwined. If you run Windows 3.1 in a network environment, turn to Chapter 16 to learn more about specific optimization considerations for networks.

16

*Strategies for Networks
and Communications*

For those of you in a hurry, this chapter starts out with a section of tips that apply to any network installation of Windows. Following that, you'll learn a number of customization techniques for both installing and using Windows on your network. In particular, I'll pay close attention to the various personalization and optimization options available to you via the many network settings in the SYSTEM.INI file.

You'll also learn some tricks for using Windows in a network environment that will enhance performance. Importantly, you'll learn some of the unique considerations required for printing on a network. The chapter ends with a number of tips, tricks, and techniques for supercharging general communications applications.

◆ TIPS FOR RUNNING WINDOWS ON ANY NETWORK

This section focuses on advice for any network user or administrator who runs Windows on a network. These are general tips only, because the tips that have to do with customization of specific SYSTEM.INI settings are grouped into their own sections later in this chapter.

MAINTAINING NETWORK PERFORMANCE

After successfully surmounting the difficulties of installing Windows on a network, you may bemoan the loss of overall performance. In the typical server

Starting Up Your Network

Things to do:

♦ Start up your network before running Windows.

♦ Log on to the network from the Network section of the Control Panel if your Windows network driver supports this feature.

Things not to do:

♦ Start your network from within Windows.

♦ Log on to your network from a DOS prompt in a Windows virtual machine.

installation of Windows, in which most Windows executable and library files are located on the network server, there is considerable network traffic to support Windows' intensive disk demands. Actually, the majority of these disk requests are read requests because code segments are read-only, as is much of the menu management logic. Here are some techniques for speeding up all of these disk requests.

Increase Workstation RAM

What can you do to reduce the burden placed on your network by Windows? Obviously, you can increase workstation RAM. Just as you've already learned for standalone Windows systems, more RAM means less swapping. The more RAM your workstation can rely on, the less Windows will have to create virtual RAM from disk space and the more efficiently Windows will run on your network.

Increase the Server's Disk Cache

Sure, but that's more easily said than done. OK, how about tuning that expensive high-performance server? How about just allocating a large disk cache (see Chapter 14) for the server? Instead of allotting a 1–2MB cache (which is typically enough to boost a standalone Windows system's performance), allot 10–12MB for a server cache.

◆ DON'T MISUSE SOPHISTICATED NETWORK HARDWARE

Some workstations and network servers contain sophisticated track-buffering disk controllers. If your hardware includes one of these, and your software setup includes disk caching, you are wasting resources by buffering data in both hardware and software. Usually, the software includes a switch to turn off caching for a particular disk.

With such a large disk cache on your network server, the most frequently requested disk information for both Windows itself and key applications is typically found in the cache. This reduces, for all workstations, the time lag involved with waiting for actual server disk reads, since the data will often be found in the cache. Overall network response time will be dramatically enhanced. You will have countered a serious drain on the network caused by Windows' disk-intensive operations.

Perform Only Local Swapping

So what else? Let's say you've put as much RAM on each workstation and bought as large a server cache as your budget allows, and the network is still much slower than before. What else can be done? Remember the discussion of swap files in Chapter 14. Swapping occurs in 386 enhanced mode when Windows creates virtual memory to sustain more running applications. The more efficiently swapping can occur, the more efficiently your network will run.

In Chapter 14, I suggested creating a permanent swap file rather than simply allowing Windows to create temporary swap files. Assuming that you have the hard-disk space, this was a better solution to performance problems.

I also suggested placing a permanent swap file on your system's fastest hard disk. In a network environment, the fastest hard disk may be on the server. Because of the slow speed of the network, however, this is never the best place

Running Windows on Diskless Workstations

If you're determined to run Windows from a workstation that does not contain a hard disk, you can do it but it won't work very well. Without a hard disk, a PC running Windows will run slowly when Windows accesses files. The time spent accessing executable files, initialization files, customization files, not to mention possible swapping and paging, will become unbearable in short order.

Most diskless workstations run Windows in standard mode, thereby avoiding the network traffic caused by virtual memory in 386 enhanced mode.

to put a swap file (permanent or temporary). Any hard disk that is local to a workstation is a better place for a swap file, because Windows will access the information faster from the local drive and network traffic will be reduced.

If you choose not to use a permanent swap file, you can still ensure that Windows will create a temporary one on a local drive. Just use the PagingDrive setting in the [386Enh] section of SYSTEM.INI.

If you have set up your network with diskless workstations, it is probably best to disable paging completely. Do this by setting Paging=No in the [386Enh] section.

Although you can decide for yourself, my opinion is that it is best to disable paging for diskless workstations. In this way, you limit the possible applications on the workstation to whatever local memory can handle. If you must run more programs, you can add more memory or a hard disk. Allowing swapping to occur will allow you to run more applications simultaneously but will hinder your network's performance.

INSTALL THE NETWORK BEFORE WINDOWS

When Setup installs Windows, it determines which type of network you have installed and copies the necessary driver files from the installation disks. It also saves information about the installation drive and the path names of any applications located on network server drives. Furthermore, Setup usually adds the necessary entries for your network in the SYSTEM.INI file.

♦ "NETWORK NOT RUNNING!"

If you see this message, don't panic. Very often, you've just started Windows on your local PC and the network it's connected to is simply not up and running. It's just an informational message.

If this message appears too often for you, you can prevent its display. If the network is running, you can select the Network icon in the Control Panel and directly turn off the message for the future. If the network is not running, make the following entry in the [Windows] section of the WIN.INI file: NetWarn=False.

As you can tell, much of the Setup installation sequence is dependent on your specific network and applications. Consequently, you should avoid changing network vendors or application file locations if possible. If you do make changes, be sure to run Setup again; otherwise, Windows will not work correctly. At the very least, Program Manager icons that were set up for your applications will not be able to launch the applications.

USE CURRENT DRIVER AND SHELL VERSIONS

On my machine, I had to update every single hardware driver for Windows 3.1. Network drivers are responsible for much of the nitty-gritty hardware details. Be aware that you may need to acquire the latest versions of your network drivers before installing Windows 3.1. Call your network vendor and ask if you need to update any files.

You may or may not need updates, but if you do, the combination of Windows and your network will not run correctly until you obtain them. You can also read the NETWORKS.WRI file (use Windows Write), located in your WINDOWS directory. It contains detailed suggestions and instructions for updating both Windows and the most popular network operating systems, such as

- ◆ 3Com Networks
- ◆ Artisoft LANtastic
- ◆ Banyan VINES
- ◆ DEC Pathworks
- ◆ IBM OS/2 LAN Server
- ◆ IBM PC LAN Program
- ◆ Invisible Software - NET/30
- ◆ Microsoft LAN Manager Networks
- ◆ Microsoft Network
- ◆ Novell NetWare
- ◆ TCS 10Net
- ◆ Ungermann-Bass Net/One

Windows 3.1 includes a number of required updates to certain driver and network shell components for these networks. For example, your Novell NetWare shell may currently be NET3.COM, NET4.COM, or even NET5.COM. You will need to replace it with the NETX.COM file on your Windows 3.1 installation disks.

You should also inquire about the latest versions of the network drivers that run outside of conventional memory: in expanded memory, extended memory, or the upper reserved memory blocks. Remember from Chapter 15 that loading drivers, files, programs, and other operating-system components in these areas can increase dramatically the conventional memory available to DOS applications on your system.

In a similar way, some network shells can load themselves into additional areas of UMBs, extended memory, or expanded memory. This placement of the network components can make all the difference in being able to run DOS applications (which may need conventional memory) under Windows.

In each case, though, you'll need to run the proper version of the network shell for where you intend to load it. For example, Novell NetWare offers separate versions of its shell program (i.e., NET5.COM) for loading into extended memory (i.e., XMSNET5.COM) and expanded memory (i.e., EMXNET5.COM). Be sure to obtain and load high the appropriate shell programs.

BEWARE OF CONFLICTS

Conflicts can take many forms. Some conflicts produce controlled crashes of a particular application (allowing you to do a local reboot). Other conflicts take down your entire Windows system. Sometimes, this will force you to reboot your workstation, and other times, you may have to restart your entire network. This depends on what crashed and on whether Windows is running completely standalone on a workstation or in shared fashion from a network server.

Conflicts with Memory Mapping

Remember that many network adapter cards contain memory that is mapped into UMB addresses. Certain adapters, like those for hard disks and scanners, require that you prevent Windows from accessing their memory. (The IBM Token Ring adapter is an example of such an adapter.)

You can use the EMMExclude line in the SYSTEM.INI file to exclude a range of addresses from Windows' consideration. Each network adapter manufacturer should include in its documentation any areas that should be excluded with EMMExclude. If you do need to use EMMExclude and you neglect to include it in SYSTEM.INI, you will have frustrating, intermittent system crashes.

Conflicts with Interrupts

On a PC, devices are not supposed to use the same interrupt lines. Although on some machines, it is possible to share IRQs (interrupt requests) between communications programs, it is safest to avoid such situations unless you know that they can be done. In general, your network card's port address should be different from all other peripheral devices.

To avoid interrupt conflicts, sit down with all the documentation for each of your peripheral devices and adapter cards. Take a piece of paper and create

Networks and Non-Windows Applications

Since Windows addresses extended memory directly, a network driver and shell loaded into conventional memory before starting Windows will not have a negative impact on Windows applications. However, non-Windows applications do use conventional memory. So loading network software in conventional memory will usually make it more difficult to run a non-Windows application under Windows successfully.

Three techniques are available for minimizing this problem on your system. Select the one that is most feasible for your combination of network and operating-system software:

◆ Load your network's driver in upper reserved blocks with a memory manager (like EMM386.EXE).

◆ Direct your network's shell to use extended memory if it can.

◆ Direct your network's shell to use expanded memory if it can.

four columns:

DEVICE/CARD   **IRQ**   **DMA**   **PORT**

In the DEVICE/CARD column, write the name of each device or adapter card on your system. In the other three columns, write down the interrupt line used, the Direct Memory Access channel used, and the port address used.

You may not be able to obtain entries for each device because not all devices require all of these. However, if you fill out these entries and discover that there is duplication, sharing, or overlap, you know that you have the makings of a conflict. If so, refer to each adapter's documentation for suggestions about solutions. Many devices can be switched (through hardware or software adjustments) from one IRQ to another, from one port to another, or from one DMA channel to another.

Be particularly alert to possible problems if the port is 300h, which is used by many boards. Also, be aware that IRQ 2 is more difficult to handle, because it is essentially the entry point to a second level of interrupt lines on an

AT-level machine. Not all software can manage the complexity of this IRQ, so avoid using it if you can use other IRQ lines.

Conflicts with Printing

Printing sometimes reveals problems on networks that use parallel printer ports for LAN connections. Windows typically prints by writing directly to a port, rather than passing the output requests to DOS for processing. This can be problematic if the LAN interface is trying to interpret the instructions that appear at the port.

To avoid this problem, send printed output to a LPTx.DOS printer port instead. This forces Windows to use a standard BIOS technique for printing rather than using direct port addressing.

◆ THE PRINT MANAGER AND NETWORKS

> If you have a local printer that you want to make available to other network users, be sure to define the printer in the Print Manager as a network printer rather than a local printer.

Conflicts with File Access

Networks usually include support services that prevent multiple applications from accessing and possibly corrupting the contents of a file. Windows is a special case. Although it is seen by a network as a single application, it is in fact a multitasking operating environment in its own right.

The network may be able to prevent one Windows session from accessing a file that has been opened from another workstation. Remember, however, that you can run more than one DOS program in virtual machines under Windows. Your network will not police simultaneous access of the same file from different DOS sessions under Windows.

The network won't assume complete responsibility for simultaneous access. Windows won't either. So it's simply up to you to remember if and when you might be accessing the same file from more than one DOS session.

Port Address, Memory, and Interrupt Conflicts

Memory conflicts usually occur in the adapter segment. Use the EMMExclude line in the [386Enh] section of your SYSTEM.INI file to minimize this problem. Consult your network's documentation to determine the memory ranges to exclude.

Memory conflicts can also occur during the processing of some parallel printer output. If output to LPTx produces a LAN adapter conflict, change the printer port to LPTx.DOS instead. Use the Printers icon from the Control Panel.

If your network has problems when you move your mouse or when serial communications are occurring, there is probably a conflict in the handling of interrupts. This could be due to multiple devices being assigned the same interrupt, or your network card's port address may be the same as some other peripheral. Although there are some techniques for handling COM port exceptions, both IRQs and port addresses must be unique.

◆ INSTALLING WINDOWS ON A NETWORK

You can install Windows on a LAN workstation in three ways:

◆ You can have all Windows files on the workstation hard disk and no Windows files on the network server.

◆ You can have workstation-specific Windows files on the local hard disk and shared Windows files on the server.

◆ You can have no Windows files on the hard disk (or a diskless workstation) and shared Windows files with private directories for each workstation on the server.

You should realize, though, that the second and third cases use Windows files that must first be loaded on the network server. To prepare for individualized workstation installation of Windows, you must first use the /A switch with the Setup program. By itself, this does not create a usable version of Windows. All the Windows files that will be shared by workstation Windows users will be copied to the network drive, then renamed, expanded, and marked as read-only.

◆ SHARING VIOLATIONS ON NETWORKS

Sharing violations can appear on some networks when users run the same application from different nodes. Be sure to mark the application's .EXE file as read-only.

Some networks are incompatible with the DOS SHARE program. This can also be a cause of some sharing violations, so you may not be able to load the program on network workstations. Your network documentation will probably alert you to this.

To install Windows in this configuration, you should place Windows 3.1 disk 1 in your floppy drive and change to that drive. Then, just type

SETUP /A

and follow the instructions for entering the desired network drive and directory.

During installation, a Microsoft Write file (named SYSADMIN.WRI) is copied to the specified server directory. If you are the network administrator, print out this file, because it contains useful information about setting up and managing Windows in your network environment.

Windows 3.1 requires 16MB on your network server disk for the shared network directory. Each private Windows network directory requires 300K.

LOAD THE WORKSTATION, NOT THE NETWORK

The three ways shown in Figure 16.1 for installing a network present significant alternatives in performance, configuration, and ease of setup. Case A uses the greatest amount of workstation hard-disk space, because it places a

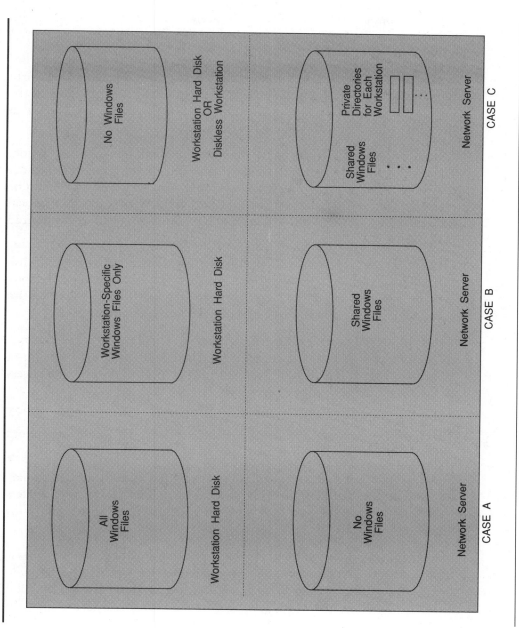

FIGURE 16.1: Three alternatives for installing Windows on a local area network

complete copy of Windows on the workstation. Because all files are local, this configuration offers the best performance.

In addition, if your network ever crashes, shuts down, or becomes disconnected from your local workstation, your version of Windows can continue to run uninterrupted. (Of course, you would be unable to access anything on the network server.) To set up your network like case A, simply type SETUP at the command prompt and follow the instructions.

Case B is the most balanced, and the most common, network installation. Shared files, such as executables and dynamic link libraries, are stored on the network server and used by each workstation as necessary. These files must be marked read-only on the server to avoid corruption. Each workstation's local hard disk only stores files that are unique to each user, such as customized .INI files.

Case B has the advantage of reducing the drain on workstation hard-disk space. This can amount to saving many megabytes *on each workstation*. However, because network traffic increases when Windows files on the server are accessed, it has the disadvantage of reduced overall performance.

To set up your network like case B, use the SETUP /N option. First, change to the server directory that contains the shared administrative version of Windows. Then, type SETUP /N to set up your local workstation for access to the shared network copy of Windows.

Case C places all the burden for running Windows on the network server. This has the advantage of requiring no hard disk on the local workstation. However, the increase in network traffic will be considerable.

You should not consider setting up your network like case C, although it may be necessary on workstations without local hard disks. If you have diskless workstations, you have no choice but to set up case C, if you wish to run Windows on them at all.

If you have a workstation that has a hard disk that simply does not have sufficient space to support even case B, you should at least create your swap file (see Chapter 14) on the local hard disk. Because swapping is a fundamental aspect of Windows operations, you should at the very least keep swapping localized to enhance performance.

Managing Directory Access on a Network

To install Windows, you must create certain directories. If the installation is on a network drive, the network usually restricts write access. If the network supervisor installs Windows, there is no problem because the supervisor normally has full privileges.

If someone other than the network supervisor installs Windows on a network drive, there are two options:

♦ Give the installer write and create privileges on the network drive.

♦ Have the network supervisor create the necessary directories (WINDOWS and WINDOWS\SYSTEM) on the network drive before the Setup installation is done.

Be aware that the installation of many applications, such as Adobe Type Manager, requires write access to the WINDOWS directory or the WINDOWS\SYSTEM directory or both.

Case C also uses the SETUP /N option for installation. Again, change to the directory that contains the shared copy of Windows before running SETUP /N. In both cases B and C, Setup will ask you to enter the path name of the directory that should contain the private Windows files (e.g., your .INI files). Typically, you specify your local hard disk (e.g., C:\WINDOWS). If your workstation is diskless, you specify a directory on the network server (e.g., Q:\ROBBINS).

There is one misconception that I'd like to clear up right now. Some people believe that if they install Windows on a high-performance server, such as a 33-Mhz 486 PC, it will result in improved performance for a group of connected, slower PCs. This is false for Windows.

In other environments, running an application with heavy resource demands (like a database manager) on a high-performance server can result in significant performance benefits. But Windows is different. The server is largely treated as a shared site for the bulk of the Windows files. Windows itself runs its primary code from each workstation's RAM. In the first case, the power of

SUPERCHARGING WINDOWS

the server gets the application's job done faster. In the second case, the power of the server is not really tapped because Windows simply transfers the necessary shared files to the workstation and then does the necessary work on the workstation's processor.

◆ FILE SERVERS AND LOCAL PCS

Do not store key Windows files on a fast file server. Although the machine itself may be much faster than your local PC, the network overhead will more than offset any gains of the faster server. Windows on each workstation executes its own code from each PC's local RAM, so it will constantly be generating network transmissions for access to its necessary files.

Regardless of the speed of your workstation, install Windows on a local hard disk. Although this consumes the largest amount of disk space, it offers the best performance for Windows in a network environment.

This means that there is ongoing and significant network traffic to support Windows, and individual workstations still run Windows locally. Not only is there no speed gain but there is an overall reduction in performance because of the overhead simply to get the necessary Windows files to the workstation before they can run.

INSTALLING WINDOWS ON MANY IDENTICAL WORKSTATIONS

The /H switch for the SETUP command provides an option for automated setup of Windows. It can be used for a single installation of Windows, or it can be used to simplify installation on multiple workstations in a network.

◆ MANAGING ICONS ON A NETWORK

Because there are so many commercial and shareware icon programs, there are thousands of icons available. Even though a single

Maintaining Windows on a Network

Although performance may suffer to some extent, if you are a network administrator, your job will be considerably easier if a single copy of each major application is maintained on a network drive. It is much easier to update software if there is only one copy of each application to update. It also may be well worth your while to create a master program group on a network drive for these shared applications. You can click on each icon in this shared group to run the application.

The trick here is to make the shared group (.GRP) read-only. This protects the integrity of the shared group from accidental updates or changes when Windows users on local workstations exit from Windows, or attempt to copy or move icons into or out of this group.

In addition, you must properly adjust the appropriate [Groups] entry in the PROGMAN.INI file for each user to point to the location of this shared group. This is considerably easier, since it is a onetime effort, than adjusting each workstation's .GRP file each time a new application is made available to network users.

icon file consumes less than 1K, thousands of them can easily consume several megabytes of disk space. As a guideline for managing disk-space usage, copy all available icons to your network file server. Then, direct each local workstation user to download just the handful of icons that he or she will use.

You can create an ASCII text file, not unlike the WIN.INI and SYSTEM.INI files, that contains settings to control the various setup options. I'll explain the structure of this file in a moment. You can create a series of such automated setup files, one for each system configuration.

Suppose that your network consists of 20 identical workstations. You can create a single settings file that contains each workstation's configuration, then follow the /N shared Windows installation sequence. In each case, you would use the /H option along with /N. For example, if your settings file is named WORKSTAT.AIF, you enter

SETUP /H:WORKSTAT.AIF /N

This assumes that both the SETUP.EXE and the WORKSTAT.AIF files are located in the same directory, or in the PATH. This will use the prepared responses and options from WORKSTAT.AIF to install a preconfigured version of Windows, using files previously loaded on the server.

Table 16.1 summarizes the purpose of each section in the setup file. You can refer to the SETUP.AIF file in your SYSTEM directory, which Windows provides as a template for creating your own customized .AIF settings file.

Figure 16.2 shows a sample .AIF file from my system. I'll briefly explain each of the possible settings.

Some sections in your automated installation file are simple and contain only one entry. The first section, [sysinfo], contains only the showsysinfo entry. In general, you should set this option to *yes*. In this way, Setup will display current system-configuration values. You can then review them and quickly determine if anything needs to be changed before continuing with the setup. However, if you know that the configuration is the same for many workstations, you can probably minimize screen clutter by setting this value to *no*.

TABLE 16.1: Automated Settings File Sections

Section Name	Purpose
[configuration]	Specifies devices on the workstation
[dontinstall]	Specifies optional Windows components to avoid installing
[endinstall]	Controls processing at end of workstation installation
[options]	Controls setup of applications and running of Tutorial
[printers]	Defines which printers are to be set up on the workstation
[sysinfo]	Displays system configuration screen
[userinfo]	Specifies user and company name
[windir]	Locates the WINDOWS directory

The [windir] section also contains only one entry. It specifies the location for the WINDOWS files. If you neglect to include this entry, Setup will display a dialog box requesting that you specify the installation directory.

The seven settings in the [configuration] section define the primary devices in the Windows workstation. Table 16.2 indicates the sections in SETUP.INF (see Chapter 2) that contain these particular variables. If any of these entries are not included, Setup uses the default device or the device actually detected.

The [userinfo] section contains two entries. The first entry, the workstation's user name, is required. The second entry, the company name, is optional; it is

```
[sysinfo]
showsysinfo=yes

[configuration]
machine = ibm_compatible
display = vga
mouse = ps2mouse
network = lanman
keyboard = t4s0enha
language = usa
kblayout = nodll

[windir]
c:\windows

[userinfo]
"Judd Robbins" ; User Name
"Computer Options" ; Company Name

[dontinstall]
accessories
readmes
games
screensavers
bitmaps

[options]
setupapps
autosetupapps
readonline
tutorial

[printers]
"HP LaserJet III",LPT1:

[endinstall]
configfiles = save
endopt      = restart
```

FIGURE 16.2: A sample network settings file

TABLE 16.2:   Sections in SETUP.INF for [configuration] Entries

Setting Name in .AIF File	Section Name in SETUP.INF
display	[display]
kblayout	[keyboard.tables]
keyboard	[keyboard.types]
language	[language]
machine	[machine]
mouse	[pointing.device]
network	[network]

usually the same on a group of workstations being installed at different sites in the same company.

In Chapter 14, you learned that there are five major optional components of a Windows installation. At any time, you can install or remove any of these components. To do so, you just double-click on the Windows Setup icon in the Program Manager, pull down the Options menu, and choose Add/Remove Windows Components.

When you set up separate workstations, you can also control whether or not these optional components are installed. Just include the names of the components in the [dontinstall] section of your .AIF file. If you do not include any names, the optional component will be included by default.

In my file, shown in Figure 16.2, I've specified all five possible names. Therefore, none of the five groups of files will be installed in my automated workstation setup. This will save roughly 2MB of disk space on each workstation's hard disk.

The [options] section controls the application icon setup for the Program Manager and execution of a Windows tutorial when setup concludes. There are four possible entries in this section:

◆ If you include *setupapps*, Setup will display all existing hard-disk applications and allow you to specify interactively which ones you want to install.

♦ If you include *autosetupapps*, Setup will automatically set up all applications that are on your hard disk. The automated choice takes precedence if you include both option lines.

♦ If you include *readonline*, Setup will automatically enable you to view online text documents during setup.

♦ If you include *tutorial*, Setup will run a special Windows tutorial when all other Setup processing is complete.

If you don't want any of these options during your workstation setup, just leave this section out completely.

The [printers] section can contain one or more entries, each one representing a printer that can be used by the installed workstation. Each line consists of a printer description followed by a port name. The printer description must match one of the valid ones found in the [io.device] section of CONTROL.INF, and the port name must match one found in the [ports] section of WIN.INI. Because most printer descriptions contain blank spaces, quotation marks are generally required.

Finally, the [endinstall] section determines several optional final steps. If you set configfiles to *save*, Setup will write any proposed modifications to CONFIG.SYS and AUTOEXEC.BAT to files named CONFIG.WIN and AUTOEXEC.WIN. You'll have to view these files and decide whether or not to make the proposed changes yourself.

Once you've figured out the entries for this automated workstation installation, you should probably just set configfiles to *modify*. This will directly update the workstation's CONFIG.SYS and AUTOEXEC.BAT files. If you do not include any configfiles entry line, the result will be the same as if you had specified *modify*.

Even though this selection will modify your CONFIG.SYS and AUTOEXEC.BAT files, Setup will save the original versions of these files in backup files named CONFIG.OLD and AUTOEXEC.OLD. If you are setting up Windows on a diskless workstation, the modify option is invalid because unique workstation versions of these DOS start-up files cannot exist.

For workstation installations, the endopt option can be either exit or restart. A third option, reboot, is only available for standalone Windows installations.

exit   Exits to DOS after setup is complete

restart   Restarts Windows after setup is complete

reboot   Reboots the computer after setup is complete

If you do not set one of these values, Setup will pause at the end of its processing and display a dialog box requesting that you select one of the possibilities.

◆ ENHANCING NETWORK PERFORMANCE

In Chapter 12, you learned how the many settings in the SYSTEM.INI file can dramatically influence your Windows environment. In particular, a number of the settings directly influence how Windows runs in a network environment. They are summarized in Table 16.3.

Some of these settings control personalization of your Windows version, such as the Network.drv setting in the [Boot] section. Most of the settings, however, have a direct performance impact on Windows. Some settings will be required on your network just to ensure that it works properly; other settings ensure that it performs optimally.

MEMORY CONSIDERATIONS FOR SYSTEM.INI SETTINGS

Standalone Windows systems depend greatly on available memory to perform efficiently and to control how many simultaneous DOS applications can be started. In a network environment, the amount of available memory can influence how many users can access a shared network copy of Windows.

Accessing Open Files Rapidly

As you've already learned earlier in this book, some memory considerations directly affect performance. Windows uses memory to store file handles for

TABLE 16.3: Network Settings in SYSTEM.INI

Name	Section	Purpose
AllVMsExclusive	[386Enh]	If True, forces exclusive full-screen mode on DOS applications
CachedFileHandles	[Boot]	Limits the number of open .EXE and .DLL files
EMMExclude	[386Enh]	Restricts Windows from searching a memory range for unused addresses (16K at a time)
FileSysChange	[386Enh]	Enables File Manager to receive messages indicating creation, renaming, or deletion of disk files
InDOSPolling	[386Enh]	Supports critical section exclusivity for memory-resident software
INT28Critical	[386Enh]	If True, enables a critical section for handling memory-resident software's INT28h interrupts
Int28Filter	[Standard]	Controls percentage of INT28h pass-through to memory-resident software loaded before Windows
NetAsynchFallback	[386Enh]	Specifies how to react to a failing NetBIOS request
NetAsynchTimeout	[386Enh]	Sets timeout period for enabled NetAsynchFallback critical sections
NetDMASize	[386Enh]	Sets DMA buffer size for network use
NetHeapSize	[386Enh] and [Standard]	Sets data-transfer buffer size

TABLE 16.3: Network Settings in SYSTEM.INI (continued)

Name	Section	Purpose
Network	[386Enh]	Defines the network in use
Network.drv	[Boot]	Specifies file name of network driver
PSPIncrement	[386Enh]	Determines additional memory to reserve when UniqueDOSPSP is on
ReflectDosInt2A	[386Enh]	Passes through (if True) or processes (if False) all INT2A interrupts
ReservedHighArea	[386Enh]	Eliminates a range of memory from Windows' scan for unused address space
TimerCriticalSection	[386Enh]	Sets up critical sections around timer interrupt code
TokenRingSearch	[386Enh]	Enables or disables recognition of token-ring network adapter card
UniqueDOSPSP	[386Enh]	Enables or disables starting of each application at unique addresses

the most recently used .EXE and .DLL files. In the [Boot] section, the number of these cached file handles is set with this option:

CachedFileHandles=x

The default value is 12, which means that Windows retains 12 open handles. The larger the value of x, the fewer users can run a shared copy of Windows on a single server. This is actually caused by networks that have limits on the number of files that can be open on a server at one time. If you discover that some users are having difficulty running Windows in a busy environment, decrease this number. The minimum value is 2.

Transferring Network Data Successfully

In both the [Standard] and [386Enh] sections, you can specify a value in kilobytes for NetHeapSize, which controls the size of the buffer that Windows uses for its network data transfers.

The default value is 8K when you are running Windows in standard mode and 12K when you are running Windows in 386 enhanced mode. This memory represents the space needed by Windows to store data that will be transmitted over the network. Windows rounds up your entry to the nearest 4K.

You should set this number to the size of the largest data block required for network transfer. However, don't set this value any larger than it has to be. As this buffer size increases, remember that less memory remains available for Windows to dole out to running applications.

Generally, you will notice an incorrect NetHeapSize setting when an application seems to fail when transferring large amounts of data over the network. If you don't know the required value, you'll have to adjust it 4K at a time, save SYSTEM.INI, and restart Windows.

Reserving Memory to Avoid Adapter Conflicts in UMBs

Remember that some network adapters conflict with Windows' use of upper memory blocks. The EMMExclude line can prevent Windows from using a particular portion of UMBs. The valid values for this option are from A000 to EFFF. If you specify hexadecimal values that fall between 16K boundaries, the starting address will be rounded down and the ending address will be rounded up.

However, if you know that your network adapter card requires a smaller range than 16K, you can use the ReservedHighArea option to define a smaller range to avoid. For example:

ReservedHighArea=C000–C300

Unique Load Addresses for Virtual Machines

Some networks identify different network processes by their memory load address. Two SYSTEM.INI settings directly bear on this issue for non-Windows applications.

The UniqueDOSPSP setting takes a Boolean value. If it is True, Windows reserves a certain amount of memory below the application each time a virtual machine is created in which to run the application.

The amount of memory reserved is defined by the PSPIncrement setting; it can have a value from 2 to 64. Its value tells Windows, in 16-byte increments, how much extra memory to reserve below the application. Essentially, if UniqueDOSPSP is True, this ensures that new applications (in different virtual machines) start at unique memory addresses. Although this consumes more overall system memory, it makes for easier network identification. Check with your network vendor or documentation to determine whether you should change UniqueDOSPSP from its default value, False.

MULTITASKING CONSIDERATIONS FOR SYSTEM.INI SETTINGS

The remaining SYSTEM.INI settings directly affect performance. You can greatly influence the performance of your Windows system and your network by controlling the values of these settings.

Passing Interrupts through to TSRs

Some applications that you load on your system before starting Windows rely on receiving interrupt 28 (INT28). This interrupt is generated when the system is idle. Under DOS, these applications would receive every INT28. Under Windows, however, passing every INT28 through to these applications would be an unacceptable burden on Windows performance.

In standard mode only, the Int28Filter setting controls how many INT28s are passed to software that loads before Windows is started. In the [Standard] section, include

Int28Filter=*n*

where *n* represents the frequency of INT28s that are passed through; every *n*th interrupt is passed. The more often an INT28 is passed through, the more Windows performance is burdened. Consequently, the lower the value of *n*, the more frequently INT28s are generated and the harsher the performance penalty.

Individual users can increase Windows performance by increasing the value of *n*. The default value is 10. You can eliminate interrupts completely by setting Int28Filter to 0. However, any reduction in the frequency of INT28s may conflict with the ability of your network TSR shell to execute properly.

But there is another downside. Communications applications on your network may suffer if you set Int28Filter too low. In this case, the frequency of INT28s increases, the system overhead increases, and the interrupt servicing may be unable to proceed successfully.

Ensuring That Non-Windows Applications Receive More CPU Time

The ALLVMsExclusive setting can be set to True or False. In 386 enhanced mode, setting this option to True is an easy way to ensure that all DOS applications run in full-screen mode. It ensures that non-Windows applications automatically receive more CPU cycles in which to execute. In theory, this should ensure that they receive the maximum possible number of CPU cycles.

However, the flip side for network users is that setting the ALLVMsExclusive option to True will slow down a typical Windows session on a network. Giving more CPU cycles to non-Windows applications reduces the number of cycles left to dole out to Windows applications. Consequently, the default value is False to balance out the typical load on the network.

The FileSysChange setting is another Boolean setting. When it is set to True, Windows sends DDE messages to the File Manager when non-Windows applications create, delete, or rename files. Although this will maintain the accuracy of File Manager windows, it also accounts for one more burden on system performance.

Unless it becomes essential to maintain completely accurate File Manager windows, disable this setting by changing it to False. Overall system overhead will decrease, and overall system performance will increase. In particular, performance of non-Windows applications will improve because the drain of alerting Windows to file system changes will be gone.

◆ HOW NON-WINDOWS SETTINGS ARE RELATED

Note how FileSysChange and ALLVMsExclusive relate to each other. You can set ALLVMsExclusive to True to run non-Windows applications in exclusive, full-screen mode. But you should also set FileSysChange to True to disable automatic file manipulation messages as well. Otherwise, the non-Windows applications will not truly be running exclusively and will not be receiving the largest possible amount of CPU time.

Dealing with Memory-Resident TSRs

Some TSRs include special code that depends on timer interrupts. To ensure that Windows will not switch away from a TSR, you can specify a fixed period of time:

TimerCriticalSection=*nnnnn*

where *nnnnn* is the desired number of milliseconds for the code section that depends on the timer interrupt. By not switching away from the DOS application during this length of time, only one DOS application (i.e., one virtual machine in 386 enhanced mode) at a time will process the timer interrupts.

Although this ensures that an older DOS application is more likely to execute correctly, system performance will suffer. At times, it may even appear that the system has completely stopped. Normal multitasking is totally inhibited while this artificially created system resource freeze occurs.

On the other hand, some network TSRs cannot work successfully unless this setting is correct. Because the default value is 0, you should check your network documentation to determine what setting may be required. If your network (or any other DOS application) fails, call the vendor and ask if TimerCriticalSection should be set to some particular value.

Special Asynchronous Windows Support

From time to time, applications make asynchronous network BIOS data requests. Windows provides a special global network buffer to handle the data for such requests. However, if there is insufficient space in the buffer for an application's NetBIOS request, Windows will normally return a code signaling a request failure.

You can help such requests to succeed more frequently by changing the setting for NetAsynchFallback to True (the default is False). Windows will attempt to satisfy the NetBIOS request by creating a local memory buffer.

However, in doing this, Windows will also prevent all virtual machines from continuing until the NetBIOS data has been received and processed. This helps one application to proceed successfully but can impede the progress and multitasking of all other non-Windows applications.

Related to this setting is the NetAsynchTimeout setting. This option specifies, in seconds to one decimal place, how long the timeout period should be for attempting to satisfy the NetBIOS request. The default is 5.0 seconds and is only meaningful when you've also set NetAsynchFallback to True. In essence, this value represents the length of a timer critical section that Windows will occasionally enter. Windows will do this to satisfy an asynchronous NetBIOS request out of local memory, which would otherwise have failed because of insufficient global buffer space.

◆ PRINTING ON A NETWORK

This section addresses the most common areas of interest concerning network printing. Chapter 13 discusses some general issues, such as print queues.

CONNECTING TO A NETWORK PRINTER

To print anything at all on a network printer, you must first establish a connection to the printer. You may have already done that before starting Windows. In that case, Windows will recognize the connection and you can print directly to the printer. If that connection has not been made, however, or if you want to modify the connection, you can use the Printers icon in the Control Panel.

If you are connected to a network, a Network button will be available in the Printer dialog box. Select this button and the printers-network connections will appear. If there is any existing connection, you will see it in the Connections field. You can change this connection, create a brand new one, or add another one. To do any of these, you must properly fill in the Port, Path, and optionally, the Password fields. If you simply want to abandon an existing connection, choose the Disconnect button.

Click on the down arrow in the Port field and choose the port that your network printer is connected to. Typically, this will be LPT1, LPT2, or LPT3. This is the output port through which your local PC will send printed output to the network.

The Path field enables you to enter a valid DOS path to your network printer, which generally consists of the server name followed by the print queue identifier. The format for this entry will change according to your network, for example,

\\SERV1\LASRJET2

If your network requires you to enter a password to gain access to the printer, you must enter it in the Password field. When all necessary fields are complete, choose the Connect button to complete the entry. This establishes the connection from your local PC's output port to the network-queuing mechanism for subsequent print requests.

PRINTING FROM A WINDOWS APPLICATION TO A NETWORK PRINTER

Printing to a network printer is no different from printing to any other printer, once you've correctly established the connection from your local PC to the printer. A Windows application still uses the File Print command to send output to a printer. The particular printer that is used is usually the default printer, as specified via the Printers icon in the Control Panel. However, as you learned in Chapter 13, the printer could also be selected from the Windows application's Printer Setup option, also on the File menu.

Presumably, this print request is going to a port that matches one that is connected to a network printer. If the connections are all made properly, the printed output flows from the Windows application, out the port, and into the queue of the network printer. You can then use the Print Manager to monitor the status of your print request.

ACCESSING THE NETWORK PRINT QUEUE

Each printer that is connected to a network controls the flow of print requests by using queuing techniques. Just as the Print Manager provides a form of queuing, or spooling, on your local PC, print managers on networks provide similar facilities.

You can view the current status of your network print requests from the Print Manager. Unlike local print requests, however, you cannot modify entries in a network queue from the Print Manager. To manage individual entries in a network queue, you will have to find out the necessary commands on your particular network.

However, you can update the status of the Print Manager's queue displays: Just select Update Net Queues from the View menu of the Print Manager. Although Windows intermittently updates the Print Manager's display via DDE messages from the network, choosing this option requests an immediate update of the Print Manager window.

◆ IMPROVING WINDOWS COMMUNICATIONS FACILITIES

Networking is really a very specialized type of communications. Not all Windows users run on networks, but many use modems and faxes and communicate regularly with bulletin boards or information services like CompuServe. This section addresses some of the special techniques for getting the most out of your Windows system when using communications facilities.

USING A MODEM UNDER WINDOWS

You may have suffered trying to get your modem connected and working on a serial port. Most modems still seem to leave the factory configured for COM2 and a specific IRQ address. Here's some advice about the most likely things you need to check or change if your modem doesn't begin working immediately.

The first thing you should do is to leave Windows and try the modem under DOS. If it works under DOS, go back to Windows and check the settings from the Ports icon in the Control Panel.

If the modem doesn't even work under DOS, check the modem's documentation for the proper IRQ address to use. Remember that this IRQ address specifies the location of the code that will handle interrupts from the software port (COM1 to COM4).

CONNECTING TO BULLETIN BOARDS AND INFORMATION SERVICES

Do you often try to log on to a busy BBS (bulletin board system)? Don't waste time hanging out in your COMM program window, calling your favorite BBS over and over again. Just set up an auto-dialer in your COMM program. Use either a script sequence or a simple switch setting in your configuration to dial your BBS repeatedly until a connection is made.

◆ LOG OFF BEFORE HANGING UP

When you are connected to a BBS or a remote information service (like CompuServe), be sure to transmit an Exit or Log Off command before hanging up the phone. Otherwise, you may continue to incur connection charges until the remote system determines that you have disconnected your computer.

After initiating the auto-dial sequence, iconize the application and go on with other work. When a connection is finally made, most COMM programs issue some form of audible signal. You can then switch back to your communications program.

AVOIDING INTERFERENCE FROM "CALL WAITING"

Does your phone have "Call Waiting"? While you are online to some BBS, has your modem software ever disconnected you when you received a call? It may be possible to prevent the interruption. Check with your local phone company to see if the following solution will work in your area.

A common dialing sequence is *70, which disables Call Waiting for a single call. In this case, the single call is the one you are about to make to Compu-Serve or your favorite computerized BBS. You can first pick up your telephone receiver and press *70 (if you have touch-tone dialing), then initiate your modem transmission. Alternatively, you can include *70 in an automated dialing sequence that your modem software transmits. For example, a sample sequence on a Hayes-compatible modem looks like

ATDT*70, 736-8343

This sends out a touch-tone *70, pauses (represented by the comma), and dials 736-8343. There may be alternative sequences in your phone area, and there may even be sequences to use if you have only rotary dialing.

LOSING CHARACTERS DURING COMMUNICATIONS

If your communications program runs in 386 enhanced mode and loses data at high baud rates, include the following line in the [386Enh] section of your SYSTEM.INI file:

COM*x*Protocol=XOFF

where *x* is the number (1 to 4) of the COM port you are using.

Be careful not to use this setting if your application is performing binary data transfers. This protocol for stopping and resuming transmission works only for text transmission. In a binary data transmission (e.g., .EXE and .COM files), the XOFF and XON characters used for stopping and restarting the transmission can themselves appear in the data. This results in characters being treated as control characters rather than as part of the data itself, causing errors in the transmission.

Remember that data can be lost if the DOS application cannot keep up with the maximum transmission rate at the port. XON/XOFF is a form of flow control. If your DOS communications program supports this protocol (most programs do), it can issue an XOFF character when its own internal buffer fills up. Windows will then wait for the application to catch up before transmitting any more characters. The application will issue a special XON character to signal when it is ready to receive data again.

USE YOUR COMMUNICATIONS PORTS IN ORDER

Many modems come configured as COM2. Many people use a bus mouse. If your system has no other serial devices, the easiest connection is simply to hook up your modem to the COM2 port, leaving COM1 unused. Don't do it.

Windows does not like to deal with a serial device on COM2 if there is no device connected to COM1. For best results (or any results in most cases), reconfigure your modem and your communications software to use COM1, leaving COM2 unused for now. In fact, Windows works better if you always use all serial ports in order.

DETECTING IDLE TIME MAY BE A MISTAKE

You may need to turn off the Detect Idle Time setting in the Advanced options portion of a non-Windows applications's PIF. Do this if your system slows down noticeably when running a non-Windows communications application, or worse still, if the application freezes or crashes.

In general, detecting idle time is an option that is set by default. With this feature, Windows notices when a DOS application is not doing anything with its available time. At these times, Windows reallocates the time to other applications. When the option is turned on, multiple applications can actually run faster and more smoothly.

If your communications program doesn't use the keyboard often, however, Windows may mistakenly assume that it is doing nothing when, in fact, it is processing COM port data. To protect against this mistake, you must uncheck the PIF's Detect Idle Time option.

Turning off Detect Idle time may also provide a cure for programs that seem to process keystrokes extremely slowly. They may be doing this because Windows has erroneously assumed that the programs were inactive and has given away the remainder of their time slice. Turning off idle-time detection means that the application remains active for its entire time slice. It can then respond more quickly to your keystrokes, albeit at the expense of overall Windows performance.

This chapter completes the discussion of how to fine-tune performance and resource usage in your Windows system. If Windows is working correctly, and you've followed the advice in the last three chapters, Windows is probably working at maximum efficiency. However, if you are having any sort of problems with your system, turn to Part V now to learn how to troubleshoot the difficulties.

Troubleshooting Windows

Part V shows you to deal with Windows problems of all kinds. In Chapter 17, you'll find answers to some of the most commonly asked questions about ways to improve Windows' performance. In Chapter 18, you'll learn how to deal with Unrecoverable Application Errors. In Chapter 19, you'll find explanations of many different types of Windows error messages.

In addition to the information in these chapters, you can turn to the following sources:

Telephone Support

Microsoft Technical Support: (206) 454-2030
Microsoft Windows Support: (206) 637-7098
Microsoft Prerecorded Windows Support: (206) 635-7245
Microsoft Customer Service: (800) 426-9400
Microsoft OnLine and OnLine Plus: (800) 443-4672
Microsoft Product Support for the Hearing Impaired: (206) 635-4948 with a TDD

Information Services

CompuServe: (800) 848-8199 (voice)
  GO MSWIN: End-user Windows issues
  GO MSAPP: Microsoft applications
  GO WINAPA: Third-party Windows applications
  GO WINAPB: Third-party Windows applications
  PC MagNet: PC Magazine
Windows OnLine Bulletin Board System: (510) 736-8343
Byte Information Exchange (BIX): (800) 227-2983 (voice)

Periodicals

Acknowledge, The Windows Letter
114 Talmadge Road
Mendham, NJ 07945
(201) 543-6033

Inside Microsoft Windows
The Cobb Group
6420 Bunsen Parkway, Ste. 300
Louisville, KY 40220
(800) 223-8720

Microsoft Systems Journal
Subscription Dept.
P.O. Box 1903
Marion, OH 43305
(800) 669-1002

The Windows Journal
WUGNET Publications, Inc.
1295 N. Providence Road, Ste. C107
Media, PA 19063
(215) 565-1861

Windows Magazine
CMP Publications, Inc.
600 Community Drive
Manhasset, NY 11030
(805) 284-3584

The Windows Power Letter
The LeBlond Group
P.O. Box 247
Soquel, CA 95073
(408) 479-9055

Windows Shopper's Guide
Whitefox Communications Inc.
P.O. Box 7125
Beaverton, OR 97005-7125
(800) 669-5612

Windows Watcher
Computhink, Inc.
15127 NE 24th, Ste. 344
Redmond, WA 98052
(206) 881-7354

WPMA View
WPMA
P.O. Box 851385
Richardson, TX 75085
(214) 234-8857

User Groups

Atlanta: (404) 393-1629 (voice)
Boston: (617) 643-0223
Houston: (713) 524-4486
Los Angeles: (213) 318-5212
New York: (714) 544-6411
Philadelphia: (215) 951-1255
San Francisco: (415) 927-2909

17

Questions Most Frequently Asked

This is an interesting chapter. It's written in the first person because it represents the most often asked questions (by me, by Microsoft, and by consultants) about Windows. I've arranged the chapter into logical groups, organizing the questions into the following categories:

- ◆ Setting Up Windows
- ◆ Running Windows Applications
- ◆ Running Non-Windows Applications
- ◆ 386 Enhanced Mode
- ◆ Memory Management
- ◆ Printing
- ◆ Video Displays
- ◆ Object Linking and Embedding
- ◆ Networking
- ◆ Communications
- ◆ Performance

◆ QUESTIONS ABOUT SETTING UP WINDOWS

I couldn't even get past the first part of the Setup program before my system locked up. What's up?

Usually, the Setup program detects your system's hardware components automatically. You probably have some unique hardware connected to your system. Rerun Setup using the /I switch. This directs Setup to skip its hardware detection step. You will have to select entries from the System Information screen to match your system's equipment.

Why is the TEMP environment variable so important?

Windows uses the TEMP environment variable as the location for temporary files. Since temporary files are usually created during printing and during application switching, you can enhance performance by specifying the right drive/directory location for the TEMP variable. (Chapter 2 discusses this topic at length.) The bottom line is to set TEMP to a first-level directory on your fastest hard disk or possibly to a directory on a RAM disk:

SET TEMP=E:\TEMP

If you set TEMP to a RAM disk, be sure to have created at least a 2MB RAM disk.

Why should I use SMARTDrive?

Any disk cache dramatically improves the performance of Windows. SMARTDrive (SMARTDRV.EXE) is a disk cache utility that is part of Windows 3.1. (It is discussed in Chapter 14.) Disk caching reduces the amount of slow disk activity (measured in milliseconds) and increases the reliance on memory activity (measured in microseconds or nanoseconds). This means that Windows and your applications can run faster.

Why should I use HIMEM.SYS?

HIMEM.SYS is an extended memory manager, which is essential to using the extended memory in your computer. In addition to managing access to the extended memory in your computer, HIMEM.SYS enables DOS itself to use part of the first 64K of extended memory (called the High Memory Area). Chapter 15 discusses how to use the HIMEM.SYS driver most efficiently. The bottom line is that this feature alone makes significantly more conventional memory available before you even start Windows.

*Why does my mouse not work at all under Windows?
It works OK for my DOS applications before I start
Windows.*

You may have installed Windows and incorrectly configured the mouse. Run Setup again to check the current mouse configuration. Or you could be using a bus mouse and not have specified the interrupt level correctly. Level 5 is a common setting, but it may conflict with other hardware on your system. Check your mouse's documentation to determine how to use an unused IRQ if the default interrupt is being used by a different device.

*Can I prevent Microsoft's logo from appearing when
Windows starts up? Can I replace Microsoft's logo
with an image of my own choosing?*

Yes to both questions. To inhibit Microsoft's logo from appearing at all, just start Windows by typing a space and a colon after WIN at the DOS prompt:

WIN :

To replace the logo with your own bit-map image, follow the explanation in Chapter 2.

*My printer is not shown in the list of supported printers.
Which of the existing drivers should I use?*

Always check your printer's documentation to answer compatibility questions. If the documentation does not specifically answer your question, follow these guidelines:

◆ If your printer is a laser printer and is LaserJet-compatible, use the HP LaserJet Plus driver.

◆ If your printer is a laser printer and is PostScript-compatible, use the Apple LaserWriter Plus driver.

◆ If your printer is a dot-matrix printer and is Epson- or IBM Proprinter-compatible, try the Epson FX-80 or IBM Proprinter driver.

◆ If your printer uses HPGL (Hewlett-Packard Graphics Language), you can use the HP Plotter driver (typically the HP 7475A driver).

◆ If your printer is incompatible with all these industry-standard models, consider buying a new one. In the meantime, use the Generic/Text Only driver.

◆ QUESTIONS ABOUT RUNNING WINDOWS APPLICATIONS

When I pull down the Help menu and choose About Program Manager, Windows tells me that I have 85 percent free system resources and over 17MB of free memory. What are system resources and how do they relate to memory?

Chapter 3 discusses this very question in depth. Briefly, system resources are essentially two 64K areas (formally called *heap space*) in the Windows' USER and GDI (Graphics Device Interface) modules. These areas contain descriptive information about running applications, windows, and icons on the desktop.

Sometimes, you run out of memory and it really means that there is insufficient memory to run any more applications. Other times, you run out of memory and it really means that there are insufficient system resources to keep track internally of any more screen or system elements.

If you receive an "Out of Memory" message, check the Help About box in the Program Manager. If the free system resource percentage is still high, you've really run out of memory. If the free system resource percentage is low, your system may still have considerable free memory, but there is no more space remaining to record additional screen and system activity. Refer to Chapter 3 for many suggestions to surmount this problem, such as closing windows and organizing Program Manager groups more efficiently.

*Is there a limit to the number of applications I can run under
Windows?*

There is no inherent limit. However, there is a practical limit imposed
by the amount of physical memory in your system and the remaining system
resources.

*I always run out of system resources after I get all my
applications going. Is there a way to determine how much
each one uses?*

Yes. Choose the About Program Manager option on the Program
Manager's Help menu before running an application. Note the percentage of
System Resources Free. After performing an application's most common
tasks, switch to the Program Manager and note the System Resources Free
percentage again.

*What are the system initialization files and why are they so
important?*

There are two critical initialization files. WIN.INI contains a wide
range of options that define the environment in which Windows runs. SYS-
TEM.INI similarly defines the hardware and execution-time environment.

Chapter 12 explains the contents of these two files. Make changes to
WIN.INI to customize your desktop, and make changes to SYSTEM.INI to
optimize the performance of your Windows system.

*How does application priority influence performance in the
background and in the foreground?*

The priority numbers are just indicators of how much CPU time to allot.
The priority number you assign determines what percentage of the entire
CPU "pie" a program receives.

Chapter 7 explains priority and performance in detail. Remember that
all Windows applications share a single time slice. Each running DOS application receives its own time slice. This actually unbalances the division of
time, assigning more CPU time to individual DOS applications than to Windows applications.

CPU time is divided up proportionately among all running applications. If a Windows application is in the foreground, the Windows foreground priority number (set in the Scheduling portion of the Control Panel's 386 Enhanced dialog box) is used. If a DOS application is in the foreground, its foreground priority number (found in the PIF) is used. Refer to Chapter 7 for detailed examples of how you can influence overall performance by adjusting priority numbers.

How can I switch to any other running application (Windows or DOS) with a single keystroke?

In 386 enhanced mode, you can define an application shortcut key in the Advanced options section of a DOS application's PIF. In the Program Manager, when you define a new icon that represents any application, you can define a shortcut key in the Program Item Properties dialog box. These two methods enable you to assign a single keystroke for switching to either a DOS or a Windows application.

If you use both methods to create a shortcut key for a non-Windows application, the Shortcut Key entry in the Program Item Properties dialog box takes precedence over any PIF entry.

♦ QUESTIONS ABOUT RUNNING NON-WINDOWS APPLICATIONS

Why won't my mouse work with a DOS application running in a 386 enhanced mode window?

In versions 3.0 and earlier, Windows controls the mouse for desktop operations in 386 enhanced mode. If you run a DOS application that uses a mouse, its use of the mouse is disabled while the application runs in a window. To use the mouse, you have to switch the application to full-screen mode.

In Windows 3.1, this is only true if you haven't properly installed the latest mouse drivers that come with Windows 3.1. These drivers, MOUSE.SYS and MOUSE.COM, can support a normal DOS application even when it is running in a 386 enhanced mode window. The only requirement is that you load the new drivers before you start Windows.

If you've upgraded to Windows 3.1 from an earlier version, your previous mouse driver may still be in place. This is especially likely if your mouse driver was provided by another vendor, like Logitech or ATI.

You will have to use the EXPAND utility on the Windows 3.1 installation disks to decompress the MOUSE.COM or MOUSE.SYS driver. Then, either load MOUSE.SYS in your CONFIG.SYS file or load MOUSE.COM in your AUTOEXEC.BAT file.

If you are now using the latest mouse driver that came with your Windows 3.1 package, and it still does not work properly with your DOS application in a 386 enhanced mode window, you may also need to update your display driver. The latest 16-color, 800×600 Super VGA driver that accompanies Windows 3.1 does support the latest mouse capabilities. You may need to use Setup to update your driver.

Can a DOS application use the Clipboard to exchange data?

Yes. In fact, a DOS application can exchange data with either Windows applications or other DOS applications. There are a variety of possibilities and some restrictions. Remember, for example, that you cannot paste graphics into a non-Windows application. Refer to the detailed discussions about the Clipboard in Chapter 5.

Can I load a device driver for a specific DOS application in the same way as I can load a TSR for a specific DOS application?

No. You can only load device drivers in your system's CONFIG.SYS file. If you're attempting to save memory, remember from Chapter 15 that you can

Having Trouble Pasting Data into a Non-Windows Application?

Pasting data, whether text or graphics, from one application into another can be an enormous time-saver. However, while it is a valuable feature of Windows, it does not always work as smoothly as you'd like. Here are some of the reasons why it does not:

♦ You cannot paste graphics into a non-Windows application. Open the Clipboard and pull down the Display menu to determine whether the stored data is text. If it is text, the Text option will appear and the problem is something else.

♦ Your application is running full screen. If you are using standard mode, you must first position the cursor at the insertion point, minimize the application, and choose Paste from the Control menu. If you are using 386 enhanced mode, you must press Alt+Enter to switch to a window, then use the Paste option from the Control menu.

♦ The application cannot handle the Fast Paste method of insertion in 386 enhanced mode. Check the PIF, and clear the check box beside this advanced option.

load device drivers in upper memory blocks (UMBs) if you use DOS 5's EMM-386.EXE UMB manager, Windows' 386 enhanced mode, and DOS 5's DEVICEHIGH command.

Do I need a PIF for every DOS application? It seems that PIFs exist only for some applications.

No, you don't need a separate PIF for each application. If Windows does not find a PIF for a program, it will use the settings in _DEFAULT.PIF. If your application requires special settings, it should have its own PIF. If you use the application frequently, you should consider creating a customized PIF for that application.

◆ TEMPORARY AND PERMANENT CHANGES TO SETTINGS

You can pull down the Control menu in the upper-left corner of a DOS application's window, then make changes to any of several settings (such as priority or display options). However, these adjustments are only temporary, affecting the application for its current invocation only. After you exit the application, the settings will be restored to their defaults (or PIF values) the next time you run the application.

If you want to change an application's settings on a permanent basis, create a customized PIF for that application by using the PIF Editor in the Main group of the Program Manager.

My DOS application uses Alt+Tab, which is one of Windows' special shortcut keys. What can I do?

In the application's PIF, you must check off that key combination in the Reserve Shortcut Keys section. Although Windows will no longer be able to use the particular key's special function, the key will be available once again to your particular application.

If you run your application in standard mode and this solution doesn't work, try checking the Directly Modifies Keyboard option. If you do this, you will be unable to switch away from your application after you've loaded it.

I frequently get "Out of Memory" messages when I start applications. What can I do?

You can use the techniques presented in Chapter 15 for increasing the amount of conventional memory that remains after you start Windows. Refer to that chapter for an in-depth discussion of memory optimization and techniques for freeing up memory in standard mode and 386 enhanced mode.

You should use DOS 5 to reduce the amount of conventional memory used by DOS itself. The DOS=HIGH line in CONFIG.SYS will place part of DOS and its buffers in the High Memory Area. Also, you can use an upper-memory manager like EMM386.EXE to load device drivers and TSRs in the

Some Non-Windows Applications Must Run Exclusively

Some applications will not run successfully in 386 enhanced mode unless they are in the foreground and no other applications are running. Support software for my fax board from the Complete Communicator is one such example. To run such an application properly, you must turn on the Exclusive switch in the Advanced section of the appropriate application's PIF.

However, the application shortcut keys may still enable you to circumvent this exclusivity, with damaging consequences. To minimize the likelihood that you will forget this requirement, you can disable almost all switching keystrokes (like Alt+Esc) in the PIF. This will make it difficult, but not impossible, to switch easily to another application.

But beware of any special-purpose shortcut keys that you may have defined for other applications. Windows will still respond to such hot keys, attempting to switch to the other non-Windows application. The exclusivity requirement for the application you have just switched from may result in a system integrity violation. You will be advised to exit from Windows and reboot your computer. Follow that advice.

reserved UMB area. These techniques are your greatest tool for increasing available conventional memory for DOS applications under Windows.

You can also free up some memory on the fly from within Windows by using some of the following techniques:

- Make PIF adjustments to the memory entries of any running non-Windows applications (see Chapter 8).

- Close unneeded applications.

- Run DOS applications in full-screen mode.

- Minimize other running Windows applications.

- Use the Clipboard Viewer to clear or save the contents of the Clipboard.

◆ Use the Desktop icon in the Control Panel to change the wallpaper selection to None. You can also use a simple and repeating pattern as a wallpaper equivalent, which uses much less memory than a complex bit map, or you can use a color choice, which uses no extra memory.

◆ Clear the Background check box for non-Windows applications that do not need to run when they are not the foreground application.

I run a non-Windows application that executes very slowly, and I've tuned the PIF as much as possible. Does this problem have anything to do with memory?

It certainly may. If the hard-disk light turns on frequently, you can bet that there is insufficient memory and Windows is doing lots of swapping to keep your non-Windows application and all other applications going. Follow the advice in the answer to the preceding question to help solve this problem.

When I create a PIF for a batch file, instead of just for a single non-Windows application, what settings are actually used for the different programs that I name in the batch file?

The PIF defines the settings used for the overall virtual machine, or DOS session, not for any one application. All DOS programs named within the batch file run under the settings established by the PIF for the entire virtual machine.

My non-Windows applications do not run when I'm connected to my network. What's up?

This problem can also arise in non-network situations. If you're running in standard mode, your application may simply be incompatible with Windows. If you're running in 386 enhanced mode, the application may have to run in an exclusive state. Remember that you can check off the Exclusive option in the application's PIF to prevent any other applications from running in the background while this application runs in the foreground.

Difficulties in Switching Applications

You may be experiencing difficulties in switching from non-Windows applications. This problem can be due to a number of causes, depending on which Windows mode you are using.

◆ If your application has a PIF, the reserve shortcut keys may be checked. This reserves certain keystrokes for the application and prevents Windows from receiving them.

◆ If your application has a PIF, the Prevent Program Switch option (in standard mode) may be set. This prevents any switching at all.

◆ You may be running the application in full-screen mode. Press Alt+Enter to change to windowed mode; then try to switch away from the application again.

◆ The application itself may be intercepting the switching keystrokes. You will need to exit the application to use Windows or another application.

I can't seem to switch away from a non-Windows
application by pressing Alt+Esc, Ctrl+Esc, or Alt+Tab.
What can I do to reactivate these switching keys?

Check your application's PIF. First, the check box beside any or all of these reserved shortcut keys may be marked. If so, you can restore Windows' use of these keys by unchecking the box beside each one. However, because these key combinations had formerly been reserved for the application's use, the application will no longer be able to use them.

Second, the Reserve Shortcut Keys boxes may not be checked. If this is the case, you may be running in standard mode and have checked the Prevent Program Switch option in the PIF. This conserves memory at the expense of being able to switch away from the application.

◆ QUESTIONS ABOUT 386 ENHANCED MODE

I have an 80386 machine but I can't get Windows to run in 386 enhanced mode. Why not?

If you are able to run Windows in standard mode, you may have insufficient conventional memory, insufficient extended memory, or insufficient disk space to run in 386 enhanced mode. If you have at least

◆ 200K free conventional memory

◆ 1MB free extended memory

◆ 2MB free disk space

you can force Windows to run in 386 enhanced mode by typing WIN /3 at the DOS prompt. However, Windows will run slowly with this configuration.

There may also be adapter area conflicts between Windows and hardware cards in your system. Add the following line to the [386Enh] section of your SYSTEM.INI file:

EMMExclude=A000–FFFF

If this enables you to bring up Windows in 386 enhanced mode, you might begin an analysis of where the conflict is (read the documentation for your add-in cards) to refine the exclusion range. You can also explore the layout of upper memory with DOS 5's MEM command or the Microsoft Diagnostics Utility (MSD.EXE) included with Windows 3.1.

There may be a problem with handling hard-disk interrupts in 386 enhanced mode. Add this line to the [386Enh] section of your SYSTEM.INI file:

VirtualHDIrq=False

This prevents Windows from managing interrupts and leaves interrupt handling to the normal system ROM routine.

My system includes a high-speed SCSI controller and drive.
What must I do to set up a permanent swap file? Windows
says that no suitable drive could be found.

Sorry, but Windows cannot perform the direct I/O necessary for a permanent swap file on SCSI drives. You'll have to settle for a temporary swap file.

I'm running low on disk space on my C drive, on which I
run Windows. Can I create a permanent swap file on my
D drive, which has much more available space?

No problem at all. Just choose the Virtual Memory button in the 386 Enhanced dialog box, select Change, and choose D: from the Drive list box.

In 386 enhanced mode, I would rather receive an
"Out of Memory" message than slow down all running
applications. What should I do?

You should set Paging=No in the [386Enh] section of your SYSTEM.INI file. This will disable paging when the system runs out of memory.

Is there a limit to physical or virtual memory in
386 enhanced mode?

16MB for both.

◆ QUESTIONS ABOUT MEMORY MANAGEMENT

What is the difference between expanded memory and
extended memory?

The terms expanded memory and extended memory are confusing to many people. Chapter 4 discusses different types of memory at length.

Windows uses extended memory for nearly everything. Extended memory comes after the 1MB conventional memory address space.

Expanded memory, on the other hand, is a more restrictive and complex form of memory that can only be addressed through a method called *bank switching*. By using special software, this extra memory can be accessed in blocks called banks, using conventional memory addresses. Different banks of expanded memory are accessed at different times, using a special section of memory called the *page frame*, which is usually located in a 64K block of reserved memory between 640K and 1MB.

Expanded memory is more difficult for applications to use than extended memory. It involves more overhead than extended memory. And it is only used by some DOS programs. In standard mode, DOS programs that require expanded memory can access true expanded memory. In 386 enhanced mode, DOS programs that require expanded memory are actually provided a form of emulated expanded memory that Windows creates from available extended memory.

How much memory do I really need to run Windows?

The documentation mentions theoretical minimums. It may say 2MB, but 3MB or 4MB will make a significant difference in performance. The extra RAM can be used for a disk cache or a RAM drive.

Windows uses memory more efficiently for Windows applications than for DOS applications. Each additional DOS application run under Windows will require an additional 750K to 1MB of RAM. Because of the way Windows allocates memory for DOS applications, your PIF settings become quite important (see Chapter 8).

I decided to use Quarterdeck's QEMM 386 and I'm having some difficulties. What do you suggest?

At least temporarily, go back to using HIMEM.SYS and EMM-386.EXE. Then contact Quarterdeck Technical Support for advice on possible incompatibilities between your version of QEMM 386 and your version of Windows.

◆ QUESTIONS ABOUT PRINTING

I know that Windows 3.1 contains TrueType fonts, but I can't seem to print them on my laser printer. What's wrong?

Applications only offer TrueType fonts if your printer driver is Windows 3.1-compatible. Your system may be using an earlier version. Use the Printers dialog box from the Control Panel to switch connections to a Windows 3.1 printer driver. If Windows doesn't contain the driver you need, try to use an alternative one. Check with your manufacturer as well; they may have a Windows 3.1 driver available.

When I try to print, the printer just spits out page after page of garbage characters. What's up?

This one's simple. You're probably using the wrong printer driver. Check the Printers dialog box for the default printer you're using. Either change it or choose Setup Printer from your application's File menu to specify the correct driver. Additionally, if you're using a serial printer, the problem could be an improperly set baud rate. To check this, choose the Ports icon in the Control Panel, and check your printer's setup for baud rate as well.

Why don't my print requests work?

This is one of the most common problems in any computer system. There are an enormous number of possible explanations, as well as actions you can take. Consider all of these possibilities:

◆ If your problems occur when printing from Windows applications, try printing from a non-Windows application. Also, exit Windows and try printing from a DOS application at a command prompt. This can help to isolate the problem's origin.

◆ The required printer driver might not have been correctly installed or connected to the printer port. Check the Printers dialog box in the Control Panel for the printer and port connections. (Chapter 13 discusses these connections.) To help identify such a problem, you can try to print to a file instead of to an LPTx or a COMx port.

◆ You've installed the incorrect driver for your printer. If all else fails, reinstall the same printer driver from the original installation disks. It may be that your disk copy of the driver has become corrupted.

◆ You are using a network printer. The Timeouts settings in the Printers Connect dialog box may need to be increased to allot more time before the print request fails. Increase the Device Not Selected value from 15 to 30, and increase the Transmission Retry value from 45 to 120.

◆ You are trying to print graphics on an HP LaserJet (or compatible printer) without sufficient memory; 512K is insufficient to print a full page of graphics. If your printer has more memory installed than this, choose the Setup button in the Printers dialog box. You may need to adjust the value for installed memory to reflect the actual amount in your printer.

◆ Your TEMP environment variable is not set correctly. Set TEMP in your AUTOEXEC.BAT file to a first-level directory on a fast hard disk or a RAM disk. The Print Manager uses the directory specified by the TEMP variable to store its temporary spool files.

◆ Some part of the physical connection between your computer and the printer has failed. This could be as simple as a cable that is not fully plugged in. To check this possibility, pull out the printer cable and plug it back in both the computer end and the printer end. Also, a switch box, print spooler, or network that intercepts print requests could be at fault. Try temporarily connecting the computer and the printer to identify or eliminate the intercepting devices as the cause. If printing works when circumventing these additional devices, you can slow down the printer output in the following way. First, choose the Printers icon in the Control Panel, then clear the Fast Printing Direct To Port check box in the Connect dialog box. Finally, try a different cable completely. Check the printer documentation for the correct configuration or wiring for your cable.

◆ The communications settings for a serial printer are incorrect. Choose Ports Settings to verify the current values or change them to correct values. The most common settings for a serial printer are 9600 for baud rate, 8 for Data Bits, None for Parity, 1 for Stop Bits,

Solving Printer Problems

One of the most frequent questions from users has to do with difficulties in printing. The following may be all you need to solve your problem immediately:

♦ Your laser printer does not have sufficient memory to print a complete page of graphic data, or you have not correctly identified the amount of memory available in your laser printer.

♦ The printer is not be plugged in, powered up, and online.

♦ The printer was not installed properly. A particular printer must be selected, and it must be connected to a particular port.

♦ The Timeouts settings in the Connections portion of the Printers section of the Control Panel are not set high enough for network printing.

♦ You have a faulty switch box, print spooler, or network cable.

♦ Your serial communications settings in the Ports section of the Control Panel are incorrect.

and XON/XOFF for Flow Control. Both your printer and the ports settings must be the same or you'll get no response at all.

♦ You forgot to download the header information for a PostScript printer.

♦ Your printer needs paper, a new ribbon, a print wheel, or toner. Start the Print Manager from the Program Manager's Main group.

How can I speed up printing from my Windows applications?

Do you want to reduce the time it takes for printing to be completed? If so, you can print directly to a port by disabling the Print Manager, or you can check the High Priority option on the Print Manager's Options pull-down menu. However, taking either of these steps will slow down other running applications.

Do you want to reduce the time it takes to return from the print request to the application for further processing? If so, consider installing a print spooler, or creating a RAM disk and pointing the TEMP environment variable to it.

◆ QUESTIONS ABOUT VIDEO DISPLAYS

My DOS application's screen display is sometimes garbled when I switch back to it. What should I do?

If you're running in standard mode, choose the Graphics/Multiple Text button in the application's PIF.

If you're running in 386 enhanced mode, you should change each of the Monitor Ports and Video Memory options. Make only one change at a time, bumping up your choice by one each time, and test your application in between changes.

If you are using a 16-color, 800 × 600 Super VGA display, you may need to update the display driver. Windows 3.1 includes a new Super VGA display driver that supports most popular displays. Run the Setup program to update to this driver.

The new Fonts option on the Control menu of my DOS applications is great, but it doesn't seem to work for all my DOS applications. Why not?

You can only change font size for a DOS application running in 386 enhanced mode when it is running in text mode. You'll have to check your application's documentation to determine whether it is running in graphics mode and whether you can control switching it back to text mode.

You also may be using an older Super VGA display driver that doesn't support this new Windows 3.1 feature. Use Setup to update to the latest Super VGA driver.

◆ USE CHARACTER MAP TO RETRIEVE SPECIAL SYMBOLS

Use the new accessory program, Character Map, to find international characters and special symbols from all available fonts. You can copy individual characters or entire typed sequences in the selected font to the Clipboard. From there, you can paste the data into other applications.

◆ QUESTIONS ABOUT OBJECT LINKING AND EMBEDDING

I tried to add sound effects to my Word document, but Word never opened when I selected Insert Object. What's wrong?

Verify that Word for Windows is still available on your hard disk and in a directory on the PATH. Windows may be unable to find your application; its absence is the only indication you're going to get.

Why can't I see a picture of my OLE object with the Object Packager?

The Picture button in the Content window of the Object Packager is only available when you transfer a graphic object to the Object Packager from the Clipboard. Furthermore, you must have created the object in the first place, before copying it to the Clipboard, with an OLE server application.

My OLE application works fine most of the time, but every once in a while, I receive a message that says the server is unavailable. What does this mean?

It means that the server application is busy doing something else. Usually, this means that you are running the server application for printing, calculating, or managing input via some dialog box.

You may occasionally receive this message when you attempt to update, edit, play, or simply create objects. In many cases, your request will be handled automatically as soon as the server becomes available. Because the server application may in fact be waiting for you to input something in another window, the server may never become available. In this special case, you will have to cancel your activating OLE request.

Why does my Paste editing command work differently in different applications?

If the application that places the information in the Clipboard supports OLE, the information can later be embedded with a Paste command. Once embedded, you can launch the creating application by double-clicking on the icon.

If the application that places the information in the Clipboard does not support OLE, using the Paste command later can only insert the data. You will not be able to launch the creating application automatically; you'll only be able to manipulate the pasted version.

◆ QUESTIONS ABOUT NETWORKING

On my network, I have several diskless workstations. How do I most efficiently set up a swap file for them?

You don't. As discussed in Chapter 16, you should disable swapping permanently for diskless workstations. Otherwise, the extra network traffic will bog down your network dramatically.

When I installed Windows on a workstation, using SETUP /N, no SYSTEM directory was created. What happened?

The SYSTEM directory is created beneath the WINDOWS directory on local installations only. On a network, the Windows system files are all located

Connecting to Network Resources

If you are having problems using network resources that you know exist, consider the following explanations:

◆ Necessary Windows network support routines were not installed. This may have happened because the network was not loaded at the time Windows was installed. To correct this, return to Windows Setup and select your system's network. Then restart Windows.

◆ The network's utility programs are out of date for the current version of Windows. Contact your network administrator to obtain updated versions of the necessary utilities.

◆ Your network is incompatible with Windows. Too bad. If Windows doesn't support your network, you are out of luck.

◆ The network driver or support software or both were not loaded before you started Windows.

◆ The network itself is not online.

on the network. The Setup program actually expands the system files on the network so that they will be accessible in shared form to all workstations.

Can I eliminate the banner that appears at the beginning of every printout?

Yes, but not from within Windows. This is a configuration option on most networks.

My print jobs sometimes just disappear. What's going on?

Once again, printing problems can have a myriad of causes. Read the earlier section "About Printing Problems." Any of these problems can cause print jobs to diappear in a network environment as well as a standalone environment. However, there are additional considerations when printing over a network.

First of all, the print request may simply be held up behind other print server requests. You may just have to wait. If you're anxious, use the Print Manager to display the status of all queues. Check the network's queue for your print job.

Also be careful to check other printer queues, since it is also possible that your print job has erroneously made its way into a different printer's queue.

You must also check that your workstation is properly logged on to the network. Naturally, the print server itself must be logged on, or else your print requests will simply be queued up but unable to print.

My network won't let me run Windows. Why not?

Do you mean that performance is unacceptable when you are running Windows? You may not have enough memory on your workstation or the network server itself. Consider installing Windows locally on your workstation's hard disk. Alternatively, use the techniques described in Chapter 16, such as creating permanent or temporary swap files on your local workstation's hard disk.

Do you mean that you can't even start Windows from a network workstation? If so, perhaps you are not using the most recent network shell that is required for Windows 3.1—check with your vendor. Or you may not have properly installed the HIMEM.SYS driver in your system's CONFIG.SYS file, or the EMM386.EXE upper-memory-block manager in your AUTOEXEC.BAT file.

You may have an IRQ conflict. Add-in boards often conflict in how they use interrupt levels. Interrupts 2 and 9 are particularly susceptible to conflicts because so many different add-in boards use them. Check the documentation for all your boards, and make sure that you follow instructions for changing IRQs to avoid conflicts.

Finally, there may be a conflict between Windows and your network adapter card. Check your network's documentation for an address range to exclude. Then use the EMMExclude option in the [386Enh] section of your SYSTEM.INI file to protect these addresses.

I know my network is there, but Windows doesn't seem to recognize it. Why not?

Is your network online? Check with the network administrator.

Is the network one of the ones supported by Windows? If not, forget it. (See Chapter 16 for a list of supported networks.)

Did you load the network before starting Windows? To check this, open the Control Panel and select Windows Setup. If your network is not named on the Network line, you will have to change the system settings to choose your network.

◆ QUESTIONS ABOUT COMMUNICATIONS

I bought a new 9600-baud modem and now I get random weird characters from my favorite BBS. Can't I communicate at that speed under Windows?

Yes, you can but it's not always easy. What you've described can even happen at 2400 baud under Windows, especially if you are running any DOS applications at the time. There is just so much CPU time to go around, and the time-slicing algorithm that Windows uses (see Chapter 7) in 386 enhanced mode limits the amount of time that a communications program is given. This limitation actually makes it more difficult for Windows communications programs than for DOS communications programs running under Windows to work successfully, because Windows is given less time to respond to serial port interrupts.

Try any or all of the following techniques to help both Windows and your communications program to correct for transmission errors:

◆ Shut down any unnecessary non-Windows applications.

◆ Clear the Background check box for any running non-Windows applications that you want to keep open.

◆ Reduce the background priority of non-Windows applications that you want to keep running in the background.

◆ Reduce the foreground priority of any non-Windows application (e.g., an older but favorite word processor) that you intend to work in while your communications program runs in the background.

◆ Set your computer to its highest speed.

◆ If you have a port that has a fast buffering 16550A UART (Universal Asynchronous Receiver Transmitter), select it for your communications connection. If you are already using such a port, try using a different one without a UART. If you have only one port, and it is a buffered UART, try disabling the buffer with the COMxFIFO option in the SYSTEM.INI file (see Chapter 12). In all of these solutions, you are either speeding up communications that are bogging down or slowing down communications that are proceeding too fast for an application to handle.

◆ If your communications program is actually a non-Windows application, and it understands the XON/XOFF protocol, try including COMxProtocol=XOFF in your SYSTEM.INI file. This will enable the application to avoid buffer overflow that is caused by data being transmitted and received faster than it can be processed.

As a final alternative, you may actually have to use a lower baud rate. If you do this, make sure that you match settings in your communications software and in the Windows Port specification, and that these settings match the speed of the remote computer, BBS, or online service.

◆ USE SERIAL PORTS IN SEQUENTIAL ORDER

Suppose that you have your modem on COM2, but you have a bus mouse rather than a serial mouse on COM1. You may have problems. Windows may not be able to handle the serial communications on COM2 properly if there is nothing on COM1. This is a consideration when you have other than a plain-vanilla system (e.g., extra boards, IRQ handling, etc.). The solution is to change the settings to use COM1 for your modem, and leave COM2 available for the next piece of equipment you acquire.

My computer freezes when I start my communications program. What's wrong?

It sounds like an interrupt conflict. Two devices are probably trying to use the same IRQ at the same time. Check your device and system documentation to determine what other equipment may be set to use the same IRQ as the modem. If possible, try to change one of these two devices to use a free IRQ.

Remember that COM1 and COM3 may be different ports, but they use the same interrupt (IRQ4) by default. The same is true for the COM2 and COM4 ports; they use IRQ3 by default. If you have more than one serial communications device (e.g., a modem, mouse, and plotter), you may have an interrupt conflict even though it appears that the devices are plugged into different ports.

It is still safest to try to reassign a free IRQ to one of the devices connected to one of these paired ports. However, if your system configuration requires that you maintain the IRQ settings as they are, you may be able to specify COMIRQSharing as True in the SYSTEM.INI file. But don't get your hopes up. This works on very few computer systems.

My communications program sometimes dies when I try to access the port. It works under DOS, and it even works sometimes under Windows. What's going on?

This conflict appears to be with another application. Check to see which other application uses the same serial port or IRQ level. It may be that the application is still retaining access to the port even though it may no longer be using it. You may have to close the other application (e.g., a scanner or fax program) to enable your communications program to access the IRQ and the serial port.

♦ QUESTIONS ABOUT PERFORMANCE

Does it matter whether I locate SMARTDRV.EXE and HIMEM.SYS in the root or in another directory in the PATH?

No. Once you've installed these files, they perform independently of their disk locations.

How large should I make the permanent swap file in 386 enhanced mode?

Chapter 14 discusses this question and the trade-offs involved. Remember that it will help your system's efficiency to defragment your disk (from outside of Windows) before creating a permanent swap file.

Initially, it is best to simply accept Windows' suggested swap file size. However, if you later run out of memory while there are free system resources, you should increase the size of the file. Add 1MB to the swap file for each additional program that you want to run simultaneously.

Is it faster to run my applications in standard mode or 386 enhanced mode?

If you must multitask any DOS applications, you must use 386 enhanced mode.

If there is significant hard-disk activity in standard mode, you should try to run in 386 enhanced mode. Paging is more efficient than standard mode's segment swapping.

If you do not run DOS applications, and your machine has sufficient physical memory to run your Windows applications without resorting to swapping, you should run in standard mode. This eliminates the overhead of 386 enhanced mode when your environment does not require it. Primarily, this eliminates the virtualization of devices and drivers to sustain multitasking in 386 enhanced mode.

Are Your Non-Windows Applications Running Very Slowly?

In standard mode, free up memory to speed up slow applications. In 386 enhanced mode, the following PIF settings can have a strong effect on memory consumption and consequently on speed:

KB Desired: Limit this value if your application doesn't profit from extra memory. Increase it if the extra memory you gain noticeably enhances performance.

KB Required: Make sure that this value is at least equal to the minimum amount needed by your application.

Priority: Increase foreground or background priority values, depending on when and how you run the application. Tune this value for all non-Windows applications.

Detect Idle Time: This setting should normally be turned on. If one non-Windows application runs particularly slowly, turn off this option and rerun that application.

Why does it take so long to start up Windows?

This problem could be due to several causes. First, your hard disk could be slow. Older hard disks may have data transfer rates greater than 50 to 100 milliseconds. Newer hard disks often have transfer rates that dip below 10 milliseconds.

Second, your processor could be slow. A 286 system is noticeably slower than a 386 system. A 386 system with a 16-Mhz processor is noticeably slower than the same system with a 33-Mhz processor.

Third, you may be directing Windows to load up or run many applications at start-up. The more programs that must be initiated at start-up, the longer it will take to complete the start-up sequence.

*Should I avoid using SMARTDRV.EXE to preserve
memory for the swap file?*

No. Use SMARTDRV to gain the performance benefits of a disk cache
(see Chapter 14). Then, whenever possible, use a swap file to gain the benefits
of virtual memory in 386 enhanced mode.

*Is there any difference in performance between using the
SMARTDRV that came with DOS 5 and the one that
came with Windows 3.1?*

The newest one (check the creation date) is better to use. That is
probably the SMARTDRV that came with Windows 3.1. Microsoft is always
working to improve their disk-caching utility software. Using the most recent
version will enhance disk operations under DOS and Windows.

*Why should I bother pointing the TEMP environment
variable to a RAM disk?*

A RAM disk is dramatically faster for all operations than a hard disk.
Operations that involve file creation, processing, and deletion can have a
great performance benefit if those files are on a RAM disk. If you set TEMP
to point to a directory on a RAM disk, any application that uses temporary
files will perform much faster than if those files are on a hard disk. This obviously includes the Print Manager, which uses the TEMP location for its
short-term spool files.

18

*Unrecoverable
Application Errors*

In the strictest sense, an Unrecoverable Application Error (UAE) is an error from which a specific application cannot recover, but from which Windows can recover. When an UAE occurs, you will see the dreaded UAE dialog box, which does no more than frustrate you by informing that the application has seriously crashed. You can continue working in Windows because after informing you of this individual crash, Windows merely terminates the application. This chapter explains why, how, and when this problem occurs.

In addition, this chapter also discusses situations in which Windows itself crashes. I consider this to be a distinct form of unrecoverable error. And I find it not only frustrating, but annoying, since all running applications crash at once.

For both of these situations, I'll discuss what kinds of actions you can take. Although there's not much you can do to recover individually from these types of severe errors, there are some steps you can take to make your life easier in the future.

◆ WHAT ARE UAE'S?

In theory, all applications in a proper multitasking environment are protected from one another. The failure of one to execute properly should not be able to affect any other running application. Also, the failure of an application to follow the ground rules set by the operating system should be detectable.

Ideally, if one application attempts to write to the address space of another application, the operating system should be able to detect the attempt. If one application attempts to execute one of the hardware instructions reserved for

All Crashes Are Not Really Crashes

Once in a while, your Windows system may seem to die or freeze up. There may be no apparent response to your keyboard or mouse, not even to Ctrl+Esc. Before pressing the Reset button or Ctrl+Alt+Del, check to see whether all hardware devices are connected, powered up, and online.

Many Windows configurations include exotic CONFIG.SYS files, which contain drivers for a variety of devices. Some programs (e.g., some hard-disk managers and BBS message readers) perform a variety of (not always essential) port/hardware checks. Sometimes, a previously powered-up device is shut down because it is no longer needed or will not be needed for a while.

As a result, some programs may freeze up while they wait for a response (i.e., a hardware interrupt signal) from the currently unavailable device. If this is the reason for your apparent system lockup, simply turning on all connected devices may unfreeze your machine.

operating-system use, the operating system should also be able to detect the attempt. After detection, the application can be terminated without any impact whatsoever on remaining applications.

In reality, all operating systems crash from time to time. Operating systems attempt to detect things like memory violations or application attempts to execute restricted instructions. If the invalid attempt is caught, Windows can display a dialog box that informs you of the unrecoverable error. This means that the application cannot continue to execute safely. Even if you are able to continue running the application (an option under Windows 3.1), you cannot be sure that it will run correctly.

In some cases, you can perform the equivalent of a local reboot, choosing to abort the application completely at that moment or to return control temporarily to the application. In some cases, you may want to return to the application to save files and then exit normally.

Most serious UAEs occur when you try to run your DOS applications under Windows. As you learned in Chapter 4, DOS applications address memory differently from Windows applications. Consequently, there is a greater possibility for unintentional yet fatal errors occurring in your Windows environment when you run DOS applications. Since these applications don't even know the rules of running under Windows, they can sometimes overwrite memory locations without even giving Windows the opportunity to catch the unintentional error.

If the problem isn't caused by a DOS application, it usually lies in some form of hardware conflict. The next section explores possible explanations.

◆ WHAT CAUSES UAE'S AND SYSTEM INTEGRITY VIOLATIONS?

There are quite a few possible explanations for integrity violations and other unrecoverable errors. Integrity violations occur when an application actually corrupts important Windows address locations, leading to a situation in which Windows may completely or partially fail to operate correctly. Unrecoverable Application Errors occur when applications themselves fail. At the very least, you should check your Free System Resources percentage in the Help pull-down menu of the Program Manager whenever you start having UAEs. A very low percentage (below 20 percent) can cause UAEs. This happens in large part because some applications don't react correctly when system resources are not readily available.

If an application attempts to access a disk file that happens to be cross-linked with another file, UAEs can occur. This rarely happens; using the CHKDSK command with the /F switch can clear up the problem. Just remember to run this command from time to time at the DOS prompt (not from within Windows itself), and you will have eliminated another possible source of system UAEs.

Remember also from the discussion in Chapter 12 that some hard disks generate interrupts in ways that Windows cannot readily handle. If Windows has problems with the interrupts, you should turn off Windows' virtualization

Identifying the Source of Unrecoverable Application Errors

Versions of Windows earlier than 3.1 could only display a frustratingly limited UAE message, telling you that the current application was being terminated. Windows 3.1 does better than that, identifying the problem to a greater extent. But the explanation can still be somewhat obscure, sometimes understandable only to programmers or technical staff.

In plain English, here are some of the most likely reasons why you may still suffer from the UAE blues:

♦ There are adapter, or page-mapping, conflicts in 386 enhanced mode. Use the EMMExclude=A000–EFFF line in the [386Enh] section of SYSTEM.INI.

♦ There is a memory management conflict between HIMEM.SYS and some other TSR or driver.

♦ You are running an older application that has not been updated for the latest version of Windows.

♦ You are not using the latest version of RAMDRIVE or SMARTDRV. Check your DOS and WINDOWS directories for the latest versions.

♦ The Windows Setup program has identified your hardware or network incorrectly.

♦ You are running a program that does not work with your high-resolution or multicolor video driver. In some of these cases, you may need to drop back to 16 colors to use a particular program.

of the interrupts. To let the ROM routine handle the interrupts, in a slower but more reliable fashion, just set VirtualHDIrq=False in the [386Enh] section of your SYSTEM.INI file.

In the following sections, I'll discuss some of the many other reasons for UAEs and some of your possible responses. In each case, remember that it is safest to save all files, reboot your computer, and restart Windows. You can no longer be sure of the integrity of your system.

INCOMPATIBLE SOFTWARE
OR HARDWARE

The CONFIG.SYS file contains nearly all your system's hardware drivers. The AUTOEXEC.BAT file contains most memory-resident programs that execute before Windows is started. Windows is incompatible with a number of these programs. A problem arises when an incompatible driver or TSR is in place when you run Windows. This could occur because Setup did not recognize the incompatibility, or because you installed the driver or TSR after setting up Windows.

Incompatible memory-resident software is a common source of UAEs when you try to run Windows. This kind of incompatibility can account for crashes, freezes, and erratic and inconsistent UAEs.

It is possible but more rare that the incompatibility is with an expansion board in your computer. If none of the other approaches in these sections solves your UAE problems, remove the suspect board and reboot your system without it. Then test whether or not the UAEs still occur.

As a first approach to identifying incompatible software as the cause of a UAE, you should revise your CONFIG.SYS and AUTOEXEC.BAT files to exclude all nonessential drivers and TSRs. If Windows then works and the application that caused the UAE also works, you can add the extra driver and TSR lines one line at a time.

Each time you revise the AUTOEXEC.BAT or CONFIG.SYS file by restoring a single TSR, device driver, or network driver, reboot your machine and restart Windows. You should then attempt to re-create the same application mix you had when the UAE appeared. When the UAE reappears, you'll know which program was the direct cause.

But don't get your hopes up too much. Some UAEs occur only when a particular combination of factors exists. You may actually have a driver and a TSR that are themselves incompatible. UAEs may only occur when the two of them are loaded simultaneously. You may need to update or replace both of them to completely surmount the problem.

Then again, a TSR may not account for a UAE except when it happens to be active at the moment you run the application. For example, the TSR may be using some portion of a UMB at precisely the same time as your application uses the UMB. Unless you can reproduce the scenario that existed when the UAE occurred, you may not be able to identify which TSR or device/network driver is the culprit.

INCORRECT VERSION OF DOS

When I first started using DOS, I quickly discovered that there were different versions of DOS. I don't mean just versions 5.0, 3.3, and so on. I mean one version from IBM, another from Hewlett-Packard, another from Panasonic. Because these OEM versions include instructions that are specific to particular hardware, it is even more crucial to use the proper version of DOS when you start Windows on your machine.

UAEs can occur solely because of internal inconsistencies that crop up between Windows, DOS, and your OEM's special hardware. Although it may appear that IBM's PC-DOS seems to work OK on your Hewlett-Packard or Toshiba computer, you can almost rely on the appearance of UAEs from time to time.

My advice is to use a manufacturer's OEM version of DOS if they have one. Even though Microsoft's MS-DOS is generic and runs on virtually all computers, it is not the best choice all the time. However, if you choose Microsoft's version, use DOS 5 if possible. DOS 3.3 is second best if you haven't yet decided to upgrade to DOS 5. Don't use any other version.

ADAPTER SEGMENT CONFLICTS

In 386 enhanced mode, Windows may run afoul of upper memory blocks (i.e., the adapter segment). Most often, this shows up when your system simply freezes up. Because 386 enhanced mode uses UMB locations to support page mapping when multitasking, this problem is also called a *page-mapping* conflict.

I've already discussed in Chapters 12 and 17 how to use the EMMExclude command to prevent Windows from using specifically defined regions of the UMB area in 386 enhanced mode. This prevents conflicts with adapters that use certain UMB areas but are not recognized automatically as using those areas. When you know exactly which areas are being used by your hardware, you can include one or more EMMExclude lines in the [386Enh] section of your SYSTEM.INI file.

To identify if a UMB area conflict is the cause of your UAEs when in 386 enhanced mode, follow these steps:

1. Run the application in standard mode. Temporarily remove the EMM386.EXE reference in your AUTOEXEC.BAT file. Then start Windows in standard mode by entering WIN /S at the DOS prompt. If you experience no UAE when you run your application, there is probably a 386 enhanced mode page-mapping conflict.

2. Edit your SYSTEM.INI file to exclude the entire UMB area that Windows normally uses for available mapping addresses:

   EMMExclude=A000–EFFF

3. Add the EMM386.EXE line back to your AUTOEXEC.BAT file. Restart Windows in 386 enhanced mode. Run your application again. If the UAE does not appear now, you can be reasonably sure that a page-mapping conflict was the cause.

Your system may now work without UAEs, but it will be inefficient. Windows cannot use any memory in the UMB region, even though some may be available. You should refine the EMMExclude line to exclude just the address ranges that produce the conflict. Remember that you can add more than one EMMExclude line to prevent mapping to multiple noncontiguous regions in the upper memory blocks. For example, suppose that your video adapter uses the two address ranges A000–AFFF and B800–CFFF. You could include these lines in the SYSTEM.INI file:

EMMExclude=A000–AFFF

EMMExclude=B800–CFFF

To decide which memory locations are used by your adapter, you can always try calling the vendors of your add-in boards, or you can check the documentation for your adapters. These methods are appropriate for typical ISA (Industry Standard Architecture) machines. If you have an IBM PS/2 or any MCA bus computer, you can also boot with the computer's reference disk to discover the adapter addresses in use.

Reserved Memory Adapter Conflicts

You may know about the EMMExclude line in the SYSTEM.INI file, and you may know about switches like /X= on your QEMM386 device-driver line in CONFIG.SYS. But many UAEs occur because of video board conflicts. Are you sure that you're excluding a sufficient portion of reserved memory?

Some boards switch modes automatically, defeating the best memory manager's attempts to determine what upper reserved blocks are really available for use. Only the board's documentation, or a call to the board manufacturer, can tell you what to really exclude. For example, the technical support staff for VGA Wonder boards suggest excluding A000–C7FF.

Yes, this sounds like more than you'd need. But they say that their driver uses it all at different times. For example, more memory is consumed as you use the board for higher video modes. Super VGA requires more reserved memory to be excluded than just plain VGA.

INCORRECT SETUP

Recall from Chapter 2 that Setup offers two primary options: Express and Custom setups. If you accept the Express option, the Setup program automatically detects your hardware and provides a set of default configuration values. Its decisions are not always correct.

In particular, some computers from Toshiba, NEC, Zenith, and others require that you use the Custom Setup option. You must select the name of your computer because the automatic detection logic does not always identify the computer correctly. This error can lead to UAEs.

In addition, the same consideration requires that you explicitly name certain networks when running Setup. Not specifying your network during Setup can also lead to UAEs.

It is safest to use the Custom option for your entire installation. Naturally, this does defeat to some extent the value of having the Express option in the first place.

If you have purchased networks and special OEM computers, you should check Setup to discover what computer and network names have been specified. It may be that Setup originally detected the incorrect computer or network type. Then again, someone may have actually chosen the wrong type during a previous custom setup.

To make changes safely, exit Windows and run the Setup program from the DOS prompt.

OUT-OF-DATE APPLICATION VERSIONS

Many applications on the market today once ran under Windows 2.x and 3.0. Although most applications that ran under Windows 3.0 will run successfully under Windows 3.1, not all will do so. Although many applications that ran under Windows 2.x may run successfully under Windows 3.1, many will not run at all.

Earlier versions of applications that were designed to run in Windows real mode (not available in Windows 3.1) will no longer work. They must have been designed to run solely in protected mode, the only mode available in Windows 3.1.

When you attempt to start one of these older programs, typically a dialog box will be displayed, containing a message warning you that the program may not work reliably in the Windows 3.1 environment. If you choose to run the program instead of canceling the Start request, you may get UAEs.

If your UAEs are the result of an older program, get an updated version of the program or a different program that performs the same task.

Some programs "mark" earlier Windows applications, which hides from Windows that the applications were written for an earlier version of Windows. You will not see the warning dialog box for such an application. This means that, unless you are sure from the application's documentation that it is Windows-3.x compatible, it is possible that you are actually running a marked Windows 2.x program. This could also account for UAEs.

What to Do If a Non-Windows Application Freezes Up

There are several possible explanations for why a non-Windows application does not respond to your input. Consider the following steps:

♦ The application itself may have crashed but Windows is up and running. To ignore the application for now, press Ctrl+Esc to display the Task List, then switch to any other running task.

♦ The application may be running in 386 enhanced mode and in a window. If so, you may have begun but not completed a marking or selection operation. Complete the operation or cancel the request.

♦ The application may be processing a very long computational or disk-intensive request. Minimize the application so that you can continue working with another task.

♦ As a last resort, if you're sure that the application has frozen up, you can forcibly terminate it by pressing Ctrl+Alt+Esc and selecting OK (you will lose changes to any open files). This is a shortcut in Windows 3.1 for opening the Control menu and choosing Terminate.

APPLICATION-SPECIFIC PROBLEMS

Most of the causes of UAEs that I've already discussed are relatively random. They can occur in almost any running application and often can occur at different points during execution.

Some UAEs occur when you run a particular application and no others. The previous section deals with older Windows 2.*x*-specific applications that may cause UAEs. Some newer applications can also cause UAEs if they contain errors in their programming.

In some cases, UAEs can appear for a specific application solely because it has been installed improperly. This is not unlike specifying the wrong hardware during the Windows setup. An individual application may have its own setup, start-up, or installation procedure. If you make mistakes, you may get UAEs.

◆ UAE'S AND ENVIRONMENT SIZE

Beware the erroneous assumption that each DOS session you open in Windows receives an environment whose size is set with your CON-FIG.SYS's SHELL command. Not so!

It may be that a DOS application under Windows requires a larger environment size. Simply upping the /E:*xxxx* parameter in the SHELL command will not do the trick. Windows allots only a default size environment for DOS applications. However, you can set up COM-MAND.PIF to run COMMAND.COM; make sure to place a larger-size parameter (i.e., /E:*xxxx*) in the Optional Parameters field of the PIF Editor.

Some UAEs can be caused by insufficiently sized environments. You may have assumed that your DOS window had a larger environment than it actually does.

If UAEs occur when you run a particular application, you should first try to reinstall that application. If that fails to eliminate the UAEs, you can try calling the application vendor. They may have an updated version or suggest a workaround.

SOLVING NETWORK CRASHES

Some system crashes occur because of the interrelationship between an application and the network that is running. You may encounter these problems in either standard mode or 386 enhanced mode, and the approach to solving the problem will depend on which mode you usually run in.

Network Application Crashes in Standard Mode

A crash may occur because of memory switching among applications. As is common, the problem may lie in a non-Windows application that is running. If possible, try to run your network application without simultaneously executing non-Windows applications. If that is impossible, try to avoid switching between applications when running an error-prone network application.

If the problem application is a Windows application, it may simply be incompatible with standard mode. Call the vendor to ascertain if this is the case. Otherwise, the most common problem occurs with switching applications or with running simultaneous DOS applications. You can eliminate this possibility by closing DOS applications or by not switching applications.

If the problem network application is a non-Windows application, you can adjust the PIF to guarantee that no switching can occur. In standard mode, you can select the Prevent Program Switch option. This controls the memory-switching problem, which will probably prevent system crashes.

Selecting this switch, however, also disables your ability to switch easily to do other work while the network application is running. To run any other Windows or non-Windows application, you'll have to exit from the network application.

Network Application Crashes in 386 Enhanced Mode

In 386 enhanced mode, a network application may crash because of an apparently unrelated application that is running simultaneously.

Just as in standard mode, the network application may encounter problems because of memory switching. If it is a non-Windows application, you can use a PIF setting to control execution. Rather than just preventing a program switch away from the network application, as in standard mode, you can set the Exclusive check box for the application. This setting suspends all background applications while the network application is running. More resources become available to your network application, and there is less contention for memory usage.

If the network application is a Windows application, you cannot adjust any PIF setting to control crashes. Another cause of crashes may be that active programs running in the background are responsible for memory switching that is interfering with your network application.

If the background applications are non-Windows applications, you can close some or all of them. If you want them to continue to be available, you can also consider changing their execution status. Disable their PIF's Background check box so they won't be executing at all when your network application is in the foreground. There will be no memory switching or resource contention.

Suppose that there are no non-Windows applications running in the background, yet your network application still crashes. Some network applications automatically send messages to Windows that define what files have been created or modified, which can interfere with network usage. You may need to ask your network administrator or read the application's documentation to determine if this is the case.

You can disable file manipulation messages by setting the FileSysChange entry in the [386Enh] section of SYSTEM.INI to False. This may solve the problem immediately. If not, you may have no other choice but to run the application in standard mode. In either case, remember that by turning off the flow of file manipulation messages in this manner, you will improve overall Windows performance.

◆ USING DIAGNOSTIC SOFTWARE

OK. You've tried everything suggested in the preceding pages to prevent UAEs. Admit it now. Did you remove any hardware boards? Did you remove all lines from CONFIG.SYS and AUTOEXEC.BAT that reference TSRs and device drivers, then restore those lines one at a time, rebooting and rerunning Windows each time?

Maybe you have. A last resort is to use some of the resources listed at the beginning of this part. Microsoft's technical support staff is very helpful. They will probably suggest one or more of the steps already outlined in this chapter. Beyond that they may suggest using their diagnostic utility programs.

USING THE DR. WATSON UTILITY

DRWATSON.EXE is a debugging utility that was originally designed to assist Microsoft programmers in determining the cause of UAEs. If it is running, it logs information to a disk file whenever a UAE occurs. This information

Use Local Reboot to Kill a Frozen Program

Press Ctrl+Alt+Del when a Windows or non-Windows application freezes up. Windows will offer several options to resume your processing:

◆ You can press Ctrl+Alt+Del once again to restart your entire system. An exception would be if a DOS application hangs up in the background. In this case, press Ctrl+Alt+Del a third time to truly restart the system, or press any other key to reactivate the frozen non-Windows application.

◆ You can press Escape to return control to a frozen application in the foreground.

◆ You can press Enter to close a frozen foreground Windows application or to terminate a frozen foreground non-Windows application.

consists of a variety of system conditions and status information that existed when the UAE occurred.

You can be ready at all times for UAEs by including an icon for Dr. Watson in your Windows 3.1 STARTUP directory. This will initiate the utility each time you start Windows. It uses very little memory and has no impact on Windows performance. If your system is stable, you can remove Dr. Watson from the STARTUP directory.

If UAEs start occurring again, you can always start Dr. Watson manually by double-clicking on its icon. Alternatively, just pull down the File menu in the Program Manager, choose Run, type in DRWATSON, and choose OK.

The file that Dr. Watson creates is named DRWATSON.LOG and appears in the WINDOWS directory after a UAE occurrs. Dr. Watson will neither prevent nor cure UAEs. But it can help Microsoft or an experienced Windows programmer to determine what may have caused a UAE. Figure 18.1 shows a typical Dr. Watson log file.

In this example from my own system, the log file gave me enough information to determine the problem and eventually solve it on my own. The report opens up with a message that identifies the program at fault (SOUND-REC.EXE), as well as the problem that occurred (An "exceed segment bounds" fault). This was actually enough for me to go back to the Sound Recorder utility and determine that I hadn't set up my hardware properly.

Had I (or Microsoft) needed more information, the log file also includes the precise contents of all CPU registers, system information, stack information, multitasking information, and my own notes about the error:

1> Just double clicked on Sound Recorder icon

2> in the Accessories program group

When a UAE occurs, Dr. Watson displays a dialog box that prompts you for information about what you did just before the UAE. As you can see at the bottom of Figure 18.1, these notes are appended to the Dr. Watson log file.

If UAEs reoccur, each subsequent UAE is logged to the same DRWAT-SON.LOG file. If UAEs occur frequently, this file can grow very large and be more difficult to work with. While you are working to solve your UAE problems, it is a good idea to rename the file daily or weekly. For instance, I could use DOS's RENAME command to change the log file from DRWAT-SON.LOG to JUL14.LOG:

RENAME DRWATSON.LOG JUL14.LOG

This will retain today's UAE information in the JUL14.LOG file. Dr. Watson will create a new DRWATSON.LOG file when the next UAE occurs and will append additional information to it for each subsequent UAE. If you seek additional help, Microsoft may ask you to send them a copy of your UAE log file.

◆ AFTER THE UAE: WHAT THEN?

You can perform a local reboot for the application that suffered the UAE, or Windows may direct you to shut down and reboot the entire system. If Windows says to do this, do it. Anything else may affect future performance of Windows or your applications.

USING THE MSD UTILITY

After a UAE occurs and Dr. Watson prompts you to enter information, one of two things can occur. Your system may be effectively dead, in which case

```
Start Dr. Watson 0.80 - Tue Jul 14 13:02:03 1992
******************************************************************************
Dr. Watson 0.80 Failure Report - Tue Jul 14 13:04:40 1992
SOUNDREC had a 'Exceed Segment Bounds (RMW)' fault at USER
INVALIDATEDCCACHE+1dee
$tag$SOUNDREC$Exceed Segment Bounds (RMW)$USER INVALIDATEDCCACHE+1dee$adc
[bx+si], al$Tue Jul 14 13:04:40 1992

CPU Registers (regs)
ax=07b7  bx=362c  cx=36e0  dx=1997  si=2b74  di=2bf8
ip=a98d  sp=22a0  bp=1997  O- D- I+ S- Z+ A- P+ C-
cs = 0487      45b00:b85f Code Ex/R
ss = 1957      5b120:303f Data R/W
ds = 1957      5b120:303f Data R/W
es = 07b7    8061fd80:443f Data R/W

CPU 32 bit Registers (32bit)
eax = 000007b7  ebx = 0000362c  ecx = 000036e0  edx = 00001997
esi = 00002b74  edi = 00002bf8  ebp = 00001997  esp = 80012290
fs = 0000          0:0000 Null Ptr
gs = 0000          0:0000 Null Ptr
eflag = 00000002

System Info (info)
Windows version 3.10
Retail build
Windows Build 3.1.061d
Username Judd Robbins
Organization Computer Options
System Free Space 17073184
Stack base 1368, top 9410, lowest 7854, size 8042
System resources:  USER: 77% free, seg 07b7  GDI: 78% free, seg 060f
LargestFree 15790080, MaxPagesAvail 3855, MaxPagesLockable 1113
TotalLinear 4924, TotalUnlockedPages 1120, FreePages 414
TotalPages 1379, FreeLinearSpace 3855, SwapFilePages 3931
Page Size 4096
11 tasks executing.
WinFlags -
   80386 or 80386 SX
   Enhanced mode
   Protect mode

Stack Dump (stack)
Stack Frame 0 is USER INVALIDATEDCCACHE+1dee  ss:bp 1957:1997
0487:a982   68 a9b6           push a9b6
0487:a985   8b 5e 10          mov  bx, [bp+10]
0487:a988   e8 0306           call near ac91
0487:a98b   8b ea             mov  bp, dx
(USER:INVALIDATEDCCACHE+1dee)
0487:a98d   10 00             adc  [bx+si], al
0487:a98f   d7
0487:a990   13 bb ffff        adc  di, [bp+di+ffff]
0487:a994   e8 03c4           call near ad5b

System Tasks (tasks)
Task  WFSOUND, Handle 1497, Flags 0001, Info  115184 10-30-91 10:54
   FileName D:\WFSOUND\WFSOUND.EXE
Task   TCLOCK, Handle 12df, Flags 0001, Info   38885 09-13-91  9:25
   FileName D:\WFSOUND\TCLOCK.EXE
Task DRWATSON, Handle 1aa7, Flags 0001, Info   26832 12-17-91  3:10
   FileName D:\WINDOWS\DRWATSON.EXE
Task WINOLDAP, Handle 1157, Flags 0003, Info   48784 12-17-91  3:10
   FileName D:\WINDOWS\SYSTEM\WINOA386.MOD
```

FIGURE 18.1:   A sample DRWATSON.LOG text file

```
Task WINOLDAP, Handle 1117, Flags 0003, Info    48784 12-17-91  3:10
  FileName D:\WINDOWS\SYSTEM\WINOA386.MOD
Task   WINCAP, Handle 10d7, Flags 0001, Info    62976 06-20-91 11:15
  FileName D:\COLLAGE\COLLAGE.EXE
Task  WINHELP, Handle 1a37, Flags 0001, Info   253616 12-17-91  3:10
  FileName D:\WINDOWS\WINHELP.EXE
Task WINOLDAP, Handle 1287, Flags 0003, Info    48784 12-17-91  3:10
  FileName D:\WINDOWS\SYSTEM\WINOA386.MOD
Task MICROPHO, Handle 14df, Flags 0001, Info    24064 12-17-91  3:10
  FileName D:\WINDOWS\SYSTEM\OLESVR.DLL
Task  PROGMAN, Handle 0647, Flags 0001, Info   113936 12-17-91  3:10
  FileName D:\WINDOWS\PROGMAN.EXE
Task SOUNDREC, Handle 19e7, Flags 0001, Info    53518 12-17-91  3:10
  FileName D:\WINDOWS\SOUNDREC.EXE

1> Just double clicked on Sound Recorder icon
2> in the Accessories program group

Stop Dr. Watson 0.80 - Tue Jul 14 13:06:12 1992
```

FIGURE 18.1: A sample DRWATSON.LOG text file (continued)

you'll have to reboot, or your system may be unstable yet seemingly usable. Don't bother using Windows any more at this point. Save what files you can and exit Windows.

At the prompt, change to the root directory and run MSD.EXE, the Microsoft Diagnostics utility. Usually, MSD.EXE is located in your WINDOWS directory, so you can just type MSD to start the utility. If you are running the utility on an LCD or a monochrome screen, type MSD /B.

Figure 18.2 shows the main screen that appears when you run the MSD utility.

Because MSD is a standard DOS program, you can actually run it anytime you like. You needn't wait until a UAE strikes. If you are investigating your system, you can even run it from within Windows at the DOS prompt. By running it inside Windows, it can provide useful information about memory usage by your applications and Windows itself. Furthermore, it can provide information about IRQs, which can be particularly useful because some IRQ usage occurs only inside Windows.

◆ IRQ CONFLICT AVOIDANCE

Plain-vanilla systems don't have IRQ conflicts. But if you have lots of extra equipment in your computer, you may have them. Say your computer has a scanner card that uses IRQ 3. Then you go out and buy a fax card that also uses IRQ 3. At some point, you'll be scanning and a fax will arrive in the background.

What can you do? Read the manuals to determine how to change the IRQ level used by one of the cards, and make sure not to use one that may be used by another device in your system.

The MSD main menu screen has a menu bar with File, Utility, and Help options. You can explore them on your own. The primary options appear in the center workspace, with brief summary information provided as well. You can see that my computer, for example, is an 80386 with an AMI (American Megatrend) BIOS. It has three COM ports and one LPT parallel port.

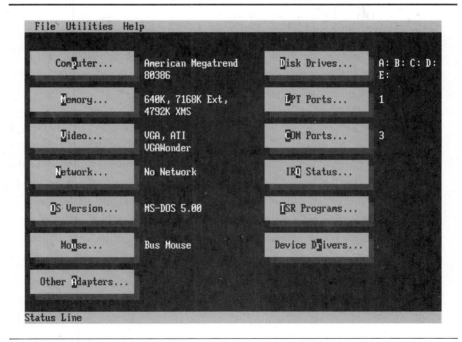

FIGURE 18.2: The main menu screen of the Microsoft Diagnostics utility

If you press the highlighted, or shortcut, key (e.g., P for Computer or C for COM Ports), MSD displays additional information about your selection. Table 18.1 summarizes the information provided by these displays.

You can also create a log of this diagnostic information. Pull down the File menu and select Print Report. This displays the screen shown in Figure 18.3.

From this screen, you can place an X beside any possible information entry. These include the choices available from the main screen (Figure 18.2) as well as other useful system aspects, available from the pull-down menus. These include such things as information about specific memory regions, your system's CONFIG.SYS and AUTOEXEC.BAT files, and your Windows initialization files.

TABLE 18.1: MSD Information Categories

Category	Information Provided About
Computer	BIOS, CPU, coprocessor, DMA, keyboard, and bus
Memory	RAM, ROM, and memory usage (640K–1MB)
Video	Video board's BIOS, adapter, type, manufacturer, and mode
Network	Network type
OS Version	OS/Windows version IDs, serial numbers, location of DOS, and current environment variable contents
Mouse	Mouse driver, type, and version information
Other Adapters	Connection, status, and version information
Disk Drives	Type, free space, and total size for local and logical drives
LPT Ports	Status and port information for all parallel ports
COM Ports	Status and configuration information for all serial ports
IRQ Status	Address, description, detection, and handling information
TSR Programs	Name, address, and size of memory-resident software
Device Drivers	Installed hardware devices and file names

You can send the report directly to your printer port, as I've done in Figure 18.3. Alternatively, you can send a copy of the report to a file. The default file name is REPORT.MSD, although you can change it to a different name, such as JUL14.MSD, if you wish.

If you are printing a copy of an MSD log for UAE diagnosis, you should include a copy along with the Dr. Watson log file when submitting information to Microsoft for assistance.

Turn to Chapter 19 now to round out your understanding of Windows errors by looking at the breadth of error conditions that can occur.

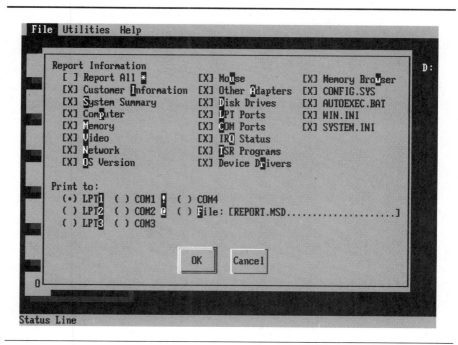

FIGURE 18.3: The MSD Print Report screen

C H A P T E R

19

Inside Windows Error Messages

Congratulations. In the first 16 chapters of this book, you learned all about the power and capabilities of Windows 3.1. In the preceding two chapters, you learned still more about what can sometimes go wrong with Windows and your applications running under Windows. In this chapter, you'll discover the meaning behind the most common error messages that you'll encounter.

The very first section of this chapter discusses the messages that apply to Windows in general, rather than only to a single aspect of your Windows environment. I've arranged the remaining messages into these classes:

- ◆ Multitasking
- ◆ File-Related
- ◆ Device
- ◆ Video
- ◆ Printing
- ◆ Multimedia

Within each section, I list and explain the primary messages that you may occasionally see. In most cases, the wording of the messages will be exactly what you'll see on your screen. In other cases, where Windows displays variations of the message, I'll vary the message slightly to apply to a range of possible cases. In either case, I'll explain the principal causes of the messages that you see.

◆ THE MAJOR SYSTEM ERROR MESSAGES

Some error situations will stop you dead in your tracks. One group, for instance, will prevent you from starting Windows at all or prevent you from starting in a preferred mode. Another group will prevent you from running a favorite application. This section will deal with these most critical error situations.

◆ "ERROR: A20 LINE ALREADY ENABLED"

If you receive this message while your computer is booting, it means that some driver is already using extended memory by the time that Windows' HIMEM.SYS is loaded. Check your CONFIG.SYS file for a DEVICE line that precedes HIMEM.SYS. Try reversing the order so that HIMEM.SYS loads first.

DIFFICULTIES STARTING WINDOWS

Most difficulties with starting Windows have to do with problems in your DOS setup (i.e., the CONFIG.SYS file) or with your DOS file system (i.e., access to necessary disk files). Here are some of the most common problems and their suggested solutions:

◆ "You tried to run in 386 enhanced mode, but your hardware configuration is insufficient." Just type WIN and Windows will start up in standard mode. If this still doesn't work, remove the reference to EMM386.EXE in your CONFIG.SYS file.

◆ "Cannot find necessary files." For example, to run in 386 enhanced mode, Windows needs access to the WIN386.EXE file. In standard mode, Windows needs access to DOSX.EXE. Check to ensure that the path is correct or reinstall Windows.

◆ "Invalid or missing HIMEM.SYS." Install it from your Windows Setup disks, or make sure that the file is in your Windows directory and that its location is correctly specified in your CONFIG.SYS file.

◆ "Incorrect version of DOS." Windows 3.1 requires DOS version 3.10 or greater.

◆ "Insufficient conventional memory to run Windows." You must reconfigure your system to increase free conventional memory and try again. This primarily means adjusting CONFIG.SYS and AUTOEXEC.BAT driver and TSR entries (see Chapter 15 for ideas).

◆ Memory is sufficient, but not enough file handles (the FILES command in CONFIG.SYS) have been specified. Make sure that FILES is set to 30 or greater.

◆ You tried to run Windows in real mode, which is no longer supported.

THIS APPLICATION HAS VIOLATED SYSTEM INTEGRITY

What an annoyance this message is. When you get it, it's almost always too late to do anything except mutter or curse. Occasionally, depending on the nature of the internal violation, Windows may inform you that you can continue working with the application but that you should save all your modified data as soon as possible. Take this advice and be thankful that you're getting a second chance.

Usually, this message means that your application is immediately terminated and any unsaved work is gone forever. There are a number of explanations for this message, most of which you can't do anything about. Receiving this message simply means that the application you were running has violated the rules of Windows programming.

Any of the following reasons can explain why Windows abruptly terminates an application:

◆ Execution of a privileged instruction

◆ Execution of an invalid instruction

- ◆ An invalid page fault
- ◆ An invalid general protection fault
- ◆ An invalid system fault

Windows recommends that you close all applications, exit Windows, and reboot your computer. Some people ignore this suggestion and blithely continue with Windows. In fact, most of the time, you can just rerun the offending application and attempt to continue working with the same document. But don't. There are actually portions of memory that may be corrupted as a result of this integrity violation. If you do not exit your other applications and Windows, then reboot your computer, you will be more likely than before to have additional integrity violations.

It is also possible that the next integrity violation may affect other data in your system. Yes, I know it's a pain in the neck to have to shut down and reboot. But it's the safest course to follow after this type of message. If you continue to receive integrity violations from the same application, you should contact the vendor to see if there is an update to the product that will solve the problem.

INSUFFICIENT MEMORY

As I've emphasized throughout this book, but particularly in Chapters 4 and 15, the performance of your system relies heavily on memory. There are many reasons why you might receive a message about insufficient memory. In each case, the message generally explains what cannot be done because of the limited amount of memory. I'll briefly remind you of some of the obvious steps that can be taken to remedy the situation.

In general, every error situation has the same underlying problem: There is not enough memory to go around. Any of the techniques discussed in Chapter 15 will help minimize the likelihood of such an error message appearing. However, when you actually receive the message, you'll want to know how best to respond.

Some of the key error messages and situations are the following:

♦ "Cannot restore screen." An attempt to restore an application's display failed when you tried to switch back to it.

♦ An application will not even begin to run. This may be because certain minimum values in the application's PIF are not being met or because there is not enough memory left to create a virtual machine in which to run a non-Windows application.

♦ "Cannot successfully paste data from the Clipboard."

♦ "A minimum PIF setting cannot be met."

♦ "A custom icon cannot be constructed for an application."

♦ "Not enough environment space for a non-Windows application." Modify the PIF to allocate more memory (i.e., use the /E switch on COMMAND.COM).

♦ "Can't change fonts."

♦ "Could not define the shortcut key for one of your applications."

♦ "Can't bring up a dialog box."

♦ "Can't repaginate or print the document."

♦ "Not enough memory to edit image."

♦ "Cannot complete an operation that has started."

♦ "Cannot copy image." Naturally, you can select a smaller image or use one of the following techniques to increase available memory.

♦ "Cannot display an entire directory."

♦ "Application cannot continue."

♦ "There is not enough memory to load the rest of the movie." An animation sequence requires more memory to complete than exists on your system.

What can you do in response to these situations? Try any of the following:

♦ Close one or more Windows applications.

♦ Decrease the size of the problem application's window.

Dealing with "Out of Memory" Messages

The obvious response to an "Out of Memory" message is to close an application that is no longer needed. But suppose that you don't want to close anything. There are two other actions you can take to free up system resources to allow your new application to execute successfully:

♦ Close unneeded child windows in an open application. This is similar to my earlier advice to reduce resource drain by minimizing program groups in the Program Manager. All child windows in any application consume extra amounts of memory to support the graphic resources used to support the display of the child windows.

♦ If you have an application that manipulates complex graphics files, close the files. Additionally, you can try switching to simpler graphics formats, if possible.

♦ Convert the application to full-screen mode (by typing Alt+Enter or by choosing Settings in the Control menu).

♦ Free up disk space, then increase the size of the swap file. In 386 enhanced mode, Windows can use disk space to manufacture virtual memory, which can then be used to relieve the burden on actual memory.

♦ Reduce the KB Required setting in the PIF. This could be a setting for conventional, expanded, or extended memory. Or it could be a specification for high MS-DOS memory or video memory.

These solutions will not always enable your application to work. If your PIF says that the application must have access to high MS-DOS memory and none is available (perhaps because of a network that was started before Windows), you will be unable to run the application.

There is a limit to the number of programs that can be running simultaneously. If, for instance, you've run out of conventional and extended memory, and certain memory areas are locked from use, Windows may not be able to construct a new virtual machine for yet another non-Windows application.

If this is the case, you will be unable to start that application until one or more currently running applications are closed.

INSUFFICIENT DISK SPACE

Some problems are caused by both insufficient memory and insufficient disk space. Given that Windows in 386 enhanced mode uses disk space to simulate physical memory, it's not too hard to see the connection. Running out of memory often causes Windows to look for disk space to help with multitasking chores.

The following error messages may be due to either insufficient disk space alone or some combination of limited memory and disk space. You'll have to consider both as a cause unless the error message clarifies it.

♦ "Cannot successfully paste data from the Clipboard." This could be because of limited memory or limited disk space, or it could even be that you are trying to paste incompatible data, such as graphics data into a text-only DOS window.

♦ "Not able to save this file." To save the file, you can free up disk space, close files from other running applications, delete files to increase available disk space, or save the specified file to a different disk.

♦ "Cannot edit a file." Many applications store backup versions of your work in disk files that are deleted after your session, so freeing up disk space is of paramount importance.

♦ MULTITASKING ERROR MESSAGES

Some errors crop up when you are multitasking applications. A communications program, for instance, may have no problems at all unless another program attempts to use the port used by the communications program.

CLIPBOARD ERRORS

Some problems with Clipboard cutting and pasting have to do with available memory and others have to do with actual Clipboard contents. Other problems have to do with the complexities involved with several programs trying to access the Clipboard at the same time. For example, you might receive the message

Cannot copy to the Clipboard

This may simply mean that another application is using the Clipboard. You'll have to wait until it is done before reattempting the copy operation.

You've already seen in this chapter that pasting from the Clipboard can be a problem because of insufficient memory. The Clipboard may also contain data in a format that cannot be processed by your application or by the mode you are running in.

For example, you may not be able to paste data as a bit map. If this is true, you should use the Clipboard Viewer program to verify that the Clipboard contains a bit map. Remember that you cannot paste graphics from the Clipboard into a non-Windows application.

♦ CHECK THE FORMAT OF DATA STORED IN THE CLIPBOARD

Before using the information stored in the Windows Clipboard, you may need to know whether it is stored as text (such as numbers and characters) or as graphics (such as bit maps). To find out, run the Clipboard Viewer program from the Main group in the Program Manager. If you see text, the Text option on the Display pull-down menu will be accessible.

There are a number of other Clipboard error messages, including "Contents of Clipboard too big for available memory." You might copy data to the Clipboard in smaller units.

FILE ACCESS ERRORS

There are many reasons why your application may be denied access to a particular file. The "Access Denied" message usually appears when another application is currently using the file you want to open and the file is locked. There's not much you can do except wait until the other application is finished using the file.

A sharing violation occurs in network and multitasking environments when a file is read-only and an application attempts to write to the file. You'll have to change the file's attributes before continuing, or you'll have to work on a different file.

Sharing violations can also occur if you bring up the PIF Editor when another program is already working on the particular PIF. You'll have to wait until the PIF is free before you can open the file.

NETWORK ERRORS

A network is probably the most complex environment you'll encounter when running Windows. It can be very difficult to obtain a complete picture of what is going on at any specific time on a network.

Any of the following error messages can occur while you are running Windows on a network:

◆ "Unable to connect to network drive." You should check the connections and status of the network drive.

◆ "Cannot find the specified file." You should ensure that the path and file name are correct.

◆ "Please verify security privileges." You may not be privileged to perform the operation (such as creating a directory) that you are attempting.

◆ "This file exists and is read-only." You should use a different file name, or make sure you are accessing the right file.

◆ "Cannot access file." The file may be write-protected. Also, you cannot save a file on a write-protected disk.

Solving Network Transfer Buffer Problems

To transfer data over a network, Windows first stores the information in conventional memory, using an area (known as the *transfer buffer*) of at least 12K. In 386 enhanced mode, the size of this area is controlled by the NetHeapSize setting in the [386Enh] section of SYSTEM.INI. If Windows displays a message that the NetHeapSize is insufficient, you must increase the transfer size by adjusting this entry.

Ask your network administrator what value to use. If no one is sure how large to make the buffer, try adjusting the setting upward by 4K at a time. You must quit and restart Windows for the new buffer setting to take effect. But be aware that every additional 4K you assign to the transfer buffers removes 4K of conventional memory from each of your non-Windows applications while you are connected to the network.

♦ "Create the file?" Your application seemingly wants to create a file on a network drive with Create but no Modify privileges. Is the file worth creating if you won't be able to save any work that you do in your application to that file? At this point, you may want to consult the network administrator.

♦ APPLICATIONS MODIFYING THE SAME DATA FILE

Use the DOS file-sharing utility, SHARE.EXE, to prevent two applications from simultaneously modifying the same disk file. SHARE is usually run from the AUTOEXEC.BAT file.

COMMUNICATIONS ERRORS

Communicating is, along with printing, one of the most common background chores on a Windows system. Some of the most common problems exist because of conflict with other programs. However, many of the following problems are caused solely because of difficulties with hardware or data transmission.

♦ "The COM port is either not supported or is being used by another device." You should select another port.

♦ "No COM ports available." You should release one of the ports that are in use and try again.

♦ "Serial port not initialized." You should check your communication settings and try again.

♦ "Already connected." You should select Hangup from your communications program's menu.

♦ "Emulation selected is not available."

♦ "Timeout if not connected has been reset to the minimum 30 seconds."

♦ "Transfer failed due to unrecognized packet." You should try sending or receiving the file again.

♦ "Transfer failed due to invalid packet number." You should try sending or receiving the file again.

♦ "Transfer failed due to too many retries." You should try sending or receiving the file again.

♦ "Transfer failed because transmission was stopped by sender."

♦ EXCESSIVE COMMUNICATIONS ERRORS

The most common reason for excessive error rates with your communications program is an incorrect baud rate. Usually, the baud rate is set too high for Windows, particularly if there are other background programs running at the same time.

Reduce the baud rate at the remote computer and in the Ports dialog box in the Control Panel. Follow the instructions in your communications software's manual to reset the baud rate, and remember to reset the modem itself to the new rate. You usually have to change switch settings on the modem board.

WARNING: TERMINATION IS A LAST RESORT

In some situations, Windows anticipates that a step that you are about to take will result in severe problems. In those cases, you'll receive a warning box that explains the consequences of what you're about to do. Read the message carefully and then consider whether or not to proceed.

You should typically end non-Windows applications by using the Quit or Exit command. Most applications will prompt you to save any work in progress. At the very least, using a Windows 3.1 termination sequence (such as a local Ctrl+Alt+Del reboot) will not save your modified data. At the very worst, direct termination of an application may result in DOS itself becoming unstable. Windows strongly recommends that you close all applications, exit Windows, and then reboot the machine.

◆ FILE-RELATED ERROR MESSAGES

The majority of file system error messages are the result of simple path-name mistakes.

GENERALIZED FILE ERRORS

Let's first take a look at the simple file messages. For example, a common message is

Cannot find file *xxxxxxxx.yyy* (or one of its components)

Typically, you must make sure that the path and file name are correct and that all required libraries are available. Most of the following messages call for the same sort of checking:

- ◆ "Your disk is full."
- ◆ "File is read only."
- ◆ "File name invalid."

◆ "Invalid filename." In this situation, you usually should check to ensure that the file name has no more than 8 characters, followed by a period and a three-letter extension.

◆ "Cannot open file." Check that the path and file name are correct.

◆ "Cannot read file." Check that the path and file name are correct.

◆ "Invalid settings file; recreate the settings file."

◆ "Cannot close file."

◆ "Cannot print file." Check that the appropriate COM port is connected.

◆ "Cannot find drive and/or directory."

Other file system errors are more subtle and less common, for example,

The specified path points to a file that may not be available during later Windows sessions.

You may receive this message if you specify a path to a file on a removable media device. The file may not be on the medium that happens to be in the drive (if one is even in the drive at all) when the application later requests the file.

Another error may occur when you receive this message:

Cannot make backup copy of this file.

You may get such a message if another file already exists with the same name as the backup name that is being used. You might be asked if you want to replace the existing file. Alternatively, the file system may be unable to make the backup copy because the file is already in use. You might respond by using a new file name or by closing the file in use by another application. Also, there simply may not be enough disk space left on the target drive. You will typically have to delete files to increase available disk space.

OBJECT LINKING AND EMBEDDING (OLE) ERRORS

In practice, a number of unique problems can arise when you try to link multiple programs and documents. (Chapter 5 discusses how OLE works.) Here are some of the most common error messages:

♦ "The linked or embedded objects in this document are not compatible with the document format in the current version of the application." Beware, because the incompatible objects will be altered or deleted when you save the file. You'll be asked whether you want to continue.

♦ "Cannot save object to document." The data associated with the object you're attempting to embed probably exceeds the 64K limit. You will first have to decrease the size of the object if you want to embed it.

♦ "Linked document is unavailable." This might be due to an improper path name, a network connection that has not been established, or a path to a removable media object.

♦ "This document contains links to other documents." These are manual links that are updated only on request. It's up to you to decide when and whether to update the links.

♦ "This selection contains open embedded objects which will be closed or deleted." Have you forgotten about the status of these open objects? Either cancel the file request and properly deal with the embedded objects, or continue with the request and risk losing data.

♦ "This document contains open embedded objects which may need updating." Have you forgotten about the status of these open objects? Cancel the current request and update the open objects before continuing.

♦ "Update open embedded objects before closing or saving?"

♦ "The action cannot be completed because the application needed by the object is busy." You'll have to try again later.

♦ "Cannot process command, server busy." The serving application is currently active performing another task; you'll have to try again later.

♦ "This action cannot be completed." Usually, this is because the application needed by the object is busy. You can try to switch to the object's application and correct the problem.

♦ CLOSING YOUR SHELL PROGRAM

You can open the System menu for your Windows shell (the Program Manager or a replacement) and select Close. Windows interprets this as a request to shut down Windows. Windows sends messages to any running Windows applications. Their responsibility is to notify you of any files to be saved or actions to take before they will end. However, non-Windows applications do not perform these types of chores by themselves. So Windows reminds you that a non-Windows application is active, and you must explicitly switch to it and shut it down normally.

NON-WINDOWS APPLICATIONS ERRORS

If you run DOS applications under Windows, there are a variety of error messages that can appear. If you still run your favorite DOS applications under Windows, this is probably one of the most annoying groups of messages you'll see.

Often, the problem does not even lie with the application as much as it lies with how you've configured the application to run under Windows. In most cases, there is some problem with one of the many settings found in the application's PIF.

For example, you might receive this message:

Start-up directory not found

All this may mean is that you should check the application's PIF to ensure that the initial directory for the application's .EXE is specified correctly.

If a non-Windows application cannot start, you may be unable to read the error message that the application displays. This is because Windows typically closes the non-Windows session as soon as the application ends. An error condition at start-up is usually equivalent to an explicit exit, so Windows interprets this as a normal application termination.

To view an error message that an application displays, remove the check mark from the Close Window on Exit toggle switch in the PIF that controls this application. In this way, Windows will retain the error message on screen in an inactive window. After you've read the message, close the application window and restore the check mark.

Before running Windows, you may have started a TSR. However, Windows knows of certain TSRs that prevent non-Windows applications from running. If this situation occurs, Windows will explicitly name the problem TSR. You'll have to decide between having the TSR continue to be active and having the ability to run some other non-Windows application from within Windows.

◆ CONFLICTS WITH ADVANCED DOS COMMANDS

Certain DOS commands enable you to create the illusion of disk restructuring. Commands like JOIN, SUBST, and APPEND change the appearance of the disk organization and may confuse Windows. Do not use these commands before starting Windows. Be sure to check your AUTOEXEC.BAT file for lines that include these commands.

◆ DEVICE ERROR MESSAGES

Some errors are caused by hardware, not by software. However, to be fair to the hardware designers, some of these errors are really caused by hardware events that were unanticipated by the software designers.

THE "APPLICATION HAS BEEN CRASHED" MESSAGE

If you see an error message that begins with "The Application Has Been Crashed," this means that Windows has placed the blame on a device rather than on the application. Either of the following reasons can account for this situation:

♦ There has been invalid hardware manipulation.

♦ The device responded in an unexpected fashion to the application.

This message has the same impact as an integrity violation. Windows may advise you to close all applications, exit Windows, and reboot your computer. Then, Windows will terminate your application peremptorily. If you're lucky, Windows will only recommend that you save all modified data as soon as possible. That's what you should do immediately.

DEVICE CONFLICT

Device conflict arises in 386 enhanced mode when two or more applications attempt to use the same port. If you've selected the Always Warn button in the Device Contention section of the Control Panel's 386 Enhanced dialog box, Windows will inform you when a second application attempts to use a port that is already in use by a different application. For example:

The LPT? (or COM?) port is currently assigned to a DOS application.

Do you want to reassign the port to Windows?

If you are sure that the previous non-Windows application is finished using the port, you can answer Yes to this query. The Windows application can then use the port. You'll receive a similar message if the non-Windows application later wants to reuse the port.

If you've specified a time lag in the Device Contention portion of the Control Panel's 386 Enhanced dialog box, there may be times when the lag is not sufficient. If so, Windows will still warn you when another application is already using the communication ports. You'll be reminded that the running application might lose characters if you decide to start or restart your application at that time. You'll be given the chance to decide about actually starting the new communications application.

◆ VIDEO ERROR MESSAGES

Your video adapter or monitor may be the cause of many problems.

THE "CANNOT INITIALIZE THE ADAPTER" MESSAGE

Generally, this message appears if an error occurs while you are trying to initialize the VGA adapter. You can press any key to continue and no data is lost. However, this usually occurs because you are trying to run Windows with a driver that requires higher resolution than your hardware adapter can support.

You may also see this message if the Windows 3.1 Super VGA display driver that you've selected does not support the adapter in your system. You should contact the adapter's manufacturer for a driver that works. Until you receive one, you should use the Windows Setup program to select a different display type, such as VGA.

THE "CANNOT FIND NECESSARY FILES" MESSAGE

Certain files are only necessary at certain times. For example, the grabber file WINOLDAP.GRB is only necessary when running a non-Windows application. If your system has trouble finding a grabber file, it may be simply that the needed grabber file is not in the SYSTEM directory. It may also be that you specified a full path name in the [Boot] section of the SYSTEM.INI file, and the 386grabber or 286grabber file name cannot be found in the specified path.

In addition to having occasional difficulties finding a specified file, Windows may also have difficulties opening a specified file. This often occurs when the file is of the wrong type. Most of you are already familiar with what happens if you try to execute an unassociated document file: You get the same result if you try to open a graphic file that turns out not to be in bit-map format:

Please verify that this is a valid bitmap image file.

This is a specific message. The more general message that occurs is

Not able to open this file because the format is not recognized.

If either of these messages is displayed, you may wish to use Windows Paintbrush, or the Paintshop program included on this book's second disk, to load the file. After loading, you'll have a better idea of what the file actually contains. In addition, you can probably convert the file format to the correct one for the application you are using.

THE "CANNOT RUN IN A WINDOW" MESSAGE

In previous versions of Windows, you couldn't run any graphic non-Windows application in a 386 enhanced mode window. This is no longer true. However, not every application can now run in a sizable window. If one can't, you will still encounter the message

This application cannot run in a window due to the way it uses the display; run the application in Full Screen mode.

Typically, this occurs when the application makes specific references to absolute screen coordinates. If you receive this message, you have no choice but to run the application in full-screen mode.

THE "CANNOT SWITCH TO A FULL SCREEN" MESSAGE

Generally, you'll be unable to switch back to full-screen mode when you've started a window-oriented operation that you have not completed. For example, you may have started to mark, copy, paste, or scroll some portion of a DOS window in 386 enhanced mode. These choices are available by selecting Edit from the Control menu.

On the Edit menu, you can select Mark to begin defining a portion of your workspace for copying to the Clipboard. With the mouse, you can click at a starting point, then hold down the left button until the entire region has been highlighted. With the keyboard, you can move the cursor to the starting point, then hold down the Shift key and move the cursor to highlight an area. While the area is being marked, the title bar is labeled with the word *Mark*.

If you select Scroll from the Edit menu, the title bar will include the word *Scroll* until you complete the scrolling operation. While scrolling, you can move the viewport into the workspace by repositioning the slider boxes in the horizontal and vertical scroll bars.

While either Mark or Scroll appears in the title bar, you cannot return to full-screen mode. You must first complete the operation. Marking can be completed in one of several ways:

♦ Press the right mouse button or the Escape key to cancel the marking request.

♦ Select Copy from the Edit menu to make a copy of the selected data in the Clipboard.

Scrolling can be completed in one of two ways: You can press the Enter key or the Escape key. Only then can you return your non-Windows application to full-screen mode by pressing Alt+Enter, or by choosing Full Screen mode from the Settings option on the Control menu.

♦ PRINTING ERROR MESSAGES

Since the early days of DOS computing, printing has been one of the major sources of error messages. Printing under Windows has become more powerful but at the same time, it has become more complex.

PROBLEMS WITH FONT AVAILABILITY

The Printers dialog box in the Control Panel manages many aspects of print output, beginning with the required steps to install a printer driver and connect it to a port. If you use soft fonts or external font cartridges, you will have to copy the fonts to each new port to which you connect a physical device. This requires that you use the Fonts button in the Printer Setup dialog box.

Only then can you be assured that the fonts will be available for output to the combination of a particular port and a printer.

PROBLEMS WITH OBTAINING A PRINTOUT

If you have problems obtaining a printout, the cause can include everything from the printer's being configured incorrectly to the printer's plug being disconnected. Here are some of the major error messages:

- ◆ "Paper width or margin value is set incorrectly." For instance, the width must be a positive integer in the legal range for the configured paper size.

- ◆ "Paper Size and Paper Source are incompatible."

- ◆ "Low on printer memory; page was printed twice."

- ◆ "Too many different fonts on page; unable to print page at all."

- ◆ "Not enough printer memory; unable to print page."

- ◆ "Invalid paper source for the paper size selected. Please change."

- ◆ "The current combination of Paper Size and Paper Source results in zero printable region. Please change."

In each case, choosing the Printers icon in the Control Panel is the easiest way to make adjustments to your printer setup. Don't forget to check that the printer is installed, connected, and powered up.

◆ SETTING THE AVAILABLE PRINTER MEMORY

Windows 3.1 printer drivers now keep track of the amount of memory that is installed in HP LaserJet Series II and III printers. This facility improves the efficiency of spooling to these printers. If your printer has more memory installed than the usual minimum (512K), you must be sure to let Windows know. Select Printers from the Control Panel, select Setup, and enter the correct memory size in the Memory section.

LIMITATIONS ON DOWNLOADED FONTS

As a rule of thumb, Microsoft recommends that the total point size of permanent fonts should add up to no more than 150 points. They say that permanent fonts work best when used for the most common typefaces, such as body text of 9 to 12 points. Hewlett-Packard printers will flash "20" or "out of memory" if you download too many fonts.

A separate issue from printer memory and downloading considerations is the issue of disk space consumed by your font files. Your disk may have enough space for more fonts, but don't forget that this will limit the amount of free space that remains for creating new documents. Consequently, you should just load and retain the fonts you expect to use.

In fact, most printer drivers can only load a limited number of fonts in either landscape or portrait orientation. If you exceed the maximum, you'll have to delete some fonts from your disk. You'll also have to remove fonts that you've installed in Windows.

THE "PRINT MANAGER WON'T PRINT" MESSAGE

The Print Manager offers a number of helpful facilities. Most important, it offers a simple spooling capacity so that your application can carry on with other work while the burden of dealing with the printer falls to the Print Manager. The following messages are some of the ones that you may see while attempting to print:

♦ "Try printing the document again." This message will appear if there are too many jobs already queued for a particular port. You can wait for one or more documents to finish printing, or you can cancel a waiting document.

◆ "Print Manager cannot print to a specified port." The port settings may not match those required by your printer. Use the Printers dialog box in the Control Panel or the Printer Setup command in Print Manager to change the port settings.

◆ "The printer is out of paper or is not connected to your computer." Check the printer cable or network connection to make sure the printer is connected properly, or refresh the paper supply.

◆ "The printer is offline or not selected." Press an online button, or select the printer.

◆ "Too many ports listed under [ports] in the win.ini file."

◆ "Not enough memory for Print Manager."

◆ "The password is not valid." Use the Control Panel to supply the correct password to the network.

◆ "Access to the network device is denied." The network is too busy. Try the operation later.

◆ "The network username is not correct." Use the Control Panel to supply a valid username.

◆ "The network is not running or is incorrectly installed."

◆ "The specified job no longer exists on the network queue." The job may have finished printing or been removed by the network administrator.

◆ MULTIMEDIA ERROR MESSAGES

In Windows 3.1, there are a range of new error messages that pertain solely to the use and misuse of MIDI and sound devices. This section presents the messages you are most likely to encounter. Some problems have to do with the hardware itself, and other problems have to do with your software settings.

CONFIGURATION OR HARDWARE PROBLEMS

Configuration or hardware error messages occur when an application attempts to send instructions to a multimedia device or port whose driver cannot understand the request. In general, you can solve problems that arise from improper device-driver setup by choosing the Drivers icon in the Control Panel to reconfigure the affected driver.

Several possible scenarios might explain the problem and suggest a solution:

♦ Your multimedia adapter card itself must be upgraded before you can use the selected driver.

♦ You must install the necessary driver for the device.

♦ You must replace the current driver with a different one that was designed for this version of Windows.

♦ You have two drivers for the same device installed in your computer. You must remove one of them.

PROBLEMS WITH ACCESSORIES

The two principal new multimedia accessories in Windows 3.1 are the MIDI Mapper and the Sound Recorder. This section discusses some of the most common error situations that can arise.

MIDI Mapper Problems

The MIDI Mapper is a sophisticated multimedia program. Several situations can arise that will prevent this application from executing properly. The error messages include the following:

♦ "Cannot find a valid MIDIMAP.CFG file in the Windows SYSTEM directory." This configuration file is required. You will be asked if you want to create and initialize a new MIDIMAP.CFG file. Answer Yes if you've never created one. Answer No if one already exists; then find it and move it to your Windows SYSTEM directory.

◆ "The current MIDI setup references a device that has not yet been installed."

◆ "The MIDI Mapper is currently in use by another application." While this is true, you will not be allowed to make changes to the current configuration.

◆ "A disk has been specified that is full or non-existent."

◆ "An invalid destination channel has been specified."

◆ "Cannot delete the current MIDI Mapper setup."

◆ "The MIDIMAP.CFG file is READ ONLY."

◆ "Low Memory." Usually, this occurs in response to the needs of a particular operation.

◆ "This format is not supported by the hardware."

◆ "There is no current MIDI map." You'll have to create one.

◆ "The port is busy outputting data." You'll have to wait.

◆ "Current setup contains non-existent device(s)." You'll have to revise the setup to reflect your system configuration accurately.

◆ "Invalid device ID."

◆ "Unknown command or command parameter."

◆ "Hardware error on media device."

◆ "The device is not open or is not known."

◆ "Error loading media device driver." The file you tried to play did not send a valid command to the driver.

◆ "Action not available for this device."

Sound Recorder Problems

The Drivers icon provides access to the MCI Sound waveform drivers. By highlighting the MCI Sound choice in the Drivers dialog box and selecting Setup, you can configure the amount of memory that *mciwave* will use for buffering audio data during playback or recording. Although this amount is 4 seconds of audio, you can increase it to 9 seconds. Be aware that each additional second requires more memory.

In addition, the following errors may crop up during your use of the Sound Recorder:

- ◆ "File format is incorrect or unsupported."
- ◆ "Cannot open waveform output or input device."
- ◆ "Your audio hardware does not support recording."
- ◆ "The file '%s' is not a valid or a supported sound file."
- ◆ "Your audio hardware cannot record into or play back files like the current file." To record, create a new document. To play back, you'll have to select a different file or a different hardware device.

P A R T

Using Applications on the Companion Disks

Part VI contains two chapters that thoroughly describe all the application programs contained on the two disks accompanying this book.

Disk 1 contains the following 17 productivity tools described in Chapter 20:

BackMenu	Pop-up Program Manager replacement
BigDesk	Expands desktop size with large virtual screen
Cachetst	Tests efficiency of cache programs
Chkmodem	Determines available communications connections
Clean (Memory)	Frees up system memory
Clean (Viruses)	Removes computer viruses
Closer	Closes running applications easily
Cpuuse	Displays processing load information
Exitw	Exits Windows quickly
Pkware	Compresses and decompresses other disk files
Run	Runs multiple programs with a single request
Scan	Identifies specific computer viruses

Sysgraph	Graphically displays system loading
Unicom	Communications program
Vshield	Inhibits viruses from entering your system
Wbar	Generates bar codes
Wincheck	Checkbook management

Disk 2 contains the following 20 tools for personalizing Windows, described in Chapter 21:

Address	Manages mailing/phone lists
Apptimer	Launches applications at specified times
Chess	Plays the game of chess
Dirnote	Attaches explanatory notes to listings of disk files
Iconmstr	Edits, views, and manages icons
Klotz	Plays a game similar to Tetris
Metcnvrt	Converts numbers between systems
Mowin	Expands the size of your virtual screen
Paintshp	Picture viewer, editor, and format converter
Quote	Displays pithy quotations
Reminder	Manages personal calendar
SnagIt	Captures and prints screen images
Stop	Exits from Windows rapidly
Taipei	Plays a version of the game of Mah-Jongg
Timefram	Displays time in the topmost window's title bar
Whiskers	Programs your mouse to simulate common keystrokes
Winclock	Screen clock with alarms and timers

Winplay	Plays music files through the PC speaker
Winpost	Displays messages at specified times, for specified operations, or in specified files
Yacht	Plays the game of Yahtzee

Some of these 37 main programs come with auxiliary programs, which are also described in the chapters. Nearly all of the programs come with additional textual information files, also included on the two disks. Most of the text files that accompany the disk's programs are in one of three forms: .WRI, .TXT, or .DOC file formats. These are typically associated with Microsoft Write, Notepad, or Word for Windows. See Chapter 7 if your system does not already connect text files with these extensions to these three common text processing programs. There are other ASCII text files that you will have to process individually, such as README, READ.ME, README.DAT, or READ-ME.PRN. Generally, these files have no embedded control codes and can be read and edited with any word or text processing program.

◆ INSTALLING THE APPLICATIONS

Both disks are in compressed format, so the actual expanded size of the included files is nearly five megabytes. Each disk contains approximately 2.5MB of compressed information.

To install all of the productivity tools described in Chapter 20, you must have approximately 2.5MB of free disk space. Then you can place Disk 1 in a disk drive, change to that drive, and run the Setup1 program from the DOS command prompt. Specify your hard disk as the first parameter.

For example, to install all 2.5MB of the productivity tools from Disk 1 onto drive C, you might place Disk 1 in drive A, then type these two instructions:

A:

SETUP1 C:

Similarly, to install all of the personalization programs described in Chapter 21, you should place Disk 2 in a disk drive, change to that drive, and run the Setup2 program from the DOS command prompt.

The SETUP1.BAT and the SETUP2.BAT batch files control the copying and decompressing of all application programs from a single floppy disk onto your hard disk. Setup1 creates a \Sybex1 directory and separate subdirectories for the productivity tools. Setup2 creates a \Sybex2 directory and separate subdirectories for the Windows personalization programs. After running Setup1 and Setup2, you will find the applications in the following subdirectories on your hard disk:

APPLICATION NAME	INSTALLED IN DIRECTORY
Address	\Sybex2\Address
Apptimer	\Sybex2\Apptimer
BackMenu	\Sybex1\BackMenu
BigDesk	\Sybex1\BigDesk
Cachetst	\Sybex1\Cachetst
Chess	\Sybex2\Chess
Chkmodem	\Sybex1\Chkmodem
Clean (Memory)	\Sybex1\Utl107
Clean (Viruses)	\Sybex1\Vclean
Closer	\Sybex1\Utl107
Cpuuse	\Sybex1\Cpuuse
Dirnote	\Sybex2\Dirnote
Exitw	\Sybex1\Utl107

Iconmstr	\Sybex2\Imstr10
Klotz	\Sybex2\Klotz
Metcnvrt	\Sybex2\Metcnvrt
Mowin	\Sybex2\Morewin
Paintshp	\Sybex2\Paintshp
Pkunzip	\Sybex1\Pkware
Quote	\Sybex2\Quote
Reminder	\Sybex2\Reminder
Run	\Sybex1\Utl107
Scan	\Sybex1\Vscan
SnagIt	\Sybex2\SnagIt
Stop	\Sybex2\Stop
Sysgraph	\Sybex1\Sysgraph
Taipei	\Sybex2\Taipei
Timefram	\Sybex2\Timefram
Unicom	\Sybex1\Unicom
Vshield	\Sybex1\Vshield
Wbar	\Sybex1\Barcodes
Whiskers	\Sybex2\Whiskers
Wincheck	\Sybex1\Wincheck
Winclock	\Sybex2\Winclock
Winplay	\Sybex2\Music
Winpost	\Sybex2\Winpost
Yacht	\Sybex2\Yacht

It is probably best to scan Chapters 20 and 21 first to decide which applications you wish to install on your disk. To selectively copy and decompress the application programs, you must create a target directory, copy the appropriate zip file into it, then use the PKUNZIP.EXE program to decompress that one application. Each disk contains a copy of PKUNZIP.EXE for your convenience. Each application listed in the preceding table is compressed into a zip file whose name is the same as the subdirectory used to store the expanded files.

For instance, the REMINDER.EXE program and its support files are zipped up in a file named REMINDER.ZIP. To install just this one application onto your C drive in a directory called Reminder, you would perform these steps:

1. Place Disk 2 into drive A.

2. Create a Reminder directory on drive C:

   C:
   MD \REMINDER

3. Copy the zip file into that directory:

   COPY A:REMINDER.ZIP C:\REMINDER

4. Change to that directory and run the PKUNZIP.EXE program:

   C:
   CD \REMINDER
   A:PKUNZIP C:\REMINDER\REMINDER.ZIP

After copying and decompressing one or more applications, you can recover space by erasing the .ZIP file from your hard drive for that application. Do not erase the original .ZIP file from the book's disks. The Setup1 and Setup2 batch files automatically copy and decompress, then erase from your hard drive, all zip files from their respective disks.

There may still be a separate procedure to follow if you want to install the application into the Program Manager environment. You should read the appropriate documentation in Chapters 20 and 21, as well as the text files accompanying each application, for instructions about installing the application into your Windows environment. Naturally, in all cases you can run any of the applications directly by using the File Run pull-down choice in the Program Manager.

The disks that accompany the book are 5¼" versions. Instructions for obtaining 3½" versions can be found on the disk envelope. The installation procedure for these 3½" versions is the same as for the 5¼" disks.

◆ SHAREWARE AND FREEWARE

Most applications on these disks are shareware, although some of the programs are freeware and others are demonstration versions of commercial products. The documentation that accompanies each application explains each product fully. If a product is commercial, it is typically sold in stores or mail order for a fixed price. The package contains a license to use the product, usually on a single computer, and has accompanying documentation.

Freeware programs have virtually no strings attached. They usually offer no restrictions on noncommercial use, although the author still retains his ownership (copyright) to the program itself. Documentation is usually minimal. Public domain software is the extreme example of freeware that is simply offered to the world with no restrictions on use of any sort, including repackaging or rewriting as a commercial product.

Shareware is a distribution method, not a type of software. Shareware products are often offered to the public in their complete, unrestricted form at no initial charge. Shareware distribution gives users a chance to try software before buying it, providing the ultimate money-back guarantee—if you don't use the product, you don't pay for it. If you try a shareware program and continue using it, you are expected to register. Individual programs differ on registration details—some politely request registration, while others require it through some programming mechanism, such as a maximum trial period after which the program will no longer operate. A common technique for encouraging registration is to display a dialog box that reminds you that you haven't yet registered the program, causing some users to dub shareware *nagware*.

After registration, you may receive the simple right to continue using the software, or you may receive an updated program with a printed manual, or you may even receive the right to free access to the author's bulletin board system, which provides free future upgrades. If your shareware product uses the dialog box reminder to register, registration usually includes receipt of a number that will disable the reminder.

Copyright laws apply to both shareware and commercial software, and the copyright holder retains all rights, with a few specific exceptions as stated below. Shareware authors are often accomplished programmers, just like commercial authors, and the programs are of comparable quality. (In both cases, there are good programs and bad ones!) The main difference is in the method of distribution. The author specifically grants the right to copy and distribute the software, either to all and sundry or to a specific group. For example, some authors require written permission before a commercial disk vendor may copy their shareware.

Nonregistered users of the shareware included with this book are typically granted a limited license to make an evaluation copy for trial use. You should use this copy to determine whether the program is suitable and desirable for continued use. At the end of this trial period, you should either register your copy or discontinue using the program.

C H A P T E R

20

Productivity Tools

◆

♦ THE BACKMENU PROGRAM

OVERVIEW

BackMenu (see Figure 20.1) is a program that allows you to define a pop-up menu on the Windows 3.0 background and use it to quickly run applications and tools. It is currently bundled with a program called BigDesk; together, they are called BackDesk. The idea for BackMenu came from using X-Windows and SunView, where the user has a root menu that can be configured.

BackMenu allows you to describe a set of actions and associate command lines with them. To bring up the menu, simply click with the mouse button (left, middle, or right) on the Windows desktop. This will bring up the description list. Selecting a description will cause the appropriate command line to be executed.

USING THE PROGRAM

You can start BackMenu either from the Run... dialog box of the Program or File Manager or by clicking on the BackMenu icon that was installed in its own program group during this book's installation sequence. A pretty box will appear in the middle of the screen along with a picture of a watch with the second hand ticking. After that, absolutely nothing!

Now move the mouse pointer to somewhere on the desktop background (outside of an application window) and click the *right* mouse button. A menu will pop up on your screen. Select any application from the menu. That's all you really need to know, but if you want to alter the contents of the menu, you can edit the configuration file BackMenu uses (this can be done with Notepad or any other text processor).

Modifying the Configuration File

By default, BackMenu looks for a file called BACKMENU.INI in the same directory as BACKMENU.EXE. The syntax for a menu item in the configuration file is

item description, application, optional start-up directory

Blank lines can be placed between items to create a line space in the menu. For example:

Wordprocessing, Write, C:\WORK

Spreadsheet, Excel, C:\WINDOWS\EXCEL\EXCEL

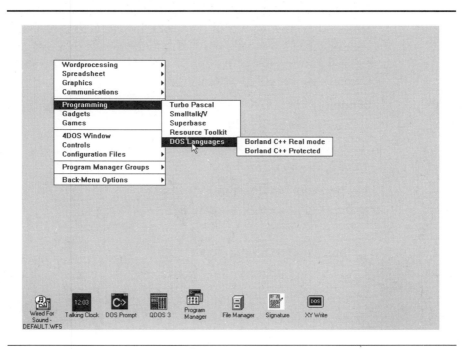

FIGURE 20.1: The BackMenu program

> **Program Manager Groups, $Groups**
>
> **>BackMenu Options**
>
> **About..., $About**
>
> **Edit Menu, NOTEPAD.EXE, C:\WINDOWS\BACKMENU.INI**
>
>
> **Exit Windows, $ExitWindows NoConfirm**
>
> **!**

BackMenu also supports cascading menus. A cascading menu item is one that has multiple options associated with it. By clicking on the item, another menu appears with the options on it. It is even possible to have further cascading menus associated with one or more items within that menu.

The submenu is enclosed between a greater-than sign and an exclamation point. The text that follows the greater-than sign is the text to appear in the menu (a description of the submenu).

In the above example, "BackMenu Options" will appear in the menu, and when clicked upon will produce a submenu with the items defined. Defining items within a submenu is done in exactly the same way as for a main menu (even to the extent of adding a submenu to this submenu). For example:

> **>Editors**
>
> **Andy's editor, AE.EXE**
>
> **Notepad, NOTEPAD.EXE**
>
> **>Word processors**
>
> **Word for Windows, WORD.EXE**
>
> **Windows Write, WRITE.EXE**
>
> **!**
>
> **Multi-Pad, MULTIPAD.EXE**
>
> **!**
>
> ...

There is no limit to the number of items you can have in any particular menu.

Using BackMenu as the Start-Up Shell

BackMenu can be used in place of Program Manager as the default shell for Windows. To install it, simply edit SYSTEM.INI in the Windows directory. In the [boot] section of the file, replace the usual line that reads

SHELL=PROGMAN.EXE

with the line

SHELL=BACKMENU.EXE

Occasionally, other installation routines will reset this shell line back to the Program Manager setting. Also, some installation routines expect the Program Manager to be running. If this is the case, just start a copy of PROGMAN.EXE before beginning the installation.

Once you've installed BackMenu as the Windows shell, you can customize your operations in a number of ways. For example, the choice of which mouse button to use dramatically changes the way BackMenu "feels." If the left mouse button is chosen, the menu pops up when the button is pressed and disappears as soon as the button is released. With the right mouse button the menu remains on screen until a bottom-level selection is made, regardless of how many times the right button is pressed.

BackMenu also supports the middle mouse button. If you choose this and find that BackMenu no longer functions, take the following steps:

1. Exit Windows, or reset if BackMenu is installed as the shell.

2. Edit WIN.INI in the Windows directory.

3. Find the line that has [BackMenu] on it. Below this is the line Button=Middle. Change this to Button=Left or Button=Right.

BackMenu now allows simple ambiguous file names as command line parameters to programs. If BackMenu finds an ambiguous file name, it prompts you for a choice with a dialog box. The path and file name are substituted into the command line. If abort is chosen, the application is not started. For example:

Word, C:\WORD\WINWORD.EXE *.DOC

In this case, paths cannot be specified, and the command line can contain only the ambiguous file name.

It is also possible to make BackMenu prompt you for a command line, which is then passed to the relevant program. To do this, place a percent sign after the program name in the menu file:

Excel, C:\EXCEL\EXCEL.EXE %

BackMenu will bring up a dialog box, which will allow the command line parameters to be typed. Anything following the % will be placed in the dialog box for editing.

BackMenu has the ability to read Program Manager group files and provide the items and groups as a pull-right menu. If you create a menu item with the keyword $Groups, BackMenu will insert a pull-right menu containing all the Program Manager groups. Pulling right on a particular group will give a list of the programs within that group.

The $CallDLL option is a powerful hook through which you can extend functionality of BackMenu. Programmers can write a DLL that performs some function, and have the DLL executed through BackMenu. Parameters are passed to the function in the form of a string, as this allows the most flexible way to pass parameters of different type. The % and * characters can be used to prompt for a parameter or get a file name from a list.

The BackMenu DLL (BACKMLIB.DLL) contains a function that allows the menu to be popped up remotely. The function is called ActivateBackMenu() and takes no parameters. By calling this function it is possible for other applications to cause the background menu to be displayed.

WINCOM.DLL is a DLL that provides standard dialog box functions for Windows applications. If you already have WINCOM.DLL from another application, BackMenu will use that version.

◆ THE BIGDESK PROGRAM

OVERVIEW

Imagine that you had nine monitors attached to your computer, all hidden behind a wall. Imagine a one-screen-sized hole in the wall. Now imagine that you can move the hole to look at any of the screens or even at parts of several of them. That unique ability to expand the size of your desktop is what Big-Desk (see Figure 20.2) offers you.

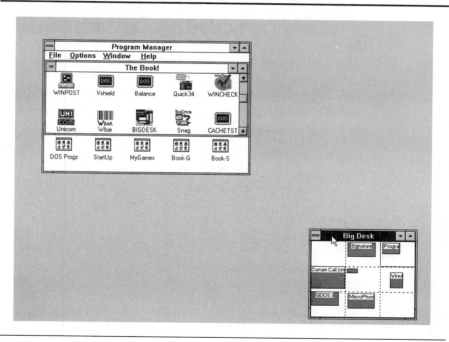

FIGURE 20.2: The BigDesk program

In order to use BigDesk to the maximum, you should use its companion program BackMenu. The two programs are now bundled together as the shareware package BackDesk. Together, they can provide you with a pop-up program menu on each of these "virtual" screens.

USING THE PROGRAM

One of the best things about Windows is that you can run several programs at once. The only real problem with this is that the screen gets awfully cluttered. BigDesk offers a solution to this problem.

There are many features to this program beyond simply offering a larger virtual desktop. In this version, you can use a computer-aided design tool called *grid snap*. When you click on the map or icon, BigDesk tries its best to keep the screen within grid boundaries. The grid does not constrain you when you are dragging things around, however. This gives the effect of having lots of separate screens.

Individual windows can be dragged around the map to other areas of the virtual desktop. The desktop size is configurable up to 8×8 times the size of the screen—you can have up to 64 screens. The map window is scalable and can also be maximized.

BigDesk keeps track of task switches, such as pressing Alt+Esc to switch between programs. It makes sure all the edges of the new window are on the screen, unless you've got grid snap enabled (see below). There is also an option to allow the BigDesk map or icon to always stay on top of the stack of windows.

BigDesk remembers its position between sessions. You can save this position at any time, or BigDesk will save it when the application is closed.

To run the program, click on the BigDesk icon in the installed Program Manager group, or use the Run command to invoke it directly. An icon will appear at the bottom of your screen; it will look like a tic-tac-toe grid. This grid represents the number of virtual screens available to you; it starts out as nine screens. Double-click on the icon, and a window will appear in the lower-right corner of your screen that contains a larger 3×3 grid in its work area.

Understanding Mouse Operations

There are several different operations that can be performed with the mouse. First, you can choose a new virtual screen at any time. You can do this by clicking on the desired virtual screen with the right mouse button. These selection clicks work on either the larger window map or the minimized icon.

To move anywhere on the BigDesk desktop, drag the mouse pointer with the right button. When you click and release the right mouse button, one of the virtual screens is selected. By default, these screens are aligned with the desktop grid. However, you can disable this alignment by turning off the Snap Desktop to Grid option. If grid snap is enabled, the selected virtual screen will be centered on the point on the map where you click. This option is discussed further below.

You are not constrained to precise alignment. If you click the right mouse button and keep the button pressed down, you can drag a small outline box around the virtual desktop. When you release the right mouse button, the outline box remains positioned in the icon or BigDesk window. This reminds you of where you are in the larger virtual desktop; the appearance of the screen windows and icons is readjusted according to the portion of this larger desktop that you are now viewing.

Manipulating Application Windows

These operations only work on the map. To activate a particular application window from the BigDesk map window, you need only double-click the left mouse button on the box representing the window.

To activate an iconized application, you must double-click the left mouse button on the box representing the icon.

Moving a window around the BigDesk desktop is possible only from the map, not from the icon. To move an application window or icon to another place on the virtual desktop, drag the box representing the window using the left mouse button.

It's a good idea to add BigDesk to your Backmenu. Even if BigDesk has already been run, subsequent invocations just activate the existing BigDesk display.

◆ THE CACHETST PROGRAM

OVERVIEW

The Cachetst program (see Figure 20.3) runs a demanding test of an existing software cache. Cachetst evolved as a response to the growing number of cache programs that all claim to be the fastest. You may have heard about different manufacturers suggesting that their product is better than SmartDrive, and perhaps better than their other competition as well. How can a person tell which product to use?

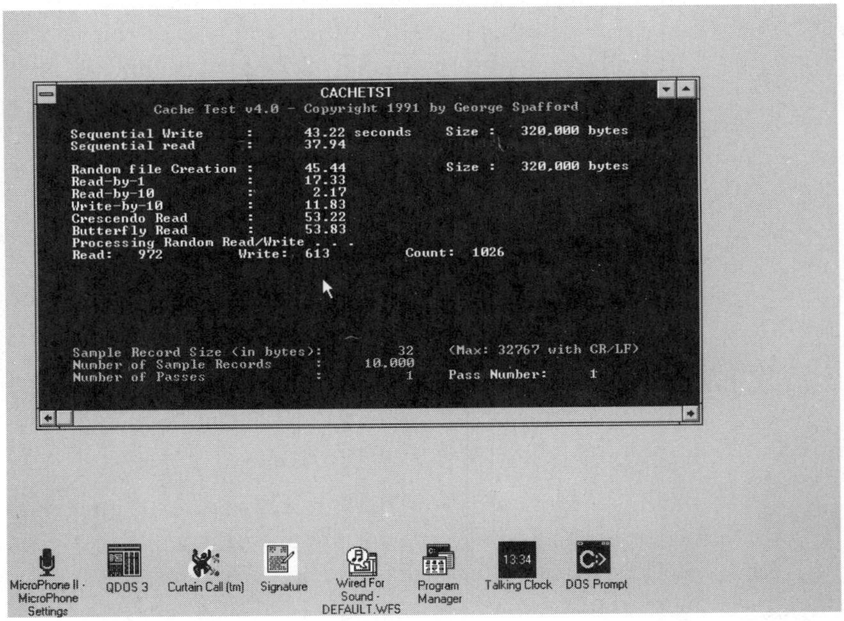

FIGURE 20.3: The Cachetst program

Running Cachetst will enable you to obtain some personal results before and after testing any cache program that you acquire for your system. Many people turn to cache programs to speed up their favorite disk-intensive application program. You can turn to CT.EXE to determine which of the available cache programs will work best in your environment.

USING THE PROGRAM

Cachetst, as it stands in version 4.0, is really just the combination of two basic file formats—sequential and random access. The timing process is actually more intricate than the disk-based processes.

The timing routine uses the 8086-class processor's clock tick as a metering device. This clock signal occurs 18.2 times per second. The Cachetst internal routines watch for this byte to change, whereupon a counter holding the byte count is incremented by one. Once the routine has completed and a score is required, the counter is divided by 18.2 to return the number of elapsed seconds.

No cache program is best in all circumstances. There are so many variables affecting cache performance that a user is best advised to try the comparison themselves. Many variables affect software caches. Some of the most obvious are:

Processor type

Memory speed

Type of memory used

Base hard-drive speed

Memory-resident software

If you're looking for powerful cache programs as an alternative to Microsoft's SMARTDrive, take a look at the latest version of the Norton Utilities, HyperDisk, or Vcache.

Operating Details of the Cachetst Program

This program is designed to help a user evaluate the impacts of a cache, or the changes to an existing cache, on a drive's performance. The test file (TEST$$CT.SPD) is written in the root directory of the target drive. If you ever see this file, don't be concerned. Cachetst usually deletes it at the end of a test. It remains only if you interrupt a test before completion.

With users increasingly using caches during a variety of tasks, it is important to find the optimal cache settings given the task at hand. Whereas a word processor might use sequential files heavily, a database might make heavy use of random access files. With this in mind, the memory requirements, sectors cached, write delays, and so forth have many possible variations.

By default, Cachetst creates a 10,000-record sequential file using 32-byte records and then a 10,000-record random access file that again uses 32-byte record lengths. Even if the default is changed, any sample string length will be increased by two bytes by the addition of a CR/LF. You may want to compensate accordingly if you wish to be exact in your measurements. The sample record-size indicator displays the TRUE sample string size.

This program uses BIOS to do all of its reads and writes, so any hardware or software cache should be able to get some good "hits." In an attempt to flush caches during the test, files are frequently opened and closed.

All of the times that this program writes are the result of subtracting the beginning time from the ending time. It's nothing fancy, so the values are relatively accurate. Note that if you do some math to compute access times per record, you will run into the age-old problem of significant digits. This program accounts for only one decimal position (0.1). As such, if you try to take the timings out to $\frac{1}{100}$th of a second, the resulting error factor can be quite high, relatively speaking.

Remember, if an outcome is in doubt, use a larger sample size! That is to say, increase the number of bytes that are written to the disk. The other alternative is to increase the number of sample passes. You'll notice that results begin to stabilize with file sizes of 5000 records, 32 bytes, and 5 passes.

Using the Command-Line Parameters

This is a non-Windows application, so you can invoke it from a command prompt or run it from the Program Manager. In this case, Windows will initiate a DOS session and automatically run CT.EXE from the command prompt.

The syntax for running the program is

CT </D:d><F:bbb></N:nnn></B></R></S></W></?>

With no parameters specified, Cachetst will test the active drive with the default record length of 32 bytes and 10,000 records. The switches have the following meanings:

/D:d	This specifies "d" as the drive to be tested. You must have at least 1.3MB available on this drive for Cachetst to be able to create all the required data.
/F:b	This specifies the number of fixed bytes per record. It must be between 1 and 32,765. The default is 32 bytes. Use this with the /N:n switch to enhance your testing. (Because of CR/LF usage in the file structure, the logical limit for a user input is 32,765 and not the allowable 32,767.)
/N:n	This specifies the number of test records. Note, the only limitation here is the available space on your test drive. You can also go as small as you want, but you will reach a point where your test will lose its validity. The default value, if this switch is not used, is 10,000 records.
/P:ppp	This specifies the number of test passes; that is, the number of times the test will repeat. If this option is greater than 1, then when the passes have all completed, a summary screen appears with average sequential, random, and total times. If there is only one pass, the summary screen will not be displayed.
/B	Test both sequential and random access records.
/R	Test random access records only.

/S	Test sequential access records only.
/W	Wait after each screen (pause).
/?	Display a registration screen.

Here are some suggestions for making the most effective use of the Cachetst program:

1. Set up a batch file that purges your cache before CT.EXE is run. This will allow the cache to have a little fairer test, as opposed to starting out partially full.

2. If you are interested in the actual hits on your cache, most cache programs have status switches that allow you to see the results from the cache's point of view.

◆ THE CHKMODEM PROGRAM

OVERVIEW

Chkmodem (see Figure 20.4) is a utility that checks either internal serial ports 1–4 or a designated port address and interrupt for the existence and response of a modem. The program is quite useful in determining the serial port to which the modem is attached. Chkmodem also determines whether the modem responds as required to Carrier Detect and Data Terminal Ready changes, as well as the minimum and maximum baud rates at which the modem will respond to commands.

USING THE PROGRAM

This program is a non-Windows application that can be run either from a command prompt or from the Run command in the Program Manager. To start the program from a command prompt, simply type CHKMODEM.

In its default state the program will check serial ports 1 through 4 with these specifications:

Com port:	COM1	COM2	COM3	COM4
Address:	3F8H	2F8H	3E8H	2E8H
Interrupt:	4	3	4	3
Hand shake:	NONE	NONE	NONE	NONE

Chkmodem sends an initialization string to each port. A response of OK is considered a confirmation. You can bypass the default settings by naming a configuration file for Chkmodem on the command line. The command

CHKMODEM @MODEM.DAT

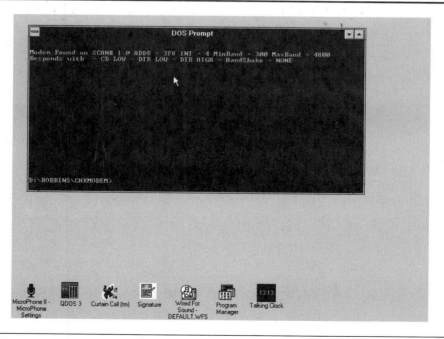

FIGURE 20.4: The Chkmodem program

will cause the program to look for a file named MODEM.DAT in the current directory on the current drive. The configuration file must have the following layout:

hex addrs; send command; expected result; hand shaking;

These four parameters have the following meanings:

Hex addrs	The hexadecimal address of the port
Send command	The modem command that is sent to the port
Expected result	The desired response from the port
Hand shaking	The type of synchronization protocol

Note that each of the four parameters is delimited by a required semicolon. For example, the default MODEM.DAT file contains the following four lines:

2F8;3;AT;OK;NONE;

2F8;3;AT;OK;XON/XOFF;

2F8;3;AT;OK;CTS;

2F8;3;AT;OK;CTS/XON/XOFF;

You can interpret this set of configuration commands as follows. The port at 2F8 Hex and interrupt 3 will be sent the message "AT" in each of the four tests. Each test merely changes the hand-shaking protocol, but expects the same OK result regardless of whether the hand shaking is NONE, XON/XOFF, CTS, or CTS/XON/XOFF.

Each time the serial port is checked, the program tries to get a response from the modem at 300, 1200, 2400, 4800, 9600, 19200, 38400, and 57600 baud. The program will report the slowest and fastest baud rates accepted by the modem.

The modem is also checked with Carrier Detect and Data Terminal Ready lines enabled and disabled. Note that with this version of Chkmodem, it is possible to redirect the program's output to a printer or file. You can use the DOS piping facility when starting the program to direct the output to any DOS device. For example, the command

CHKMODEM > RESULT.TXT

will cause the program's output to be routed to a file called RESULT.TXT. The command

CHKMODEM @MODEM.DAT > LPT1:

will cause the program to use configuration file MODEM.DAT and route output to the printer connected to LPT1.

You should be careful to allow the program to complete normally, since the program does grab interrupt vectors. Your computer may lock up the next time you try to use the same interrupt if you exit abruptly before completion and normal restoration of the internal interrupt chain.

If you do not exit the Chkmodem program normally and you have a serial mouse or serial printer, you may have to reboot your system in order to restore the normal actions of these devices.

◆ THE CLEAN PROGRAM (MEMORY)

One of the four programs on the disk from Dragon's Eye Software Company (the others are Closer, Exitw, and Run), Clean will increase your available memory under Windows. Just use the Program Manager or the File Manager to run Clean, and it cleans the Clipboard, globally compacts memory, and returns. It doesn't display any window at all. You can pull down the Help About choice before and after running Clean to discover how much Windows memory was freed up. Just note the entry that displays KB Free Memory. Since this program does not perform any otherwise visible task, you can test it on your system after a particularly busy session. Alternatively, you can just note the available memory, press the PrintScreen key, and note the available memory again. After running Clean, the memory taken up by contents of the Clipboard (the screen image) should have been returned to Windows for other uses.

◆ THE CLEAN PROGRAM (VIRUSES)

OVERVIEW

CLEAN.EXE (see Figure 20.5) is a virus disinfection program for IBM PC and compatible computers. Clean will search through the partition table, boot sector, or files of a PC and remove the virus specified by the user. In most instances Clean is able to repair the infected area of the system and restore it to normal usage. Clean works on all viruses identified by the current version of the Viruscan (Scan) program. Clean runs on any PC with 256KB and DOS 2.00 or above.

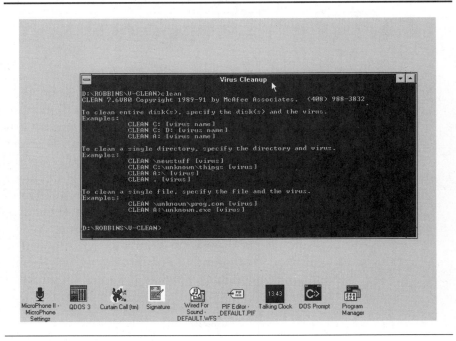

FIGURE 20.5: The Clean program

USING THE PROGRAM

Clean runs a self-test when executed. If Clean has been modified in any way, a warning will be displayed. It is always possible that a crafty new virus program will attempt to subvert your virus management utilities (Clean and Scan) themselves. If Clean reports that it has been damaged after future disk work, you should obtain a new, clean copy. The best advice for future clean-up operations is to make a copy of the CLEAN.EXE program on a disk, then write-protect the disk. Subsequently, you can run the Clean program from this write-protected disk to prevent infection of the program itself.

Authenticating the Validity of Clean Itself

Clean is packaged with the Validate program to ensure the integrity of the CLEAN.EXE file. You can also use this program to check other programs for signs of tampering. Validate uses two discrete methods to generate cyclic redundancy checks (CRCs). The results are then displayed for the user to compare against the known value for the program(s) validated. The known validation data can be published by the author of the program or obtained from a trusted information database. The dual CRC checking provides a high degree of security.

The Computer Virus Industry Association (CVIA) provides an online database of validation values for shareware authors at no cost. You are encouraged to call the CVIA's BBS at (408) 988-4004 to access current validation data for McAfee Associates' Clean and Scan, California Software Concepts' Shez, Vern Berg's List, and other shareware programs.

If the validation data produced by Validate matches the data published by the program author or obtained from a trusted database, it is highly improbable (less than one in sixty-four quadrillion) that the program has been modified.

To run Validate, type

VALIDATE D:\PATH\FILENAME.EXT

The validation results for Version 80 of CLEAN.EXE should be as follows:

Size: 119,999

Date: 06-24-1991

File Authentication

Check Method 1: F8AE

Check Method 2: 05DD

If your copy of CLEAN.EXE differs, it may have been modified. The latest version of Clean can always be obtained from the McAfee Associates' bulletin board system at (408) 988-4004.

The validation results for VALIDATE.COM itself are:

With CRC Checking: Size is 6495

Without CRC Checking: Size is 6485

Date: 10-31-1989

File Authentication

Check Method 1: 4637 CB21

Check Method 2: 1214 13B7

If you have an older version of Validate, it may be ten bytes shorter. This is because it was not processed by Scan's CRC-checking feature, added in Version 66 of Scan. The validation code can be removed from VALIDATE.COM by running Scan against it with the /RV remove validation option. However, this is not recommended.

New Virus Protections

If you are concerned about virus contamination of your system, you should register your version of Clean and endeavor to obtain the latest release. For example, this release includes protection from the Loa Duong, Michelangelo, Tequila, V801, Form, Empire, and Nomenclature viruses. In each case, the /Report option now displays version number, options used, date and time, and cleaning results.

◆ AN IMPORTANT WARNING ABOUT THE STONED VIRUS

Removing the Stoned virus can cause loss of the partition table on systems with nonstandardly formatted hard disks. As a precaution, back

> up all critical data before running Clean. Loss of the partition table can result in the loss of all data on the disk!

The Loa Duong virus is a memory-resident floppy-disk and hard-disk boot-sector infector. It is named after the Laotian funeral dirge it plays after every 128 disk accesses.

The Michelangelo virus is a floppy-disk boot-sector and hard-disk partition-table infector based on the Stoned virus. On March 6, Michelangelo's birthdate, it formats the hard disk of infected PCs.

The Tequila virus originated in Switzerland. It is a memory-resident multipartite virus that uses stealth techniques and attaches to the boot sector of floppies, the partition table of hard disks, and .EXE files. It contains messages saying "Welcome to T.TEQUILA's latest production.", "Loving thoughts to L.I.N.D.A", and "BEER and TEQUILA forever!".

The Telephonica virus is a memory-resident multipartite virus that infects the boot sectors of floppy disks, the hard-disk partition table, and .COM files. The virus infects .COM files at about 15-minute intervals, and keeps a counter of the number of reboots that have occurred. When 400 reboots have occurred, the virus displays the message "VIRUS ANTITELEFONICA (BARCELONA)" and formats the hard disk. The virus has been reported at multiple sites in Spain and England.

The V801, Form, Empire, and Nomenclature viruses are older viruses that have been reported with increasing regularity in Canada and England.

Your program group contains a VIRLIST.TXT text file, which includes a detailed listing of the latest viruses and their characteristics.

How Viruses Work

Hundreds of viruses and variants of them have been identified as of this date, and creative computer science people all over the world continue to create them. Read the VIRLIST.TXT file for information about each of them. Some are destructive, some are just humorous, while others are just annoying. Each uses one of a variety of techniques:

- ◆ Infects hard-disk partition table
- ◆ Infects hard-disk boot sector
- ◆ Infects floppy-disk boot
- ◆ Infects overlay files
- ◆ Infects .EXE files
- ◆ Infects .COM files
- ◆ Infects COMMAND.COM
- ◆ Installs itself in memory
- ◆ Uses self-encryption
- ◆ Uses stealth techniques

One of the identifiable characteristics of each virus may be an increase in the infected program's size. Many viruses attach themselves surreptitiously to your COMMAND.COM file. In all applicable cases, the VIRLIST.TXT file lists the size increase for each virus. In addition, this file identifies other invasive characteristics of each virus.

For example, sometimes the virus does not attach to files but simply wreaks some havoc with your system. In other cases, the virus does attach itself to the file (but to the tag-end of it) but does not change file's size. Still again, some viruses overwrite the beginning of the infected file, so no file-size change can be noted.

◆ **VIRUSES CAN BE TRICKY WITH OVERLAY FILES**

Sometimes viruses that infect .EXE files cannot be removed successfully. This usually occurs when the .EXE file loads internal overlays. Instead of attaching to the end of the .EXE file, the virus attaches to the beginning of the overlay area, and program instructions are overwritten.

> Clean will truncate files infected in this manner. If a file no longer runs after being cleaned, replace it from the manufacturer's original disk.

The best thing that can be said about viruses is that they demonstrate creativity on the part of the authors. The damage can take several forms:

♦ Boot sector is corrupted or overwritten.

♦ Data files are corrupted.

♦ All or part of the disk is formatted or overwritten.

♦ File linkage is directly or indirectly corrupted.

♦ System run-time operation is affected.

♦ Program or overlay files are corrupted.

In most cases, the Clean program can disinfect your system of an attacking virus. In some cases, you will have to use the Scan program also included on Disk 1. Running Scan with the /D option will overwrite and then delete the entire infected program. The program must then be replaced from the original program disk.

Safely Running the Clean Program

Clean searches the system looking for the virus you wish to remove. When an infected file is found, Clean isolates and removes the virus, and in most cases repairs the infected file and restores it to normal operation. If the file is infected with a less common virus, Clean will display a warning message asking the user whether it should overwrite and delete the infected file. Files erased in this way are nonrecoverable.

You should verify the suspect virus infection with the Scan program before running Clean. Scan will locate and identify the virus and provide the I.D. code needed to remove it. The I.D. is displayed inside the square brackets [and]. For example, the I.D. code for the Jerusalem virus is displayed as "[Jeru]". This I.D. must be used with Clean to remove the virus. The square brackets must be included.

You should first power-down the infected system and boot from a clean, write-protected system disk. This step will ensure that the virus is not in control of the computer and will prevent reinfection. After cleaning, power-down the system again, reboot from the system disk, and run the Scan program to make sure the system has been succesfully disinfected.

After cleaning the hard disk, remember to also run the Scan program on any floppies that may have been inserted into the infected system. In this way, you can determine if they also have been infected. Clean will display the name of the infected file and the virus found in it, and report a successful disinfection when the virus is removed.

If a file has been infected multiple times by a virus, Clean will report that the virus has been removed successfully for each infection. Multiple infections are possible if the virus does not check whether it has already infected a file.

The syntax for running Clean is

CLEAN d1: ... d10: [virus ID] /A /E .xxx /FR /MANY /M

/REPORT d:filename /NOPAUSE

The first argument indicates the drives to be cleaned. The second argument is the virus identification code, provided by the Scan program when it detects a virus. The possible options are:

/A	Examine all files for viruses. This should be used if an overlay-infecting virus is detected.
/E .xxx .yyy .zzz	Clean overlay extensions .xxx .yyy .zzz. Extensions must be separated by a space after the /E and between each other. Up to three extensions can be added with this option. For more extensions, use the /A option.
/FR	Display messages in French.

/MANY	Check and disinfect multiple floppies. If the user has more than one floppy disk to check for viruses, this option allows you to check them without having to run Clean multiple times.
/NOPAUSE	Disables the "More…" prompt that appears when Clean fills a screen with data. This allows Clean to run on a machine with multiple infections without requiring operator intervention when the screen fills up with messages from the Clean program.
/REPORT d:filename	The /REPORT option is used to generate a listing of disinfected files. The resulting list can be saved to disk as an ASCII text file. To use the report option, specify /REPORT on the command line, followed by the device and file name.

Here are some sample command lines:

CLEAN C: D: E: [JERU] /A

This will disinfect drives C, D, and E of the Jerusalem virus, searching all files for the virus in the process.

CLEAN A: [STONED]

This will disinfect the floppy disk in drive A of the Stoned virus.

CLEAN C:\MORGAN [DAV] /A

This will disinfect the MORGAN subdirectory on drive C of the Dark Avenger virus, searching all files for the virus in the process.

CLEAN B: [DOODLE] /REPORT C:YNKINFCT.TXT /A

This will disinfect the floppy disk in drive B of the Yankee Doodle virus, searching all files in the process, and creating a report of disinfected files named YNKINFCT.TXT on drive C.

◆ THE CLOSER PROGRAM

CLOSER.EXE (see Figure 20.6) is a small program whose sole purpose is to close other windows. To run it, just copy the CLOSER.EXE file to your Windows directory and then double-click on it. A menu appears with a list of currently open windows (including Closer). You can then select any program with the mouse and close it by selecting the Close Program button. Closer takes less than 8K of memory while running.

Closer now deselects any current selections in the list box when the focus moves to another window. This was done so that if you open another application you don't have to worry about closing the wrong window when returning to Closer. A radio button in Closer enables you to force Closer to update the application list box. Closer does not always update the list box correctly when an application is closed and Closer later regains the input focus.

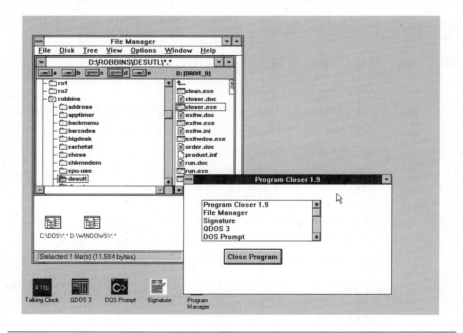

FIGURE 20.6: The Closer program

◆ THE CPUUSE PROGRAM

OVERVIEW

The Cpuuse program (see Figure 20.7) provides you with a CPU Usage meter. This utility program keeps track of how much of your CPU's time is being used while you're in Windows. When you run it, an icon will appear at the bottom of your screen, in which you'll see a number representing the percentage of CPU time being utilized. This number will be updated approximately every three seconds.

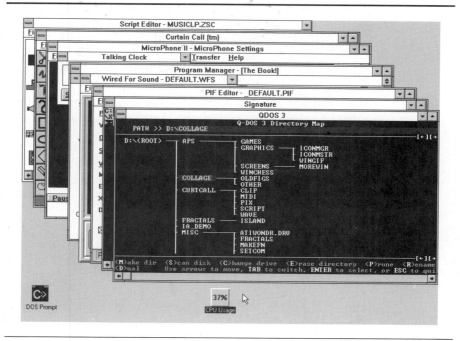

FIGURE 20.7: The Cpuuse program

USING THE PROGRAM

If you want to run the CPU Usage meter automatically every time you run Windows, move the CPU-USE icon from the CPU-USE program group to the STARTUP group. Alternatively, if you have removed the Windows 3.1 STARTUP group, you can always edit the WIN.INI file. Under the [Windows] section, look for a line that starts "load=". If there isn't one already, make one. Add "cpuuse.exe" to the end of the line.

If you want to have the CPU Usage meter automatically keep itself in front of any other windows, select "Keep in front" from the System menu. When a checkmark appears next to that option, it is enabled. The setting will be stored and recalled the next time you run the program.

There are a few annoying little things about the CPU Usage meter. When you first run it, it'll take about six seconds to determine how fast your CPU is so that it can give you an accurate reading.

Another minor annoyance is due to the way Windows handles menus. When you click on the CPU-USE icon to display the menu, the CPU Usage meter will no longer be able to measure usage properly until you complete the menu operation. During this time, a double question mark (??) will appear in the icon.

Lastly, at particular combinations of screen resolutions, icon sizes, and font sizes, the text will not fit properly inside the icon space. None of these problems causes any harm or affects the information being displayed.

◆ THE EXITW PROGRAM

OVERVIEW

EXITW.EXE allows you to close down Windows without the Program Manager or File Manager arguing about it. It will also allow you to pass back a DOS error-level code or to set a DOS environment variable.

USING THE PROGRAM

Exitw can display a message before exiting to DOS that presents both an OK and a Cancel button so the user can cancel or continue the exit process. Using Exitw, the user can pass back an error-level code to DOS. The user can also set a specific DOS environment string.

A new program called EXITWDOS.EXE is used to parse the parameters that are included on the Exitw command line, once control is returned to DOS. Either an error-level code or environment strings can be set using the unique combination of Exitw and ExitwDOS.

You can specify several command-line parameters for EXITW.EXE when you execute the program, using the syntax

Exitw <parameters>

Each parameter should be preceded by a dash (–) character. These are the possible parameters:

M <message>   where <message> is a string contained within quotes that you want displayed to the user before exiting Windows. The message box that will be displayed to the user will have both Cancel and OK buttons. If the user presses Cancel, Exitw will not shut down Windows. Quotes are required so that dashes can be included in the message text. For example:

Exit –M "Now running Autocad – Click on Cancel to abort"

E <num>   where <num> is the error-level number that should be returned to DOS when the program EXITWDOS.EXE is executed. This number should fall between 1 and 200. An error-level code of 200 is used by Exitwdos to indicate a data file error. For example:

EXITW –E 10

S <string>   where string is an environment variable string that should be added to or changed within the set of current MS-DOS environment settings. For example:

EXITW –S PATH=C:\;C:\DOS

When you run EXITWDOS.EXE, the program sets your path equal to C:\;C:\DOS.

If no parameters are given on the Exitw command line, Exitw will not create a data file. It will merely cause Windows to exit to DOS.

The following two lines should be present in the WIN.INI file for Exitw to operate properly:

[EXITW]

FILENAME=<path>

where <path> is a full path name to a file in which you want Exitw to store the commmand-line parameters. For example:

FILENAME=C:\WINDOWS\EXITW.DAT

If this entry is not found, Exitw will save the parameters to a file called EXITW.DAT in the root directory of the current drive.

Here is a complete example for using this program:

EXITW –M "Exiting Windows" –S PATH=C:\ –E 10

causes Exitw to write to disk the options

–S PATH=C:

–E 10

When Exitwdos is executed, it parses the data file created by Exitw, changes the path to equal C:\, and returns an error-level code of 10. When executing Exitwdos, you must specify the location and name of the file created by Exitw. Without this specification, Exitwdos will not know where to find the file. For example:

EXITWDOS C:\WINDOWS\EXITW.DAT

causes Exitwdos to look in the directory \WINDOWS on drive C for the file EXITW.DAT. If this file exists, Exitwdos will parse the file and return the information contained within it.

◆ THE PKWARE PROGRAMS

Pkware is a package of utility files that primarily perform file compression and decompression. Pkzip is the program that shrinks files. This shrinking process is often referred to as data compression. Pkunzip performs the unshrinking, or decompressing, function.

OVERVIEW

Pkzip also handles all file maintenance, including adding and deleting files, as well as reporting on technical information from within the compressed file.

Pkunzip is the program that decompresses or extracts compressed files. In addition to extracting a complete Zip file, it can selectively release individual files, show files on the screen for fast viewing, or print them out on a printer.

The term *compression* means to reduce in size. Computer file compression refers to reducing files in size so that they take up less storage space on disk. Pkzip will perform this reduction quickly and easily. The compressed files are then stored in a special file (which has a .ZIP extension) called a Zip file.

Zip files have three distinct benefits:

1. They use less disk space than normal files. Storing files in compressed form increases the life and storage availability of your expensive hard disk.

2. Many individual files can be compressed into a single Zip file. This makes file-group identification, copying, and transporting faster and easier.

3. Compressed files travel faster via modem, which reduces telecommunication transmission and reception. Many BBS (computer bulletin board services) use Pkware files as their standard. This enables the BBS to store more files and enables you to transfer files faster and easier.

USING THE PROGRAMS

The Pkware programs have a wide range of features and options, each of which is extensively explained in the .DOC files found in your Pkware directory after installation of this book's software. In this section, I'll explain the most common use of the Pkzip and Pkunzip programs.

To zip up one or more files into a smaller .ZIP file, you should use the following syntax:

PKZIP <newname>.ZIP <filenames>

The name of the compressed .ZIP file will be NEWNAME.ZIP. If you do not include the .ZIP extension, Pkzip will add it automatically. The files that are compressed into the single .ZIP file are listed on the remainder of the line. Just replace <filenames> with a series of file names or wildcard expressions.

Let's take a look at a couple of typical examples. First, suppose that you enter the following at a command prompt:

PKZIP A:NEWFILE *.*

This creates a file named NEWFILE.ZIP, which contains compressed versions of all files from the current directory. If you wanted to zip up just two specific files (let's say BUDGET1.WK1 and BUDGET2.WK1), you might use the following command:

PKZIP BUDGET.ZIP \LOTUS\Budget1.wk1 \LOTUS\Budget2.wk1

This creates a ZIP file named BUDGET.ZIP, which contains two files from the \LOTUS directory.

Decompressing a .ZIP file is even easier. You just use this syntax:

PKUNZIP <filename>.ZIP

For example, all the files for the Reminder application on Disk 2 are zipped up into REMINDER.ZIP. After creating a Reminder directory, copying the zipped file into it, and changing to that directory, the following line decompresses the entire application:

PKUNZIP REMINDER.ZIP

If you take a look at the batch files that install the applications from the book's disks, you'll see that all applications are decompressed with a similarly straightforward command line. Creating the .ZIP file in the first place was just as simple, since I had arranged all files for each application in a separate directory. Compressing each group of files only required a *.* file specification.

◆ THE RUN PROGRAM

OVERVIEW

RUN.EXE is a Windows program that executes other Windows programs. What makes Run so useful is that you can run any number of applications at the same time and give each application its own command line.

USING THE PROGRAM

To use Run, execute it from the DOS command line when you start Windows. For example:

WIN RUN <APPNAME...>

where APPNAME... can be one or more application names separated by commas that are either in the current directory or along the DOS path. For example:

WIN RUN CONTROL, CLOCK.EXE, TERMINAL

will execute the Control Panel, Windows Clock, and the Windows Terminal program in that order, as though you had double-clicked on them from the File Manager. Run assumes that the program has an extension of .EXE if no extension is supplied.

To use Run from the Program Manager, select File/Run and type

RUN <APPNAME...>

as before. You can also add a command line to the program that you are telling Run to execute. For example:

RUN CONTROL, WRITE TEST.DOC, CLOCK

will execute the Control Panel first. Then Run will execute Write with the command line "TEST.DOC" so that Write will open the file TEST.DOC upon startup. Finally, Run will execute the Clock application.

You can also add an entry to WIN.INI that will cause Run to start up with a default command line. If you start Run with no command line and the two lines

[DE-RUN]

Command="write, control, notepad win.ini"

are in your WIN.INI, Run will automatically use the string in quotes as the command line to execute. You should replace this quoted string with any set of programs you want executed.

If you do not have the above entry in WIN.INI and you start Run with a blank command line, Run will attempt to open your WIN.INI file using the Notepad application. To prevent this, you should add the two lines shown above to your WIN.INI file and set Command to "". For example:

[DE-RUN]

Command=""

causes Run to do nothing at all if started with a blank command line.

If you see the message "Invalid WIN.INI Entry" and the Notepad opens with your WIN.INI file displayed, Run could not find the Command entry in the [DE-RUN] section of your WIN.INI file. To prevent this from happening again, be sure the section for Run in WIN.INI matches that shown above.

◆ THE SCAN PROGRAM

OVERVIEW

SCAN.EXE (see Figure 20.8) is a virus detection and identification program for the IBM PC and compatible computers. Scan will search a PC for known computer viruses in memory, the boot sector, the partition table, and the files of a PC and its disks. Scan will also detect the presence of unknown viruses.

Scan works by searching the system for instruction sequences or patterns that are unique to each computer virus, and then reporting their presence if found. This method works for viruses that Scan recognizes. Scan can detect unknown viruses in files and boot sectors by appending validation (CRC) codes to .COM and .EXE files and then checking the files against their codes for changes, warning that an infection may have occurred if the file has been modified in any way, and by checking boot sectors for generic routines that a boot-sector virus must have. Scan can check for new viruses from a user-supplied list of virus search strings.

Scan runs on any PC with 256KB and DOS version 2.00 or higher.

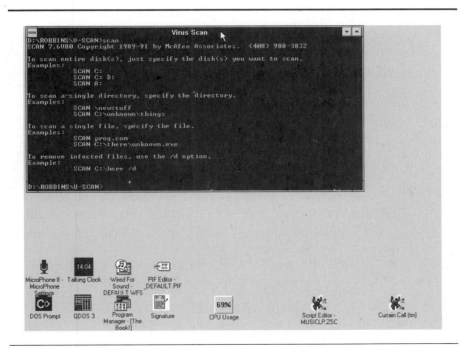

FIGURE 20.8: The Virus Scan program

USING THE PROGRAM

Scan runs a self-test when executed. If Scan has been modified in any way, a warning will be displayed, but the program will still continue to check for viruses. If Scan reports that it has been damaged, you should obtain a clean copy.

Understanding Virus Infections

Scan scans disks or entire systems for preexisting computer virus infections. It will identify the virus infecting the system and tell what area of the system (memory, boot sector, file) the virus occupies. An infected file can be removed with the overwrite-and-delete option, /D, which will erase the offending file. The Clean program is also available to disinfect the system and repair damaged areas whenever possible. The Clean program is described in a section earlier in this chapter. It includes a discussion of the nature of viruses, the types of attacks they make on your system, and the manner in which they can be identified.

Scan Version 80 identifies all 293 known computer viruses along with their variants. Some viruses have been modified so that more than one "strain" exists. Counting such modifications, there are 714 virus variants. The accompanying VIRLIST.TXT file describes all new, public domain, and extinct computer viruses identified by Scan. The number of variants of each virus is listed in parentheses after the virus name.

All known computer viruses infect one or more of the following areas: the hard-disk partition table (also known as the master boot record); the DOS boot sector of hard disks and floppy disks; or one or more executable files within the system. Executable files include operating system files, .COM files, .EXE files, overlay files, or any other files loaded into memory and executed. A virus that infects more than one area, such as a boot sector and an executable file, is called a *multipartite virus*.

Scan identifies every area or file that is infected, and indicates both the name of the virus and the CLEAN.EXE ID code used to remove it. Scan will check the entire system, an individual disk, a subdirectory, or individual files for existing viruses. Scan can also check files for unknown viruses with the Add Validation and Check Validation options. This is done by computing a code for a file, appending it to the file, and then validating the file against that code. If the file has been modified, the check will no longer match, indicating that viral infection may have occurred.

Scan uses two independently generated CRCs (cyclic redundancy checks) that are added to the end of program files to do this. Files that are self-checking should not be validated, because this will "set off" the program's self-check. Files that are self-modifying may have different values for the same program depending upon the modifications. Scan adds validation codes to .COM and .EXE files only.

The validation codes for the partition table, boot sector, and system files are kept in a hidden file called SCANVAL.VAL in the root directory. To detect boot-sector viruses, Scan checks the boot sector for signs of viral code. If suspicious code is found, Scan will report that it has found a suspicious boot-sector virus.

Scan can also be updated to search for new viruses via an External Virus Data File option, which allows the user to provide the Scan program with new search strings for viruses. Scan can display messages in either English or French.

Scan works on stand-alone and networked PCs, but not on a file server. For networks, the NetScan server-drive scanning program must be used.

Safely Operating the Scan Program

It is safest to create a bootable floppy disk and include the SCAN.EXE program on that disk. Prior to running the Scan program from that disk, write-protect it to prevent infection of the Scan program during the scanning process.

You can run Scan on the designated drive(s) that could be host to a virus. If a virus is found, a message is displayed telling the name of the infected file or system area and the name of the identified virus. Scan will examine files for viruses based on their extensions. The default file extensions supported by Scan are .APP, .BIN, .COM, .EXE, .OV?, .PGM, .PIF, .PRG, .SWP, .SYS, and .XTP. Additional extensions can be added to Scan, or all files on disk can be selected for scanning.

To run Scan, use the following syntax:

SCAN d1: ... d10: /A /AV /CV /D /E .xxx .yyy .zzz

    /EXT d:filename /FR /MANY /NLZ /NOBREAK /NOMEM /NOPAUSE

    /REPORT d:filename /RV /SUB

These are the possible parameter options:

A simple slash (\ ) scans root directory and boot area only.

The /A option scans all files, including data, for viruses. This should be used only if a file-infecting virus has already been detected or when checking a new program. The /A option will add substantial time to scanning. This option takes priority over the /E option.

The /AV option allows the user to add validation codes to the files being scanned. If a full drive is specified, Scan will create validation data for the partition table, boot sector, and system files of the disk as well. Validation adds ten bytes to files; the validation data for the partition table, boot sector, and system files are stored separately in a hidden file in the root directory of the scanned drive.

The /CV option checks the validation codes inserted by the /AV option. If the file has been changed, Scan will report that the file has been modified, and that a viral infection may have occurred. Using the /CV option adds about 25 percent more time to scanning.

You should be aware that some older Hewlett Packard and Zenith PCs modify the boot sector or partition table each time the system is booted. This will cause Scan to continually notify the user of boot-sector or partition-table modifications if the /CV switch is selected. Check your system's manual to determine whether your system contains self-modifying boot code.

The /D option tells Scan to prompt the user to overwrite and delete an infected file when one is found. If the user selects Y, the infected file will be overwritten with hex code C3 (the return-to-DOS instruction) and then deleted. A file erased by the /D option cannot be recovered. It is recommended that the McAfee Associates' Clean program be used to remove the virus instead of Scan, because in most cases it will recover the infected file. Boot-sector and partition-table infectors cannot be removed by the /D option and require the Clean virus disinfection program.

The /E option scans the files with overlay extensions .xxx, .yyy, and .zzz. The /E option allows the user to specify an extension or set of extensions to scan. Extensions should include the period character (.) and should be separated by a space after the /E and between each other. Up to three extensions can be added with /E. For more extensions, use the /A option.

The /EXT option allows Scan to search for viruses from a text file containing user-defined search strings in addition to the viruses Scan already checks for. The syntax for using the external virus data file is /EXT d:filename, where d: is the drive name and filename is the name of the external virus data file.

Note that the /EXT option is intended for users to add strings for detection of computer viruses on an interim or emergency basis. When used with the /D option, it will delete infected files. This option is not recommended for general use and should be used with caution.

The /FR option displays messages in French.

The /M option tells Scan to check system memory for all known computer viruses that can inhabit memory. By default, Scan checks memory only for critical and "stealth" viruses, which are viruses that can cause catastrophic damage or spread the infection during the scanning process.

It is these types of viruses that absolutely require that you use Scan from a floppy disk. If one of these viruses is found in memory, Scan will stop and advise the user to power down. This protects you from further damage if you've run Scan directly from your hard disk's Vscan installation directory. You can then reboot the system from a virus-free system disk.

Using the /M option with another antiviral software package may result in false alarms if the other package does not remove its virus search strings from memory. The /M option will add 6 to 20 seconds to the scanning time.

The /MANY option is used to scan multiple disks placed in a given drive. If the user has more than one floppy disk to check for viruses, the /MANY option allows the user to check them without having to run Scan multiple times. If a system has been disinfected, the /MANY and /NOMEM options can be used to speed up scanning of disks.

The /NLZ option tells Scan not to look inside files compressed with the LZEXE file compression program. Scan will still check the programs for external infections.

The /NOBREAK option disables your ability to stop Scan while it is running by disabling Ctrl+C/Ctrl+Brk.

The /NOMEM option is used to turn off all memory checking for viruses. It should be used only when a system is known to be free of viruses.

The /NOPAUSE option disables the "More..." prompt that appears when Scan fills up a screen with data. This allows Scan to run on a machine with multiple infections without requiring operator intervention when the screen fills up with messages from the Scan program.

The /REPORT option is used to generate a listing of infected files. The resulting list is saved to disk as an ASCII text file. To use the report option, specify /REPORT on the command line, followed by the device and file name.

The /RV option is used to remove validation codes from a file or files. It can be used to remove the validation code from a disk, subdirectory, or file(s). Using /RV on a disk will remove the partition-table, boot-sector, and system-file validation. This option cannot be used with the /AV option.

The /SUB option allows Scan to scan subdirectories (d1: ... d10: indicates the drives to be scanned). Previously, Scan would recursively check subdirectories only if a logical device (e.g., drive C) was scanned.

Examples of Running the Scan Program

The following examples demonstrate how to run Scan in a variety of situations:

SCAN C:

This scans drive C.

SCAN A:R–HOOPER.EXE

This scans the file "R–HOOPER.EXE" on drive A.

SCAN A: /A /CV

This scans all files and checks validation codes for unknown viruses on drive A.

SCAN B: /D /A

This scans all files on drive B and prompts for erasure of any infected files.

SCAN C: D: E: /AV /NOMEM

This adds validation codes to files on drives C, D, and E, and skips memory checking.

SCAN C: D: /M /A /FR

This scans memory for all known and extinct viruses, as well as all files on drives C and D, and outputs all messages in French.

SCAN C: D: /E .WPM .COD

This scans drives C and D, and includes files with the extensions .WPM and .COD.

SCAN C: /EXT A:SAMPLE.ASC

This scans drive C for known computer viruses and also for viruses added by the user via the external virus data file option.

SCAN C: /M /NOPAUSE /REPORT A:INFECTN.RPT

This scans for all viruses in memory and drive C without stopping, and creates a log on drive A called INFECTN.RPT.

SCAN C: D: /NOPAUSE /REPORT B:VIRUS.RPT

This scans drives C and D for viruses without stopping, and creates a log on drive B called VIRUS.RPT.

SCAN E:\DOWNLOADS /SUB

This scans all subdirectories under DOWNLOADS on drive E.

In each of these cases, Scan may return one of several exit codes. If you program a batch file with Scan, you can use the following error-level values:

VALUE	DESCRIPTION
0	No viruses found
1	One or more viruses found
2	Abnormal termination (program error)

If a user stops the scanning process, Scan will set the error level to 0 or 1, depending on whether a virus was discovered prior to termination of the Scan program. The /NOBREAK option can be used to prevent scanning from being stopped.

How to Remove Viruses That Scan Finds

What do you do if a virus is found? You can contact McAfee Associates by BBS, FAX, telephone, or Internet for help with removing viruses. There is no charge for support calls to McAfee Associates. Alternatively, or additionally, the Clean universal virus disinfection program is part of this book's disk software. It will disinfect the majority of reported computer viruses. It is updated with each release of the Scan program to remove new viruses.

It is strongly recommended that you get experienced help in dealing with viruses, especially critical viruses that can damage or destroy data. Improper removal of partition-table or boot-sector viruses could result in the loss of all data and use of the infected disk(s). For qualified assistance in removing a virus, please contact McAfee Associates directly. Alternatively, but for a possible fee, you can check the enclosed AGENTS.TXT file in the Vscan directory for an authorized McAfee Associates agent in your area.

◆ THE SYSGRAPH PROGRAM

OVERVIEW

Sysgraph (see Figure 20.9) is a Windows program that graphically displays the CPU loading of your current mix of applications. It includes a number of display settings that enable you to select the graph's updating rate, as well as decide whether to display relative system loading or free time.

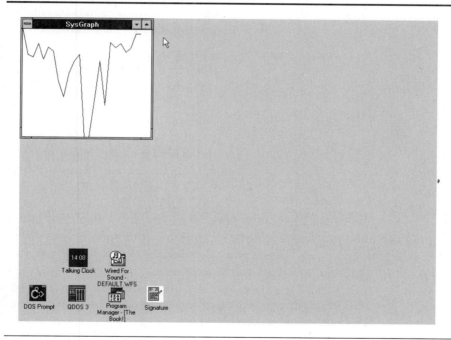

FIGURE 20.9:   The Sysgraph program

USING THE PROGRAM

Sysgraph initially displays the load in the Windows system queue in an icon at the bottom of the screen; you can enlarge the icon to a sizable screen window (as seen in Figure 20.9) by double-clicking on it. Additional system load is shown by dips in the graph. You can choose between two primary automatic ways to scale and display the information: continous autoscaling or scaling based on the largest recorded value. A user option exists for selecting between them.

The graph will automatically rescale to accommodate the largest values recorded. Two commands are available on the system menu:

Rescale	A one-time rescaling of the graph is performed, based on the data points currently displayed. This command is enabled only when Auto Rescale is turned off.
Auto Rescale	This mode is turned on and off by selecting this menu option. When it is on, a checkmark is placed by the menu item and the Rescale command is disabled. When the option is enabled, the graph is continually rescaled based on the displayed data points. Otherwise, the scaling is changed only to accommodate new maximum data points or when the Rescale command is used.

By default, SysGraph updates the graphical display at one-second intervals and provides a relative indication of the system CPU free time as obtained from system queue cycles. By selecting the About option, you can modify the update rate to two or five seconds. From the About box you can also choose to view a relative free-time indicator, rather than a relative loading indicator. When you change from a slower update rate to a faster update rate (i.e., five seconds to one second), you may need to select the Rescale option from the pull-down menu to correct the graph scaling. I prefer the two-second update rate with a relative free-time indicator. This produces a graph that rises with increasing system load. It also is an update rate that averages out momentary system load peaks, thereby providing a more meaningful indication of system load.

◆ THE UNICOM PROGRAM

OVERVIEW

Unicom (see Figure 20.10) is a data communications application specifically designed for users of Microsoft Windows. Unicom can perform all data communication tasks in the background while other applications are running. You can switch to another Windows application at any time.

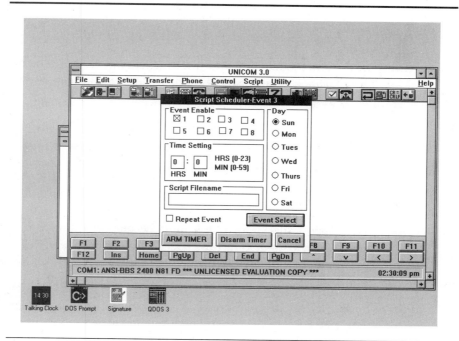

FIGURE 20.10: The Unicom communications program

USING THE PROGRAM

Hardware and Software Requirements

Unicom requires Microsoft Windows Version 2 or 3 to be installed and properly configured on your computer. Before installing Unicom on your computer, check the following:

1. If a bus mouse is installed in your computer, make sure the mouse interrupt level does not conflict with interrupts reserved for serial port operation. The bus mouse interrupt is set via a jumper on the interface board. Consult your mouse installation manual.

2. Your serial port(s) (COM1 and COM2) or (COM3 and COM4) should be set for interrupt operation using IRQ4 and IRQ3 respectively. The interrupt levels are typically selected via jumpers located on your serial interface board or on the motherboard. Consult your computer reference manual.

3. A Hayes-compatible modem must be present to support Unicom's directory-assisted dialing and call hang-up features.

4. The modem dip-switch settings should be set to the manufacturer's default positions. The modem must be configured to return verbose responses.

Please note that certain operations such as Clipboard-to-Clipboard transfers require enough temporary memory and disk storage to hold the data being transferred. This storage is released after the transfer operation is completed.

Getting Started

The support file UCLIB.DLL must be placed in a directory listed in your search path as defined by the DOS PATH environment variable. This PATH environment variable is typically set in the DOS AUTOEXEC.BAT file.

You can start Unicom by clicking on the icon in the Unicom program group created during installation. You can also modify the program properties of this icon (see Chapter 9) to activate Unicom with the following syntax:

Unicom [configfile]

When Unicom is activated for the first time, a file path setup window will appear which prompts you to enter names for Unicom files directory, as well as names for the upload and download directories.

The files directory should be set to the drive and directory where Unicom has been installed. The download directory should be set to the drive and directory where files received from data transfers are to be stored. The upload directory should be set to the drive and directory where Unicom will first look to locate files for upload selection.

Enter the path names into the edit fields within the dialog box. Paths defined here are valid only for the current Unicom session. To make the paths permanent, activate the Save Setup option from within the Setup menu. Paths are stored in your Windows WIN.INI file.

An error message will be displayed if any of the path fields contain an invalid directory or if Unicom could not locate its executable files in the directory specified in the Files Directory field.

At the start of each program run, the UNICOM.CFG configuration file is accessed (from the file path set previously) to determine which communication port will be used as well as other operating parameters. If Unicom cannot locate this file, the port will default to COM2, 1200 baud, no parity, 8 data bits, and 1 stop bit.

Should a communication port fail to open, Unicom will display a message box to indicate the failure. The port configuration dialog window will be displayed automatically. A valid communication port should be selected.

When a communication port is opened successfully, Unicom tries to initialize the Hayes-compatible modem if the port is configured for a modem connection. If the message "Modem Not Responding" appears, Unicom could not get the modem's attention. Make sure the communications port and modem are configured properly. Ensure that the modem is set to return verbose responses.

To select and configure a communications port, select the COMM PORT option from the Setup menu. A setup window will appear displaying the current port configuration. Select the communication characteristics desired from this window using a mouse or keyboard. COM1 through COM4 are shown as available options. If your computer system does not support a particular port, an error message will be displayed if an attempt is made to configure it.

◆ THE VSHIELD PROGRAM

OVERVIEW

Vshield (see Figure 20.11) is a virus prevention program for IBM PC and compatible computers. It will prevent viruses from infecting your system. When Vshield first loads, it searches for known computer viruses in memory, the partition table, boot sector, system files, and in itself. It then installs itself as a terminate-and-stay-resident (TSR) program.

Next, it scans all programs before allowing the system to execute them. If any program contains a virus, Vshield refuses to allow it to execute. Nor does it allow the system to be warm-booted from any disk that contains a boot-sector virus.

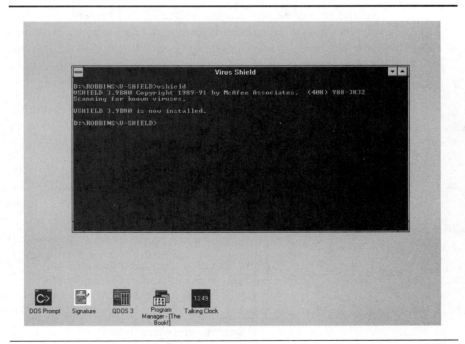

FIGURE 20.11: The Vshield program

Two separate programs are available. The first, VSHIELD.EXE, checks for known viruses as well as unknown viruses by checking validation codes added with the Scan program. The second program, VSHIELD1.EXE, does validation-code checking only.

The Vshield programs monitor all program loads, regardless of what disk they occur from, unless otherwise specified. Vshield optionally provides access-control functions to reduce the risk of introducing computer viruses from unknown software. Vshield will run on any PC with 256KB and DOS version 2.0 or greater. Vshield1 uses 6KB of system memory, while Vshield uses 31KB of system memory in nonswap mode, or 3KB if swapping to disk is specified.

USING THE PROGRAM

Vshield is packaged with the Validate program to ensure the integrity of the VSHIELD.EXE and VSHIELD1.EXE files. Validate is explained in the description of the Clean program earlier in this chapter. The Validate program is distributed with Vshield and can be used to check all future versions of Vshield.

The validation results for Vshield Version 80-B and Vshield1 Version 0.2 should be as follows:

File Name: VSHIELD.EXE VSHIELD1.EXE

Size: 33,723 11,281

Date: 07-01-1991 02-14-1991

File Authentication

Check Method 1: 9B2B 6B40

Check Method 2: 097C 103E

When Vshield is placed in the AUTOEXEC.BAT file, it installs itself each time the system is turned on or rebooted. It proceeds to check the memory, partition table, boot sector, system files, and itself for viruses and then installs itself as a terminate-and-stay-resident (TSR) program. It then monitors all program loads for viruses.

Establishing Levels of Protection

Vshield has four levels of user-selectable protection:

Level I protection   Provided by the Vshield1 program, this level checks the cyclic redundancy check (CRC) validation-code values added to programs by the Scan program's /AV option. If a program no longer matches its validation code, Vshield1 will not allow it to execute. Vshield1 will also check the partition-table and boot-sector validation codes, if present. Level I protection provides a minimal degree of protection, and it is recommended that level II protection or above be used if system resources permit.

Level II protection   Provided by the Vshield program, this level checks program files for *virus signatures*, pieces of code or patterns unique to each computer virus strain. Vshield will check the memory, partition table, boot sector, system files, and itself for viruses before installing itself as a TSR program. It then monitors all program loads and if a virus is found, Vshield does not allow the program to execute. Vshield also does not allow a computer to be warm-booted from a disk infected with a partition-table or boot-sector vius.

Level III protection   Combines level I and level II protections.

Level IV protection   This level provides access control by enabling a user to specify which programs will be allowed to run. Level IV protection can be set up so that only programs that are listed in a certification file can be run on a given system. It can also be set up so that only those programs that have been validated by Scan can be run.

Each level of protection has its advantages and disadvantages. Level I protection requires the least amount of system overhead, using 6KB of system memory. However, it provides minimal protection. Level II, III, and IV protections require 31KB of system memory, but this can be reduced to 3KB by using the /SWAP option.

Vshield1 adds an average of only one second to each program load. Vshield adds an average of three seconds to each program load and six seconds to each reboot. Vshield does not degrade the performance of the system in any way once a program has been loaded. Vshield and Vshield1 should not be used simultaneously. You should select either one or the other.

The /SWAP option leaves a Vshield kernel in memory that swaps the main body of the program in and out of memory as needed. Using the /SWAP option adds an additional 600 milliseconds to each program load.

◆ PROTECT YOUR VERSION OF VSHIELD

Create a backup disk by copying the Vshield programs to a blank floppy and write-protecting it before running the programs. This gives you a valid backup in case the Vshield programs themselves become infected by a sophisticated virus.

Vshield and Vshield1 both monitor your system for attempts to load an infected program. If an infected program is loaded, Vshield displays a message stating the name of the file and the virus infecting it. It then prevents the file from being executed. Vshield1 does the same except that it does not identify the infecting virus.

Running Vshield with Options

Vshield allows a variety of options. Use the following syntax at a DOS command prompt before running Windows:

Vshield /CERTIFY filename /CHKHI /CONTACT message

/CV /F pathname /IGNORE d1:...d26: /LOCK /M

/NB /NOMEM /SWAP pathname /WINDOWS

The /CERTIFY option allows a systems administrator to control access to executable files. This can be used to prevent the running of unauthorized software. When run with the /CV option, /CERTIFY allows only those files that have had validation codes inserted into them with the Scan program to execute.

You can also create an exception list of "trusted" files to allow a particular list of files to be executed. If /CERTIFY is used without the /CV option, only the programs in the exception list are allowed to run. For instructions on how to create an exception list, see the last section of this description of Vshield. Be aware that running /CERTIFY without the /CV option or an exception list will prevent all programs other than DOS internal commands from being run.

The /CHKHI option checks the high memory area (HMA) on AT and 386 machines for viruses. The message "Scanning 1088K RAM" is displayed. This option cannot be used with the /NOMEM option.

The /CONTACT option displays a contact name and phone number when a virus is found. The name and number message can be 50 characters long and can contain any characters. If the message begins with a slash or a hyphen, the message must be placed in quotation marks.

The /CV option checks validation codes inserted by the Scan program to provide level III protection as defined above. If a file no longer matches its validation code, Vshield reports that the file has been modified and that viral infection may have occurred, and does not allow the program to execute. If the /CV option is not specified, Vshield provides only level II (virus signature) checking. For information about the installation of CRC validation codes, please refer to the Scan program documentation.

The /F option is required if the user wishes to use the /SWAP command and is running DOS 2.0 or earlier. The /F option tells Vshield where it has been loaded from. The complete path name must be specified.

The /IGNORE option specifies the drives from which to ignore program loads. Drives that are ignored will *not* be checked for viruses. Up to 26 drives can be ignored. This option is for use with network operating systems that have existing virus protection; it is not recommended for use on standalone PCs or networks that have no antiviral features in use.

The /LOCK option will halt the system if a virus is found so that processing cannot continue.

The /M option tells Vshield to check system memory for all known computer viruses that are memory resident before installing itself. By default, Vshield checks memory only for critical and "stealth" viruses, which can cause damage or spread during the scanning process. If a critical or "stealth" virus is found, Vshield stops the system and advises the user to cold-boot the machine from a clean copy of DOS and scan the system for viruses.

The /NB option tells Vshield not to look at the partition table and boot sector.

The /NOMEM option is used to turn off all memory checking for viruses during installation. It should be used only when a system is known to be free of viruses. This option cannot be used with the /M or /CHKHI options.

The /REMOVE option uninstalls the Vshield program and removes it from memory. If other memory-resident programs prevent Vshield from being uninstalled, an error message appears.

The /SWAP option tells Vshield to install only its kernel as memory resident. The Vshield program will then be swapped in and out of memory as needed from a hard disk or RAM disk. The placement of a path after the /SWAP command is optional, and should be used only if Vshield is to be swapped from a path other than the one from which it is being executed. It is recommended that Vshield be used without the /SWAP option whenever memory permits, because /SWAP may cause conflicts with programs that fail to allocate memory properly. If conflicts occur, remove the /SWAP option and reboot the machine. If there is not enough memory to load Vshield in non-swap mode, the Vshield1 program should be used instead.

The /WINDOWS option enables checking of DOS processes under Windows. On the assumption that you will be running Windows on your system, you should always include this switch.

Vshield1 can be run with only two options:

Vshield1 /NB /REMOVE

The /NB option tells Vshield1 not to look at the partition table and boot sector. This option should be used only if Vshield1 continually reports that the boot sector has been modified. This occurs on some old Hewlett Packard and Zenith systems because they modify the boot sector each time the system is booted. Check your system's manual to determine whether your system contains self-modifying boot code.

The /REMOVE option uninstalls the Vshield1 program and removes it from memory. If other memory-resident programs prevent Vshield1 from being uninstalled, an error message appears.

Here are some examples of using either Vshield or Vshield1:

Vshield1

installs Vshield1 (level I protection).

Vshield

installs Vshield (level II protection).

Vshield /CV

installs Vshield (level III protection).

Vshield /CV /CERTIFY EXCPTN.LST

installs Vshield (level IV protection) with CRC and exception-list checking.

Vshield /SWAP

installs only the Vshield kernel as memory resident and swaps the program in and out of memory from the root directory of the disk on a DOS 3.0 (or higher) system.

Vshield /SWAP /F C:\Vshield.EXE

installs only the Vshield kernel as memory resident and swaps the program in and out of memory from the root directory of the disk on a DOS 2.0 system.

Vshield /CV /CONTACT "Please Contact the PC Help Desk"

installs Vshield using level III protection and displays the quoted message if a virus is found.

Installation and Batch File Techniques

Vshield and Vshield1 should normally be placed at the end of your system's AUTOEXEC.BAT file. The exception to this is any AUTOEXEC.BAT that contains a menu program, such as MS-DOS's DOSSHELL program, PC Tools' PC Shell, or Norton Commander. If using such a program, Vshield or Vshield1 should be loaded before it.

If network drivers are being used, Vshield must be loaded after the network drivers, preferably at the end of the AUTOEXEC.BAT file. This is because network drivers replace normal DOS functions in a manner that prevents Vshield from recognizing program loads if Vshield is loaded first. Running Vshield after network drivers have been loaded will ensure proper virus protection.

◆ THE WBAR PROGRAM

OVERVIEW

Wbar (see Figure 20.12) is a program that generates bar codes (i.e., 3 of 9, UPC, PostNet, etc.) that can be copied to the Windows Clipboard. Once in the Clipboard, you can paste the bar code into other programs such as Windows Write, Microsoft Word for Windows, Paintbrush, or any other Windows program that can accept bitmaps or metafiles from the Windows Clipboard.

USING THE PROGRAM

Upon execution, Wbar displays a typical Windows program window. The menu consists of File, Edit, Action, Type, Special, and Help. When first

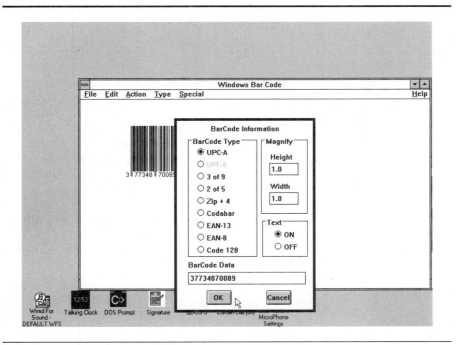

FIGURE 20.12: The Wbar program

loaded, the About Wbar dialog box appears if you have an unregistered copy of Wbar; otherwise, a blank window appears. The cursor takes on the shape of a bar code while in the workspace of the Wbar window.

To make a bar code, you simply position the cursor in the window where you want to place the bar code and click the left button on your mouse. A dialog box will appear allowing you to toggle various options, select what type of bar code to produce, and to input the bar code data. After all this is done, clicking on OK will produce the desired bar code on the display. If you have the Auto-Meta mode on, a metafile of the bar code is copied to the Clipboard.

If you wish to copy a bitmap representation of the bar code to the Clipboard, choose Action from the main menu. Clicking on Select from the Action sub-menu will toggle the cursor to a cross. You then press the left mouse button and drag a box around the bar code. After releasing the left mouse button, clicking on Copy from the Edit menu copies the selected box area to be pasted in bitmap form to the Windows Clipboard.

The main Wbar menu contains six primary choices: File, Edit, Action, Type, Special, and Help. Each has a series of subchoices. The most common choice, File, includes a New and an Exit choice. New clears the Wbar window of any bar codes, while Exit closes the window and exits the Wbar program.

The Edit menu offers the traditional Clipboard functions of Copy, Paste, and Clear. Copy copies a selected area to the Clipboard, Paste pastes from the Clipboard to the upper-left area of the Wbar window, and Clear erases the Wbar window.

The Action menu offers two choices: Barcode and Select. Barcode sets the cursor to bar-code mode, while Select sets the cursor to the area-select mode.

The Type menu offers three choices: Color, Monochrome, and Auto Metafile. If Color is checked, all copies sent to the Clipboard will be in color bitmap format. If Monochrome is checked, all copies sent to the Clipboard will be in monochrome bitmap format.

Finally, if Auto Metafile is checked, all bar codes produced on the display will be automatically copied to the Clipboard in the Windows MetaFile format.

This last choice can be very useful for producing bar codes of exact size. Also, this is the best way to paste bar codes into CorelDRAW or to produce PostNet bar codes suitable for printing on envelopes. Metafiles pasted into other applications may not look correct on the display, but they should print correctly.

The Special menu contains three useful subchoices: Default Barcodes, Bookland Barcode, and FIM Codes. Selecting Default Barcodes will display a dialog box that enables you to specify a variety of options. With this dialog box you can choose among the following bar codes:

UPC-A

3 of 9

2 of 5

Zip + 4

Codabar

EAN-13

EAN-8

Code 128

Select Bookland Barcode on the Special menu to produce the special bar codes typically found on or in most books sold today. With this option checked, the Bookland EAN bar code dialog box will appear when you click on the main work area of the window. You can then input various options such as ISBN number, magnification, and pricing.

The last choice on the Special menu is FIM (Facing Identification Mark) codes. FIM patterns are typically used on reply mail envelopes and cards to further help the Postal Service in sorting mail.

Finally, as is now common on Windows applications, the Help choice appears on the menu bar. It displays two selections: Help and About. Selecting Help invokes the Wbar online help system, while selecting About displays a dialog box containing information about the Wbar program.

◆ THE WINCHECK PROGRAM

WinCheck (see Figure 20.13) is a personal finance manager for Microsoft Windows that makes it possible to enter and track the following transactions for multiple checking, checking and savings, or credit card accounts:

Transaction types

Interest accrued

Cash machine advances

Miscellaneous bank charges

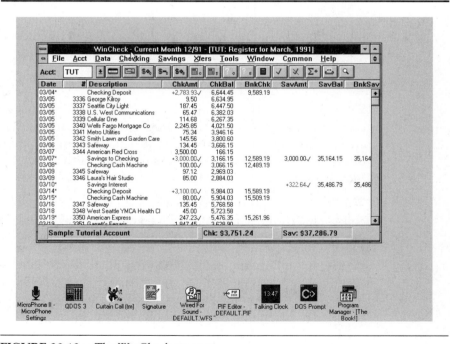

FIGURE 20.13: The WinCheck program

Transfers to or from savings and checking

Debit and credit cards

OVERVIEW

WinCheck will manage all of these transactions, making it easy to balance your checkbook, record a savings account's history, or keep track of credit card transactions. When you first start the WinCheck program, the Load Account dialog box contains the intials TUT. This is the account ID for the WinCheck tutorial file.

USING THE PROGRAM

The WinCheck program does not modify your AUTOEXEC.BAT or CON-FIG.SYS files. You may want to add WinCheck to your path if you will be running the program from the Windows command line.

Getting Started with WinCheck

Start WinCheck by double-clicking with the mouse on the WinCheck icon in Program Manger. The icon is located in the group called WinCheck (created during installation).

If WinCheck is on your path, it is also possible to start WinCheck by choosing Run from the File menu of Program Manager and then typing WINCHECK. Otherwise, type the full path name for WinCheck (such as C:\WINCHECK\WINCHECK).

Upon startup, you are prompted for the account to load. The tutorial account included with WinCheck is an excellent place to begin learning to use the program. The WinCheck tutorial file includes sample data for January, February, and March of 1991. To load the Tutorial account, choose TUT from the drop-down list box (click on the down arrow or press Alt+↓). Then click on OK or press Enter. If you have already started the WinCheck program and need to load the TUT account, choose Load Account from the File menu and choose TUT from the drop-down list box.

When loading the Tutorial file, the Balances dialog box appears with the balance values for savings and checking as well as the date of the last transaction. Press OK to exit the Balances dialog box and view the account register for March of 1991. WinCheck automatically loads the account register that is closest to the current date. In the case of the TUT account, March 1991 is the last month with transactions.

The WinCheck Screen   There are two visual aids besides the menu at the top of the screen: the control bar of icons across the top of the screen (mouse required) and the status line along the bottom of the WinCheck screen. The control bar allows for quick operation of the program by placing icon buttons of common operations below the menu. There are 15 buttons that execute common WinCheck operations and an "Acct:" list box on the far left that lists open accounts. TUT is listed now, to indicate that the Tutorial file is open. The status line displays the description of the account (Sample Tutorial Account) and the current balance information. The caption just above the menu lists the open month, the account ID, and whether the open window is a statement or a register. For example:

WinCheck – Current Month 12/91 – [TUT: Register for March, 1991]

The menu bar is just below the description information. One letter of each menu item is underlined to indicate the Alt combination needed to activate the menu. That is, to activate the File menu from the keyboard, you would type Alt-F (for File). To activate the File menu using the mouse, click on the word File.

There are three arrow buttons in the upper-right corner of the WinCheck screen. The top two buttons are used to control the size of the WinCheck program screen; the third button below is used to control the size of the Register or Statement window.

Click on the third button (the up and down arrow) and the Register window will be reduced in size. Click on the down arrow along the title of the Register window and the window will be reduced to an icon at the bottom of the screen.

Double-click on the check icon or press Enter to restore the Register window. Finally, click on the up arrow along the frame of the Register window to maximize the window to its original position.

Writing Your First Check   To write a check, click on the check icon (the tiny blue check) on the control bar, or press F3, or choose Check from the Checking menu. Any of these actions will bring up a blank check transaction.

Click only once when clicking on an icon. Double-clicking will bring up a message stating that only one new open transaction can be open at a time. If this message box appears, press OK and continue.

In the resulting check, click on the down arrow or press Alt+↓ to view current transaction categories. Categories are a means of classifying your transactions into certain groups such as Entertainment or Business.

To complete the check, follow these steps:

1. Select the Health Club category from the drop-down list box (click on the down arrow).

2. Press the Tab key twice to jump to the Date field and type 03/30/91. (For the purpose of this example, I've changed the date to be within the month of March to match the other tutorial data. Normally, you would leave the current date that is automatically inserted with a new transaction.)

3. Press the Tab key again to advance to the To field.

4. Type NorthWest Fitness.

5. Press the Tab key once to advance to the dollar amount field and type 23.34. The check is now complete.

6. Click on OK or press Enter to record the check transaction.

To view the check in the Register window, use the vertical scroll bar to scroll to the end of the month (or use the Page Down key when Num Lock is off).

Sorting the Register and Statement Data   The default sorting routine for the Register window is by date, so the transaction you just entered will appear near the end of the Register window data. To sort on a different key, choose Sort from the Data menu and pull to the right with the mouse to view the sorting options. The current sorting option is by date, as indicated by the check mark. Choose Number as the sorting method for the data in the

Register window. When the Register is sorted by number, all transactions without check numbers (such as deposits) will appear at the top of the Register window, with the checks below in ascending order.

Viewing Check Statement and Register Windows

WinCheck is capable of viewing several statements and registers from the same or different accounts at one time. To view a check statement, choose Display Check Statement from the Acct menu. In the resulting dialog box, WinCheck displays the available months (in this case January 1991–March 1991). Available months are those months that actually contain data. For example, April will appear in the "Pick a month to view" dialog box once a transaction has been made with an April date.

Choose January 1991 and press Enter or click on OK. The statement differs from the register in that the transactions are grouped according to type (deposits, checks, etc). Click on the Window menu or press Alt-W. At the bottom of the Window menu is a listing of the open Register and Statement windows.

The two open windows are listed, with a check mark by number 2. This indicates that the Statement window for January, 1991 is the active window:

1: TUT: Register for March, 1991

2: TUT: Statement for January, 1991

Choose Tile (from the Window menu) and view both windows at the same time. Switch back and forth between windows by clicking with the mouse anywhere in the January Statement window or the March Register window. Choose TUT: Register for March, 1991 from the Window menu to activate the March window. Now click on the Up arrow to the left of the window title bar to maximize the Register window.

These are the column headings for this register:

HEADING	COLUMN CONTENTS
ChkAmt	The amount of the checking transaction
ChkBal	Your running balance for checking
BnkChk	The "bank's opinion" on your running balance

HEADING	COLUMN CONTENTS
SavAmt	The amount of the savings transaction
SavBal	Your running balance for savings
BnkSav	The "bank's opinion" on your running balance

The Calculator Icon   If you need to manipulate numbers not necessarily within transactions, click on the calculator icon located on the control bar (it's the sixth icon from the right) or choose Calculator from the Data menu. To close the Calculator, press Alt+F4 or click twice on the close bar in the upper-left corner.

Essential WinCheck Operations

To start a new account, double-click on the WinCheck icon in Program Manager or choose Load Account from the File menu if the program is already running.

Once you have started your account with WinCheck, there are a few activities you may do quite often. These are among the most frequent daily activities:

♦ Entering checks you wrote while away from your computer. This can be done by pressing F3, by clicking on the Check icon on the control bar, or by choosing Check from the Checking menu.

♦ Paying bills and other regular expenses. WinCheck can print checks on any available blank check that will fit in your printer. WinCheck can also keep track of an endless number of common transactions. For example, payday can be entered as a common transaction, allowing you to make your payroll deposit with a single menu choice. Also, regular bills such as mortgage and car payments can be automatically paid. Refer to the section on common transactions for more information.

♦ Entering deposits, transfers, ATM (cash machine) withdrawals, or miscellaneous transactions.

Additional activities that you will perform, but not as frequently, may include:

♦ Reconciling and balancing your account(s).

♦ Creating common transactions. Here you can define a transaction that will happen on a regular basis (for example, a mortgage or car payment).

♦ Creating or loading check form templates. The WinCheck Form Designer allows you to create templates to print on any check.

♦ Printing reports. WinCheck's Report Generator has a list of reports you can choose from, or you can create custom reports.

♦ Changing WinCheck settings.

♦ Designing a budget and printing budget reports.

Writing Checks   WinCheck has two dialog boxes for entering checks: Endstub and conventional. The only difference between the two types of checks is the tab ordering of the fields and the title bar for the dialog box. To select Endstub tab ordering, choose Select Checkbook from the Acct menu and mark the box labeled Endstub. If the box is clear, you are using conventional tabbing order.

If you are using the Endstub ordering, the check dialog boxes have the following text in the title bar:

TUT: Endstub Check #101

where TUT is the account ID and #101 is the next blank check number. Conventional checks use a title bar as follows:

TUT: Check #101

where TUT is the account ID and #101 is the next blank check number.

1. In the dialog box, click on the down arrow to drop down a list of available categories or tab to the list box and press Alt+↓.

2. Select a category from the list or type in a name to create a new category.

3. Press the Tab key twice to jump to the Date field. You can leave the current date (automatically inserted with a new transaction) or

manually change the date (F5 moves the date back a day; F6 advances the date forward a day). If you enter an invalid date, WinCheck provides the following error message:

The date is incorrect. Please use MM/DD/YY format.

4. Press the Tab key to advance to the To: field and type the name of the check recipient, such as Safeway.

5. Press the Tab key once to advance to the dollar amount field ($) and type the transaction amount, such as 34.00.

The check is now complete. Choose OK to record the check transaction, Another to record the transaction and write another check, or Print to print the check. Choosing Details brings up the Transaction Details dialog box.

If you enter an invalid dollar amount, such as 6g5.78, WinCheck will inform you of its interpretation of the number in a dialog box titled Amount Verification. Here WinCheck lists the Original Entry (6g5.78) and its Corrected Amount (65.78). Type in the correct value for the transaction and press Enter or click on the OK button.

It is very common to have to enter checks that were written while you were away from home. For example, suppose that you went shopping at the grocery store, picked up some videos at the video rental outlet, and had an espresso at the coffee shop.

1. Select Check from the Checking menu, press F3, or click on the check icon on the control bar.

2. Select a category from the drop-down list box of categories. You might want to add a category called Groceries or make groceries be a subcategory of Personal, Personal:Groceries.

3. Let's say that you wrote the check for groceries two days ago. So, with the focus on the Date field (click on the Date field or press the Tab key until the Date field is selected) press the F5 key twice to decrement the current date by two days.

4. Type in the name of the grocery store in the To: field and the amount of the check beside the dollar sign ($).

5. When the fields are complete, click on the Another button or press Alt+A from the keyboard.

6. Repeat steps 2–5 for the check written to the video store, except the category should be something like Personal:Videos, Personal, or Video Rentals.

7. Repeat steps 2–5 for the check written to the coffee shop, except press the OK button instead of Another.

Setting Up WinCheck for Bill Paying   Bill paying is quickest and easiest if you add periodical bills (i.e., monthly and/or weekly bills) to the Common menu. As an example, the following steps describe how to add your monthly mortgage or rent payment to the Common menu:

1. Choose Add from the Common menu and select Check as the transaction type.

2. In the resulting check, choose a category for the transaction, such as Personal:Rent or Mortgage.

3. The day of the month in the Date field is normally the day that the bill is paid (the check is written). Leave the month and year as is and change the *day* to 1 (if the payment is due on the first of the month.

4. Fill in the check recipient in the To: field (for example, the name of the mortgage company or landlord).

5. In the $ field type the transaction amount. If the dollar amount varies, fill in a dollar amount of 0.00 or leave the amount blank.

6. Press OK to add the transaction to the Common menu.

The following steps describe how to add a monthly checking account service fee to the Common menu:

1. Choose Add from the Common menu and select Checking Misc as the transaction type.

2. The day of the month in the Date field should be the approximate date your bank statement arrives. So if your bank statement arrives

on the 13th of the month, leave the month and year as is and change the day to 13.

3. In the Description field, type Service Fees or Monthly Checking Fees.

4. In the $ field, type the rate you are charged each month or leave the field blank to indicate that the amount varies from month to month.

5. Choose a category for the transaction, such as Service Fees or Bank Fees.

6. Press OK to add the transaction to the Common menu.

7. Press Alt+O or click on the Common menu to see the items listed below the Common menu. The Common menu should now have a transaction with the date indicated in the steps above and the description entered above (Service Fees).

You can use similar steps to add a monthly Visa payment from your Checking account to your Credit Card account. To make (recall) any of the common transactions, simply select the transaction from the Common menu. In addition to adding transactions to the menu (by default), there are several other common transaction facilities, such as Remind and Automatic.

Reconciling Your Bank Statement   Note the beginning date for your statement and choose Account Settings from the Acct menu. In the field labeled Bank Statement Starts, type the starting day for your bank statement (a number from 1–31).

Open up a Statement window for the month of your bank statement. If you have transactions from the previous month that did not clear, you may need to open last month's Statement window as well. Choose Display Check Statement from the Acct menu and pick a month to view.

Then Choose Display Uncleared Only from the Data menu for each of the open Statement windows. The top line in the Statement window now lists the open month and the text UNCLEARED CHECKS. If your bank statement starts on a day other than 1, there will be two headings for uncleared checks, for example, May, 1991 UNCLEARED CHECKS and June, 1991 UNCLEARED CHECKS. This is a list of the transactions that have not yet cleared the bank. In the Statement window you have two options for sorting the checks: Checks by Date or Checks by Number. Both are available by selecting Sort from the Data menu. Other items, such as Checking Deposits, Transfers, and Savings Misc items are sorted by date in the Statement window.

Compare the transaction amounts on the bank's statement with your statement to make sure the amounts agree. For example, make sure that check number 234 is recorded as a debit of $34.00 on the bank's statement as well as your WinCheck statement. If the amounts disagree, either contact your bank or change your transaction amounts to reflect the bank's statement.

Once the transaction amounts agree (checks, deposits, transfers, and anything else), clear the transactions that are listed on the bank's statement. To do this select an item to clear and click with the mouse on the check mark icon on the control bar or press Ctrl+C. You can select multiple continuous transactions by holding down the Shift key while using the arrow keys. Discontinuous selections are made by holding down the Ctrl key and clicking on transactions with the mouse.

Continue to clear items until all of the items on the bank statement are marked as cleared in the WinCheck program. Cleared transactions disappear from the Statement window.

Enter any bank service fees by using the Misc Checking transaction dialog. Choose Misc from the Checking menu.

Check your balance by pressing F2, or choose Display Current Balance from the Acct menu. The bank's balance should match your balance if you have not made any transactions that do not appear on the bank statement. If you have made deposits or written checks that do not yet appear on the bank statement, your balance will not match with the bank's. Open the month's register to examine the Bank's Balance figure on the closing day of your bank statement.

21

Tools for
Personalizing Windows

◆ THE ADDRESS PROGRAM

OVERVIEW

The Address Manager, or AM, program is a full-featured Windows application that will manage your address book for you. This program includes the following features:

- ◆ Supports almost an infinite amount of data, limited only by the size of your hard disk.
- ◆ Offers full support for dot matrix and laser labels. Templates provided for some Avery laser labels.
- ◆ Prints directly to any size envelope, up to $8\frac{1}{2}" \times 11"$.
- ◆ Works with up to 32 user-defined lists (subsets of the names in the file).
- ◆ Provides all the typical database support—i.e., add/modify/delete names, searching, and sorting.
- ◆ Dials the phone for you, provided you have your modem on COM1, COM2.
- ◆ Prints in single or double columns on normal $8\frac{1}{2}" \times 11"$ paper.
- ◆ Offers several ways to view the data.
- ◆ Customizable fonts and colors.
- ◆ DDE Support.

USING THE PROGRAM

If this is the first time you are running AM, you should select New from the File pull-down menu (shown in Figure 21.1). This brings up a dialog box that prompts you for the name of your data file. You can give your address book any valid DOS file name. The extension .ADD is the default.

Once you have specified a name for your address book, you will immediately be taken into the Add mode. Because this is the first time you're running AM, enter the information that is shown in each field in the Edit/Modify dialog box. (This information will be displayed only when there are no entries in your address book.)

Use the Another button to add additional names. When you have entered the last name, choose OK to return to the main display.

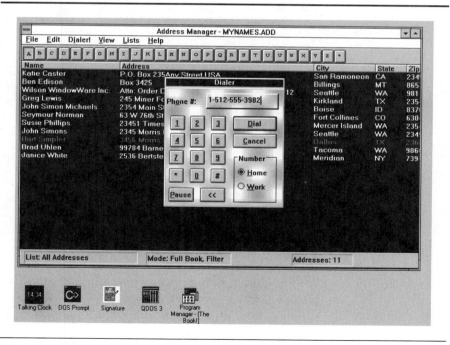

FIGURE 21.1: The Address Manager (AM) program

Hints and Tips

Because it is possible to create your own user-defined lists, it is less efficient to keep separate files for customer addresses, supplier addresses, personal addresses, etc. Instead, just maintain one file and create subsets of it as user-defined lists. Be sure to keep backup copies of your data, using the File/Save As feature.

Use the slider to adjust columns of data. Set the column headings in each of the view modes the first time you run Address Manager, then use Save Heading Columns to save the current settings. The next time you load Address Manager, the saved settings will be used. Alternatively, select Best Fit Columns on the File/Settings menu to have AM dynamically adjust the columns to the best fit for the current data.

When entering names in your book, you can use the up and down arrow keys to help minimize the number of keystrokes you type. AM will remember the last three entries for the Last Name field and the City field; thus, you don't have to type "Seattle" for all of your friends who live there—just use the arrow keys when you get to the City field.

◆ THE APPTIMER PROGRAM

OVERVIEW

AT.EXE (the Apptimer program, shown in Figure 21.2) launches programs at a specified time or at regular intervals. It can be used to automate backups, asynchronous communications, CPU-intensive calculations, etc. It is an easy program to use. Just set the time, date, and the program to be launched, and as long as Apptimer is running, it will launch your program. It will launch DOS programs as well as Windows programs.

USING THE PROGRAM

If you plan to use AT.EXE for daily or weekly program launching, you should have the program automatically load when you run Windows. To have AT.EXE automatically load as an icon, you should first associate the .AT extension with the AT.EXE program (see Chapter 7). Then put your .AT file on the load= line of your WIN.INI file. For example, suppose that you've created a .AT file that specifies the application programs to load and run. To automatically initiate the AT.EXE program, using the program names found in the data file, you could type

load= C:\AT\RUNAUTO.AT

in the [Windows] section of the WIN.INI file. The AT.EXE program does not have to be the foreground task to launch applications.

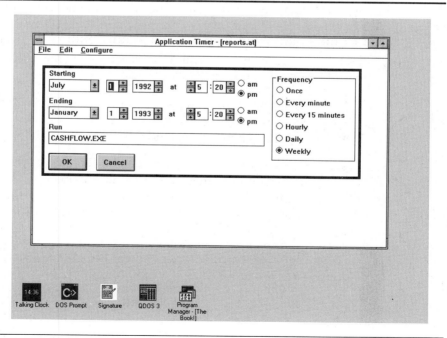

FIGURE 21.2: The Apptimer (AT.EXE) program

The program uses a minimal amount of CPU time. It periodically checks your system's clock, and you may specify the frequency for which the computer checks for a program to launch. The time entry is the number of milliseconds to wait before checking.

The recommended time is 100 (1 second). With the default setting, you will probably not notice any slowdown on the system. If your computer experiences any slowdown, or if the operations to be controlled by AT.EXE are not time-critical, you may want to increase the number. This means that AT.EXE will check the system clock less frequently, thereby imposing less overhead on your system. Be sure your system clock is correct, because the AT program compares the time against your system clock.

Working With a .AT File

To create a .AT file, you must choose Add on the Configure pull-down menu, then fill in the name of the program (in the Run field) and the time and date that you would like to have the program launched (in the Starting field). The default Frequency in autostart mode is set to Once. If you would like the program to be launched at regular intervals, choose one of the other intervals, and then fill out the Ending field.

For example, suppose that you chose Daily frequency. In this case, the program will launch every day at the same time until it passes the Ending Time. You may specify an entire command line in the Run field.

To edit an existing entry in the created .AT file, select an entry in the work area by clicking on it, then choose Edit; alternatively, you may double-click directly on any entry. This will allow you to make any modifications you like. The item that you are editing will be deactivated until you have made your modifications and pressed OK.

To delete a .AT file entry, select any entry, then choose Delete. But be careful, since you will not be asked for a confirmation.

◆ THE CHESS PROGRAM

OVERVIEW

CHESS.EXE (see Figure 21.3) is a Windows version of the historically popular game. There are literally hundreds of books about this game, so I'll assume that you know the rules. I'll describe only how to use this particular program version to best advantage.

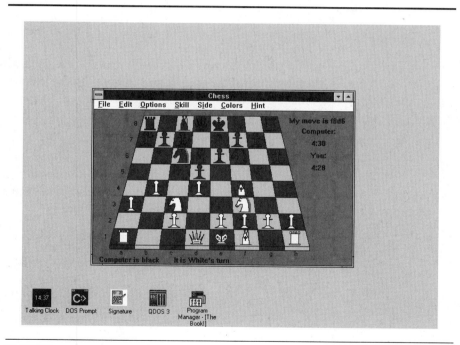

FIGURE 21.3: The game of Chess

USING THE PROGRAM

The program requires at least 282K of memory.

There is no help file, so this documentation is all you'll have. The file GNUCHESS.BOO must be in the same directory as the executable CHESS.EXE. The program creates a CHESS.INI file in your Windows directory to store various settings.

There are seven main menu options. As noted above, the conventional Help choice is not among them:

File

Six choices appear on the main File menu. The New choice resets the board and begins a new game, with you (White) given the first move. The Open choice reads a saved game from disk and picks up the game where it was left off. You can save any game to disk by selecting Save and either typing in a new file name, selecting an existing file name, or accepting the default, CHESS.CHS.

The List choice offers you a way to store, move by move, a record of the program's decision analyses. For each move in the game to the point you save a .LST file with this choice, Chess will store information about the move, an internal scoring value, the depth of analysis, the number of analytical nodes, and the time taken to compute this move.

Exit immediately ends the game, while About Chess displays a message box with traditional copyright information.

Edit

The Edit menu contains five choices. Use the Setup Board choice to construct a customized layout of the chess pieces. This is typically used to recreate an actual chess contest, from a book, the newspaper, or historical records. It can also be used to attempt to solve checkmating puzzles.

Use the Review Game option to display a detailed listing of both player's moves to this point in the game. It includes a white/black player indication, the actual board move, and the score, depth, and time taken for each move.

Each move by either player (you or the computer) can be taken back by selecting the Undo choice on this menu. Each time you select Undo, Chess redraws the board positions for the prior move. You can select Undo successively to move backwards in the contest as far as you like.

Choose Remove to quickly undo the last two game moves (one by each player). The board is restored to the positions prior to the preceding two moves.

Lastly, choose Force to switch from automatic mode to manual mode. The computer will analyze each position and will play the pieces for best possible gain each time you click on Force. It will play for whichever player's turn it is.

Options

This menu allows you to specify a number of settings, such as whether or not the computer speaker beeps with each move and whether or not the coordinates (a–h, and 1–8) of the board squares are visible.

Two of the most interesting options on this menu are Both and Book. When you select Both, Chess switches the game into fully automatic mode. The computer automatically analyzes each position and plays for both players. It is comparable to pressing Force over and over again, with no pause other than to make the decision-tree analysis of the best move.

To gain a better feel for Chess's internal analysis depth, you should select Search Stats, then move the resulting dialog box to another portion of your screen while you continue to play Chess. Each move is reflected in the search statistics displayed in this box.

At any point, you can select Book. Just as a Bookie might place or accept a bet on the game, this option displays the computer's analysis of the two positions. It will indicate such things as which player is ahead, which is likely to mate, how soon it is to take place, and whether or not a draw is likely.

Skill

Use the choices on this menu to determine how tough a chess game to play. The Time choice defines the limits of the game, in terms of either a number of moves or a maximum number of minutes for each player. This time limit is displayed in countdown fashion while you are playing the game, as you can plainly see in Figure 21.3.

Choose Depth to enlarge or shrink the number of levels used during the move analysis. The larger the number you use for the depth value, the better the move that will eventually be selected. The tradeoff is that the deeper the analysis, the more time is consumed. This will make for longer time periods between moves.

To have the computer analyze its potential responses before you even make your move, select Easy from the menu. Choosing Random will vary the depth and quality of the computer's analysis. Clicking on any square to take your turn will abort the look ahead.

Side

Four choices on this menu determine whether you play the white or the black pieces. Just click on White or Black to make the obvious choice. Normally, the white pieces are on the user's side of the board, and the black pieces are on the back side of the board. This is a typical position, much like it would be if you were playing a real opponent on the other side of the board.

By clicking on Switch, you can take control of the black pieces at the rear of the board, while the computer switches places with you and controls the moves made by the white pieces.

When you click on Reverse, the computer retains control of the black pieces but the board is rotated. The black pieces are now in the foreground of the window, played by the computer, and the white pieces are in the rear of the window, played by you. Naturally, both Switch and Reverse attend to their switching or reversal chores without regard to what color pieces you are actually playing. This is controlled by the Black and White choices. The Reverse and Switch choices are more appropriate to controlling the seating of the players.

Colors

Multiple choices on this menu enable you to control all aspects of your chess game. After selecting any of the following choices, Chess displays a color palette from which you can choose the individual colors for each aspect of the game. You can separately control the color of the window background, the squares, the pieces, and all displayed text.

◆ THE DIRNOTE PROGRAM

OVERVIEW

WDN.EXE runs the Dirnote program (see Figure 21.4), which offers the ability to add annotations to directory listings. The program is similar to the DOS program DIRNOTES.COM.

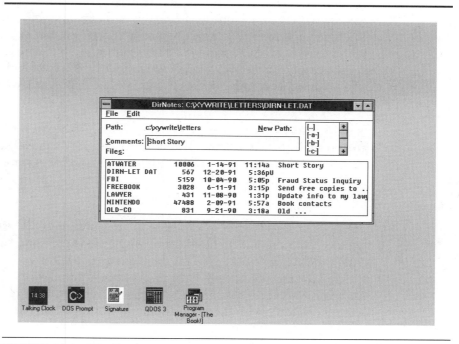

FIGURE 21.4: The Dirnote program

USING THE PROGRAM

The menu for this app is simply

File

    Exit/Update

    Quit/NoUpdate

    About

Edit

    Undo

    Cut

    Copy

    Paste

To annotate a file name, click on the drive you want in the New Path list box, then on the file name in the Files box. Then type your comments (up to 38 characters) in the Comments field. You can also edit existing comments in the same field. As soon as you click on another file name in the Files box, or use any one of the arrow keys to highlight a different file name, the notation is immediately added to the entry in the Files box. The Up/Dn/PgUp/PgDn arrows scroll the box.

Each directory's notes are stored in a file called DIRN-*xxx*.DAT, where the *x*'s are replaced by the first three letters of the directory name. If the name is less than 3 letters, hyphens are used to indicate blanks. For example, the note file for the root directory is called

DIRN----.DAT

The format for this file is identical to that used by DIRNOTES.COM, a popular DOS program. The Files box displays the file name, extension, size, date, time, a marker indicating if the file is an update of a previously existing file, and the comment itself. If the program was started with a specific file, the list box is scrolled to that entry. Note that directories are included in the listing, as contrasted with the results from the DOS program DIRNOTES.COM.

◆ THE ICONMSTR PROGRAM

OVERVIEW

Sooner or later, every Windows' user encounters the need to manipulate icons. The need may be to create personalized icons, to edit existing icons, or just to sort and manage multiple icons.

Windows does not include an icon editor or icon management facilities. The method of installing icons in the Program Manager by typing file names and then clicking sequentially through all of the icons in the file to make a selection is both awkward and inefficient.

ICONMSTR.EXE, or the IconMaster program (see Figure 21.5), is a complete Windows icon editor, viewer, and management system. It enhances your Windows environment in the following ways:

- ◆ It provides a quality graphics editor, including transparent and inverse color attributes.

- ◆ It makes it easy to edit and enhance existing icons, and allows you to capture screen images into an icon.

- ◆ It makes it possible to manage hundreds of icons without having to click through them one at a time.

- ◆ It makes it possible to use all of the icons a user may already have without having to worry about special file formats or custom libraries.

- ◆ It makes it possible to install icons into the Program Manager by using drag-and-drop—without entering file names and without clicking through multi-icon files.

USING THE PROGRAM

As with the other programs on this book's diskettes, you can execute Icon-Master by double-clicking its icon in the ICONMSTR program group. You can also execute IconMaster using the Program Manager's Run command. In this case, IconMaster accepts a single command-line argument for a single icon file to edit upon opening.

If you use Associate in the File Manager to assign ICONMSTR.EXE as the program for .ICO files, you can invoke IconMaster to edit an icon file by simply double-clicking on the icon file. When you invoke the program by double-clicking on a .ICO file, or using RUN with a file name with a .ICO extension, IconMaster starts up the Edit window and displays the desired icon. When you invoke it by clicking on IconMaster's icon in the Program Manager, or by typing RUN without a file name, IconMaster starts up with an empty Preview window.

The primary vehicle for managing icons in IconMaster is the Preview window. A Preview window is analogous to a files window in the File Manager, except that you can see all of the actual icons along with their file names. Up to four separate Preview windows can be open at one time. You can drag and

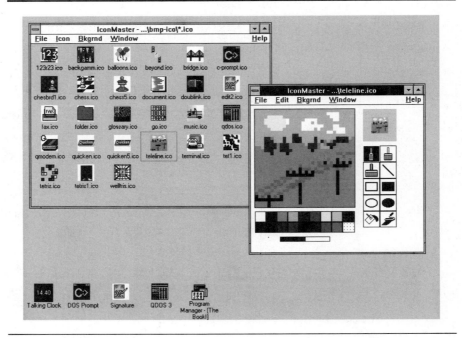

FIGURE 21.5: The IconMaster program

drop icons between Preview windows just like you drag files in the File Manager. You can also drag icons into the Program Manager (Install) to replace whatever icon was previously used for a program or file. Double-clicking on an icon in a Preview window opens the icon for editing in the Edit window.

◆ THE KLOTZ PROGRAM

OVERVIEW

KLOTZ (see Figure 21.6) is a game of falling pieces, similar to TETRIS. You must arrange the falling pieces into solid rows. When you maneuver a piece

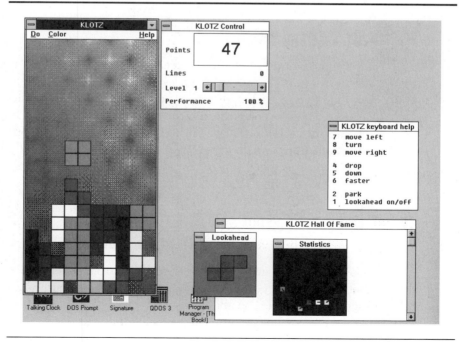

FIGURE 21.6: The game of Klotz

in such a way as to complete a row, the row is removed and you score additional points. If a piece falls and doesn't fill a row, the piece simply remains where it has fallen. New pieces may land on top of settled pieces, raising the height of a column. If a column of pieces grows high enough to prevent a new piece from falling, the game ends. The object is to obtain the highest score before the game ends.

USING THE PROGRAM

The program is named KLOTZ.EXE. It stores the scorebook in a file named KLOTZ20.DAT in the current directory or the network directory. This allows you to have more than one scorebook. The position and size of the main window and the position of the dialog boxes can be saved into WIN.INI. Saved positions are used automatically for all subsequent games. If you want KLOTZ to size and place the windows for you, don't use the Store Desktop function. You will have to edit WIN.INI with an editor and delete the [KLOTZ] section in order to get the automatic positioning back.

Rules of the Game

You get points for every settled piece. How much you get depends on the playing level, i.e., on how fast the pieces move down. If you force a piece down in less than five seconds you can get up to 12 extra points. At level 0 you have 30 seconds before the piece falls the distance of a single line, but you get only 3 points for each piece placed at the bottom. At level 1 the piece falls at the rate of one line per second, and at level 9 it moves over the whole field in one second. At this speed you get 25 points per piece. All pieces start at the top of the playing field—same place, same orientation.

The game has a clock. You can hear it ticking if you have switched Sound to On. At each tick the piece moves down one line. How fast the clock ticks depends on the level; the higher the level, the faster the clock.

You can make as many as five actions (keystrokes) per line. Any more than that have no effect other than to diminish your score: unsuccessful keystrokes count against you. The ability to turn a piece depends on the target position, not on the possibility to turn it physically into the desired position.

Use Key 1 to switch the Lookahead (preview) box on and off. When the Lookahead box is displayed, any points you receive are awarded as if you were playing one level down.

Use Key 2 to *park* (freeze) the current piece in mid-fall and drop the next piece, which starts from the usual place at the top of the playing field. After this piece is settled, the parked piece automatically resumes its fall. If you have parked more than one piece, the pieces are reactivated in the order they were parked. If a full line is removed, parked pieces above the line are shifted down along with other, settled pieces. If part of a parked piece is removed in the process of removing a full line, it cannot be reactivated anymore.

If you release a piece manually with Key 4, there is a lag time between the key press and the drop. The drop will occur on the next beat. You can use the extra time to move the piece (Keys 7, 8, and 9).

Key 5 triggers the next tick. You will find this useful on level 0. At the tick, rows that are already filled will be removed immediately. All rows above the filled ones will be moved down. Although you do not get any points for removing lines per se, it is the only way you can get space for new pieces. For every ten lines you remove, your level is incremented (—through level 9; you can reach level 10 only with Key 6 or the Level control in the KLOTZ Control box).

If you want to increase the game's speed, you can increment your level instantly by using Key 6. If you want to decrease the speed, you must use the Level control in the KLOTZ Control box, which has the unfortunate effect of terminating your current game and throwing away your score. This means you cannot actively lower your level within a game.

There is one main application window for the playing field. All other windows are modeless dialog boxes. You can open and close the dialog boxes at any time. The only required window is the main (playing field) window.

You can resize the playing field and open, close, and move the other windows as you wish. The game starts with a full-screen playing field (with icons). When you invoke the other windows they appear to the right of the playing field. If you prefer a specific layout, you can save it using the menu entry Store Desktop. This saves your window layout into WIN.INI.

If Square Pieces is checked before resizing, the size of the playing field is adjusted to keep the pieces square by adjusting the horizontal size.

The menu entry Grid is not stored into WIN.INI, but Sound and Background Color are.

If you start KLOTZ and then start another Windows application, KLOTZ will start to play for itself. This is KLOTZ's Attract mode. It continues in this mode until you go back to KLOTZ (by clicking into the playing field, for example), at which point it will return to the game that was interrupted.

KLOTZ.EXE is callable from within DOS. If you have Windows and KLOTZ in your path, it starts Windows and then KLOTZ. KLOTZ20.DAT is protected using a CRC scheme, so please don't mess around with it. It ensures that text and data in the Hall Of Fame aren't modified.

If your computer is too slow for KLOTZ, you will not be able to play at higher levels.

◆ THE METCNVRT PROGRAM

OVERVIEW

Metric Converter, or METCNVRT.EXE (see Figure 21.7), handles 14 frequently needed conversions between American and metric (SI) systems. Metcnvrt also converts American to American and metric to metric.

USING THE PROGRAM

Metcnvrt simplifies conversions by offering the user two sets of menus: one for "From" units and the other for "To" units. Both menus are implemented as radio buttons. The user enters a value in Metcnvrt's From window using either the keyboard or the Clipboard. To convert the value, the user simply selects one radio button from either of the From boxes and one radio button from either of the To boxes. The From window value can be entered in either floating point or scientific notation. Metcnvrt figures out the format from the value entered.

The user triggers a conversion by doing any of the following:

♦ Pressing the Enter key after typing the From value,

♦ Clicking on the Convert button,

♦ Selecting any radio button, or

♦ Typing *c*, C, or ^C.

Metcnvrt's Quantities menu lists 14 quantities. By selecting a quantity, the user causes Metcnvrt to display radio-button menus for both the American and metric units of that quantity.

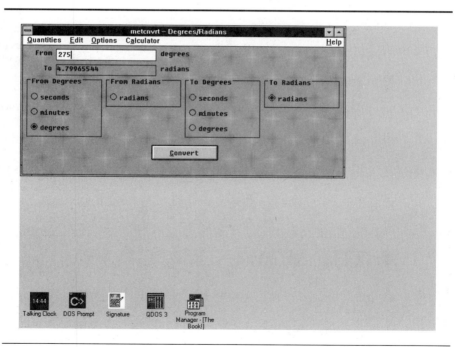

FIGURE 21.7: The Metric Converter program

The Options menu allows the user to display the output conversion in any of three formats: floating point, scientific notation, or general. General format implies that the program will select whichever format is more compact for the number of digits and precision.

The Options menu also allows the user to select the To and From system(s) for the conversion. When a system is checked, that system's group of radio buttons is displayed in the main window.

The Save entry on the Options menu writes

◆ the quantity selected,

◆ the system(s) selected, and

◆ the format type selected

to the WIN.INI file.

The Calculator menu item spawns a Windows calculator. The user may specify the calculator program by creating a [metcnvrt] section within the WIN.INI file and adding a string similar to CALC=CALC.EXE. The default calculator is, of course, CALC.EXE.

When either Scientific or General format is selected, Metcnvrt displays converted values to nine significant digits. When Floating Point format is selected, Metcnvrt displays converted values to nine decimal places.

Internally, most Metcnvrt conversion table factors are accurate to ten significant digits.

◆ THE MOWIN PROGRAM

OVERVIEW

MOWIN.EXE, or the More Windows program (see Figure 21.8), dramatically increases the screen size of smaller EGA and VGA screens by simulating larger screens to handle the Windows desktop. This larger, or virtual, screen is much larger than your real screen. For example, the real screen size on a

VGA monitor is 640 pixels wide by 480 pixels high. More Windows simulates a virtual screen that is 66 percent larger than your VGA screen and up to 110 percent larger than an EGA.

More Windows offers you the ability to move the mouse against the screen edges to bring a different portion of the virtual screen instantly into view. This feature is called *panning*. With panning, you can place more icons and windows on your desktop, each of which will have more space around it for easier viewing and manipulation.

USING THE PROGRAM

Do not run the More Windows program (MOWIN.EXE) before running the special installation program. To install MOWIN.EXE properly, double-click on the INSTALL icon in the MOREWIN program group. Select a video

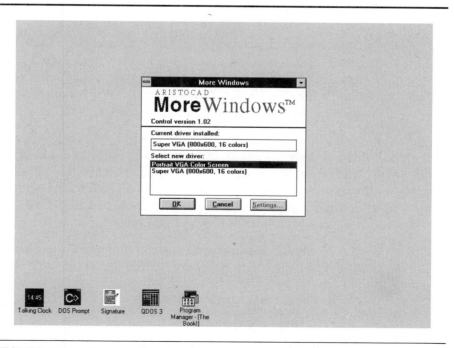

FIGURE 21.8: The More Windows program

adapter (EGA or VGA) and then click on Install. All necessary files will be automatically copied to the Program Manager's Main group. You will then be asked if you wish to create icons in the Program Manager's Main group for MOWIN.EXE and SK.EXE files. Click on OK and the main installation is done.

Now if you wish to run Windows under the auspices of the MOWIN program, click on Yes. A dialog box appears that displays the type of video driver that Windows is currently using. In the version of More Windows included with this book's diskettes, there is only one choice of driver: Portrait VGA Color Screen. In the full commercial version of the product, you have more choices:

- ◆ Full-page color (1024 x 1024)
- ◆ Full-page paper-white (1024 x 1024)
- ◆ Landscape color (1024 x 511)
- ◆ Portrait color (640 x 800)
- ◆ Square color (800 x 600)

If you make a choice (full commercial version only), More Windows will inform you that you must restart Windows for your new video choice to take effect. If DOS applications are running, you will be directed to exit from them and then return to the More Windows dialog box to finally leave the Windows product and return to the DOS prompt.

If you have any difficulties when installing More Windows, you can always return your system to its previous configuration by copying the SYSTEM.BAK file (saved by More Windows during the installation process) to overwrite SYSTEM.INI in your \WINDOWS subdirectory. Additionally, you can back out of the installation sequence at any time by choosing the Cancel button in the ongoing dialog box.

If you followed the instructions above and you cannot restart Windows because your video appears to have locked up, follow these instructions:

1. Change your current directory to \WINDOWS.

2. Type the command

   COPY SYSTEM.BAK SYSTEM.INI

3. Restart Windows by typing

WIN

◆ THE PAINTSHP PROGRAM

OVERVIEW

Different graphics programs usually create different file formats. Consequently, to port a picture from one painting program to another often requires a tool to convert the picture to the new format. PAINTSHP.EXE, or Paint Shop (see Figure 21.9), was designed to be that tool. But Paint Shop goes beyond that.

In its simplest form, Paint Shop can be used as a picture viewer. Taking it a step further, Paint Shop may be used as a file format converter. Recognizing the need for some picture manipulation, Paint Shop includes capabilities to alter the picture and its colors. And finally, for those with specialized needs, Paint Shop can be used as a screen capture utility.

As a Windows user you already have the programs necessary to create quality documents. As an example, you can use Paint Shop to open a TIFF file: Dither the picture to black-and-white, mark off the area of the picture to be used, copy that area to the Clipboard, then paste the picture into Microsoft's Write. Use Write to put the text into your document, and then print the document.

USING THE PROGRAM

Due to the large amounts of memory demanded by large pictures, Paint Shop works best in 386 enhanced mode. Paint Shop can be run in Windows' standard mode, but remember that large pictures take quite a bit of memory; if you do not have enough memory to handle a picture, a message telling you so will appear.

Pictures are handled by Paint Shop in one of two ways. After Paint Shop has read the picture's data from the file, it is up to your video driver to create a picture that can be displayed on your system. This picture will be referred to as a *bitmap*.

In some cases the video driver will not be able to create the bitmap. The most common reasons are lack of memory or the picture is too large. If the bitmap cannot be created, Paint Shop will use its only alternative: it will *draw* the picture. Drawing the picture is slower than displaying a bitmap. You will be able to tell the difference from the way the picture is displayed. A bitmap will be displayed from the top down. A drawn picture will be drawn from the bottom up.

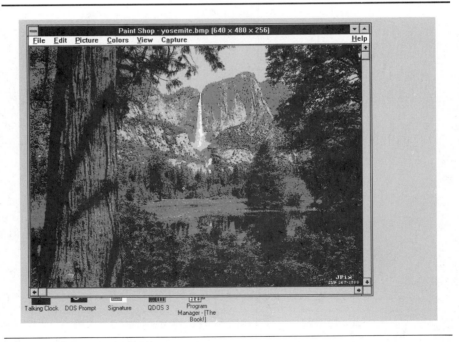

FIGURE 21.9: The Paint Shop program

The picture drawing method will be used for all 24-bit pictures. The reason for this is the large amount of time that is required for most video drivers to create a bitmap of a 24-bit picture. As an example, it took less than a second for my video driver to create the bitmap for a 640 × 480 picture with 256 colors. But the same video driver took more than a minute to create the bitmap for a 24-bit picture.

Some Paint Shop operations require additional memory. If additional memory is not available Paint Shop will attempt to recover the current picture and inform you that there was not enough memory to complete the operation.

If Paint Shop cannot recover your original picture the program will reset. Paint Shop resets by clearing the present picture from memory and from the client area. Just reopen the picture file to get the original picture back into Paint Shop.

Loading and saving GIF pictures, and dithering of any picture, are done in the background, allowing you to continue to work in Windows while Paint Shop processes your picture.

Although Paint Shop allows for multiple instances of itself, you should not attempt to run more than one copy of the program at the same time.

◆ THE QUOTE PROGRAM

OVERVIEW

The QUOTE, or Quote for the Day, program (see Figure 21.10) displays in a window one quotation selected at random from a database of quotes. Quote for the Day can be configured to pick another random quotation at regular intervals, to minimize to an icon, or to close itself after a specified period. It can also find quotations based on a fragment of text that you give it, and can copy the currently shown quotation into the Clipboard so that you can insert it into a word processor or other program. A simple menu controls all these operations.

USING THE PROGRAM

You can install this program to appear when you first load Windows (copy it to the START program group), or you can launch it as you would any other application via the Program Manager or File Manager.

Understanding the Menu Options

In addition to the standard Windows options, the menu attached to Quote for the Day contains the following:

New Quote	Randomly chooses a new quotation when selected. Click on this for a new quotation.
Find Quote	Invokes the Find dialog, which can be used to find quotations based on text contained within them.

FIGURE 21.10: The QUOTE program

Copy Quote	Copies the quotation into the Clipboard, to be subsequently pasted into another application.
Options	Invokes the Options dialog, which is used to set various operating features of Quote for the Day.
About	Invokes the About dialog, giving version information.

The other menu choices are provided by Windows, and perform their usual operations.

Understanding the QUOTE File Format

The file that Quote for the Day uses is an ordinary text file. As such, it can be prepared and edited using any text editor or word processor. If you use a word processor, make sure that it doesn't insert formatting codes.

Each quotation in the database must be on its own line (each line must end in a carriage return). That line can be any length up to 1,023 characters, counting letters, spaces, and everything. A quotation consists of two parts: the body of text and the name of the person the quotation is attributed to. Quote for the Day expects these to be separated by the three characters *space-dash-space*. For example:

"Balanced, like a child's seesaw." - Judd Robbins

In this case "Balanced, like a child's seesaw" is the quotation, and Judd Robbins is the author. Anything that follows the author's name is also considered part of the name. This makes it easy to include biographical information. Surrounding the quotation in quotation marks is purely cosmetic; they can be omitted.

Quote for the Day will separate the two parts of the quotation, displaying the body of the quotation in a large font and the author's name in a smaller font, justified to the right margin.

Quote for the Day will treat the quotation so that word-wrapping is done automatically. You don't and can't insert any of your own carriage returns anywhere within the quotation. However, you can force a line-break by typing the | (vertical bar) character where you want the line to break. In this way, you may control how lines break for a short poem or verse.

◆ THE REMINDER
PROGRAM

OVERVIEW

Windows Reminder (see Figure 21.11) is a time-management program written exclusively for Windows 3.0 and 3.1. The program is simple to use yet powerful enough to do your work for you without you having to be there!

Reminder is a Windows application that maintains a "To Do" list or task list of items that you want to be reminded of. An "item" can be thought of as a specific event, such as

Dinner at 6:00 with Fred

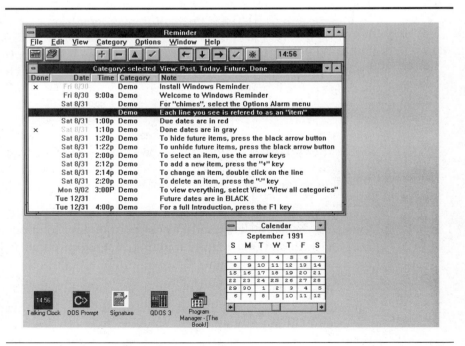

FIGURE 21.11: The Reminder program

or

       Bank Open new account

Since the time is not required, you can make a list of errands to do for any day, and print it out to take it along with you, or give to others as a reminder for them. This list can be used by you or by others in your family or work to keep track of your items. If you choose not to delete items as you take care of them, you will have a log of the items you accomplished. This comes in handy when you need to give a status report of your work or progress on a project.

Reminder was designed to let you set up and view your appointments as easily as possible. Items or tasks are sorted by date and time. This places all the items needing attention at the top so you can easily see what is next on your list. The time is not required; you can still enter a task that needs to be done that day. If you do enter a time, Reminder will automatically set an alarm to display your message or run your programs. When running as an icon, Reminder displays the current clock time so you can always keep track of what time it is.

USING THE PROGRAM

The program offers many features that are at once functional and easy to use.

Entering and Editing Reminders

Reminder makes it as simple as possible to enter and edit items by taking full advantage of a Control Bar with three-dimensional buttons, full keyboard support, a Calendar program, Pen Windows support, and sophisticated online help complete with "jump words" for easy access and look-up.

Reminder's Control Bar gives you quick access to editing and viewing items and displays keyboard equivalents to allow you the same access. The current time is displayed on the right side of the Control Bar, and if there is a time item for the current day an alarm picture is displayed.

The Edit section of the Control Bar allows you to quickly edit an item. To create a new item to be reminded of, you can do any of the following:

    ◆ Click on the + button on the Control Bar.

♦ Click on the + key on the keyboard.

♦ Choose the Edit Add menu item.

♦ Press F5.

♦ Double-click on the day you want in the Calendar program.

The View section of the Control Bar allows you to quickly view the items by past, present, future, and done dates. To view just the items you need to do from the past and today, select the left arrow (for past) and the down arrow (for now or today). If you also want to view what you have done for the same time frame, click on the Check button. You can use the F9 through F12 keys to "press" the same buttons on-screen or use the View menu commands. The asterisk at the end is for viewing everything at once (the same effect as pressing all the buttons).

Reminder comes with a Calendar program (also found in the REMINDER program group) that lets you view the days in a month and scroll to other months and years. If Reminder isn't running, the Calendar will start it for you if you double-click on a date. The Enter New Item dialog is automatically brought up for you with the selected date already placed in the date field. Any time the Edit Item dialog is up, you can use Calendar to enter or change the date and time just by clicking the mouse on the date you want and using the right mouse button to select the time.

Adding Music to Your Reminders

Reminder can automatically start up other applications at a specific time and run macros to further automate your job. Reminder can start two different kinds of applications:

♦ A regular Windows or MS-DOS application

♦ A Windows application with DDE commands

To start a regular Windows or MS-DOS application, just supply the name of the program and optional data file to be passed to the application. For example, to start WinWord, just type **WinWord** in the Run field's Note2 section, set the "Action" to Run, and it's set to start at the specified time.

As another example, suppose that you want to remind yourself of a certain event with more than just a windowed message. You could run the WINPLAY program discussed earlier in this chapter. For example, you might have borrowed your neighbor's car last month when your car was in the shop. In return, your neighbor may have asked you to help him paint his new baby's nursery.

You enter a reminder to yourself to go to your neighbor's house on the agreed-upon day. For fun, you set the alarm action to play the theme from *The Godfather*. You set the action to Run (rather than the default Show Message), and you enter the following in the Run field:

WINPLAY C:\ROBBINS\MUSIC\GODFATHR.POL

This runs the WINPLAY program, presuming that it has been placed on the DOS PATH, as it would be if you moved it into the WINDOWS directory. Since the current directory (if you are running the REMINDER program) is C:\ROBBINS\REMINDER, you must either move the melody files into the Reminder directory, or specify the full path name for the melody parameter.

◆ THE SNAGIT PROGRAM

OVERVIEW

SnagIt (see Figure 21.12) is, among other things, a great documentation tool. With SnagIt you can include printed screen shots and images from Windows 3.0 and 3.1 in your documentation. One of SnagIt's key features is its full support for Windows' Dynamic Data Exchange (DDE). With DDE SnagIt may be integrated with any application that supports DDE.

Creating documentation for your applications can be a frustrating task. Importing Windows screens or images into your manual, report, or proposal is a cumbersome, time-consuming task that can try the patience of the most adept user. SnagIt simplifies the documentation process. Windows programmers can quickly create printouts of program screens, windows, and icons for presentation and review. SnagIt also provides DOS users with "Print Screen" capability for applications running in a DOS session under Windows.

With SnagIt, Windows users can capture an entire screen, a portion of the screen, or a single window or icon. SnagIt sends the captured area to a printer, the Windows Clipboard, or a file. These images can be pasted into other Windows applications such as word processors and desktop publishing programs.

USING THE PROGRAM

To use SnagIt, you need:

♦ An IBM PC or 100% Compatible

♦ Microsoft Windows 3.x

♦ A mouse or other pointer device

♦ Any printer that supports bitmaps, such as an HP LaserJet or a Postscript printer

FIGURE 21.12: The SnagIt program

A mouse is required when using SnagIt. The left mouse button is used to select SnagIt menu options and to select screen regions and windows. The right mouse button is used to cancel a region or window selection.

The following keyboard commands are used:

Ctrl+Shift P   Activates SnagIt printing.

Ctrl+Shift X   Makes the SnagIt icon or window disappear from the screen. Pressing Ctrl+Shift X a second time causes the icon or window to reappear.

The SnagIt menu bar has five choices: Input, Output, Format, Options, and Help.

The Input option allows you to select the particular screen image, icon, window, bitmap file, or Clipboard content that you want SnagIt to capture.

The Output option allows you to select an output destination for images captured by SnagIt.

The Format option allows you to change how the SnagIt image will appear in finished form: monochrome, color, or gray-scale. The Options choice allows you to select from a number of additional features offered by the SnagIt program, including alert beeps, color boost, scaling, and Clipboard chaining.

The Help option provides information about each menu selection.

◆ THE STOP PROGRAM

OVERVIEW

The STOP.EXE program (see Figure 21.13) offers a convenient way to quickly exit from Windows. Rather than have to switch back to the Program Manager and then choose Exit from the File menu, you only need click on the stop-sign icon. This offers an equivalent shutdown service.

One of the nicest features of Windows is its ability to communicate between tasks. STOP takes advantage of this by essentially requesting all open applications to close themselves. This allows each application to execute its own shutdown procedure. For instance, a Windows program that has an open file that has been modified can take this opportunity to ask the user to save the file before exiting.

DOS programs cannot process the DDE messages from Windows. Consequently, Windows displays a message directing you to close the non-Windows application yourself.

USING THE PROGRAM

When STOP is iconized, you can exit Windows and all open Windows applications merely by clicking on the STOP icon. To run STOP automatically,

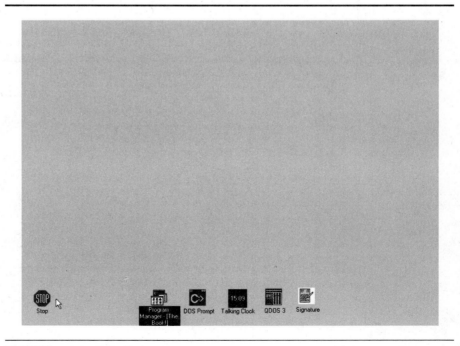

FIGURE 21.13: The Stop program

you can either add it to your Startup group in the Program Manager, or add it to the load= line in your WIN.INI file. The STOP program transmits the correct termination codes to all running Windows programs. If you are currently running a non-Windows application, you will receive a message explaining that the application is still active:

Application still active:

Exit the application and then try closing Windows.

You must then switch to each running DOS application and properly exit from it, saving all necessary files and following each program's individual exit sequence.

◆ THE TAIPEI PROGRAM

OVERVIEW

Taipei (see Figure 21.14) is a modern, solitaire version of the Chinese game Mah-Jongg. The board displays a beautiful layout of intricate, attractively designed playing tiles. You must find and click on matching tiles in order to remove them from the board. Winning a game is much like solving a complex puzzle. One false move at the beginning could ruin your chances at victory. And, while every game has a solution, finding it often takes hours of diligent play.

USING THE PROGRAM

Playing Taipei is simple. The object of Taipei is to remove all of the tiles from the board. Tiles are removed from the board in matching pairs. Tiles can only be removed if they are "free." A tile is free if:

1. It has no tiles on top of it, and

2. You can "slide" the tile out to the right or left.

Understanding the Menu Commands

There are two menus in Taipei. The one that is first displayed when you start the game is called the Play menu. The one that is displayed while you are creating new tile layouts is called the Edit menu.

The Play Menu There are four major pull-down menus in the Play menu: File, Move, Options and Background.

The File pull-down menu offers these commands:

Load Layout	Loads a new tile layout
Edit	Brings up the tile layout editing screen
Exit	Abandons the game

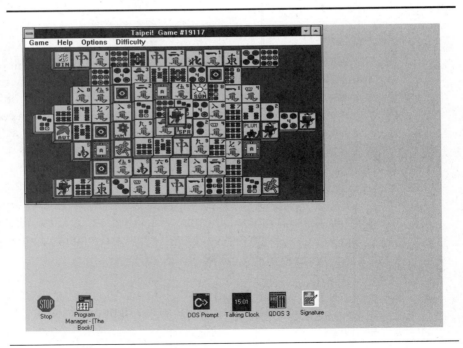

FIGURE 21.14:   The game of Taipei

The Move menu presents the main game commands:

New Game
: Starts a new game. A random game number is selected and the tiles are arranged according to the selected tile layout.

Backup
: Allows you to take back moves all the way up to the start of the game.

Hint
: If you're stuck, Taipei will show you a pair of tiles that match and are free. Taipei does this by flashing the two matching tiles on the board. Select Hint again and Taipei will show another matching set. Selecting Hint will display all matching pairs successively until all of the possibilities are exhausted.

Start Over
: If you want to try the same board over again, use this command.

Select Game
: Allows you to select a specific game number to play. Each of the seven tile layouts has 65,536 different games to play.

Autoplay
: When in Autoplay mode, the computer will begin playing the board and removing tiles for you.

The Options menu allows you to set various parameters:

Color
: Toggles the tiles from color to black-and-white. Normally, Taipei selects either the color or the black-and-white tile set automatically according to the type of display you have.

Messages
: Directs Taipei to display detailed error messages.

Watch Builds
: If checked, Taipei will display each tile as it builds a particular board layout.

The Background menu lets you change the background of the Taipei screen:

Bitmap	Allows you to load your own custom bitmap. The bitmap can be centered in the middle of the Taipei playing field, or can be repeated to create a pattern effect. Many of the standard Windows background bitmaps such as PYRAMID.BMP can be used this way. Taipei will automatically save this bitmap name in the WIN.INI file so you don't have to re-enter it every time you play.
Solid	Uses the standard felt green background.

The Edit Menu   The Edit menu includes its own File menu. The File menu has the following commands:

Load	Loads a previously saved tile layout.
Save	Saves the current tile layout.
Save As	Saves the current tile layout, prompting for a file name first.
Play	Returns to the Play menu using the current tile layout.
Clear	Removes all tiles from the current tile layout.
Level	Selects the level (1–7) on which to place new tiles.

Using the Keyboard Effectively

A mouse is required to play Taipei. However, the following keys may be helpful in addition to using the mouse:

F1	Help
F2	New Game
ESC	Minimize
H	Hint
Backspace	Back up one move

Here are some final hints for you if you are having difficulty solving the Taipei puzzles:

1. Remove the end tiles as soon as you can, especially those tiles that block more than one other tile.

2. If all four tiles in a matching set are free, you can remove all four safely.

3. Work from the outside in.

◆ THE TIMEFRAM PROGRAM

OVERVIEW

TimeFrame (see Figure 21.15) is a small Windows utility that adds a digital clock display to the right-hand side of the topmost window's title bar. (Most clock utilities display the time in just another window on the screen.) After you've created a complex group of running tasks, it can often be difficult to find the window or even icon that is showing the time. TimeFrame always shows the current time in the topmost window's title bar.

USING THE PROGRAM

The author of this program named it TimeFrame because it displays the time in the frame part of a window. It does not display the time when the window is a dialog box.

The two key files installed in your TIMEFRAM directory by this book's installation program are TFRAME.DLL and TIMEFRAM.EXE. You can permanently run this program at Windows startup by including an icon in your STARTUP directory. Make sure that the program directory is \ROBBINS\TIMEFRAM, or that you've moved both files into your WINDOWS directory.

Once you restart Windows, you should see the clock display in the topmost window.

◆ THE WHISKERS PROGRAM

OVERVIEW

Whiskers (see Figure 21.16) is a utility that lets you assign keys of the keyboard to the right and/or middle buttons of the mouse. By using the Shift and Ctrl keys, two mouse buttons can have eight combinations. Assign "Enter" to a mouse button and you'll be able to activate default OK buttons

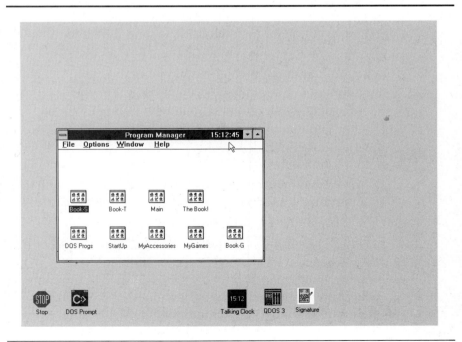

FIGURE 21.15:   The TimeFrame program

without clicking on them and your hand will stay on the mouse. Whiskers can do a left double-click in one click and simulate a middle button on two-button mice.

USING THE PROGRAM

To run Whiskers, double-click on its icon in the WHISKERS program group that was created during the book's installation sequence. A new Whiskers icon will appear at the bottom of your screen. At this point the Whiskers icon will have bars showing. This means that Whiskers is running. The bars indicate that the mouse-button clicks are being captured and processed as the default settings. To view or change the default settings, see the "Programming the Mouse Buttons" section below.

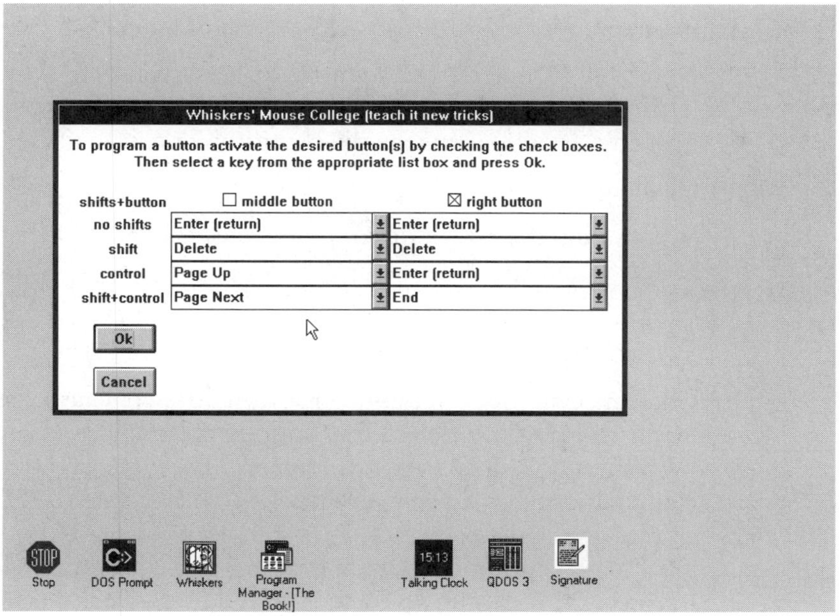

FIGURE 21.16: The Whiskers program

Whiskers requires a minimum of 18K of memory to run. When using either of the Hideit options described below, the minimum memory required to run Whiskers is 7K.

You can run Whiskers by clicking on the mouse icon in the WHISKERS program group that was created during this book's installation sequence. You can also put Whiskers on the load= line of the WIN.INI file in order to load Whiskers as an icon when Windows is first started. The authors recommend that you make the Whiskers entry on the WIN.INI's load= line as opposed to the Run line.

Using the Hideit Feature

The Hideit option allows you to hide the Whiskers icon, thereby reducing screen clutter. This option requires that a Whiskers entry be made or adjusted in your WIN.INI file. In the WIN.INI file, scroll to the [Whiskers] section and make an entry that reads

hideit=on

Now close Whiskers, then restart Whiskers again by double-clicking the icon in the Program Manager. Whiskers will load, but the icon will be hidden. To turn off this option, change the hideit=on line in the WIN.INI file to

hideit=off

When using the Hideit option, the memory required to run Whiskers drops to approximately 7K.

Programming the Mouse Buttons

Click once on the Whiskers icon at the bottom of your screen and the system menu will pop up. Select the Buttons command and a dialog box titled "Whiskers Mouse College" will appear. The right and middle buttons' key combinations have been programmed with default key values. You may change any of these defaults. For example, to program the right button to be the Delete key, turn the check box on, then click on the down arrow of the list box that is in the No Shifts row and in the Rightbutton column. Scroll the list box until you find the Delete entry. Select it and click on the OK button.

To program the Shift+RightArrow button combination, follow the same steps as above, but make your selection in the list box in the Shift row and Rightbutton column. Follow these steps for programming each of the combinations. Repeat these steps for programming the middle button on a three-button mouse.

If you have a Logitech bus mouse you will need to call Logitech Tech Support at 415-795-8100 to get a new LMOUSE.DRV file. This file will support the middle button of your mouse.

◆ THE WINCLOCK PROGRAM

OVERVIEW

WinClock (see Figure 21.17) is a digital clock, with the following features:

- ◆ Display of time and date in many different formats
- ◆ Ten daily or specified date alarms
- ◆ Runs programs at specified times
- ◆ Optional hourly beep
- ◆ Allows user to set date and time easily
- ◆ Optionally stays in front of other applications
- ◆ Remembers its position on the screen
- ◆ Two stopwatches
- ◆ Two countdown timers
- ◆ Optional blinking colon separating hours and minutes
- ◆ Context-sensitive help
- ◆ Auto-detect active screen saver
- ◆ Cascade and Tile compatibility

USING THE PROGRAM

The three key files needed to run WinClock are WINCLOCK.EXE, WCHOOK.DLL, WINCLOCK.HLP. If you choose to run WinClock from a different directory than the one created by this book's installation diskette, be sure to keep these files together. It will be easiest to copy the WinClock icon (from the book's WINCLOCK program group) into your Windows STARTUP directory. In this way, WinClock will always be available to you when you start Windows.

Explaining the WinClock Options

To bring up a list of options, click once on the WinClock date/time icon.

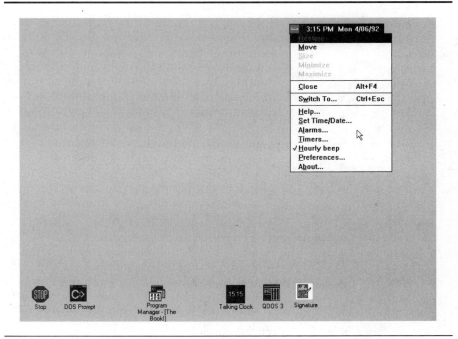

FIGURE 21.17: The WinClock program

Help   This will bring up help about WinClock and explain how to use context-sensitive help. It will also display an index of all help available for WinClock.

Set Time/Date   This allows you to easily update the current time and date. When the window pops up, enter the correct time and date.

Alarms   This allows you to configure one or both of WinClock's alarms. To set an alarm, click on the radio button for the alarm that you want to set (one through ten). When you have made your choices, click on OK. (If you want to leave the alarms the way they were, click Cancel.)

In the Time field, enter the time for the alarm to go off.

In order to cause the alarm to beep when the specified time/date arrives, select the Beep check box so that there is an × in the box.

WinClock offers two alarm actions. You can have a simple note displayed in a message box, or you can cause a specified program to execute. If you want a note to appear in a message box, click on the Note radio button and type a note into the field box beside the radio button. If you want to run a program at the time for which you have set the alarm, select the Run Program radio button.

Timers   WinClock has two stopwatches and two countdown timers. By selecting different options you can have WinClock display some or all of the timers as well as the time and date.

The settings that you make in the Timer dialog box only affect the WinClock display while one or more timers are running. The settings will be saved while WinClock is running but will be reset to the default when WinClock is restarted.

Hourly Beep   Select this option if you want WinClock to sound a short beep and flash on the hour.

Preferences   Preferences allows you to change how the date and time are displayed. Select the options you want and click on OK.

About   Select About to display WinClock ownership information.

◆ THE WINPLAY PROGRAM

OVERVIEW

WINPLAY (see Figure 21.18) is a Windows polyphonic music player. It will play any of a series of musical files through your PC's speaker.

USING THE PROGRAM

The WINPLAY program will play any of the following music files:

> FATUM.POL
>
> GODFATHR.POL
>
> LYRICS.POL
>
> MORIA.POL
>
> TCHAYK.POL
>
> ZHIVAGO.POL

However, be aware that WINPLAY does not play by the Windows rules. Since it does not readily give up the focus when it is playing music, you should not use this program in a system that is already burdened with many time-dependent applications. Also, since each song takes a portion of a minute, you should be prepared to sit back and listen since you will not be able to do much else once you start a music file.

You can also specify the name of a particular polyphonic music filename (?7E.POL) as the first parameter when you start WINPLAY. For example, you would enter the following command line:

WINPLAY *filename*

to play the melody stored in *filename*. If you run WINPLAY without a parameter, WINPLAY creates a window and you must then pull down the Play menu to bring up the screen window seen in Figure 21.18. You can then highlight the desired melody name in the File box and click on Play.

The easiest way to use WINPLAY is to install it in the Program Manager using New on the File menu. At a command line, type

WINPLAY *melodyfilename*

and then type the actual melody name as a comment. This way you will have a separate icon for each melody.

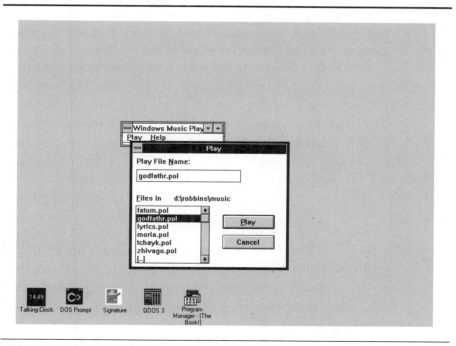

FIGURE 21.18:   The WINPLAY program

Another unique use for WINPLAY is to combine it with the REMINDER program discussed earlier in this chapter. When done correctly, the Reminder program can run Winplay using any of these songs. Rather than just receive a windowed reminder message, you can be reminded of a meeting or any other event by a message and/or a melody of your choice. See the end of the Reminder discussion below for an explanation of how to combine these two programs.

◆ THE WINPOST PROGRAM

OVERVIEW

WinPost (see Figure 21.19) provides an easy-to-use facility for managing reminder notes for the Microsoft Windows 3.0 environment. Up to 100 "notes" can be in use at any given time. WinPost will save the state of all notes upon program termination so that the next time the program is started, the notes will look exactly the same as when the program was exited.

Some of WinPost's many features include:

- ◆ Large number of configuration parameters, including note size, color, text font, etc.

- ◆ Each note provides a complete editing facility, including cut, copy, and paste operations.

- ◆ Notes can be manipulated very easily through the use of mouse shortcuts and/or accelerator keys.

- ◆ Print facility allows the user to print a single note or all notes.

- ◆ Alarm Note feature allows the user to set a note to be displayed at a specified date/time, accompanied by an optional alarm tune.

- ◆ Search facility provides a way to sort through numerous notes rapidly.

♦ Layout feature allows the user to organize notes into various categories.

♦ A note can be configured as Always On Top, which causes the note to always rise to the top of a stack of windows automatically.

♦ Auto Saver feature saves all information to disk periodically so that not all data is lost in case of a Windows crash.

USING THE PROGRAM

While there are numerous files in the distribution form, only two files are actually needed: WINPOST.EXE and WINPOST.HLP. WinPost can be started by using one of several methods:

1. Clicking on the WINPOST icon in the Program Manager.

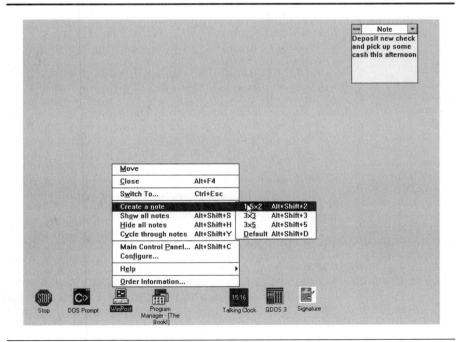

FIGURE 21.19: The WinPost program

2. Using the File Run choice in the Program Manager.

3. Copying the WINPOST icon into the Windows STARTUP program group.

Creating a Note

You can create three different sizes of notes: 1.5" × 2", 3" × 3" and 3" × 5". Note size selected during the process of creating a note simply indicates its starting size—the user is able to resize notes by turning on the Resizable Note option.

Up to 100 notes can be created. If the user attempts to create more than 100 notes, an error message box will be displayed.

When a note is created, it is assigned by default to the current layout. If the current layout is "All," the note will not be assigned to any layout.

To create a note, perform one of the following:

1. Choose Create a Note from the Controller Icon menu. This causes a cascading menu to be displayed. Simply choose the desired note size.

2. Or double-click on the Controller icon. This causes a default-size note to be created.

3. Or use one of the possible accelerator keys:

   ♦ Alt+Shift+2 to create a 1.5" × 2" note
   ♦ Alt+Shift+3 to create a 3" × 3" note
   ♦ Alt+Shift+5 to create a 3" × 5" note
   ♦ Alt+Shift+D to create a default-size note.

Editing a Note

The Note window is a fully editable window, with standard Windows editing conventions. Undo, Cut, Copy, and Paste operations are available through the Note window system menu. In addition, a Copy All operation provides a shortcut whereby all text in the note window is copied to the Clipboard.

Deleting a Note

To delete a note, perform any of the following procedures:

1. Choose Delete This Note from the Note window system menu.

2. Or Double-click on the Note window system menu icon.

3. Or use the accelerator key Alt+F4.

Printing Out Your Notes

The content of the notes may be printed, either individually or all notes at one time. The print facility makes use of the default Windows printer font (typically Courier). Printer output contains the note title, date/time of last modification, date/time of alarm (if set), and the actual note text.

Printing a Note

To print a note, choose either of these procedures:

1. Choose Print This Note from the Note window system menu.

2. Or use the accelerator key Alt+P.

Printing All Notes

Print from the Main Control Panel prints all notes that are assigned to the current layout. It also prints all alarm notes that have expired. If the Show All Note option in the Configuration dialog is turned on, unexpired notes are also printed.

Saving Data to Disk

WinPost automatically saves information about all notes (size, position, configuration, edit window content) whenever WinPost is closed or a Windows session is terminated. However, the user may choose to save data to disk to ensure that important changes are saved.

To save data to disk, click on the Save button in the Main Control Panel.

◆ THE YACHT PROGRAM

OVERVIEW

Windows Yacht (see Figure 21.20) is a Windows version of the popular board game Yahtzee. The object of the game is to reach the highest possible point score by rolling and scoring dice.

USING THE PROGRAM

A new game begins by rolling the dice. To discover how many points a roll is worth, click on any scoring category. The potential score appears, and the Roll button changes to a Score button. When you are ready to select a score and a scoring category, click on the Score button. The turn ends, the score is entered permanently in that category, and all the dice roll for the next turn.

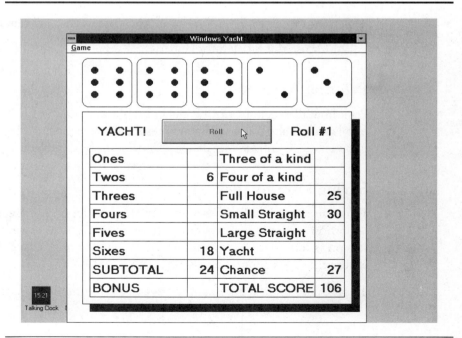

FIGURE 21.20:   The game of Yacht

After the first and second rolls, some or all of the dice may be rolled again. To roll the dice, click on the individual dice that you wish to reroll, then click on the Roll button. After the third roll of a turn, a score must be selected.

The keyboard may be used instead of a mouse. Use the Tab key to move between the dice, scores, and the Roll/Score button. Use the arrow keys to move from die to die, or from score to score. Use the spacebar to select and deselect dice and scores. Finally, use the Enter key to press the Roll/Score button.

At the end of the game, the total of all scores gives the final score. If the total of all the scores on the left side of the score card (Ones through Sixes) is greater than or equal to 63 points, an additional 35-point bonus is added.

The following lists the different types of scores, and how their points are computed:

CATEGORY	SCORE
Ones	1 × the number of dice that came up 1
Twos	2 × the number of dice that came up 2
Threes	3 × the number of dice that came up 3
Fours	4 × the number of dice that came up 4
Fives	5 × the number of dice that came up 5
Sixes	6 × the number of dice that came up 6
Three of a kind	Sum of all dice values
Four of a kind	Sum of all dice values
Full House	25 points if three dice have come up the same and the remaining two match each other
Small Straight	30 points if four dice are in a straight sequence
Large Straight	40 points if all five dice are in a straight sequence
Yacht	50 points if all dice have come up the same
Chance	Sum of all dice values

Glossary

This glossary defines all of the important Windows- and DOS-related terms used in this book. Although most of these terms are defined in the text when they are introduced, this glossary offers concise definitions that will refresh your memory when you read a chapter later in the book, or when you simply can't remember the meaning of a particular term.

◆

accelerator key   *See* shortcut key.

adapter segment   *See* reserved memory.

address   A numeric identification of a particular location in computer memory.

allocation   The assignment of memory locations during the creation of graphical objects.

allocation unit   *See* cluster.

ANSI driver   A device driver that provides additional support for advanced console features.

anti-aliasing   A technique used in Continuous Edge Graphics (CEG). Pixel colors along the edges of an image are blended to create a smoother appearance.

API   *See* Application Programming Interface.

applets   A diminutive term that is used to describe the collection of small, special-purpose utility programs that are part of the Windows 3.1 package.

application   *See* application program.

application icon   The rectangular graphic that appears on the desktop to represent an application that has been initiated, then minimized.

application program   A program that performs a manual function, such as balancing a checkbook or managing inventory.

Application Programming Interface (API)   The set of all operating-system service calls.

application shortcut key   In 386 enhanced mode, a key combination that returns a background task to the foreground.

application swap file   In standard mode, a temporary hidden file used to store information about a suspended non-Windows application.

application window   A screen window that contains the output of a running application.

archive attribute   A bit used to indicate whether the file in question needs to be backed up.

assembly language   A symbolic form of computer language used to program computers at a fundamental level.

associate   To connect all file names having a particular extension to a specified application. When a file name having the extension is opened in the File Manager, the associated application is executed.

asynchronous communications   *See* serial communications.

attribute   A characteristic of a disk file. *See also* archive attribute, read/write attribute, hidden attribute, system attribute.

audio-video interleaving (AVI)   Displays digital TV in a window on your VGA (or better) monitor.

authoring system   The computer system used to develop a multimedia presentation.

AUTOEXEC.BAT   A batch file executed automatically whenever the computer is booted up.

automatic link   An OLE link that forces Windows to update the object's icon image automatically in all documents containing an occurrence of the linked object.

AVI   *See* audio-video interleaving.

backfill   To use some memory from an EMS board as conventional memory.

background   All the screen area behind the active window; also refers to all processing that occurs for other than the foreground task.

background application (or task)   Any program that has been started but is currently not the foreground task.

bank switching   A method of providing expanded memory by switching blocks (called *banks*) of memory into and out of the addressable range under 1MB.

batch program (or batch file)   An ASCII file containing a sequence of DOS commands that will be executed when you invoke the program.

baud rate   The speed of serial data transmission.

BBS   Stands for *bulletin board system*. An information system that offers file access and conference services. It is accessible via a modem and communications software.

binary   A numbering system based on powers of 2.

binary file   Any file that is not composed solely of ASCII characters.

binary transfer   A method for sending data files between computers. It transmits all data without processing any of the data as control characters.

bit   One-eighth of a byte. A bit is a binary digit, either 0 or 1.

bitblt   Stands for *bit block transfer*. Refers to a graphics function that copies a group of pixels from memory to the screen or to another memory location.

bit-mapped font   Any font that is fixed in size, device-specific, and stored as a group of bit values (i.e., a *bit map*).

bit mapping   The process of using memory to represent the color and intensity of portions of graphic images.

Boolean   A logical indicator of one of two possibilities, such as True/False or On/Off.

booting   The process in which the computer is turned on, performs a series of hardware and memory validity checks, and then loads the operating-system code into memory from disk. *See also* warm booting, cold booting.

boot record   The section on a disk that contains the minimum information DOS needs to start the system.

branch   A subportion of a directory tree.

branching   The transfer of control or execution to another statement in a batch file.

buffer   An area in memory set aside to speed up the transfer of data, allowing more data to be transferred at once.

byte   The main unit of memory in a computer. A byte is an 8-bit unit. One ASCII character is usually stored in one byte.

cache   A portion of memory reserved for the contents of disk sectors. It facilitates faster access to the same sectors. It can be implemented with the SMARTDRV.EXE device-driver program.

cascade   To arrange windows so that each one overlaps another but with the title bar always visible for each window.

CAV   Stands for *constant angular velocity*. One of the two principal techniques used for recording on videodiscs; with this technique, the rotational speed of the disk remains constant.

CD-I   Stands for *compact disc-interactive*. A set of standards for merging data of various sorts (text, graphics, audio, video) on a single compact disc.

CD-ROM/XA   Stands for *Compact Disc Read-Only Memory Extended Architecture*. An extension to the standard CD-ROM format that specifies how to merge (*interleave*) audio with other data.

chaining   A process in which the control of execution is passed from one batch file to another.

channel map   A specification table that defines, for source MIDI channel messages, the destination channels, output devices, and patch maps.

check box   A square box that appears in dialog boxes. When selected, an X appears to indicate that the option has been turned on.

child window   A secondary window, wholly contained within a screen window. For example, the directory window in the File Manager is a child window of the File Manager application. Sometimes called a *document window*.

client application   In a DDE conversation, the program that accepts the pasted link. In an OLE conversation, the program that starts a server application to manipulate linked or embedded data.

Clipboard   The name given to the memory area assigned to temporary storage duties for data transfer between applications.

Clipboard Viewer   The name of the Windows Accessory program that offers direct access to the Clipboard memory area.

close   To terminate an application and remove its window from the screen.

cluster   A group of contiguous sectors on a disk. Also known as an *allocation unit,* this is the smallest unit of disk storage that DOS can manipulate.

CLV   Stands for *constant linear velocity*. One of the two principal techniques for recording video on videodiscs; with this technique, the speed of the data as it passes the laser pickup remains constant. To do this, the hardware varies the rotational rate of the disk.

code page   A character set that redefines the country and keyboard information for non-U.S. keyboards and systems.

cold booting   The process in which DOS is booted by turning the computer's power on. *See also* booting.

collapse   To remove from view, in the File Manager directory tree display, all subdirectories below the currently highlighted one. When the subdirectory structure is hidden in this way, a plus (+) sign appears in the icon just to the left of a directory name.

color pattern   A combination of two colors to form a third in the Color Palette of the Windows Paintbrush program.

color scheme   One of several groups of defined colors used for the various screen elements on the desktop.

command button   A button in a dialog box that contains a selectable option, such as Cancel or OK.

COMMAND.COM   The command processor that interprets your internal and external command requests.

command line   The line on which a command is entered, along with all its associated parameters and switches.

command processor   The program that translates and acts on commands.

command prompt   A visual indicator that DOS is waiting for input.

COM port   Shorthand phraseology for a communications port. Windows and DOS support four serial ports, named COM1, COM2, COM3, and COM4.

composite video   A video signal that contains all necessary color and timing information in a single input connection.

compound device   An MCI (Media Control Interface) device that uses instructional files to control its multimedia outputs.

compound document   An OLE document that contains multiple kinds of data, which are stored in multiple formats. Each data object also includes information about the object that originally created the data so that the application can be restarted automatically.

CONFIG.SYS   An ASCII text file containing system configuration commands.

configuration   An initial set of system values, such as the number of buffers DOS uses, the number of simultaneously open files it allows, and the specific devices that are supported.

context switching   The process in which an inactive program is made into the active (i.e., foreground) program.

contiguity   The physical adjacency on a disk of the disk sectors used by a file.

CONTROL.INI   The Windows initialization file that contains the specifications for your desktop color patterns.

Control menu   The menu that lists options that affect the overall size, shape, and activity of applications and the windows that display them. It appears when you click on the Control-menu box in the upper-left corner of any application window. It also appears when you click on any application icon.

Control-menu box   The icon in the upper left-corner of an application window.

Control Panel   A principal Windows application program, located in the Main group of the Program Manager, that enables customization of a variety of Windows hardware and software settings.

conventional memory   Physical memory located below the 640K DOS addressing limit (also called *low DOS memory*).

conversation   A DDE transaction between two Windows applications.

CPU   Stands for *central processing unit*. The main chip that executes all individual computer instructions.

CRC   *See* cyclic redundancy check.

cyclic redundancy check   A method of determining whether or not an error has occurred during a data transmission. In this method, a single character is computed from the data itself by an industry-standard algorithm. If the receiver calculates the same CRC character as the transmitter (which embeds the CRC character in the data), it is assumed that no error has occurred.

cylinder   Two tracks that are in the same place on different sides of a double-sided disk. It may be extended to include multiple platters. For example, side 0 track 30, side 1 track 30, side 2 track 30, and side 3 track 30 form a cylinder.

DASD   *See* direct access storage device.

data area   Tracks on a disk that contain user, as opposed to system, information.

data bits   The number of bits that make up a transmitted or received character in serial communications.

data disk   A disk that has been formatted without the /S switch. The disk can contain only data; no space is reserved for system files.

data file   A named storage area, used by applications to store a group of related information, such as a spreadsheet. Also called a *document*.

data stream   The data transmitted between two components or computers.

DDE   Stands for *Dynamic Data Exchange*. The predecessor standard to OLE for simultaneously updating data in one application with information from another executing application. It is based on a low-level message-passing protocol for application communications.

DDEML   Stands for *Dynamic Data Exchange Management Library*. A function-based set of API service calls that is built on the earlier message-based DDE.

deallocation   The return of memory space to the operating-system pool for subsequent use by other applications or by the operating system itself.

deferred writes   *See* staged writes.

delimiter   A special character, such as a comma or space, used to separate values or data entries.

delivery system   The computer system used to play back a multimedia presentation.

demand loading   The process in which a disk file is read into memory when, and only when, the module is actually needed by the currently executing program.

desktop   The screen area that contains windows, icons, and dialog boxes.

destination document   An OLE document that contains an iconic link to a data object in a source document.

device   Any internal or external piece of hardware.

device contention   In 386 enhanced mode, a situation that occurs when two or more devices attempt to use the same device.

device context   A special data structure used by applications to connect the Windows API with a hardware-specific device driver.

device driver   A special program that must be loaded at boot-up to use a device (also known as an *interrupt handler*).

Device Independent Bitmap (DIB)   A monitor-independent format for graphic images.

device name   The name that DOS uses to refer to a device.

dialog box   A rectangular window that displays information and usually prompts you to make choices or to enter data.

DIB   *See* Device Independent Bitmap.

digital signal processor (DSP)   A computer chip that performs specialized operations on digitized waveforms to support rapid sound and video processing.

Digital Video Interactive (DVI)   A proprietary technology from Intel Corporation for storing highly compressed, full-motion video information on compact discs.

direct access storage device (DASD)   A disk drive.

direct memory access (DMA)   The very fast transfer of data between memory and a device, such as a disk drive, using a dedicated high-speed I/O channel.

directory   A named group of files on disk. As part of DOS's file system, this group may include other directories called *subdirectories*.

directory icon   A mini-icon in the File Manager that represents a disk directory.

directory path   A series of directory names that locate a particular file on a disk. Also called a *full path* or *path name*.

directory tree   In the File Manager, a graphic depiction of the directories and subdirectories that represent the organization of files on a disk.

Directory Tree window   In the File Manager, a child window that lists information about the files contained within the current (i.e., highlighted) directory.

disk cache   *See* cache.

disk drive   A hardware device that reads and writes the data stored on a disk.

disk-drive icon   A graphic icon that depicts a particular type of drive in the Directory Tree window of the File Manager. Windows uses different icons for floppy, hard, RAM, network, and CD-ROM drives.

disk optimizer   A program that rearranges files stored on a disk to make the files contiguous.

disk-resident command   *See* external command.

display adapter   An add-in hardware board that sends video output signals to your monitor.

DLL   *See* Dynamic Link Library.

DMA *See* direct memory access.

document *See* data file.

document file Any document that is associated with an application.

document file icon An icon that looks like a dog-eared piece of paper. It appears in the File Manager's Directory Tree window beside any document file. Clicking on such an icon starts the application associated with this document.

document window *See* child window.

DOS Stands for *disk operating system*. The main disk and file management software that facilitates computer/user interaction.

DOS environment A part of memory set aside to hold variables used by DOS and applications, such as COMSPEC, PATH, and LASTDRIVE.

DOS maximizer A memory manager that uses the protected mode of 80386 (and higher) processors to relocate code to maximize the available conventional memory for DOS applications.

DOS memory Sometimes used to refer to the first 640K of conventional memory, used by the typical DOS application.

DOS prompt *See* command prompt.

DOS Protected Mode Interface (DPMI) A formal specification for how multiple protected-mode applications are to run safely in a DOS-based multitasking environment.

dot pitch The size in millimeters of each pixel on a video monitor. The smaller the dot pitch, the higher the allowable screen resolution and the clearer the colors.

double-click speed The time frame within which two mouse button presses are registered as a double click, as opposed to two successive single clicks.

downloadable font   A printer font that can be copied from a disk file, or from system RAM, into a printer's memory. Also called a *soft font*.

DPMI   *See* DOS Protected Mode Interface.

DRAM   Stands for *dynamic random access memory*. A memory chip that uses capacitive techniques for storing data. This method requires constant refresh cycles every second to maintain data integrity. During the refreshing, the processor cannot read the data and is forced to wait.

drive icon   *See* disk-drive icon.

drive identifier   A single letter assigned to represent a drive, such as A or B. It usually requires a colon after it, for example, A:.

driver   *See* device driver.

DRIVER.SYS   A device driver used to facilitate assigning logical drive identifiers to extra physical disk drives.

drop-down list box   A box that contains a single column of choices.

drop-down menu   A menu that appears in a window, located just below a selected option from a window's menu bar. Also called a *pull-down menu*.

DSP   *See* digital signal processor.

DVI   *See* Digital Video Interactive.

Dynamic Data Exchange   *See* DDE.

Dynamic Link Library (DLL)   A collection of executable procedures, grouped into one file on disk, that can be shared at run time by multiple Windows applications. The procedures need not be separately linked to each application's .EXE file.

EEMS   Stands for *Enhanced Expanded Memory Specification*. Improved on the earlier EMS by allowing program code in addition to data to be mapped. In addition, it allowed mapping to occur anywhere within the 1MB addressing range of conventional memory.

8514   The 1987 high-resolution video standard introduced by IBM. It offers both 640 × 480 VGA resolution with 256 colors and interlaced 1024 × 768 resolution with either 16 or 256 colors.

EISA   Stands for *Extended Industry Standard Architecture*. A computer industry bus design that enables adapter memory addresses to be modified with simple configuration change requests, rather than by resetting switches on the adapter boards themselves.

embed   To insert a data object created by one OLE application into a document created by another (or the same) OLE application.

embedded object   A document file created in one application and inserted iconically into another document.

EMM   Stands for *expanded memory manager*. A device driver that manages expanded memory, using either the physical characteristics of a memory board or the facilities of the 386/486 chip to emulate expanded memory.

EMM386.EXE   A device driver for 80386 and 80486 computers that manages the allocation of upper memory blocks, as well as the emulation of expanded memory from extended memory.

EMS   Stands for *Expanded Memory Specification*. Memory that conforms to the LIM (Lotus-Intel-Microsoft) specification for addressing memory beyond the 1MB maximum addressable DOS limit. LIM 4.0 is the current standard version, although LIM 3.2 (its predecessor) is still adhered to by many applications and hardware boards.

emulation mode   A machine state in which one device (usually a printer or terminal) mimics the behavior of another device.

environment variable   A symbolic name, such as PROMPT or PATH, that contains system data. Values are assigned to these names with the SET command in DOS.

EPS   Stands for *Encapsulated PostScript*. This is a Page Description Language (PDL) that was developed by Adobe Systems. PostScript offers both resolution and device independence and is supported by the largest number of software and hardware companies.

error level   A code, set by programs as they conclude processing, that tells DOS whether an error occurred, and if so, the severity of that error.

exclusive application   In 386 enhanced mode, a foreground application that uses virtually all CPU resources.

executable file   Any runnable application with a file extension of .COM, .EXE, .BAT, or .PIF.

expand   In the File Manager, to redisplay subportions of the directory tree.

expanded memory   Extra physical memory, generally found on separate, add-in boards, which is designed to conform to the industry-standard LIM EMS (Lotus-Intel-Microsoft Expanded Memory Specification). This memory is not directly addressable and must be mapped into pages of conventional memory.

expanded memory emulation   The simulation of expanded memory with extended memory, typically performed by a device driver.

expanded memory manager   *See* EMM, EMM386.EXE.

Expanded Memory Specification   *See* EMS.

expansion card   An add-on circuit board that can increase the power of the system, such as adding extra memory or a modem.

expansion slot   A connector inside the computer in which an expansion card is placed so that it ties in directly to the system.

extended DOS partition   A disk partition, beyond the first hard-disk drive C: partition, which can be divided into further logical disk drives (D:, E:, and so on).

extended memory   Additional physical memory beyond the DOS 1MB addressing limit for 80286, 80386, and 80486 computers. It is used by Windows to support multiple, simultaneously started programs. This memory is directly accessible in protected mode, using 24-bit (on 80286 computers) or 32-bit (on 80386/80486 computers) linear addresses.

extended memory manager   Any device driver (e.g., HIMEM.SYS) that manages extended physical memory.

Extended Memory Specification   *See* XMS.

external buffer   A device, connected between a computer and another device, that acts as a temporary storage area for data transmitted from the computer.

external command   A command whose procedures are read from disk into memory, executed from memory, and then erased from memory when finished.

file   A collection of bytes, representing a program or data, organized into records and stored as a named group on a disk.

FILE   One of the possible print destinations, available through the Control Panel's Printers dialog box, that directs printed output to a specified disk file.

file allocation table (FAT)   A table of sectors stored on a disk that tells DOS whether a given sector is good, bad, continued, or at the end of a chain of records.

file attribute   One of several bits that denotes whether a file is read-only, system, hidden, or archived.

File Manager   The main Windows application for the management of files and disk structures.

filter   A program that accepts data as input, processes it in some manner, and then outputs the resulting data.

fixed-width font   Any font whose characters all have the same width.

flag   A single bit, usually part of a byte indicating a status. For example, the *accessed* flag in the Virtual Memory Manager's page table indicates whether an application has read from or written to a page since it was first loaded into physical memory.

flicker   A condition in which the video rewrite speed is too slow to create the visual illusion of a steady image; caused by either a slow refresh rate (the screen seems to blink) or by interlacing of the horizontal line output (one or more extraneous lines seem to move down the screen).

flow control   The method used to control the starting and stopping of data transmission during serial communications.

font   The set of all characters in a given typeface at a given point size and with an attribute (or stroke weight), such as italic. In Windows, a font may not have a specific point size. *See also* vector font.

font cartridge   A casing that plugs into a printer slot and contains a set of hardware fonts.

foreground application (or task)   The program running in the active (or foreground) window.

formatting   The placement of timing marks on a disk to distinguish tracks and sectors.

fragmentation   A condition in which a file is stored in noncontiguous sectors on a disk.

full-motion video   A sequence of video displays (at least 30 frames per second) that create the illusion of smooth motion.

full-screen mode   The mode in which a non-Windows application runs as it does under DOS alone. It uses the entire screen for its display rather than appearing within a window.

GDI   Stands for *Graphics Device Interface*. Windows' graphic language used for programming window-oriented applications.

General MIDI specification   A set of standard definitions for MIDI files. These include instrument patch settings, key assignments, and channel settings.

GIF   *See* Graphics Interchange Format.

gigabyte (GB)   1024 megabytes.

global descriptor table (GDT)   A table of address entries that enables the Windows operating environment to convert logical segment addresses into actual physical memory locations. Also used to maintain addressability to information used by multiple applications as well as the operating system.

global memory   Random access (RAM) memory that Windows uses for information that may be accessed by all applications.

granularity   The invisible spacing grid used by Windows to line up windows and icons on the desktop.

graphical user interface (GUI)   A screen display in which executing programs can appear in windows. All programs use a consistently appearing group of pull-down menus, dialog boxes, and graphical elements, such as icons and scroll bars.

graphics coprocessor   An additional processing chip, usually found on high-end video adapters, that takes over time-consuming graphics operations from the main CPU.

Graphics Device Interface   *See* GDI.

Graphics Interchange Format (GIF)   CompuServe's compressed, device-independent, color image format. It also supports gray-scale images and is used as a popular exchange mechanism by many electronic bulletin board users.

graphics mode   The mode in which all screen pixels on a monitor are addressable and can be used to generate images. Contrasts with text mode, which allows a fixed number of rows and columns of characters.

graphics resolution   The degree of detail used to display or print any image, measured in number of dots. Higher resolutions require special-purpose video or printer equipment.

group   In the Program Manager, a named collection of applications. The entire group can be iconized or enlarged to appear within a child window.

group icon   The small graphic icon that appears in the Program Manager that, when maximized, displays the individual applications located within the group.

group window   A child window within the Program Manager that displays the application icons (or data files associated with applications) that appear within the group.

GUI   *See* graphical user interface.

hardware interrupt   A signal from a device to the CPU, indicating that an event has taken place.

head   A disk-drive mechanism that reads data from and writes data to the disk.

hexadecimal   A numbering system in base 16.

hidden attribute   A bit used to indicate whether the file in question is to be hidden from view and from all commands that search the DOS directory table.

hidden file   A file whose name does not appear in a directory listing. This term usually refers to DOS's internal system files, disk labelling file, deletion-tracking file, and partition table image file. It can also refer to certain files used in copy-protection schemes.

high DOS memory   *See* reserved memory.

High Memory Area (HMA)   Refers to the first 64K of extended memory; can be used by DOS 5 to load internal tables and buffers, thereby freeing up additional conventional memory.

High Performance File System (HPFS)   The advanced file system, currently available in OS/2 but not in DOS, that supports long file names (up to 256 characters) and extended file attributes (e.g., the name of the application that created the file).

high-resolution mode   The mode on a video monitor in which a large number of pixels are used to provide the most detailed screen image possible. On a color monitor, this mode reduces the possible range of colors that can be output.

HIMEM.SYS   The extended memory manager used by both DOS 5 and Windows.

hinting   The process in which a TrueType instruction, contained within each TrueType font file, redefines the outline for a particular character at a particular size to ensure the best graphic result at a lower resolution.

HMA   *See* High Memory Area.

horizontal frequency   A measure of the time required to draw one horizontal line of pixels across the screen.

hot key   A key combination used to signal that a memory-resident program should run.

hot link   A DDE connection between two applications that accounts for information in one application (the *client*) being automatically updated when data in the other application (the *server*) changes.

hue   The fundamental color of a portion of the screen.

hypermedia   A term commonly used to describe multimedia applications that have interactive, hypertext-like linkage to various multimedia elements.

I-beam   The vertical pointer, shaped like the letter *I*, that replaces the mouse pointer whenever you move the mouse pointer into a screen area that can accept input.

icon   A small screen image (32 × 32 pixels) that represents an element in Windows, such as a running application or an available disk drive.

icon view   A small screen drawing that represents embedded or linked information. Selecting the icon view runs the appropriate application, which then displays the actual embedded or linked data.

import   To create an OLE package by reading an existing file into the Object Packager utility.

Industry Standard Architecture   *See* ISA.

insertion point   The location, represented by a flashing vertical bar, in a window where typed text will be displayed.

interlaced video   A method of video image generation that draws every other line on the screen, then rescans the screen to fill in the intervening lines.

interleaving   The sequencing of sectors on the tracks of a hard disk. A 1:1 interleave means that each numbered sector is physically located just after the one that precedes it. A 2:1 interleave means that each numbered sector is located at every other physical sector.

internal command   *See* resident command.

interprocess communication (IPC)   The term that encompasses the primary methods of passing information from one application to another. In Windows, IPCs include Clipboard operations, Dynamic Data Exchange (DDE), and Object Linking and Embedding (OLE).

interrupt   *See* hardware interrupt.

I/O address   A memory location used for communicating information between a program and a hardware device.

IRQ   Stands for *interrupt request*. The hardware line that carries the interrupting signals (for sending or receiving data) from devices.

ISA   Stands for *Industry Standard Architecture*. Refers to the most common hardware bus design used by the IBM PC/AT and compatibles.

ISO   Stands for *International Standards Organization*. Reponsible for defining many computer industry standards, such as the High Sierra (or ISO-9660) format for CD-ROM disks.

Joint Photographic Experts Group (JPEG)   An industry organization that created a standard for compressing still images.

key map   A table of translation information that converts source key numbers in MIDI messages into destination key numbers for a particular MIDI device.

key repeat rate   The rate at which a character will be redisplayed if you keep the key depressed.

kilobyte (K)   1024 bytes.

landscape mode   A printer mode in which characters are printed horizontally along the length of the page. *See also* portrait mode.

large page frame   A term that refers to the existence of memory pages in conventional memory that can be switched between different banks of expanded memory. This facilitates access to extra physical expanded memory pages beyond the 64K limit provided by the standard page frame, which must always be located in reserved memory (between 640K and 1MB).

LDT   *See* local descriptor table.

Least Recently Used (LRU)   The algorithm used by Windows in 386 enhanced mode to decide which pages of physical memory are copied out to a swap file to make room for new pages associated with the currently running application.

LIM EMS   Standards for *Lotus-Intel-Microsoft Expanded Memory Specification*. A specification for managing expanded memory.

LIM 4.0   Version 4.0 of LIM EMS, which provides for a maximum expanded memory window of 1MB (sixty-four 16K pages).

LIM 3.2   Version 3.2 of LIM EMS, which provides for a maximum expanded memory window of 64K (four contiguous 16K pages).

link   As a noun, it means a reference in a destination document to a preexisting object from a source document. As a verb, it means to insert an icon or bit map into a destination document that represents an editable source object.

linked object   An icon or bit map that represents, in a destination document, an embedded OLE object.

list box   A child window within a dialog box that displays a list of available choices.

local descriptor table (LDT)   A table of address entries that enables Windows programs to convert logical segment addresses to actual physical memory addresses.

local printer   A printer that is connected to a port on your computer in contrast to a network printer that may be connected to a port on another computer in the network.

logical drive   A disk drive, created in an extended DOS partition, that does not physically exist but that DOS thinks exists. It is a means for DOS to access a physical disk that has more than 32MB available.

look-ahead buffer   A 512-byte buffer used by DOS or a cache program to read successively positioned disk sectors before they are actually referenced by a program, thereby improving performance.

low DOS memory   *See* conventional memory.

LPT port   A parallel communications port. Windows supports up to three such ports, which are named LPT1, LPT2, and LPT3.

LRU   *See* Least Recently Used.

luminosity   The degree of brightness of a color, ranging from minimum luminosity (black) to maximum luminosity (white).

manual link   A link that is not updated automatically when you make changes to the linked object.

mark   To select a portion of the screen in a non-Windows application by using the Edit/Mark option on the Control menu.

maximize   To increase the size of a window to its largest size.

Maximize button   The up arrow located to the right of the title bar in Windows. Clicking on this button expands the window to its largest possible size.

MCI   *See* Media Control Interface.

MDI   *See* Multiple Document Interface.

Media Control Interface (MCI)   A specification for controlling multimedia devices and files. Windows includes drivers for MIDI devices and outputting sound (.WAV) files.

media file   A disk file that contains multimedia instructions for creating sound, animation, or video output.

medium-resolution mode   The mode on a Color/Graphics Adapter (CGA) in which only 320 × 200 pixels of resolution are allowed.

megabyte (MB)   1024 kilobytes.

memory cache   *See* cache.

memory-resident   Located in physical memory, as opposed to stored in a disk file. *See also* TSR.

menu bar   The horizontal bar, located just below the title bar, that contains the names of an application's menus.

message passing   The non-preemptive, cooperative method of multitasking used in Windows.

MIDI   Stands for *Musical Instrument Digital Interface*. A set of specifications for communication between computers and musical instruments.

MIDI file   A file that contains the necessary instructions for outputting sounds on a MIDI device. *See also* channel map, key map, and patch map.

MIDI setup   A translation table that specifies the type of MIDI device and the correspondence between source channel numbers and destination channels, as well as port and patch map names.

minimize   To decrease the size of a window to a representative icon.

Minimize button   The down arrow located to the right of the title bar in Windows. Clicking on this button removes the window from the screen, replacing it with an icon at the bottom of the screen.

monochrome   A display using two colors only.

monospaced font   *See* fixed-width font.

mouse pointer   The screen symbol representing the symbolic location of the mouse. In graphics mode, the mouse pointer appears as an arrow; in text mode, it appears as a solid movable rectangle.

MPC   *See* multimedia PC.

MPEG   Stands for *Motion Picture Experts Group*. An industry organization that has defined a technique for compressing full-motion video data.

multimedia   A technology that displays words or graphics on screen that provide immediate access to underlying video, sound, graphics, or character information.

Multimedia Extensions   A set of system function calls that can be found in new dynamic link libraries (DLLs) and that support the control of multimedia hardware.

multimedia PC (MPC)   A personal computer that contains the necessary hardware and software to run multimedia applications.

Multiple Document Interface (MDI)   A set of specifications that define how an application manages multiple child windows within the visual client area of a single Windows application.

multitasking   The condition in which two or more applications execute simultaneously.

multithreading   The condition in which multiple independent code sequences (threads) run simultaneously within a single program.

Musical Instrument Digital Interface   *See* MIDI.

network   A setup in which computers are connected together, combined with software that facilitates sharing of data files and peripheral devices.

network device   Any shared device (e.g., a disk drive or laser printer) located on a network whose contents are available to any user logged on to the network.

noninterlaced mode   A video display pattern in which an entire screen is drawn in one pass by drawing all horizontal screen lines in order from top to bottom.

non-Windows application   Any application not designed to use the features of Windows. Typically, this term refers to an older DOS application that may or may not have a Windows version available.

NTSC   Stands for *National Television Standards Committee*. The industry organization that produced the standards for color television displays in the United States. The U.S. standard consists of 525 horizontal lines per frame, displayed at a rate of 30 frames per second, using interlaced scan techniques.

object   Any group of data created by an application, such as a block of worksheet cells, a data graph, or a sound file. This collection of data can be linked to or embedded in another document created by a different OLE application.

object handler   A dynamic link library, normally provided by an OLE server application, that provides rapid and specialized services to OLE client applications. These services may handle the most common requests, thus saving the time of initiating the full-blown server application.

Object Linking and Embedding   *See* OLE.

OEM Text   The text format used when pasting text into a non-Windows application.

OLE   Stands for *Object Linking and Embedding*. The successor protocol to DDE for application communications. Based on high-level dynamic link libraries rather than on simple intertask communications, it facilitates the connection of tasks by enabling one task to connect dynamically to another task for application initiation as well as data updating.

OLE client application   Any program that can store and display an OLE object.

OLE object   An icon or some other graphic element that represents an encapsulated data or file item in an OLE client application.

OLE server application   Any program that can begin executing and activate an OLE object when that OLE object is selected by double clicking in an OLE client application.

open   In the File Manager, to run a highlighted program or to run an executable program that has been previously associated with a file extension.

optimization   The mechanism of improving the speed and performance of the overall Windows system.

option button   A small circle in a dialog box that appears beside each of several mutually exclusive options. Also called a *radio button*.

OS/2   Stands for *Operating System/2*. An advanced 32-bit multitasking operating system from IBM, which is interrupt-driven and manages all computer/user interaction, enhanced-memory features, and true multitasking.

overhead   The additional bytes required to manage global memory objects.

overlay area   A portion of memory reserved for storage and execution of overlay file instructions.

overlay file   A file containing additional portions of a sophisticated and complex program. An overlay file is usually too large to fit into memory along with the main .EXE or .COM file.

overlay manager   A program that controls loading (during execution) of independent and mutually exclusive code segments. This capability allows older DOS programs, which are constrained by a 640K address maximum, to include more instructions than can fit at one time into conventional memory.

package   An application icon (or small bit map) that represents embedded or linked information. When you select the package in the document that contains it, the original application that created it is opened for editing, displaying, or playing (depending on the type of data represented by the object).

page frame   The reserved memory area (limited to 64K in upper memory blocks) used for access to expanded memory pages.

paging   A feature of 80386 (and later) processors that organizes all possible memory into 4K blocks. Each block is assigned a table-resident base address (which effectively maps the virtual address location into available memory addresses) and an access status (e.g., paged to disk).

palette   The set of colors offered by Windows for its desktop or by an application (like Paintbrush) for its own display.

parallel communications   Data transmission in which several bits can be transferred at one time.

parallel port   Any one of three computer connections (named LPT1, LPT2, and LPT3) used for parallel communications.

parameter   Information given on a command line that determines how a command executes.

parameter passing   The process of using variable parameters (%0 to %9) to pass information to a program.

parity bit   The bit, added to the end of a sequence of data bits and used to improve error checking, that makes the total of the data bits and the parity bit odd or even.

partition   A section of a hard disk. (The maximum number on one hard disk is four.)

password   A sequence of characters that allows entry into a protected system or program.

patch map   The translation table for a MIDI device that defines destination patches, volume percentage, and key map names for the source patch numbers used in an output channel.

path   The list of disks and directories that DOS searches to find a command file ending in .COM, .BAT, or .EXE.

path name   *See* directory path.

PCM   *See* pulse code modulation.

pel   A synonym for pixels. Originally, *pel* was an abbreviated form of *picture element*.

peripheral   Any physical device connected to a computer.

permanent swap file   A fixed, hidden swap file. It allows Windows to write directly to a known disk location, thereby enhancing performance as compared with writing to the disk with conventional DOS file calls.

PIF (program information file)   A file of specifications that defines how a non-Windows application runs from within Windows.

PIF Editor   The Windows application, found in the Main group of the Program Manager, that enables you to create and modify a .PIF file.

piping   The process of making the output of one program the input to another program.

pixel   The smallest unit of display on a video monitor—in short, a dot—which can be illuminated to create text or graphics images.

pixel depth   The number of video memory bits required to specify a pixel's color. Four bits are required for 16 ($2^4 = 16$) colors, eight bits are required for 256 ($2^8 = 256$) colors, and so on.

plotter font   A font generated by scalable lines, or dots. Also called a *vector font*.

port   A connection for transferring data to and from external devices.

portrait mode   A printer mode in which characters are printed horizontally along the width of the page. *See also* landscape mode.

Presentation Manager   The windowing interface of OS/2, which displays executing programs within separate screen windows on the same display monitor.

primary DOS partition   The first disk portion of a hard disk. It contains the boot record and other DOS files.

printer driver   The software that manages the interface between your computer and a particular printer.

Print Manager   The Windows application that manages spooled output to your printer for all Windows applications.

print queue   The list of file names to be printed by a particular printer.

priority   Refers to the relative proportion of time (out of all possible processor time) that is to be allocated to an application.

processor time   The overall CPU time available to divide up among applications. *See also* priority and time slice.

program file   A .PIF, .EXE, .COM, or .BAT file that can run an application.

program group   In the Program Manager, a collection of like objects (typically applications) contained within one child window.

program information file   *See* PIF.

program-item icon   In the Program Manager, a graphic symbol that represents a runnable and selectable application.

Program Manager   The primary Windows shell program, which manages program execution and application switching.

proportional font   Any font whose characters have variable widths for printing and display.

protected mode   An operating mode of an Intel 80286, 80386, or 80486 chip, which supports multitasking and advanced memory management.

protocol   The conventions that govern data transfer between computers.

pull-down menu   A vertical list of command choices that appears when you select an option from a menu bar.

pulse code modulation (PCM)   A method of sampling and digitizing sound.

QEMM 386   An expanded memory manager program, available from Quarterdeck. It is often used as an alternative to Microsoft's EMM386.EXE.

queue   A series of files waiting in line to be processed. *See also* print queue.

radio button   A small circle in a dialog box or an options box that indicates whether an option has been selected. A dot appears in the circle if the adjacent option has been selected. Also called an *option button*.

RAM   Stands for *random access memory*. The part of the computer's memory to which you have access; it stores programs and data while the computer is on.

RAM disk   An area of RAM that acts as if it were a disk drive. All data in this area of memory is lost when the computer is turned off or warm-booted. Also known as a *virtual disk*.

RAMDRIVE.SYS   Microsoft's device driver that emulates a physical disk drive in memory (i.e., a RAM disk).

raster font   A single-size character font created from a fixed pattern of dots.

read-after-write verification   An extra level of validity checking; it is invoked with the VERIFY command or the /V switch. Data is reread after being written to disk and is compared with the original information.

read-ahead buffer   A portion of memory reserved to hold additional data that is read for performance enhancement purposes during disk caching and buffering operations.

read-only attribute   A file attribute that prevents a file from being updated or deleted. The file can still be read.

read/write attribute   The bit that indicates whether a file can accept changes or deletions, or can only be accessed for reading.

real mode   The operating environment that runs Windows with less than 1MB of extended memory. It is not available in Windows 3.1.

redirection   Causing output from one program or device to be routed to another program or device.

refresh rate   *See* vertical frequency.

REM statement   A line of text in a QBasic program, CONFIG.SYS file, or batch file that contains remarks or comments for program explanation or clarification.

reserved memory   System memory (between 640K and 1MB). DOS can use it (with the appropriate system configuration) for device drivers, memory-resident programs (TSRs), and ordinary applications. Also known as the *adapter segment* or *high DOS memory*.

resident command   A command located in random access memory.

resolution   The density in dots per inch of a printout or video display. *See also* graphics resolution.

resource compiler   A special program used in the preparation of .RES files and Windows .EXE files. The .RES file contains information about the graphic resources used by a Windows program, and the final Windows .EXE program combines the code and data information for the application with the graphic resource information used by that application.

Resource Interchange File Format (RIFF)   A Microsoft standard (compound document format) for storing and managing all multimedia data types.

Restore button   A small rectangular box (containing a double-headed up and down arrow) that appears at the right side of a title bar to indicate that a window has been maximized. Clicking on this button will return the window to its former screen size.

reverse video   Black letters on a white background.

RGB monitor   A type of monitor that uses three separate signals to control the red, green, and blue portions of the image.

Rich Text Format (RTF)   A text format, generally used in Clipboard transfers that retain the original text arrangement, that includes both the text and its associated formatting information.

RIFF   *See* Resource Interchange File Format.

ROM   Stands for *read-only memory.* The section of memory that you can only read from. This contains a small portion of the basic computer operating system, as well as certain hardware support routines.

root directory   The top-level directory on any disk.

RTF   *See* Rich Text Format.

SAA   *See* Systems Application Architecture.

sans-serif font   Any font whose characters do not have extra strokes above or below the main body of each character.

saturation   The purity of a screen color. It signifies how much of the actual color is used in the mix of pixels used and how much gray is blended in.

scalable font   *See* vector font. Also called a *scalable typeface.*

screen capture   A copy of the current screen image or active window image in the Clipboard or in a disk file.

screen saver   A variable pattern of colors or images that appears on your screen after a certain amount of time in which no keystrokes or mouse movements have been detected.

scroll arrow   An arrow at either end of a scroll bar that enables you to move the workspace contents by one line each time you click on the arrow.

scroll bar   A vertical or horizontal bar that appears at the right or bottom of a window that is not large enough to display all necessary data. At either end of the scroll bar is an arrow that indicates the scrolling direction.

scroll box   A small, movable rectangle that moves within a scroll bar to indicate your relative position within the data that appears inside the window's workspace. Also called a *slider box*.

SCSI   Pronounced "scuzzy" and stands for *small computer system interface*. This 50-pin parallel interface is a fast data transfer (approximately 4MB per second) standard for daisy-chain connection of up to seven disk and/or tape drives to a single controller board. Many of the newest hard disks and CD-ROM drives use this interface.

secondary command processor   A second copy of COMMAND.COM, invoked either to run a batch file or to provide a new context for subsequent DOS commands.

sector   A division of a disk track; usually 512 bytes.

segment   A separately defined and managed block of code or data. Segments are combined into applications and are separately managed by the addressing mechanisms of the operating system.

select   To specify, by highlighting, a screen item for a subsequent action (e.g., moving or copying) to be performed.

selection cursor   The extended highlighting that indicates that an item or a screen area has been selected.

serial communications   Data transmission in which data is transferred and processed one bit at a time.

serial port   A connection between your computer and one of up to four separate serial data devices. The ports are named COM1, COM2, COM3, and COM4.

serif font   A font whose characters have finishing strokes above or below the main body of the characters.

server   On a network, a computer that processes requests from multiple nodes (computers) on the network. Also, in a DDE or OLE transaction, the program that handles requests for source data.

server application   Any Windows program that creates OLE objects.

shadow RAM   Any portion of RAM into which has been written a copy of instruction code from read-only memory (ROM). Typically, this is done to be able to execute the code from these faster RAM locations rather than the normally slower ROM locations.

shareware   Copyrighted software that may be tried first and paid for (and registered) later.

shell   An application that enables you to select and execute other applications.

shortcut key   A single key combination that replaces a sequence of steps to effect some program action.

simple device   Any Media Control Interface (MCI) device (e.g., an audio-only CD player) that generates output from direct instructions rather than from media files.

slider box   *See* scroll box.

small computer system interface   *See* SCSI.

small page frame   A term that simply refers to a standard 64K page frame located in upper reserved memory.

SMARTDRV.SYS   A disk-caching device driver that speeds up disk access and overall Windows performance. Also know as the *SMARTDrive utility*.

snapshot program   A program used in debugging to store the status of system or application program variables.

soft font   *See* downloadable font.

software interrupt   A signal from a program that calls up a routine that is resident in the computer's basic programming. It is also a signal to the computer that the program has finished, has a problem, and so on.

sound board   An add-in controller card that enables you to produce multimedia output of high-quality recorded music and voice.

sound driver   A device controller that enables Windows and applications to generate sounds on appropriate hardware.

sound file   A disk file that contains audio data that represents playable sounds; it has a .WAV extension.

source document   An OLE document that contains the object that is linked or embedded elsewhere.

special characters   A group of unique graphic, mathematical, and international character symbols that cannot be generated from single key-presses. You can create such characters with the Character Map accessory program in Windows 3.1.

split bar   A vertical line in a File Manager window that separates the directory tree (on the left) from the contents window (on the right).

spooling   Using a high-speed disk to store input to or output from low-speed peripheral devices while the CPU does other tasks.

staged writes   A caching technique in which data is held in the cache until the CPU is free to write the data to disk, or until a fixed length of time passes.

standard mode   The most common operating mode of Windows. It provides task-switching ability and supports access to protected-mode operations as well as up to 16MB of extended memory. It does not allow for multitasking of non-Windows applications but does allow context switching.

start bit   The bit sent at the beginning of a data stream to indicate that data bits follow.

status bar   Any line of miscellaneous information placed by an application on a line at the bottom of a window.

stop bit   The bit sent after the data bits, indicating that no more data bits follow.

subdirectory   A directory contained within another directory or subdirectory. Technically, all directories other than the root directory are subdirectories.

Super VGA   Any video resolution that exceeds the standard 640 × 480 VGA resolution. Most commonly, this term refers to 800 × 600 resolution with 16 colors.

swap file   In 386 enhanced mode, a disk file used to store portions of running applications that have been temporarily swapped to make room for other portions. *See also* application swap file.

switch   A parameter included in DOS commands, usually preceded by the slash (/) symbol, that clarifies or modifies the action of the command.

synchronization   The coordination of a sending device and a receiving device so that both simultaneously send and receive data at the same rate.

system attribute   A bit used to indicate whether the file contains special system information.

system disk   A disk containing the necessary DOS system files for booting.

system font   The type size and style used as the Windows default for desktop elements.

SYSTEM.INI   The Windows initialization file that specifies characteristics of the hardware and internal operating environment.

System menu   *See* Control menu.

Systems Application Architecture (SAA)   A standard developed by IBM for a graphic interface, which defines most of the elements of the Windows and OS/2 desktops.

Tagged Image File (TIF)   A format (sometimes known as TIFF) used by most scanner and page layout applications. It includes compression techniques and the ability to store multiple images in a single file. It provides color, gray-scale, and black-and-white capabilities.

task   An active Windows or DOS application, and the set of system resources that it uses.

Task List   The Windows control program that displays a list of running applications and facilitates switching, termination, and window/icon arrangement.

task switching   The process in which the foreground focus is switched from one active program to another. *See also* context switching.

temporary swap file   In 386 enhanced mode, a hidden file is created only during Windows activities. No disk space is consumed when Windows is not running.

terminate-and-stay-resident program   *See* TSR.

terminal emulator   A program that enables your computer to appear to a remote system as a terminal.

text box   A small box (or field) within a dialog box that allows text input for clarifying how to process a specified action. You can type parameters, switches, or actual commands, depending on the request from the dialog box.

text file   Any file that consists only of characters in the 256-character ASCII set.

text mode   The mode in which characters can be displayed on a monitor.

386 enhanced mode   The most advanced of Windows' three operating modes. In this mode, Windows accesses the protected mode of the CPU chip for extended memory management and multitasking of both Windows and non-Windows applications.

386 expanded memory manager   *See* EMM386.EXE.

386MAX.SYS   A popular expanded memory manager program, available from Qualitas Corp. Often used as an alternative to Microsoft's EMM386.EXE.

throughput   A term used to indicate how efficiently Windows is performing. It refers to the amount of work that is done by the running applications. The less time wasted by individual applications and by switching between applications, the higher the throughput.

TIF   *See* Tagged Image File.

tile   To adjust the position and size of all open windows so that they are adjacent to one other and do not overlap.

timeout   The amount of time that an application will wait for an event to occur before designating an error condition.

time slice   The smallest unit of time that is allocated by Windows to each non-Windows application. This same unit of time is allocated to the Windows kernel and is therefore divided up among all running Windows applications.

title bar   The thin rectangular portion at the top of a window that contains the name of the window.

track   A concentric circular stream of data on the disk. It is similar to a track on a record, only it does not spiral.

TrueType fonts   Fonts that can be sized to any height to appear the same on the printed page as they appear on your screen. Depending on your printer, a TrueType font may be generated as a bit map or as a soft font.

TSR   Stands for *terminate-and-stay-resident* program. A program that is read into memory the first time it is used and then continues to reside in memory.

UAE   Stands for *Unrecoverable Application Error*. A fatal error from which an executing program is unable to recover. Sometimes, UAEs can even disable Windows itself.

UART   Stands for *Universal Asynchronous Receiver Transmitter*. A buffering device that speeds up data communications in serial ports.

UMB   Stands for *upper memory blocks*. A reserved 384K area of system memory in the range 640K to 1MB. *See also* reserved memory.

utility   A program designed to carry out a specific operation, usually to modify the system environment or perform housekeeping tasks.

variable parameter   A named element, following a command, that acts as a placeholder; when you issue the command, you replace the variable parameter with the actual value you want to use.

VCPI   *See* Virtual Control Program Interface.

vector font   A character font that consists of a series of line definitions, representing the linear strokes necessary to create the desired character or symbol. Also called a *plotter font*.

vertical frequency   A measure of the time required to draw, from top to bottom, all the horizontal lines on a screen. Also called *refresh rate*.

VESA   *See* Video Electronics Standards Association.

Video Electronics Standards Association (VESA)   Organization responsible for setting manufacturer guidelines for video boards and displays.

Virtual Control Program Interface (VCPI)   An interface specification for 80386 computers, written by Phar Lap Systems, to establish protocols for systems that contain both a DOS extender and an expanded memory manager. This specification eliminates conflict when processor modes must be switched or memory must be allocated.

virtual disk   *See* RAM disk.

virtual 8086 mode   The memory access facility of a 80386 processor that allows separately accessible, and independent, virtual 1MB 8088/8086 processors. This enables the execution of multiple DOS applications in completely separate and protected address spaces. Also know as V86 *mode*.

virtual machine   In 386 enhanced mode, the simulated software environment for each separately running application that creates the illusion to each application that it is running independently on its own computer.

virtual memory   In 386 enhanced mode, the apparent (but not actual) memory available to running applications. It is composed of actual free memory plus a disk file (see *swap file*) used to simulate extra physical memory.

Virtual Memory Manager   *See* VMM.

VMM   Stands for *Virtual Memory Manager*. The management code built into Windows' 386 enhanced mode for managing virtual memory; it uses a page table to map logical application pages to actual physical memory pages.

VRAM   Stands for *video RAM*. A modified form of DRAM on video boards that permits much faster displays because of two data access paths.

wallpaper   The graphic pattern that appears on the screen desktop as a backdrop behind windows, icons, and dialog boxes.

warm booting   Resetting the computer by using the Ctrl+Alt+Del key combination. *See also* booting.

warm link   A DDE connection between two applications in which information in one application (the *client*) is updated only when data in the other application (the *server*) changes, and only if the client program requests the update.

window   A rectangular portion of the screen that forms the fundamental graphic area in which Windows displays applications.

Windows application   An application that uses Windows' conventions for window management, display, and arrangement and connections to the internal API (Applications Programming Interface).

Windows Setup   A primary application (included in the Main group of the Program Manager) that allows access to the principal hardware and desktop settings stored in the SYSTEM.INI and WIN.INI files.

WIN.INI   The Windows initialization file that contains specifications for desktop customization, among other things.

workspace   The central portion of a window, which is used for the primary information display area.

write caching   An algorithmic technique that analyzes disk write requests to reduce the amount of disk activity. This technique embodies a variety of techniques, implemented by different manufacturers, for preventing multiple writes of unchanged data and for ordering the actual writes to minimize disk-head movement when writing changed data to disk.

XMM   See *extended memory manager*.

XMS   Stands for *Extended Memory Specification*. The set of conventions that govern the use of extended memory.

I N D E X

A

A-B switches, 61, 583
About Program Manager option, 80–81, 729–730
accelerator keys. *See* shortcut keys
accessed flag, 164
Accessories group, 21
Action! program, 244–247
active drives, 415
active windows, 302
adapter segment. *See* upper memory blocks (UMB) area
adapters, 554–555, 759, 761–763, 945. *See also* monitors; screens; video
ADC (analog-to-digital conversion), 212, 231, 234–236
Add Fonts dialog box, 570
Address program (companion disks), 882–884
addresses, 116, 936
    with A20 line, 120–122, 779
    for expanded memory, 133–142
    I/O, 483, 955
    lines for, 13
    and processors, 28
    in protected mode, 122–128
    in real mode, 117–120
Advanced Settings for COM1 dialog box, 482
After Dark program, 300–301
alarms, 909, 925
aligning
    with BigDesk, 821
    icons, 472–473
    menu items, 519
allocation, 84, 936
Alt key
    interrupt processing for, 549
    in macros, 423–424
    for menus, 108–109
    for special characters, 571–572

Alt+Esc, 303, 351, 374, 737
Alt+Tab, 303, 350–351, 373–374, 469–470, 734, 737
alternative memory managers, 666–669, 740
AM program (companion disks), 882–884
amplitude of sound, 236
analog clocks, 429
analog sound, 211–212
analog-to-digital conversion (ADC), 212, 231, 234–236
analog video, 210
animation, 219
annotating directories (Dirnote), 891–892
ANSI driver, 936
anti-aliasing, 448, 936
APPEND command, 793
applets, 296, 936
"Application Has Been Crashed" message, 793–794
Application Programming Interface (API), 17–19, 937
applications, 936
    automatic launching of, 884–886
    background, 637, 938
    backing up, 290–295
    Clipboard for, 178–179
    directories for, 277, 475
    documentation for, 911–913
    DOS. *See* DOS applications; .PIF files
    foreground, 7, 951
    icons for, 473, 476–478, 936
    installing, 46–47, 628–629
    limit on, 730
    limiting, 638
    loading, 286–288, 415, 477, 519
    marked, 295–296, 764, 958
    priority of, 730–731
    properties for, 275–278
    removing, from disk, 630–631
    resources for, 83

running, 286–288, 296–299, 477, 519, 637, 884–886
shortcut keys for, 277–278, 470–471, 734, 737, 937
starting, 157, 264–278, 288, 734–736
swap files for, 614, 937
switching, 6–7, 301–306, 348, 469–471, 731, 737, 972
translating between, 398–399
UAEs from, 764–766
versions of, 764–765
windows for, 937
Windows vs. non-Windows, 266–267
appointment manager, 908–911
Apptimer program (companion disks), 884–886
archive attribute, 937
Arial typeface, 559–560, 565
ASCII files, 579, 585
assembly language, 10, 937
Associate dialog box, 271–272
associating data files, 937
with File Manager, 406
with icons, 274–275
in Macintosh, 27
with menus, 271–273
with WIN.INI, 289, 396, 520–523
asynchronous communications. *See* serial ports and communications
asynchronous network support, 712–713
AT program (companion disks), 884–886
atoms, 189–190
attributes, 559, 937, 950, 953, 971
A20 line, 120–122, 779
audio. *See* sound
audio-video interleaving (AVI) technology, 211, 241, 937
authoring packages, 247–249
authoring platforms and systems, 207, 937
Auto Clipboard format, 176
AUTOEXEC.BAT file, 282, 937
on bootable disks, 40
for conventional memory, 44–45
editing, 425–427, 509, 513
for installation, 42
LOADHIGH in, 654–655

SHARE in, 92, 265, 787
SMARTDRV.EXE in, 607
virus protection program in, 866
Windows equivalent for, 287
AUTOEXEC.WIN file, 705
automatic launching, 884–886
automatic links, 937
AVI (audio-video interleaving) technology, 211, 241, 937

B

Back-It 4 utility, 39, 293
BackDesk programs, 814
backfilling memory, 138–139, 153, 938
background, 7
applications in, 359–361, 637, 639, 938
communications in, 857–859
priority settings for, 313–314, 363–364, 389–391
backgrounds, 465–469, 520, 938
BackMenu program (companion disks), 143, 297, 814–818
BACKMENU.INI file, 815
backups, 38–41
for applications, 290–295
problems with, 384
speed of, 636
bandwidth on networks, 213–214
bank switching, 133–136, 740, 938
banners, network, 747
bar codes, 867–869
base addresses, 118
base-level synthesizers, 492
batch files, 938
icons for, 331–332
for mouse drivers, 384
and multiple instances, 327–329
in .PIF files, 337, 677, 736
on RAM disks, 674
for TSRs, 379–382
for video drivers, 446
baud rates, 482, 553, 717
for modems, 749–751
for printers, 742

problems with, 788
Beep setting, 512–513
beeping, clock with, 925
BigDesk program (companion disks), 814, 819–821
binary files, 88–89, 91, 938
binary numbers, 938
binary transfers, 938
BIOS requirements, 35–38
bit block transfers, 107, 938
bit maps, 938
    with Clipboard, 174, 177
    for fonts, 563–564, 938
    for map graphics, 434–437
    with Paint Shop, 904–905
    and .RLE files, 73
    for wallpaper, 467–469
Bitmap Clipboard format, 177
bits, 938
blink rate for cursor, 483–484, 516
[blowaway] section (SETUP.INF), 70
.BMP files. See bit maps
boldface fonts, 559
Bookshelf for Windows, 229
Boolean values, 506–507, 939
boot record, 939
[Boot] section (SYSTEM.INI)
    drivers and devices in, 533–535
    fonts in, 455, 567–568
    network entries in, 707–708
    screen savers in, 516
    Setup program for, 50
    shells in, 143, 297
[Boot.description] section (SYSTEM.INI), 533
bootable disks, 39–40, 971
booting, 939–940, 975
borders, window, 12, 474, 516
branches, directory, 414–419, 939
branching, 939
buffers, 939. See also disk caching
    for CD-ROM drives, 223
    for communications, 553
    external, 950
    for networks, 537, 709
    printer, 590

transfer, 131–132, 155, 787
translation, 150–152
unnecessary, 612–613
BUFFERS command (CONFIG.SYS), 42, 44, 650
bulletin board systems (BBS), 172, 716–717, 938
burn-in, monitor, 299–301, 423, 516, 968
buttons, mouse, 485, 920–923
bytes, 939

C
caches, 939. See also disk caching
    font, 567
    hardware, 600–601, 612–614
    hits and misses in, 610, 616
    memory, 29
    software, 600–606, 822–826
Cachetst program (companion disks), 822–826
calculator, 875, 900
Calendar program (companion disks), 910
CALIBRAT program, 636
Call Waiting, 717
"Cannot Find File" message, 267
"Cannot Find Necessary Files" message, 795–796
"Cannot Initialize the Adapter" message, 795
"Cannot Run in a Window" message, 796
"Cannot Switch to a Full Screen" message, 796–797
capturing screen and window images, 433–434, 968
    to Clipboard, 174–175, 180–181, 433, 912–913
    with IconAuthor, 249
    with SnagIt (companion disks), 911–913
carets (^)
    in [Extensions] section of WIN.INI, 522
    in macros, 423
Carrier Detect, checking, 826, 828
cartridges for fonts, 951

cascading menus, 816

cascading windows, 939

CD Technology, CD-ROM drives by, 225

CD-I standards, 939

CD-ROM drives, 207, 209, 939
    advantages of, 218–219
    choosing, 223–227
    controllers for, 224–226
    operation of, 232–234
    software for, 228–230
    sound with, 211, 217–218, 234–237
    speed of, 221, 224
    writing to, 219–220

CEG (Continuous Edge Graphics) video standard, 447–448, 458–459

CGA, 447–448

chaining, 940

Change Icon dialog box, 324–325, 401

channel maps, 495–497, 940

Character Map utility, 21, 560, 572–574, 745

check boxes, 940

checking account manager (Wincheck), 870–880

Chess program (companion disks), 887–891

CHESS.INI file, 888

child windows, 940
    capturing, 434
    and MDI, 107–109
    resources for, 80, 83, 85

CHKDSK program (DOS), 45
    and defragmentation, 627, 629
    for lost clusters, 630–632
    problems with, 384–385

Chkmodem program (companion disks), 826–829

Clean program (memory—companion disks), 829

Clean program (viruses—companion disks), 830–837, 848, 854

clicking, 394–395

client applications, 19–20, 187–189, 940, 961

client area, 108

Clipboard, 19, 169, 940
    for bar codes (Wbar), 868

    button for, 420
    with Curtain Call, 244
    vs. DDE and OLE, 199
    with DOS applications, 99, 101, 179–184, 359, 371–373, 732–733
    error messages for, 785
    formats with, 99, 175–177, 200, 399, 785
    for graphics, 169, 172, 175, 183
    memory for, 157, 169, 173, 829
    and .PIF files, 183, 348, 371–372
    for quotes (Quote program), 905
    for screen images, 174–175, 180–181, 433, 912–913 (SnagIt)
    selecting data for, 170–173
    for special characters, 21, 573–574
    translating between applications with, 398–399
    for Windows applications, 178–179

Clipboard Viewer, 172–173, 175–178, 940

CLIPBRD.EXE file, 175

Clock utility, 429

clocks, 429, 919–920, 923–926

Closer program (companion disks), 838

closing, 940
    DOS applications, 372–373
    on exiting, 349, 361–362
    windows, 108, 838
    Windows 3.1, 840–842

clusters, 630–632, 940

code pages, 62, 940

[codepages] section (SETUP.INF), 62

cold booting, 940

Collage Plus program, 434, 437

collapsing directories, 941

Color dialog box, 438, 478–479

colors, 437, 941
    for Chess program, 890–891
    for desktop, 478–481
    for Help window, 528–529
    number of, 454–456
    palettes for, 438–442, 962
    for screen, 481, 529–530
    and speed, 427, 442–445
    with Windows 1.0, 9

[Colors] section (WIN.INI), 480, 529–530

columns for Terminal, 427–428
COM ports, 941. *See also* serial ports and communications
command buttons, 941
command-line parameters, 329–330
command lines, 941
command processors, 941, 968
command prompts, 941
COMMAND.COM program, 941
    extended memory for, 648–649
    on RAM disks, 674
    and viruses, 834
COMMDLG.DLL file, 22
comments in .INI files, 506–507, 678
communications, parallel, 525, 962. *See also* serial ports and communications
compaction utilities, 625–627, 629
compatibility
    of disk-caching programs, 602
    of drivers, 41, 52, 68, 760–761
    of hardware, 71, 760–761
    of memory managers, 668, 740
    of printers, 728
    of Windows 3.1, 16
[compatibility] section (SETUP.INF), 41, 68
compiling resource files, 91, 966–967
Complete Communicator board, 71
composite video, 941
compound devices, 258, 941
compound documents, 941
compressing data
    files, 628, 843–845
    in multimedia, 210–211, 214, 230–231, 237–240
Compton's Multimedia Encyclopedia, 228–229
computer-based training (CBT), 249
Computer Virus Industry Association (CVIA), 831
COMSPEC environment variable, 385–386, 674
CONFIG.SYS file, 942
    on bootable disks, 40
    editing, 425–427, 509, 513
    incompatible drivers in, 52, 68

    for memory optimization, 43–44, 645, 647–650
    multiple, 153
    setting up, 41–45, 68–70
    SHARE in, 266
CONFIG.WIN file, 705
configuration, 942
    automatic, 20
    of serial ports, 481–483
confirmation messages, 410–411, 413
conflicts
    with direct memory access, 69, 945
    with file access, 694
    with hardware, 155–157, 554–555, 661, 748, 759
    with interrupts and IRQ lines, 69, 483, 553–554, 692–695, 738, 748, 751, 772–773, 955
    with page frames, 157–158, 661
    with pages, 761
    with printing, 694
    UAEs from, 759, 761–763
    with UMBs, 155–158, 554–555, 661–662, 692, 695, 738, 748, 759, 761–763
    with video, 155–157, 554–555, 661, 748, 759
constant angular velocity (CAV) method, 232, 939
constant linear velocity (CLV) method, 232, 940
context switching, 942
contexts, 105–106, 944
contiguity, 942
Continuous Edge Graphics. *See* CEG
Control-menu box, 942
Control menus, 942
    changing settings with, 388–389, 734
    for copying data, 371
    for fonts, 744
    and full screens, 796
    for pasting Clipboard data, 181–184
    for printers, 797
    for priorities, 312, 639
    in windows, 358
Control Panel, 942
    changing, 509–510

improvements to, 21
for international settings, 497–499
for multimedia, 220–222
for printers, 577
Screen Saver on, 21
for time slice allocation, 308–310
CONTROL.INF file, 705
CONTROL.INI file, 502, 942
controllers for CD-ROM drives, 224–226
conventional memory, 129–132, 942
adding, 117
AUTOEXEC.BAT settings for, 44–45
CONFIG.SYS settings for, 43–44
for DOS applications, 131–132
High Memory Area for, 367–368
in .PIF files, 346, 353–355
in 386 enhanced mode, 146–152
and UMBs, 151–152
conversations, DDE, 185, 187–189, 942
converting
analog and digital signals, 212, 231, 234–236
extended memory to expanded, 280
formats, 903
metric measurements, 898–900
vector graphics, 437
cookies, 71
cooperative multitasking, 88
copies, printing, 580–581
coprocessors for video, 457–458, 952
Copy command, 170–172, 183
copying
to Clipboard, 170–172, 183
files, 56–58, 65–67, 419–420
graphics, 169
icons, 407
objects, 198–199
packages, 202
corrupted files, 40
country settings. See international settings
CPU (central processing unit), 942
and CD-ROM drives, 224
load on, 855–857
usage meter for, 839–840
Cpuuse program (companion disks), 839–840

crashes. See conflicts; error messages; Unrecoverable Application Errors (UAE)
CRC. See cyclic redundancy checks (CRC)
CreateWindow function, 286
cross-linked files, 758
CT.EXE file, 822–826
Ctrl key
in macros, 423
for selecting files, 416
Ctrl+Alt+Del, 17, 102, 675, 757, 765, 769–770, 789
Ctrl+Esc, 6, 302–303, 350–351, 374, 737, 765
currency, international, 497, 523
cursors, 483–484, 516, 968
Curtain Call program, 242–244
Custom Color Selector dialog box, 438
Custom Setup, 45, 763
Cut command, 170–172, 181, 187
cyclic redundancy checks (CRCs), 942–943
with Clean, 831
in .EXE files, 97
with Scan, 847, 849
with Vshield, 862
cylinders, 943

D

DAC (digital-to-analog conversion), 212, 231, 234–236
DASD, 945
data
compressing. See compressing data
on disks, 943
in .EXE files, 94
protecting. See protecting data
sharing. See Clipboard; Dynamic Data Exchange; Object Linking and Embedding
data bits, 482, 742, 943
data files, 943
associating. See associating data files
extensions for, 518–519
loading, 270–271
OLE with, 19, 941
[data] section (SETUP.INF), 55–56

data streams, 943
Data Terminal Ready, checking, 826, 828
dates
    international, 497, 523
    setting, 925
DDE. *See* Dynamic Data Exchange
DDEML (Dynamic Data Exchange Management Library), 18, 190–192, 943
deallocation, 943
debugging utilities, 768–775
default printer, 581–582
default settings
    for installation, 45–48
    for .PIF files, 25, 311, 313–314, 332, 335–338, 637, 733
    for swapping, 618–620
    in [386Enh] section of SYSTEM.INI, 548
_DEFAULT.PIF file, 25, 311, 313–314, 332, 335–338, 637, 733
deferred disk writes, 605–606, 609, 970
defragmentation utilities, 625–627, 629
delay, keyboard repeat, 484–485, 513, 956
delayed disk writes, 605–606, 609, 970
Delete commands, 173
deleting
    confirmation messages for, 411
    groups and icons, 404–405
    notes, 931
    printer queue entries, 589–590
    sound, 254
    temporary swap files, 630
    WIN.INI entries, 511, 513
delimiters, 943
delivery platforms and systems, 207, 217, 944
demand loading, 944
demand paging, 160–162
descenders, 560–561
descriptions for applications, 276
descriptor tables, 112, 123–127, 129, 952, 957
desktop, 464, 944
    backgrounds for, 465–469, 520
    colors for, 478–481
    customizing, 519–521

for icon spacing, 471–472
for keyboard, 396–398
for mouse, 394–396
size of, 819–821
sizing grid for, 472–474, 520
for switching applications, 469–471
for translating between applications, 398–399
Desktop dialog box, 466, 516
[Desktop] section (WIN.INI), 519–521
DesQ operating environment, 8
DESQview and DESQview 386
    expanded memory with, 137–138
    running under, 8, 101–103
destination documents, 944
device independence, 11, 104
Device Independent Bitmap (DIB) format, 219, 944
DEVICEHIGH command, 43, 151, 652–653, 655–656, 663
devices, 944
    conflicts with, 483, 553–554, 772–773, 794, 944
    contexts for, 105–106, 944
    drivers for (*See* drivers)
    error messages for, 793–794
    fonts in, 576
    names of, 944
    for networks, 960
    powering up, 586
    simple and compound, 258, 941, 969
    support for, 37
    SYSTEM.INI entries for, 533–535
    timeouts for, 516, 743, 973
[Devices] section (WIN.INI), 516, 531
diagnostic software, 768–775
dialog boxes, 22, 54–55, 944
[dialog] section (SETUP.INF), 54–55
digital clocks, 429, 919–920, 923–926
digital signal processor (DSP), 212–213, 944
digital sound, 211–213
digital-to-analog conversion (DAC), 212, 231, 234–236
digital video, 210–211

Digital Video Interactive (DVI) technology, 210–211, 944
direct access storage device (DASD), 945
direct access to ports, 347–348
direct memory access (DMA), 368, 945
    conflicts with, 69, 945
    with file backups, 292–293
    problems with, 384
directories, 945
    annotating, 891–892
    for applications, 277, 475
    changing, 415
    displaying, 408, 412–414, 941, 949
    for drivers, 72–73
    icons for, 945
    on networks, 699
    paths for, 637, 945
    in .PIF files, 343–344
    pruning and grafting, 416–419
    for RAM disks, 75, 676
    shortcut keys with, 412–413
    for swapping, 536
    SYSTEM, 49, 57, 746–747
    WINDOWS, 49, 637
Directory Tree window, 412–413, 945
Dirnote program (companion disks), 891–892
DIRNOTES.COM program, 892
dirty flag, 164
disk caching, 598–599, 939
    and BUFFERS, 650
    concepts of, 600–602
    drivers for, 41
    with file backups, 292
    and fragmentation, 603, 626
    hardware-based, 612–614
    of read requests, 603–605
    for servers, 687–688
    using SMARTDRV.EXE, 606–612
    software-based, 602–606
    testing, 822–826
disk drives. See drives; hard disks
[diskcache] section (SEUPT.INF), 41
diskless workstations, 689, 746–747
disks. See also hard disks; RAM disks and RAMDRIVE.SYS driver

backing up, 290–293
bootable, 39–40, 971
commands for, confirming, 411
crashes on, 39–40
for expanded memory, 139–142
high-density, 31
icon files on, 402
optimizers for, 945
space available on, 55, 627–632, 784, 843
swapping to (See swapping and swap files)
[disks] section (SEUPT.INF), 56–57
display adapters, 554–555, 759, 761–763, 945. See also monitors; screens; video
display contexts, 105
[display] section (SETUP.INF), 58, 65
DISPLAY.DRV driver, replacing, 445
.DLL files. See dynamic link libraries (DLLs)
DMA. See direct memory access
documentation
    for applications, 911–913
    for .INI files, 506–507, 678
documents. See associating data files; data files
DOS, 946
    DOS 5, 646–647
    environment for. See environment
    High Memory Area for, 43, 648–649, 734
    maximizers for, 946
    memory for, 946
    Setup program for, 48–51, 56–58
    versions of, 36, 48, 761
DOS applications, 320–321, 960
    in background, 359–361, 639
    batch files for, 331–332
    Clipboard with, 99, 101, 179–184, 359, 371–373, 732–733
    closing, 372–373
    custom start-ups for, 329–330
    under DESQview 386, 102
    display problems with, 744
    drivers for, 732–733
    enhancing, 97–101

environment for, 385–388, 682–684, 946
error messages for, 789, 792–793
fonts for, 536, 569–570, 744
icons for, 100, 322–325, 400–403
installing, 322–325
memory for, 131–132, 280–281, 684
memory-resident. *See* TSR
mouse with, 383–384, 731–732
multiple instances of, 326–329
multitasking, 20
with networks, 693, 711–712, 736
performance of, 638–641
.PIF files for. *See* .PIF files
problem commands in, 384–385
speed of, 638–641, 753
switching, 737
SYSTEM.INI entries for, 535–536
terminating, 24, 390, 765, 769, 789
in 386 enhanced mode, 266–267, 281
in windows, 357–359
vs. Windows applications, 266–267
DOS directory, 637
DOS=HIGH (CONFIG.SYS), 43–44, 47, 648–649, 734
DOS Protected Mode Interface (DPMI), 110–114, 946
DOS=UMB directive, 43–44, 651, 668
[dos.mouse.drivers] section (SETUP.INF), 63
DOSAPP.INI file, 536
DOS Protected Mode Interface (DPMI), 110–114, 946
dot-matrix printers, 561, 728
dot pitch, 449–450, 946
double buffering with disk caches, 612–613
double clicking
speed of, 486, 517, 946
uses of, 305, 395
downloadable fonts, 575, 947, 970
limits on, 799
PostScript, 573
DPMI (DOS Protected Mode Interface), 110–114, 946
drag-and-drop method, 22, 270–271

DRAM (dynamic random access memory), 147, 456, 947
DRIVER.SYS driver, 947
drivers
on bootable disks, 39–40
directories for, 72–73
for DOS applications, 732–733
icon for, 21
incompatible, 41, 52, 68, 760–761
installing, 58–61, 69
for keyboards, 61–62
memory for, 147, 677–678
for mouse, 44, 62–63, 383–384, 677–678, 732
for multimedia, 220
for networks, 63–64, 690–692
for nonstandard hardware, 53
for printers, 585, 741–742, 964
for screen, 58–61, 65
for sound, 487–489, 970
SYSTEM.INI entries for, 533–535
in UMB, 43–45, 150–151, 647, 650–656, 662–666
for video, 58–61, 65, 445–446
Windows, 105–107
Drivers dialog box, 487–488
[Drivers] section (SYSTEM.INI), 533
drives, 945, 957. *See also* CD-ROM drives; hard disks
changing, 415
icons for, 945
identifiers for, 947
moving files between, 419
with SMARTDRV.EXE, 607
for swapping, 536, 739
drop-down list boxes, 947
drop-down menus, 947
DRWATSON.EXE utility, 768–771
DSP (digital signal processor), 212–213, 944
DRWATSON.LOG file, 769
dual-ported architecture, 456–457
DVI (Digital Video Interactive) technology, 210–211, 944
Dynamic Data Exchange (DDE), 12–13, 18–20, 184–186, 943

vs. Clipboard and OLE, 199
conversations in, 185, 187–189, 942
functions for, 190–192
with SnagIt, 911
and visibility, 84
Dynamic Data Exchange Management
Library (DDEML), 18, 190–192, 943
dynamic font caching, 567
dynamic link libraries (DLLs), 947
for dialog boxes, 22
limit on files in, 533
for multimedia, 220
dynamic RAM (DRAM), 147, 456, 947

E

EBIOS, 72
[ebios] section (SETUP.INF), 72
echoes with sound, 256
Edit menu
for Chess program, 888–889
for Packager, 202
for Taipei program, 918
Edit Pattern dialog box, 466–467
editing
MIDI key maps, 492–494
notes, 930
patterns, 466–467
sound files, 253–254
system files, 104, 425–427, 509–511,
513
EEMS. *See* Enhanced Expanded Memory
Specification
EGA, 447–448
8514 font files, 568
8514 video standard, 447, 452, 948
80286 processor, 26–28
80386 processor, 28
80486 processor, 28–30
EISA (Extended Industry Standard
Architecture), 554, 948
embedded objects, 20, 194–198, 200, 204,
420, 948
[Embedding] section (WIN.INI), 531

EMM386.EXE driver
for expanded memory, 14, 136, 141–
142, 152–153, 280, 684
installing, 43–44, 651–652
parameters for, 43–44, 141, 150, 652–
653, 659–661
for UMBs, 151, 646, 650–655, 948
EMS standard, 133–135, 138–139, 948
emulating
expanded memory, 14, 136, 139–142,
152–153, 280, 684, 949
text mode, 369–370
emulation mode, 948
encyclopedias on CD-ROM, 228–229
Enhanced Expanded Memory Specification (EEMS), 136–138, 947
environment
for DOS applications, 385–388, 682–
684, 946
inheriting, 149
size of, 387, 650, 683, 766
variables in, 344, 948
EPS (Encapsulated PostScript), 948–949
equipment flag, 283
errand manager, 908–911
"Error: A20 Line Already Installed" message, 779
error-level codes, 840–842, 949
error messages, 778. *See also* Unrecoverable Application Errors (UAEs)
for Clipboard, 785
for communications, 787–788
for devices, 793–794
for disk space, 784
for DOS applications, 789, 792–793
for file access, 786
for files, 789–793
improvements in, 17–19
for integrity violations, 780–781
for memory, 154, 288, 729, 734–736,
739, 781–784
for multimedia, 800–803
for multitasking, 784–789
for networks, 786–787
for OLE, 790–792

for printing, 797–800
at start-up, 779–780
for video, 795–797
events, 11
and multitasking, 86
sound for, 489–490, 528
evolution of Windows, 7–8
future of, 22–24
and OS/2, 23–26
Windows 1.0, 9–12
Windows 2.0, 12–13
Windows/286 and Windows/386, 13–14
Windows 3.0, 14–15
Windows 3.1, 15–22
exchanging information. See Clipboard;
Dynamic Data Exchange (DDE); Object
Linking and Embedding (OLE)
exclamation points (!) for hidden files, 409–410
excluding UMBs, 155–157, 554–555, 661–662, 692, 695, 738, 748, 759, 761–763
exclusive applications, 360, 391, 551–552, 640, 735, 949
executable (.EXE) files, 505, 949
building, 88–92
limit on, 533
structure of, 94–97
execution modes. See standard mode; 386
enhanced mode
exiting, 840–842
closing on, 349, 361–362
shutdown program for, 913–915
Exitw program (companion disks), 840–842
EXITWDOS.EXE program, 841–842
EXPAND utility, 732
expanded directories, 414, 949
expanded memory, 15, 949
adding, 117
addressing, 133–142
converting extended to, 280
with DOS 5, 646
for DOS applications, 280, 684
emulating, 14, 136, 139–142, 152–153, 280, 684, 949
as extended, 14

vs. extended, 739–740
locking, 366–367, 551, 681–682
page frames for. See page frames
in .PIF files, 356–357, 680–681
for RAM disks, 671–673
in standard mode, 143–145
in 386 enhanced mode, 152–158
using, 132–133
in Windows/286, 13
Expanded Memory Manager (EMM.SYS), 135–136, 948
expansion cards and slots, 949
exporting data, 8
Express Install program, 20
Express Setup, 45, 763
Extended Basic Input/Output System (EBIOS), 72
extended DOS partitions, 949
extended-level synthesizers, 492
extended memory, 949–950
adding, 117, 131–132
converting, to expanded, 280
for disk caches, 600, 609
for DOS, 648–649
with DOS 5, 646
vs. expanded, 739–740
expanded memory as, 14
HIMEM.SYS for, 122, 646–648, 727
locking, 366, 551
managers for, 950
and page frames, 150–151
in .PIF files, 346–347, 357, 680–681
for RAM disks, 671, 673
for shadow memory, 155
in standard mode, 145–146
in 386 enhanced mode, 158–159
Extended Memory Specification (XMS), 122, 145, 976
extenders
DOS, 110
memory, 137
extensions for files, 74
associating files by. See associating
data files
default, 406
for documents, 518–519

for graphic images, 436
[Extensions] section (WIN.INI), 272–273, 289, 396, 406, 519–523, 678
external buffers, 950
external CD-ROM drives, 223
external commands, 950

F

far pointers, 189
FASTOPEN command (DOS), 42
FAT. *See* file allocation table
fax boards in background, 361
FDISK program (DOS), 40
fields
    limit, 127
    video, 451
file allocation table (FAT), 292, 385, 950
File Manager, 406, 950
    for confirmation messages, 410–411
    finding files with, 407–410
    improvements to, 20–21
    moving and copying files with, 419–420
    quick operations with, 415–416
    shortcut keys with, 412–414
    starting applications from, 269
File menu
    for Chess program, 888
    for PIF Editor, 334
FILE port, 579, 582–585, 950
files, 950
    accessing, 636–638, 694, 786
    associating. *See* associating data files
    attributes for, 559, 937, 950, 953, 971
    backing up, 290–295
    batch. *See* batch files
    binary, 88–89, 91, 938
    compressing, 843–845
    copying, 56–58, 65–67, 419–420
    corrupted, 40
    cross-linked, 758
    error messages for, 789–793
    extensions for, 74, 406, 436, 518–519
    finding, 407–410
    group. *See* groups and .GRP files

handles for, 52, 708
help, 425
hidden, 409–410, 953
for macros, 421
media, 958
MIDI, 958
moving, 419–420
on networks, 52, 57, 533, 706–708
output to, 526
overlay, 675, 834–835, 851, 961–962
.PIF. *See* .PIF files
printing to, 579, 582–585
read-only, 294–295, 966
renaming, 419
resource, 88–89, 91–93
saving Clipboard contents to, 177
searching for, 407–410
selecting, 415–416
Setup program for, 51
sharing, 92–93, 95, 265–266, 696, 787
sound, 250–254, 527–528, 970
speed of accessing, 636–638
swap. *See* swapping and swap files
SYSTEM.INI entries for, 555
text, 416, 972
in Windows 1.0, 9–10
FILES command (CONFIG.SYS), 649
filters, 950
finance manager (Wincheck), 870–880
finding files, 407–410
fixed-function chips, 230
fixed-width fonts, 64–65, 561, 568, 950
[fixedfonts] section (SETUP.INF), 64–65
flags, 164, 283, 327–329, 951
flicker, 951
flow control, 718, 742, 750, 951
Font dialog box, 552
Font Selection dialog box, 536
fonts, 558, 951
    availability of, 797–798
    bit-mapped, 563–564, 938
    boldface, 559
    cartridges for, 951
    for DOS applications, 536, 569–570, 744
    downloadable, 573, 575, 799, 947, 970

fixed-width, 64–65, 561, 568, 950
hinting with, 566–567, 954
for icons, 520
improvements in, 22
installing, 64–65, 67, 569–571
italic, 559
memory for, 575–576, 679
new, 19
outline, 22
plotter, 561–564, 575, 964
for printers, 22, 575–576, 741, 797
proportional, 561, 965
raster, 561–563, 965
sans-serif, 560, 967
scalable, 22, 967
for screen, 22, 552, 561–564, 567–571
serif, 560, 969
Setup program for, 50, 52, 67
size of, 455, 559–561, 744
soft. *See* soft fonts
special characters from, 571–574
in standard mode, 567–568
system, 971
temporary, 575–576
for Terminal, 428
terminology of, 559–561
TrueType. *See* TrueType fonts
vector, 561–564, 974
weight of, 559
width of, 560
WIN.INI for, 526–527
WYSIWYG, 564–565
Fonts dialog box, 569–570
[fonts] section (SETUP.INF), 67
[Fonts] section (WIN.INI), 526, 678
[Fontsubstitutes] section (WIN.INI),
526–527
footprints, DOS, 149
foreground applications, 7, 313–314, 363–
364, 389–391, 549–550, 639–640, 951
foreign languages. *See* international settings
FORMAT program (DOS), 40
formats
Clipboard, 99, 175–177, 200, 399, 785
converting, 903
with Curtain Call, 243

for screen images, 434–437
formatted ASCII files, printing, 579
formatting, 40, 951
fragmentation, 951
and disk caching, 603, 626
optimizing, 625–627
and swap files, 616, 620–622, 626
frames, clock in, 919–920
Framework IV program, 8
full-motion video, 951
full-screen mode, 358, 640, 711–712, 796,
951

G

games (companion disks)
Chess, 887–891
Klotz, 895–898
Taipei, 915–919
Yacht, 932–933
GDI. *See* Graphics Device Interface
GDI.EXE program, 57–58, 79
GDTs. *See* global descriptor tables
General MIDI specification, 952
general protection faults, 781
gigabyte (GB), 952
GIF (Graphic Interchange Format), 952
global atoms, 189–190
global descriptor tables (GDTs), 123–126,
952
global memory, 84, 188–190, 952
GNUCHESS.BOO file, 888
grafting directories, 416–419
granularity bit for segments, 127–128
granularity of desktop, 472–473, 520, 952
graphical user interface (GUI), 4, 952
graphics
Clipboard for, 169, 172, 175, 183
coprocessors for, 457–458, 952
mode for, 345, 352–353, 952
multimedia for, 210–211, 219, 230
in opening screens, 330
printing, 742
resolution of, 435–437, 953
resources for, 83
for screen images, 434–437

Graphics Device Interface (GDI), 11–12, 104–107, 951
    managing, 57–58
    rasterizer for, 567
    resources for, 79, 83, 85
    with TrueType fonts, 575
Graphics Interchange Format (GIF), 952
grayed Clipboard entries, 399
grid, sizing, 472–474, 520, 820–821
groups and .GRP files, 953, 964
    backing up, 38, 40, 293–294
    with BackMenu, 818
    deleting, 404–405
    icons for, 405, 474–476, 953
    moving icons between, 407
    for networks, 701
    protecting, 294–295
    resources for, 80–81
    Setup program for, 67–68
    windows for, 953
GUI (graphical user interface), 4, 952
Guinness Disc of Records, 229

H

handlers
    message, 86
    object, 960
handles
    for files, 52, 708
    for global memory blocks, 188
hard disks, 623–624. See also disks; drives
    backing up, 40
    caches for. See disk caching
    vs. CD-ROM drives, 232–234
    interleaving on, 632–636, 955
    interrupts for, 550, 758–759
    for laptops, 17
    for multimedia, 217
    optimizing, 384, 625–627, 629
    requirements for, 36
    space available on, 55, 627–632, 784, 843
    and system upgrades, 31
    for virtual memory, 162–165
    for Windows 1.0, 11

hardware
    conflicts with, 155–157, 554–555, 661, 748, 759
    drivers for, 50, 53, 107
    fonts for, 576
    incompatibility of, 71, 760–761
    interrupts from, 953
    for multimedia, 801
    nonstandard, 53
    and setup problems, 727
    Setup program for, 49–50, 70–72
    sharing, 347–348
    SYSTEM.INI entries for, 532
    for Windows, 35–38
hardware caches, 600–601, 612–614
headers in .EXE files, 94, 96–97
heads, 953
heap space, 79, 83, 85, 729
height of fonts, 560
help, 425
    for Setup program, 49–50
    WIN.INI entries for, 528–529
hexadecimal numbers, 953
hidden files and attributes, 409–410, 953
hiding menus, 520
High Memory Area (HMA), 122, 953
    for DOS, 43, 648–649, 734
    in .PIF files, 367–368
High Performance File System. See HPFS
High Sierra standard, 220
high-density disks, 31
high-resolution mode, 954
HIMEM.SYS driver, 43, 954
    and A20 line, 779
    benefits of, 727
    for extended memory, 122, 646–648, 727
    loading, 44
    location of, 752
    and shadow memory, 155
    in standard mode, 145
    versions of, 35
hints for TrueType fonts, 566–567, 954
hits, cache, 610, 616
HMA. See High Memory Area
horizontal scan rate, 451, 954

hot keys. *See* shortcut keys
hot links, 186, 954
HPFS (High Performance File System), 23–24, 27, 954
HPGL printers, 729
hue, 438, 440–441, 954
HyperCard program, 209
hyperlinks, 202–203
hypermedia, 208–209, 954
hypertext, 208–209

I

I-beam pointer, 954
icon view, 955
IconAuthor program, 247–249
Iconmastr program (companion disks), 324, 400, 476, 893–895
icons, 955
    aligning, 472–473
    appearance of, 476–478
    for applications, 473, 476–478, 936
    for associating data files, 274–275
    for batch files, 331–332
    changing, 400–402
    for Clock, 429
    deleting, 404–405
    for directories, 945
    for DOS applications, 100, 322–325, 400–403
    for drives, 945
    for groups, 405, 474–476, 953
    labels for, 341, 472, 475–476, 520
    loading with, 415, 477
    for macros, 424
    managing, 893–895
    moving and copying, 407
    on networks, 700–701
    for Program Manager, 474–477
    program-item, 965
    resources for, 80–81, 85, 395
    spacing, 471–472, 520
    for starting applications, 267–268, 322, 415
idle time for DOS applications, 100, 753
    with communications, 718–719

detecting, 364–365
    setting, 641
importing data, 8, 955
incompatibility. *See* compatibility
[incompTSR1] section (SETUP.INF), 68
[incompTSR2] section (SETUP.INF), 68
information access with multimedia, 219
inheriting environments, 149
.INI files, 502. *See also* SYSTEM.INI file; WIN.INI file
    backing up, 38, 40, 293–294
    Boolean values in, 506–507
    documenting, 506–507
    editing, 104, 425–427, 509–511, 513
    structure of, 504–505
[ini.upd.31] section (SETUP.INF), 70
insertion point, 955
[Installable.Drivers] section (SETUP.INF), 69
installing
    applications, 46–47, 628–629
    default values with, 45–48
    DOS applications, 322–325
    drivers, 58–61, 69
    EMM386.EXE, 43–44, 651–652
    fonts, 64–65, 67, 569–571
    hardware-specific entries, 70–72
    networks, 46, 63–64, 689–690
    printers, 576–582
    required files, 65–67
    Windows, 20, 35, 53, 695–706
instances, multiple, 326–329
integrated applications, 8
integrity violations, 758, 780–781
Intel processors, 26–30
intensity of color, 440
interactive multimedia, 209, 241
    Action!, 244–247
    advantages of, 215–216
    Curtain Call, 242–244
    IconAuthor, 247–249
interactive video, 210
interlaced monitors, 451–452
interleaving, 632–636, 955
internal CD-ROM drives, 223
International dialog box, 497–498

international settings, 497–499
    for keyboards, 62
    resource files for, 91–93
    Setup program for, 72
    WIN.INI section for, 522–525
interprocess communication (IPC), 955.
    See also Clipboard; Dynamic Data
    Exchange (DDE); Object Linking
    and Embedding (OLE)
interrupt 28, and networks, 710–711
interrupts and IRQ lines, 955
    changing, 483
    conflicts with, 69, 483, 553–554, 692–
    695, 738, 748, 751, 772–773, 955
    for hard disks, 550, 758–759
    hardware, 953
    and lost keystrokes, 305–306
    multiplex, 98–99
    nonmaskable, 156
    for serial ports, 483
    software, 970
    SYSTEM.INI entries for, 549–550
    for TSRs, 710–712
[Intl] section (WIN.INI), 522–525, 679
invalid instructions, 780
I/O addresses, 438, 955
IPC. *See* interprocess communication
IRQ (interrupt request) lines. *See* inter-
    rupts and IRQ lines
ISA (Industry Standard Architecture), 955
ISO (International Standards Organization),
    956
ISO–9660 CD-ROM standard, 220
italic fonts, 559

J

JOIN command, 793
Joint Photographic Experts Group (JPEG),
    231, 239–240, 956
joystick functions, 221

K

kernel, 56, 58, 79, 307–308, 313–315
key maps with MIDI, 492–494, 956

Keyboard dialog box, 484, 513
[Keyboard] section (SYSTEM.INI), 50, 533
KEYBOARD.DLL file, 533
[keyboard.drivers] section (SETUP.INF),
    61–62
[keyboard.tables] section (SETUP.INF), 62
[keyboard.types] section (SETUP.INF), 62
keyboards
    for child windows, 109
    with Clipboard, 170, 172
    desktop for, 396–398
    direct access to, 347–348, 680
    drivers for, 61–62
    installation options for, 46
    macros for, 420–424
    mouse button assignments for,
    920–923
    multiple, 61
    settings for, 483–485, 513
    SYSTEM.INI for, 533
    with Taipei program, 918
keystrokes
    lost, 305–306
    priority for, 549–550
    repeat rate for, 484–485, 513, 956
kilobyte (K), 956
Klotz program (companion disks), 895–898
KRNL286.EXE file, 56, 58, 79
KRNL386.EXE file, 56, 58, 79

L

labels for icons, 472, 475–476, 520
landscape orientation, 580, 956
[language] section (SETUP.INF), 72
laptops, 17
large drivers, memory for, 662–666
large page frames, 153, 956
laser printers
    compatibility of, 728
    fonts for, 741
    memory for, 743
LASTDRIVE command
    (CONFIG.SYS), 44
    for CD-ROM drives, 227
    for RAM disks, 674

LCD displays
colors for, 481
mouse trails for, 63, 486
readability on, 454
LDTs. *See* local descriptor tables
Least Recently Used (LRU) algorithm, 162–164, 956
left-handed mouse settings, 485
.LGO files, 285
lifetime of objects, 84
LIM EMS standards, 13–14, 133–135, 138–139, 948, 956
[lim] section (SETUP.INF), 41
limit fields, 127
Linker program, 89
links, 957, 975. *See also* Dynamic Data Exchange (DDE); Object Linking and Embedding (OLE)
list boxes, 947, 957
Loa Duong virus, 833
LOADHI programs (QEMM), 667–669
LOADHIGH (LH) command, 44–45, 151, 647, 654–656, 663–664
loading
applications, 286–288, 415, 477, 519
data files, 270–271
demand, 944
drivers, 43–45, 150–151, 647, 650–657, 662–666
Windows, 96
workstations, 696–700
local descriptor tables (LDTs), 112, 123–126, 129, 957
local heap, 83, 85
local printers, 957
local queues, 587–588
local reboots, 17, 765, 769–770
and DESQview 386, 102
and devices, 757
and RAM disks, 675
warnings for, 789
local swapping, 688–689, 698
locking memory, 365–367, 551–552, 680–682
log files for UAEs, 768–771, 774–775
logging off information services, 716

logical drives, 957
logical memory, 128–129
logical pages, 137, 164
logical sectors, 632
logo screen, 282–285, 728
look-ahead buffers, 603, 608, 957
losses in compression, 239
lost clusters, 630–632
lost keystrokes, 305–306
Lotus 1-2-3, expanded memory for, 367, 681
LPT ports, 591, 957
LRU (Least Recently Used) algorithm, 162–164, 956
luminosity of color, 438, 440–441, 957

M

M9 parameter for EMM386.EXE, 659–660
[machine] section (SETUP.INF), 70–72
Macintosh computers, 5, 27
MacroMind Director files, 219
macros, 420–424
Mah-Jongg program (companion disks), 915–919
Manifest program, 121
manual links, 957
mapping memory, 128–129, 136–137, 164, 761
MARK.EXE utility, 296, 764
marked applications, 295–296, 764, 958
maximizing windows, 958
maximum memory option in .PIF files, 354–355
MCGA video standard, 447
MCI. *See* Media Control Interface
[MCI Extensions] section (WIN.INI), 527
mci multimedia functions, 221–222
[MCI] section (SYSTEM.INI), 535
MCI Waveform Driver Setup dialog box, 489
MDA video standard, 447–448
MDI (Multiple Document Interface), 107, 959
measurements
converting, 898–900
international, 497, 523

Media Control Interface (MCI), 219, 221–222, 958
media files, 958
Media Player, 21, 257–260
medium-resolution mode, 958
megabyte (MB), 958
MEM command (DOS), 43, 654–655, 659
memory, 644–645. *See also* addresses
    for adapters, 155, 554–555, 661–662, 759, 761–763
    adding, 117, 131–132
    alternative managers for, 666–669, 740
    backfilling, 138–139, 153, 938
    boards for, 131
    buying, 147, 159
    cleaning, 829
    for Clipboard, 157, 169, 173, 829
    CONFIG.SYS settings for, 43–44, 645, 647–650
    conventional. *See* conventional memory
    and disk access, 598–599
    for DOS, 648–649, 946
    for DOS applications, 131–132, 280–281, 684
    DOS 5 management of, 646–647
    DPMI management of, 112
    for drivers, 147, 677–678
    error messages for, 154, 288, 729, 734–736, 739, 781–784
    for .EXE files, 97
    expanded. *See* expanded memory
    extended. *See* extended memory
    extenders for, 137
    for fonts, 575–576, 679
    global, 84, 188–190, 952
    HMA. *See* High Memory Area
    locking, 365–367, 551–552, 680–682
    mapping, 128–129, 136–137, 761
    for multimedia, 217
    for networks, 687, 706–710
    physical, 128–129
    and .PIF files, 145, 152, 346–347, 352–353, 356–357, 365–368, 679–682
    for printers, 575–576, 743, 798–799
    and processors, 28
    QEMM 386 management of, 103, 121
    RAM disks in. *See* RAM disks and RAMDRIVE.SYS driver
    requirements for, 36, 740
    reserved. *See* upper memory blocks (UMB) area
    and resolution, 442–443
    and resources, 79, 84–85, 729
    for screen redrawing, 550
    in standard mode, 36, 142–146
    for starting applications, 157, 288, 734–736
    and system upgrades, 31
    in 386 enhanced mode, 36, 146–159, 281–282, 738–739
    for TSRs, 150, 368, 376–377, 385, 650–655, 678, 682
    types of, 129–133
    UMB. *See* upper memory blocks (UMB) area
    for vector graphics, 435
    for video, 147, 345, 352–353, 370–371, 442–444, 454–457, 641, 681, 975
    virtual. *See* virtual memory
    for virus protection program, 862
    for wallpaper, 154, 157, 469, 677
    WIN.INI and, 678–679
    for windows, 358
    for Windows 1.0, 9–11
Memory Commander program, 137
memory-resident programs. *See* TSR (terminate-and-stay-resident) programs
menu bars, 958
menus
    aligning, 519
    defining, 814–818
    drop-down, 947
    hiding, 520
    pull-down, 965
    shortcut keys for, 397–398
message handlers, 86
message loops, 86–87
messages
    confirmation, 410–411, 413
    for DDE conversations, 188–189
    error. *See* error messages

passing, 18, 86–89, 958
queues for, 11, 86, 188
Metafile Clipboard format, 177, 868
Metcnvrt program (companion disks), 898–900
MFT program, 121
MGA video standard, 447
Michelangelo virus, 833
Microsoft System Diagnostics (MSD.EXE) program, 20, 770–775
MIDI (Musical Instrument Digital Interface), 217, 958
  channel maps with, 495–497, 940
  extensions for, 212
  key maps with, 492–494, 956
  with Media Player, 257–259
  operation of, 237–238
  patch maps with, 494–495, 963
  ports for, 217, 220, 237–238, 497
  setup for, 491–492
  for sound effects, 490–497
  specifications for, 952
MIDI Key Map dialog box, 492–493
MIDI Mapper, 21, 494, 801–802
MIDI Mapper dialog box, 494
MIDI Patch Map dialog box, 494–495
minimizing windows, 959
minimum memory option in .PIF files, 353–354
MIRROR.EXE file, loading high, 656–657
MIRROR/PARTN command (DOS), 41
misses, cache, 610
mixing sound, 254–255
mmio multimedia functions, 221
Mode menu for PIF editor, 333, 343
modems, 716–718
  baud rates for, 749–751
  checking, 826–829
  compressed files for, 843
modes, execution. See protected mode; real mode; standard mode; 386 enhanced mode
money manager (Wincheck), 870–880
monitors. See also screens; video
  multiple, 61, 453–454
  ports for, 368–369

refresh rates for, 451, 954, 974
requirements for, 37
screen savers for, 299–301, 423, 516, 968
selecting, 449–454
monochrome, 959
More Windows program (companion disks), 445, 900–903
Motion Picture Experts Group (MPEG), 231, 239–240, 959
mouse
  with BackMenu, 817
  with BigDesk, 821
  with Clipboard, 170
  confirmation messages for, 411
  desktop for, 394–396
  with DOS applications, 383–384, 731–732
  drivers for, 44, 62–63, 383–384, 677–678, 732
  installation options for, 46
  keys assigned to, 920–923
  left-handed settings for, 485
  in macros, 420
  pointer for, 959
  problems with, 728
  settings for, 485–486, 517–518
  with SnagIt, 913
Mouse dialog box, 485, 517–518
mouse trails, 63, 486, 518
MOUSE.COM file, 383, 732
MOUSE.DRV file, 383
moving
  directories, 416–419
  files, 419–420
  icons, 407
  objects, 198–199
  printer queue entries, 590
  windows, 473, 519, 821
Mowin program (companion disks), 445, 900–903
MPEG (Motion Picture Experts Group), 231, 239–240, 959
MS-DOS Executive, 10–11
MSCDEX program, 226–227, 246
MSD utility, 20, 770–775

MSDOS.EXE shell, 143
multimedia, 206–207, 486
    applications for, 214–216
    CD-ROM drives for, 223–227,
    232–237
    chips and boards for, 230–231
    compression in, 210–211, 214, 230–
    231, 237–240
    error messages for, 800–803
    extensions for, 211, 219–222, 527–
    528, 959
    future of, 24
    hardware for, 801
    history of, 208–209
    interactive, 209, 241–250
    Media Player for, 257–260
    and MPCs, 216–222, 959
    on networks, 213–214
    RIFF for, 240–241
    software for, 228–230
    sound with, 209, 219, 250–256, 487–
    497, 527–528
    SYSTEM.INI entries for, 535
    video graphics, 210–211
Multimedia Beethoven, 230
multimedia personal computers (MPCs),
    216–222
multipartite viruses, 848
Multiple Document Interface (MDI), 107,
    959
multiple instances, 326–329
multiple monitors, 61, 453–454
multiple .PIF files, 338–339
multiple printers, 583, 587
multiplex interrupt, 98–99
multiscanning monitors, 454
multitasking, 5, 85, 959
    cooperative, 88
    data protection in, 92–93, 95, 265–266
    with DESQview, 8, 101–103
    DOS applications, 20
    error messages for, 784–789
    LIM EMS for, 138–139
    memory for, 36
    message passing for, 86–89
    modes for, 26

    with networks, 710–713
    in OS/2, 23–25
    paging for, 28
    .PIF files for, 25, 363–365
    preemptive, 23–25, 88–89, 102
    printing with, 517
    priorities for. *See* priorities
    programming models for, 88–92
    swapping for, 614–623
    386 enhanced mode for, 281
multithreading, 23, 25, 960
music. *See also* MIDI
    for appointment manager, 910–911
    multimedia for, 219
    player for, 926–928
Musical Instrument Digital Interface. *See*
MIDI

N

names
    in DDE, 187, 190
    for devices, 944
    for icons, 341, 472, 475–476, 520
    for .PIF files, 339
National Geographic's Mammals, 229
Native Clipboard format, 200
NEC, CD-ROM drives by, 225
NetScan virus-scanning program, 849
"Network Not Running" message, 690
[network] section (SETUP.INF), 63
[Network] section (WIN.INI), 531
networks, 960
    bandwidth of, 213–214
    buffers for, 537, 709
    CD-ROM drives with, 226–227
    copying files for, 52, 57
    crashes of, 766–768
    devices for, 960
    directories on, 699
    disk caching on, 613–614, 687–688
    diskless workstations with, 689,
    746–747
    DOS applications with, 693, 711–
    712, 736
    drivers for, 63–64, 690–692

error messages for, 786–787
future of, 24
groups on, 701
icons on, 700–701
improvements to, 21
installing, 46, 63–64, 689–690
limit on open files for, 533
memory for, 687, 706–710
multimedia on, 213–214
multitasking with, 710–713
performance of, 686–689
printing on, 517, 592, 694, 713–715, 742, 747–748, 957
problems with, 746–769
protecting data on, 696–698
queues for, 587–588
setup problems with, 764
SHARE in, 92, 95, 787
shells for, 691–692
starting, 687
swapping on, 688–689, 698
virus scanning on, 849, 864, 866
WIN.INI entries for, 531
Windows installed on, 695–706
New Grolier Electronic Encyclopedia, 228
NOEMS parameter for EMM386.EXE, 43–44, 141, 150, 652
non-Windows applications. *See* DOS applications
noninterlaced monitors, 451–452, 454, 960
nonmaskable interrupts, 156
nonstandard hardware, 53
[NonWindowsApp] section (SYSTEM.INI), 535–536, 622
notes, reminder, 928–931
[Novell_net] section (SETUP.INF), 64
NTSC (National Television Standards Committee), 960
number formats, international, 497, 523

O

object files, 88–89
Object Linking and Embedding (OLE), 18–20, 190, 192–193, 961
    advantages of, 197
    embedding vs. linking in, 194–198
    error messages for, 790–792
    with file copying, 420
    objects in, 193–194, 198–200, 961
    packages with, 200–204
    problems with, 745–746
    sound effects for, 745
    WIN.INI entries for, 531
Object Packager, 21, 200–204, 745–746
ObjectLink Clipboard format, 200
objects, 960
    embedded, 20, 194–198, 200, 204, 420, 948
    global memory, 84
    handlers for, 960
    OLE, 193–194, 198–200, 961
OEM fonts, 64–65, 568
OEM Text format, 176, 960
OEMANSI.BIN file, 533
[oemfonts] section (SETUP.INF), 64–65
offset registers, 118–120
OLE. *See* Object Linking and Embedding
on-board memory caches, 29
open process, 961
opening screen
    bypassing, 282–283, 728
    graphics in, 330
    replacing, 283–285, 728
optimization, 961
    of hard disks, 384, 625–627, 629
    of memory, 43–44, 645, 647–650
option buttons, 961
optional Window components, 47, 66–67, 628–629
Options menu
    for Chess program, 889
    for Taipei program, 917
order of loading in upper memory blocks, 656–657, 662–663
orientation of printer, 580, 956, 964
OS/2 operating system, 5–6, 961
    failure of, 14–15
    vs. Windows, 23–26
"Out of Memory" messages, 154, 288, 729, 734–736, 739, 783
outline fonts, 22

overhead, 84, 961
overlapping windows, 10, 12, 973
overlay area, 961
overlay files, 961
    managers for, 962
    on RAM disks, 675
    viruses in, 834–835, 851
Owner Display Clipboard format, 177
OwnerLink Clipboard format, 200

P

packagers, 21, 200–204, 745–746, 962
page faults, 160–163, 781
page frames, 740, 962
    allocating, 154
    conflicts with, 157–158, 661
    EMM386.EXE for, 141
    and extended memory, 150–151
    large and small, 153, 956, 969
page mode RAM, 147
page tables, 162
pages
    conflicts with, 761
    DPMI management of, 112–113
    and granularity, 128
    mapping, 137, 164, 761
    for video, 345
paging, 962
    demand, 160–162
    disabling, 739
    with diskless workstations, 689
    SYSTEM.INI entries for, 556
    virtual memory for, 28, 160–162
Paintshp program (companion disks), 285,
    434–435, 903–905
Paintbrush program, 434
palettes, 438–442, 962
panning, 901
paper problems, 798
paragraphs, 118
parallel ports and communications, 525,
    694, 962
parallel-to-SCSI adapters, 225
parameters, 962
    for DOS applications, 329–330

    for EMM386.EXE, 43–44, 141, 150,
    652–653, 659–661
    in .INI files, 504
    in .PIF files, 342–343
    for RAMDRIVE.SYS, 673
    testing, 19
    for variables, 974
parity bits, 482, 742, 962
partition tables
    saving, 41
    and viruses, 832–833
partitions, 949, 963–964
passing messages, 86–89
passwords, 963
    for macros, 424
    for network printers, 714
    for screen savers, 300, 423
Paste command, 170–172, 181, 183–184,
    187, 371–372, 733, 746
Paste Link command, 186–187
patch maps with MIDI, 494–495, 963
PATH command and paths, 963
    for directories, 637, 945
    guidelines for, 637–638
    for .PIF files, 336–337
    for RAM disks, 675
    Setup program for, 49
    software versions in, 35
    WIN.INI for, 531
patterns for desktop, 465–467, 520
pausing printer queues, 589
paying bills, 875, 878–879
PCL (Printer Control Language), 575
PCM (pulse code modulation), 965
pels, 963
pen recognition, 24
percent signs (%) in macros, 423–424
peripherals, 963
permanent fonts, 576
permanent swap files, 163–164, 615, 963
    drives for, 739
    settings for, 618–620
    size of, 611, 752
    vs. temporary, 616–617
persistence of vision, 451
PFB files, 573

PFM files, 573
PGA video standard, 447
physical memory, 128–129
physical sectors, 632
picture viewer, 903
.PIF files, 100–101, 320–321, 332, 733, 963
   backing up, 38
   batch files for, 337, 677, 736
   for Clipboard, 183, 348, 371–372
   for closing applications, 372–373
   for closing on exiting, 349, 361–362
   creating, 333–335
   default settings for, 25, 311, 313–314, 332, 335–338, 637, 733
   environment variables in, 344
   for fax boards, 361
   memory for, 145, 152, 346–347, 352–357, 679–682
   for memory control, 365–368
   multiple, 338–339
   for multitasking, 363–365
   parameters in, 342–343
   for priority settings, 101, 308, 311–314, 316–317, 363–365, 388–391, 639–640, 753
   program file names in, 340–341
   for program switching, 348, 680
   for running in background, 359–361
   for running in windows, 357–359
   saving, 334
   for screen management, 348–350, 368–371
   for sharing hardware, 347–348
   for shortcut keys, 350–351, 373–376
   standard mode options for, 332–333, 336, 344–351, 679–680
   start-up directory in, 343–344
   for 386 enhanced mode, 332, 334, 337–338, 351–376, 680–682
   for TSRs, 379–382
   video mode in, 345–346, 352–353, 680–681
   window titles in, 341–342
piping, 963
pitch
   of dots, 449–450, 946

of fonts, 561
pixels, 455–456, 963–964
Pkunzip program, 843–845
Pkware program (companion disks), 843–845
Pkzip program, 843–845
Plasma Power Saver colors, 481
plotter fonts, 561–564, 575, 964
plus signs (+)
   with directories, 414
   in macros, 423
pointers
   in .EXE files, 97
   far, 189
   I-beam, 954
   for mouse, 959
   in resource files, 91
[pointing.device] section (SETUP.INF), 62
points and point sizes, 561
pop-up menus, 814–818
portable CD-ROM drives, 225
portrait orientation, 580, 964
ports, 964
   for MIDI, 217, 220, 237–238, 497
   parallel, 525, 694, 962
   for printers, 531, 580–582, 585, 714
   serial. See serial ports and communications
   for video, 368–369
   WIN.INI entries for, 525–526
Ports dialog box, 525
[Ports] section (WIN.INI), 516, 525–526, 678
PostScript fonts, 22, 573
PostScript printers, 948–949
   compatibility of, 728
   drivers for, 585
power failures, 40
preemptive multitasking, 23–25, 88–89, 102
preparing for Windows, 34
   backups, 38–41
   CONFIG.SYS file, 41–45
   hardware, 35–38
present bit, 128–129
Presentation Clipboard format, 200

Presentation Manager (PM), 25, 964
presentation software, 241
    Action!, 244–247
    Curtain Call, 242–244
    IconAuthor, 247–249
PrevInstance parameter, 326
primary DOS partitions, 964
Print Manager, 517, 585–586, 964
    bypassing, 591–593
    for networks, 694
    problems with, 799–800
    for queue management, 587–591
    for speed of printing, 591–593
"Print Manager Won't Print" message,
    799–800
Print Screen key, 174, 433
Print To File dialog box, 583–584
Printer Control Language (PCL), 575
Printer dialog box, 714
Printer Setup dialog box, 581, 584, 797
[PrinterPorts] section (WIN.INI), 531
printers, 574
    drivers for, 585, 741–742, 964
    fonts for, 22, 575–576, 741, 797
    installing, 576–582
    memory for, 743, 798–799
    nonsupported, 728–729
    ports for, 531, 580–582, 585, 714
    settings for, 516–517
    for workstations, 705
Printers Connect dialog box, 742
Printers dialog box, 516
    and Control Panel, 577–578
    for drivers, 741
    for fonts, 797
    for ports, 580, 585
    for Print Manager bypassing, 592
    Setup button in, 580
    and WIN.INI, 531
printing, 585–586
    conflicts with, 694
    error messages for, 797–800
    to files, 579, 582–585
    improvements to, 21–22
    on networks, 517, 592, 694, 713–
    715, 742, 747–748, 957

notes, 931
problems with, 741–744
queues for, 587–591, 715, 748, 964
speed of, 589, 591–593
text files, 416
PrintQ LAN program, 592
priorities, 287, 730–731, 964
    algorithm for, 313–317
    and baud rates, 749
    of DOS applications, 101, 308, 311–
    314, 316–317, 363–365, 388–391,
    639–640, 753
    of keystrokes, 549–550
    and preemptive multitasking, 89
    of printing, 591–593, 743
    settings for, 308–310
    time slices for, 306–308
privilege levels, 122–124, 127
privileged instructions, 780
processor time, 964
processors, 26–30
    for multimedia, 217
    requirements for, 36
profile names, 62
[progman.groups] section (SETUP.INF),
    52, 67
PROGMAN.INI file, 502
"Program Cannot Be Run from DOS
    Mode" message, 321
program code in .EXE files, 94
program file names in .PIF files, 340–341
program files, 964. See also applications
program groups. See groups and .GRP files
program information files. See .PIF files
Program Item Properties dialog box, 276
    for icons, 323, 325, 332, 401, 473
    for keyboards, 397
Program Manager
    associating data files with, 274–275
    deleting groups and icons with,
    404–405
    and icons, 400–402, 474–477
    improvements to, 21
    introduction of, 15
    properties with, 275–278
    protecting groups with, 294–295

replacing, 143
settings for, 402–404
Setup program for, 52, 67–68
program-item icons, 965
programmable chips, 230
programming models, 88–92
programs. *See* applications
[Programs] section (WIN.INI), 531
PROMPT command (DOS), 386
prompts, 386, 941
properties for applications, 275–278
proportional fonts, 561, 965
protected mode, 18, 27, 965
addresses in, 122–128
interface for, 110–114
protecting data. *See also* viruses
.GRP files, 294–295
on networks, 696–698
with SHARE, 92–93, 95, 265–266,
787
protection faults, 122–123, 127, 781
protocols, 965
pruning directories, 416–419
pull-down menus, 965
pulse code modulation (PCM), 965

Q

QEMM 386 memory manager, 103, 666–
669, 965
versions of, 35
with Windows, 47, 121, 740
queues, 965
for messages, 11, 86, 188
for printing, 587–591, 715, 748, 964
Quote program (companion disks),
905–907

R

radio buttons, 965
RAM (random access memory), 965. *See
also* memory
RAM disks and RAMDRIVE.SYS driver,
41, 669, 965
creating, 670–674

parameters for, 673
in PATH, 637
for printing, 589, 744
Setup program for, 52
size of, 611, 670–671, 673
for swapping, 163, 623–624, 671
for temporary files, 75, 291, 676–677,
754
using, 674–676
versions of, 35, 759
[ramdrive] section (SETUP.INF), 41
random access time of CD-ROM drives, 224
raster fonts, 561–563, 965
rasterizers, 565–567
.RC files, 89, 91
read requests, disk caching of, 603–605
read-after-write verification, 966
read-ahead buffers, 603, 608, 966
read-only files, 294–295, 966
read/write files, 966
real mode, 16, 117–120, 966
.REC files, 421
Recorder utility, 420–424
recording sound, 250–256
red-green-blue (RGB) color model,
438–441
redirection, 966
redrawing screen, 550–551
reference materials, multimedia for,
214–215
refresh rates for monitors, 451, 954, 974
REGEDIT.EXE program, 531
Registration Info Editor, 531
Relocatable Screen Interface Specification
(RSIS), 137
relocation tables, 94, 96–97
REM statements, 506, 966
Reminder program (companion disks),
908–911
renaming files, 419
repeat rate, keyboard, 484–485, 513, 956
repetitive keystrokes, 420–424
replacing
confirmation messages for, 411
DISPLAY.SYS, 445
opening screen, 283–285, 728

shells, 143
Requested Privilege Level (RPL), 123
required files, installing, 65–67
.RES files, 91, 93
reserved memory. *See* upper memory
  blocks (UMB) area
resident commands, 966
resolution, 966
    of graphics, 435–437, 953
    of monitors, 453
    and printing, 592
    of raster fonts, 563
    and speed, 442–445, 592
Resource Interchange File Format (RIFF),
  240–241, 967
resources, 78
    compilers for, 91, 966–967
    consumption of, 79–82, 85, 395
    determining, 730
    files for, 88–89, 91–93
    load on, 855–857
    and memory, 79, 84–85, 729
    types of, 89
    and UAEs, 758
    using, 82–85
Restore button, 967
resuming printer queues, 589
reverse sound, 256
reverse video, 967
Revert option (Sound Recorder), 251–252
RGB color mode, 438–441
RGB monitors, 967
Rich Text Format (RTF), 177, 967
RIFF (Resource Interchange File Format),
  240–241, 967
.RLE files, 73, 285
ROM (read-only memory), 155, 967
root directory, 967
RPL (Requested Privilege Level), 123
RSIS (Relocatable Screen Interface
  Specification), 137
Run command, 269
Run Length Encoded (RLE) files, 285
Run program (companion disks), 845–846
[run] section (SETUP.INF), 54

running
    applications, 286–288, 296–299, 477,
    519, 637
    automatic, 884–886
    TSRs, 44, 265, 376–379
RUNONCE.BAT file, 327

S

SAA (Systems Application Architecture),
  12–13, 170, 395, 972
sampled waveform audio, 220
sampling rates, 236–237
sans-serif fonts, 560, 967
saturation of color, 438, 440–441, 967
saving
    Clipboard contents, 177
    color settings, 480
    partition tables, 41
    .PIF files, 334
    Program Manager settings, 402–404
    RAM disk contents, 675
    screen images, 349–350
scalable fonts, 22, 967
scales with Media Player, 259
Scan program (companion disks), 830,
  835–836, 846–854
screen images, 432
    capturing. *See* capturing screen and
    window images
    Clipboard for, 174–175, 180–181
    formats for, 434–437
    saving, 349–350
screen savers, 21, 299–301, 423, 516, 968
screens. *See also* monitors; video
    backgrounds for, 465–469
    colors for, 481, 529–530
    drivers for, 58–61, 65
    exchanging, 348, 680
    fonts for, 22, 552, 561–564, 567–571
    installation options for, 46
    for multimedia, 217
    opening, 282–285, 330, 728
    .PIF files for, 348–350, 368–371
    redrawing, 550–551

size of, 900–903
scripting for presentations, 242
scroll arrows, 968
scroll bars, 10, 968
scroll boxes, 968
SCSI drives and interface, 968
    for CD-ROM drives, 224–226
    interrupt conflicts with, 69
    permanent swap files for, 739
searching for files, 407–410
secondary command processors, 968
sectors, 632–636, 968
segments and segment registers, 118–120,
  127–128, 968
selecting, 968
    data for Clipboard, 170–173
    files, 415–416
    monitors, 449–454
selection cursor, 968
selectors, 123, 127
semaphores, 327–328
semicolons (;) in .INI files, 506
serial ports and communications, 715–
  719, 969
    background, 857–859
    checking, 826–829
    Clipboard with, 172
    configuring, 481–483
    conflicts with, 483, 553–554, 693–
  694, 696, 751, 794
    direct access with, 347–348
    error messages for, 787–788
    for modems, 716, 718, 750–751
    problems with, 749–751
    setting, 525–526
    SYSTEM.INI entries for, 552–554
    Terminal for, 427–428
    for Unicom, 857–859
serif fonts, 560, 969
server applications, 19–20, 187–189, 961
servers, 969
    disk caching for, 687–688
    speed of, 700
SET command, 344, 385–386
Settings dialog box, 390

Setup program and SETUP.INF file, 53, 976
  and CONFIG.SYS, 41, 68–70
  default values with, 45–48
  and DOS applications, 322
  DOS portion of, 48–51, 56–58
  for DOS version, 48
  and files, 51
  and groups, 67–68
  and hardware-specific entries, 70–72
  help for, 49–50
  and incompatible files, 68–70
  and networks, 63–64
  questions about, 726–729
  sections in, 54–56
  switch options for, 48
  and SYSTEM directory, 48
  UAEs from, 763–764
  Windows portion of, 51–53, 65–67
  and workstations, 700–706
[setup] section (SETUP.INF), 54
SETVER command (CONFIG.SYS), 42
shadow RAM, 155–156, 969
SHARE command (DOS), 92–93, 95,
  265–266, 696, 787
shareware, 969
sharing hardware, .PIF file option for,
  347–348
sharing violations, 786
SHELL command (CONFIG.SYS), 387,
  650
[shell] section (SETUP.INF), 58
shells, 969
    BackMenu as, 817–818
    for networks, 691–692
    replacing, 143
    Setup program for, 52, 58
    specifying, 289, 297–299
Shift key
    in macros, 423
    for selecting files, 416
shortcut keys, 969
    for applications, 100, 277–278, 470–
  471, 731, 734, 737, 937
    for Clipboard, 172
    with File Manager, 412–414

for menus, 397–398
in .PIF files, 350–351, 373–376
for TSRs, 149, 376–378
ShowWindow function, 286
shutdown program, 913–915
SideKick utility, 265
signatures, virus, 862
SIMM (single in-line memory module), 147
simple media devices, 258, 969
single applications, running, 296–299
SIP (single in-line package) memory chips, 147
size
of child MDI windows, 108
of Clipboard contents, 99
of desktop, 819–821
of disk caches, 608, 611–612, 687–688
of environment, 387, 650, 683, 766
of fonts, 455, 559–561, 744
of programs with viruses, 834
of RAM disks, 611, 670–671, 673
of swap files, 611, 616, 618, 752
of wallpaper images, 468
of windows, 285–286, 900–903, 958–959
sizing boxes, 12
sizing grid, 472–474, 520
SK.EXE file, 902
slide shows, 244, 249
small page frames, 153, 969
SMARTDrive. See SMARTDRV.EXE driver
SMARTDRV.EXE driver, 970
benefits of, 727
compatibility of, 602
in CONFIG.SYS file, 42
extended memory for, 600
with file backups, 292
loading, 659–660, 662
location of, 752
Setup program for, 52
and swap files, 754
using, 606–612
versions of, 35, 754, 759
SnagIt program (companion disks), 175, 433, 437, 911–913
snapping to sizing grid, 472

snapshot programs, 970
sndPlaySound system call, 220
soft fonts, 575, 947, 970
limits on, 799
PostScript, 573
software
diagnostic, 768–775
incompatible, 760–761
interrupts from, 970
for multimedia, 228–230
versions of, 35
software caches, 600–606, 822–826
Software Carousel program, 6
Sony, CD-ROM drives by, 224
sorting
Action! scenes, 245–246
financial information (Wincheck), 873–874
international settings for, 498
sound
amplitude of, 236
analog and digital, 211–213
for appointment manager, 910–911
Beep setting for, 512–513
boards for, 970
with CD-ROM drives, 211, 217–218, 234–237
drivers for, 487–489, 970
files for, 250–254, 527–528, 970
icon for, 21
in multimedia, 209, 219, 487–497, 527–528
music player for, 926–928
in presentations, 243
recording, 250–256
Sound Blaster Pro, 213, 487
Sound dialog box, 489, 528
sound effects, 489–490
MIDI for, 490–497
with OLE, 745
Sound Recorder, 21
playing and editing with, 253–254
problems with, 802–803
recording with, 250–253
special effects with, 255–256
Sound Recorder dialog box, 251

[Sound] section (WIN.INI), 528
source code, 88, 93
source documents, 970
spacing icons, 471–472, 520
special characters, 21, 560, 571–574, 745, 970
special effects for sound, 255–256
[special_adapter] section (SETUP.INF), 72
speed
    of backups, 636
    of CD-ROM drives, 221, 224
    and colors, 427, 442–445
    of DOS applications, 638–641, 753
    of double clicking, 486, 571, 946
    of file access, 636–638
    of memory chips, 147, 456–457
    and modes, 752–753
    of printing, 589, 591–593
    for screen redrawing, 551
    of servers, 700
    for sound, 255–256
    of standard mode, 26, 752
    of start-up, 753
    and system upgrades, 31
    of 386 enhanced mode, 752
    of video RAM, 456–457
    of Windows 1.0, 9
SPINRITE II program, 636
split bars, 970
spooling, print, 517, 587–592, 715, 748, 964, 970
square brackets ([]) for sections, 54
SRAM (static random access memory), 31, 147
Stacker program, 628
STACKS command (CONFIG.SYS), 42
staged disk writes, 605–606, 609, 970
standard mode, 970–971
    addressing in, 116–117
    fonts in, 567–568
    memory for, 36, 142–146
    network crashes in, 766–767
    and PIF Editor, 332–333, 336, 344–351, 679–680
    speed of, 26, 752
    swap files in, 614, 620–623

SYSTEM.INI entries for, 536–537
    vs. 386 enhanced mode, 278–282
    for 286 PCs, 26–27
[Standard] section (SYSTEM.INI), 537, 707, 709
standards for video, 446–448
start bits, 971
start-up
    custom, 329–330
    directory for, 343–344
    error messages at, 779–780
    loading and running applications at, 267–269, 286–288
    macros executed at, 421–423
    opening screen for, 282–285, 330, 728
    shell selection at, 289
    speed of, 753
    window size on, 285–286
starting
    applications, 157, 264–278, 288, 734–736
    networks, 687
StartUp group, 21, 505
    and resources, 82–83
    running programs in, 267–269, 286–287
static RAM, 31, 147
status bar, 971
Stoned virus, 832–833
stop bits, 482, 742, 971
Stop program (companion disks), 913–915
subdirectories, 971
submenus, 816
SUBST command (DOS), 793
Super VGA, 447–448, 452, 971
swapping and swap files, 11, 971
    for applications, 614, 937
    default settings for, 618–620
    deleting, 630
    disk space for, 628
    drives and directory for, 536, 739
    and fragmentation, 616, 620–622, 626
    installation options for, 46
    and multitasking, 614–623
    for networks, 688–689, 698
    and paging, 28, 160–162

permanent vs. temporary, 616–617
and .PIF file settings, 354
and present bit, 128–129
preventing, 365–367
and RAM disks, 163, 623–624, 671
size of, 611, 616, 618, 752
and SMARTDRV.EXE, 754
in standard mode, 614, 620–623
SYSTEM.INI entries for, 556, 621–622
TEMP environment variable for, 622–623
in 386 enhanced mode, 615–620
virtual memory for, 162–165, 616, 618–619
switches, 329–330, 342–343, 971
switching
    banks, 133–136, 740, 938
    tasks and applications, 6–7, 301–306, 348, 469–471, 731, 737, 972
switching boxes, 61, 583
synchronization, 219, 971
synthesizers, 492
SYSADMIN.WRI file, 696
Sysedit program, 104, 425–427, 509
[sysfonts] section (SETUP.INF), 64–65
Sysgraph program (companion disks), 855–857
SysInfo program, 280
SYSINI.WRI file, 503, 556
system attributes, 971
System Configuration Editor, 104, 425–427, 509
SYSTEM directory
    copying files to, 57
    with networks, 746–747
    Setup for, 49
system disks, 39–40, 971
system files. *See* .INI files
system fonts, 971
system integrity violations, 758, 780–781
system resources. *See* resources
[system] section (SETUP.INF), 70
system support files, installing, 52
SYSTEM.INI file, 503, 532, 971
    corruption of, 294

DOS application entries in, 535–536
driver and device entries in, 533–535
editing, 425–427, 509–511
exclusivity and locking entries in, 551–552
file entries in, 555
font entries in, 455, 552, 567–568
importance of, 730
interrupt processing, 549–550
memory entries in, 706–710
multimedia entries in, 535
multitasking entries in, 710–713
port entries in, 552–554
screen redrawing via, 550–551
screen savers in, 516
Setup program for, 50, 52
shells, 143, 297–299
standard mode entries in, 536–537
swapping entries in, 556, 621–622
386 enhanced mode entries in, 538–556
Systems Application Architecture (SAA), 12–13, 170, 395, 972

T

Tagged Image File (TIF) format, 972
Taipei program (companion disks), 915–919
Task List and task switching, 6–7, 301–306, 469–471, 731, 737, 972
    with BigDesk, 820
    displaying, 6–7
    with DOS applications, 101, 348, 680
tasks, 972
Telephonica virus, 833
TEMP directory, 629
TEMP environment variable
    in batch files, 328
    importance of, 727
    for printing, 742, 744
    for RAM disks, 75, 291, 676–677, 754
    setting up, 386, 536
    for swapping, 622–623
temporary fonts, 575–576

temporary swap files, 163–164, 615, 972
  deleting, 630
  vs. permanent, 616–617
  settings for, 618–620
Tequila virus, 833
terminal emulators, 972
Terminal utility, 427–428
terminating DOS applications, 24, 390, 765, 769, 789
testing
  disk caching, 822–826
  parameters, 19
text
  Clipboard for, 172, 175
  transferring, 169
text boxes, 972
Text Clipboard format, 176
text files, 416, 972
text mode, 369–370, 972
TFRAME.DLL file, 919
third-party memory boards and managers, 131, 666–669, 740
386 Enhanced dialog box, 310, 549
386 enhanced mode, 20–21, 973
  addressing in, 116–117
  checking for, 98
  cut-and-paste operations in, 179, 181–182
  demand paging in, 160–162
  DOS applications in, 266–267, 281
  interrupt conflicts in, 69
  memory for, 36, 146–159, 281–282, 738–739
  multiple instances with, 326
  network crashes in, 767–768
  for Paint Shop, 903
  for .PIF files, 332, 334, 337–338, 351–376, 680–682
  problems in running, 738–739
  SHARE in, 92
  speed in, 752
  vs. standard mode, 278–282
  swapping in, 615–620
  SYSTEM.INI entries for, 538–556
  time slices in, 306–317

[386Enh] section (SYSTEM.INI), 538–548
  communications entries in, 717
  DOS application memory and, 131–132
  exclusivity and locking and, 551–552
  expanded memory and, 684
  files and, 555
  fonts and, 455, 552, 569
  interrupts and, 69, 549–550, 738, 759
  networks and, 707–709
  page frames and, 154
  ports and, 552–554
  screen redrawing and, 550–551
  shells and, 817–818
  swapping and, 556, 621, 689
  temporary files and, 291
  transfer buffers and, 787
  translation buffers and, 152
  UMBs and, 155–158, 554–555, 661–662, 692, 695, 738, 748, 759, 761–763
386MAX.SYS memory manager, 666, 973
386SPART.PAR file, 163, 615, 617
throughput, 973
TIF format, 972
tiling windows, 10, 12, 973
time
  displaying, 429, 919–920, 923–926
  international, 497, 523
  setting, 925
time lines with Action!, 244–245
time slices, 306–308, 973. See also priorities
Timefram program (companion disks), 919–920
timeouts, 516, 743, 973
timers, clock with, 925
title bars, 973
track-buffering disk controllers, 688
tracks, 232, 973
training
  computer-based, 249
  multimedia for, 216
  and Windows, 5, 23
transfer buffers, 131–132, 155, 787
transfer rate of CD-ROM drives, 224

transferring data, 8. *See also* Clipboard; Dynamic Data Exchange (DDE); Object Linking and Embedding (OLE)
translating between applications, 398–399
translation buffers, 150–152
trees for directories, 412–413, 945
true color cards, 456
TrueType fonts, 19, 561–562, 973
   with Curtain Call, 244
   hinting with, 566–567, 954
   as outline fonts, 22
   for printers, 575, 741
   Setup program for, 52, 67
   and WYSIWYG, 564–565
TrueType rasterizer, 565–567
[TrueType] section (WIN.INI), 526–527, 678
TSR (terminate-and-stay-resident) programs, 974
   addresses with, 120
   background processing for, 637
   batch files for, 379–382
   and defragmentation, 627
   incompatible, 68, 760–761
   interrupts for, 710–712
   managing, 149
   memory for, 150, 368, 376–377, 385, 650–655, 678, 682
   running, 44, 265, 376–379
   shortcut keys for, 149, 376–378
TTY.DRV driver, 585
two-way linking. *See* Object Linking and Embedding (OLE)
.TXT files, 556
typefaces. *See* fonts

U

UAE. *See* error messages; Unrecoverable Application Errors (UAEs)
UART device, 553, 750, 974
UMB. *See* upper memory blocks (UMB) area
UMB providers and loaders, 668
Undo commands, 173
unformatted ASCII files, printing, 585

Unicom program (companion disks), 857–859
Unix operating system, 6
Unrecoverable Application Errors (UAEs), 756–757, 974. *See also* error messages
   API services for, 17–19
   from application versions, 764–765
   from application-specific problems, 765–766
   diagnostic software for, 768–775
   from DOS versions, 761
   file corruption from, 40
   from incompatibilities, 760–761
   from network crashes, 766–768
   from setup problems, 763–764
   sources of, 758–759
[Update.Files] section (SETP.INF), 69
updating
   linked data, 186–187
   network drivers, 690–691
   printer queues, 588, 715
   WIN.INI file, 68–69
upgrading, 31, 131, 457
upper memory blocks (UMB) area, 151, 650–655, 966, 974
   available space in, 657–662
   conflicts in, 71, 155–158, 554–555, 661–662, 692, 695, 738, 748, 759, 761–763
   and expanded memory, 133–134
   for fax boards, 361
   linking, 43–44, 651, 668
   loading in, 43–44, 150–151, 647, 650–657, 662–666
   with networks, 709
   order of loading in, 656–657, 662–663
   and QEMM 386, 47
   using, 150–152
User (USER.EXE) program, 58, 79, 83, 85
utilities, 674, 974
UTILITY directory, 637

V

[v7e] section (SETUP.INF), 60
[v7vga] section (SETUP.INF), 60

Validate program
    for Clean, 831–832
    for Vshield, 861
vaporware, 9
variable parameters, 974
Vclean program (companion disks), 830–837, 848, 854
Virtual Control Program Interface (VCPI), 112–113, 974
VDISK.SYS file, 68
vector fonts, 561–564, 974
vector graphics, 434–437
V86 mode, 13, 28, 975
versions
    of applications, 764–765
    of DOS, 36, 48, 761
    and marked applications, 295–296, 764
    of RAMDRIVE.SYS, 759
    of SMARTDRV.EXE, 754, 759
    of software, 35
vertical refresh rate, 451, 974
VESA (Video Electronics Standards Association) video standard, 452, 974
VGA, 447–448, 452, 971
[VGA.3gr] section (SETUP.INF), 60
VGALOGO.RLE file, 59, 73, 285
video. See also screens; monitors
    analog and digital, 210–211
    buffers for, 137
    colors for, 454–456
    conflicts with, 155–157, 554–555, 661, 748, 759
    Continuous Edge Graphics for, 447–448, 458–459
    coprocessors for, 457–458, 952
    with DESQview 386, 103
    direct access to, 368
    drivers for, 58–61, 65, 445–446
    error messages for, 795–797
    memory for, 147, 345, 352–353, 370–371, 442–444, 454–457, 641, 681, 975
    monitors for, 449–454
    standards for, 446–448
video boards
    for multimedia, 217

and system upgrades, 31
video mode in .PIF files, 345–346, 352–353, 680–681
video RAM (VRAM), 147, 456–457, 975
VIRLIST.TXT file, 833–834, 848
virtual 8086 mode, 13, 28, 975
Virtual Control Program Interface (VCPI), 112–113, 974
virtual disks. See RAM disks and RAM-DRIVE.SYS driver
virtual machines, 975
    memory for, 146–149, 281–282
    with networks, 709–710
    for TSRs, 378–379
virtual memory, 20–21, 159, 280–282, 975
    paging with, 28, 160–162
    for swapping, 162–165, 616, 618–619
Virtual Memory dialog box, 618–619
Virtual Memory Manager (VMM), 160–165, 281–282, 975
virus signatures, 862
Viruscan program, 830
viruses
    detecting and identifying, 846–854
    preventing, 860–866
    removing, 830–837, 848, 854
visibility of objects, 84
VisiOn operating environment, 7–8
visual effects, 242
VMM. See Virtual Memory Manager
voice (MIDI), 238
VOPT program, 625
VRAM (video RAM), 147, 456–457, 975
Vshield program (companion disks), 860–866

W

wallpaper, 975
    memory for, 154, 157, 469, 677
    selecting, 467–469, 520
Wallpapers, Misc. dialog box, 629, 631
warm booting, 975
warm links, 186, 975
.WAV (waveform) files, 250–253, 489
Wbar program (companion disks), 867–869

WCHOOK.DLL file, 924
WDN.EXE file, 891
weight of fonts, 559
Whiskers program (companion disks),
  920–923
width of fonts, 560
wildcards in file searches, 409
[win.apps] section (SETUP.INF), 66
[win.bmps] section (SETUP.INF), 66
WIN.CNF file, 50, 285
WIN.COM program, 50–51, 73, 283–285
[win.copy] section (SETUP.INF), 51, 65
[win.copy.386] section (SETUP.INF), 52
[win.copy.net] section (SETUP.INF), 52, 65
[win.copy.win386] section
  (SETUP.INF), 65
[win.dependents] section (SETUP.INF),
  66–67
[win.games] section (SETUP.INF), 66
WIN.INI file, 503, 507, 531, 976
  associating data files by using, 272–
    273, 289, 396, 406, 520–523
  color entries in, 479–480, 529–530
  corruption of, 294
  deleting entries from, 511, 513
  desktop entries in, 516, 519–521
  and document files, 519
  editing, 425–427, 509–511
  executable programs and, 505
  font entries in, 526–527
  help entries in, 528–529
  importance of, 730
  international settings in, 522–525
  memory entries in, 678–679
  mouse settings in, 517–518
  multimedia sound file entries in,
    527–528
  port entries in, 525–526
  printer settings in, 516–517, 531
  and resources, 82–83
  Setup program for, 52
  and start-up applications, 21, 267,
    269, 286–288
  updating, 68–69
  use of, 508–511

[Windows] section in, 511–519
[win.readme] section (SETUP.INF), 66
[win.scrs] section (SETUP.INF), 66
[win.shell] section (SETUP.INF), 65
WIN386.SWP file, 163, 615
Wincheck program (companion disks),
  870–880
Winclock program (companion disks),
  923–926
WINCLOCK.HLP file, 924
WINCOM.DLL file, 818
window titles in .PIF files, 341–342
windows, 940, 975
  active, 302
  for applications, 937
  borders of, 12, 474, 516
  capturing, 174–175, 434
  cascading, 939
  closing, 108, 838
  DOS applications in, 357–359
  for groups, 953
  and MDI, 107–109
  maximizing, 958
  minimizing, 959
  moving, 473, 519, 821
  overlapping, 10, 12, 973
  resources for, 80, 83, 85
  size of, 285–286, 900–903, 958–959
  tiling, 10, 12, 973
Windows 1.0, 5, 9–12
Windows 2.0, 12–13
Windows/286 and Windows/386, 13–14
Windows 3.0, 14–15
Windows 3.1, 15
  closing, 840–842
  compatibility of, 16
  data sharing in, 18–20
  error handling in, 17–18
  improvements in, 20–22
  on networks, 695–706
  new features of, 16
  vs. OS/2, 23–26
  processors for, 26–30
  Setup program for, 51–53, 65–67
WINDOWS directory, 49, 637

[windows] section (SETUP.INF), 57
[Windows] section (WIN.INI), 511–515
    desktop and, 516
    mouse settings in, 517–518
    network entries in, 64
    Print Manager entries in, 679
    printer settings in, 516–517
    and start-up applications, 286–287
[Windows Help] section (WIN.INI), 528–529
Windows Setup dialog box, 628–630
[windows.system] section (SETUP.INF), 57
[winexec] section (SETUP.INF), 56
Winhelp utility, 425
WININI.WRI file, 503, 556
[wininiupdate] section (SETUP.INF), 68–69
WINOLDAP.GRB file, 795
WINOLDAP.MOD program, 99, 101
Winplay program (companion disks), 926–928
Winpost program (companion disks), 928–931
WINPOST.HLP file, 929
WINVER.EXE file, 49
Wired For Sound program, 211
workspace, 976
workstations
    diskless, 689, 746–747

installing Windows on, 700–706
loading, 696–700
multimedia, 215
printers for, 705
WORM (Write Once, Read Many times) CD-ROM drives, 220
wraparound with addressing, 121
.WRI files, 556
write caching, 605–606, 976
WYSIWYG and TrueType fonts, 564–565

X

x height of fonts, 561
XGA video standard, 447, 452
XMS (Extended Memory Specification), 122, 145, 976
XON/XOFF flow control, 718, 742, 750

Y

Yacht program (companion disks), 932–933

Z

[zen396_cookz] section (SETUP.INF), 71
Zip files (Pkware), 843–845
zoom boxes, 10

Selections from The SYBEX Library

OPERATING SYSTEMS

The ABC's of DOS 4
Alan R. Miller
275pp. Ref. 583-2

This step-by-step introduction to using DOS 4 is written especially for beginners. Filled with simple examples, *The ABC's of DOS 4* covers the basics of hardware, software, disks, the system editor EDLIN, DOS commands, and more.

The ABC's of DOS 5
Alan Miller
267pp. Ref. 770-3

This straightforward guide will haven even first-time computer users working comfortably with DOS 5 in no time. Step-by-step lessons lead users from switching on the PC, through exploring the DOS Shell, working with directories and files, using essential commands, customizing the system, and trouble shooting. Includes a tear-out quick reference card and function key template.

ABC's of MS-DOS
(Second Edition)
Alan R. Miller
233pp. Ref. 493-3

This handy guide to MS-DOS is all many PC users need to manage their computer files, organize floppy and hard disks, use EDLIN, and keep their computers organized. Additional information is given about utilities like Sidekick, and there is a DOS command and program summary. The second edition is fully updated for Version 3.3.

The ABC's of SCO UNIX
Tom Cuthbertson
263pp. Re. 715-0

A guide especially for beginners who want to get to work fast. Includes hands-on tutorials on logging in and out; creating and editing files; using electronic mail; organizing files into directories; printing; text formatting; and more.

The ABC's of Windows 3.0
Kris Jamsa
327pp. Ref. 760-6

A user-friendly introduction to the essentials of Windows 3.0. Presented in 64 short lessons. Beginners start with lesson one, while more advanced readers can skip ahead. Learn to use File Manager, the accessory programs, customization features, Program Manager, and more.

DESQview Instant Reference
Paul J. Perry
175pp. Ref. 809-2

This complete quick-reference command guide covers version 2.3 and DESQview 386, as well as QEMM (for managing expanded memory) and Manifest Memory Analyzer. Concise, alphabetized entries provide exact syntax, options, usage, and brief examples for every command. A handy source for on-the-job reminders and tips.

DOS 3.3 On-Line Advisor
Version 1.1
SYBAR, Software Division of SYBEX, Inc.
Ref. 933-1

The answer to all your DOS problems. The DOS On-Line Advisor is an on-screen reference that explains over 200 DOS error messages. 2300 other citations cover all you ever needed to know about DOS. The DOS On-Line Advisor pops up on top of your working program to give you quick, easy help when you need it, and disappears when you don't. Covers thru version 3.3. Software package comes with 3½" and 5¼" disks. **System Requirements:** IBM compatible with DOS 2.0 or higher, runs with Windows 3.0, uses 90K of RAM.

DOS Instant Reference
SYBEX Prompter Series
Greg Harvey
Kay Yarborough Nelson
220pp. Ref. 477-1

A complete fingertip reference for fast, easy on-line help:command summaries, syntax, usage and error messages. Organized by function—system commands, file commands, disk management, directories, batch files, I/O, networking, programming, and more. Through Version 3.3.

DOS 5: A to Z
Gary Masters
900pp; Ref. 805-X

A personal guru for every DOS 5 user! This comprehensive, "all you need to know" guide to DOS 5 provides detailed, A-to-Z coverage of DOS 5 commands, options, error messages, and dialog boxes—with syntax, usage, and plenty of examples and tips. It also includes hundreds of informative, in-depth articles on DOS 5 terminology and concepts.

DOS 5 Instant Reference
Robert M. Thomas
200pp. Ref. 804-1

The comprehensive quick guide to DOS—all its features, commands, options, and versions—now including DOS 5, with the new graphical interface. Concise, alphabetized command entries provide exact syntax, options, usage, brief examples, and applicable version numbers. Fully cross-referenced; ideal for quick review or on-the-job reference.

The DOS 5 User's Handbook
Gary Masters
Richard Allen King
400pp. Ref. 777-0

This is the DOS 5 book for users who are already familiar with an earlier version of DOS. Part I is a quick, friendly guide to new features; topics include the graphical interface, new and enhanced commands, and much more. Part II is a complete DOS 5 quick reference, with command summaries, in-depth explanations, and examples.

Essential OS/2
(Second Edition)
Judd Robbins
445pp. Ref. 609-X

Written by an OS/2 expert, this is the guide to the powerful new resources of the OS/2 operating system standard edition 1.1 with presentation manager. Robbins introduces the standard edition, and details multitasking under OS/2, and the range of commands for installing, starting up, configuring, and running applications. For Version 1.1 Standard Edition.

Essential PC-DOS
(Second Edition)
Myril Clement Shaw
Susan Soltis Shaw
332pp. Ref. 413-5

An authoritative guide to PC-DOS, including version 3.2. Designed to make experts out of beginners, it explores everything from disk management to batch file programming. Includes an 85-page command summary. Through Version 3.2.

Graphics Programming
Under Windows
Brian Myers
Chris Doner
646pp. Ref. 448-8

Straightforward discussion, abundant examples, and a concise reference guide to graphics commands make this book a must for Windows programmers. Topics range from how Windows works to programming for business, animation, CAD, and desktop publishing. For Version 2.

SYBEX

FREE BROCHURE!

Complete this form today, and we'll send you a full-color brochure of Sybex bestsellers.

Please supply the name of the Sybex book purchased.

_____

How would you rate it?

_____ Excellent   _____ Very Good   _____ Average   _____ Poor

Why did you select this particular book?

_____ Recommended to me by a friend

_____ Recommended to me by store personnel

_____ Saw an advertisement in _____

_____ Author's reputation

_____ Saw in Sybex catalog

_____ Required textbook

_____ Sybex reputation

_____ Read book review in _____

_____ In-store display

_____ Other _____

Where did you buy it?

_____ Bookstore

_____ Computer Store or Software Store

_____ Catalog (name: _____)

_____ Direct from Sybex

_____ Other: _____

Did you buy this book with your personal funds?

_____ Yes   _____ No

About how many computer books do you buy each year?

_____ 1-3   _____ 3-5   _____ 5-7   _____ 7-9   _____ 10+

About how many Sybex books do you own?

_____ 1-3   _____ 3-5   _____ 5-7   _____ 7-9   _____ 10+

Please indicate your level of experience with the software covered in this book:

_____ Beginner   _____ Intermediate   _____ Advanced

Which types of software packages do you use regularly?

_____ Accounting	_____ Databases	_____ Networks
_____ Amiga	_____ Desktop Publishing	_____ Operating Systems
_____ Apple/Mac	_____ File Utilities	_____ Spreadsheets
_____ CAD	_____ Money Management	_____ Word Processing
_____ Communications	_____ Languages	_____ Other _____

(please specify)

Which of the following best describes your job title?

_____ Administrative/Secretarial   _____ President/CEO

_____ Director   _____ Manager/Supervisor

_____ Engineer/Technician   _____ Other _____
                                                    (please specify)

Comments on the weaknesses/strengths of this book: _____

_____

_____

_____

_____

Name _____

Street _____

City/State/Zip _____

Phone _____

PLEASE FOLD, SEAL, AND MAIL TO SYBEX

SYBEX, INC.
Department M
2021 CHALLENGER DR.
ALAMEDA, CALIFORNIA USA
94501

SYBEX

SEAL

Applications on the Companion Disks

Disk 1: Productivity Tools

BackMenu	Pop-up Program Manager replacement
BigDesk	Expands desktop size with large virtual screen
Cachetst	Tests efficiency of cache programs
Chkmodem	Determines available communications connections
Clean	Frees up system memory
Closer	Allows for easy closing of running applications
Cpuuse	Displays processing load information
Exitw	Allows you to exit quickly from Windows
Pkware	Compresses and decompresses other disk files
Run	Runs multiple applications with a single request
Scan	Identifies specific computer viruses
Sysgraph	Graphically displays system loading
Unicom	Communications program
Vclean	Removes computer viruses
Vshield	Inhibits viruses from entering your system
Wbar	Generates bar codes
Wincheck	Manages your checkbook

Disk 2: Tools for Personalizing Windows

Address	Manages mailing/phone lists
Apptimer	Launches applications at specified times
Chess	Plays the game of chess
Dirnote	Attaches explanatory notes to disk files
Iconmstr	Edits, views, and manages icons
Klotz	Plays the game of Tetris
Metcnvrt	Converts numbers between systems
Mowin	Expands the size of your virtual screen
Paintshp	Picture viewer, editor, and format converter
Quote	Displays pithy quotations
Reminder	Manages personal calendar
SnagIt	Captures and prints screen images
Stop	Rapid exit from Windows
Taipei	Plays the game of Taipei
Timefram	Displays time in topmost window's title bar
Whiskers	Programs mouse to simulate common keystrokes
Winclock	Screen clock with alarms and timers
Winplay	Plays music files through the PC speaker
Winpost	Displays on-screen messages
Yacht	Plays the game of Yahtzee